ENGLAND

PLAYER BY PLAYER

A compilation of every player ever to have played for England

Foreword by Sir Bobby Robson

WRITTEN BY GRAHAM BETTS

ENGLAND
PLAYER BY PLAYER

This edition first published in the UK in 2006 by Green Umbrella

www.greenumbrella.co.uk

Publishers Jules Gammond, Tim Exell, Vanessa Gardner

Printed and bound in Italy

ISBN 1-905009-63-1

CONTENTS

FOREWORD

Sir Bobby Robson

As one of a very select few who has had the privilege and honour to both play for and manage the national side, I am still hard pressed to decide which gave me the greater satisfaction. Most professionals will tell you that nothing ever beats the thrill of actually playing, but many managers will also tell you that seeing a side that you selected scale heights previously undreamed of generates a special feeling all of its own. You will therefore appreciate my dilemma!

My first match as a player for England came against France in 1957 when I partnered Tommy Taylor up front and we both scored twice in the 4-0 victory. Neither of us could really fail to score since we were being supplied with chances on the day by the likes of Tom Finney, Johnny Haynes and Duncan Edwards. We weren't to know it at the time, but what was my first England appearance turned out to be the last for both Duncan and Tommy, along with defender Roger Byrne, all of whom were so sadly to die three months later in the Munich disaster.

The following summer I appeared in the World Cup finals for the first and last time, an experience I have never forgotten. We failed to win any of our matches, although there was still a sense of pride in holding the eventual winners Brazil to a goalless draw in the group stage. By the time the next World Cup came around, in Chile in 1962, a certain Bobby Moore had claimed my new position of half back and I don't think he did too bad a job of it, all things considered!

Twenty years after making my final playing appearance for England I was honoured to become the manager of the side. It is of course the two World Cup campaigns, in Mexico in 1986 and Italy four years later that people still remember, with Maradona's goals in Mexico City and the penalty shoot out in Turin the usual subjects for debate. Regardless of our wretched luck in both campaigns, I derive immense pride in knowing that we were certainly one of the most entertaining sides, especially in 1990.

It is now nearly fifty years since I first played for England and sixteen since I managed the side, but of course I have continued to be involved in the beautiful game and follow the nation's fortunes with great interest. I count myself extremely fortunate to have played alongside at international level and against at club level with many of the players featured in this book and, of course, as manager was responsible for selecting a considerable number too. This is one of those books that you flick through to find your own personal favourites, looking to see what happened to them after they finished with football. Since the book features all of the players who have played for England over the course of more than one hundred and thirty years, there are some great names from bygone days whose contributions to England are just as valid and vital as those who will be competing in Germany this summer. I am sure you will enjoy reading about each and every one of them.

Bobby Robson

INTRODUCTION

England and Scotland met in the world's very first official football international in 1872, the game in Glasgow finishing a goalless draw. For seven years England versus Scotland was the only international match on the calendar, although in 1879 the English and Scottish both accepted an invitation from the Welsh for a series of annual fixtures, followed three years later by the Irish. The subsequently-named British championship could therefore lay claim to being the oldest international football competition, although the World Cup and European Championship surpassed it in terms of importance and the competition was abandoned in the early 1980s.

Since 1872 England have gone on to play well over 800 full international matches against countries from all around the globe. The importance of football around the world can be gauged by the fact that FIFA, the Federation of International Football Associations, currently has more members than the United Nations! England has yet to meet each and every one, but as befits the oldest established national association they have met more than most. England has been represented by well over 1100 players during that time (Neil Webb in 1987 became the 1000th English player to be officially 'capped' by his country) and this book details the exploits of each and every one of them. To be selected to represent England is the pinnacle of every player's career, be it in a friendly match on an end-of-season tour or a World Cup Final; every player who has put on the shirt of England has derived immense pride in so doing.

Whilst the FA Challenge Cup (to give it its full title) may strike more at the romanticism of the game, pitting David against Goliath on an almost regular basis, international football is no less short of passion. It does not matter whether an international career lasted for eight minutes, as in the case of Steve Perryman, or 125 games, such as played by Peter Shilton; representing your country was what you spent your life building towards.

It has been my intention to supply the following information on each player to have appeared for England; their full names (the Everton full-back who played for England in the 1966 World Cup Final may well have gone through his entire career known as Ray Wilson, but he was christened Ramon), the place and date of birth, the place and date of death where applicable, the clubs played for during his career, the opponents, date and venue of their debuts and the total number of appearances made. I have also included the goal tallies for those who have netted for England, and appearances in unofficial matches.

It is, of course, almost impossible to pay full tribute to the likes of Bobby Charlton, Billy Wright, Peter Shilton and others of their ilk whose contributions to England are perhaps more worthy of an entire volume, and I apologise in advance for this. I can only trust that the reader is sufficiently aware of the full extent of these players' careers to accept the shortness of their entries. Equally, I hope providing details of some of the long forgotten players will more than compensate; Morton Peto Betts is assured his place in football's history as the scorer of the very first goal in an FA Cup Final (for Wanderers against the Royal Engineers in 1872) but had to wait five years before making his one and only appearance for England. That one appearance is made all the more interesting by the fact that he turned out as goalkeeper!

Before we consider those players who have represented England, it is worth reminding ourselves of how football progressed before England and Scotland met for the very first time, so let's go back more than 150 years to the 1840s. Football in England in the 1840s bore little relation to the game that now enjoys global appeal. To begin with, there were not yet universal rules that all clubs could agree upon and invariably inter-school matches were impossible to organise. One school might favour or allow handling of the ball, others tripping and hacking and there were often heated debates conducted through the letter pages of The Times on the respective merits of each style. It was in Cambridge that the first move towards establishing a fixed set of rules was undertaken, with 'The

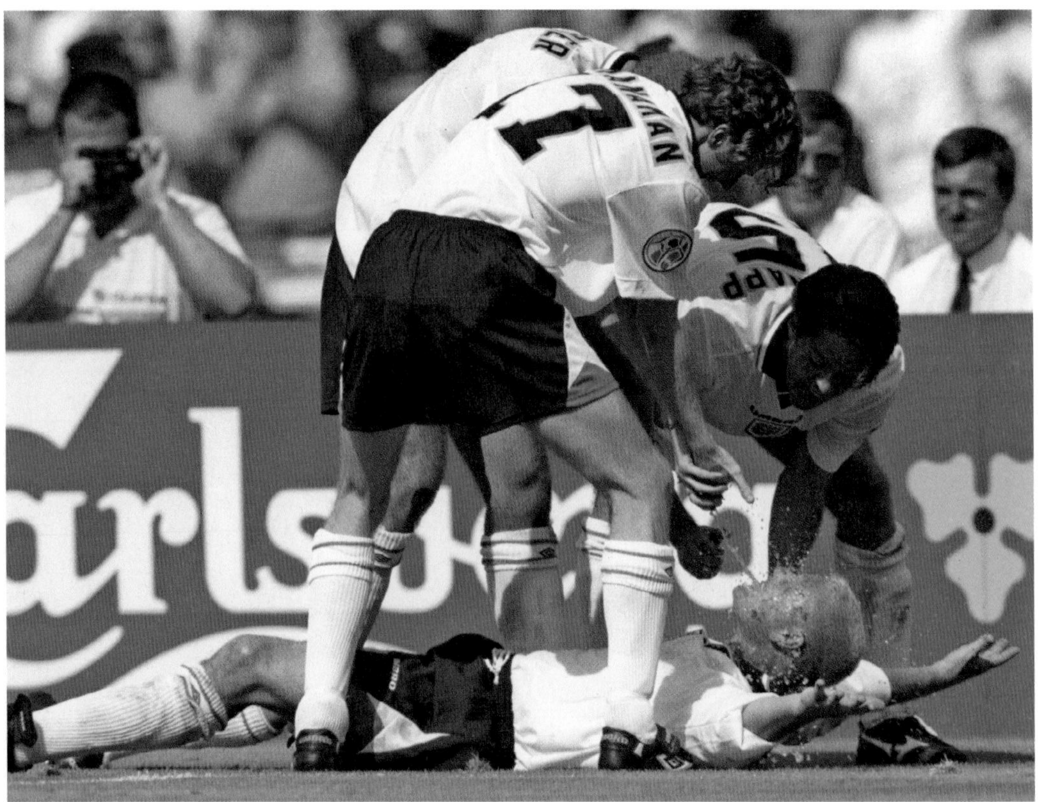

Cambridge Rules' being drawn up in 1846. Whilst no copy of these rules still exist, word of their content quickly spread across the country, with graduates from the university returning to their hometowns and forming clubs who eagerly adopted the new rules. In 1862 the rules were refined into a simple set of ten laws governing the game and the following year, in October, were amended once again. There was still no one body responsible for the rules or the game, a fact duly reported in The Field by journalist John D Cartwright, but already the captains and secretaries of some dozen or so clubs were making moves to address this situation. On the evening of Monday 26th October 1863 a body of gentlemen gathered at the Freemasons Tavern in Great Queen Street in London's Lincoln Inn Fields 'for the purpose of forming an Association with the object of establishing a definite code of rules for the regulation of the game.' Eleven of the twelve clubs present became founder members (the one refusal was from the Charterhouse club) and a further six meetings took place over the next month and a half to establish the laws of the game.

Despite the formation of the Football Association matters were still not all plain sailing, for some, like Blackheath, favoured a game similar in style to that which we now know as rugby, complete with tripping and hacking and an abundance of bodily contact. Blackheath duly withdrew from the FA and helped set up another body, the Rugby Union. For those who preferred kicking the ball rather than the man, the new set of rules was first put to the test in a friendly match on Saturday 19th December 1863 between Barnes and Richmond. The Field noted that the new set of rules was easy to follow for both sides, the match was played in good spirit and resulted in a goalless draw. The success of the rules led to most clubs in and around the London area adopting them as the definitive laws of the game and the popularity of football was on the up.

By 1865, however, the FA could still only boast one member outside of the capital city; Sheffield, which had also played an important part in the development of the game. It was the Sheffield club that suggested a match between themselves and London, an offer eagerly accepted by the FA as a way of expanding the popularity of the game. Thus, on 31st March 1866 the very first representative match was played at Battersea Park, with London winning one goal to nil thanks to a goal from the FA's own secretary, Ebenezer Cobb Morley.

The Football Association was still not a fully established body; it had no permanent home, holding its meetings at the aforementioned Freemasons Tavern and the offices of the Sportsman newspaper and Cricket Press as and when such meetings were required. The first permanent home was established in 1881 at 28 Paternoster Row, some fifty yards or so from St. Paul's Cathedral. It had no full time staff either, with the officers undertaking their duties on an honorary basis. By 1870 these officers had also changed; Mr. Morley had retired as secretary in 1866 and been replaced by Mr. R. W. Willis, who held the position for two years before handing over to Mr. R. G. Graham, who in turn retired after two years to be replaced by Mr. C. W. Alcock. Mr. Morley had become President of the FA in 1867, replacing the first incumbent Mr. A. Pember.

Charles William Alcock proved himself to be a more than capable secretary of the Association and it was he who suggested the introduction of the FA Challenge Cup in 1871, based in part on the inter-house knockout competitions he had participated in whilst at school at Harrow. He was also responsible for the launch of international football, organising a match at Kennington Oval on 5th March 1870, although the Scottish side featured all London-based players. In order to get Scottish players further interested in his proposal, he penned a letter to the Glasgow Herald that duly appeared on 3rd November 1870. It read:

ENGLAND VERSUS SCOTLAND

Sir,-Will you allow me a few lines in your paper to notify to Scottish players that a match under the above title will take place in London on Saturday, 19th inst., according to the rules of the Football Association? It is the object of the Committee to select the best elevens at their disposal in the two countries, and I cannot but think that the appearance of some of the more prominent celebrities of football on the Northern side of the Tweed would do much to disseminate a healthy feeling of good fellowship among the contestants and tend to promote to a still greater extent the extension of the game. In Scotland, once essentially the land of football, there still should be a spark left of the old fire, and I confidently appeal to Scotsmen to aid to their utmost the efforts of the committee to confer success on what London fondly hopes to found, an annual trial of skill between the champions of England and Scotland. Mr. A. F. Kinnaird, 2 Pall Mall East, London, will be glad to receive the names of any Scottish players who will take part against England in the match in question.

Although the letter was read by members of Glasgow's Queen's Park club with interest and they informed Robert Smith, a former player who had recently moved to London, the 'Scottish' side was still drawn up entirely from London-based players, with Kinnaird himself playing in the side that went down 1-0 to 'England'. Three other unofficial matches were also played over the next two years, each carefully noted by Queen's Park. In the absence of a Scottish Football Association, which was not formed until 1873, it was generally accepted that the Queen's Park club was the voice of Scottish football. They entered the very first FA Challenge Cup, were exempt until the semi final stage and held Wanderers to a draw. Lack of funds to travel back to London for the replay caused them to scratch from the competition, but in light of their exceptional performance against one of the leading English sides of the day, it prompted them to suggest to Alcock that they could organise a proper England and Scotland fixture.

Queen's Park offered to guarantee the expenses of the English side, a risky venture given that they had some months earlier been unable to travel to London themselves for an FA Cup semi final, but it was a risk their committee felt worth taking. They approached the West of Scotland Cricket Club, whose ground at Hamilton Crescent was the biggest enclosed sports field in Glasgow at the time, and made arrangements to hire the ground for 30th November 1872. A down payment fee of £10 was agreed, with a further £10 being payable should the 'gate' amount to over £50. In the event the day was a successful one; a crowd of over 4,000 (including, it was reported, a fair number of ladies) paid £102 19s 6d in admission money. Ground rent and match expenses accounted for £69 11s 6d with the balance of £38 8s being set aside by Queen's Park for the purposes of an 'International Fund'. The game itself ended in a goalless draw, but contemporary accounts report that the difference in styles, with Queen's Park preferring the passing game to the individual dribbling talents of their opponents, was much appreciated by the crowd. The differing styles owed much to the formations of the two sides; Scotland played in something close to the goalkeeper, two full-backs, three half-backs and five forwards that was to dominate British football for the next few decades, whilst England played with a goalkeeper, one full-back, one half-back and eight forwards! The Scottish side was also advantaged by the fact they were all members of the Queen's Park club and therefore were familiar with each other's style. England, for their part, drew their team from eight clubs, with Charles Clegg of Sheffield the only northern representative. Clegg was later to claim that he hated the whole affair, with the 'southern snobs' refusing to talk to him on the train journey up to Glasgow or pass to him out on the pitch!

England, it was noted, played in 'white jerseys with the arms of England as a badge on the left breast' whilst their Scottish counterparts donned blue jerseys, thus establishing their colours which have remained constant ever since. Notwithstanding the experience of Clegg, the match itself was a success and led to an agreement between the Football Association and Queen's Park (and subsequently the Scottish Football Association) that the match be played on an annual basis, with the two sides hosting the game in alternate years. Despite the historic nature of the match there are no photographs of either the two teams or the action. Although a photographer was approached, neither side would give any guarantee as to how many prints they would order and the photographer therefore reached the conclusion that it probably wasn't worth him turning up. If only he had known.

Ninety-nine years later I saw my first 'live' England match, a dour 0-0 draw against Wales at Wembley in 1971. Despite this inauspicious start, I was hooked enough to return to Wembley three days later, buy a ticket off a tout and take my place as England beat Scotland 3-1. As a Spurs fan there was the added bonus of seeing all three England goals being netted by Spurs players, with the Martins - Chivers and Peters - scoring two and one respectively to secure the victory and the Home International Championship into the bargain.

WARTIME

As a Spurs fan I have always had an interest in the careers of those who wore the white shirt of both Tottenham Hotspur and England, but as time progressed my interest extended beyond the white club shirt – I wondered about the careers of those who had represented the nation over the more than 100 years, even those who wore the red and white shirt of Arsenal! That interest eventually led me to putting together a book detailing the careers of all 1141 who had played for their country up to and including 1st March 2006, together with the 45 players whose only international appearances came in the wartime and Victory fixtures held in 1919 and between 1939 and 1946.

Whilst there is extensive coverage of international matches today, with every fan the length and breadth of the country being knowledgeable about the metatarsal problems encountered by the likes of David Beckham, Wayne Rooney and Michael Owen, coverage even twenty or so years ago was nowhere near as intensive. Go back even further, beyond two World Wars and into the Victorian era and there was sometimes virtually no interest whatsoever, as we have seen with the lack of a photographer at the 1872 meeting.

It is probably the Victorian era that interested me most, with players turning out for their country on one or two occasions before going on to become Reverends and Canons. About the closest we have come in the last fifty or so years is Peter Knowles, brother of England international Cyril, who was tipped to become an international player himself but gave the game up in order to become a Jehovah's Witness. Had he waited until after he had won a cap, then the story would have been even more interesting!

Players in that Victorian era almost all played for either Oxford or Cambridge Universities, where not only the brightest minds but seemingly the best sportsmen were also gathered. You will find numerous references to players earning a Blue in some sport or another whilst attending these two universities. This refers to a player being selected to play for Oxford against Cambridge and vice versa and being able to wear a Blue blazer in recognition of their selection.

These players were also all amateurs, with James Forrest of Blackburn Rovers believed to have been the first professional player to represent England. Certainly, the Scottish opposition objected enough to his professional status that he was forced to wear a different coloured jersey from his team-mates! At the time James was believed to have been earning £1 a week from Blackburn, considerably less than today's stars! Forrest's first cap was awarded in 1884 and he remained at Blackburn until 1895, when he left the club acrimoniously claiming they had asked him to revert back to amateur status in order to save the club paying his wages, although this was denied by the club. By then more and more professional players were being called up to represent England, although there was still seemingly room in the side for a number of amateurs, with former schoolteacher and journalist (when he wasn't playing for Arsenal) Bernard Joy being the last in 1936 against Belgium.

It was NL Jackson, founder of the amateur side The Corinthians, that first suggested the awarding of 'caps' in 1886 (players often wore them whilst playing in this era) and the first awarded were royal blue in colour with a rose on the front. Each player is given one cap per season, on to which is embroidered the initial letter of the country he has played against during that campaign. The caps are currently made by Toye, Kenning & Spencer and what follows are potted biographies of the 1141 players who have earned them by representing their country.

A

ABBOTT, Walter
A'COURT, Alan
ADAMS, Tony Alexander
ADCOCK, Hugh
ALCOCK, Charles William
ALDERSON, John Thomas
ALDRIDGE, Albert James
ALLEN, Albert
ALLEN, Anthony
ALLEN, Clive Darren
ALLEN, Henry
ALLEN, James Phillips
ALLEN, Ronald
ALSFORD, Walter John
AMOS, Reverend Andrew
ANDERSON, Rupert Darnley O.B.E.
ANDERSON, Stanley
ANDERSON, Vivian Alexander
ANDERTON, Darren Robert
ANGUS, John
ARMFIELD, James Christopher
ARMITAGE, George Henry
ARMSTRONG, David
ARMSTRONG, Kenneth
ARNOLD, Johnny
ARTHUR, John William Herbert
ASHCROFT, James
ASHMORE, George Samuel
ASHTON, Claude Thesiger
ASHURST, William
ASTALL, Gordon
ASTLE, Jeffrey
ASTON, John
ATHERSMITH, William Charles
ATYEO, Peter John Walter
AUSTIN, Samuel William

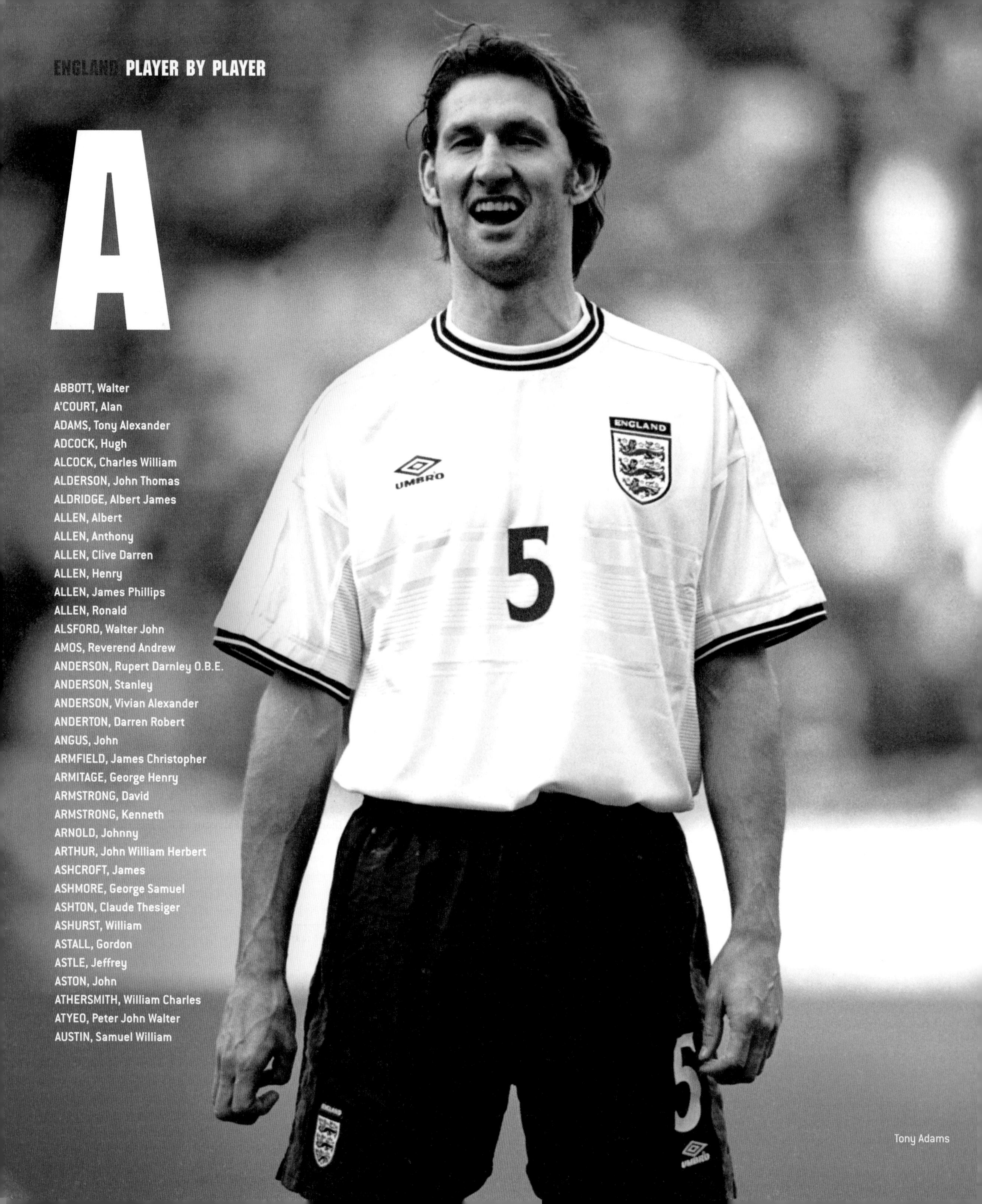

Tony Adams

Walter ABBOTT

Born: Birmingham, 7th December 1878
Died: 1st February 1941
Role: Inside-Forward
Career: Rosewood Victoria, Small Heath, Everton, Burnley, Birmingham City
Debut: v Wales (a) 3-3-1902
Appearances: 1

Walter began his career as an inside-forward for Small Heath and soon attracted the attention of Everton, who made numerous visits to see him in action, finally taking him to Goodison Park in June 1899. There he was converted to wing-half and went on to make nearly 300 appearances for the first team and got called up for England in 1902. Strangely, England used him as a centre-half, a position he had never played in before, but he did sufficiently well on the day even if he was not called upon again. He did get to represent the Football League on four occasions however, and also helped Everton reach two FA Cup Finals (in 1906 and 1907), collecting a winners' medal in 1906. In the summer of 1908 he was sold to Burnley and two years later returned to Small Heath, by now known as Birmingham, where his career was ended by injury during the 1910-11 season. He remained in Birmingham and worked in the motor industry in its formative years. His son, also named Walter, played for Grimsby Town immediately after the First World War.

Alan A'Court

Alan A'COURT

Born: Rainhill, Lancashire, 30th September 1934
Role: Left-Winger
Career: Liverpool, Tranmere Rovers, Norwich City
Debut: v Northern Ireland (a) 4-10-1958 (scored once)
Appearances: 5 (1 goal)

Despite coming from a family of Rugby League fans, Alan excelled at football as a youngster and represented Liverpool County at schoolboy level. After playing for Prescot Celtic and Prescot Cables he was snapped up by Liverpool in September 1952 and went on to make over 350 League appearances for the Anfield club, scoring 64 goals. During this time he helped Liverpool win the Second Division championship, represented the Football League on two occasions and collected seven caps for England at Under-23 level in addition to his full caps. He initially broke into the England team as a replacement for the injured Tom Finney. In October 1964 he was sold to local rivals Tranmere Rovers for £4,500 and made 50 appearances for the club before being released in the summer of 1966. He signed with Norwich City as a player-coach but did not play first team football for the Canaries, concentrating on the coaching side. He was made assistant manager of Chester in 1969, later serving Crewe Alexandra and Stoke City in a similar capacity before trying his luck overseas. After a spell as coach to Ndola United of Zambia he returned for a second spell with Crewe Alexandra.

Tony Alexander ADAMS

Born: Romford, Essex, 10th October 1966
Role: Defender
Career: Arsenal
Debut: v Spain (a) 18-2-1987
Appearances: 66 (5 goals) + 1 unofficial appearance

Tony joined Arsenal as an apprentice and signed professional forms in January 1984 having already made his League debut for the club the previous September. He quickly established himself as a pillar of the Arsenal defence and became club captain, guiding them to four League titles, three FA Cups, two League Cups and the European Cup Winners' Cup as well as runners-up in both the League Cup and European Cup Winners' Cup. After making his England debut in 1987 and playing in the 1988 European Championships in Germany he looked set to become a regular for many years, but a series of personal problems, culminating in a spell in prison for a drink-driving offence cost him his place in the side and he missed the squad for the 1990 World Cup Finals in Italy. He later admitted to being an alcoholic, an admission that set him on the road to recovery and the resumption of his international career. He was an integral part of the England side in the 1996 European Championship Finals held in England although he carried a knee injury throughout the tournament that was enough to keep him out of the Arsenal side until September 1996. He fully recovered however and reclaimed his place in the England side, going on to be one of England's best performers in the 1998 World Cup finals in France. He made over 400 League appearances for Arsenal, a model of consistency. In 1988 against Holland, Tony became the first player to score both for and against England, netting for England first and later turning past his own goalkeeper. Later the same year he may well have repeated the feat; he definitely scored against the USSR in the European Championship finals and also appeared to get the final touch to a low cross into the England penalty area that ended up in the net. He retired from playing at the end of the 2001-2002 season having helped Arsenal to a second double in four years. He returned to the game in November 2003, taking over as manager of Wycombe Wanderers but resigned at the end of the season.

Hugh ADCOCK

Born: Coalville, Leicestershire, 10th April 1903
Died: 16th October 1975
Role: Right-Winger
Career: Coalville Town, Loughborough Corinthians, Leicester City, Bristol Rovers, Folkestone
Debut: v France (a) 9-5-1929
Appearances: 5 (1 goal)

Hugh Adcock

After playing schoolboy football in his hometown of Coalville, Hugh signed as an amateur with Loughborough Corinthians in April 1921 and over the next two years impressed enough to be offered terms by Leicester City, signing as a professional in March 1923. He remained with the club for the next twelve years and proved himself to be one of the most consistent performers of all time, setting a record of 119 consecutive appearances in 1929. As well as helping Leicester City to the Second Division championship in 1925, Hugh was selected for the Football League and made his England breakthrough on the end of season tour of Europe in 1929. He was released by Leicester in 1935 and joined Bristol Rovers in July of that year, spending a season at the club before finishing his playing career with non-League Folkestone. Upon retiring as a player he became a publican in Sileby in Leicestershire before returning to Coalville where he worked as a maintenance engineer. He was a cousin of Birmingham City and England player Joe Bradford.

Charles William ALCOCK

Born: Sunderland, 2nd December 1842
Died: Brighton, 26th February 1907
Role: Forward
Career: Wanderers, Surrey
Debut: v Scotland (h) 6-3-1875
Appearances: 1 (1 goal) + 5 unofficial appearances

Charles William Alcock is probably the most important sports legislator of all time and whilst football has much for which to thank him, other sports also owe him considerable gratitude. Born in Sunderland and educated at Harrow he joined the FA committee in 1866 and was appointed secretary in 1870. Almost immediately he organised the first unofficial international match with Scotland, thus setting in motion the launch of a series of official matches in later years and in 1871 put forward the suggestion for the FA Cup, captaining Wanderers to victory in the very first final. He remained secretary of the FA until 1896, subsequently becoming vice-president the following year, a position he held until his death. He also played cricket for Essex, was secretary of the Surrey Cricket Club from 1872 until his death (which accounts for the use of Kennington Oval as

Tony Allen

the venue for the FA Cup Finals in the competition's early years), organised the first test match between England and Australia in 1880 and also served as chairman of the Richmond Athletic Association, was vice-president of the Surrey Golf Club and a Justice of the Peace. He also found time to launch the first Football Annual (1868) and two further magazines, Football and Cricket, the latter of which he was editor until 1905. This quite remarkable man contributed to The Sportsman and The Field and helped found the Referees' Association. He captained England in his only appearance for his country, a week before refereeing the FA Cup Final and also refereed the 1879 final. It is believed, however, that he selected himself on no fewer than five occasions, but only played the once (although he did play in all five unofficial matches in 1870 and 1871). According to press reports he was determined to ensure he made an impact; a report of his goal stated 'There it was breasted by the England captain, and he perniciously adhered to it until he had got it securely over the Scottish goal-line.'

John Thomas ALDERSON

Born: Crook, County Durham, 28th November 1891
Died: 17th February 1972
Role: Goalkeeper
Career: Crook Town, Shildon Athletic, Middlesbrough, Newcastle United, Crystal Palace, Pontypridd, Sheffield United, Exeter City
Debut: v France (a) 10-5-1923
Appearances: 1

Jack Alderson first impressed as an amateur with Crook Town and Shildon Athletic and signed amateur forms with Middlesbrough in the close season of 1912. Newcastle United paid £30 for his transfer in January 1913 and he made one appearance for the first team before the outbreak of the First World War brought a temporary halt to his career. At the end of hostilities he was sold to Crystal Palace for £50 in May 1919 and quickly developed into one of the best goalkeepers outside the top two divisions, helping Palace win the Third Division championship in 1921. He was especially talented as a penalty stopper, saving 11 out of 12 whilst with Palace, including two in one match against Bradford City. After five years with Palace he was surprisingly allowed to join non-League Pontypridd, but a year later returned to League action with Sheffield United, where he remained for four years. He then spent a season with both Exeter City and Torquay United before winding down his playing career with Crook Town. He owed his place in the England side to the withdrawal of Hubert Pearson from the squad. In all he made 354 post-War League appearances for his various clubs and became a farmer upon his retirement as a player.

Albert James ALDRIDGE

Born: Walsall, 13th April 1864
Died: May 1891
Role: Full-Back
Career: Walsall Swifts, West Bromwich Albion, Walsall Town Swifts, Aston Villa
Debut: v Ireland (a) 31-3-1888
Appearances: 2

Albert Aldridge joined Walsall Swifts in 1882 and proved a valuable acquisition by the club, not least for his ability to play on either flank with equal skill. In four years he had developed into one of the best full-backs in the game and prompted a transfer to West Bromwich Albion in 1886. At the end of his first season at the club he had helped them reach the FA Cup Final against Aston Villa at Kennington Oval, where they were beaten 2-0, Albion's second successive cup final defeat. In 1888 they made it third time lucky, beating Preston North End 2-1 at the same venue, with Aldridge being singled out for having a particularly good game against the lively Preston forward line. A week later Albert collected his first cap for England, helping them to a 5-1 win over Ireland in Belfast. In the summer he was surprisingly allowed to return to Walsall, signing for the newly formed Walsall Town Swifts (in effect the amalgamation of two clubs, Walsall Town and Walsall Swifts) and thus missed out on playing in the Football League's inaugural season. His international career suffered little for the move, for he earned a second England cap in March 1889 as England beat Ireland 6-1 and his performance was such that Aston Villa signed him the following month. Sadly, Albert was to enjoy only one season of League football, for at the end of the 1888-90 season he was released by Villa owing to illness and died the following year.

Albert ALLEN

Born: Aston, Birmingham, April 1867
Died: 13th October 1899
Role: Winger
Career: Aston Villa
Debut: v Ireland (a) 31-3-1888
Appearances: 1 (3 goals)

Albert Allen scored a hat-trick for England against Ireland on what was his only appearance for his country, England going on to win 5-1 in Belfast. He then played in Villa's first-ever League match and became the first Villa player to score a League hat-trick for the club, a feat achieved against Notts County in the 9-1 win in September 1888. He was top scorer at the end of the season, netting 18 goals in 21 appearances, having formed an extremely good understanding with Dennis Hodgetts, and the following season was joint top goalscorer and seemingly on his way to becoming a legend for both club and country, but sadly illness forced him to retire from the game at the age of just 24 and, although he was able to work, he died in October 1899 at just 32 years of age. Albert is one of five players to have netted a hat-trick on their one and only appearance for England, the others being Frank Bradshaw, Walter Gilliat, John Veitch and Jack Yates.

Anthony ALLEN

Born: Stoke-on-Trent, 27th November 1939
Role: Left-Back
Career: Stoke City, Bury, Hellenic (South Africa), Stafford Rangers
Debut: v Wales (a) 17-10-1959
Appearances: 3

After playing for local schools and the boys' brigade, Tony Allen was signed by Stoke City as an amateur, turning professional in November 1956. Having earned England honours at Youth and Under-23 level (he went on to win seven caps at this level) he collected his first full cap before he had turned 20. Selection at such a relatively young age seemed to affect his later career, and after winning only three caps for England he was effectively discarded at international level. He did, however, represent the Football League on two occasions and helped Stoke City to the

Clive Allen

Second Division championship in 1963 and to the final of the League Cup the following year. He remained with Stoke until 1970 when he was sold to Bury for a fee of £10,000 and switched to half-back but spent only a year at Gigg Lane before going off to South Africa to play for Hellenic. He returned to England in October 1973 and finished his playing career with non-League Stafford Rangers. When his playing career came to an end he became a publican in the Stoke area.

Clive Darren ALLEN

Born: Stepney, London, 20th May 1961
Role: Striker
Career: Queens Park Rangers, Arsenal, Crystal Palace, Queens Park Rangers, Tottenham Hotspur, Bordeaux (France), Manchester City, Chelsea, West Ham United, Millwall, Carlisle United
Debut: v Brazil (a) (substitute) 10-6-84
Appearances: 5

The son of former Spurs player Les Allen, Clive began his career with Queens Park Rangers despite having trained with Spurs as a schoolboy. He made an immediate impact as a striker with Rangers and in July 1980 was transferred to Arsenal for a fee of £1,250,000. Less than two months later and having made only three appearances in friendlies, Clive was on the move again, this time in a swap deal with Kenny Sansom of Crystal Palace. With the Palace manager Terry Venables departing two months later Clive found it difficult to settle at Selhurst Park and moved back to Loftus Road and Queens Park Rangers in 1981. In 1982 he was part of the QPR team that reached the FA Cup final against Spurs, although it was a match Clive would like to forget; injured after only two minutes he hobbled on for a further eight minutes until substituted and was forced to miss the replay. He continued to score at a prolific rate and was awarded his first England cap in 1984 shortly before a £700,000 move took him to White Hart Lane. He was particularly lethal when playing as a lone striker in front of a five-man midfield and rattled in an unprecedented 49 goals in the 1986-87 season. It was always going to be impossible for Clive to register similar goalscoring exploits and in March 1988 he was on his way once again, this time a £900,000 fee taking him to Bordeaux. A year later he returned home to join Manchester City, remaining 18 months before he joined another of his father's former clubs Chelsea. He later played for West Ham United, Millwall and Carlisle United and had a brief spell playing American football as a kicker for the London Monarchs before retiring to become a television pundit, also joining the coaching staff at Spurs. Clive holds the record for having scored most goals in the League Cup in a single season, with a tally of 12 in 1986-87.

Henry ALLEN

Born: Walsall, 19th January 1866
Died: Wolverhampton, 23rd February 1895
Role: Half-Back
Career: Walsall Town Swifts, Wolverhampton Wanderers
Debut: v Wales (h) 4-2-1888
Appearances: 5

Harry Allen spent his brief football career playing in the Black Country, signing for Wolves in 1886 from Walsall Swifts. Whilst with Wolves he became acknowledged as being an excellent header of the ball and able to set up a number of attacks from his half-back position, collecting his first cap for England in 1888 and the following year helping Wolves reach the FA Cup Final where they were beaten by a Preston side completing the very first double of FA Cup and Football League. Harry received compensation in 1893 when Wolves beat Everton at Fallowfield, scoring the only goal of the game on the hour mark. That proved to be the pinnacle of his career, for the following year after 153 League appearances for Wolves he was forced to retire and took jobs as a licensee and a coal merchant before his early death. Although Harry never scored for England, he may well have scored against them in the 1889 clash with Scotland, for some reports state that James Oswald's shot was pushed out by Billy Moon and bounced back into the goal off Harry Allen.

James Phillips ALLEN

Born: Poole, 16th October 1909
Died: February 1995
Role: Centre-Half
Career: Poole Central, Poole Town, Portsmouth, Aston Villa
Debut: v Northern Ireland (a) 14-10-1933
Appearances: 2

Jimmy Allen made his name with Portsmouth, helping them to the FA Cup Final in 1934 where they were beaten 2-1 by Manchester City and earned two caps for England. In the summer of 1934 a then record fee of £10,775 (Portsmouth used the money to build a new stand which is still known as the Jimmy Allen Stand) took him to Villa Park and Aston Villa and although he was unable to break back into the national side, he was a regular for his club for the next two seasons. Although he was forced to sit out much of the 1936-37 season owing to injury, he returned the following season to help Villa win promotion back into the First Division. He made 160 appearances for the Villa first team before the outbreak of the Second World War brought his professional career effectively to an end, although he guested for Birmingham City, Fulham and Portsmouth during the hostilities before retiring in 1944. He then had a brief spell working for a Birmingham firm as a welfare officer before taking over as manager of Colchester United, finally finishing with football for good in 1953 and becoming a publican in Southsea. His England career came to an end following his second appearance, against the Welsh in 1933, for he was taken off injured during the game and never selected again.

Jimmy Allen

Ronnie Allen

Ronald ALLEN

Born: Fenton, Staffordshire, 15th January 1929
Died: 9th June 2001
Role: Forward
Career: Port Vale, West Bromwich Albion, Crystal Palace
Debut: v Switzerland (a) 28-5-1952
Appearances: 5 (2 goals)

Ronnie Allen played both rugby and football at school, representing Hanley High at both codes but concentrating on the Association game when he left. After playing for the Bucknall Boys Brigade and Wellington Scouts he signed as an amateur with Port Vale in March 1944, turning professional in January 1946. He made over 100 League appearances before West Bromwich Albion paid £15,000 to take him to the Hawthorns in March 1950. Whilst with the club he won an FA Cup winners' medal in 1954 and scored over 200 League goals in 415 appearances, represented the Football League on one occasion and won two England B caps as well as his full tally of five full appearances. In May 1961 he was allowed to join Crystal Palace, subsequently becoming player-coach in 1964. He returned to the Midlands in 1965 as coach at Wolverhampton Wanderers, becoming caretaker manager in January 1966 following the departure of Andy Beattie, the appointment becoming permanent in July the same year. He remained in charge at Molineux for two years before jetting off to Spain to try his luck at Atletico Bilbao in February 1969. He left the post in November 1971, returned to the Iberian peninsular in April 1972 to take over at Sporting Lisbon and landed the Walsall job in July 1973. He was in charge at Walsall less than six months and subsequently became a consultant at West Bromwich Albion. He had two spells in charge at the Hawthorns, taking over when Johnny Giles and then Ron Atkinson left for pastures new. Ronnie also had a spell as manager of the Saudi Arabian national side.

Wally Alsford (right)

Walter John ALSFORD

Born: Edmonton, London, 6th November 1911
Died: Bedford, 3rd June 1968
Role: Left-Half
Career: Northfleet, Tottenham Hotspur, Nottingham Forest
Debut: v Scotland (a) 6-4-1935
Appearances: 1

A graduate of the Spurs nursery at Northfleet, Wally made his debut in the London FA Charity Cup tie against Chelsea in 1930, although his League debut did not come until two months later, at Reading on December 27th. Although not a regular at any time during the six years he spent with Spurs, he did make a total of 81 League appearances, including being almost a regular in the second half of the 1934-35 season which culminated in Spurs being relegated from the First Division, and winning an England cap in April 1935 against Scotland, effectively replacing the unavailable Wilf Copping and John Bray. In January 1937 Spurs transferred the half-back to Nottingham Forest where, twelve months later, he was found to be suffering from osteomyelitis and told his career was at an end. He retired in May 1938 but made a number of guest appearances for Forest and other clubs during the early months of the Second World War. At the end of the war he became a publican.

Reverend Andrew AMOS

Born: Southwark, London, 20th September 1863
Died: Rotherhithe, London, 2nd October 1931
Role: Half-Back
Career: Cambridge University, Old Carthusians, Hitchin Town, Corinthians, Hertfordshire
Debut: v Scotland (h) 21-3-1885
Appearances: 2 (1 goal)

After being educated at Charterhouse School, for whose school team he played in 1882, he attended Cambridge University and was awarded his Blue in 1884. He then played for Old Carthusians and joined Corinthians in 1885, going on to make 45 appearances for the famous amateur club, a remarkable figure given that they never played in competitions. For many years his contribution to England was believed to be restricted to just two appearances, but contemporary reports suggest that he scored England's second goal against Wales in the 3-1 win in 1886. Modern record books have therefore been amended to include his goalscoring exploits. He was ordained in 1887 and ministered in London from 1889 until 1922, when he became Rector of Rotherhithe until his death in 1931. He also served as a councillor on the Bermondsey Borough Council and was later elected an alderman.

Rupert Darnley ANDERSON O.B.E.

Born: Liverpool 29th April 1859
Died: 23rd December 1944
Role: Goalkeeper
Career: Old Etonians
Debut: v Wales (h) 18-1-1879
Appearances: 1

Although Rupert's only cap for England saw him playing in goal, he was better known as a forward player, having represented Eton College, Cambridge University and Old Etonians in this position. He was only selected for England because the original player selected, the Reverend W. Blackmore, pulled out shortly before the game. Neither Rupert nor Blackmore were ever selected for England again, whilst Rupert's international career lasted barely an hour; a snowbound pitch forcing the game to be terminated early. He was injured soon after his only appearance for England and was thus forced to sit out the 1879 FA Cup Final as Old Etonians beat Clapham Rovers. After his playing career ended he emigrated to America, working as an orange planter in Florida before returning home to England to live in Staffordshire and then Surrey. During the First World War he was active with both the Territorial Army and newly-formed Air Force, for which he was awarded the OBE.

Stanley ANDERSON

Born: Horden, County Durham, 27th February 1934
Role: Wing-Half
Career: Horden Colliery Welfare, Sunderland, Newcastle United, Middlesbrough
Debut: v Austria (h) 4-4-1962
Appearances: 2

Stan Anderson had played schools football in Durham and for Horden Colliery Welfare before being offered amateur forms with Sunderland in June 1949. Although he signed as a professional in February 1951 he continued his apprenticeship as a plumber until he was 21, just in case his football career didn't pan out. He need not have worried, for he went on to make over 400 appearances for Sunderland during his twelve years with the club before switching to Newcastle United in a £19,000 move in November 1963. He spent two years at St. James's Park before going on to play for the third of the big north east clubs, signing for Middlesbrough in November 1965 for £11,500 and combining his playing career with coaching. He retired as a player in April 1966 and took over as manager, remaining in charge until January 1973. He then spent a spell in Greece as manager of AEK Athens before returning to England to become coach at Queens Park Rangers. Stan was briefly caretaker manager at Loftus Road for one month and then went on to manage Doncaster Rovers for three years. He joined Bolton

Stan Anderson

Wanderers as assistant to Ian Greaves in November 1978 and stepped up to the position of manager in February 1980, holding the post until May 1981. In addition to his two full caps for England, Stan also represented his country at B level and won four caps for the Under-23 side.

Vivian Alexander ANDERSON

Born: Nottingham, 29th August 1956
Role: Full-Back
Career: Nottingham Forest, Arsenal, Manchester United, Sheffield Wednesday, Barnsley, Middlesbrough
Debut: v Czechoslovakia (h) 29-11-1978
Appearances: 30 (2 goals)

Viv began his professional career with Nottingham Forest in 1974 and helped the club to the First Division title in 1978, the European Cup in 1979 and 1980 and League Cup honours in 1979 and 1980. By then he had earned the first of his 30 caps for England, becoming the first black player to represent the country after more than one hundred years of fixtures. He then signed with Arsenal in 1984 where he won a further League Cup winners' medal and was signed by Manchester United in July 1987 for £250,000. Although he failed to add to his medal tally he was a more than capable

Viv Anderson

squad member and was given a free transfer in January 1991 upon which he joined Sheffield Wednesday. After a spell in charge as player-manager at Barnsley he linked up with Bryan Robson at Middlesbrough as assistant manager.

Darren Anderton

Darren Robert ANDERTON

Born: Southampton, 3rd March 1972
Role: Midfield
Career: Portsmouth, Tottenham Hotspur, Birmingham City, Wolverhampton Wanderers
Debut: v Denmark (h) 9-3-1994
Appearances: 30 (7 goals) + 1 unofficial appearance

Darren joined Portsmouth as a trainee in 1990 and quickly graduated through the ranks to become a professional. He was an integral part of the side that reached the FA Cup semi finals in 1992, putting in some outstanding performances that soon alerted the bigger clubs to his potential, and in June 1992 he was signed by Spurs for a fee of £1.75 million. Although he took a while to settle in at the club, when he found his form and consistency England honours beckoned, finally earning him selection for the full side after collecting 12 caps at Under-21 level. He faced a race against time in order to be fit for the European Championships in 1996 but was one of the star England performers during the tournament. The next two seasons were also wrecked by injury but once again he recovered in time for the 1998 World Cup Finals in France and confounded his critics with another series of stunning performances, including scoring England's opening goal in the match against Colombia. In 1999 he won his first major domestic medal, helping Spurs win the Worthington Cup. Injuries continued to blight his career and at the end of the 2003-04 season he was given a free transfer by Spurs, subsequently signing with Birmingham City on a 'pay as you play' basis in order to prove his fitness. At the end of the 2004-05 season he moved to Wolverhampton Wanderers on a similar deal.

John ANGUS

Born: Amble, Northumberland, 2nd September 1938
Role: Right-Back
Career: Burnley
Debut: v Austria (a) 27-5-1961
Appearances: 1

John played for Amble Boys' Club before coming to the attention of Burnley, signing amateur forms in 1954 and turning professional in September 1955. He remained with the club, his only professional club, for the next seventeen years. He represented England at Youth and Under-23 level, collecting seven caps at the latter level, and the Football League on one occasion. He was an integral part of the fine Burnley side of the early 1960s, a side that won the League title in 1960 and were runners-up in both the League and FA Cup in 1962, to Ipswich and Spurs respectively and therefore missed out on a possible double. Despite such fine club form, John was unfortunate that Ray Wilson had effectively made the right-back position his own for England, retaining his place for the 1966 World Cup finals. John's sole appearance, therefore, came when Ray was unavailable. Tendon trouble forced John to retire in May 1972 after 438 League appearances for the Turf Moor club and having scored three goals. His uncle, also named John Angus, played for Exeter City between 1930 and 1948 - the Angus family was obviously loyal to their respective clubs.

John Angus

Jimmy Armfield

James Christopher ARMFIELD O.B.E.

Born: Denton, Manchester, 21st September 1935
Role: Right-Back
Career: Blackpool
Debut: v Brazil (a) 13-5-1959
Appearances: 43

Jimmy had played for Blackpool youth clubs St. Peter's and Highfield (and also excelled at rugby, playing for Lancashire Schools) before being offered amateur forms with Blackpool in 1951, subsequently turning professional in September 1954. He remained with the club for the next seventeen years, making 568 League appearances, representing the Football League on 12 occasions, collected nine Under-23 caps and played for the full England side on 43 occasions. He was unfortunate that his time at Blackpool coincided with the club's fluctuating fortunes, moving up and down between the First and Second Divisions without every seriously threatening for the game's major honours, especially after the departure of Stanley Matthews. In February 1971 Jimmy was appointed player-coach at Bloomfield Road, although three months later he decided to retire from playing and accept the position of manager at Bolton Wanderers. He remained in the post for just over three years before taking over at Elland Road, bringing some stability to Leeds United after the brief and turbulent reign of Brian Clough. He guided Leeds to the final of the European Cup in 1975, although debatable refereeing decisions and rioting by Leeds supporters ruined what should have been a great night. He left Leeds in July 1978 and although he had a number of other offers within the game (including, it was said, the position of England manager) he concentrated on a career in broadcasting. He has, however, served the FA in a consultancy capacity and was responsible for the selection of Terry Venables as England's manager in succession to Graham Taylor.

George Henry ARMITAGE

Born: Stoke Newington, London, 17th January 1898
Died: 28th August 1936
Role: Centre-Half
Career: Wimbledon, Charlton Athletic, Leyton
Debut: v Northern Ireland (a) 24-10-1925
Appearances: 1

George played for Hackney schools in 1912 before joining St. Saviour's FC, subsequently signing as an amateur with Wimbledon. He made the step up to League level with Charlton in March 1924 and spent seven years with the club, helping them win the Third Division South championship in 1929. He was, therefore, one of the first Third Division players to gain full England recognition, a feat achieved in 1925. He also represented England at amateur level on five occasions and toured with the FA side in South Africa in 1929, playing twice on the tour. He moved on to Leyton in January 1931 where he finished his playing career, having also represented Surrey and the London FA during his career.

David ARMSTRONG

Born: Durham, 26th December 1954
Role: Midfield
Career: Middlesbrough, Southampton, Bournemouth
Debut: v Australia (a) 31-5-1980
Appearances: 3

David joined Middlesbrough as an apprentice straight from school, signing in July 1970 and being upgraded to the professional ranks in January 1972. He spent nine years at Ayresome Park and was a remarkably consistent performer for the club, making a record run of 356 consecutive appearances for Middlesbrough. Having already represented England at Under-23 and B level he broke into the full squad during the tour to Australia in 1980. He was transferred to Southampton for £600,000 in August 1981, a then record fee for the south coast club and spent six years at The Dell. In July 1987 he was transferred to Bournemouth where he finished his playing career.

David Armstrong

Ken Armstrong

Kenneth ARMSTRONG

Born: Bradford, 3rd June 1924
Died: New Zealand, 13th June 1984
Role: Right-Half
Career: Bradford Rovers, Chelsea, Easter Union (New Zealand), North Shore United (New Zealand), Gisborne (New Zealand)
Debut: v Scotland (h) 2-4-1955
Appearances: 1

Ken Armstrong was spotted by Chelsea whilst playing alternately for Bradford Rovers and the Army and was signed to professional forms in December 1946. A solid and reliable right-half, he went on to amass a new record of appearances for Chelsea, turning out in 362 League games and 39 appearances in the FA Cup after making his debut against Blackpool in August 1947. He also scored 25 League goals and five in the FA Cup, collecting a League championship medal in 1954-55. He might have won more caps for England but for a series of injuries that restricted his availability for the national side. At the end of his Stamford Bridge career he emigrated to New Zealand, turning out for a number of local sides and earning 13 caps for the New Zealand national side before retiring to concentrate on coaching. He died in New Zealand in 1984. His son Ron also represented New Zealand, collecting 27 caps.

John ARNOLD

Born: Cowley, Oxfordshire, 30th November 1907
Died: 3rd April 1984
Role: Left-Winger
Career: Oxford City, Southampton, Fulham
Debut: v Scotland (a) 1-4-1933
Appearances: 1

John played cricket and football whilst at school in Oxford and excelled at both sports. He signed with Oxford City to play football and with Oxfordshire for cricket, but as Oxfordshire was one of the minor counties arranged a transfer to Southampton in July 1928 in order that he might play cricket for Hampshire. He remained associated with Hampshire County Cricket Club between 1929 and 1950 when he was forced to retire on health grounds. He appeared in one Test Match, against New Zealand at Lord's in 1931 (although he was out for a duck!) and in February 1933 joined Fulham, two months before making his one and only appearance for England at football. From 1961 he was a first class umpire at cricket.

John William Herbert ARTHUR

Born: Blackburn, 14th February 1863
Died: 27th November 1930
Role: Goalkeeper
Career: Lower Bank Academy Blackburn, King's Own Blackburn, Blackburn Rovers, Southport Central
Debut: v Ireland (h) 28-2-1885
Appearances: 7

Herbie Arthur signed with Blackburn Rovers in 1880 after playing for minor sides in the area. He was originally a right-half and only changed position to goalkeeper when volunteering for the Rovers reserve side when they were short. He proved to be so good that he soon displaced the first team goalkeeper and helped Rovers win the FA Cup in three consecutive seasons; 1884, 1885 and 1886. He was then able to transfer this reliability to the international stage, for England did not lose any of the seven matches in which he kept goal. He remained with Rovers until 1890, having received a benefit from the club (although he was supposedly an amateur throughout his career!), and signed for Southport Central where he finished his career. Herbie was a mill furnisher and commercial traveller by occupation.

James ASHCROFT

Born: Liverpool, 12th September 1878
Died: 9th April 1943
Role: Goalkeeper
Career: Gravesend United, Woolwich Arsenal, Blackburn Rovers, Tranmere Rovers
Debut: v Ireland (a) 17-2-1906
Appearances: 3

Jimmy Ashcroft

John Arnold

After playing for Garston Copper Works in Liverpool, Jimmy Ashcroft came south to play for Gravesend United in 1899. Less than a year later he was snapped up by Woolwich Arsenal and went on to give the club eight years' excellent service. In 1906, at a time when he was widely regarded as the best goalkeeper in the country, he became the first Arsenal player to earn England recognition and also went on to represent the Football League twice. He was transferred to Blackburn Rovers in May 1908 and was a regular for the Ewood Park club for three years until ill health restricted his first team opportunities. Indeed, he was forced to sit out as Rovers won the League title in 1911-12, the closest he came to club honours during his career. In 1913 he was allowed to sign for Tranmere Rovers where he finished his career.

George Samuel ASHMORE

Born: Plymouth, 5th May 1898
Died: 19th May 1973
Role: Goalkeeper
Career: Nineveh Wesley, West Bromwich Albion, Chesterfield
Debut: v Belgium (a) 24-5-1926
Appearances: 1

George represented South Devon Schools as a youngster before moving with his family to the Midlands and was playing for Ninevah Wesley in the Handsworth League when he was spotted by West Bromwich Albion. He signed for Albion in November 1919 and soon replaced Hubert Pearson as the first choice goalkeeper at the Hawthorns. He went on to make 268 appearances for the first team during his twelve years at the club before being replaced by Harry Pearson, Hubert's son! George left to join Chesterfield in October 1931 and was a regular for two seasons before announcing his retirement in 1933.

Claude Thesiger ASHTON

Born: Calcutta, India, 19th February 1901
Died: 31st October 1942 (Killed on active service)
Role: Centre-Forward
Career: Cambridge University, Corinthians, Old Wykehamists
Debut: v Northern Ireland (a) 24-10-1925
Appearances: 1

Claude was born in India but educated at Winchester College, playing for and later captaining the college football side. He then went on to Cambridge University and earned his Blue at hockey, cricket and football, although he was absent from the 1923 clash with Oxford University. Upon graduating he combined a football career with Corinthians and Old Wykehamists with playing cricket for Essex CCC, representing the county between 1921 and 1938. He was made captain for his only appearance for the full England side, the last player to have done so, although he did not have a particularly memorable game, with contemporary reports stating 'he failed in giving cohesion to his line and his shooting was weak' in the goalless draw with Northern Ireland. It may well have been that centre-forward was not his best position, for although he was a good tackler and dribbler, he was weak in the air. He had better luck as an amateur international, however, earning 12 caps for his country. He retired from football in 1933 and then assisted the Beckenham hockey club and even managed to make the England trials at this sport. A chartered accountant by profession he later worked in the Stock Exchange, joining up with the RAF at the outbreak of the Second World War. He lost his life in 1942 when the plane he was piloting crashed at Caernavon in Wales.

William ASHURST

Born: Willington, County Durham, 4th May 1894
Died: 26th January 1947
Role: Right-Back
Career: Durham City, Leeds City, Lincoln City, Notts County, West Bromwich Albion, Newark Town
Debut: v Sweden (a) 21-5-1923
Appearances: 5 + 1 unofficial appearance

After starring for Willington Schools and Durham City, Bill Ashurst was signed by Leeds City in the close season of 1919, although the subsequent enforced closure of the club meant he was sold to Lincoln City for £500 in October of the same year. He had less than a year at Sincil Bank before Notts County paid £1,000 to take him to Meadow Lane in June 1920. He developed into a fine right-back whilst with

Bill Ashurst

County, earning selection for the Football League and helping his club win the Second Division title in 1923, the same year he won his first cap for England. By the time he left for West Bromwich Albion in November 1926 he had won five caps for England and his value had escalated to £3,100. Although he was not able to return to the national side he did give Albion good service during his two years with the club, leaving for Newark Town in August 1928 and retiring a year later. After his playing career came to an end he joined his father and three brothers as a miner, although the family also ran a small firm.

Gordon Astall

Gordon ASTALL

Born: Horwich, Lancashire, 22nd September 1927
Role: Right-Winger
Career: Plymouth Argyle, Birmingham City, Torquay United
Debut: v Finland (a) 20-5-1956 (scored once)
Appearances: 2 (1 goal)

Gordon had played schools football in Horwich and had an unsuccessful trial with Bolton Wanderers before playing army football with the Royal Marines in Plymouth. Here he came to the attention of Plymouth Argyle, signing as an amateur in 1947 and being upgraded to the professional ranks following his demobilisation in November the same year. He helped Plymouth to the Third Division South championship in 1952 before a £14,000 move to Birmingham City in October 1953. He collected a second championship medal, this time from the Second Division in 1955 and the following year was at Wembley with City in the FA Cup, picking up a runners-up medal as Manchester City won 3-1. That same year he accompanied England for their summer tour, ostensibly because Stanley Matthews was unavailable, and won his two caps for England in the process. He remained with Birmingham City until May 1961 when he was transferred to Torquay United, finishing his career with the club two years later. Upon retiring he worked in the insurance industry as well as coaching minor League sides in Devonshire.

Jeffrey ASTLE

Born: Eastwood, Nottinghamshire, 13th May 1942
Died: 19th January 2002
Role: Centre-Forward
Career: Notts County, West Bromwich Albion
Debut: v Wales (h) 7-5-1969
Appearances: 5 + 1 unofficial appearance (2 goals)

Jeff signed with Notts County as an amateur player in 1958 and had a spell playing for the works side of John Player before signing professional forms with County in October 1959. He went on to make over 100 League appearances for the club, netting 32 goals and then was sold to West Bromwich Albion for £25,000 in September 1964. He proved an immediate success at the Hawthorns, helping them win the League Cup in 1966, reach the final of the same competition in 1967, win the FA Cup in 1968 and finish runners-up again in the League Cup in 1970. He represented the Football League on two occasions and having broken into the England side in 1969 was taken to the World Cup in Mexico the following year, having finished the season as top goalscorer in the First Division. It was for a miss, against Brazil, that he is perhaps best remembered, for he shot wide when it appeared easier to score and England lost the match, with Jeff making his last appearance for England in the final group match against Czechoslovakia. He remained with West Bromwich until July 1974 when he joined Dunstable Town and he finished his career in the non-League game, turning out for Weymouth, Atherstone Town and Hillingdon Borough before retiring in 1977.

Jeff Astle

John Aston (2nd left)

John ASTON

Born: Manchester, 3rd September 1921
Died: 31st July 2003
Role: Right-Back, Left-Back
Career: Clayton Methodists, Manchester United
Debut: v Denmark (a) 26-9-1948
Appearances: 17

After turning out for Clayton Methodists and Mujacs John signed with Manchester United as an amateur in May 1939, although he was not able to turn professional until August 1946. Thereafter he made nearly 300 appearances for the first team and appeared in both the 1948 FA Cup and 1952 championship winning teams as well as being called to represent the Football League twice. Initially an inside-forward he achieved his greatest success as a full-back, but was able to return to an inside-forward position during the 1950-51, when injuries decimated the United side, and scored 16 goals during the season. After making his last appearance for the club in April 1954 he retired

Charlie Athersmith

from playing in June 1955 on health grounds and promptly became junior coach, later serving the club as chief scout from 1970 until 1972. John also won one cap with the England B team and represented the Football League on two occasions. His son John junior also played for United, appearing in their 1968 European Cup success.

William Charles ATHERSMITH

Born: Bloxwich, Staffordshire, 10th May 1872
Died: 18th September 1910
Role: Right-Winger
Career: Bloxwich Strollers, Unity Gas Depot, Aston Villa, Small Heath, Grimsby Town
Debut: v Ireland (a) 5-3-1892
Appearances: 12 (3 goals)

Charlie Athersmith joined Aston Villa in 1891, joining the club a month before John Devey. The pair linked up and formed a devastating right-wing partnership for Villa, helping the club win five League titles and two FA Cups, including the coveted double in 1897. In addition to his twelve international caps for England, Charlie also represented the Football League on nine occasions. His best season was undoubtedly 1896-97 which saw him collect every award then available; winners' medals in both the League and FA Cup and selection for England in all three international matches that season, against Scotland, Ireland and Wales. The following season it was claimed he played in one match for Villa whilst carrying an umbrella, thoughtfully handed to him by a spectator in order to shield him from the rain! He remained at Villa Park until 1901 and after 308 appearances in the claret and blue. He joined fellow Birmingham club Small Heath (the forerunners of Birmingham City) and made over 100 appearances for them before finishing his career with Grimsby Town. At the end of his playing career in 1907 he became a trainer at Grimsby.

Peter John Walter ATYEO

Born: Dilton Marsh, Wiltshire, 7th February 1932
Died: 9th June 1993
Role: Inside-Right, Centre-Forward
Career: Westbury United, Portsmouth, Bristol City
Debut: v Spain (h) 30-11-1955 (scored once)
Appearances: 6 (5 goals)

John Atyeo was a centre-forward in the old style and became one of the few players from the lower divisions to represent England. He played schools and junior football before signing as an amateur with Portsmouth in 1950, although he made only two appearances for the League side and decided to move on in search of more regular football. He therefore signed as a professional with Bristol City in June 1951 and remained with the club for the next fifteen years. During that time he set most of City's individual records, including most League appearances (597) and most League goals (315), a remarkable return. He represented England at Youth, Under-23 and B level as well as his six full caps and also made the Football League side on two occasions. His only club honour came in 1955 when he helped City win the Third Division South championship. John retired from playing in 1966 and later became a teacher.

Samuel William AUSTIN

Born: Arnold, Nottinghamshire, 29th April 1900
Died: 2nd April 1979
Role: Right-Winger
Career: Arnold United, Arnold St. Mary's, Norwich City, Manchester City – Chesterfield – Kidderminster Harriers
Debut: v Northern Ireland (a) 24-10-1925
Appearances: 1

Sam had originally failed a trial with Sheffield United and seemed lost to the professional game until taken on by Norwich City in October 1920. At The Nest (Norwich's home until 1935) he developed into one of the best wingers outside the top divisions and was also able to weigh in with vital goals of his own. In May 1924 therefore, Manchester City paid £2,000 to take him to Maine Road and within a year he had earned England recognition. Whilst with City he helped the club to the Second Division title in 1928 and the FA Cup Final in 1926, where they were beaten by Bolton Wanderers. Sam remained with City until December 1931 when he signed for Chesterfield. He played for the club until the close season of 1933 when he joined Kidderminster Harriers, his last club.

John Atyeo

BACH, Philip
BACHE, Joseph William
BADDELEY, Thomas
BAGSHAW, John James
BAILEY, Gary Richard
BAILEY, Horace Peter
BAILEY, Michael Alfred
BAILEY, Norman Coles
BAILY, Edward Francis
BAIN, John
BAKER, Alfred
BAKER, Benjamin Howard
BAKER, Joseph Henry
BALL, Alan James
BALL, John
BALL, Michael J
BALMER, William
BAMBER, John
BAMBRIDGE, Arthur Leopold
BAMBRIDGE, Edward Charles
BAMBRIDGE, Ernest Henry
BANKS, Gordon
BANKS, Herbert Ernest
BANKS, Thomas
BANNISTER, William
BARCLAY, Robert
BARDSLEY, David J
BARHAM, Mark Francis
BARKAS, Samuel
BARKER, John William
BARKER, Richard Raine
BARKER, Robert
BARLOW, Raymond John
BARMBY, Nicholas Jonathan
BARNES, John Charles Bryan
BARNES, Peter Simon
BARNET, Horace Hutton
BARRASS, Malcolm Williamson
BARRETT, Albert Frank
BARRETT, Earl Delisser
BARRETT, James William 'Tiny'
BARRY, Gareth

BARRY, Leonard James
BARSON, Frank
BARTON, John
BARTON, Percival Henry
BARTON, Warren Dean
BASSETT, William Isiah
BASTARD, Segal Richard
BASTIN, Clifford Sydney
BATTY, David
BAUGH, Richard
BAYLISS, Albert Edward James Matthias 'Jem'
BAYNHAM, Ronald Leslie
BEARDSLEY, Peter Andrew
BEASANT, David John
BEASLEY, Albert Edward 'Pat'
BEATS, William Edwin
BEATTIE, James S
BEATTIE, Thomas Kevin
BECKHAM, David Robert

BECTON, Francis
BEDFORD, Henry
BELL, Colin
BENNETT, Walter 'Cocky'
BENSON, Robert William
BENT, Darren Ashley
BENTLEY, Roy Thomas Frank
BERESFORD, Joseph
BERRY, Arthur
BERRY, Reginald John
BESTALL, John Gilbert

BETMEAD, Harry A.
BETTS, Morton Peto
BETTS, William
BEVERLEY, Joseph
BIRKETT, Ralph James Evans
BIRKETT, Reginald Halsey
BIRLEY, Francis Hornby
BIRTLES, Gary
BISHOP, Sidney Macdonald
BLACKBURN, Frederick
BLACKBURN, George Frederick
BLENKINSOP, Ernest
BLISS, Herbert
BLISSETT, Luther Loide
BLOCKLEY, Jeffrey Paul
BLOOMER, Stephen
BLUNSTONE, Frank
BOND, Richard
BONETTI, Peter Philip
BONSOR, Alexander George
BOOTH, Frank
BOOTH, Thomas Edward
BOULD, Stephen Andrew
BOWDEN, Edward Raymond
BOWER, Alfred George 'Baishe'
BOWERS, John William
BOWLES, Stanley
BOWSER, Sidney
BOWYER, Lee D
BOYER, Philip John
BOYES, Walter Edward
BOYLE, Thomas Wilkinson
BRABROOK, Peter
BRACEWELL, Paul William

Philip BACH

Born: Ludlow, Shropshire, 1872
Died: 30th December 1937
Role: Full-Back
Career: Middlesbrough, Reading, Sunderland, Middlesbrough, Bristol City
Debut: v Ireland (h) 18-2-1899
Appearances: 1

Phil played junior football in Middlesbrough and was signed by the local club straight from school. He was transferred to Reading in 1895 and spent two seasons with the club playing in the Southern League before joining Sunderland in June 1897 and two years later made his only appearance

Phil Bach

for England. Two months later he signed to Middlesbrough for a second time, although he was on the move again a year later when he joined Bristol City. He spent four years at St. John's Lane and in 1904 was reinstated as an amateur, although he did not play again. Having developed hotel interests in Cheltenham and later Middlesbrough, Phil returned to Middlesbrough a third time and served as a director from February 1911. He was chairman between July 1911 and 1925 and again from 1931 to 1935. He also served as an FA Councillor from 1925 to his death in 1937 and was on the international selection committee from October 1929.

Joseph William BACHE

Born: Stourbridge, 8th February 1880
Died: 10th November 1960
Role: Inside-Left
Career: Bewdley Victoria, Stourbridge, Aston Villa, Mid Rhondda, Grimsby Town
Debut: v Wales (h) 2-3-1903 (scored once)
Appearances: 7 (4 goals)

Joe Bache was spotted by Aston Villa whilst playing for Stourbridge and was signed as a professional in 1901, making his debut for the club in a friendly against the German club Berlin FC. Just as Charlie Athersmith and John Devey had earlier formed an effective right-wing partnership, so Joe and Albert Hall linked exceptionally well on the left-wing. Joe replaced Howard Spencer as captain of Villa and during his fourteen seasons with the club won two FA Cup and one League championship medals, as well as seven caps for England. The outbreak of the First World War effectively brought his career to an end, although he made a handful of wartime appearances for Villa before leaving in 1920 to become player-manager of Mid-Rhondda. He later coached Grimsby Town and the Rot Weiss club of Frankfurt in Germany and returned to Villa Park as reserve team coach in 1927. A boilermaker by trade he also worked as a publican after his involvement with football came to an end.

Thomas BADDELEY

Born: Bycars, Staffordshire, 2nd November 1874
Died: Stoke, 24th September 1946
Role: Goalkeeper
Career: Burslem Swifts, Burslem Port Vale, Wolverhampton Wanderers, Bradford, Stoke
Debut: v Ireland (h) 14-2-1903
Appearances: 5

Despite standing only 5' 9" tall Tom Baddeley made up for his lack of height with his agility, proving extremely difficult to beat irrespective of whether it was by long or short range shooting. He began his career with Burslem Swifts and joined the Port Vale club in 1892, spending five years with them before joining Wolves for £40 in 1896. Having already represented the Football League on four occasions Tom was awarded his first cap for England in 1903 on his own home ground of Molineux and went on to collect five caps, with glowing reports accompanying his performances. He remained with Wolves for ten years, making over 300 appearances before accepting an invitation to join the newly formed Bradford club (in time they would become known as Bradford Park Avenue), one of the first players engaged by the club. He stayed with the club until 1910 when he spent a brief spell with Stoke before retiring.

John James BAGSHAW

Born: Derby, 25th December 1885
Died: 25th August 1966
Role: Right-Half
Career: Graham Street Primitives, Derby County, Notts County, Watford, Grantham, Ilkeston United
Debut: v Ireland (a) 25-10 1919
Appearances: 1 + 1 War appearance

Like many of his generation, Jimmy Bagshaw was unfortunate that the best years of his career were swallowed up by the First World War. He had joined Derby County in October 1906 and helped the club win the Second Division title in both 1912 and 1915 and was widely regarded as one of the best centre-backs of the day. He was able to play equally competently at right-half or centre-half, with the key to his ability being his stamina and speed. The First World War robbed him of both, and after playing in one Victory International he was selected for the full England side in the first official international after the war. Up against Patsy Gallagher Jimmy struggled and never got close to England selection again. He remained at Derby until February 1920 when he joined Notts County, a club he had guested for during the war, spending a little over a year with the club before joining Watford in May 1921. He drifted out of the League game at the end of the year, signing first for Grantham and then Ilkeston United. During the Second World War he was trainer at Nottingham Forest and later scouted for both Forest and Coventry City. Away from the game Jimmy was employed by the engineering company Raleigh Industries.

Gary Bailey

Gary Richard BAILEY

Born: Ipswich, 9th August 1958
Role: Goalkeeper
Career: Manchester United, Kaiser Chiefs (South Africa)
Debut: v Republic of Ireland (h) 25-3-1985
Appearances: 2

The son of former professional footballer Roy Bailey, Gary was born in Ipswich but living in Johannesburg when he was recommended to Manchester United in 1978 and quickly impressed, earning a contract and making his debut in November 1978 against Ipswich! A regular in goal thereafter, he won FA Cup winners' medals in 1983 and 1985 and broke into the England squad, although it was an injury sustained during an England training session in February 1986 that effectively ended his career. The goalkeeping position then became something of a problem for United, one that was not properly resolved until the arrival of Peter Schmeichel. Meanwhile, Gary was released by United in September 1987 and returned to South Africa to play for the Kaiser Chiefs.

Horace Peter BAILEY

Born: Derby, 3rd July 1881
Died: Biggleswade, 1st August 1960
Role: Goalkeeper
Career: Derby County, Ripley Athletic, Leicester Imperial, Leicester Fosse, Derby County, Birmingham
Debut: v Wales (a) 16-3-1908
Appearances: 5

Horace Bailey coupled his full time job as a rating official with the Midland Railway at Derby with a playing career, signing with Derby County in 1899 and coming to prominence whilst with Leicester Fosse who he joined in 1907. The following year saw Horace earn a great number of accolades and awards, helping Leicester win promotion to the First Division for the very first time and become the first player to be capped for England whilst with the club. In February 1908 he won his first amateur cap for England against Wales and was elevated to full status three weeks later against the same opposition (Horace even saved a penalty taken by none other than Billy Meredith). That summer he was a member of the full England side that toured Central Europe and returned home in time to link up with the United Kingdom amateur side that won the Olympic Games at White City in London, conceding only one goal during the tournament, and even that was an own goal scored by Frederick Chapman. He returned to Derby County in 1910 to help the Baseball Ground club out of an injury crisis and a year later joined Birmingham where he finished his career. In addition to his five full caps he won eight caps at amateur level.

Michael Alfred BAILEY

Born: Wisbech, Cambridgeshire, 27th February 1942
Role: Midfield
Career: Charlton Athletic, Wolverhampton Wanderers, Minnesota Kicks (USA), Hereford United
Debut: v USA (a) 27-5-1964
Appearances: 2

After playing schools and junior football in Gorleston, Mike was taken on to the Charlton Athletic ground staff in June 1958, subsequently turning professional in March 1959. Over the next seven years he developed into a powerful and resilient midfield player, vying with Alan Mullery for a regular place in the England set-up. It was a battle ultimately won by Mullery, although both players missed out on the 1966 World Cup finals in England. Mike was transferred to Wolves in February 1966 for £40,000 and soon made captain, leading the club by example. During his time with Wolves he was captain when they won the League Cup in 1974 and reached the final of the UEFA Cup in 1972, although Alan Mullery of Spurs scored the goal that won the cup! He remained with Wolves until January 1977 when he went to play in America, costing the Minnesota Kicks club £15,000. Eighteen months later he returned to England to take over as player-manager at Hereford United, spending a little over a year at the club before going back to Charlton Athletic as team manager and then manager. He served Brighton as manager between June 1981 and December 1982, assembling most of the side that went on to reach the FA Cup Final at the end of the season. As well as his club honours Mike also collected five caps for England at Under-23 level and represented the Football League on three occasions.

Norman Coles BAILEY

Born: Streatham, London, 23rd July 1857
Died: 13th January 1923
Role: Half-Back
Career: Old Westminsters, Clapham Rovers, Corinthians, Wanderers, Swifts, Surrey
Debut: v Scotland (a) 2-3-1878
Appearances: 19 (2 goals)

Considering that opposition to England was restricted to Scotland, Wales and Ireland when Norman Bailey was playing, his final tally of 19 caps was a remarkable achievement, his caps being won over a nine year period. He played for Westminster School, Old Westminsters, Clapham Rovers, Wanderers, Swifts and Corinthians as well as earning representative honours for Surrey and London. He helped Clapham Rovers reach successive FA Cup Finals, finishing runners-up to Old Etonians in 1879 and winning the following year against Oxford University. At his peak he was described as 'A very safe half-back, with plenty of dash and judgement; has both strength and pace and never misses his kick.' Norman was also inspirational, captaining England in his final 15 appearances to set a then record. A solicitor by profession, having been admitted in 1880, he served on the FA Committee from 1882 to 1884 and was a vice-president between 1887 and 1890.

Norman Bailey

Edward Francis BAILY

Born: Clapton, London, 6th August 1925
Role: Inside-Forward
Career: Tottenham Hotspur, Port Vale, Nottingham Forest, Leyton Orient
Debut: v Spain (Rio de Janeiro) 2-7-1950 (WC)
Appearances: 9 (5 goals)

Although he signed amateur forms with Spurs during the Second World War he was later reported missing in action and Spurs therefore allowed his registration to lapse. Upon arriving back in England he was persuaded by Chelsea to sign amateur forms with them, and it was only when he popped into White Hart Lane to collect his boots that the situation became clear. To their credit, Chelsea agreed to tear up their contract and Baily re-signed with Spurs in February 1946, being upgraded to professional status in October the following year. He made his League debut in January 1947 at home to West Bromwich and quickly became a permanent fixture in the first team. It was around his passing skills and vision that 'push and run' centred, bringing player after player into play and carving opening after opening. More than a few fell to Baily himself, all dispatched with aplomb. He won a total of nine caps for England and also represented the Rest of the UK and the Football League. In 1956 he moved on to Port Vale for £6,000, but after only nine months moved to Nottingham Forest and helped them gain promotion to the First Division. He finished his playing career with Leyton Orient and then switched to coaching, returning to White Hart Lane in 1963 as Bill Nicholson's assistant. Nicholson's resignation in 1974 also saw the departure of Eddie Baily and he joined West Ham as chief scout, a position he held until his retirement in 1992.

John BAIN

Born: Bothwell, Lanarkshire, 15th July 1854
Died: 7th August 1929
Role: Forward
Career: Oxford University
Debut: v Scotland (h) 3-3-1877
Appearances: 1

Despite being born in Scotland John Bain was qualified to play for England and finally did so in 1877, thus becoming the first Scottish-born player to represent England. He was educated at Sherborne School, Winchester College and Oxford University, earning his Blue in 1876 and the following year helping Oxford to the final of the FA Cup, where they were beaten 2-1 after extra time by Wanderers. Whilst his only appearance for England saw him playing in the forward line, he was more normally a half-back, his position for the 1877 FA Cup Final. He qualified as a barrister and was called to the Bar in 1880 and also served as Master of Marlborough College between 1879 and 1883 and again from 1886 to his retirement in 1913.

Alfred BAKER

Born: Ilkeston, 27th April 1898
Died: 1st April 1955
Role: Right-Half
Career: Ilkeston, Cossall St. Catherine's, Long Eaton, Eastwood Rangers, Chesterfield, Crystal Palace, Huddersfield Town, Arsenal
Debut: v Wales (h) 28-11-1927
Appearances: 1

Alf Baker

Alf Baker was one of the original utility players, appearing in just about every position for Arsenal, including goalkeeper in an emergency. The First World War broke out before he had linked with any one club and so during the hostilities he guested for Chesterfield, Crystal Palace and Huddersfield Town, signing with Arsenal in May 1919 just before normal League football resumed. Over the course of twelve years at Highbury he helped the club win the FA Cup in 1930 having already collected a runners-up medal in 1927 and represented the Football League on two occasions. He announced his retirement in May 1931 and spent a spell scouting for the club, although he later worked as a groundsman for a London sports club upon leaving the game.

Ben Howard Baker

Benjamin Howard BAKER

Born: Aigburth, Liverpool, 13th February 1892
Died: Warminster, 10th September 1987
Role: Goalkeeper
Career: Blackburn Rovers, Preston North End, Liverpool, Everton, Northern Nomads, Chelsea, Everton, Oldham Athletic, Lancashire County, Corinthians
Debut: v Belgium (a) 21-5-1921
Appearances: 2

Ben Howard Baker first came to prominence as an athlete and represented Great Britain at the 1912 Olympics in Stockholm in the high jump and later went on to set a new British record of 6' 5", a record which remained unbeaten for twenty-six years. He also competed in the same event at the 1920 Olympics in Antwerp, where he finished in sixth place; had he repeated his British record at either Olympics he would have won the gold medal. In 1920 he also competed in the triple jump (finishing eighth) and the discus. He began his football career with Marlborough Old Boys and Liverpool Balmoral and was on the books of Blackburn Rovers immediately before the First World War. His first taste of success came whilst he was signed to Northern Nomads, helping them win the Welsh Amateur Cup in 1921 as well as earning the first of 10 caps for England at amateur level. A couple of months later he was capped for England at full level during the country's tour of Europe. He also represented the Football League on one occasion and collected his second full cap for England in 1925. Another good all-round sportsman, he played cricket for Liverpool Cricket Club, was considered international level at water polo and was more than competent at the hurdles and discus. He played at Wimbledon in the men's doubles tennis event and also won the Welsh covered courts doubles in 1929 and 1932. There is still some confusion as to his name, for some reference books show his surname as Howard-Baker, others as Baker.

Joseph Henry BAKER

Born: Liverpool, 17th July 1940
Died: 6th October 2003
Role: Centre-Forward
Career: Coltness United, Armadale Thistle, Hibernian, Torino (Italy), Arsenal, Nottingham Forest, Sunderland, Hibernian, Raith Rovers
Debut: v Northern Ireland (h) 18-11-1959 (scored once)
Appearances: 8 (3 goals)

Joe Baker was the first player to be capped by England whilst playing outside the country; he was on the books of Scottish club Hibernian at the time of his appearance against Yugoslavia in 1960, and he went on to make a further four appearances whilst still in Scotland. He had begun by playing schools football in Scotland and joined the Chelsea ground staff at the age of 15, although soon became homesick and was released and joined Hibernian in June 1956. His performances for both Hibernian and

Joe Baker

Alan Ball

later England alerted others clubs to his talents and Italian giants Torino paid £73,000 to take him to Turin in May 1961. Unable to properly settle in Italy he was sold to Arsenal in July 1962 for £67,500, spending four years at Highbury before a further move to Nottingham Forest for £60,000 in February 1966. Three years later he joined Sunderland for £30,000 and spent two years at Roker Park before returning to Scotland and Hibernian for £12,000 in 1971. He finished his playing career with Raith Rovers, playing for the club between 1972 and 1974. Aside from his eight full caps for England Joe also collected six caps at Under-23 level, represented Scotland at Schoolboy level and helped Hibernian reach the Scottish FA Cup Final in 1958 where they were beaten by Clyde. His brother Gerry was also a professional footballer and although he was born in Scotland went on to make international appearances for the United States of America!

Alan James BALL

Born: Farnworth, Lancashire, 12th May 1945
Role: Midfield
Career: Blackpool, Everton, Arsenal, Southampton, Vancouver Whitecaps (Canada), Blackpool, Southampton, Bristol Rovers
Debut: v Yugoslavia (a) 9-5-1965
Appearances: 72 (8 goals) + 1 unofficial appearance

He began his career with Blackpool in 1962 and made 162 appearances for the Seasiders before joining Everton for a six-figure sum in August 1966, by which time he was holder of a World Cup winner's medal. He won a League championship medal with Everton and then in December 1971 joined Arsenal for £220,000, then the biggest transfer fee in Britain. After five years with Arsenal and a runners-up medal in the 1972 FA Cup Final he joined Southampton and gave them near on four years' good service before landing his first managerial post with his first club, Blackpool. After he was sacked he returned briefly to playing with Southampton before trying his hand at management once again, this time with better results. He returned Portsmouth to the First Division in 1988 (although they went straight back down) and performed a financial miracle at Exeter before accepting an offer to team up with Lawrie McMenemy at Southampton in 1994 and subsequently going on to Maine Road and Manchester City and finally returning to Fratton Park. His father, also named Alan, was a former professional footballer and manager.

John BALL

Born: Hazel Grove, Stockport, 29th September 1900
Role: Inside-Left
Career: Silverwood, Sheffield United, Bristol Rovers, Wath Athletic, Bury, West Ham United, Coventry City, Stourbridge
Debut: v Ireland (a) 22-10-1927
Appearances: 1

Jack Ball began his professional career with Sheffield United during the close season of 1919, shortly before the resumption of League football following the First World War. He spent two years with the club before moving on to join Bristol Rovers. He spent just one season with the club before dropping out of League football with Wath Athletic, but Bury rescued him in May 1923 for a fee of £350. His six years at Bury represented the most successful of his career, culminating in his selection for England in 1927. At half time Jack had to go in goal following an injury to Ted Hufton and conceded Ireland's second goal in their 2-0 win and was never selected for England again. Jack joined West Ham United in May 1929 and spent a year at Upton Park before moving on to Coventry City and finished his playing career with Stourbridge. He scored 109 goals in 268 League matches for his five clubs, a good return.

Michael John BALL

Born: Liverpool, 2nd October 1979
Role: Defender
Career: Everton, Glasgow Rangers, PSV Eindhoven
Debut: v Spain (h) 28-2-2001
Appearances: 1

Michael Ball

A graduate from the youth ranks at Everton and an England international at Youth level, Michael Ball was one of the first beneficiaries of new England manager Sven Goran Eriksson's 'clean slate' policy of judging for himself each player's abilities rather than relying on reputations and previous involvement with the full England set-up. Thus Michael's reliable performances for Everton in those early months earned him a call-up for Eriksson's first England squad for the match against Spain and a substitute appearance when he replaced Chris Powell. Whilst Michael has not come close to the full England side since, his club performances did alert attention from elsewhere and in the summer of 2001 he switched to Glasgow Rangers in a deal worth £6.5 million. He was a regular in the side until the 2004-05 season when he was used less and less by Rangers, mainly because his continued presence in the side would have triggered additional payments to Everton. He was allowed to leave at the end of the season on a free transfer and subsequently signed a two year deal with PSV Eindhoven.

William BALMER

Born: Liverpool, 1877
Role: Right-Back
Career: Aintree Church, South Shore, Everton, Croydon Common
Debut: v Ireland (h) 25-2-1905
Appearances: 1

The older of the two Balmer brothers to play for Everton by four years (his younger brother Robert joined the club in 1902) he joined the club in 1897 and went on to make over 300 appearances for the first team, partnering first Jack Crelley and then his own brother at full-back. In 1905 he won his only cap for England and the following year collected a winners' medal in the FA Cup and also represented the Football League on one occasion. He remained at Everton until 1908 when he went to join Croydon Common, later serving Huddersfield Town as coach. There appears to be some confusion as to his real first name, for whilst England historians refer to him as William, in most Everton books he is named Walter! His nephew Jack Balmer played for Liverpool between 1935 and 1952.

William Balmer

John BAMBER

Born: Peasley Cross, 11th April 1895
Died: 1971
Role: Left-Half
Career: St. Helens, Liverpool, Leicester City, Tranmere Rovers, Prescot Cables
Debut: v Wales (a) 14-3-1921
Appearances: 1

Jack Bamber gave great service to all three of his League clubs, playing right-half for Liverpool, left-half with Leicester City and at centre-half for Tranmere Rovers, although his one appearance for England saw him at left-half. He had joined the professional ranks in December 1915 with Liverpool, with the First World War delaying his League debut until the 1919-20 season. A succession of injuries meant he missed out as Liverpool twice won the League title and did not get to represent his country on more occasions, for he undoubtedly possessed the abilities to have collected many more caps. In February 1924 he was transferred to Leicester and helped them to the Second Division championship in 1925. He moved on to Tranmere Rovers in July 1927 and spent three years with the club before moving into non-League circles. In addition to his one cap for England, Jack did represent the Football League on two occasions and was part of the FA touring side to South Africa in 1920.

Arthur Leopold BAMBRIDGE

Born: Windsor, 16th June 1861
Died: 27th November 1923
Role: Full-Back, Forward
Career: Clapham Rovers, Berkshire, Corinthians
Debut: v Wales (h) 26-2-1881
Appearances: 3 (1 goal)

One of five brothers who played football to a high standard (three played for England) he was educated at St. Mark's School and Windsor and played for the Windsor XI in 1877. He joined Upton Park in 1879 and later served Swifts, Clapham Rovers and Corinthians as well as representing Berkshire. According to the 1881 Football Annual he was 'useful; plays with judgement and is difficult to pass.' Injury brought his playing career to an end in 1884 after which he travelled the world studying art.

Edward Charles BAMBRIDGE

Born: Windsor, 30th July 1858
Died: Wimbledon, 8th November 1935
Role: Left-Winger
Career: Windsor Home Park, Swifts, Streatham, Berkshire, Upton Park, Clapham Rovers
Debut: v Scotland (h) 5-4-1879 (scored twice)
Appearances: 18 (11 goals)

The most capped of the three Bambridge brothers to represent England, Charles was educated at St. Mark's School in Windsor and later went on to play for Malvern College, Windsor Home Park, Streatham, Upton Park, Clapham Rovers, Swifts and Corinthians and played representative football for Berkshire. He was one of the first 'stars' of the England side; on his debut England were 4-1 down at half time and he scored twice in the second half, his second goal winning the match 5-4 for England. He was the first player to score as many as 10 goals for his country and also scored in eight consecutive games, a record that was not equalled until 1966 by Bobby Charlton. Known throughout his career as Charlie Bam he was an extremely fast winger and went on to serve on the FA Committee between 1883 and 1886. In 1882 he was one of the founders of the Corinthians and was honorary secretary between 1923 and 1932.

Ernest Henry BAMBRIDGE

Born: Windsor, 16th May 1848
Died: 16th October 1917
Role: Forward
Career: Swifts, Windsor Home Park, East Sheen, Berkshire, Corinthians
Debut: v Scotland (a) 4-3-1876
Appearances: 1

The first of the three Bambridge brothers to represent England, Ernie also had the shortest international career, earning just one cap for his country. His playing career was spent with Windsor Home Park, Swifts, East Sheen and the Corinthians and representative honours with Berkshire. He, like his brother Charles, served on the FA Committee between 1876 and 1882 and was a member of the Corinthians committee in 1882. Aside from his football exploits Ernie also worked in the Stock Exchange.

Gordon BANKS O.B.E.

Born: Sheffield, 30th December 1937
Role: Goalkeeper
Career: Millspaugh Steelworks, Rawmarsh Welfare, Chesterfield, Leicester City, Stoke City
Debut: v Scotland (h) 6-4-1963
Appearances: 73

Gordon Banks

One of the greatest goalkeepers in English history Gordon began his career playing schools football in Sheffield before signing for Chesterfield in September 1955. He made 23 League appearances in four years at the club but was immediately targeted by bigger clubs, finally signing for Leicester City for £6,000 in May 1959. Whilst at Leicester he helped the club to the finals of both the FA Cup and League Cup on two occasions, although only one of these, the League Cup in 1964 ended in victory. Having represented England at Under-23 level on two occasions he was handed his first full cap in 1963 and went on to become first choice, at least at national level, for the next nine years and was described 'Banks of England' in deference to his safe goalkeeping - he kept 35 clean sheets in his 73 appearances. Goalkeeper when England won the World Cup in 1966, his reputation worldwide was effectively made with his performances in the 1970 tournament, especially one stunning save from a Pele header in a group match that was acclaimed 'the greatest save ever'. Unfortunately Gordon's World Cup ended amid speculation that he had been 'got at', for he was forced to miss the quarter final clash with West Germany owing to a mystery illness; no one else in the squad suffered and England slid out of the competition. Whilst Gordon may have been first choice for England, at club level it was a different story, for the emergence of Peter Shilton at Leicester prompted the club to believe that Shilton was a better prospect and Gordon was sold to Stoke City for £52,000 in April 1967. He helped the Potteries club win the League Cup in 1972, the same year he was named Footballer of the Year and awarded the O.B.E. The following year he was involved in a car accident that cost him the sight of one eye and his career, although he did attempt something of a comeback in America with Fort Lauderdale Strikers. Once his playing career ended he became club coach at Stoke, later serving Port Vale and non-League Telford United in a similar capacity. After a spell as general manager at Telford he returned to Stoke City to become specialist goalkeeper coach for the club. Away from the game he has been a partner in a plant hire company and run a sports promotions company.

Tommy Banks

Herbert Ernest BANKS

Born: Coventry, 1874
Died: 1947
Role: Inside-Left
Career: Everton, Third Lanark, Millwall Athletic, Aston Villa, Bristol City, Watford
Debut: v Ireland (h) 9-3-1901
Appearances: 1

Herbert Banks played junior football in Leamington before enlisting with the Seaforth Highlanders. Posted to India he represented his unit in numerous competitions, helping them win the Simla Regimental Cup twice. Upon returning to England he signed with Everton, although a couple of months later joined Third Lanark in time for the 1897-98 season. He spent two years in Scotland before returning south of the border and signed for Millwall Athletic. Although Millwall played in the Southern League, Herbert's performances were of such quality he was selected for England in March 1901 against Ireland. Herbert gave a good account of himself, even if he was never selected again, for a month later he joined Aston Villa, then one of the major clubs in the country. He proved unable to settle at Villa Park and left for Bristol City in November 1901, finishing his playing career with Watford who he joined in the 1903 close season. After his retirement he moved to Birmingham where he worked for an engineering company.

Thomas BANKS

Born: Farnworth, Lancashire, 10th November 1929
Role: Left-Back
Career: Prestwich's XI, Bolton Wanderers, Altrincham, Bangor City
Debut: v USSR (a) 18-5-1958
Appearances: 6

Tommy Banks was one of the toughest full-backs of his age and a player feared throughout the game, for the ferocity of his tackling was legendary. Indeed, in one game he was heard to tell Chelsea and England winger Peter Broadbent 'If thou tries to get past me, lad, thou will get gravel rash!' Tommy first began to attract attention whilst playing for Farnsworth Boys' Club, going on to represent both England and Great Britain Boys' Clubs. He also represented the Army whilst on national service and joined Bolton Wanderers in October 1947. He spent virtually his entire professional career at Burnden Park, helping the club win the FA Cup in 1958 and made 233 appearances in the League for the club, scoring twice, although he was more often than not entirely concerned with preventing goals! He was released by Bolton in the 1961 close season and signed for Altrincham, spending two years with the club before switching to Bangor City and helping them to win the Welsh FA Cup Final in 1964. Tommy represented the Football League once in addition to his six caps for England. He was also a leading advocate in the move to abolish the maximum wage for players. Indeed, at one meeting he turned on a player who claimed footballers were already well paid with the retort "Tha can tell tha father from me that if he fancies chasing Brother Matthews [Stanley Matthews] here around for ninety minutes, then I'll swap jobs with tha father anytime and I'll have his wages and he can have mine!"

Bobby Barclay

William BANNISTER

Born: Burnley, 1879
Died: 26th March 1942
Role: Centre-Half
Career: Earley, Burnley, Bolton Wanderers, Woolwich Arsenal, Leicester Fosse, Burnley
Debut: v Wales (h) 18-3-1901
Appearances: 2

Billy Bannister joined Burnley from Earley in 1899 and proved a worthwhile acquisition by the club, earning a call-up to the England squad within eighteen months of his signing. He collected his first cap for England owing to the unavailability of Frank Forman through injury, but Billy did well enough in the 6-0 win to suggest it might not be his last performance. In November 1901 he was sold to Bolton Wanderers for £75, a ridiculously low figure given his stature, and he was selected for his second England cap in the 1-0 win over Ireland in March 1902. He spent just over a year at Bolton before moving south to join Woolwich Arsenal and a little over a year later moved on to Leicester Fosse. He remained with Leicester six years before rejoining Burnley for a season before retiring. Billy, who also represented the Football League on two occasions, became a licensee upon his retirement, first in Burnley and later back in Leicester.

Robert BARCLAY

Born: Scotswood, Newcastle-upon-Tyne, 27th October 1906
Died: 13th July 1969
Role: Inside-Forward
Career: Allendale, Scotswood, Derby County, Sheffield United, Huddersfield Town
Debut: v Scotland (h) 9-4-1932 (scored once)
Appearances: 3 (2 goals)

Bobby played junior football in the Scotswood area as a youngster and signed with Derby County in February 1927. At a time when inside-forwards were expected to do little other than score goals, Bobby was an extremely useful player to have in the side; creative and aware of others in better positions and just as likely to deliver a killer pass as score a goal himself. He spent four years with Derby before moving to Sheffield United in June 1931 and the following year collected his first cap for England. He helped United reach the FA Cup Final in 1936, where they were beaten by Arsenal and in March 1937 moved on again, this time joining Huddersfield Town. He reached his second FA Cup Final the following year although he had to settle for another runners-up medal as Preston North End won in the last minute of extra time thanks to a penalty. The outbreak of the Second World War brought Bobby's playing career to an end after 369 League appearances for his three clubs, scoring 106 goals.

David Bardsley

David John BARDSLEY

Born: Manchester, 11th April 1964
Role: Full-Back
Career: Blackpool, Watford, Oxford United, Queens Park Rangers
Debut: v Spain (a) (substitute) 9-9-1992
Appearances: 2

First signed by Blackpool he represented England at Youth level before a £150,000 move to Watford in 1983 where he helped the club to the FA Cup Final at the end of his first season. He moved on to Oxford United in 1987 for £265,000 but made his name when signing for Queens Park Rangers in 1989, a move that cost the Loftus Road club £500,000. Capped by England on two occasions he then suffered a succession of injuries, culminating in some 20 months out of the game until re-appearing for QPR in February 1998. At the end of the season he was released by the club.

Mark Francis BARHAM

Born: Folkestone, 12th July 1962
Role: Midfield
Career: Norwich City, Huddersfield Town, Middlesbrough, West Bromwich Albion, Brighton & Hove Albion, Shrewsbury Town
Debut: v Australia (a) 12-6-1983
Appearances: 2

Mark was taken on as an apprentice by Norwich in June 1978 and turned professional in April 1980. Having represented England at Youth level he was taken on the end of season tour to Australia by the full side in 1983 and appeared twice against the home side, his international career lasting three days. Whilst it was difficult to get back into England contention Mark did turn in some sterling performances for Norwich, helping them win the League Cup in 1985. Although Norwich were relegated from the First Division the same year, they bounced back as Second Division champions in 1986. Sadly Mark suffered a severe knee injury during the 1985-86 season and was seldom the same player thereafter, being sold to Huddersfield Town in July 1987 for £25,000. A little over a year later he moved on again, this time to Middlesbrough, although after only three League appearances he was transferred to West Bromwich Albion. His stay at the Hawthorns was equally brief, taking in four League matches and another move, this time to Brighton. He remained with them nearly three years before joining Shrewsbury where he finished his League career. Mark had earlier represented England at roller-hockey, a unique sports double.

Samuel BARKAS

Born: Wardley Colliery, Northumberland, 29th December 1909
Died: 10th December 1989
Role: Left-Back
Career: Bradford City, Manchester City
Debut: v Belgium (a) 9-5-1936
Appearances: 5

One of four brothers to have played League football professionally, Sam played junior football for Middle Dock FC whilst working as a miner before being signed by Bradford City midway through the 1927-28 season. He was something of a utility player whilst at City, for he played at left-half during the 1928-29 season when the club won the Third Division (North) championship and later converted to full-back, the position at which he enjoyed his greatest success. He was sold to Manchester City for £5,000 in April 1934 and remained with the Maine Road club for the rest of his career, finally retiring in May 1947. In-between times he had collected a League championship medal in 1937 and a Second Division championship medal in 1947, something of a unique treble. He was probably at his best between 1936 and 1938, gaining five England caps and representing the Football League three times during this period. Upon retiring as a player he took over as manager of Workington

Mark Barham

Town, later holding the reins at Wigan Athletic and scouting for Manchester City and Leeds United. He later returned to Bradford City, running the club's pools scheme during the mid 1960s. Sam was also selected for England for the match against Scotland on 2nd December 1939 but the car carrying him and fellow player Eric Brook crashed on route to Newcastle, thus forcing England to select Tommy Pearson, a Scotsman, in his place.

John William BARKER

Born: Denaby, Yorkshire, 27th February 1907
Died: 20th January 1982
Role: Centre-Half
Career: Denaby Rovers, Denaby United, Derby County
Debut: v Wales (a) 29-9-1934
Appearances: 11

Jack Barker was another player who combined playing junior football with full time work as a miner, experiencing a pit roof collapse during his time underground. After playing in the Rawmarsh League with Denaby Rovers he joined Denaby United for one season and was then spotted by Derby County, costing the club £200 when they signed him in April 1928. He remained with County until the outbreak of the Second World War, at which point he announced his retirement as a player having collected 11 caps for England and made three appearances for the Football League. He captained the England team in his last international,

Richard Barker

against Wales in 1936, although the Welsh won 2-1. At the end of the hostilities he took over at Bradford City as manager, a post he held until January 1947 when he journeyed to Ireland to take over at Dundalk. He returned to England in November 1948 to become trainer and coach to Oldham Athletic, although this position lasted three months. He later had a second spell at Derby County, serving as manager between November 1953 and May 1955.

Richard Raine BARKER

Born: Kensington, London, 29th May 1869
Died: 1st October 1940
Role: Wing-Half
Career: Casuals, Corinthians
Debut: v Wales (h) 18-3-1895
Appearances: 1

Richard was educated at Repton School and played for the school team in 1887, joining the Casuals when he left. He helped them reach the FA Amateur Cup in 1894 and was also linked with Corinthians between 1894 and 1900. He was one of three debutants in the match against Wales which was drawn 1-1, and the general consensus about Richard was that he was much too slow to be an international player, even if he could pass a ball accurately and kick exceptionally well. He was an engineer by profession and was later manager of the Bromley Electric Light Company.

Robert BARKER

Born: Wouldham, Kent, 19th June 1847
Died: 11th November 1915
Role: Goalkeeper, Forward
Career: Hertfordshire Rangers, Middlesex, Kent
Debut: v Scotland (a) 30-11-1872
Appearances: 1

Educated at Marlborough College, Robert also played rugby as well as football and joined Hertfordshire Rangers in order to concentrate on football when he left. He also represented both Middlesex and Kent during his career and was also believed to have turned out for Westminster School and Wanderers during his career. He was selected in goal for England's first international against Scotland, although switched with William Maynard at half time. The original choice, Alex Morten was unavailable on the day and it is believed Barker was chosen because he was the biggest and slowest player in the England team and because his rugby experience and handling of the ball would come in useful. He kept a clean sheet during his spell in goal, as did Maynard. Robert Barker was a civil engineer by profession and later served as Chief Assistant Engineer to the London, Chatham and Dover Railway and the South Eastern Railway.

Raymond John BARLOW

Born: Swindon, 17th August 1926
Role: Left-Half
Career: West Bromwich Albion, Birmingham City, Stourbridge
Debut: v Northern Ireland (a) 2-10-1954
Appearances: 1

Ray Barlow

Ray played schoolboy football in Swindon and later at junior level for Garrad's FC before linking with West Bromwich Albion as an amateur in June 1944. He was upgraded to the professional ranks the following November and made his debut for the club in the first season after the Second World War. He remained an Albion player until August 1960, by which time he had made 403 appearances for the League side, scoring 31 goals. He helped Albion win the FA Cup in 1954 and later the same year made his only appearance for England, the presence in the side of Jimmy Dickinson and Duncan Edwards preventing further appearances. He went on a month's trial with Birmingham City and joined the club permanently in August 1960 but was to make only five appearances in the League side before retiring in March 1961. He was then associated with non-League Stourbridge, finally retiring for good in the summer of 1962. As well as one appearance for the full England side Ray turned out for the B side twice and for the Football League four times. He was a newsagent in Stourbridge after his retirement.

Nicholas Jonathan BARMBY

Born: Hull, 11th February 1974
Role: Midfield
Career: Tottenham Hotspur, Middlesbrough, Everton, Liverpool, Leeds United, Nottingham Forest, Hull City
Debut: v Uruguay (h) (substitute) 29-3-1995
Appearances: 23 (4 goals)

Nick signed with Spurs as a trainee in 1991 after graduating from the England School of Excellence and was soon established as an integral part of the team, linking up exceptionally well with Teddy Sheringham as the team reached the FA Cup semi final in 1993. The arrival of Jurgen Klinsmann threatened that partnership and Nick expressed his wish to return to the north, finally joining Middlesbrough for £5.25 million in August 1995. A little over a year later a £5.75 million fee took him to Goodison Park and Everton. Having broken into the England set-up whilst at Spurs, he has since suffered from considerable competition for places. He re-

Nick Barmby

Peter Barnes

discovered something approaching his previous form in 1997-98, earning a recall to the England B side and captaining Everton, but he suffered a groin injury that was to prove crucial. After further appearances for the B side he was unable to earn selection for the full side, but a switch across Stanley Park to Liverpool brought about a change in fortunes and a recall to the England side. He rejoined Terry Venables at Leeds United in 2002 but signed for his hometown club Hull City in the summer of 2004 after a loan spell at Nottingham Forest.

John Charles Bryan BARNES

Born: Kingston, Jamaica, 7th November 1963
Role: Forward, Winger
Career: Sudbury Court, Watford, Liverpool, Newcastle United, Charlton Athletic
Debut: v Northern Ireland (a) (substitute) 28-5-1983
Appearances: 79 (11 goals)

Watford signed John Barnes on a free transfer from Sudbury Court in July 1981 and he was to prove one of the key players that earned Watford their promotion to the then First Division for the first time in their history and a place in the 1984 FA Cup Final. By then he was already an England international, but he will forever be remembered for a goal he scored against Brazil at the Maracana Stadium in Rio de Janeiro that summer, dribbling his way through the defence before stroking the ball home. Such form, even if it was explosive rather than consistent was always likely to earn him a big money move and in 1987 Liverpool paid £900,000 to take him to Anfield. There he developed into one of the best midfield players of the age, helping the club win two League titles, the FA Cup, League Cup and two Charity Shields and a Footballer of the Year award on a personal level. Whilst his form at club level was never in question, for England he remained something of an enigma, disappearing from games for spells and then lighting up proceedings with a touch of brilliance. A member of the side that reached the World Cup finals in 1986 and 1990 he made his last appearance for England in 1996. The following year, after ten years at Anfield he was given a free transfer and immediately linked up with former manager Kenny Dalglish at Newcastle United (along with another former Anfield favourite in Ian Rush), where his experience was put to good use as Newcastle reached the FA Cup Final in 1998. He came off the bench at Wembley to become part of an exclusive club; representing three different sides in the FA Cup Final. In February 1999 he joined Premiership strugglers Charlton Athletic on a free transfer.

Peter Simon BARNES

Born: Manchester, 10th June 1957
Role: Winger
Career: Manchester City, West Bromwich Albion, Leeds United, Real Betis (Spain), Leeds United, Coventry City, Manchester United, Manchester City, Bolton Wanderers, Port Vale, Wimbledon, Hull City, Bolton Wanderers, Sunderland, Stockport County
Debut: v Italy (h) 16-11-1977 (WCQ)
Appearances: 22 (4 goals)

The son of former Manchester City professional Ken Barnes, Peter played schools football in Manchester and signed with Manchester City as an associate schoolboy, being offered an apprenticeship in July 1972 and being upgraded to the professional ranks in July 1974. He was considered a huge prospect as a youngster, being capped for England at Youth and Under-21 level, winning nine caps at that level

John Barnes

and also being named the PFA Young Footballer of the Year in 1975. Two years later he had broken into the full England side, collecting the first of 22 caps for his country. In July 1979 West Bromwich Albion paid their record fee of £748,000 to take him to the Hawthorns where he continued his form and kept his place in the England set-up. Albion received their record fee for him in August 1981 with Leeds United paying £930,000 for his signature. He spent a year at Elland Road before a £1.15 million move to Real Betis of Spain in the summer of 1982, although he was back at Leeds twelve months later. In October 1984 he joined Manchester United, spending two years as a squad player at Old Trafford and then across the city to rejoin Manchester City in January 1987 for £30,000. His career thereafter saw him at Bolton Wanderers, Port Vale, Wimbledon, Hull City, Sunderland and Stockport County. Peter also represented England at B level during his career.

Horace Hutton BARNET

Born: Kensington, London, 6th March 1856
Died: London, 29th March 1941
Role: Right-Winger
Career: Royal Engineers, Corinthians
Debut: v Ireland (a) 18-2-1882
Appearances: 1

Horace Barnet joined the Royal Engineers in 1875 and quickly represented the unit at football, appearing in the 1878 FA Cup Final against Wanderers which was lost 3-1. He later played for Corinthians and made his only appearance for England in 1882, at the time being known as a forward who was comfortable when dribbling with the ball but prone to erratic passing and shooting. This was probably best exemplified by his only appearance for England; Ireland were beaten 13-0 and only one of England's forwards failed to get on the scoresheet or play for their country again; Horace Barnet. He retired from the Royal Engineers during the early 1900s having attained the rank of Colonel but was recalled for service during the First World War. He later lived in London.

Earl Barrett

Malcolm Williamson BARRASS

Born: Blackpool, 15th December 1924
Role: Centre-Half
Career: Bolton Wanderers, Sheffield United, Wigan Athletic, Nuneaton, Pwliheli
Debut: v Wales (a) 20-10-1951
Appearances: 3 + 1 War appearance

The son of former Sheffield Wednesday and Manchester City player Matt Barrass, who won two Second Division championship medals during the 1920s, Malcolm was spotted by Bolton Wanderers whilst playing for Ford Motors in Manchester during the Second World War. He signed for Bolton Wanderers in early 1944 and made an immediate impact, being called up by England for the wartime international against Wales in 1945. He had to wait six years before making his full debut for his country but by then he was an established member of the Bolton side, going on to make 329 League appearances for the Trotters. A member of the side that reached the FA Cup Final in 1953, where they were beaten by Blackpool, Malcolm remained with Bolton until September 1956 when he was sold to Sheffield Wednesday for £5,000. He made just 18 League appearances for the Hillsborough club before being released in July 1958 in order to take over as player-manager at Wigan Athletic, a post he held for barely six months. He finished his playing career in the non-League game, turning out for Nuneaton Borough and Pwllheli before becoming trainer to Hyde United in the summer of 1962. As well as his three full caps for England, Malcolm also represented the Football League on two occasions.

Albert Frank BARRETT

Born: West Ham, London, 11th November 1903
Role: Left-Half
Career: Fairbairn House, Leytonstone, Essex, West Ham United, Southampton, Fulham
Debut: v Ireland (a) 19-10-1929
Appearances: 1

Albert played for West Ham Schools and represented England at schoolboy level before signing with Leytonstone in 1921, linking with West Ham United as an amateur in 1923. He made one League appearance during the 1924-25 season for Southampton and made four appearances for the England amateur side before signing as a professional with Fulham in June 1925. His only appearance for the full England side came at a time when Fulham were still in the Third Division. Known as Snowball in recognition of his extremely blond hair, he remained with Fulham until his retirement in 1937. During his playing career Albert had continued to work as an accountant and immediately after the Second World War worked as secretary to a wholesale firm based in Romford.

Earl Delisser BARRETT

Born: Rochdale, 28th April 1967
Role: Full-Back
Career: Manchester City, Chester City, Oldham Athletic, Aston Villa, Everton, Sheffield United, Sheffield Wednesday
Debut: v New Zealand (a) 3-6-1991
Appearances: 3

Earl began his career with Manchester City but after two years and only three first team appearances was sold to Oldham for £35,000. Oldham's FA Cup exploits and Second Division title win alerted other clubs to his talents and he was sold to Aston Villa for £1.7 million in February 1992, going on to help his new club win the League Cup in 1994. He was sold to Everton for £1.7 million in January 1995 but was ineligible for the FA Cup Final that season having already appeared for Villa earlier in the competition. In 1998 his position at Everton came under threat and he joined Sheffield United on loan, with a view to the move becoming permanent should he prove his fitness. This he accomplished with little trouble, but before Sheffield United could finalise his move he was snapped up by city neighbours Sheffield Wednesday on a free transfer.

Jim Barrett

James William 'Tiny' BARRETT

Born: Stratford, London, 19th January 1907
Died: 25th November 1970
Role: Centre-Half
Career: Fairbairn House, West Ham United
Debut: v Northern Ireland (h) 22-10-1928
Appearances: 1

Although Jim Barrett played for Fairbairn House and West Ham United at almost exactly the same time as Albert Barrett, they are not believed to have been related. Jim had signed as a professional with West Ham in the summer of 1923 when aged only 16 and went on to appear in every position for the senior and reserve sides. He was also capped by England at schoolboy level, making two appearances, and was something of a schoolboy star, scoring over 200 goals for his school team over two seasons and 98 for West Ham Schools in season 1920-21. Jim holds the record for the shortest ever international career for England; after only four minutes of the match against Northern Ireland he was injured, and although he struggled on for a further four minutes he was carried off the field and never selected again. He remained with West Ham United until his retirement in 1945 and then had a spell in charge of the A team at Upton Park. His son, also named Jim, played for West Ham between 1949 and 1954 and returned to the club in 1960 after playing for Nottingham Forest and Birmingham City.

Gareth BARRY

Born: Hastings, 23rd February 1981
Role: Defender
Career: Aston Villa
Debut: v Ukraine (h) 31-5-2000
Appearances: 8

A graduate from the YTS scheme at Aston Villa, Gareth turned professional in February 1998 and made his League debut for the club before the season was out. Initially a midfield player, Gareth found greater success as a defender and during the 1998-99 season his progress was such that he was able to oust Republic of Ireland international Steve Staunton from the left-back berth, going on to make 32 League appearances over the course of the season. Despite his youth, Aston Villa felt sufficiently confident in his promise they offered him a five year contract on his 18th birthday. In May 2000, having helped Aston Villa reach the FA Cup final for the first time since 1957 (although they were beaten by Chelsea) he was awarded his first cap for England. Although he has not been selected for the England side since 2003, he is still young enough to make a return.

Gareth Barry

Leonard James BARRY

Born: Sneinton, Nottinghamshire, 27th October 1901
Died: 17th April 1970
Role: Left-Winger
Career: Notts County, Leicester City, Nottingham Forest
Debut: v France (a) 17-5-1928
Appearances: 5

Len Barry played schools football in Nottingham and even transferred back to his old school in order to continue playing the sport, having found the rugby playing school he had gone to not to his liking. He joined Notts County as an amateur in 1921 and turned professional two years later after winning one cap for the England amateur side. He remained with County until September 1927 when he cost Leicester City £3,300 and less than a year later had collected the first of his five caps for the full England side. He remained with Leicester until the summer of 1933 when he left to join Nottingham Forest and retired the following year. After giving up football he worked at RAF Chilwell on transport and later at two civilian airfields.

Frank BARSON

Born: Sheffield, 10th April 1891
Died: Birmingham, 13th September 1968
Role: Centre-Half
Career: Albion FC, Cammell Laird FC, Barnsley, Aston Villa, Manchester United, Watford, Hartlepool United, Wigan Borough, Rhyl Athletic
Debut: v Wales (h) 15-3-1920
Appearances: 1

A legendary character within the game, Frank began his playing career with Barnsley having previously been a blacksmith. He had a disagreement with the Barnsley board in 1919 and was allowed to join Aston Villa for £2,850 in October 1919. His time at Villa Park was both successful and confrontational, for although he helped Villa win the FA Cup in 1920 and collected his only cap for England the same year, he was frequently at loggerheads with the board of directors at Villa Park over his refusal to move house into the Birmingham area. It was also rumoured that during one row with the manager he had pulled out a gun! After three years of battling with the board he was allowed to join Manchester United and it was the FA Cup semi final in 1926 for which he is best remembered; an alleged foul on Manchester City's Sam Cowan left the City player unconscious, and although the referee had not seen the incident and took no action, the FA later banned Frank for two months. He also spent six months banned whilst at Watford. He left United on a free transfer in 1928 after helping the club attain its First Division status. Indeed, in 1925 Frank was promised a pub if he helped the club win promotion. When they did he was given the keys to a hotel in Ardwick Green, but got so fed up with the flattery being handed out by his customers on the first day he handed the keys to the head waiter and telegraphed his wife to stop the delivery of their furniture!

Frank Barson

John BARTON

Born: Blackburn, 5th October 1866
Died: Blackburn, 22nd April 1910
Role: Right-Half
Career: Witton, Blackburn West End, Blackburn Rovers
Debut: v Ireland (a) 15-3-1890
Appearances: 1 (1 goal)

Jack joined Blackburn Rovers in 1887 having played for local junior sides Witton and Blackburn West End and was said to have modelled his playing style on another Rovers player, Jimmy Forrest. Indeed, with Jack at right-half and Jimmy at left-half, Blackburn Rovers were one of the outstanding sides of the era, winning the FA Cup five times between 1884 and 1891. Jack appeared in two of those finals, helping Rovers overcome Sheffield Wednesday 6-1 in 1890 and Notts County 3-1 in 1891. His only appearance for England came in the 9-1 win over Ireland, with Jack being credited in some sources with England's ninth goal, although the Irish have always claimed that the shot went over the bar, not into the goal. Jack seemed set for a lengthy and successful career for both club and country but was forced to retire through injury towards the end of 1891. He later had a spell as trainer to Preston North End and then became a licensee in his hometown of Blackburn.

Percival Henry BARTON

Born: Edmonton, London, 19th August 1895
Died: October 1961
Role: Left-Half
Career: Tottenham Thursday, Sultan FC, Birmingham, Tottenham Hotspur, Stourbridge
Debut: v Belgium (a) 21-5-1921
Appearances: 7

Percy Barton played schools football for Montague Road in Edmonton, the same school that would later produce Spurs and England winger Jimmy Dimmock. When Percy left school he joined Tottenham Thursday and was widely expected to link with Spurs but instead Birmingham nipped in to sign him in 1913 and he made his League debut for the club in January 1914. With the outbreak of the First World War, Percy returned to London and made 87 appearances for Spurs in wartime football, rejoining Birmingham at the end of the hostilities. He helped Birmingham win the

Second Division title in 1921 and collected his first cap for England the same year, having previously appeared in two trial matches. He and Arthur Grimsdell, another Spurs player, competed for a regular place at left-half, with Percy collecting seven caps and Arthur six. Percy remained with Birmingham until 1929 and had switched to full-back when he went to play for non-League Stourbridge, finally retiring in 1933.

Warren Barton

Warren Dean BARTON

Born: Stoke Newington, London, 19th March 1969
Role: Defender
Career: Leytonstone, Maidstone United, Wimbledon, Newcastle United, Derby County, Queens Park Rangers, Wimbledon
Debut: v Republic of Ireland (a) 15-2-1995 (abandoned)
Appearances: 3

First spotted by Maidstone United whilst playing for Leytonstone, Warren cost the Kent club £10,000 when he signed in 1989. Less than a year later he was sold to Wimbledon for £300,000 and developed into one of the best defenders in the game as the so-called 'Crazy Gang' continued to confound the critics and maintain their top flight status. In June 1995 he was sold to Newcastle United for £4.5 million, having already broken into the England side, albeit in the abandoned match in Dublin. He made a further two appearances for his country although competition for places was at its fiercest. The closest he came to domestic honours was an appearance in the 1998 FA Cup Final in which Newcastle were beaten 2-0 by Arsenal, with the London club completing the domestic double. Warren left St James Park in February 2002 and later played for Derby County, QPR and Wimbledon before retiring.

William Isaiah BASSETT

Born: West Bromwich, 27th January 1869
Died: West Bromwich, 8th April 1937
Role: Right-Winger
Career: West Bromwich Strollers, West Bromwich Albion
Debut: v Ireland (a) 31-3-1888
Appearances: 16 (8 goals)

Billy Bassett was widely regarded as one of, if not the greatest right-wingers of the nineteenth century, a reputation established with West Bromwich Albion and confirmed with England. He played schoolboy football in the West Bromwich area and then went on to sign for Oak Villa, Old Church FC and West Bromwich Strollers before joining the senior club in the area, West Bromwich Albion in 1886. Two years later Billy had collected both his first FA Cup winners' medal and England cap, adding a second winners' medal in 1892. He made one further appearance in the final, finishing on the losing side when Albion lost to Aston Villa in 1895. Standing just over 5' 5" Billy's game relied heavily on his speed and accurate centres into the penalty area. His reputation was such that during an FA tour in 1899 to Germany, one defender was detailed to man-mark Billy throughout the entire game. Billy realised what his opponent's instructions were and so decided to have a little fun; midway through the game he went walking behind the goal, amused to see the defender follow him every step of the way! Billy retired as a player soon after although this did not mean relinquishing his connections with West Bromwich Albion, joining the board of directors in March 1905 and becoming chairman in September 1908, a position he held until his death. Billy also served on the FA Council between 1930 and 1937 and the Football League Management Committee during the same period. As well as his 16 caps for England, Billy represented the Football League on three occasions and was also a noted cricketer, turning out for West Bromwich Dartmouth cricket club. When he died in 1937 the FA asked for two minutes' silence in his honour before the West Bromwich Albion and Preston North End FA Cup semi final. They also requested, despite appeals from Albion, that the traditional cup final hymn Abide With Me be sung. Albion were so overcome with emotion they crashed to a 4-1 defeat.

Billy Bassett

Cliff Bastin

Segal Richard BASTARD

Born: Bow, London, 25th January 1854
Died: Epsom, 20th March 1921
Role: Winger
Career: Upton Park, Corinthians, Essex
Debut: v Scotland (a) 13-3-1880
Appearances: 1

Segal Bastard was another of the Victorian all-round sportsmen, having developed skills at cricket, rugby and football whilst at the City of London School. He became a solicitor in London in 1879 yet managed to combine his full time job with playing cricket for Essex County Cricket Club and football for Upton Park, helping the latter win the London Senior Cup in successive seasons; 1882-83 and 1883-84. He served on the FA Committee from 1877 to 1882 and refereed the 1878 FA Cup Final and the England and Wales clashes of 1879 and 1880, although whether he was indirectly responsible for the chant aimed at referees ever since has never been fully established! He was, however, one of only two men to have both played for and refereed an England match and officiated at an FA Cup Final, an honour he shares with Charles Clegg. The success of his business meant that in later years he was able to follow another interest, that of horse racing and he owned a number of racehorses. Indeed, he collapsed and died of a heart attack whilst at Epsom station, following a day at the races.

Clifford Sydney 'Boy' BASTIN

Born: Exeter, 14th March 1912
Died: Exeter, 4th December 1991
Role: Forward
Career: St. Mark's Exeter, St. James Exeter, Exeter City, Arsenal
Debut: v Wales (h) 18-11-1931
Appearances: 21 (12 goals)

Cliff played for Exeter schools and was something of a child prodigy, signing as an amateur with Exeter City in 1926 and as a professional in October 1928. By then he had already appeared in the first team, making his debut at the age of 15. He was spotted by Herbert Chapman of Arsenal whilst playing for Exeter at Watford; Chapman had gone to look at another player but was so taken by the young wing-forward that he forgot all about his original target and set about acquiring Cliff. He joined for £2,000 in May 1929, although when he arrived at Highbury to sign for the club an over zealous doorman assumed from his age that he was an autograph hunter and nearly sent him on his way; this led to Cliff being dubbed 'Boy' by his team-mates. He was a member of the side that won the League title on five occasions (1931, 1933, 1934, 1935 and 1938) and the FA Cup twice (1930 and 1936) as well as reaching the final on one other occasion. He represented the Football League four times and was capped by England at full level by the age of 19, making his last appearance in 1938. He was troubled by his hearing which affected his later career, although he managed to appear for Arsenal after the Second World War and retired in 1947 having made 350 appearances in the League, scoring a record 150 goals. He returned to Devon to become a licensee.

David BATTY

Born: Leeds, 2nd December 1968
Role: Midfield
Career: Leeds United, Blackburn Rovers, Newcastle United, Leeds United
Debut: v USSR (h) (substitute) 21-5-1991
Appearances: 42

David first signed as a trainee with Leeds in 1987 and quickly established himself as a tigerish midfield player, helping the club win the Second Division title in 1990 and reclaim their top flight status after an absence of eight years. Two years later he was the cornerstone of the side that won the First Division title and had also broken into the full England side after five appearances for the B side and seven Under-21 appearances. In October 1993 he was surprisingly sold to Blackburn Rovers for £2.75 million and he helped them win the Premier League title in 1994-95, although the following season he and team-mate Graham Le Saux were involved in an on-pitch fight among themselves as Blackburn slipped out of the European Cup. A further move in March 1996 to Newcastle United for £3.75 million followed and he was a member of the side that finished runners-up in the 1998 FA Cup. He subsequently returned to Elland Road in December 1998 and finished his playing career in 2003. A member of the England side that competed in the 1998 World Cup finals in France, he had the misfortune to miss the vital penalty in the clash with Argentina. It was, however, the very first penalty he had ever taken in professional football!

David Batty

Richard BAUGH

Born: Wolverhampton, 14th February 1864
Died: Wolverhampton, 14th August 1929
Role: Right-Back
Career: Rose Villa, Wolverhampton Rangers, Stafford Road, Wolverhampton Wanderers, Walsall
Debut: v Ireland (a) 13-3-1886
Appearances: 2

Dickie Baugh was educated at St. Luke's school in Blakenhall (the school that was to play a major part in the formation of Wolverhampton Wanderers) and began his playing career with Rose Villa, spending a number of seasons with them before joining Wolverhampton Rangers in 1880. Soon after he joined Stafford Road and was with this club when he collected his first cap for England against Ireland. During the 1886 close season he joined Wolverhampton Wanderers and spent ten years with the club, being described as 'a solid full-back, tough, determined, quick and a sound tackler'. He helped the club reach the FA Cup Final on three occasions, collecting a winners' medal in 1893 when Everton were beaten and in 1890 earned a recall to the England side, appearing for a second time against Ireland. He remained with Wolves until 1896 when he joined Walsall and spent a year with the club before retiring at the age of 33 years. His son, also named Dickie, played for Wolves, West Bromwich Albion and Exeter either side of the First World War.

Albert Edward James Matthias 'Jem' BAYLISS

Born: Tipton, Staffordshire, August 1863
Died: 19th August 1933
Role: Wing-Half
Career: Tipton Providence, Wednesbury Old Athletic, West Bromwich Albion
Debut: v Ireland (h) 7-3-1891
Appearances: 1

James Bayliss was known as Jem throughout his career, the name being derived from his initials. After playing for Great Bridge Schools he joined Tipton Providence, finally signing for West Bromwich Albion in August 1884 after a season with Wednesbury Old Athletic. He initially played as a centre-forward but was later successfully converted to wing-half, earning his only cap for England in this position. He helped West Bromwich reach the FA Cup Final in three successive years, finally collecting a winners' medal in 1888 after disappointments in 1886 and 1887. He remained a player at Stoney Lane (Albion's home until 1900) until his retirement in 1892, although by this time he was also a member of the Albion board of directors. He later became chairman of the club, a position he retained until his resignation in 1905, although in June 1909 he was elected a life member of the club.

Ron Baynham

Ronald Leslie BAYNHAM

Born: Birmingham, 10th June 1929
Role: Goalkeeper
Career: Erdington Rovers, Bromford Amateurs, Worcester City, Luton Town
Debut: v Denmark (a) 2-10-1955
Appearances: 3

Ron Baynham did not even begin to play competitive football until he joined the Army but proved to be an extremely agile goalkeeper, exceptionally brave and particularly good at dealing with crosses. He joined Erlington Rovers in 1946 and Worcester City in 1949, finally playing League football after joining Luton Town in November 1951 for £1,000. After seeing off the challenge of Bernard Streten, another England international at Kenilworth Road, Ron made the first team spot his own, appearing in the 1959 FA Cup Final which Luton lost 2-1 to Nottingham Forest. As well as three appearances for the full England side, Ron also played for the B side once and the Football League twice. He was forced to retire through injury in 1965 having made 388 League appearances for the Hatters and then became a painter and decorator in Bedfordshire.

Peter Andrew BEARDSLEY

Born: Longbenton, Newcastle-upon-Tyne, 18th January 1961
Role: Forward
Career: Wallsend Boys Club, Carlisle United, Vancouver Whitecaps (Canada), Manchester United, Vancouver Whitecaps (Canada), Newcastle United, Liverpool, Everton, Newcastle United, Bolton Wanderers, Manchester City, Fulham
Debut: v Egypt (a) (substitute) 29-1-1986
Appearances: 59 (9 goals)

Peter began his career with Carlisle and then went to Canada to play for Vancouver Whitecaps, subsequently being recommended to Manchester United. After one substitute appearance he was released on a free transfer, returning to Canada and then trying in England once again with Newcastle United. Here he developed into an exceptional player, linking well with Kevin Keegan and Chris Waddle as Newcastle returned to the top flight. His subsequent emergence in the England side brought the best out of players like Gary Lineker, with Beardsley seen as the perfect foil for one of the deadliest strikers in the modern game. In 1987 he was sold to Liverpool for £1.9 million, going on to help the Anfield club win two League titles and the FA Cup as well as two Charity Shields. He was sold to Everton for £1 million in 1991 but quickly proved that Liverpool may have been too hasty to show him the door, for he remained a vital club and country player during his time at Goodison Park. In 1993 he returned to Newcastle United, costing the St. James' Park club £1.4 million and held his place for the next four years, finally leaving for Bolton in 1997 for a fee of £450,000 in search of regular first team football. After a number of substitute appearances he was on the move again, joining Manchester City on loan as they tried to avoid relegation into the Second Division for the first time in their history and later Fulham as they attempted to get out of the same division. The move to Fulham was subsequently made permanent and he linked up once again with Kevin Keegan.

Peter Beardsley

David John BEASANT

Born: Willesden, 20th March 1959
Role: Goalkeeper
Career: Wimbledon, Newcastle United, Chelsea, Grimsby Town, Wolverhampton Wanderers, Southampton, Nottingham Forest, Portsmouth, Bradford City, Wigan Athletic, Brighton
Debut: v Italy (h) (substitute) 15-11-1989
Appearances: 2

Dave Beasant began his career with non-League Edgware Town, costing Wimbledon £1,000 when he signed in August 1979. He helped the club win the Fourth Division title in 1983 and was later captain when they pulled off the biggest ever shock in the history of the FA Cup, beating Liverpool in the 1988 final. Indeed, Dave Beasant became the very first goalkeeper to captain a winning side in the competition and had further cause to remember the day with affection, saving a penalty from John Aldridge. Such form prompted an £800,000 move to Newcastle in June 1988, although he was unable to settle in the North East and returned to the capital with Chelsea, costing the Stamford Bridge club £725,000 in January 1989. At the end of the season he had a Second Division championship medal as Chelsea returned to the top flight. The following season he had also broken into the England set-up, but a loss of form and public criticism from his then manager spelt the end of his days at Chelsea and he was loaned to Grimsby and Wolves before being sold to Southampton in 1993 for £300,000. Here he rediscovered something approaching his earlier form and confidence and served the club with distinction for four years. Released on a free transfer in the summer of 1997 he was snapped up by Nottingham Forest and helped then win the First Division title at the end of his first season. His height (he stands 6' 4") led to him often being called Lurch by his team-mates.

Dave Beasant

Albert Edward 'Pat' BEASLEY

Born: Stourbridge, 16th July 1913
Died: Taunton, 27th February 1986
Role: Left-Winger
Career: Cookesley, Stourbridge, Arsenal, Huddersfield Town, Fulham, Bristol City
Debut: v Scotland (a) 15-4-1939 (scored once)
Appearances: 1 (1 goal)

Pat Beasley played for Brierley Hill Schools and then junior football with Cookesley and Stourbridge, costing Arsenal £550 when he signed in May 1931. He was a member of the side that won the League championship in 1934 and 1935 before being sold to Huddersfield Town for £750 in October 1936. He appeared in the 1938 FA Cup Final, which was won by Preston North End and collected his only cap for England in April 1939, later accompanying the touring FA side to South Africa, appearing twice against the national side. In December 1945 he was released to sign for Fulham, helping them win the Second Division title in 1949 and then joined Bristol City as player-manager in July 1950. He retired from playing in May 1952 and retained his managerial position until January 1958, guiding the club to the Third Division South championship in 1955. He then joined Birmingham City, initially as joint manager with Arthur Turner and then held the job solely between September 1958 until May 1960. After a spell scouting for Fulham, Pat returned to management with non-League Dover, holding the reins between 1961 and April 1964.

William Edwin BEATS

Born: Wolstanton, Staffordshire, 13th November 1871
Died: Reading, 13th April 1939
Role: Centre-Forward
Career: Porthill, Port Vale Rovers, Burslem Port Vale, Wolverhampton Wanderers, Bristol Rovers, Burslem Port Vale, Reading
Debut: v Wales (h) 18-3-1901
Appearances: 2 + 1 unofficial appearance

Billy Beats was an all-action type of centre-forward who invariably brought other colleagues into the game with his unselfish attitude. He began his career with Porthill and signed for Port Vale Rovers in 1889, and joined Wolverhampton Wanderers from Burslem Port Vale in 1895. He spent eight years at Molineux, helping the club reach the final of the FA Cup in 1896 where they were beaten by Sheffield Wednesday and later collected two caps for England. Billy's unofficial appearance for England came in the Ibrox disaster match of 1902 and he subsequently played in the replayed game a month later.

He was transferred to Bristol Rovers in May 1903 and helped his new club win the Southern League championship in 1905 before returning to the Potteries and Port Vale in May 1906. A year later he joined Reading where he became player-trainer, retiring from the playing side in 1911. He then returned to Bristol Rovers, spending three years as trainer and finally a second spell with Reading, joining them in 1914 and retiring in 1917 in order to become licensee of the Truro public house in Castle Street, Reading, a position he held until 1936.

James Beattie

James Scott BEATTIE

Born: Lancaster, 27th February 1978
Role: Striker
Career: Blackburn Rovers, Southampton, Everton
Debut: v Australia (h) 12-2-2003
Appearances: 5

Educated at a public school James considered pursuing a career in medicine until taken on as a trainee at Blackburn Rovers, being upgraded to the professional ranks in 1994. He had to wait two years before making his first team debut, finally being given an outing during the 1996-97 season and making just three appearances the following term. Although he was a prolific goalscorer for Rovers' reserve side, where he averaged a goal every other game, he found the Premiership a much different proposition and was unable to score in Rovers' colours. In July 1998 he was valued at £1 million in the deal that saw Kevin Davies leave Southampton for Blackburn Rovers and James Beattie make the opposite journey. At The Dell he finally found his scoring boots, finishing his first season as the club's Player of the Year and winning selection for the England Under-21s. Injuries restricted his progress during the 1999-2000 season, but once fully fit he returned to terrorise Premiership defences once again. His exploits at club level finally earned him a call-up for the full England side in February 2003 against Australia and he was briefly a regular in the squad. However, with Southampton involved in a battle against relegation, whilst his rivals for a place in the England forward line were competing in Europe on a regular basis saw him slip down the pecking order. In January 2005 he was transferred to Everton for a reported fee of £6 million, the move designed to get him back into England contention.

Thomas Kevin BEATTIE

Born: Carlisle, 18th December 1953
Role: Defender
Career: Ipswich Town, Colchester United, Middlesbrough
Debut: v Cyprus (h) 16-4-1975 (ECQ)
Appearances: 9 (1 goal)

A succession of injuries prevented Kevin's career from reaching the heights previously promised, although he still managed to attain a good standard. After playing school and junior football in Carlisle he was taken on as an apprentice at Ipswich Town in 1970, subsequently turning professional in July 1971. He spent ten years with Ipswich, representing England at Youth, Under-23 and full level and helping the club to the FA Cup in 1978. First capped in April 1975 he made nine appearances for the full side, the last coming in October 1977, but already injuries were beginning to interrupt his career. He officially retired through injury in December 1981 but returned with Colchester United in July 1982, later turning out for Middlesbrough before retiring as a player for a second and final time in October 1983. He later had a spell coaching Norwegian side Kongsverg. At the time he broke into the England side he was being acclaimed as the new Duncan Edwards.

David Robert BECKHAM

Born: Leytonstone, London, 2nd May 1975
Role: Midfield
Career: Manchester United, Real Madrid
Debut: v Moldova (a) 1-9-1996 (WCQ)
Appearances: 87 (16 goals)

Although David trained with Spurs as a youngster he was signed by Manchester United as a trainee in January 1993 after helping the youth side win the FA Youth Cup in 1992. Loaned to Preston in February 1995 he broke into the United first team in 1994-95 and was soon established as a regular in the side. He helped the club win the Premier League in 1996 and 1997 and the FA Cup in 1996 and the following year was named PFA Young Footballer of the Year. By then he had already broken into the England side on a regular basis and was part of the side that took the country to the World Cup finals in France in 1998. His World Cup experience was not exactly as had been planned, for he sat out the first game with the manager claiming 'he wasn't focused enough', made a substitute's appearance in the second game and then sparkled in the third and crucial group match against Colombia, scoring England's second goal with a stunning free-kick. The next game was little short of a personal disaster as he was dismissed early in the second half against Argentina and effectively limited England's chance of success. The following few months saw him the subject of verbal abuse from spectators around the country, but David Beckham had the ability to override such criticism and win fans over, and within the space of two years he had become the fans' favourite, not least for his ability to weigh in with vital goals, especially in the crucial World Cup qualifier against Greece in 2001. He exorcised the Argentinean ghost with the only goal of the game from the penalty spot in England's second group match in Japan, a goal that went some considerable way towards removing Argentina from the competition. Having helped United to six League titles, two FA Cups and the European Champions League, he was surprisingly deemed surplus to requirements at Old Trafford and sold to Real Madrid for £25 million in the summer of 2003. It was said that manager Alex Ferguson had grown tired of the media circus that often accompanied David and his wife, former Spice Girl Victoria, but his actions on the field have always overshadowed his exploits off it. In the World Cup qualifier against Poland in 2005, David became the first England player to have been sent off twice, earning his marching orders after two yellow card offences.

David Beckham

Francis BECTON

Born: Preston, 1873
Died: 6th November 1909
Role: Inside-Forward
Career: Fishwick Ramblers, Preston North End, Liverpool, Sheffield United, Bedminster, Preston North End, Swindon Town, Ashton Town, New Brighton Tower
Debut: v Ireland (h) 9-3-1895 (scored twice)
Appearances: 2 (2 goals)

Frank Becton joined Preston North End in 1891 having previously played schools football in the town and junior football with Fishwick Ramblers. He was awarded his first cap for England whilst with Preston, making his debut in the match against Ireland that also saw Steve Bloomer making his first appearance; both players scored twice in the 9-0 win. In March 1895 he was sold to Liverpool for £100, collecting a second cap for England against Wales in 1895 and the following year helped Liverpool win the Second Division title. He remained with Liverpool until October 1898 when he signed with Sheffield United, although eight months later he joined Bedminster. He returned to Preston in September 1900 and spent a year with the club before switching to Southern League club Swindon Town. He then finished his career with a spell with Ashton Town and New Brighton Tower before ill health brought his playing career to an end.

Henry BEDFORD

Born: Calow, 15th October 1899
Died: 24th June 1976
Role: Centre-Forward
Career: Grassmoor Ivanhoe, Nottingham Forest, Blackpool, Derby County, Newcastle United, Sunderland, Bradford, Chesterfield, Heanor Town
Debut: v Sweden (a) 23-5-1923
Appearances: 2 (1 goal)

Harry Bedford was a much travelled and vastly experienced centre-forward who proved an important acquisition for all his clubs. He played for Grassmoor Ivanhoe in the Chesterfield League before signing with Nottingham Forest as an amateur in 1919, subsequently turning professional in August the same year, just as League football was about to resume after the First World War. In March 1921 he cost Blackpool £1,500 and went on to make both his appearances for England whilst with the club. He then joined Derby County for £3,500 in September 1925, spending just over five years at the Baseball Ground before switching to Newcastle United for £4,000 in December 1930. In January 1932 he cost Sunderland £3,000 but spent just four months with the club before moving on to Bradford, and a year later finished his League career with Chesterfield. By the time he joined non-League Heanor Town as player-coach in August 1934 he had scored 308 goals in 486 League appearances for his various clubs and had been top goalscorer in the Second Division in both 1922-23 and 1923-24 and the League's top goalscorer the same year with a tally of 34 goals. He rejoined Newcastle United as trainer and coach in October 1937 and was then briefly masseur at Derby County in May 1938. Aside from his two full caps for England, Harry also represented the Football League on two occasions. After his football career came to an end he became a licensee in Derby and then Chesterfield, although he had a brief spell as manager of Heanor Town in 1956.

Colin Bell

Colin BELL

Born: Heselden, County Durham, 26th February 1946
Role: Midfield
Career: Horden Colliery, Bury, Manchester City
Debut: v West Germany (a) 1-6-1968
Appearances: 48 (9 goals) + 1 unofficial appearance

After playing schools and junior football in County Durham, Colin was invited along to both Sunderland and Newcastle United for trials but failed to impress, eventually signing with Bury in July 1963. He made his League debut the following season, ironically against Manchester City and quickly impressed, finishing his one full season with the club as top goalscorer, despite playing in midfield. This prompted a £47,500 move to Manchester City and he made the transition from a side struggling at the bottom of the Second Division to one challenging for honours at the top of the First with consummate ease. He helped City win the League title in 1968, the FA Cup in 1969, the European Cup Winners' Cup and League Cup in 1970 and added a runners-up medal in the same League Cup competition in 1974. His non-stop effort in midfield led to him being nicknamed Nijinsky, after the racehorse, and also earned him considerable representative recognition, with two appearances for the Under-23 side, four Football League appearances and 48 caps for the full England side. He suffered serious injuries to a thigh and both knees in 1976, forcing him to miss the entire 1976-77 season for his club, and although he subsequently returned to the side his best days were already behind him. He was forced to retire in August 1979 having made over 460 appearances for the Manchester City first team and became a restaurateur in partnership with Colin Waldron, a former Burnley player. He returned to Maine Road in 1990 as youth team coach.

Walter 'Cocky' BENNETT

Born: Mexborough, Yorkshire, 1874
Died: 6th April 1908
Role: Right-Winger
Career: Mexborough, Sheffield United, Bristol City, Denaby United
Debut: v Wales (h) 18-3-1901
Appearances: 2

Known throughout his playing career as Cocky, he began working life as a miner and playing part-time football with Mexborough when Sheffield United persuaded him to turn professional in February 1896. He helped the club win the League title in 1898 and the following year collected a winners' medal in the FA Cup as Sheffield United overwhelmed Derby County 4-1, with Cocky scoring the first goal of the game. In 1901 he helped United reach the final, although this time had to settle for a runners-up medal as Spurs won after a replay. His third and last appearance came in the 1902 final, which Sheffield United won after a replay against Southampton, but Cocky badly injured a leg in the first game and was forced to sit out the replay. He did, however, get to receive a medal. He remained with Sheffield United until April 1905 and at the end of his first season had collected a Second Division championship medal. He left Bristol City in the summer of 1907 and signed with Denaby United, also returning to his former career of miner. He lost his life when a pit-roof collapsed.

Robert William BENSON

Born: Whitehaven, 9th February 1883
Died: London, 19th February 1916
Role: Left-Back
Career: Newcastle United, Southampton, Sheffield United, Arsenal
Debut: v Ireland (a) 15-2-1913
Appearances: 1

Bobby Benson began his career with Swalwell FC before being spotted by Newcastle United and signed as a professional in December 1902. He proved unable to break into the first team with any regularity and so was transferred to Southampton for £150 in the close season of 1904. He did sufficiently well during his one season at The Dell to attract the interest of Sheffield United where he developed into a strong tackler and expert penalty taker. A member of the FA touring party to South Africa in 1910 and called to represent the Football League on one occasion, he was finally awarded a full cap for England in 1913 shortly before being transferred to Woolwich Arsenal. With the outbreak of the First World War he found work at the local munitions factory and gave up playing football altogether. In February 1916 he was at Highbury watching Arsenal play Reading in a London Combination match when the home team discovered they were a man short and asked Benson to help them

Bobby Benson

out. He had not played for over two years and midway through the game complained of feeling unwell and retired to the dressing room. He died soon after from a burst blood vessel.

Darren Ashley BENT

Born: Wandsworth, 6th February 1984
Role: Striker
Career: Ipswich Town, Charlton Athletic
Debut: v Uruguay (h) 1-3-2006
Appearances: 1

Darren joined Ipswich Town as a trainee and was upgraded to the professional ranks in July 2001, going on to make his League debut the following season. He became a regular in the first team in 2002-03 and hit 12 goals in 35 League matches, earning him selection for the England Under-21 side in 2003. At club level he formed a particularly effective partnership with Shefki Kuqi, with the pair netting 39 goals during the 2004-05 season. Continued good form for the England Under-21 side had a number of bigger clubs taking a look and he finally moved on to Charlton Athletic in the summer of 2005 for £2.7 million, having scored 56 goals in 116 games for Ipswich. The step up to the top flight was one he took to almost immediately, hitting a good run of form and eventual selection for the full England side in the last match before the World Cup squad would be announced.

Roy Bentley

Roy Thomas Frank BENTLEY

Born: Bristol, 17th May 1924
Role: Centre-Forward
Career: Bristol Rovers, Bristol City, Newcastle United, Chelsea, Fulham, Queens Park Rangers
Debut: v Sweden (a) 13-5-1949
Appearances: 12 (9 goals)

One of the greatest names in Chelsea's history, Roy Bentley started with local club Bristol Rovers in 1937 but spent only a year on their books before joining rivals Bristol City and then, after the Second World War, Newcastle United for £8,500. In 1948 Chelsea paid £12,500 for his services, switching him from inside-forward to centre-forward and reaping the benefits as he became leading goalscorer for eight consecutive seasons, one of the club's best ever buys. He captained the 1955 Football League Championship winning team and made 366 League and Cup appearances in which he scored 149 goals. He also netted in the 1955 FA Charity Shield. He departed Stamford Bridge for Fulham in August 1956 with the Blues receiving £8,500 as his transfer fee, meaning he had cost them the princely sum of £4,000 for his services! He spent just under five years at Craven Cottage, during which time he helped the club win promotion to the First Division and was transferred to Queens Park Rangers in May 1961. He finished his playing career at Loftus Road in January 1963 when he joined Reading as manager, remaining in charge at Elm Park until February 1969. After a brief spell scouting for Bradford City, Roy was lured back into management by Swansea Town in August 1969 and guided the club to promotion from the Fourth Division in 1969-70. A poor start to the 1972-73 season saw Roy being relieved of his position in October 1972 and he moved into non-League circles before returning to Reading as club secretary in the summer of 1977. He remained at Elm Park for seven years and later served in a similar capacity at Aldershot. In addition to his 12 full caps Roy made two appearances for the England B side and represented the Football League on three occasions.

Joseph BERESFORD

Born: Chesterfield, 26th February 1906
Died: 1978
Role: Inside-Forward
Career: Bentley Colliery, Mexborough Athletic, Mansfield Town, Aston Villa, Preston North End
Debut: v Czechoslovakia (a) 16-5-1934
Appearances: 1

Joe Beresford began his career with Mansfield Town and was transferred to Aston Villa in 1927. Able to play at either inside-forward or centre-forward, he fired home a hat-trick in only his second appearance for the club, thus establishing himself as a favourite with the crowd. In 1930-31, during which time Villa rattled in a record tally of 128 League goals, Joe weighed in with 14 of them. His form in the early 1930s continued and in 1934 he won his only cap for England, and also netted a total of 73 goals for Villa in 251 first team appearances. The arrival of Jimmy McMullan, Villa's first ever manager, saw Joe surprisingly sold to Preston North End, but he was an integral part of the side that reached the FA Cup Final in 1937 where they were beaten by Sunderland. At the end of his playing career he ran a fish shop.

Arthur BERRY

Born: Liverpool, 3rd January 1888
Died: Liverpool, 15th March 1953
Role: Left-Winger
Career: Oxford University, Liverpool, Fulham, Everton, Wrexham, Oxford City
Debut: v Ireland (h) 13-2-1909
Appearances: 1

Arthur Berry first showed ability at the oval code game, captaining the Denstone College rugby team and only began to concentrate on football when he moved on to Wadham College. Indeed, his impact was little short of remarkable, for in 1908 he won his Blue, his first cap at amateur level and was a member of the United Kingdom side that won the football gold medal at the Olympic Games held in London. The following year he won his only full cap for England in the match against Ireland but continued to be a regular in the amateur side until 1913 by which time he had 32 caps to his credit. He also collected a second gold medal in the Olympic Games at Stockholm in 1912, a feat which only Vivian Woodward has achieved (in the same finals!), although Berry had been dropped for the semi final in preference to Gordon Wright, only to regain his place for the final. In 1913 he was a member of the Oxford City side that reached the FA Amateur Cup Final (a side that also featured the Reverend Kenneth Hunt, another member of the 1908 United Kingdom side) and seemed set for a long and illustrious career in the game, only to retire the same year when he was called to the Bar. Commissioned into the Liverpool Regiment in 1916 and serving as Adjutant of the Lancashire Fusiliers he settled in Liverpool after the First World War and joined the family law firm, headed by his father Edwin Berry who was a director of Liverpool FC and Chairman of the club between 1904 and 1909.

Johnny Berry

Reginald John BERRY

Born: Aldershot, 1st June 1926
Died: 15th September 1994
Role: Winger
Career: Birmingham City, Manchester United
Debut: v Argentina (a) 17-5-1953 (abandoned)
Appearances: 4

Johnny Berry was first spotted whilst playing in the Army and recommended to Birmingham City by Fred Harris, himself a Birmingham player who played alongside Johnny in service representative games. He signed professional forms in September 1944 and finally established himself as a regular on the wing in 1948, having made his debut a year previously. In August 1951 he was targeted by Matt Busby as the ideal replacement for Jimmy Delaney on Manchester United's right wing and cost the club £15,000, money that was to be extremely well spent. In his first season at Old Trafford he helped United win the League title for the first time since 1910-11, and whilst in the following years it was 'Busby's Babes' who gained most of the accolades, the experience of the likes of Johnny Berry was vital to the club. He collected further League title medals in 1956 and 1957 and also helped United to the FA Cup Final in 1957 where they were surprisingly beaten by Aston Villa. He made his England debut against Argentina, a match that was abandoned owing to rain, alongside another United debutant in Tommy Taylor. Unlike Tommy, however, Johnny survived the Munich air crash of February 1958 but the injuries sustained meant he never played again. He later opened a sports goods business. His brother Peter played for Crystal Palace and Ipswich Town between 1952 and 1961.

John Gilbert BESTALL

Born: Beighton, Yorkshire, 24th June 1900
Died: 11th April 1985
Role: Inside-Forward
Career: Rotherham United, Grimsby Town
Debut: v Northern Ireland (a) 6-2-1935
Appearances: 1

Jackie Bestall gave such good service to Grimsby Town during his twelve years with the club that they named a street in Cleethorpes in his honour. After playing schools football in Sheffield, Jackie played for Beighton Miners' Welfare before linking with Rotherham United during the 1924-25 season. In November 1926 he was transferred to Grimsby for £700 and he went on to set a new record number of League appearances for the Mariners, appearing in 427 League games (the record was overtaken in 1968 by Keith Jobling) by the time he retired from playing in June 1938. He then joined Birmingham City as coach and chief scout, remaining at St. Andrews throughout the Second World War. In March 1946 he became manager of Doncaster Rovers, a position he held until April 1949 when he took over at Blackburn Rovers. He was in charge at Ewood Park for four years and then spent a little over a year at Nelson, later returning to Doncaster Rovers as chief scout in August 1958, although he was team manager between March 1959 and August 1960. As well as his one cap for the full England side Jackie represented the Football League on three occasions and won a Second Division championship medal with Grimsby in 1934.

Jackie Bestall

Harry Betmead

Harry A. BETMEAD

Born: Grimsby, 11th April 1912
Died: 26th August 1984
Role: Centre-Half
Career: Hay Cross, Grimsby Town
Debut: v Finland (a) 20-5-1937
Appearances: 1

After playing schools football in Grimsby Harry went to work as a railway porter and played junior football with Hay Cross FC when he was offered professional terms with Grimsby Town, signing in October 1930. He went on to play for the club for the next seventeen years, helping them win the Second Division title in 1934. Although a number of clubs made enquiries about taking Harry elsewhere, the Grimsby board managed to turn them all down, with the result Harry spent his entire career with the club, finally retiring in December 1947. In addition to his one full cap for England Harry also toured South Africa with the FA in 1939, appearing twice against the national side. Harry was also a competent cricketer, playing minor counties cricket for Lincolnshire. At the end of his playing career Harry went into business in Hertfordshire.

Morton Peto BETTS

Born: London, 30th August 1847
Died: 19th April 1914
Role: Full-Back, Forward, Goalkeeper
Career: Wanderers, West Kent, Old Harrovians
Debut: v Scotland (h) 3-3-1877
Appearances: 1 + 2 unofficial appearances

In 1872 Morton Peto Betts was playing for Harrow Chequers, a club formed by former pupils of the Harrow school. This club entered the very first FA Cup competition and were drawn against Wanderers in the first round, although they scratched from the competition before the game could be played. The Wanderers secretary, Charles William Alcock, invited Betts to play for Wanderers in the subsequent rounds, reasoning that as Harrow Chequers had not played a game in the competition Betts was not cup-tied. Wanderers went on to reach the final, where Betts played under the pseudonym of 'A H Chequer', thus reflecting his earlier allegiance. He scored the only goal of the game against Royal Engineers to win the cup for Wanderers, the first of five occasions they won the trophy. Betts, however, made no further appearances for Wanderers, returning to the Harrow club and subsequently earning his only cap for England five years later in a 3-1 defeat at Kennington Oval, although in this match he played in goal! He did, however, make two further appearances in the FA Cup final, acting as linesman in 1888 and 1890. Morton later served on the FA committee and was connected with Preston North End. He was also a cricketer of some note, having represented Middlesex, Kent and Essex during his career and was secretary of Essex from 1887 to 1890. He also played in goal in the two unofficial matches against Scotland in 1871. He was named after the designer of Nelson's Column in Trafalgar Square, Samuel Morton Peto.

William BETTS

Born: Sheffield, 1864
Died: 8th August 1941
Role: Left-Half
Career: Sheffield Wednesday, Lockwood, Sheffield Wednesday
Debut: v Wales (h) 23-2-1889
Appearances: 1

Billy Betts played junior football in Sheffield before signing with the local Wednesday club in 1883, although later the same year he joined the works club Lockwood Brothers. Two years later, in 1885, he returned to Wednesday, helping them win the Football Alliance in 1890 and reach the final of the FA Cup the same year, although they were beaten at Kennington Oval 6-1 by Blackburn Rovers. He remained on the playing staff until his retirement in 1895 and later became groundsman for the club. In 1922 he had a spell as assistant trainer. His grandson, Dennis Woodhead also played for Sheffield Wednesday between 1944 and 1955. Billy usually played centre-half at club level but was utilised at left-half for England in his only international, deputising for the absent David Weir.

Joseph BEVERLEY

Born: Blackburn, 12th November 1856
Died: Blackburn, 21st May 1897
Role: Full-Back
Career: Black Star, Blackburn Olympic, Blackburn Rovers, Blackburn Olympic, Blackburn Rovers
Debut: v Ireland (a) 23-2-1884
Appearances: 3

Joe Beverley was a stalwart of Blackburn football, helping set up Blackburn Olympic in 1876. Although the two senior Blackburn clubs, Olympic and Rovers, won the FA Cup four times and reached the final once in a five season spell between 1882 and 1886, Joe was often at the wrong club at the wrong time and thus won only one winners' medal, with Rovers in 1884. He had remained with Olympic until

October 1882 and then switched to Rovers, helping them win the FA Cup in 1884. He then returned to Olympic during the close season and spent another three years with the club. In late 1887 he went back to Blackburn Rovers where he finished his playing career in 1889. Upon his retirement he went to work at the Albion Mill in Blackburn where in 1897 he lost his life following an accident.

Ralph James Evans BIRKETT

Born: Newton Abbott, Devon, 9th January 1913
Role: Right-Winger
Career: Dartmouth United, Torquay United, Arsenal, Middlesbrough, Newcastle United,
Debut: v Northern Ireland (a) 19-10-1935
Appearances: 1 + 1 War appearance (1 goal)

After playing in the Plymouth & District League with Dartmouth United, Ralph was signed as an amateur by Torquay United in 1929, turning professional in March 1930. Three years later he was signed by Arsenal, although stiff competition from Pat Beasley and then Alf Kirchen restricted first team opportunities at Highbury and he was sold to Middlesbrough in March 1935 in search of a regular place. He did well enough at Middlesbrough to have earned selection for the full England side, appearing against Northern Ireland in 1935 and represent the Football League on two occasions. According to some reports, Ralph may even have scored in that game, although the goals have usually been credited to Fred Tilson. Ralph was selected for the next international match, against Germany at Tottenham, but was injured shortly before the game and replaced by Stanley Matthews. Nor surprisingly, Ralph proved unable to oust Matthews from the side. In July 1938 he joined Newcastle United in a £5,900 deal and in 1941 he was selected for the England side to face Scotland in a wartime international at Newcastle, scoring once in the 3-2 defeat. He retired later the same year having made 231 first team appearances for his clubs, scoring 63 goals.

Reginald Halsey BIRKETT

Born: London 28th March 1849
Died: 30th June 1898
Role: Goalkeeper
Career: Lancing Old Boys, Clapham Rovers, Surrey
Debut: v Scotland (h) 5-4-1879
Appearances: 1

Reg Birkett was educated at Lancing College and played for the college football team between 1866 and 1867, later playing for Lancing Old Boys when he left the college. He then joined Clapham Rovers and helped them reach the FA Cup Final in both 1879 and 1880, collecting a winners' medal in 1880 as Oxford University were beaten 1-0. He made his name as a goalkeeper and was widely regarded as being a fearless 'keeper with a strong kick, although he could also play outfield and was particularly noted as a forward or back. His goalkeeping experience proved especially useful, however, for he appeared in the very first rugby international, between England and Scotland in 1871, the first player to have been capped by England at both football and rugby, a feat that has since been equalled by only two other players, Charles Wilson and John Willie Sutcliffe. He was a member of the original Rugby Union Committee and his brother and son later represented England at the oval code. After his playing career finished he worked as a hide and skin broker in the City.

Francis Hornby BIRLEY

Born: Chorlton, Lancashire, 14th March 1850
Died: 1st August 1910
Role: Half-Back
Career: Oxford University, Wanderers, Middlesex
Debut: v Scotland (a) 7-3-1874
Appearances: 2

Francis Birley was educated at Winchester College and then went to Oxford University to study law, qualifying as a barrister and being called to the Bar in January 1876. He was another all-round sportsman, with 1874 perhaps the pinnacle of his career, for he was awarded a Blue for both football and athletics and helped Oxford University win the FA Cup, beating the Royal Engineers 2-0. That same year he also collected his first cap for England and held his place for the match against Scotland twelve months later. He appeared in four FA Cup finals in total, finishing on the losing side in 1873 with Oxford University and collecting two additional winners' medals with Wanderers in 1876 and 1877. He also played cricket for Lancashire, appearing in four matches between 1870 and 1872, Surrey for one match in 1879 and later for Cheshire. He also played representative football for Middlesex.

Gary Birtles

Gary BIRTLES

Born: Nottingham, 27th July 1956
Role: Centre-Forward
Career: Long Eaton United, Nottingham Forest, Manchester United, Nottingham Forest, Notts County, Grimsby Town
Debut: v Argentina (h) (substitute) 13-5-1980
Appearances: 3

Gary was spotted playing for Long Eaton United by Nottingham Forest and joined the professional ranks in 1976. He proved to be a quality striker for the club, helping them win the League Cup in 1979, the same season they also lifted the European Cup following their League title in the previous campaign. Gary also collected a second European Cup medal in 1980 and earned selection for the full England side, having already been capped at Under-21 and B level. His exploits with Nottingham Forest had not gone unnoticed by other clubs and he was transferred to Manchester United for £1.25 million in 1980. Unfortunately, like a few strikers who have made the move from Forest to United, he found the going more difficult, struggling to rediscover the form that had made him such a potent force at the City Ground. He remained at Old Trafford until September 1987 when he was sold back to Forest for a cut price fee of £250,000. He spent five years with Forest the second time around before crossing the Trent Bridge to play for local rivals Notts County, finally finishing his career with Grimsby Town.

Sid Bishop

Sidney Macdonald BISHOP

Born: Stepney, London, 10th February 1900
Died: Chelsea, London, 4th April 1949
Role: Wing-Half
Career: Ilford, Crystal Palace, West Ham United, Leicester City, Chelsea
Debut: v Scotland (a) 2-4-1927
Appearances: 4 (1 goal)

Sid Bishop began his career as a centre-forward, playing schools football in London and for Ilford and Crystal Palace in that position. His conversion to half-back came whilst he was playing for Crystal Palace reserves, and his success in the new position saw his career take off. He was sold to West Ham United in May 1920 and went to help the club reach the very first FA Cup Final to be played at Wembley Stadium, where they were beaten by Bolton Wanderers 2-0. In November 1926 Leicester City paid a then club record fee of £3,500 to take him to Filbert Street and five months later he had collected his first cap for England, only the second player to be honoured by England whilst on Leicester's books. His performance in the match against Scotland earned him a place on the end-of-season European tour, appearing in all three matches. He might have won more caps for England, for he was originally named as captain for the 1928 clash with Scotland at Wembley and for the 1929 match against Northern Ireland but had to withdraw from both sides owing to injury and was never selected again. In June 1928 he was transferred to Chelsea, remaining with the club until his retirement in May 1933. In addition to his four full caps for England Sid also represented the Football League once.

Fred Blackburn

Frederick BLACKBURN

Born: Mellor, Lancashire, September 1879
Role: Left-Winger
Career: Mellor, Blackburn Rovers, West Ham United
Debut: v Scotland (h) 30-3-1901 (scored once)
Appearances: 3 (1 goal)

Fred Blackburn was born in Mellor near Blackburn and played for Mellor FC before signing with Blackburn Rovers in 1897. After making his debut for England in 1901 he was much sought after by several other clubs but chose to remain with Blackburn, with whom he won all three of his caps, until May 1905 when he signed with West Ham United. He was on West Ham's books for the rest of his playing career, retiring during the close season of 1913. He then went to sea and little was heard of him, at least as far as football is concerned, until 1931 when he was appointed coach at Barking Town. Aside from his three full caps for England Fred also represented the Football League once.

George Frederick BLACKBURN

Born: Willesden Green, London, 8th March 1899
Died: 3rd July 1957
Role: Left-Half
Career: Hampstead Town, Aston Villa, Cardiff City, Mansfield Town, Cheltenham Town
Debut: v France (a) 17-5-1924
Appearances: 1

George Blackburn represented Willesden and London Schools before signing with Willesden Juniors. Aston Villa spotted him whilst he was playing youth football for Hampstead Town and signed him to amateur forms in December 1920, upgrading him to the professional ranks in January 1921. By then he had already represented the London FA and Middlesex FA. He helped Villa reach the final of the FA Cup in 1924, the season in which he made his only appearance for England, and remained at Villa Park for six years, making 145 appearances for the first team. He was sold to Cardiff City in 1927 and helped his new club win the Welsh FA Cup on two occasions and finish runners-up once before finishing his playing career with Mansfield Town. He then turned to training and joined Birmingham City in 1937, remaining with the club for nine years. When normal League football resumed at the end of the Second World War he joined the club's coaching staff. Aside from his one full cap for England, George was also named as reserve for another match but in the event was not needed.

Ernest BLENKINSOP

Born: Cudworth, Yorkshire, 20th April 1902
Died: Sheffield, 24th April 1969
Role: Left-Back
Career: Cudworth United Methodists, Hull City, Sheffield Wednesday, Liverpool, Cardiff City
Debut: v France (a) 17-5-1928
Appearances: 26

Ernie Blenkinsop was noticed by Hull City whilst playing for Cudworth United Methodists in October 1921 and sold to the Boothferry Park club for £100 and 80 pints of beer! A little over a year later a four figure fee took him to Hillsborough and Sheffield Wednesday and he developed into one of the most consistent full-backs of the age. It took five years at Hillsborough before he was selected for England but once in he became a permanent fixture and ever present for five years. He helped Wednesday win the Second Division in 1926 and then successive League titles (1929 and 1930) as well as representing the Football League on eight occasions. He remained at Hillsborough until March 1934 when he was sold to Liverpool for a reported £5,000 to resume his England partnership with Tom Cooper. In November 1937 he joined Cardiff City, spending one season with the club before moving into the non-League game. During the Second World War he assisted both Bradford and Hurst before retiring and then became a licensee in Sheffield.

Ernie Blenkinsop

Bert Bliss

Herbert BLISS

Born: Willenhall, Staffordshire, 29th March 1890
Died: Wood Green, 14th June 1968
Role: Inside-Left
Career: Willenhall Swifts, Tottenham Hotspur, Clapton Orient, Bournemouth & Boscombe Athletic
Debut: v Scotland (a) 19-4-1921
Appearances: 1

Bert Bliss was spotted by Spurs playing junior football in March 1912 and immediately snapped up, making his League debut in April the same year at home to Manchester City. A diminutive inside-forward, he made up for his lack of height (he stood only 5' 6" tall) with a knack of finding the net with regularity, hitting 91 goals in only 195 appearances, including netting 21 goals in the 1914-15 campaign that saw Spurs finish bottom of the First Division. Unfortunately, the First World War robbed Bert of four seasons of League Football, although he did score regularly for the club in the various wartime Leagues. Upon the resumption of League football in 1919, Bert carried on where he left off, netting 31 goals as Spurs romped to the Second Division title. The following season he scored 17 League goals, but from January onwards most minds were concentrated on the FA Cup. He appeared in all six of Spurs games in the competition, scoring four goals, including both in the 2-1 win over Preston North End in the semi final. As well as picking up an FA Cup winners' medal, April of 1921 saw Bert collect his only full England cap, against Scotland. His appearances at Spurs became sporadic thereafter and in December 1922 he was transferred to Clapton Orient before finishing his career with Bournemouth.

Luther Loide BLISSETT

Born: West Indies, 1st February 1958
Role: Forward
Career: Watford, AC Milan (Italy), Watford, Bournemouth, Watford, West Bromwich Albion, Bury, Mansfield Town
Debut: v West Germany (h) 13-10-1982
Appearances: 14 (3 goals)

Luther Blissett was a powerful centre-forward who was first noticed by Watford whilst playing Sunday League football for Kingfisher Youth in the Brent Sunday League. He signed with Watford in July 1975 and helped the club rise through the Football League, collecting a Fourth Division championship medal in 1978 and helping them reach the First Division in season 1982-83. He proved just as capable of scoring goals in the top flight, finishing the season as the First Division's top goalscorer with 37 goals to his credit and helping Watford finish second behind Liverpool at the top of the table, thereby qualifying for Europe. By then Luther had collected his first cap for England and attracted interest from around Europe, subsequently signing for AC Milan in June 1983 for £1 million, then the record transfer fee received by Watford. His time in Italy was not a successful one (upon arriving at the San Siro Stadium he was reported to have said 'It's a bit different from Watford; where's the dog track?') and a year later Watford paid £550,000 to bring him back to England, a then record fee paid by the club. In November 1988 he joined Bournemouth for £60,000 although he later returned to Watford for a third time, joining the coaching staff. Luther was the first black player to score for England and then became the first to have scored a hat-trick, a feat achieved against Luxembourg in 1982.

Lurther Blissett

Jeffrey Paul BLOCKLEY

Born: Leicester, 12th September 1949
Role: Defender
Career: Coventry City, Arsenal, Leicester City, Notts County
Debut: v Yugoslavia (h) 11-10-1972
Appearances: 1

Jeff played schoolboy football in Leicester and had trials with both Arsenal and Leicester City without success, subsequently signing with Midland Athletic and playing junior football in Leicester. He then came to the attention of Coventry City and joined the club as an apprentice, turning professional in June 1967. Over the next five years he

Jeff Blockley

became a commanding centre-half and attracted the attentions of numerous clubs, including Arsenal who signed him for £200,000 in October 1972. It was with Arsenal that Jeff earned his only cap for England, although his opposing centre-forward Franjo Vladic scored Yugoslavia's goal in the 1-1 draw and Jeff was not selected for his country again. In January 1975 Leicester City, the other club who had turned him down as a youngster, paid £100,000 to take him to Filbert Street and he spent a little over three years with the club, going on loan to Notts County in January 1978 before a full time switch in June. He retired from the game in the close season of 1980. Apart from his full cap for England Jeff represented his country on 10 occasions at Under-23 level.

Stephen BLOOMER

Born: Cradley Heath, Worcestershire, 20th January 1874
Died: 16th April 1938
Role: Inside-Right
Career: Derby Swifts, Derby County, Middlesbrough, Derby County
Debut: v Ireland (h) 9-3-1895
Appearances: 23 (28 goals) + 1 unofficial appearance

Steve Bloomer was spotted by Derby County whilst playing for Derby Swifts and signed in 1892, making his debut the same year. He remained with County for fourteen years and was revered as one of the finest players ever to have played for the club. In 1906 he was surprisingly allowed to join Middlesbrough, but such was his affection for Derby that he returned four years later and finished his career at the club in 1914. Although almost all of his records have since been surpassed, Bloomer was undoubtedly one of the best goalscorers of any age- he amassed 352 League goals for his two clubs; scored 28 goals for England in only 24 appearances (his tally for England was not overtaken until 1956), including five in one match against Wales, and was known as 'God's gift to football' for much of his playing career. All he had to show from his domestic career, however, were two runners-up medals in the FA Cup from 1898 and 1899 - he missed the 6-0 battering from Bury in 1903 - and a Second Division championship medal in 1912. After retiring as a player in 1914 he took up a coaching appointment in Germany and was interred for the duration of the First World War. Fortunately, however, the commandant of the Ruhleben Camp was a keen football follower and allowed Bloomer to set up a mini-League among the other prisoners. Derby County, captained by the great Steve Bloomer, finally won a League title and matches were played each and every day for the duration of the war! Upon returning to England he coached at Derby and had spells in Canada, Spain and Holland. In 1938 his health was in rapid decline (due, it was said, to something of a drink problem) and he was sent by Derby on a cruise in order to recuperate, although he died three weeks later. His son-in-law Alfred Quantrill also played for England. Whilst Steve is in the record books for having scored five times in one game against Wales in 1896, he may have achieved the feat again in 1901 against the same opposition, for whilst most sources credit him with four of England six goals, others claim he netted five. He might have made it six too, but Ernest Nudger Needham insisted on taking a penalty England were awarded and promptly missed.

Steve Bloomer

Frank Blunstone

Frank BLUNSTONE

Born: Crewe, 17th October 1934
Role: Left-Winger
Career: Crewe Alexandra, Chelsea
Debut: v Wales (h) 10-11-1954
Appearances: 5

Frank Blunstone joined the local Crewe Alexandra side straight from school and was soon regarded as one of the best left-wing talents in the lower Leagues, prompting numerous enquiries from other clubs during his early career. A fee of £7,000 took him to Chelsea in 1953 and he proved more than capable of making the grade in the higher level, earning the first of his five caps for England in 1954 and helping Chelsea win the League championship for the first time in their history at the end of the same season. He remained with Chelsea until his retirement in June 1964, having helped restore the club to the First division in 1962-63. During his time at Stamford Bridge he scored over 50 goals in nearly 350 appearances, but it was the goals he created for a host of strikers, including the likes of Roy Bentley and Jimmy Greaves for which he is better known.

Richard BOND

Born: Garstang, Lancashire, 14th December 1883
Died: 25th April 1955
Role: Right-Winger
Career: Royal Artillery, Preston North End, Bradford City, Blackburn Rovers, Lancaster Town, Garstang
Debut: v Ireland (h) 25-2-1905
Appearances: 8 (2 goals)

Dicky Bond joined the Army after leaving school and represented his unit at football, subsequently coming to the attention of Preston North End and signing in August 1902. He helped them win the Second Division championship in 1904 and the following year collected his first cap for England, going on to earn five whilst with the club. In May 1909 he was transferred to Bradford City and the following February earned a recall to the England side, having collected his last cap in April 1906. Dicky made two further appearances for England whilst with Bradford City and remained with the club until May 1922, although he lost four years of League football owing to the First World War. He rejoined the Army during the hostilities and was captured and held as a prisoner of war before being repatriated. He cost Blackburn Rovers £450 when he signed in May 1922 and remained at Ewood Park for a year before slipping into the non-League game with Lancaster Town. Although he retired in 1924 he later played for Garstang FC during the 1926-27 season. Upon finally retiring as a player he ran a fish and chip business in his hometown of Garstang. As well as his 10 full caps for England Dicky represented the Football League once.

Peter Philip BONETTI

Born: Putney, London, 27th September 1941
Role: Goalkeeper
Career: Chelsea, St. Louis Stars (USA), Chelsea, Dundee United
Debut: v Denmark (a) 3-7-1966
Appearances: 7

Peter Bonetti spent two spells at Stamford Bridge, making a record number of 728 appearances for Chelsea during that time. He made his debut for the club in 1960 and after seeing off competition from the likes of Alec Stepney was established as first choice goalkeeper, helping the club win the League Cup in 1965, the FA Cup in 1970 and the European Cup Winners' Cup in 1971. He also collected runners-up medals in the FA Cup in 1967 and the League Cup in 1972 and his athleticism led to him being dubbed 'The Cat.' He made his first appearance for England in 1966 but was not selected for the squad for the World Cup finals that year. He was, however, a member of the squad for the 1970 finals in Mexico and played in the quarter final clash with West Germany after Gordon Banks had been mysteriously taken ill. Ever since that game Peter has had to live with criticism over the three goals England conceded which signalled the end of their reign as world champions, but in fairness to him tiredness had set into the entire side in the final 20 minutes or so of normal time and there was little he could have done to prevent the goals. The continued brilliance of Gordon Banks restricted Peter Bonetti's chances at international level but he still managed to finish his career with seven caps. The curtain came down on Peter's first lengthy spell with Chelsea when he went to play in America for St. Louis Stars, but after a brief spell with Dundee United he returned to Stamford Bridge to finish his career. He is still with the club, serving as specialist goalkeeping coach.

Peter Bonetti

Alexander George BONSOR

Died: 17th August 1907
Role: Forward
Career: Old Etonians, Wanderers, Surrey
Debut: v Scotland (h) 8-3-1873 (scored once)
Appearances: 2 (1 goal) + 1 unofficial appearance

Alexander Bonsor was educated at Eton College and then played for Wanderers and Old Etonians during his career. He appeared in four FA Cup finals, collecting winners' medals with Wanderers in 1872 (the very first final) and 1873 and runners-up medals with Old Etonians in 1875 and 1876, the latter final against Wanderers! He also scored in two finals, both for Old Etonians in games that were drawn 1-1. He also scored on his England debut, netting England's second goal after 10 minutes in the 4-2 win over Scotland in 1873. He played the first 15 minutes of the match against Scotland in 1875 in goal, for William Henry Carr turned up at Kennington Oval late. He might have won more from the game but for the fact that he was apparently sidelined during the 1873-74 season, being 'in-between clubs.' After his playing career came to an end he became a brewer, with his company subsequently being bought by Watney's.

Frank Booth

Frank BOOTH

Born: Hyde, Cheshire, 1882
Died: 22nd June 1919
Role: Left-Winger
Career: Hyde, Glossop, Stockport County, Manchester City, Bury, Clyde, Manchester City
Debut: v Ireland (h) 25-2-1905
Appearances: 1

Frank Booth made his name with Manchester City, joining the club in April 1902 after being on the books of Hyde, Glossop and Stockport County. He helped City win the FA Cup in 1904 and the following year made his only appearance for England, but with the game finishing a 1-1 draw against opposition that were not considered highly, he was not selected again. He remained with City until January 1907 when he joined Bury, subsequently moving to Scotland with Clyde in June 1909. He helped the club reach the Scottish Cup final in 1910, where they were beaten 2-1 by Dundee in a second replay. He returned to Manchester City in July 1911 and spent a further season with the club before retiring.

Thomas Edward BOOTH

Born: Ardwick, Manchester, 25th April 1874
Died: 7th September 1939
Role: Centre-Back
Career: Hooley Hill, Ashton North End, Blackburn Rovers, Everton, Carlisle United
Debut: v Ireland (a) 5-3-1898
Appearances: 2

After playing non-League football with Hooley Hill and Ashton North End, Tom Booth signed professional forms with Blackburn Rovers and soon developed into a dependable centre-back and collected his first cap for England. He might well have spent his entire career with Rovers but for a financial crisis at the club which dictated that it sold a number of players in order to raise much needed funds. Tom was sold to Everton and went on to make 185 appearances for the club but had to sit out the FA Cup Finals of 1906 and 1907, the first through injury and the second for tactical reasons. He remained with Everton until 1908 when he joined Preston, but before playing a single game for them moved on to Carlisle United, retiring in 1909.

Tom Booth

Stephen Andrew BOULD

Born: Stoke-on-Trent, 16th November 1962
Role: Defender
Career: Stoke City, Torquay United, Arsenal
Debut: v Greece (h) 15-5-1994
Appearances: 2

Signed by Stoke City as an apprentice in 1980 Steve Bould spent a brief spell on loan to Torquay United before breaking into the Stoke City side on a regular basis. An uncompromising and reliable performer, he was sold to Arsenal for £390,000 in 1988 and quickly slotted into the defence, helping the club win three League titles, the FA Cup and the European Cup Winners' Cup. More importantly, Steve had continued to defy the odds, for with almost all and sundry claiming that it was time the Arsenal defence was changed as the likes of Adams, Winterburn, Dixon, Keown and Bould himself aged together, the five continued to prove miserly when it came to giving goals away. The arrival of manager Arsene Wenger appeared to give Steve a new lease of life in the Arsenal defence and although he did not play in the 1998 FA Cup Final, his performances earlier on in the season helped the club on its way to a second double.

Steve Bould

Edward Raymond BOWDEN

Born: Looe, Cornwall, 13th September 1909
Role: Forward
Career: Looe, Plymouth Argyle, Arsenal, Newcastle United
Debut: v Wales (a) 29-9-1934
Appearances: 6 (1 goal)

Ray Bowden joined Plymouth Argyle from non-League Looe and developed into an extremely confident inside-forward for the club, helping them win the Third Division (South) after they had narrowly missed out on six occasions. He became one of Herbert Chapman's last signings for Arsenal, costing the Highbury club £4,500 when transferred in March 1933 and added two First Division championship medals and an FA Cup winners' medal in consecutive seasons whilst with the club. He was transferred to Newcastle United for £5,000 in 1937, but the Second World War effectively brought his playing career to an end. The success of players such as Cliff Bastin, Ted Drake and Alex James has tended to overshadow the often vital contributions made by players like Ray Bowden at Arsenal, but his final tally of six caps for England is indicative of how important he was as a player for both club and country. He made two appearances for the Football League and at the end of his playing career returned to Plymouth where he was employed as a sports outfitter, although he had originally begun working life as an auctioneer's clerk.

Alf Bower

Alfred George 'Baishe' BOWER

Born: Bromley, Kent, 10th November 1895
Died: 30th June 1970
Role: Right-Back, Left-Back
Career: Old Carthusians, Chelsea, Casuals, Corinthians
Debut: v Northern Ireland (a) 20-10-1923
Appearances: 5

Educated at Charterhouse School, Alf Bower only began to excel at football after leaving school and joining Old Carthusians. At the end of the First World War he joined the Corinthians and developed into an extremely dependable half-back, able to play on either flank. He was capped by the England amateur side on 13 occasions and is the last amateur player to have captained the full England side, a feat he achieved against Wales on 28th February 1925. He also made nine League appearances for Chelsea during the 1920s and finished his playing career with Casuals, going on to serve on the FA Council between 1928 and 1933. After serving in the Army during the First World War he worked in the Stock Exchange in London between 1919 to 1954 and then was welfare officer for a company in Croydon until his retirement in 1960.

John William BOWERS

Born: Low Santon, Scunthorpe, 22nd February 1908
Died: 4th July 1970
Role: Centre-Forward
Career: Scunthorpe & Lindsey United, Derby County, Leicester City
Debut: v Northern Ireland (a) 14-10-1933 (scored once)
Appearances: 3 (2 goals)

Jack Bowers played for Scunthorpe works side Appelby Works before signing with Scunthorpe United in December 1927, spending barely six months at the club before he joined Derby County. He spent over six years at the Baseball Ground, representing the Football League twice and winning three caps for England before a £6,000 move to Leicester City in November 1936. His arrival at Filbert Street galvanised Leicester's promotion push and at the end of the season he had helped the club win the Second Division championship. He remained at Leicester until his retirement in August 1943, by which time he had made 285 League appearances for his three clubs, scoring 220 goals. In August 1943 he was appointed coach to the Notts County colts' side, remaining with the club until 1945 when he returned to Derby County as assistant trainer, a position he held for over twenty years. His son Jack junior was on the books of Derby between 1957 and 1966, making 65 League appearances in that time.

Stanley Bowles

Stanley BOWLES

Born: Manchester, 24th December 1948
Role: Midfield
Career: Manchester City, Bury, Crewe Alexandra, Carlisle United, Queens Park Rangers, Nottingham Forest, Orient, Brentford
Debut: v Portugal (a) 3-4-1974
Appearances: 5 (1 goal)

Stan Bowles was a maverick player whose career promised much but delivered considerably less, not least because the player himself was often found wanting in his application. He played schools football in Manchester and was taken on as an apprentice by Manchester City in July 1965, turning professional in January 1967. He failed to make the grade at Maine Road and went on trial to Bury in July 1970, making just five League appearances for the club before being released to join Crewe Alexandra. He initially spent a month on trial at Gresty Road and went on to make 51 appearances before Carlisle United paid £12,000 in October 1971 to take him north. Here his career at last began to take off and in September 1972 Queens Park Rangers paid £110,000 to bring him to London. Here he won his five caps for England and in 255 League appearances scored 80 goals, as well as being selected for the Football League once. He remained at Loftus Road until December 1979 when he joined Nottingham Forest for £210,000, seemingly with a chance to redeem his career and appear in a European Cup final, but eight months later he was on his way again, this time joining Orient. A little over a year later he moved across London to join Brentford for £40,000, remaining with the club until 1984. During his career he managed to cause just about every one of his manager's apoplexies, not least because of his activities off the field. Indeed, one was heard to remark 'If Stan Bowles could pass a betting shop the same way he passes a ball he'd be a world beater.' Certainly, on his day he was as gifted a player as previous QPR greats, including Rodney Marsh.

Sidney BOWSER

Born: Handsworth, Birmingham, 6th April 1892
Died: 25th February 1961
Role: Centre-Half
Career: Astbury Richmond, West Bromwich Albion, Distillery, West Bromwich Albion, Walsall
Debut: v Ireland (a) 25-10-1919
Appearances: 1

Sid Bowser was a versatile player able to play at inside right, inside left or centre half and played in all three positions during his career at West Bromwich Albion. After playing schools football in Birmingham he signed with junior clubs Astbury Richmond and then Willenhall. After an unsuccessful trial with Birmingham he signed for West Bromwich Albion in 1908 and helped the club win the Second Division championship in 1911 and reach the FA Cup final in 1912, although they were beaten by Barnsley after a replay. In April 1913 he went to play in Ireland for Belfast Distillery and represented the Irish League once during his fourteen month stay with the club. He returned to West Bromwich Albion in February 1914 and spent a further ten years with the club, winning a League championship medal in 1919-20, the same season he won his only cap for England against Ireland in the first official match after the First World War. He joined Walsall in August 1924 for £1,000 and spent a year with the club before retiring from playing. He then became a licensee in Dudley and many years later managed an off-licence at Acocks Green.

Lee David BOWYER

Born: London, 3rd January 1977
Role: Midfield
Career: Charlton Athletic, Leeds United, West Ham United, Newcastle United
Debut: v Portugal (h) 7-9-2002
Appearances: 1

An aggressive and tenacious midfielder, Lee began his career with Charlton Athletic as a trainee and signed professional forms during the 1993-94 season. Over the next two years his progress at Charlton was considerable, earning him caps for England at both Youth and Under-21 level, before a £2.6 million transfer took him to Leeds United in July 1996, making him the most expensive teenager in the process. He settled in well at Elland Road, winning a nomination for the PFA Young Player of the Year at the end of the 1998-99 season and going on to help Leeds qualify for European competition four years in succession. It was during this period he earned his full England cap, starting the match against Portugal in September 2002 at Villa Park. In January 2003 he left Leeds to return to London with West Ham United, where he became involved in the battle for Premiership survival. Following West Ham's relegation at the end of the season, Lee joined Newcastle United. Unfortunately Lee's career has been blighted by a series of misdemeanours, both on and off the pitch, culminating in a number of court appearances for his activities off the pitch and several bans for his actions on it. These reached new lows when he was sent off during the Newcastle United and Aston Villa match at St. James' Park for fighting with his own team-mate Kieron Dyer. Banned by the FA, he was subsequently heavily fined by the club and put on the transfer list. A proposed move to Birmingham City during the summer of 2005 fell through after a number of City fans made their feelings about the player known via the internet.

Lee Bowyer

Philip John BOYER

Born: Nottingham, 25th January 1949
Role: Forward
Career: Derby County, York City, Bournemouth, Norwich City, Southampton, Manchester City
Debut: v Wales (a) 24-3-1976
Appearances: 1

Phil Boyer came to prominence in the same Bournemouth side as Ted MacDougall, supplying the Scottish striker with an abundance of chances that were duly converted and made the reputations of both players. Whilst MacDougall went to Manchester United and found life tough, Phil's career continued to rise. He had joined Derby County as an apprentice in August 1965 and been upgraded to the professional ranks in November 1966, although he failed to make a single League appearance and was sold to York City for £3,500 in July 1968. He made 109 appearances for the club, scoring 27 goals before a £20,000 move to Bournemouth in December 1970. In a little over three years he made 141 appearances and scored 46 goals, prompting a £145,000 move to Norwich City, then a club record for the Canaries, in February 1974. A member of the side that reached the League Cup final in 1975 he became the first Norwich player to be capped at full level for England when he made his only appearance in 1976. In August 1977 he cost Southampton £125,000 and helped them to the League Cup final in 1979. He registered his fourth century plus League appearances with Southampton (he appeared 116 times for Norwich) by the time of his transfer to Manchester City in November 1980, only the third player to have appeared in over one hundred League games for four different clubs. He cost City £220,000 and later had a spell on loan to Bulovas in Hong Kong before leaving to join Grantham in July 1983. After further appearances in the non-League game with Stamford and Shepshed Charterhouse he returned to Grantham to become joint manager in December 1985. In addition to his full cap for England, Phil also represented the country twice at Under-22 level.

Walter Edward BOYES

Born: Sheffield, 5th January 1913
Died: 16th September 1960
Role: Left-Winger
Career: Woodhouse Mills United, West Bromwich Albion, Everton, Notts County, Scunthorpe United, Retford Town
Debut: v Holland (a) 18-5-1935
Appearances: 3 + 1 unofficial appearance

Despite having one leg longer than the other Wally excelled at football whilst at school and represented Sheffield Schoolboys before joining Woodhouse Mills United. He joined West Bromwich Albion as an amateur in February 1931 and was upgraded to the professional ranks a month later, going on to score in the FA Cup Final of 1935 against Sheffield Wednesday, although Wednesday went on to win the cup 4-2. As well as his three full caps for England Wally made two appearances for the Football League and played in the Jubilee Fund match between England and Scotland in 1935, a game designated unofficial. He joined Everton in February 1938 and won a League championship medal in 1939, the last full season before the outbreak of the Second World War. He remained at Goodison until 1949 when he joined Notts County as player-coach, but having made only three appearances for the Magpies joined Scunthorpe

Wally Boyes

United where he finished his League career. Wally joined Retford Town as player-manager in 1953 and was appointed manager at Hyde Town in April 1958, subsequently becoming trainer at Swansea Town in 1959. He retained the position until June 1960 when he was forced to quit owing to ill health and three months later died at the comparatively young age of 47 years.

Thomas Wilkinson BOYLE

Born: Hoyland, 29th January 1888
Died: 5th January 1940
Role: Centre-Back
Career: Hoyland Star, Elsecar, Barnsley, Burnley, Wrexham
Debut: v Ireland (a) 15-2-1913
Appearances: 1

Despite standing only 5' 7" tall Tommy Boyle proved his lack of height was no handicap, even at centre-half where it was perhaps more traditional to be approaching six foot. He had played for junior clubs Hoyland Star and Elsecar before signing with Barnsley in May 1906, going on to help the club reach the FA Cup Final in 1910 against Newcastle United, although United won 2-0 after a replay. In September 1911 Tommy was sold to Burnley for £1,150, becoming club captain and collecting his only cap for England in 1913. The following year he collected a winners' medal in the FA Cup as Burnley overcame Liverpool 1-0 at the Crystal Palace. This was the first FA Cup final at which the reigning monarch was present and Tommy thus became the first player to receive the trophy from the monarch, King George V. After the First World War Tommy helped Burnley win the League championship in 1921 and in 1922 was appointed player-coach. He left Burnley for Walsall in the close season of 1923 and then coached in Germany for a spell. As well as his one full appearance for England Tommy represented the Football League on four occasions.

Peter BRABROOK

Born: East Ham, London, 8th November 1937
Role: Right-Winger
Career: Chelsea, West Ham United, Orient, Romford, Woodford Town
Debut: v USSR (Gothenburg) 17-6-1958 (WC)
Appearances: 3

Peter joined Chelsea as an amateur in 1953 and was upgraded to the professional ranks two years later, making his debut in March 1955 as Chelsea were about to lift the League title for the first time in their history. After seven seasons at Stamford Bridge he was allowed to join West Ham for £35,000 and became part of the side that won the FA Cup in 1964, the European Cup Winners' Cup in 1965 and reached the final of the League Cup in 1966. He then joined Orient and helped them win the Third Division title in 1970 before finishing his playing career in non-League circles with Romford and Woodford. As well as his three full caps for England he also represented the country at Youth and Under-23 level, collecting nine caps at this latter level.

Peter Brabrook

Paul William BRACEWELL

Born: Heswall, 19th July 1962
Role: Midfield
Career: Stoke City, Sunderland, Everton, Sunderland, Newcastle United, Sunderland, Fulham
Debut: v West Germany (Mexico City) (substitute) 12-6-1985
Appearances: 3

Paul began his career as an apprentice at Stoke City before graduating to the professional ranks, going on to make over 125 appearances for the first team before a £250,000 move to Sunderland in 1983. Less than a year later he was on the move again, joining Everton for £450,000 and helping them to the League title and European Cup Winners' Cup in 1985 and narrowly missing out on the treble as they were beaten in the FA Cup Final. He was injured when they again won the title in 1987 and in 1989 returned to Sunderland in a deal worth £250,000. Three years later he joined local rivals Newcastle United and helped them win the First Division title in 1993 and consolidate their position

Paul Bracewell

in the top flight. He returned to Roker Park for a third time in 1995 for £100,000 and collected a second First Division championship medal in 1996, although they were relegated back at the end of the following season. In October 1997 he joined Kevin Keegan for a second time, this time at Fulham where he combined playing with a role on the coaching staff. In addition to his three full caps he also represented England on 13 occasions at Under-21 level.

Geoffrey Reginald William BRADFORD

Born: Frenchay, Bristol, 18th July 1927
Died: 31st December 1994
Role: Inside-Forward
Career: Soundwell, Bristol Rovers
Debut: v Denmark (a) 2-10-1955 (scored once)
Appearances: 1 (1 goal)

Geoff Bradford represented Bristol as a schoolboy and joined Soundwell FC before being invited for trials by both Blackpool and Blackburn Rovers. Neither club offered him a contract and so he signed with the local Bristol Rovers club in May 1949 and went on to register a number of records for the club. He helped them win the Third Division South championship in 1953, scoring 33 of their 92 League goals that season, both of which were records. He was selected for England two years later whilst still a Second Division player and scored England's last goal in the 5-1 win over Denmark. He remained with the club until his retirement in 1964, by which time he had made 461 League appearances and scored 245 goals, the latter tally another club record. His League appearance figure might have been higher too but for a series of injuries that punctuated his career. Unfortunately, by the time of his retirement Rovers were back in the Third Division. After leaving the game Geoff went to work in the oil industry, working for a company in Avonmouth.

Joseph BRADFORD

Born: Peggs Green, Leicestershire, 22nd January 1901
Died: 6th September 1980
Role: Centre-Forward
Career: Peggs Green Victoria, Birmingham, Bristol City
Debut: v Northern Ireland (a) 20-10-1923 (scored once)
Appearances: 12 (7 goals)

Joe joined the local Peggs Green Victoria club at the age of 12, playing in the Leicester Senior League and being invited along for trials by both Aston Villa and Derby County during his time with the club. He eventually signed with Birmingham in February 1920 for £125 and during the course of his fifteen years with the club became known as Gentleman Joe because of his sportsmanship. He helped Birmingham reach the FA Cup final in 1931 and although Joe scored in the final they were beaten 2-1 by local rivals West Bromwich Albion. He won his first cap in 1923 and scored England's goal in the 2-1 defeat by Northern Ireland and remained a fixture within the England side until 1931. He joined Bristol City in May 1935 and retired a year later. He initially worked as a licensee and later ran a sports shop in the Birmingham area.

Joe Bradford

Warren BRADLEY

Born: Hyde, Cheshire, 20th June 1933
Role: Right-Winger
Career: Durham City, Bolton Wanderers, Bishop Auckland, Manchester United, Bury, Northwich Victoria, Macclesfield, Bangor City, Macclesfield
Debut: v Mexico (substitute) (a) 24-5-1959
Appearances: 3 (2 goals)

Signed by Manchester United from Bishop Auckland in February 1958, along with Bob Hardisty and Derek Lewin, Warren was initially expected to bolster the reserve side in the aftermath of the Munich air disaster. However, his performances were of such quality he was offered a contract as a full professional and signed in November 1958, making his League debut the same month. At the end of the season his progress had been such that he was capped by England three times, scoring in the matches against the USA and Italy. He was never part of Matt Busby's long term plans, however, and in March 1962 he was sold to Bury for £40,000 and subsequently went back to playing non-League football. In addition to his three full caps for England, Warren earned 11 caps at amateur level and helped Bishop Auckland win the FA Amateur Cup in both 1956 and 1957. Prior to becoming a professional footballer he had been a schoolteacher.

Francis BRADSHAW

Born: Sheffield, 31st May 1884
Role: Inside-Left
Career: Sheffield Wednesday, Northampton Town, Everton, Arsenal
Debut: v Austria (a) 6-6-1908 (scored three times)
Appearances: 1 (3 goals)

Frank represented Sheffield Schools between 1895 and 1897 and then played Sunday school football in the city before linking with Sheffield Wednesday as an amateur in 1904. He was upgraded to the professional ranks the following year and in 1907 helped the club win the FA Cup against Everton. A year later he made his only appearance for England and became the last of five players to have netted a hat-trick on their one and only appearance for England, the earlier players being Albert Allen, Walter Gilliat, John Veitch and Jack Yates. By 1910 a series of serious knee injuries led Wednesday to believe his first class career was at an end and he was sold to Northampton Town for £250, but Frank proved his detractors wrong by earning selection for the Southern League. He was then transferred to Everton for £1,250 in November 1911 and he later represented the Football League on four occasions. He joined Arsenal during the close season of 1914 and went on to make 132 League appearances for the club before his retirement in 1923. He then spent a year as manager of Aberdare Athletic before retiring from the game altogether and reverting to his original trade of silversmith.

Thomas Henry BRADSHAW

Born: Liverpool, 24th August 1873
Died: London, 25th December 1899
Role: Left-Winger
Career: Northwich Victoria, Liverpool, Tottenham Hotspur, Thames Ironworks
Debut: v Ireland (h) 20-2-1897
Appearances: 1 + 1 Unofficial appearance

Tom Bradshaw first came to prominence whilst with Liverpool, helping them to the Second Division championship in 1894 and 1896, earning his only cap for England and representing the Football League twice. In May 1898 he signed for Spurs of the Southern League and was almost ever-present during his one season with the club. He also returned to the fringes of the international scene, representing the United League, playing for the South against the North in an amateur trial match and playing for an England XI against a team of Scottish counterparts in a match to raise funds for the Players Union. He then joined Thames Ironworks during the close season of 1899, but was taken ill shortly before Christmas and subsequently died on Christmas Day at the age of just 26 years. The following April Spurs met Thames Ironworks in a match to raise funds for his dependants.

William BRADSHAW

Born: Padiham, Lancashire, 1885
Role: Left-Half
Career: Padiham, Accrington Stanley, Blackburn Rovers, Rochdale
Debut: v Ireland (a) 12-2-1910
Appearances: 4

Although Bill Bradshaw played at left-half he was extremely adept at joining the attack. Indeed, one report referred to him as being as good as having a sixth forward. He played for Padiham and Accrington Stanley before joining Blackburn Rovers in May 1903 for £20 and spent seventeen years at the club, helping them win the League championship in 1912 and 1914. He collected his first cap for England in 1910 and his last in 1913 and also represented the Football League on three occasions. In April 1923 he was released in order to become player-manager of Rochdale, holding the position until September the same year. His abilities up front were as a direct result of having previously played on the left-wing and he was also an expert penalty taker.

Warren Bradley

George BRANN

Born: Eastbourne, 23rd April 1865
Died: 14th June 1954
Role: Right-Winger, Inside-Right
Career: Swifts, Slough, Corinthians
Debut: v Scotland (a) 27-3-1886
Appearances: 3 (1 goal)

George was educated at Ardingly College and represented the college at football, subsequently joining Swifts, Slough and the Corinthians upon graduating. Aside from his undoubted football abilities he was also an exceptional cricketer, representing Sussex at county level between 1883 and 1905 where he scored 25 centuries and undertaking tours of Australia, South Africa and North America. He was also a good golf player, serving as secretary to the Home Park Golf Club in Surbiton for twenty years. Away from sport George was a schoolteacher, teaching at his former college of Ardingley.

William Frederick BRAWN

Born: Wellingborough, 1st August 1878
Died: London, 18th August 1932
Role: Right-Winger
Career: Wellingborough Town, Northampton Town, Sheffield United, Aston Villa, Middlesbrough, Chelsea, Brentford
Debut: v Wales (a) 29-2-1904
Appearances: 2

Billy Brawn began his career with the local Wellingborough side, playing non-League football until persuaded to signed professional forms with Northampton Town, then in the Southern League. He made his Football League debut with Sheffield United in 1900 but his career began to take off when he signed with Aston Villa, arriving at Villa Park in December 1901. Unfortunately he was badly injured on his debut for the club against Blackburn Rovers in January 1902 and was out of the side for the rest of the season. After recovering he used his height (6' 1") and weight (13st 5lbs) to good effect on the Villa right wing, helping them to win the FA Cup in 1905 and earned two caps for England. In March 1906 he left Villa for Middlesbrough and the following November moved down south to London, signing for Chelsea. He finished his playing career with Brentford, joining them in August 1911 and retiring two years later, although he continued to serve the club as a director. He was briefly coaxed back into playing five years later; Spurs arrived at Griffin Park for a London Combination fixture in November 1918 with only nine players and so Billy Brawn played on the right wing for Spurs against his own club! After retiring a second time he became a publican, an occupation he maintained until his death.

John BRAY

Born: Oswaldtwistle, Lancashire, 22nd April 1909
Died: 20th November 1982
Role: Left-Half
Career: Clayton Olympia, Manchester Central, Manchester City
Debut: v Wales (a) 29-9-1934
Appearances: 6 + 1 unofficial appearance

Jack Bray played schoolboy football in East Lancashire and junior football with Clayton Olympia, joining Manchester Central in 1928. A year later he was taken on as a professional by Manchester City and served as understudy to the Scottish international Jimmy McMullan. Eventually Jack forced his way into the first team on a regular basis and was a member of the side that reached the FA Cup final in 1933 when City were beaten by Everton. They returned the following year to beat Portsmouth and by then Jack was being hailed as one of the best left-halfs in the country, a view confirmed later the same year when he won his first cap for England. As well as six full caps for England Jack appeared in the Jubilee international in Glasgow and represented the Football League on five occasions. He helped City win the League championship in 1937 and finally retired from playing during the Second World War. In February 1947 he took over as manager of Watford, a position he held for twelve months before moving to Nelson where he served as coach for seven months. He was also a good class cricketer, turning out for Accrington Cricket Club in the Lancashire League.

Edward BRAYSHAW

Born: Kirkstall, Leeds, 1863
Died: 20th November 1908
Role: Full-Back
Career: Walkley All Saints, Sheffield Wednesday, Grimsby Town
Debut: v Ireland (h) 5-2-1887
Appearances: 1

Teddy Brayshaw joined Sheffield Wednesday from local club Walkley All Saints in 1883 and therefore made the majority of his appearances for the club in friendly matches. He was, however, deemed good enough to earn selection for the England side that beat Ireland 7-0 in 1887, although he was surprisingly overlooked thereafter. Whilst with Wednesday he helped the club win the Football Alliance title in 1890 and reach the FA Cup final the same season, although the final was little short of a disaster as Blackburn Rovers strolled to a 6-1 win. Teddy officially retired owing to injury in 1891 but was lured out of retirement during the 1892-93 season, making a couple of appearances for Grimsby Town. Upon his final retirement he became a licensee in Sheffield but was forced to give up in 1907 owing to ill health.

Wayne Bridge

Wayne Michael BRIDGE

Born: Southampton, 5th August 1980
Role: Defender
Career: Southampton, Chelsea, Fulham
Debut: v Holland (h) 13-2-2002
Appearances: 22

Wayne joined his local club as a trainee and moved up to the professional ranks in 1997. Originally a midfield player, he made sufficient progress at The Dell to break into the first team and earn caps for England at Youth and Under-21 level. During the 1999-2000 season, with the club having an abundance of midfield players, Wayne was tried out in the defence, playing as a left-back. He proved something of a revelation, becoming one of Southampton's most consistent players and earning selection for the full England side in February 2002. Stiff competition from the likes of Ashley Cole for the left-back berth has often meant Wayne's best chance of representing his country on a regular basis has been in more of a midfield role, in the supposedly troublesome left hand side area. In the summer of 2003 he was transferred to Chelsea in a deal worth £7 million with Graeme Le Saux, whom Wayne had replaced in the England side, making the opposite journey. At Stamford Bridge Wayne developed into a versatile left sided player, equally at home at left-back and in midfield. Indeed, it was his forays in midfield that enabled Chelsea to overcome Arsenal in the 2003-04 Champions League quarter final, with Wayne scoring the winning goal. A member of the side that won the Premiership in 2004-05, Wayne's season was brought to a halt with a broken ankle sustained against Newcastle United. In January 2006 he went on loan to Fulham.

Barry Bridges

Barry John BRIDGES

Born: Horsford, Norwich, 29th April 1941
Role: Forward
Career: Chelsea, Birmingham City, Queens Park Rangers, Millwall, Brighton & Hove Albion, Highland Park (South Africa), St. Patrick's Athletic (Eire)
Debut: v Scotland (h) 10-4-1965
Appearances: 4 (1 goal)

After playing for Norwich Schools, Barry was signed to the Chelsea ground staff in July 1956, turning professional in May 1958. An important member of the first team squad for eight years he clocked up over 200 appearances and scored 93 goals. He won a Football League Cup winners' medal with the Blues in 1965 and also four England International caps, before being sold to Birmingham City for £55,000 in May 1966. He was subsequently sold to Queens Park Rangers for £50,000 in August 1968, moved across London to Millwall for £40,000 in September 1970 and finished his League career with a £28,000 move to Brighton & Hove Albion in August 1972. Two years later he joined Highland Park in South Africa and then became player-manager of St. Patrick's Athletic. Barry then had a spell managing Sligo Rovers before returning to his native Norfolk, combining management roles at Dereham Town, King's Lynn and Horsford Town with a milk round in Horsford.

George Arthur BRIDGETT

Born: Forsbrook, Staffordshire, 1883
Died: 1954
Role: Left-Winger
Career: Burslem Park, Trentham, Stoke, Sunderland, Port Vale
Debut: v Scotland (h) 1-4-1905
Appearances: 11 (3 goals)

Arthur Bridgett joined Stoke after playing schoolboy and junior football in the area, signing with the club in October 1902. Barely three months later he was sold to Sunderland where he made his name, collecting an England cap in 1905 and representing the Football League on two occasions. He had to wait over three years before making his second appearance for England, but once in the side he proved difficult to dislodge, going on to win 11 caps in total. A good crosser of the ball he was also more than capable of scoring himself, netting three goals for his country. He joined South Shields as player-manager in May 1912 and later switched to North Shields as manager. He then had a lengthy absence from the game although he returned during the 1923-24 season as a player with Port Vale, netting seven goals in just 14 League appearances for the club. A deeply religious man, Arthur objected to playing on Good Friday and Christmas Day throughout his career.

Thomas BRINDLE

Born: Darwen, Lancashire, 1861
Died: 15th April 1905
Role: Left-Back
Career: Darwen, Blackburn Olympic
Debut: v Scotland (a) 13-3-1880
Appearances: 2 (1 goal)

Tommy Brindle played junior football in the Darwen area before signing with the local club, then considered one of the major forces in the game. He helped them win the Lancashire Cup in its inaugural seasons of 1879-80, beating Blackburn Rovers 3-0 in the final. He then collected his first cap for England, in the 5-4 defeat to Scotland. Two days later he played in the match against Wales and scored one of England's goals in the 3-1 win, the first full-back to score for England in open play. Whilst the feat has been equalled many times since, at the time it caused something of a sensation, for full-backs were rarely to be found in the opposition's half of the field. During the mid 1880s he switched to Blackburn Olympic.

Arthur Bridgett

John Thomas BRITTLETON

Born: Winsford, Cheshire, 23rd April 1882
Died: 22nd February 1955
Role: Right-Half
Career: Winsford Celtic, Winsford United, Stockport County, Sheffield Wednesday, Stoke, Winsford United
Debut: v Ireland (a) 10-2-1912
Appearances: 5

Some sources give his name as James, others Tom and Charlie Buchan always referred to him as Jack; what is not in dispute is the versatility of his play, for he was found at right-half, outside-right, inside-right and even full-back at various stages during his career. He played junior football in Winsford and then joined Winsford Celtic and Winsford United before linking with Stockport County in 1902. Stockport converted him from a forward player to a half-back, the position he probably excelled at, and within two years he had attracted considerable attention from bigger clubs. He was transferred to Sheffield Wednesday in September 1904 and helped the club win the FA Cup in 1907, beating Everton 2-1 in the final. He represented the Football League twice during his time with the club and also collected five full caps for England between 1912 and 1914. He remained with Sheffield Wednesday until May 1920 when he joined Stoke City, carrying on playing League football until he was 43 years of age. He rejoined Winsford United as player-coach in 1925, his final club. His son Tom junior was on the books of Aston Villa between the two World Wars.

Cliff Britton

Clifford Samuel BRITTON

Born: Hanham, Bristol, 27th August 1909
Died: 1st December 1975
Role: Right-Half
Career: Hanham Athletic, Hanham United Methodists, Bristol St. George, Bristol Rovers, Everton
Debut: v Wales (a) 29-9-1934
Appearances: 9 (1 goal) + 12 War appearances + 1 unofficial appearance

Cliff Britton spent over 45 years in the game, serving as a player and manager for a host of clubs. As a player he began his career as an amateur with Bristol Rovers in 1926, being upgraded to the professional ranks in the summer of 1928. In June 1930 he was transferred to Everton for a four figure fee and went on to make 240 League appearances for the Goodison club before the outbreak of the Second World War effectively brought his League career to an end. Whilst with the club he won an FA Cup winners' medal in 1933, represented the Football League on four occasions and was a member of the FA touring party to South Africa in 1939, appearing three times in matches against the national side. He made his final full appearance for the England side in May 1937 but returned to the side in the representative games played during the Second World War, making 12 appearances. He guested for Aldershot during the Second World War and announced his retirement as a player in October 1945, subsequently taking over as manager of Burnley. He took them to the FA Cup final and promotion to the First Division in 1947, finishing runners-up to Charlton Athletic in the cup and behind Manchester City in the League. In September 1948 he returned to Everton as manager, a position he was to hold until February 1956. During that time Everton were relegated into the Second Division in 1951, although they were promoted back into the First Division in 1954. He learned that the club planned to appoint a temporary manager whilst he was away with the side on tour and therefore resigned, although he resurfaced as manager of Preston North End six months later. He spent five years at Deepdale and then joined Hull City as manager in July 1961. In November 1969 he was promoted to general manager, a post he held until his retirement in October 1971.

Peter Frank BROADBENT

Born: Elvington, Kent, 15th May 1933
Role: Inside-Forward
Career: Dover, Brentford, Wolverhampton Wanderers, Shrewsbury Town, Aston Villa, Stockport County, Bromsgrove Rovers
Debut: v USSR (Gothenburg) 17-6-1958 (WC)
Appearances: 7 (2 goals)

Peter was educated at and played for Deal County Modern school and was briefly associated with Dover before signing professional forms with Brentford in May 1950. He had made just 16 League appearances for the Bees when Wolves paid £10,000 to take him to Molineux in February 1951, a fee repaid many times over during the following fourteen years. He made 453 League appearances for the Molineux club between 1951 and 1965 and helped them win three League titles (1954, 1958 and 1959) and the FA Cup in 1960, narrowly missing out on the double in 1960 when Wolves finished runners-up in the League. He also collected one cap for the England B side, one cap for the Under-23 side and two appearances for the Football League in addition to earning seven caps for England. After a brief spell with Shrewsbury he was signed by a Villa side desperate for some firepower up front, although the club's problems at the time he signed lay more with the defence! He spent three years with Villa before winding down his League career with Stockport County. At the end of his career he took over a children's clothes shop in Halesowen, whilst his son Gary is a professional golfer.

Peter Broadbent

Ivan Arthur 'Ivor' BROADIS

Born: Poplar, London, 18th December 1922
Role: Inside-Forward
Career: Finchley, Northfleet, Finchley, Carlisle United, Sunderland, Manchester City, Newcastle United, Carlisle United, Queen of the South
Debut: v Austria (h) 28-11-1951
Appearances: 14 (8 goals)

Whilst many players lost their best years to the two world wars, the Second World War proved to be something of a benefit for Ivor Broadis, for it gave him playing experience he might not otherwise have received. He had joined Spurs as a junior and played for Finchley and Northfleet, Spurs nursery club and then assisted Spurs during the Second World War. After playing regularly for eighteen months he enlisted in the armed forces and thereafter guested for Bradford Park Avenue, Manchester United and Millwall before joining Carlisle United during the 1945-46 season. He proved such a success at Carlisle that they offered him professional forms as both player and manager in August 1946. In February 1949 he transferred himself to Sunderland for £18,000, then a record fee for the club. In October 1951 he cost Manchester City £20,000 and a month later collected his first cap for England. Whilst at City he represented the Football League three times and collected a further seven caps for England before joining Newcastle United for £17,000 in October 1953. He won his final six England caps whilst at St. James' Park and then returned to Carlisle United as player-coach in July 1955, costing the club £3,500. He finished his playing career with Queen of the South in the Scottish League, joining the club in June 1959 and retiring in 1960 but continued as coach until 1962. He then returned to live in Carlisle and worked as a sports journalist.

Ivan Broadis

John BROCKBANK

Born: Whitehaven, Cumberland, 22nd August 1848
Died: 4th February 1896
Role: Forward
Career: Cambridge University
Debut: v Scotland (a) 30-11-1872
Appearances: 1

John Brockbank was educated at and represented the Shrewsbury School before going on to Cambridge University. He won his only cap for England in the first international match, even though he had yet to earn his Blue at university. He was eventually awarded two Blues, appearing in the matches in 1874 and 1875 and also represented London between 1872 and 1874. His football prowess was achieved despite suffering from a weak knee and he was also a good cricketer, playing at club level and representing the MCC on one occasion in 1874. By profession he was an actor.

John Brant BRODIE

Born: Wightwick, Wolverhampton, 1862
Died: 16th February 1925
Role: Forward
Career: Wolverhampton Wanderers
Debut: v Ireland (h) 2-3-1889
Appearances: 3 (1 goal)

Jack Brodie was educated and later taught at St. Luke's school in Blakenhall and was a founding father of Wolverhampton Wanderers, the club he served in one capacity or another for the rest of his life. He helped amalgamate Blakenhall St. Luke's Football Club with Blakenhall Wanderers Cricket Club into Wolverhampton Wanderers FC in 1879 and was a player until his retirement in 1891. During that time he helped them reach the FA Cup Final in 1889 where they were beaten by Preston four weeks after Jack had collected his first cap for England. Upon retiring as a player in 1891 Jack became a referee, combining this with his position of assistant headmaster of St. Peter's school in Wolverhampton. He joined the Wolves board in 1913 and remained a member until his death.

Thomas George BROMILOW

Born: Liverpool, 7th October 1894
Died: 4th March 1959
Role: Left-Half
Career: United West Dingle Presbyterian Club, Liverpool
Debut: v Wales (a) 14-3-1921
Appearances: 5

Tom Bromilow had played for West Dingle Presbyterian Club and then joined the Army during the First World War, going on to represent his unit. His success prompted him to approach Liverpool for a trial when League football resumed in 1919, and after successfully coming through a match against Chelsea in October of that year was taken on as a professional player. He was to remain with the club for eleven years, making 374 League appearances and collecting League championship medals in 1922 and 1923 as well as representing the Football League six times. He finally retired as a player in May 1930 and then went into coaching, including a spell in Amsterdam before his return to England in 1932 in order to take over as manager of Burnley in October of that year. He was in charge at Turf Moor for almost three years and then took charge at Crystal Palace between July 1935 and July 1939, although he briefly resigned for six months in 1936. He spent the Second World War at Leicester City, being in the manager's chair between July 1939 and May 1945, and after a year out of the game returned as manager of Newport County in May 1946. He left Newport in 1950 and then scouted for Leicester City, a position he retained until his death.

Tom Bromilow

General Sir William BROMLEY-DAVENPORT

Born: London, 21st January 1863
Died: 6th February 1949
Role: Forward
Career: Oxford University, Old Etonians
Debut: v Scotland (a) 15-3-1884
Appearances: 2 (2 goals)

William Bromley-Davenport was educated at Eton College and played for the school team from 1881 until he moved on to Oxford University. He was awarded his Blue in the same year he earned the first of his two caps for England and later played for Old Etonians. He was elected Member of Parliament for Macclesfield in 1886 and held the seat until 1906, being made Financial Secretary to the War Office in 1903 and holding the post for two years. At the turn of the century he served in the British Army in the Boer War, for which he was awarded the DSO. During the First World War he served as a Brigadier in Egypt in 1916 and the following year was in France as assistant Director of Labour. He was appointed Lord Lieutenant of Cheshire in 1920 and held the post until his death in 1949. He was knighted in 1924 for his services to his country.

Eric Frederick BROOK

Born: Mexborough, Yorkshire, 27th November 1907
Died: Manchester, 29th March 1965
Role: Left-Winger
Career: Swinton Primitives, Mexborough, Wath Athletic, Barnsley, Manchester City
Debut: v Northern Ireland (a) 19-10-1929
Appearances: 18 (10 goals) + 1 War appearance

Eric played schools football in Mexborough and local football thereafter before signing with Barnsley in February 1926, costing the club £200 from Wath Athletic. Two years later he and colleague Fred Tilson were sold to Manchester City in a £4,000 deal and both went on to play for England. Eric helped City reach the FA Cup Final in successive seasons, winning the trophy in 1934, and the League title in 1937. First capped in 1929 he was both a creator and taker of goal chances, netting twice in the notorious match against the Italians in 1934, the game which became known as the Battle of Highbury. In addition to his England caps, Eric represented the Football League on seven occasions. By the time he retired during the Second World War he had made 453 League appearances for City, scoring 158 goals. Upon retiring as a player Eric settled in Manchester and worked as a crane driver.

Eric Brook

Trevor Brooking

Sir Trevor David BROOKING M.B.E., C.B.E.

Born: Barking, Essex, 2nd October 1948
Role: Midfield
Career: West Ham United
Debut: v Portugal (a) 3-4-1974
Appearances: 47 (5 goals) + 1 unofficial international

Trevor spent eighteen years as a professional at West Ham United, his only senior club, a remarkable length of time given that many of his peers were regularly moving between clubs. After being spotted playing schools and representative football for Ilford, Essex and London, Trevor was taken on as an apprentice by West Ham in July 1965 and was upgraded the following year. He went on to make 528 League appearances for the Hammers, scoring 88 goals and helped the club win the FA Cup in 1975 and 1980, scoring the only goal of the game in the latter final against Arsenal. His goal was made all the more special by the fact it was a header; only the third headed goal of his career! He also appeared in the final of the European Cup Winners' Cup in 1976, the League Cup Final in 1981 and won a Second Division championship medal in 1981. Having represented England at schoolboy, Youth and Under-23 level he was awarded his first full cap in 1974 and remained a regular until the 1982 World Cup, appearing as a substitute in the last match against Spain as England drew 0-0 and went out of the competition - England lost only seven of the 47 games Trevor appeared in. Trevor retired as a player in May 1984 and then went into journalism and is currently a member of the BBC Match of the Day team. Having previously been made an MBE for his service to football Trevor was awarded the CBE in the 1999 New Year's Honours List and was later knighted.

John BROOKS

Born: Reading, Berkshire, 23rd December 1931
Role: Inside-Forward
Career: Reading, Tottenham Hotspur, Chelsea, Brentford, Crystal Palace, Stevenage Town, Knebworth
Debut: v Wales (h) 14-11-1956 (scored once)
Appearances: 3 (2 goals)

After signing for his local club Johnny was transferred to Spurs for a fee of £3,000 in February 1953, with Dennis Uphill and Harry Robshaw making the opposite journey as part of the deal. Johnny's career at Spurs covered the transitional period between the 'push and run' side of the early 1950s and the great double side of the early 1960s, but Johnny was a highly creative player and came into his own following the departure of Eddie Baily in 1956. The subsequent emergence of Alfie Stokes put Johnny's position under threat and he was subsequently swapped with Chelsea's Les Allen, finishing his career with Brentford and then Crystal Palace. Whilst with Spurs he won three England caps, but despite scoring in two of those games, could not dovetail with Johnny Haynes and was not selected again.

Frank Henry BROOME

Born: Berkhamstead, Hertfordshire, 11th June 1915
Died: September 1994
Role: Winger, Forward
Career: Boxmoor United, Berkhamstead Town, Aston Villa, Derby County, Notts County, Brentford, Crewe Alexandra, Shelbourne
Debut: v Germany (a) 14-5-1938 (scored once)
Appearances: 7 (3 goals) + 1 War appearance

Frank Broome

Frank was discovered by Aston Villa whilst playing Spartan League football for Berkhamstead Town and given a trial, scoring six goals in a Colts match and thus being offered professional forms (even though both Spurs and Arsenal had rejected him for being too small at 5' 7"). He made his debut in 1935 as an inside-forward but was injured for much of the following season as Villa were relegated into the Second Division. He scored 28 goals in 1936-37 but manager Jimmy Hogan converted him to outside-right the following campaign as Villa won the Second Division title and at the end of the season he was invited to join England's European tour. His debut came in the infamous match in Berlin at which the England players were instructed to give the Nazi salute by the then British ambassador. As it happened, Aston Villa were also touring Germany at the time and the following day Frank Broome returned to the same stadium, this time with his club, but the Villa players made sure their arms were kept very firmly down by their sides! Frank remained with Villa during the Second World War and played in the first League match of 1946-47 before being transferred to Derby County. In 1949 he was sold to Notts County, helping them win the Third Division (South) title in his first season. He finished his Football League career with Crewe Alexandra after a brief spell with Brentford and then went over to Ireland to finish his playing career with Shelbourne. He then turned to management, taking over at Exeter City and Southend United, coached in Australia and then had a second spell in charge at Exeter. He finished his career coaching in the Middle East.

Tony Brown

Anthony John 'Bomber' BROWN

Born: Oldham, 3rd October 1945
Role: Forward
Career: West Bromwich Albion, Torquay United
Debut: v Wales (h) 19-5-1971
Appearances: 1

After representing both Manchester and Lancashire at schools level, Tony was signed as an apprentice by West Bromwich Albion in April 1961 and joined the professional ranks in October 1963. He made his debut for the club the same year and over the next seventeen years went on to set a number of records for the club which remain to this day; the most League appearances (a total of 574) and most League goals (218 scored) by an individual player. In all, Tony made 819 appearances for the Albion first team, scoring 312 goals, and helped the club win the League Cup in 1966 and the FA Cup in 1968, as well as reach the final of the League Cup in both 1967 and 1970. He represented the Football League twice and in 1971 was called up by Alf Ramsey for the England side to face Wales at Wembley, but was substituted after 74 minutes, although he was not injured, and he was not selected again. In 1980 Tony went to play in America, turning out for the New England Teamen and Jacksonville over the next two years, finally returning to England to sign with Torquay United for £6,000 in October 1981. He made 38 League appearances and seven substitute appearances for the club, scoring 11 goals before drifting into the non-League game with Stafford Rangers. He returned to the Hawthorns to serve as Albion's coach between 1984 and 1986.

Arthur 'Digger' BROWN

Born: Birmingham, 1859
Died: 1st July 1909
Role: Inside-Right
Career: Aston Cross, Aston Unity, Aston Comrades, Aston Villa, Mitchell St. George's, Birchfield Trinity, Excelsior, Aston Villa
Debut: v Ireland (a) 18-2-1882 (scored four)
Appearances: 3 (4 goals)

Arthur 'Digger' Brown began his career playing junior football with local sides Aston Cross, Aston Unity and Aston Comrades before being signed by the more senior club Aston Villa in 1878. He stayed only a matter of weeks, however, before leaving to join Mitchell St. George's. He rejoined Aston Villa two years later, having also turned out for Birchfield Trinity and the Excelsior club. Known as Digger during his time at the club, he was able to play equally well at either outside-right or centre-forward for Villa and scored 15 goals in just 22 FA Cup ties for the club. He collected his first cap for England in 1882, scoring four goals in the 13-0 demolition of Ireland and seemed set for a lengthy career, but instead all three of his caps came within a month of each other in 1882. By 1886 he had been forced to retire from the game owing to ill health and thus missed out on playing for Villa when they became founder members of the Football League. His younger brother Albert Brown also played for Villa, appearing in the 1887 FA Cup winning side.

Arthur Brown

Arthur Samuel BROWN

Born: Gainsborough, Lincolnshire, 6th April 1885
Died: 27th June 1944
Role: Centre-Forward
Career: Gainsborough Trinity, Sheffield United, Sunderland, Fulham, Middlesbrough
Debut: v Wales (a) 29-2-1904
Appearances: 2 (1 goal)

Arthur was something of a boy prodigy, being discovered by Gainsborough Trinity whilst playing for the Church Lads Brigade and signing for the Second Division side early in 1902, initially as an amateur. He immediately impressed watching scouts from other clubs and during the same summer was transferred to Sheffield United, costing the Bramall Lane club £350. His impact at United was no less remarkable and in February 1904 he won his first cap for England, one of the youngest to have been so honoured. Although he won a second cap two years later against the Irish, his career seldom hit such heights again, although he was transferred to Sunderland in June 1908 for £1,000. Arthur's time at Roker Park was not a success and he was subsequently released by the club. It took some time before he was able to fix himself up with another club, finally signing for Fulham in October 1910. In the summer of 1912 he returned to the North East, signing for Middlesbrough for one season. Away from football his profession was given as master builders' merchant and monumental mason.

George BROWN

Born: Mickley, Northumberland, 22nd June 1903
Died: 10th June 1948
Role: Inside-Right, Centre-Forward
Career: Mickley Colliery, Huddersfield Town, Aston Villa, Burnley, Leeds United, Darlington
Debut: v Northern Ireland (h) 20-10-1926
Appearances: 9 (5 goals)

George Brown was working as a miner at the Mickley Colliery and playing for the works side when he asked Huddersfield Town manager Herbert Chapman for a trial. He did well enough to be offered professional forms and then became a regular fixture in the side that won three successive League titles, the first time this feat had been achieved since the formation of the Football League in 1888, and helped them to the FA Cup Final in 1928 as well as collecting eight caps for England. The following year he was sold to Aston Villa for £5,000 and proved as inspirational at Villa Park as he had been at Leeds Road, netting 30 goals in 41 games. Known as Bomber Brown during his career he also returned to the England side, collecting his last cap for his country in 1933 and then joined Burnley in October 1934 for £1,400. He spent one year at Turf Moor before joining Leeds United for a season, costing the Elland Road club £3,100, ending his career with two years as player-manager at Darlington in 1938. As well as his eight caps for England, George also represented the Football League on three occasions. George, who was a cousin of Manchester United and England player Joe Spence, became a publican in Birmingham after retiring from the game.

James BROWN

Born: Blackburn, 31st July 1862
Died: Blackburn, 4th July 1922
Role: Centre-Forward
Career: Blackburn Rovers
Debut: v Wales (h) 26-2-1881
Appearances: 5 (3 goals)

Jimmy Brown was another exceptionally talented youngster who developed as a schoolboy in his hometown of Blackburn. He then played for the town's Mintholme College side and the Law Club before signing with Blackburn Rovers in August 1879. He was a highly talented forward player, at home in almost any position and particularly noted for his dribbling skills, with one early Blackburn historian reckoning that the ball was tied to his bootlaces. A member of the Blackburn side that won the FA Cup three years in succession (in 1884, 1885 and 1886) he also collected a runners-up medal in 1882 as Blackburn were beaten by Old Etonians. Jimmy also achieved the honour of scoring in both the 1885 and 1886 finals, against Queen's Park and West Bromwich Albion respectively, the latter in the replay at the Baseball Ground, Derby. He remained a player with Blackburn Rovers until 1889 when he retired and then was employed as a solicitor's managing clerk. Jimmy's two goals in the 13-0 win over Ireland in 1882 made him the only teenager to have scored two goals in a match for England.

John Henry BROWN

Born: Hodthorpe, Derbyshire, 19th March 1899
Died: 10th April 1962
Role: Goalkeeper
Career: Manton Colliery, Worksop Town, Sheffield Wednesday, Hartlepool United
Debut: v Wales (a) 12-2-1927
Appearances: 6

After playing for Manton colliery Jack Brown was signed by non-League Worksop Town immediately after the First World War and continued working as a miner. He first came to prominence after starring in the Worksop side that reached the FA Cup first round proper in 1923 and then proceeded to hold Spurs to a goalless draw at White Hart Lane (although they lost the replay 9-0), signing for Sheffield Wednesday the following month. He was to remain with Wednesday for the next fourteen years, helping them win the Second Division title in 1926, the League championship in 1929 and 1930 and the FA Cup in 1935. In between times he represented the Football League twice and won six caps for England, appearing on the winning side on five occasions and drawing the other match (on his debut England were held 3-3 by Wales), a remarkable run for a goalkeeper who didn't join the professional ranks until he was over 23 years of age. In September 1937 he was released by Sheffield Wednesday after making 465 League appearances for the club and signed for Hartlepool United, although he was released two weeks later having made only one appearance for the 'Pool. He retired from playing immediately following his brief sojourn with Hartlepool and returned to Sheffield to concentrate on running his confectionery shop in the city.

Kenneth BROWN

Born: Forest Gate, London, 16th February 1934
Role: Centre-Half
Career: Neville United, West Ham United, Torquay United, Hereford United
Debut: v Northern Ireland (h) 18-11-1959
Appearances: 1

Ken Brown represented Dagenham Schools and then joined Neville United, playing in the Dagenham League before being spotted by West Ham United. He signed for the Upton Park outfit in October 1951 and made his debut the following year, going on to make a total of 386 League appearances for the Hammers. He remained with West Ham until May 1967, by which time he had helped the club win the Second Division title in 1958, the FA Cup in 1964 and the European Cup Winners' Cup in 1965. The following year he helped West Ham reach the final of the League Cup, although they were beaten by West Bromwich Albion over two legs in the final. He made his only appearance for England in 1959 and was perhaps unfortunate not to have won more caps, the consistency of Billy Wright limiting him to just one appearance. Indeed, Ken did not win his cap until Billy had been retired from the international scene. In May 1967 Ken left West Ham and signed for Torquay United, making a total of 42 League appearances. He finished his playing career with the then non-League Hereford United, signing for the Edgar Street club in the summer of 1969. The following year he began his coaching and management career, joining Bournemouth as assistant to John Bond (whose playing career had also encompassed West Ham and Torquay). The pair then moved to Norwich City in 1973 and enjoyed a successful seven year spell in partnership before John Bond left to take over at Manchester City. Although he wished to take Ken with him to Maine Road, Ken decided to remain at Carrow Road and enter in management in his own right, accepting the manager's job at Norwich City. He spent seven years in charge, guiding them to the League Cup in 1985 before being replaced by Dave Stringer in November 1987.

Wes Brown

Wesley Michael BROWN

Born: Manchester, 13th October 1979
Role: Defender
Career: Manchester United
Debut: v Hungary (a) 28-4-1999
Appearances: 9

Considered something of an unsung hero at Old Trafford, Wes Brown has had to deal with almost constant rumours that Manchester United were about to buy one big name after another that would spell the end of his United career; Wes has seen off all of them. A graduate from the trainee

Charles Buchan

ranks at Old Trafford, Wes was capped by England at schoolboy level before joining the professional ranks. He then went on to win Youth and Under-21 caps for his country and also made his initial break into the Manchester United first team. He began to make more regular appearances during the 1998-99 season, making enough appearances to collect a Premiership medal but sat out as United added the FA Cup and Champions League trophies to their tally. His cause was not helped by a ruptured cruciate ligament that left him sidelined for fifteen months, but he returned to continue his pursuit of a regular place within the United defence. Indeed, it appears at times as though he is more appreciated within the England setup than he is at club level, for he has been something of a regular feature within the England squad, injuries permitting, since his debut in 1999.

William BROWN

Born: Fencehouses, County Durham, 22nd August 1900
Died: January 1985
Role: Inside-Right
Career: Hetton, West Ham United, Chelsea, Fulham, Stockport County, Hartlepool United
Debut: v Belgium (a) 1-11-1923 (scored once)
Appearances: 1 (1 goal)

It was not until he became a professional player with West Ham United during the 1920-21 season that Bill Brown settled into one position, that of inside-right, for during his formative years he played almost anywhere on the pitch. West Ham spotted him whilst he was playing for Hetton FC in a local Durham league and signed him immediately, and he soon formed an excellent partnership with fellow West Ham player Victor Watson. Indeed, both Bill and Victor went on to represent England. Bill was a member of the West Ham side that reached the FA Cup final of 1923, the first to be played at Wembley, although Bolton Wanderers proved too strong on the day and won 2-0. Bill remained with West Ham until February 1924 when he moved across London to sign for Chelsea, making his debut on 1st of March at West Bromwich Albion. Injuries and loss of form restricted him to just 57 League appearances in a five year stay at Stamford Bridge and in May 1929 he was transferred to near-neighbours Fulham. A little over a year later he was on the move again, this time signing for Stockport County. He finished his playing career with Hartlepool United, joining the club in September 1931. Upon retiring as a player he became a baths superintendent at the Easington Colliery.

John BRUTON

Born: Westhoughton, Bolton, 21st November 1903
Died: 13th March 1986
Role: Right-Winger
Career: Hindley Green, Horwich RMI, Burnley, Blackburn Rovers
Debut: v France (a) 17-5-1928
Appearances: 3

Jack Bruton played schools football in Westhoughton and then for Hindley Green in the Lancashire Alliance, combining part-time football with a job down the mines. After a brief spell linked with Wigan Athletic as an amateur he joined Horwich during 1924, subsequently costing Burnley £125 when he signed in March 1925. During the course of his four years with the club he graduated to the full England side, winning all three of his caps whilst with the Turf Moor outfit, representing the Football League twice and prompting a £6,500 move to Blackburn Rovers in December 1929. He was to remain with Rovers for over ten years, finally retiring as a player during the Second World War. This did not spell the end of his involvement with Blackburn however, for in September 1947 he was appointed assistant-secretary and two months later elevated to club manager, a position he held until May 1949. He then took over as manager of Bournemouth in March 1950 and remained in charge until March 1956. Although this signalled the end of his full time involvement with football he did have spells scouting for Blackburn Rovers, Bournemouth and Portsmouth, combining these positions with employment with a lamp company.

William Ingram BRYANT

Born: Ghent, Belgium, 1st March 1899
Died: 21st January 1986
Role: Centre-Half
Career: Clapton, Millwall Athletic, Clapton
Debut v France (a) 21-5-1925
Appearances: 1

An amateur player throughout his career Bill Bryant was educated at St. Olave's Grammar School in Chelmsford and played football for the school team before joining Clapton. He helped the club win the FA Amateur Cup in successive seasons, 1924 and 1925, and was persuaded by Millwall Athletic to play in the Football League in August 1925, although he retained his amateur status. Whilst with Millwall he helped the club win the Third Division South championship in 1928 and made a total of 132 League appearances for the club during his six years, scoring 30 goals and finally returning to play for Clapton in May 1931. He retired from playing in the summer of 1933, by which time he had won seven amateur caps for England to compliment his one full appearance. He was later a reporter for The Sunday Referee and served as a director of a wholesale seed company.

Charles Murray BUCHAN

Born: Plumstead, London, 22nd September 1891
Died: Monte Carlo, Monaco, 25th June 1960
Role: Inside-Right
Career: Plumstead FC, Woolwich Arsenal, Northfleet, Leyton, Sunderland, Arsenal
Debut: v Ireland (a) 15-2-1913 (scored once)
Appearances: 6 (4 goals) + 1 War appearance

Although many believed Charles Buchan to have been one of the greatest inside-forwards of his day, the cleverness of his play often confused both the opposition and his teammates in equal measure and was largely responsible for him only collecting six caps for his country. He played schoolboy and junior football in Woolwich (then the home of Arsenal) and signed with Woolwich Arsenal as an amateur in December 1908. After a brief spell with Northfleet he joined Southern League club Leyton as a professional in March 1910, quickly establishing himself within the side and attracting interest from the big League clubs of the day. He signed with Sunderland for £1,250 in March 1911 and maintained his progress, inspiring Sunderland to the League title and winning his first cap for England the same year. Sunderland nearly collected the double that season too, for they were beaten in the FA Cup Final by League runners-up Aston Villa 1-0 in front of a record crowd; the presence of so many illustrious names on both sides ensured 121,919 were present. Charles also made 10 appearances for the Football League and one war-time international appearance and seemed set to finish his career at Roker Park when Arsenal came in to persuade him to return in July 1925. Charles, who had established a sports goods business in Sunderland was reluctant to move down to the south (although it was believed that Arsenal chairman Henry Norris offered to make good any losses Buchan's business suffered) but Herbert Chapman was persuasive. He finally cost Arsenal a down payment of £2,000 and additional payments of £100 for each goal he scored during his first season; he scored 21 times for the Highbury club to add a further £2,100 to his fee. Although Charles was 33 when he returned to Arsenal he was to prove an inspirational purchase for the club, devising the 'third-back' game with which Arsenal were to dominate the game during the 1930s. Charles's only glimpse of glory at Arsenal came in 1927 when he captained the club to their first FA Cup Final, although he had to settle for another runners-up medal as Cardiff won 1-0. He retired from playing in 1928 and went into sports journalism with the Daily News and News Chronicle, later commentating for BBC Radio and in 1951 founded the still popular Football Monthly. He had previously been an accomplished cricketer, playing for Durham in 1920. Charles was on holiday with his wife in Monte Carlo in Monaco in 1960 when he collapsed and died.

Walter Scott BUCHANAN

Born: Hornsey, London, 1st June 1855
Died: Hammersmith, London, 11th November 1926
Role: Forward
Career: Clapham Rovers, Barnes, Surrey
Debut: v Scotland (a) 4-3-1876
Appearances: 1

Another one of the mystery men to have represented England, for his true identity has yet to be established beyond all doubt, although the WS Buchanan who played in the England and Scotland match of 1876 is almost certainly the Walter Scott Buchanan who was born in Hammersmith on 1st June 1855. That being the case, then his career took him from Clapham Rovers to Barnes and he also represented Surrey, although evidence suggests that he had already left Clapham by the time that club reached the FA Cup finals of 1879 and 1880.

Franklin Charles BUCKLEY

Born: Urmston, Manchester, 9th November 1883
Died: 22nd December 1964
Role: Centre-Half
Career: Aston Villa, Brighton & Hove Albion, Manchester United, Manchester City, Birmingham, Derby County, Bradford City
Debut: v Ireland (h) 14-2-1914
Appearances: 1

Although he ultimately achieved greater fame and success as a manager, Frank Buckley was no mean footballer himself, as his England cap proves. He began his playing career with Aston Villa in 1903, signing as a 16-year-old but was unable to break into the first team and so joined Brighton & Hove Albion in 1905. He spent just one season with the club, joining Manchester United in 1906 and then moving across the city to sign for Manchester City in September 1907. Two years later he joined Birmingham and then moved to Derby in May 1911. Here he won a Second Division championship medal in 1912 and his only cap for England, moving on again two months later to join Bradford City. As soon as the First World War broke out he enlisted with the Footballers Battalion of the Middlesex Regiment, rising to Commanding Officer, although he suffered wounds during the Battle of the Somme in August 1916 which were to bring his playing career to an end. He was appointed manager of Norwich City in March 1919, holding this position for a year before becoming a commercial traveller in London. He was lured back into football with Blackpool in June 1923, serving as manager for four years before joining Wolves in 1927, initially on a three year contract. Known as Major Frank Buckley he was something of a rival to Herbert Chapman at Arsenal; progressive, ambitious, a disciplinarian and an easy communicator, although sometimes his ideas were the opposite of his great rival in London, for where Chapman favoured the use of the white football, Major Frank was bitterly opposed. He introduced a new strip to the Wolves side, bringing in black and gold vertical stripes, brought through a number of youth players and totally transformed Wolves from an also ran Second Division side into one that could challenge for honours. He slowly set about getting them back into the First Division, earning an extended contract into the bargain, and finally won promotion in 1932, winning the Second Division title into the bargain. In 1939 he guided them to the FA Cup Final, their first appearance since 1921, although they froze on the day and were surprisingly beaten by Portsmouth 4-1. In 1938 his contract was extended for another ten years, then almost unheard of, but the outbreak of the Second World War meant much of his activity during the hostilities was little more than biding time until normal football could be resumed, especially as his application to enlist in the armed forces was turned down (he was well into his fifties at the time!). He did, however, take Wolves to the Wartime League Cup in 1942. In 1944 he surprisingly left Wolves for 'private and personal' reasons, resurfacing as manager of Notts County in March of that year. He spent two years with County before joining Hull City for a similar period, then taking over at Leeds United. He was in charge at Elland Road for five years before joining Walsall where he finished his career in June 1955.

Stephen Bull

Stephen George BULL

Born: Tipton, Staffordshire, 28th March 1965
Role: Forward
Career: West Bromwich Albion, Wolverhampton Wanderers
Debut v Scotland (a) (substitute) 27-5-1989 (scored once)
Appearances: 13 (4 goals)

West Bromwich Albion signed Steve Bull on a free transfer from non-League Tipton Town in August 1985 but he was unable to enjoy an extended run in the side, making just seven appearances for the club. He was sold to Wolves for £35,000 in November 1986 whilst the club were languishing in the Fourth Division, but fired by his goals began a march back up the League. In 1989 he won the first of his thirteen caps for England, becaming the first Third Division player to be capped by England since Peter Taylor, and he noted the occasion by scoring on his debut. Whilst with Wolves he helped the club to the Fourth and Third Division titles and the Associate Members' Cup as well as setting a new League goalscoring record for the club; a total of 250 goals. Although Graham Taylor tried to sell him during his spell in charge at Wolves, Steve Bull remained a folk hero to the fans in the Black Country, even after his retirement in 1998.

Frederick Edwin BULLOCK

Born: Hounslow, Middlesex, 1886
Died: Huddersfield, 15th November 1922
Role: Left-Back
Career: Hounslow Town, Ilford, Huddersfield Town
Debut: v Ireland (h) 23-10-1920
Appearances: 1

Fred played schools football for Isleworth Schools and Hounslow Town in Middlesex before joining Ilford in Essex in the summer of 1909. Eighteen months later he was spotted by Huddersfield Town and persuaded to join the club as an amateur, subsequently being upgraded to the professional ranks soon after. He was to remain with the club for the next twelve years and proved an extremely reliable full-back for the club, helping them reach the FA Cup final in 1920 although they were beaten by Aston Villa 1-0 at Stamford Bridge. Having represented Middlesex and won an amateur cap for England, Fred was awarded his only full cap for England the same year as his FA Cup final appearance and helped England to a 2-0 win over Ireland. He retired from playing during the summer of 1922 and promptly became a publican in Huddersfield, although barely six months later he was dead.

Harry Burgess

Norman BULLOCK

Born: Monkton, Manchester, 8th September 1900
Died: 27th October 1970
Role: Centre-Forward
Career: Sedgley Park, Bury
Debut: v Belgium (h) 19-3-1923 (scored once)
Appearances: 3 (2 goals)

Norman played schools and representative football in Salford and then for junior sides Broughton St. John's and Sedgley Park before linking with Bury as an amateur in 1920. He was upgraded to the professional ranks in February 1921 and was to remain a player with the club for the next fourteen years, although all he had to show for his time at Gigg Lane was one appearance for the Football League and his three caps for England. By the time he retired from playing in 1935 he had made a total of 506 League appearances for the club, a record that survives to this day. He had been appointed player-manager in the summer of 1934 and continued as manager only for three years following his retirement from playing. In June 1938 he accepted an offer to take over as secretary-manager of Chesterfield, a position he held until the end of the Second World War. At the end of hostilities he returned to Gigg Lane as manager for a second time, remaining in charge between July 1945 and December 1949. He was then appointed manager of Leicester and was to reign at Filbert Street until February 1955, thus completing an unbroken spell of 21 years in management without a pause. Despite his lengthy involvement with football administration he had also briefly worked as an analytical chemist!

Harry BURGESS

Born: Alderley Edge, Cheshire, 20th August 1904
Role: Inside-Forward
Career: Alderley Edge, Stockport County, Sandbach Ramblers, Stockport County, Sheffield Wednesday, Chelsea
Debut: v Northern Ireland (h) 20-10-1930 (scored twice)
Appearances: 4 (4 goals)

After playing for the local Alderley Edge club, Harry was signed by Stockport County and sent on loan to Sandbach Ramblers in order to get experience. He returned to Stockport in 1926 and quickly established himself as a regular in the side, attracting the attentions of bigger clubs in the process. He was transferred to Sheffield Wednesday in June 1929 and helped them win the League championship at the end of his first season with the club and then collected his first cap for England. Harry managed to represent his country on four occasions, netting two goals in both his first and last appearances, so it was something of a surprise that he was not selected again after the Belgium match of 1931. He remained with Wednesday until March 1935 when he moved south to sign for Chelsea, and by the time the Second World War broke out in 1939 could claim a total 473 League appearances for his three clubs, scoring 173 goals. He retired from playing during the war.

Herbert BURGESS

Born: Openshaw, Manchester, 1883
Died: 1954
Role: Left-Back
Career: Glossop, Manchester City, Manchester United
Debut: v Wales (a) 29-2-1904
Appearances: 4

Herbert Burgess played junior football in and around Manchester, turning out at various times for St. Francis, Gorton, Openshaw United and Moss Side before being snapped up by the then Second Division side Glossop in 1900. Despite his small size (he stood barely 5' 4" tall) he proved himself to be an exceptional tackler and was converted from wing-half to full-back and soon came to the attentions of bigger neighbours Manchester City, joining the club in July 1903. His impact on City was no less impressive, for he soon made the first of his seven representative appearances for the Football League and helped City win the FA Cup in 1904. That same year he picked up the first of his four caps for England, helping them to a 2-2 draw against the Welsh. Manchester City seemed assured of further honours but in 1906 suddenly became embroiled in controversy over illegal bonus payments to players. A number of directors were banned for life from having any involvement in football whilst all 17 players on the club's books were suspended until 1st January 1907 and ordered to be sold thereafter. Four of them - Herbert Burgess, Jimmy Bannister, Sandy Turnbull and Billy Meredith - were sold to Manchester United in a combined deal worth £1,700, although the deal itself was not without controversy, for United were known to have negotiated directly with the four players before a proposed auction involving other interested parties and were actually transferred before their suspensions had expired. Herbert Burgess and the other three players carried on with their careers, with Herbert subsequently helping United win the League championship in 1908. Herbert retired from playing in 1910 and then headed for the continent to become a coach, holding positions in Spain, Italy and Hungary.

Cuthbert James BURNUP

Born: Blackheath, Kent, 21st November 1875
Died: 5th April 1960
Role: Left-Winger
Career: Cambridge University, Old Malvernians, Corinthians
Debut: v Scotland (a) 4-4-1896
Appearances: 1

Cuthbert was educated at Malvern College and played for the college football team in 1893. He then went on to Cambridge University, collected a Blue between 1895 and 1898 inclusively and in 1896 earned a call-up for the full England side owing to the unavailability of Steve Bloomer and Ernest Needham, both of whom were injured. Cuthbert's lone appearance for England was little short of a disaster, for Scotland ended a twenty match unbeaten run and Cuthbert was widely acknowledged as having been somewhat out of his depth at international level. Although he never came close to the England side again, Cuthbert resumed his career and went on to play for Old Malvernians and Corinthians, playing for the latter club between 1895 and 1901. As with most amateur players of the day, he excelled at other sports and had been captain of the Malvern College cricket and racquets teams. He also earned a Blue for cricket whilst at Cambridge University and represented both Kent and the MCC in later years. However, in one match for the MCC in 1900, he bowled a ball that was hit for 10 runs by Samuel Hill-Wood of Derbyshire, a record for first class cricket! On the positive side, however, he holds the distinction of scoring the first double century for Kent, a feat achieved in 1900 at Old Trafford. Away from sporting activities Cuthbert worked in the City of London as a stockbroker and later in commerce.

Horace BURROWS

Born: Sutton-in-Ashfield, Nottinghamshire, 11th March 1910
Died: Sutton-in-Ashfield, 22nd March 1969
Role: Left-Half
Career: Sutton Junction, Coventry City, Mansfield Town, Sheffield Wednesday
Debut: v Hungary (a) 10-5-1934
Appearances: 3

Horace represented Nottinghamshire Schools before joining Sutton Junction and was then snapped up by Coventry City in February 1930. Three months later he was transferred to Mansfield Town where he had better luck, and within a year the First Division clubs were paying the adaptable wing-half more than a passing glance. He was sold to Sheffield Wednesday for a paltry £350 in May 1931 and continued his development, helping Wednesday win the FA Cup in 1935 and collecting his first cap for England during the continental tour of Europe in 1934. He also joined the touring party the following year, appearing in the match against Holland. Horace remained a Wednesday player until the outbreak of the Second World War when he retired and later concentrated on running a sports outfitters business in his native hometown. His son Adrian was later a professional player, appearing for Mansfield, Northampton Town, Plymouth Argyle and Southend United between 1979 and 1987.

Frank Ernest BURTON

Born: Nottingham, 18th March 1865
Died: 10th February 1948
Role: Inside-Right
Career: Notts County, Nottingham Forest
Debut: v Ireland (h) 2-3-1889
Appearances: 1

Frank attended Nottingham High School and represented the school at football, subsequently signing for local club Notts County in October 1886. He spent barely a year with the club before joining local rivals Nottingham Forest in November 1887 and was to remain with Forest until November 1891. Despite his short career Frank did manage to play some form of League football, turning out for Nottingham Forest in the Football Alliance when it was formed in 1889, although by the time Forest took their place in the Football League, in 1892, he had already departed. It appears that he gave up the game in order to join the family business, Joseph Burton & Co Ltd, a grocery chain which had been founded by his father. Frank joined as manager and worked his way up the company, subsequently serving as managing director and later chairman.

Lindsay BURY

Born: Withington, Manchester, 9th July 1857
Died: Bradford, 30th October 1935
Role: Full-Back
Career: Cambridge University, Old Etonians
Debut: v Scotland (h) 3-3-1877
Appearances: 2

Lindsay was educated at Eton College and played for the college football team between 1875 and 1876. He then went on to study at Cambridge University and earned a Blue in both 1877 and 1878, as well as earning a Blue in cricket in 1877 and athletics in 1878, 1879 and 1880 (he was especially noted for his sprinting and hammer throwing). Lindsay had also turned out on a regular basis for Old Etonians since 1877 and helped them win the FA Cup in 1879, beating Clapham Rovers 1-0 in the final at Kennington Oval. He served on the FA Committee from 1878 and also turned out once for Hampshire County Cricket Club in 1877. In later life Lindsay was an orange planter in Florida in America, which throws up an interesting link with another former England player Rupert Anderson, who also attended Eton College and Cambridge University and became an orange planter in Florida. As both players were certainly at Cambridge at the same time and played in the same England international (against Wales in 1879), the chances are that both players emigrated to America at the same time. Both subsequently returned to England, with Lindsay settling near Bradford were he died in 1935.

Terence Ian BUTCHER

Born: Singapore, 28th December 1958
Role: Defender
Career: Ipswich Town, Glasgow Rangers, Coventry City, Sunderland
Debut: v Australia (a) 31-5-1980
Appearances: 77 (3 goals)

Although Terry was born in Singapore he attended school in Lowestoft and signed with Ipswich in August 1976. A towering centre-half (he stood 6' 4") he became one of the key players in a side that challenged for the top honours, collecting a winners' medal in the UEFA Cup in 1981. In 1986 he was the subject of interest from many clubs, finally signing for Rangers and becoming part of the English revolution at the Scottish giants. Made captain he guided the club to the Scottish League title in 1987, 1989 and 1990 and three consecutive League Cups in 1987, 1988 and 1989. In 1990 he had a row with manager Graeme Souness which prompted a return south of the border, joining Coventry City as player-manager. Two years later Coventry wished to amend the contract to that of manager only and Terry subsequently resigned, going on to play for Sunderland before becoming manager at Roker Park for a spell. He later returned to Scotland and club management with Motherwell.

Terry Butcher

Nicky Butt

John Dennis BUTLER

Born: Colombo, Ceylon, 14th August 1894
Died: London, 5th January 1961
Role: Centre-Half
Career: Fulham, Dartford, Arsenal, Torquay United
Debut: v Belgium (h) 8-12-1925
Appearances: 1

Jack was brought to England soon after his birth and was educated in London, attending school in West London and representing the area at that level. He then joined Fulham on amateur forms in 1913, although he was unable to break into the first team, playing for the club's Thursday XI. He then signed professional forms with Southern League Dartford, although at the end of the 1913-14 season joined Arsenal. Although he was to remain at Highbury until 1930 the closest he came to domestic honours was an appearance in the 1927 FA Cup final in which Arsenal lost to Cardiff City 1-0, the only occasion the FA Cup has been taken out of England. Two years previously Jack had won his only cap for England against Belgium, but according to Bernard Joy, Jack was one of those players who had most difficulty adapting to the change in the offside law that required only two defending players to be between the attacker and the goal. That accounted for his further lack of international honours, but Jack was a mainstay of the Arsenal defence as Herbert Chapman set about rebuilding the club. Jack was transferred to Torquay United in May 1930 and was to spend two years with the Plainmoor club, finally retiring as a player in 1932. He then took to coaching on the continent and accepted a position with Daring FC of Brussels in Belgium, and later combined this with coaching duties to the national side. Indeed, in 1936 he helped Belgium beat England 3-2 in a friendly in Brussels. He remained with Daring FC until 1939 when the unstable political situation and impending war in Europe prompted him to return to England. In October 1940 he was appointed coach to Leicester City, a position he held until 1946 when he returned to Torquay, this time as manager. He spent a year with Torquay before accepting an invitation to take over at Crystal Palace in the summer of 1947 and was in charge at Selhurst Park for two years before joining another former club, this time Daring FC in Belgium as manager in May 1949. He returned once again to England in June 1953 to become manager of Colchester United, a position he held until January 1955.

William BUTLER

Born: Atherton, Bolton, 27th March 1900
Died: 11th July 1966
Role: Right-Winger
Career: Howe Bridge FC, Atherton Colliery, Bolton Wanderers, Reading
Debut: v Scotland (h) 12-4-1924
Appearances: 1

Bill Butler played junior football for Howe Bridge and then enlisted in the Army during the First World War, turning out regularly for his unit during the campaign. At the end of the war he became a miner and played for the Atherton Colliery before being signed by Bolton Wanderers. He was initially signed as a centre-forward but was later converted to right-winger, a position he would excel in. Whilst with Bolton he helped the club win the FA Cup on three occasions; 1923, in what was the first final to be held at Wembley as Bolton overcame West Ham 2-0, 1926 and again three years later in 1929. Wembley was something of a happy home for Bill, for his only appearance for England, against Scotland in 1924, was the first to be held at the stadium. He remained with Bolton until June 1933 when he was transferred to Reading, remaining a player at the Elm Park club for two years before announcing his retirement. He was then appointed manager of the club, an appointment that apparently made him the youngest manager in the League. He held the position until February 1939 and four months later took over as manager of non-League Guildford City, remaining in charge for the duration of the Second World War. At the end of hostilities he took over as manager of Torquay United and was at Plainmoor until May 1946 when he emigrated to South Africa. He went on to manage Johannesburg Rangers and coached the Pietermaritzburg & District FA before moving to Rhodesia where he became coach to the national FA. He died on the day England opened their 1966 World Cup campaign at Wembley against Uruguay.

Nicholas BUTT

Born: Manchester, 21st January 1975
Role: Midfield
Career: Manchester United, Newcastle United, Birmingham City
Debut: v Mexico (h) (substitute) 29-3-1997
Appearances: 39

Nicky Butt joined Manchester United straight from school and progressed through the ranks to become a mainstay of the youth side, helping them win the FA Youth Cup in 1991-92 with a two-goal display in the first leg win against Crystal Palace. He made his first team debut in November 1992 against Oldham Athletic and following the subsequent departure of Paul Ince became a permanent fixture in the United midfield. He collected six Premiership medals, two FA Cup winners medals, three Charity Shields and a winners medal in the European Champions League. He was sold to Newcastle United for £2.5 million in July 2004 and later joined Birmingham City on loan. In addition to his full caps he has also collected seven caps at Under-21 level and represented the country at schoolboy and youth level.

Gerald Bryne

Gerald BYRNE

Born: Liverpool, 29th August 1938
Role: Full-Back
Career: Liverpool
Debut: v Scotland (h) 6-4-1963
Appearances: 2

A Liverpool player through and through, Gerry represented the city at schoolboy level before signing amateur forms with Liverpool and subsequently being upgraded to the professional ranks in August 1955. He made his first team debut in 1957 and went on to make 274 League appearances for the club, scoring just two goals. He did, however, help the club win the Second Division championship in 1962, the First Division championship in 1964 and 1966 and the FA Cup in 1965, as well as reaching the final of the European Cup Winners' Cup in 1965 where they were beaten by Borussia Dortmund. A year earlier, in the FA Cup final against Leeds United at Wembley, Gerry had played for 117 minutes with a broken collar bone but managed to hold on and help Liverpool to an extra time 2-1 victory over Leeds United. Despite his bravery, at international level Gerry was unable to displace Ray Wilson from the England side, although he did manage to collect two caps at full level to go with the single cap he had previously won at Under-23 level. Gerry was forced to retire from playing owing to injury in December 1969 and almost immediately joined the coaching staff at Anfield.

John Joseph BYRNE

Born: West Horsley, Surrey, 13th May 1939
Role: Inside-Forward
Career: Epsom Town, Guildford City, Crystal Palace, West Ham United, Crystal Palace, Fulham, Durban City
Debut: v Northern Ireland (h) 22-11-1961
Appearances: 11 (8 goals)

After playing junior football for Epsom Town and Guildford City at Youth level, Johnny signed with Crystal Palace as an amateur in 1955, being upgraded to the professional ranks in May 1956. He quickly impressed as an intelligent ball-playing inside-forward and in 1961 was rewarded with his first cap for England, only the second player since the Second World War to be capped by England whilst playing in the Third Division. Under such circumstances a move to a higher club was always likely and in March 1962 West Ham United paid £58,000 plus another player to take Johnny to Upton Park, a then record fee between two English League clubs. Johnny quickly slotted into the Hammers first team and helped them win the FA Cup in 1964. In the meantime he held his place in the England side, although he was badly injured in the fixture with Scotland in April 1965. This signalled the end of his international career and may therefore have cost him a place in the England side that won the World Cup in 1966. It certainly kept him out of the West Ham side that won the European Cup Winners' Cup in 1965, although he was a member of the West Ham side that reached the League Cup final in 1966 only to lose to West Bromwich Albion. In February 1967 he returned to Crystal Palace for a fee of £45,000, spending a little over a year at Selhurst Park before a £18,000 move to Fulham in March 1968. He was at Craven Cottage for another year and took his tally of League appearances for his three clubs to 414, scoring 161 goals before moving to South Africa, playing for and later managing Durban City. Johnny, who was known as Budgie throughout his career in recognition of the fact that he seldom stopped talking, became a tyre company representative whilst with the South African club.

Roger William BYRNE

Born: Manchester, 8th February 1939
Died: Munich, 6th February 1958
Role: Left-Back
Career: Manchester United
Debut: v Scotland (a) 3-4-1954 (WCQ)
Appearances: 33

Signed by Manchester United in March 1949 he began his career at inside-forward before finding his more favoured position at full-back. He made his League debut in 1951 and played sufficient games to collect his first League championship medal, but he had ended the season at outside-left. When he was selected in the same position the following season he put in a transfer request, but Matt Busby soon put him back in the team at full-back, made him captain in succession to Johnny Carey and he became one of the most accomplished players the game has seen. Capped for England in 33 consecutive games he captained United to two further League titles and the FA Cup final in 1957 where United lost to Aston Villa. After the match Roger commented 'Never mind, we'll be back next year', which United duly did, but by then Roger was one of the seven United players who lost his life in the Munich air disaster of February 1958. In addition to his 33 full caps, Roger played for the England B team three times and represented the Football League on six occasions. Roger never scored for the full England team but did miss two penalties, both in 1956. One of these came in the Wembley clash with Brazil which England won 4-2 despite two missed penalties. Gylmar saved the first from John Atyeo and then Roger's effort, both penalties having been awarded for handball against Zozino.

Roger Bryne

C

CALLAGHAN, Ian Robert
CALVEY, John
CAMPBELL, Austin Fenwick
CAMPBELL, Sulzeer Jeremiah
CAMSELL, George Henry
CAPES, Arthur John
CARR, Jack
CARR, John
CARR, William Henry
CARRAGHER, James Lee
CARRICK, Michael
CARTER, Horatio Stratton 'Raich'
CARTER, Joseph Henry
CATLIN, Arthur Edward
CHADWICK, Arthur
CHADWICK, Edgar
CHAMBERLAIN, Mark Valentine
CHAMBERS, Henry
CHANNON, Michael Roger
CHARLES, Gary Andrew
CHARLTON, Jack
CHARLTON, Robert Sir
CHARNLEY, Raymond O
CHARSLEY, Charles Christopher
CHEDGZOY, Samuel
CHENERY, Charles John
CHERRY, Trevor John
CHILTON, Allenby C
CHIPPENDALE, Henry
CHIVERS, Martin Harcourt
CHRISTIAN, Edward
CLAMP, Edwin
CLAPTON, Daniel Robert
CLARE, Thomas
CLARKE, Allan John
CLARKE, Harold Alfred
CLAY, Thomas
CLAYTON, Ronald
CLEGG, John Charles Sir
CLEGG, William Edwin Sir O.B.E.
CLEMENCE, Raymond Neal M.B.E.
CLEMENT, David Thomas
CLOUGH, Brian Howard
CLOUGH, Nigel Howard
COATES, Ralph
COBBOLD, William Nevill
COCK, John Gilbert
COCKBURN, Henry
COHEN, George Reginald
COLE, Andrew Alexander
COLE, Ashley
COLE, Joe
COLECLOUGH, Henry
COLEMAN, Ernest Herbert
COLEMAN, John George 'Tim'
COLLYMORE, Stanley Victor
COMMON, Alfred
COMPTON, Leslie Harry
CONLIN, James
CONNELLY, John Michael
COOK, Thomas Edwin Reed
COOPER, Colin Terence
COOPER, Norman Charles
COOPER, Terence
COOPER, Thomas
COPPELL, Steven James
COPPING, Wilfred
CORBETT, Bertram Oswald
CORBETT, Reginald
CORBETT, Walter Samuel
CORRIGAN, Joseph Thomas
COTTEE, Anthony Richard
COTTERILL, George Huth
COTTLE, Joseph Richard
COWAN, Samuel
COWANS, Gordon Sidney
COWELL, Arthur
COX, John
COX, John Davies
CRABTREE, James William
CRAWFORD, John Forsyth
CRAWFORD, Raymond
CRAWSHAW, Thomas Henry
CRAYSTON, William John
CREEK, Frederick Norman Smith
CRESSWELL, Warneford
CROMPTON, Robert
CROOKS, Samuel Dickinson
CROUCH, Peter
CROWE, Christopher
CUGGY, Francis
CULLIS, Stanley
CUNLIFFE, Arthur
CUNLIFFE, Daniel
CUNLIFFE, James Nathaniel
CUNNINGHAM, Laurie
CURLE, Keith
CURREY, Edward Samuel
CURRIE, Anthony William
CURSHAM, Arthur William
CURSHAM, Henry Alfred

Bobby Charlton

Ian Robert CALLAGHAN M.B.E.

Born: Liverpool, 10th April 1942
Role: Right-Winger, Midfield
Career: Liverpool, Swansea City
Debut: v Finland (a) 26-6-1966
Appearances: 4

After playing schools football Ian was taken onto the Liverpool ground staff in 1957, signing professional forms in March 1960. He made his debut for the club as the 1959-60 season came to a close, appeared four times in 1960-61 and was something of a regular when the Second Division title was won in 1961-62. Once restored to the First Division, Liverpool were on their way to becoming the dominant force in the English and European game and Ian collected winners' medals from the FA Cup in 1965 and 1974, the League championship in 1964, 1966, 1973, 1976 and 1977, the UEFA Cup in 1973 and 1976, the European Cup in 1977 and runners-up medals for the European Cup Winners' Cup (1966), FA Cup (1971 and 1977) and the League Cup (1978). He was first introduced into the England side in 1966 and was a member of Alf Ramsey's squad for the World Cup finals being played in England, appearing in the match against France and even setting up the second goal for Roger Hunt in the 2-0 win. He then lost out to Alan Ball as the side made its way to the final and his international career appeared to be over. He was sensationally recalled to the England team in 1977, eleven years after his last appearance, and added another two caps to his tally for the full side. He had previously collected four caps for England at Under-23 level and represented the Football League on two occasions as well as winning the Football Writers' Player of the Year Award in 1974. His Anfield career finally came to an end in September 1978 after over twenty years' association with the club, joining former Liverpool player John Toshack at Swansea after more than 800 appearances for Liverpool. He spent over two years at Vetch Field and later played for Cork United, Soudifjord of Norway and Crewe Alexandra before his glorious playing career was brought to an end in 1982. A year earlier he had begun planning for his retirement, opening a restaurant in Rainford in Lancashire. He was awarded an MBE in 1975 in recognition of his services to football.

Ian Callaghan

John CALVEY

Born: South Bank, Middlesbrough, 23rd June 1876
Died: January 1937
Role: Centre-Forward
Career: South Bank, Millwall Athletic, Nottingham Forest, Millwall Athletic
Debut: v Ireland (a) 22-3-1902
Appearances: 1

John Calvey played for South Bank as a junior prior to signing with Millwall Athletic for the first time as a professional during the 1895-96 season. In May 1899 he was transferred to Nottingham Forest and was to remain with the club for five years. According to Forest historians, John Calvey's time at the club was something of a disappointment, although in addition to winning his one full cap for England he was also selected to represent the Football League. His performance in that one international against Ireland was not a successful one either, but in his defence it must be noted that John was not a centre-forward (he was an inside-forward) and was therefore played out of position. He returned to Millwall Athletic in the summer of 1904 and finished his career with the club. After his retirement as a player he became a dock worker.

Austen Fenwick CAMPBELL

Born: Hamsterley, County Durham, 5th May 1901
Died: 8th September 1981
Role: Left-Half
Career: Coventry City, Leadgate Park, Blackburn Rovers, Huddersfield Town, Hull City
Debut: v Northern Ireland (h) 22-10-1928
Appearances: 8

Austen made his first attempt at becoming a professional player with Coventry City during the 1919-20 season, joining them from non-League Leadgate Park. He returned to Leadgate in June 1921, his playing career seemingly at an end and returned to his occupation of pit boy, but he worked hard at the non-League club and was given a second chance with Blackburn Rovers, joining the club in February 1923. He was to spend six and half years at Ewood Park, helping the club win the FA Cup in 1928 with a 3-1 win over Huddersfield Town. Austen obviously impressed the Yorkshire club on the day, for in September 1929 they bought him from Blackburn Rovers and he was a member of the side that reached the FA Cup final in 1930, this time losing out to Arsenal at Wembley. Austen remained at Leeds Road until November 1935 when he was transferred to Hull City, retiring from the game in the summer of 1936. In addition to his eight caps for England, collected whilst he was on the books of Blackburn Rovers and Huddersfield Town, he represented the Football League on five occasions. His cousin Alan Brown represented Burnley and the Football League and later became a highly successful manager.

Sulzeer Jeremiah CAMPBELL

Born: Newham, 18th September 1974
Role: Defender
Career: Tottenham Hotspur, Arsenal
Debut: v Hungary (h) (substitute) 18-5-1996
Appearances: 66 (1 goal) + 1 unofficial appearance

Signed by Spurs as a trainee in 1992 one of Sol's key strengths is his ability to slot into any position and perform as though he were made for the role. Indeed, he made his debut in a match against Chelsea, coming on as a substitute and played up front, scoring one of Spurs goals. He then became a regular in the side playing at full-back, but subsequent injuries to other players saw him in midfield and back up front! He is at his happiest playing in central-defence, and it was in this position that he forced his way into the full England side. He gave particularly commanding performances in the win over Georgia and the goalless draw in Italy that confirmed England's presence in the World Cup finals and then went on to become one of the country's star performers during the finals themselves. He was made captain of Spurs and guided them to victory in the 1999 Worthington Cup final, but two years later, having resisted offers to sign a new contract at White Hart Lane, left on a free transfer and signed for local rivals Arsenal. Whilst at Highbury he has helped the club win the Premiership twice and the FA Cup twice, but has suffered from a series of niggling injuries that has restricted both his domestic and international appearances.

Sol Campbell

George Henry CAMSELL

Born: Framwellgate Moor, Durham, 27th November 1902
Died: Middlesbrough, 7th March 1966
Role: Centre-Forward
Career: Tow Law Town, Esh Winning, Durham City, Middlesbrough
Debut: v France (a) 9-5-1929 (scored twice)
Appearances: 9 (18 goals)

But for a Dixie Dean hat-trick in the final match of the 1927-28 season, George Camsell would be remembered as the scorer of most League goals in a single season, for in 1926-27 he hit 59 for Middlesbrough in the Second Division. George was a late developer as a player, working in the coal pits and not taking up football seriously until he was 18. He signed as a professional with Durham City in June 1924 and quickly became noted as an exceptional goalscorer. Middlesbrough paid £800 to take him to Ayresome Park in October 1925 and he soon repaid the fee, netting a new record tally of 59 goals as Middlesbrough won the Second Division title in 1927. Although they were relegated the following season George scored 30 goals in 1928-29 to ensure an immediate return, again as champions. George continued as a player with Middlesbrough until the Second World War and finished his career with a record of 344 goals in 444 appearances for his two League clubs. He remained associated with Middlesbrough until December 1963, serving the club as coach, chief scout and assistant secretary. His record for England, which saw him net 18 goals in just nine appearances, ranks alongside the best of all time, scoring twice on his debut, hitting four on his second appearance and an additional hat-trick three matches later, and netting at least once in every England match he played.

George Camsell

Arthur John CAPES

Born: Burton-upon-Trent, 23rd February 1875
Died: 26th February 1945
Role: Inside-Left
Career: Burton Wanderers, Nottingham Forest, Stoke, Bristol City, Swindon Town
Debut: v Scotland (h) 14-4-1903
Appearances: 1

Arthur spent a very brief spell with Burton Wanders, a club who played their fixtures at Derby Turn and were Football League members between 1894 and 1897. In the summer of 1896 Arthur, who was known as 'Sailor' during his career, moved to Nottingham Forest and two years later helped Forest win the FA Cup, scoring two of their goals in the 3-1 win over near-neighbours Derby County. He was sold to Stoke City during the close season of 1902 and subsequently collected his only cap for England the following year, appearing in a 1-0 defeat by Scotland at Sheffield. Arthur was to remain with the club for two years, subsequently joining Bristol City in May 1904 and a year later moved on again, this time joining Swindon Town. He retired from playing in the summer of 1906. Aside from his one full cap for England Arthur also represented the Football League once. His brother Adrian also played for Burton Wanderers and Nottingham Forest.

John CARR

Born: Seaton Burn, Northumberland, 1876
Died: 17th March 1948
Role: Left-Back
Career: Seaton Burn, Newcastle United
Debut: v Ireland (h) 25-2-1905
Appearances: 2

Jack Carr joined Newcastle United in December 1899 and went on to become an integral part of the side that dominated the English game in the first decade of the twentieth century. Jack helped United win the League championship in both 1905 and 1907 and also won the FA Cup in 1910, replacing Whitson in the replay after United and Barnsley had drawn at Crystal Palace and helping United to a 2-0 replay win at Goodison Park. Jack was also a member of the side that reached consecutive finals in 1905 and 1906, finishing runners-up to Aston Villa and Everton respectively at their bogey ground of Crystal Palace (United failed to win once in four visits to the venue for the final). Jack also represented the Football League once in addition to his two full caps for England. He retired as a player in 1912 and promptly joined the Newcastle United training staff, remaining on the staff for a further ten years. In February 1922 he accepted the position of team manager of Blackburn Rovers, subsequently assuming the position of secretary-manager in September 1925. He remained in the position until December 1926. Jack was also an accomplished cricketer, having represented Northumberland during his career.

John CARR

Born: South Bank, Middlesbrough, 26th November 1892
Died: 10th May 1942
Role: Inside-Forward
Career: South Bank, Middlesbrough, Blackpool, Hartlepool United
Debut: v Ireland (a) 25-10-1919
Appearances: 2

Jackie Carr grew up in the South Bank area of Middlesbrough and played schoolboy and junior football in the region, subsequently signing for South Bank and helping the club reach the final of the FA Amateur Cup in 1910. He was then spotted by Middlesbrough and joined the club in January 1911, remaining on the club's books for the next nineteen years, one of the most loyal servants the club has ever had. In fact, the Carr family was almost synonymous with Middlesbrough, for two brothers also played for the club at some point during Jackie's time; William, who was on the club's books between 1910 and 1924 and George, who was signed in 1919 and left in 1924 for Leicester. Thus only Jackie was still with Middlesbrough when they won the Second Division championship in both 1927 and 1929. Jackie also represented the Football League on three occasions and finally brought his Middlesbrough career to an end in 1930, signing for Blackpool in May of that year. A year later he accepted the position of player-coach to Hartlepool United in his native North East and remained in this position until April 1932 when he was appointed manager. He was in charge at Victoria Park until April 1935 when he moved on to take over at Tranmere Rovers and was to spend three years at Prenton Park before resigning in 1938. Jackie then took over as manager of Darlington, a position he held until his death in 1942.

William Henry CARR

Born: Sheffield, 1848
Died: 22nd February 1924
Role: Goalkeeper
Career: Walkley, Owlerton, Sheffield, Sheffield FA
Debut: v Scotland (h) 6-3-1875
Appearances: 1

William Carr played for various clubs in and around the Sheffield area during his career, including Walkley, Owlerton and the Sheffield club. At the time of his only appearance for England he was secretary of the Owlerton club and a player with Sheffield, with an 1874 annual commenting 'Carr has again and again vindicated his right to the first place among custodians of the goal.' Whilst his goalkeeping was not in question, his time keeping certainly was, for he turned up fifteen minutes late for the clash with Scotland at Kennington Oval, forcing England to play with only 10 men until his arrival! The game subsequently finished a 2-2 draw and William was not selected for his country again. He was also known to have been a more than adequate performer out on the field during his career.

James Lee Duncan CARRAGHER

Born: Bootle, 14th January 1976
Role: Defender
Career: Liverpool
Debut: v Hungary (a) 28-4-1999
Appearances: 23

Jamie Carragher

A product of Liverpool's trainee scheme, Jamie Carragher signed professional forms with the Anfield club in 1995 and made his debut against Aston Villa during the 1996-97 season, scoring once in the 3-0 win. Initially used as a midfield player, where his fierce tackling was the springboard for many an attack, he was later successfully converted into a more than useful full-back. Having represented England at Youth level he was first capped by the Under 21s during the 1997-98 season and also played for the England B team. In April 1999 Kevin Keegan brought him into the full England side for the first time, bringing him on in place of Rio Ferdinand. Just as his club used him in both midfield and defence, so did England, whose need for versatile players was often greater than at club level. A member of the side that won three trophies during the 2000-01 season (FA Cup, League Cup and UEFA Cup, with Jamie playing in all but four matches that season), he achieved his greatest moment in club football at the end of the 2004-05 season helping Liverpool win the UEFA Champions League against all odds. His tally of England appearances might have been greater had he not suffered a knee injury that required surgery just prior to the 2002 World Cup finals in Japan and Korea.

Michael CARRICK

Born: Wallsend, 28th July 1981
Role: Midfield
Career: West Ham United, Swindon Town, Birmingham City, Tottenham Hotspur
Debut: v Mexico (h) 25-5-2001
Appearances: 5

Michael Carrick

Although born in the North East of England, Michael Carrick was taken on as a trainee by West Ham United and signed professional forms in August 1998. He made his debut during the 1999-2000 season and also had spells on loan at Swindon Town and Birmingham City before becoming a regular within the West Ham side. Alongside Frank Lampard and Joe Cole he blossomed as a midfield player of true craft and made his England debut, along with Cole, in the match against Mexico in 2001. The sale of Frank Lampard to Chelsea following the dismissal of West Ham manager Harry Redknapp signalled the break up of the midfield trio, with Joe Cole following Lampard to Chelsea following West Ham's relegation. Michael Carrick remained at Upton Park to try and help the Hammers regain their Premiership status. After defeat in the 2003-04 play-offs Michael seemed set for another season spent battling to get out of the First Division, but in August 2004, just before the transfer window closed, he was signed by Spurs. The transfer was masterminded by Spurs' then director of football Frank Arnesen, with first team coach Jacques Santini announcing that he didn't think Spurs needed Carrick. Michael didn't get a first team look in whilst Santini remained in charge, but the promotion of Martin Jol in November 2004 saw Michael become something of a regular. He rediscovered his form and by the end of the season was recalled into the England squad for the mini tour of the United States. His performances, alongside those of Kieran Richardson, were the chief positive points gained during the tour, fuelling hopes that Michael Carrick may well have a long term future for England.

Horatio Stratton 'Raich' CARTER

Born: Hendon, Sunderland, 21st December 1913
Died: 9th October 1994
Role: Inside-Forward
Career: Whitburn St. Mary, Sunderland Forge, Esh Winning, Sunderland, Derby County, Hull City, Cork Athletic
Debut: v Scotland (h) 14-4-1934
Appearances: 13 (7 goals) + 17 War appearances (19 goals) + 1 unofficial appearance

Along with Tommy Lawton and Stanley Matthews, Raich Carter is the only player to have been capped by England on either side of the Second World War, a remarkable feat given the duration of the war and standards of fitness required to compete at the highest levels, but Raich also managed to win FA Cup winners' medals either side of the hostilities, a unique achievement. He had first come to prominence as a schoolboy, representing England against both Wales and Scotland during 1927-28 and alerting a number of clubs as to his potential. Although Leicester were widely tipped to be on the verge of signing him in 1930, he linked with the local Sunderland side the following year and soon became established as club captain. Inspired by Raich and his goals (he hit 118 in 246 League appearances for the Roker Park club) Sunderland romped to the First Division title in 1935-36, finishing eight points ahead of Derby in second place. The following year he scored one of the goals that enabled Sunderland to lift the FA Cup, 3-1 at the expense of Preston North End at Wembley. In addition to his 13 official appearances for England Raich played in 17 war internationals and on 5th May 1945 against Wales scored his only international hat-trick in the 3-2 win in Cardiff. At the end of the war Raich resumed his League career with Derby and was a

Raich Carter

member of the side that won the FA Cup in 1946 against Charlton Athletic. In April 1948 he became player-manager of Hull City and took them to the Third Division North championship the following year. In 1951 he resigned as manager but remained playing for the club until 1952 when he went to play for Cork Athletic and collected a winners' medal in the FA of Ireland Cup in 1953. Upon returning to England he took over as manager of Leeds United, a post he held for five years. He later took charge at Mansfield (1960 to 1963) and Middlesbrough (1963 to 1966) and lost his job at Ayresome Park following Middlesbrough's relegation into the Third Division. He was also an accomplished cricketer, having represented both Durham and Derbyshire during his career.

Joseph Henry CARTER

Born: Aston, Birmingham, 16th April 1901
Died: 21st January 1977
Role: Inside-Right
Career: Westbourne Celtic, West Bromwich Albion, Sheffield Wednesday, Tranmere Rovers
Debut: v Belgium (a) 24-5-1926 (scored once)
Appearances: 3 (4 goals)

After playing schoolboy football in Birmingham Joe joined junior side Westbourne Celtic of the Handsworth League and was subsequently signed by West Bromwich Albion in April 1921. Joe enjoyed a lengthy and successful career with the club, helping them win the FA Cup in 1931 against local rivals Birmingham City and reach the final in 1935, where they were beaten 4-2 by Sheffield Wednesday. The opponents proved to be ironic, for in February 1936 Joe signed for the Sheffield club after nearly fifteen years an Albion player, but just six days later the deal was cancelled after Joe suffered a domestic accident! He did move on in June 1936, joining Tranmere Rovers but this move lasted barely five months before he returned to the Midlands with Walsall, joining the club in November 1936. Joe then became player-manager of Vono Spots in 1937, subsequently retiring during the close season of 1940. He then returned to Hansdworth where he became a publican. Joe represented the Football League once during his career and also achieved the honour of scoring England's 500th official goal, this coming in the 5-1 win over Belgium in 1929.

Joe Carter

Arthur Edward CATLIN

Born: South Bank, Middlesbrough, 11th January 1911
Died: 28th November 1990
Role: Left-Back
Career: South Bank, Sheffield Wednesday
Debut: v Wales (a) 17-10-1936
Appearances: 5

Ted Catlin represented Middlesbrough at schoolboy level before joining amateur club South Bank, subsequently signing professional forms with Sheffield Wednesday in October 1930. A member of the side that won the FA Cup in 1935 against West Bromwich Albion, Ted remained with Wednesday for his entire career, although he did turn out for Charlton Athletic as a guest during the Second World War. It was whilst playing for Wednesday, however, that he suffered the injury that was to bring his career to an end, a knee injury sustained in the 1943 League North Cup Final first leg against Blackpool. As well as his three full caps for England he represented the Football League on one occasion. Ted subsequently became a publican in Sheffield.

Arthur CHADWICK

Born: Church, Lancashire, 1875
Died: Exeter, 21st March 1936
Role: Centre-Half
Career: Church, Accrington, Burton Swifts, Southampton, Portsmouth, Northampton Town, Accrington, Exeter City
Debut: v Wales (a) 26-3-1900
Appearances: 2

A cousin of England winger Edgar Chadwick, Arthur began his career with Church FC and Accrington before signing with Burton Swifts in 1895. He left the club in 1897 when they had finished in the re-election spots in the Second Division, signing for Southern League club Southampton. He helped the Saints win the Southern League championship three times (1898, 1899 and 1901) and reach the FA Cup Final in 1900, being beaten 4-0 by Bury in the final at Crystal Palace. After Southampton's third title success Arthur moved down the coast to join Portsmouth and helped them become Southern League champions in 1902. In the summer of 1904 he joined Northampton Town and spent two years with the club before returning to Accrington for a second spell. In 1908 he was transferred to Exeter City and finished his playing career in 1910 when he was appointed manager of the St. James' Park club which was then playing in the East Devon League. He was manager at Exeter until December 1922 and was thus in charge when they became founder members of the Third Division of the Football League in 1920. From Exeter he joined Reading as manager and held the post until October 1925 when he returned to Southampton as manager. He was in charge until retiring in April 1931 and he died five years later whilst watching a match at Exeter City's ground.

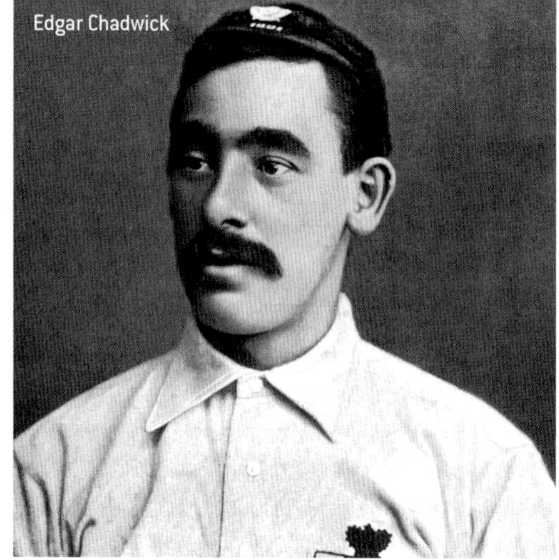
Edgar Chadwick

Edgar Wallace CHADWICK

Born: Blackburn, 14th June 1869
Died: Blackburn, 14th February 1942
Role: Inside-Left
Career: Blackburn Olympic, Blackburn Rovers, Everton, Burnley, Southampton, Liverpool, Blackpool, Glossop, Darwen
Debut: v Wales (h) 7-3-1891
Appearances: 7 (3 goals)

Edgar Chadwick began his career playing junior football for Little Dots FC in 1884 and was subsequently signed by the local Blackburn Olympic club in 1886. At the end of the 1886-87 season he was transferred to local rivals Blackburn Rovers, then one of the most successful clubs in the country, having won the FA Cup three times in succession between 1884 and 1886. He spent one season with the Leamington Road (where Rovers then played) outfit before transferring to Everton in July 1888. He played in Everton's very first Football League match and was ultimately to help them win the League title in 1891. He also collected runners-up medals from the FA Cup in 1893 and 1897 as Everton were beaten by Wolverhampton Wanders and Aston Villa respectively. In 1899 Edgar returned to the north west and signed for Burnley, although a year later he was on the move again, this time linking up with his cousin Arthur Chadwick at Southampton. Edgar collected a championship medal as Southampton won the Southern League at the end of his first season and a year later returned to the final of the FA Cup as Southampton won through to Crystal Palace. Unfortunately it was not a case of third time lucky either, for Sheffield United won 2-1 after a 1-1 draw. Soon after the final Edgar returned to Merseyside, signing for Liverpool although he was unable to win further honours whilst with the club. In May 1904 he joined Blackpool for a season, then switched to Glossop and finished his playing career with former League side Darwen. Thereafter he had coaching spells in Germany and Holland before returning to Blackburn to become a baker.

Mark Valentine CHAMBERLAIN

Born: Stoke-on-Trent, 19th November 1961
Role: Forward
Career: Port Vale, Stoke City, Sheffield Wednesday, Portsmouth, Brighton & Hove Albion, Exeter City, Fareham
Debut: v Luxembourg (h) (substitute) 15-12-1982 (scored once) (ECQ)
Appearances: 8 (1 goal)

Mark Chamberlain played junior football in the Potteries before signing with Port Vale as an apprentice, subse-

Mark Chamberlain

Mick Channon

quently turning professional in April 1979. After nearly 100 League appearances and having impressed a host of watching scouts, he was sold to local rivals Stoke City, costing them £125,000 in August 1982. His impact at Stoke and in the First Division was little short of sensational and before the year was out he had collected his first cap for England, coming on as a substitute in the match against Luxembourg and scoring. At the end of the 1984-85 season Stoke were relegated and immediately speculation mounted that Mark would be on his way, although he was not transferred to Sheffield Wednesday until September 1985, costing £350,000 even though it had been nearly a year since he had last represented England. He was unable to force his way back into the side either, although he went on to make 66 League appearances for the club (although over half of these were as a substitute) before being sold to Portsmouth for £200,000 in August 1988. He remained at Fratton Park for six years, making well over 150 first team appearances before moving further down the coast to sign for Brighton. A year later he was on the move, this time signing for Exeter City with whom he finished his League career, although he did briefly play with non-League Fareham. In addition to his eight full caps for England Mark represented his country at schoolboy and Under-21 level, collecting four caps at the latter level. His older brother Neville also played for Port Vale and Stoke City during a career that also took in Newport County, Plymouth Argyle, Mansfield Town and Doncaster Rovers.

Henry CHAMBERS

Born: Willington Quay, Northumberland, 17th November 1896
Died: 29th June 1949
Role: Centre-Forward
Career: Tynemouth, Willington United Methodists, North Shields Athletic, Liverpool, West Bromwich Albion, Oakengates Town
Debut: v Wales (a) 14-3-1921
Appearances: 8 (5 goals)

After being educated at and representing Tynemouth Schools, Harry played for Willington United Methodists and North Shields Athletic and was working in a shipyard until persuaded to sign for Liverpool in April 1915, just as the Football League was to be suspended for the duration of the First World War. As such Harry made guest appearances for Belfast Distillery and Glentoran during the hostilities. He returned to Anfield at the end of the war and helped them win successive League titles in 1922 and 1923 as well as representing the Football League on five occasions. Harry might have added further caps to his tally too but for a series of injuries that forced him to withdraw from the squad on occasions. In March 1928 he was transferred to West Bromwich Albion, who promptly converted him to centre-half for his final season of League football. He moved on to Oakengates Town as player-manager in July 1929 and he was still playing well into middle age. Harry also won two caps for England at schoolboy level.

Michael Roger CHANNON

Born: Orcheston, Wiltshire, 28th November 1948
Role: Forward
Career: Southampton, Manchester City, Southampton, Caroline Hills (Hong Kong), Newcastle United, Bristol Rovers, Norwich City, Portsmouth
Debut: v Yugoslavia (h) 11-10-1972
Appearances: 46 (21 goals) + 1 unofficial international

Southampton first spotted Mick whilst he was representing Wiltshire Schools and signed him as an associate schoolboy in 1963, subsequently offering him apprentice forms in March 1964. He was upgraded to the professional ranks in December 1965 and went on to make 392 League appearances for the club, scoring 155 goals. He also helped them win the FA Cup in 1976 and collected 45 of his England caps whilst with the club, as well as appearing for the Football League twice and earning nine appearances for the Under-23 side. In July 1977 he was sold to Manchester City for £300,000, spending three seasons with the Maine Road club and collecting his final England cap before returning back to The Dell in a move worth £200,000 in September 1979. During his second spell with Southampton he netted another 30 League goals to establish a new record for the club. He spent the summer months of 1982 playing for Caroline Hills FC in Hong Kong and returned to England in September to sign for Newcastle United. A month later he joined Bristol Rovers but remained in the West Country only two months before moving to Norwich City. A member of the side that won the League Cup in 1985 he joined Portsmouth in August 1985 where he finished his career. Since 1990 he has been a racehorse trainer and combines this with running a chain of shops and offering the occasional expert opinion on television.

Gary Andrew CHARLES

Born: London, 13th April 1970
Role: Defender
Career: Nottingham Forest, Leicester City, Derby County, Aston Villa, Benfica (Portugal)
Debut: v New Zealand (a) 8-6-1991
Appearances: 2

Taken on by Nottingham Forest as a trainee in 1987 Gary spent a brief spell on loan to Leicester before rising through the ranks to become a key part of the side that reached the

Gary Charles

FA Cup Final in 1991 and won the Full Members Cup the following year (although Gary is perhaps best known for being the player fouled by Paul Gascoigne in the FA Cup final, a foul that forced Paul out of the game for a year!). In July 1993 he was sold to Derby County for £750,000 but less than two years later was on the move again, this time joining Aston Villa. Here he helped the club win the League Cup in 1996 before suffering a string of injuries, fortunately fighting his way back into contention for the first team in 1997. In January 1999 he left to join Benfica of Portugal in a deal worth a reported £1.5 million.

John CHARLTON O.B.E.

Born: Ashington, Northumberland, 8th May 1935
Role: Centre-Half
Career: Ashington YMCA, Ashington Welfare, Leeds United
Debut: v Scotland (h) 10-4-1965
Appearances: 35 (6 goals) + 1 unofficial appearance

The elder brother of Bobby Charlton, Jack first impressed in local football before being signed by Leeds United as an amateur in 1950, subsequently turning professional in May 1952. It was the arrival of Don Revie as manager at Elland Road that turned Jack's playing fortunes around, for as a member of a side that struggled in the Second Division he did not get the chance to shine on the international scene. With Leeds subsequently restored to First Division status and challenging for a succession of honours, Jack became a high profile player and had a dual role within the side; cutting out danger in defence and using his height to extremely good effect up front, especially when Leeds won a corner. The multiple fracture suffered by Maurice Norman meant a vacancy in the England side for a centre-half and Jack was awarded his first cap at the age of 30 years. More importantly, he was given the chance to establish himself in the side just as Alf Ramsey was beginning to finalise his squad for the 1966 World Cup finals in England. Both Jack and Bobby helped England win the cup and Jack's reputation was assured. By the time he retired as a player in May 1973 (ironically on the same day that brother Bobby officially brought the curtain down on his playing career, although he later returned to the field for Preston) he had collected winners' medals from the Inter-Cities Fairs Cup twice (1968 and 1971), the League championship (1969), the FA Cup (1972), the League Cup (1968) and the Second Division championship, as well as a plethora of runners-up medals in various competitions. His playing career even survived a charge of bringing the game into disrepute after he revealed during a television interview that he kept a 'little black book' in which were recorded the names of opponents who had transgressed against him and against whom he wished to gain revenge! Jack became manager of Middlesbrough the same month he retired and fashioned a side good enough to win the Second Division title at the end of his first season in charge. He left in May 1977 to take over the reins at Sheffield Wednesday and spent six years at the club, restoring them to the Second Division during his tenure. He had a second spell at Middlesbrough as caretaker manager in March 1984 before taking over at Newcastle United in June 1984. After a couple of games into the 1985-86 season and with the fans voicing their displeasure with the style of play at St. James' Park he resigned, seemingly finished with football, although in February 1986 he accepted an offer to take control of the Republic of Ireland side. He spent ten highly successful years in charge, guiding them to the finals of the 1990 and 1994 World Cup and the 1988 and 1992 European Championships, the first time the country had qualified for the final stages of any competitions. Their failure to qualify for the 1996 finals of the European Championship, beaten in a play-off against Holland, brought his reign to an end, but he is as fondly remembered by the Irish supporters for his efforts on their behalf as he is by English fans for his exploits in an England shirt.

Bobby and Jack Charlton

Sir Robert CHARLTON, O.B.E., C.B.E.

Born: Ashington, Northumberland, 11th October 1937
Role: Centre-Forward, Inside-Forward
Career: Manchester United, Preston North End
Debut: v Scotland (a) 19-4-1958 (scored once)
Appearances: 106 (49 goals) + 1 unofficial appearance

As befitted a relative of the famous Milburn footballing family, Bobby Charlton was a child prodigy, representing England at schoolboy and Youth level before signing professional forms with Manchester United in 1954. After helping the United Youth team win the FA Youth Cup in three successive seasons (1954-1956) he became an integral part of the famed 'Busby Babes' and effectively came to the fore after surviving the Munich crash of 1958. At domestic level he won three League championship medals, a winners' medal in the FA Cup and, perhaps most importantly, led the side to victory in the 1968 European Cup final against Benfica, scoring two of the goals in the 4-1 victory. The importance of this victory to United in general and Busby in particular was revealed in the immediate aftermath; Busby reserved his longest and most heartfelt hug for Charlton. Two years previously Charlton had been a member of the England team that won the World Cup at Wembley, the same year he was declared Footballer of the Year and European Footballer of the Year. He finished his playing career as player-manager of Preston North End, but found he was perhaps not cut out for management. He won a then record 106 caps for England, scoring a record 49 goals (which has yet to be beaten) and as well as collecting a CBE was made a knight in 1994. In addition to his 106 full caps for England, Bobby also represented the country at schoolboy, Youth and Under-23 level and the Football League on eight occasions. Contrary to popular belief, Bobby was booked twice during his playing career, both within a matter of months. In 1998 it was revealed that he had been booked during the England and Argentina World Cup quarter final of 1966, although no one in the England camp had any recollection of the incident during the game. Then, in the curtain raiser to the 1966-67 season, the FA Charity Shield between Manchester United and Spurs at Old Trafford, he was booked for time-wasting, even though United were behind in the match at the time! He currently combines running a travel agency with serving Manchester United as a director.

Raymond Ogden CHARNLEY

Born: Lancaster, 29th May 1935
Role: Centre-Forward
Career: Bolton-le-Sands, Preston North End, Morecambe, Blackpool, Preston North End, Wrexham, Bradford Park Avenue, Morecambe
Debut: v France (h) 3-10-1962 (EC)
Appearances: 1

Ray played junior football for Bolton-le-Sands and was briefly signed with Preston North End as an amateur before becoming a professional with non-League Morecambe. He cost Blackpool £750 when he signed in May 1957 and went on to give the club ten years sterling service, making 363 League appearances and scoring 193 goals, a useful return for the era. He was unfortunate to make only one appearance for England, making his debut in the first match after England's disappointing showing in the 1962 World Cup finals in Chile. In December 1967 he returned to Preston North End, costing the club £11,000, although he made only 23 League appearances before moving on again, this time to Wrexham in July 1968 for £10,000. In January 1969 he was swapped with another player and joined Bradford Park Avenue, a team constantly battling at the bottom end of the Fourth Division table. That battle was finally lost during the summer of 1970 when they were voted out of the League in favour of Cambridge United. Although Bradford struggled on for a further few seasons in the Northern Premier League, Ray left soon after their dismissal from the League and joined Morecambe, having played a total of 465 League games for his four clubs and scored 217 goals.

Charles Christopher CHARSLEY

Born: Leicester, 7th November 1864
Died: Weston-super-Mare, 10th January 1945
Role: Goalkeeper
Career: Stafford Town, Stafford Rangers, Small Heath, West Bromwich Albion, Small Heath
Debut: v Ireland (h) 25-2-1893
Appearances: 1

After playing schools football in Stafford, Charles Charsley joined Stafford Town in 1881 and then moved on to the more senior Stafford Rangers. He also had a very brief spell guesting for Aston Villa before joining Small Heath, forerunners to the current Birmingham City club, in 1886. In August 1891 he was transferred to West Bromwich Albion, although he made only one League appearance for the club before returning to Small Heath in December the same year. It was during this second spell at Small Heath that he collected his only cap for England and helped the club win the Second Division championship (in their first season as a League club, the Second Division having been added in 1892), his only major domestic honour from the game. Unfortunately, Small Heath were unsuccessful in the Test Matches and thus were not promoted into the First Division (automatic promotion and relegation were not introduced until the 1898-99 season), with Charles announcing his retirement after Small Heath's 5-2 defeat at the hands of Newton Heath in Sheffield. At the end of the following season, however, Small Heath finished second in the Second Division and again qualified for the Test Matches and persuaded Charles to come out of retirement and he helped them beat Darwen 3-1 and gain promotion into the First Division for the first time in their history. Charles had joined the Birmingham City police force in 1884 and worked his way through the ranks to become Chief Constable of Coventry in 1899, a position he held until his retirement in 1918. Upon retirement he moved to Weston-super-Mare and was appointed a borough councillor in 1933, serving until his death in 1945. Charles was also deputy Mayor of Weston-Super-Mare between 1939 and 1940.

Sam Chedgzoy

Samuel CHEDGZOY

Born: Ellesmere Port, Cheshire, 27th January 1890
Died: Montreal, 15th January 1967
Role: Right-Winger
Career: Everton, New Bedford (USA), Carsteel FC (Canada)
Debut: v Wales (h) 15-3-1920
Appearances: 8

Sam played for Birnell's Ironworks in Ellesmere Port before signing with Everton in December 1910 and was to remain a player with the club for the next sixteen years. A member of the side that won the last League championship before League football was suspended for the duration of the First World War, he returned to the club at the end of the hostilities and towards the end of his career was setting up chances for Dixie Dean. For all his accomplishments, however, Sam is best remembered for getting the law changed regarding the corner kick. In April 1924, during a match against Spurs, Sam took a corner kick and dribbled the ball along the line, past bemused Everton and Spurs players alike and put the ball into the net. Despite protestations from the Spurs players, the goal was allowed to stand, for the rules in force at the time, whilst stating that a goal could be scored direct from a corner did not stipulate that the player taking the kick could only play the ball once. Not surprisingly, at the end of the season the law was changed! Sam remained with Everton until May 1926 when he moved to America and played for four years for New Bedford. In 1930 he crossed the border to play for Canteel FC of Montreal and was still turning out for the club in 1940, when in his fifties, although quite how far into his fifties is a matter of some debate, for some sources give his year of birth as 1889. His son Sidney meanwhile had played for Millwall, among a few clubs, during the 1930s.

Charles John CHENERY

Born: Lambourn, Berkshire, 1st January 1850
Role: Centre-Half
Career: Crystal Palace, Barnes, Wanderers, Surrey
Debut: v Scotland (a) 30-11-1872
Appearances: 3 (1 goal) + 1 unofficial appearance

Charles Chenery was educated at Marlborough Grammar School and became another multi-talented sportsman, playing football for England and representing a couple of counties at cricket. He was first capped by England whilst playing for the original Crystal Palace club (no relation to the side that currently bears that name) and appeared in the unofficial match between England and Scotland in February 1872. It will be remembered that the Scotland side for this and the previous three matches were entirely drawn from London and thus could not be considered a national side. Charles was, however, retained in the England side that played in the historic first match in Glasgow later the same year. Charles went on to play for the leading side Wanderers (although he did not appear in any of their five FA Cup winning sides) and also served as Secretary to the club in 1871. He also won representative honours from London and Surrey as well as representing the latter county at cricket. He also played for Northants before that county's elevation to first class status. In 1877 he was believed to have moved abroad, although no details exist as to which country and therefore his date of death is unknown (assuming he has died, of course!).

Trevor John CHERRY

Born: Huddersfield, 23rd February 1948
Role: Full-Back
Career: Huddersfield Town, Leeds United, Bradford City
Debut: v Wales (a) 24-3-1976
Appearances: 27 + 1 unofficial international

Trevor Cherry

Trevor Cherry represented Huddersfield at schools level and then played for the local YMCA before signing professional forms with Huddersfield Town in July 1965. Here he developed into a highly polished left-half and made 188 League appearances for the Terries, scoring 12 goals and helping the club win the Second Division championship in 1970. In June 1972 he was sold to Leeds United for £99,000 and successfully converted to full-back, the position he played in for most of his international appearances. Whilst at Leeds he helped the club win the League championship in 1974 and reach the finals of the FA Cup in 1973 (beaten 1-0 by Sunderland in one of the biggest cup final upsets of all time) and the European Cup Winners' Cup in 1973, where they were beaten, as much by the referee as they were by their opponents AC Milan, 1-0. After exactly 400 League appearances for Leeds Trevor was sold to Bradford City for £10,000 in December 1982 and made player-manager, helping the club win the Third Division championship in 1985. Of course, the celebrations at Valley Parade at the final game of the season, where the trophy was to be handed over following the match against Lincoln City, were completely overshadowed by the fire that engulfed the main stand, killing 59 people. Trevor's role in restoring morale within the city in the aftermath has been since overlooked and there was considerable criticism of the club and its chairman when Trevor was dismissed in January 1987. An earlier dismissal had similarly caused controversy; in 1977 he and Daniel Bertoni were sent off following an incident during the England and Argentina match in Buenos Aires, although Trevor was undoubtedly an innocent party to the event.

Allenby CHILTON

Born: South Hylton, County Durham, 16th September 1918
Died: 16th June 1996
Role: Centre-Half
Career: Seaham Colliery, Manchester United, Grimsby Town
Debut: v Northern Ireland (a) 7-10-1950
Appearances: 2

Allenby joined Manchester United in November 1938 and made his debut for the club in the 1939-40 season, although the outbreak of the Second World War meant that this result was expunged from the records. During the war he guested for United and Charlton Athletic, helping both clubs win wartime cup competitions before resuming his League career with United at the end of hostilities. A member of the side that won the FA Cup in 1948 Allenby collected his first cap for England in 1950 and his second the following year. In 1952 he won a League championship medal with United and continued to be a regular in the side until March 1955 when he was allowed to join Grimsby Town as player-manager. At the end of his first season in charge they were Third Division (North) champions and promoted to the Second Division. Allenby retired from playing in October 1956 and continued as manager for the Mariners until April 1959, taking over at Wigan Athletic in May 1960. He later had a spell scouting for Hartlepool United and then took over as manager in July 1962, remaining in charge for a little under a year before leaving the game altogether.

Allenby Chilton

Henry CHIPPENDALE

Born: Blackburn, 2nd October 1870
Died: 29th September 1952
Role: Right-Winger
Career: Nelson, Blackburn Rovers
Debut: v Ireland (a) 1-3-1894
Appearances: 1

After a brief spell with Nelson, Harry Chippendale signed with Blackburn Rovers in the summer of 1891 and was to serve the club for six years, collecting his only cap for England in the match against Ireland in partnership with club colleague Jimmy Whitehead. Part of his success was that although he operated on the wing he was physically big and strong, making him extremely difficult to knock off the ball, whilst his shooting and crossing were particularly accurate. After his playing career was at an end Harry went to work for Hornby's Brookhouse Mill in Blackburn and rose to become manager of the firm. He also performed as a linesman and in 1908 was added to the Football League list.

Martin Harcourt CHIVERS

Born: Southampton, 27th April 1945
Role: Centre-Forward
Career: Southampton, Tottenham Hotspur, Servette (Switzerland), Norwich City, Brighton & Hove Albion
Debut: v Malta (a) 3-2-1971 (ECQ)
Appearances: 24 (13 goals)

He was signed by Southampton in 1962 and quickly established himself as an exceptional striker, partnering Ron Davies in the side that won promotion to the First Division in 1967. After scoring 97 goals in 175 League appearances for the Saints he was signed by Spurs for £125,000, with Frank Saul making the opposite journey. His Spurs career got off to a blistering start, scoring on his debut and then grabbing two in the cup tie against Manchester United, but a serious injury sustained in September 1968 ended his season. When he returned he struggled for form and confidence and was dropped, but the subsequent sale of Jimmy Greaves and the arrival of play maker Martin Peters coincided with a return to form, and it was his goals more than anything else that enabled Spurs to win the 1971 League Cup (he scored both goals in the final) and 1972 UEFA Cup (both goals again in the first leg of the final), as well as the 1973 League Cup. After 268 League appearances for Spurs and 118 goals, he was sold to Servette in Switzerland for £80,000, later returning to England and Norwich City and Brighton. He retired from playing in 1982 to run a hotel and restaurant business in Hertfordshire.

Martin Chivers

Edward CHRISTIAN

Born: Malvern, Worcestershire, 14th September 1858
Died: 3rd April 1934
Role: Full-Back
Career: Cambridge University, Old Etonians
Debut: v Scotland (h) 5-4-1879
Appearances: 1

Educated at Eton College, Edward Christian had a brief but highly successful football career. He went on to Cambridge University and also played for Old Etonians, although he did not earn a Blue. He did, however, collect a winners' medal in the FA Cup in 1879 as Old Etonians beat Clapham Rovers 1-0 at Kennington Oval. A week later Edward was at the same venue representing England in the annual clash with Scotland and helped the home nation bounce back from 4-1 down to win 5-4, although this was to be Edward's only appearance for his country, with a further six players being dropped from the team at the same time. In 1881 Edward's career was effectively brought to an end when he emigrated to Ceylon, working in the country until 1904.

Harold Edwin CLAMP

Born: Coalville, Leicester, 14th September 1934
Died: November 1995
Role: Wing-Half
Career: Wolverhampton Wanderers, Arsenal, Stoke City, Peterborough United, Worcester City, Lower Gornal
Debut: v USSR (a) 18-5-1958
Appearances: 4

Eddie Clamp

Eddie Clamp played schools football in Coalville before signing as an amateur with Wolverhampton Wanderers in 1950, subsequently being upgraded to the professional ranks in April 1952. Over the next nine years he helped the club win two League titles and the FA Cup as they became the chief challengers to Manchester United. Having earned a single cap for England at schoolboy level Eddie was awarded four caps for the full England side and also represented the Football League on one occasion. After 213 appearances for the Molineux club he was sold to Arsenal in November 1961 for £34,500, remaining at Highbury until September 1962 when he signed for Stoke City for £14,000. His experience proved invaluable to Stoke, helping them win the Second Division title in 1963 and establish themselves back in the First Division. Eddie was sold to Peterborough United for £5,000 in October 1964 but less than a year later left League football to play for Worcester City. He was then out of the game for a year before finishing his career with Lower Gornal.

Daniel Robert CLAPTON

Born: Aldgate, London, 22nd July 1934
Died: Homerton, London, 24th May 1986
Role: Right-Winger
Career: Leytonstone, Arsenal, Luton Town, Corinthians FC (Australia)
Debut: v Wales (h) 26-11-1958
Appearances: 1

After playing for Hackney Schools and Leytonstone, Danny Clapton was working as a porter in Smithfield meat market when he was persuaded to sign professional forms with Arsenal in August 1953. Over the next nine years he was to make 207 League appearances for the Gunners, scoring 25 goals but setting up a considerable number of chances for his colleagues. In 1958 Tom Finney's long and illustrious international career was brought to an end and Danny was the first player given the opportunity of replacing him on the wing, although England drew 2-2 with Wales and Danny was not selected again. In September 1962 he was sold to Luton Town for £6,000, unfortunate that his Arsenal career had realised nothing in the way of domestic honours as Arsenal were in a lengthy period of consolidation and rebuilding, although he did represent the Football League on one occasion. He remained with Luton until the summer of 1963, having made only 10 League appearances for the club, and in late 1964 emigrated to Australia, later assisting the Corinthians club of Sydney.

Thomas CLARE

Born: Congleton, Cheshire, 1865
Died: Vancouver, Canada, 27th December 1929
Role: Right-Back
Career: Talke, Goldenhill Wanderers, Stoke, Burslem Port Vale
Debut: v Ireland (h) 2-3-1889
Appearances: 4

Tommy Clare was first linked with Talke FC of Staffordshire before signing for Goldenhill Wanderers and in 1883 became Stoke's first professional when he joined them. He was a member of the side that won the Football Alliance in 1891 and earned election into the expanded Football League the following season. Although their first season as a League club was something of a struggle (they finished the season second last in the League, three points ahead of Darwen but four points behind West Bromwich Albion) and they had to apply for re-election, subsequent seasons saw an improvement in the club's fortunes. The key to Stoke's success was a defence that featured Tommy, Bill Rowley and Alf Underwood, all three of whom went on to represent England (including one match when they were all in the same side). Tommy remained with Stoke as a player until 1897, having also represented Staffordshire on many occasions, and then became coach to Burslem Port Vale, later serving the club as manager. He emigrated to Canada shortly before the outbreak of the First World War and died there in 1929.

Allan John CLARKE

Born: Willenhall, Staffordshire, 31st July 1946
Role: Forward
Career: Walsall, Fulham, Leicester City, Leeds United, Barnsley
Debut: v Czechoslovakia (Guadalajara) 11-6-1970 (WC) (scored once)
Appearances: 19 (10 goals) + 1 unofficial appearance (2 goals)

Allan played schools football for Birmingham and South East Staffordshire before being offered an apprenticeship with Walsall in 1961, subsequently turning professional in August 1963. He quickly established a reputation for being an exceptional goalscorer, netting 41 goals in just 72 League appearances and in March 1966 Fulham paid £35,000 to take him to Craven Cottage. Although Fulham were involved in a constant battle against relegation from the First Division Allan still managed to register some vital goals, hitting 45 in 86 appearances for the club. In June 1968, following Fulham's relegation, Allan moved on to Leicester City for £100,000, although his one season was to see the Filbert Street club relegated at the end of the campaign, despite also being able to boast the likes of Peter Shilton in the line-up! Leicester did, however, reach the FA Cup Final at the end of the season before being narrowly beaten 1-0 by Manchester City. During the summer Allan moved on again, costing Leeds United £165,000. Here he found his true vocation, linking up front with the likes of Mick Jones and Peter Lorimer and converting a host of chances created by the likes of Billy Bremner and Johnny Giles. During the course of his nine years with the club Allan collected winners' medals in the League championship in 1974, the FA Cup in 1972 and the Inter-Cities Fairs Cup in 1971, as well as runners-up medals in the European Cup in 1975 and the FA Cup in 1970 and 1973. Having collected six caps for England at Under-23 level Allan earned his first full cap for the country during the 1970 World Cup campaign. He also represented the Football League on two occasions. In May 1978 he was sold to Barnsley for £45,000 and became player-manager, retiring as a player in 1980, having made 514 League appearances and scored 223 goals for his five clubs. He continued as manager of Barnsley until September 1980 when he returned to Leeds United as manager. Unfortunately he was unable to restore the club to earlier glories and they were relegated from the First Division at the end of the 1981-82 season and he was dismissed shortly after. Allan then became manager of Scunthorpe United in February 1983 and was later appointed to the board of directors, remaining at the club until August 1984. In July 1985 he was appointed manager of Barnsley for a second time, remaining in charge until 1989. Allan came from a noted footballing family, with his brother Wayne being a member of Everton's 1987 championship winning side. Indeed, Wayne also scored the goal that stopped Liverpool from beating Leeds United's record for the longest unbeaten run in a season!

Allan Clarke

Harold Alfred CLARKE

Born: Woodford Green, Essex, 23rd February 1923
Died: 16th April 2000
Role: Centre-Half
Career: Lovell's Athletic, Tottenham Hotspur, Llanelli
Debut: v Scotland (a) 3-4-1954 (WCQ)
Appearances: 1

After playing schools football in Woodford, Harry Clarke enlisted in the RAF during the Second World War and played representative football during service. He was signed by Welsh club Lovell's Athletic and helped them win the Welsh FA Cup in 1948 and successive Welsh League titles before being signed by Arthur Rowe of Spurs in March 1949. He quickly established himself in the side and helped Spurs to successive League titles, the Second Division in 1950 and the First Division the following year.

He retired from playing midway during the 1956-57 season but remained at Spurs as coach to the junior side, a post he held until February 1959 when he accepted the position of manager of Llanelli. He later managed Romford for a spell and then worked as an officer for a security company. His son-in-law was John White, the Spurs and Scotland player killed by lightning whilst sheltering under a tree on a golf course during a storm.

Tommy Clay

Thomas CLAY

Born: Leicester, 19th November 1892
Died: Southend, 21st February 1949
Role: Right-Back
Career: Leicester Fosse, Tottenham Hotspur, Northfleet
Debut: v Wales (h) 15-3-1920
Appearances: 4

Tommy Clay joined Leicester Fosse in April 1911 and made his debut for the club at the age of 19 years, thereafter holding his place in the side for two years. It was his performances against Spurs in the FA Cup first round in 1914 that so impressed Spurs' manager Peter McWilliam and prompted a transfer immediately after the replay. At Spurs Tommy became a key member of the side, although the outbreak of the First World War saw him enlist in the services and he made a number of guest appearances for Notts County, among others, during the hostilities. When the war came to an end he took part in his first representative match, playing in an international trial match, although he had to wait a year before making his England debut. He was Spurs' captain when they ran away with the Second Division title in 1919-20 but handed over to Arthur Grimsdell the following season when Spurs won the FA Cup. In 1921 Tommy played a League match in goal for Spurs; with both the club's regular goalkeepers injured he took over in goal at Sunderland and kept a clean sheet in a 1-0 win. In addition to his four full caps for England he also represented the Football League on one occasion and remained at White Hart Lane until 1929 when he was released, subsequently taking over as player-coach at Northfleet, Spurs' nursery side. He became a publican in St. Albans as well as joining the local non-League club as trainer and coach and later returned to his initial trade of bricklayer.

Ronald CLAYTON

Born: Preston, Lancashire, 5th August 1934
Role: Right-Half
Career: Blackburn Rovers, Morecambe, Great Harwood
Debut: v Northern Ireland (h) 2-11-1955
Appearances: 35

Ronnie Clayton was first spotted, along with his elder brother Ken, whilst playing schools football in Preston and for Lancashire, the pair signing amateur forms in July 1949. Ronnie was upgraded to the professional ranks in August 1951 having already made his first team debut for the club, appearing in the final game of the 1950-51 season. National Service obligations meant he was not able to claim a regular place in the Blackburn side until the 1954-55 season, but once he had forced his way into the side he was there to stay. In September 1955 he was awarded his first cap for the England Under-23 side, collecting his first B international cap later the same month. He maintained his progress at club level to such an extent that two months later he had graduated to the full side, collecting his first full cap in the match against Northern Ireland. Whilst his brother Ken's career was brought to an end by a broken leg, Ronnie's showed little sign of diminishing, and he went on to become an integral part of the side that returned Blackburn to their First Division status, reached the FA Cup Final of 1960 and earned 35 caps for England. He remained at Ewood Park until July 1969 after making a record number of appearances for the club; 579 League appearances (including two as substitute), a record that stood for seventeen years. He then spent a year as player-manager of Morecambe before finishing his playing career with Great Harwood. Ronnie then went into business, running a newsagents shop and then becoming a representative for a tie manufacturing company.

Ronnie Clayton

Charles Clegg

Sir John Charles CLEGG

Born: Sheffield,15th June 1850
Died: Sheffield, 26th June 1937
Role: Forward
Career: Sheffield Wednesday, Sheffield FC, Norfolk FC
Debut: v Scotland (a) 30-11-1872
Appearances: 1 + 1 unofficial appearance (1 goal)

Like Charles Alcock, Charles Clegg's true vocation came off the field, subsequently serving the FA as chairman and then President from 1923 until his death in 1937. As a player he tended to play as a forward, where his speed was used to good effect; he could run the 100 yards in 10 seconds and won over 120 prizes for his running, especially in 100 and 440 yard events. He was selected to play in the very first international match ever staged but later announced to have found the experience extremely distasteful, complaining that 'the southern snobs' wouldn't talk to him on the train journey up to Glasgow or pass to him out on the pitch! Thereafter he refereed two FA Cup Finals (1882 and 1892) and also took charge of the England and Scotland match of 1886. A solicitor by profession, he joined the FA committee in 1886 and three years later was appointed chairman. He held this position for three years, becoming vice-president in 1889 and was made president in 1923 until his death in 1937. Aside from his positions within the game's governing body he also served on the boards of both Sheffield United and Sheffield Wednesday and was president of the Sheffield FA. He was knighted in 1927, the first man to be so honoured for their services to football. His younger brother William Clegg also played for England.

Sir William Edwin CLEGG O.B.E.

Born: Sheffield, 21st April 1852
Died: Sheffield, 22nd August 1932
Role: Half-Back
Career: Sheffield Wednesday, Sheffield Albion
Debut: v Scotland (h) 8-3-1873
Appearances: 2

The younger brother of Charles Clegg, William also played for a number of clubs in and around Sheffield, including Sheffield Wednesday, Perseverance and Sheffield Albion, collecting his first cap for England in the second international match with Scotland. His second appearance came six years later against Wales, although in 1880 he was forced to retire from playing owing to injury. Like his elder brother he also served on the boards of both Sheffield United and Sheffield Wednesday, was an exceptionally good runner and was a solicitor by profession, having qualified in 1874. He was knighted in 1906, some 21 years before his brother, although he earned his accolade for his public service work, serving as Lord Mayor of Sheffield from 1893 to 1899. During the First World War he served the Sheffield Munitions Tribunal, for which he was subsequently awarded an OBE. According to legend, he arrived twenty minutes late for his second international because he was involved in the trial of the famous thief Charlie Peace, although there is little evidence to support this story, since contemporary reports make no mention of it.

Raymond Neal CLEMENCE M.B.E.

Born: Skegness, Lincolnshire, 5th August 1948
Role: Goalkeeper
Career: Notts County, Scunthorpe United, Liverpool, Tottenham Hotspur
Debut: v Wales (a) 15-11-1972 (ECQ)
Appearances: 61 + 1 unofficial international

Ray Clemence

Although he was briefly connected with Notts County, making an appearance in their 'A' team, he signed professional forms with Scunthorpe United in August 1965 and made just 50 senior appearances for them before joining Liverpool for £18,000 in June 1967. Signed initially as cover for Tommy Lawrence he took over the first team berth in 1970 and in the next eleven seasons missed just six League games as Liverpool dominated the domestic game. Ray collected five championship medals, three in the European Cup, two UEFA Cup medals and winners' medals in both the FA Cup and League Cup. In the summer of 1981 he was surprisingly sold to Spurs for £300,000, making his debut for the club in the FA Charity Shield against Aston Villa at Wembley. At the end of his first season at Spurs he picked up a further winners' medal in the FA Cup and a runners-up medal in the League Cup, where Spurs were beaten by Liverpool! A bad injury sustained in the FA Cup 3rd round match at Fulham in the 1983-84 season sidelined him for a considerable time and he was unable to reclaim his position when fully fit, sitting on the bench when Spurs won the UEFA Cup in 1984. He was restored to the first team the following season and held his place as Spurs reached the FA Cup final in 1986-87, losing for the first time at this stage against Coventry. A further serious injury in October effectively ended his playing career, but Ray had passed the 1,000 mark for senior games (only fellow goalkeepers Peter Shilton and Pat Jennings have achieved a similar figure) and was awarded the MBE in the 1987 Birthday Honours List in recognition of his services to football. He won 61 caps for the full England side, a figure that would have been considerably higher had it not been for having to compete with the equally competent Peter Shilton, and on retiring from playing in March 1988 was appointed specialist goalkeeping coach at White Hart Lane. In June 1989 he was upgraded to reserve team coach and made assistant first team coach, in tandem with Doug Livermore, in May 1992. The arrival of Ossie Ardiles in the summer of 1993 brought Ray's Spurs career to an end and he subsequently took over at Barnet as manager, later resigning to become a part of Glenn Hoddle's England set up. His son Stephen later played for Spurs and Birmingham City. During his brief spell with Scunthorpe, Ray supplemented his wages by spending the summer season working on the beach at Skegness as a deck chair attendant!

David Thomas CLEMENT

Born: Battersea, London, 2nd February 1948
Died: 31st March 1982
Role: Defender
Career: Queens Park Rangers, Bolton Wanderers, Fulham, Wimbledon
Debut: v Wales (a) (substitute) 24-3-1976
Appearances: 5

Dave represented South London at schoolboy level and was invited along to Loftus Road to sign schoolboy forms for Queens Park Rangers as a result. In July 1965 he was taken on as a professional by the club, even though he had not been an apprentice, and went on to make his debut in 1966. Over the course of the next thirteen years Dave made 407 League appearances for the club, scoring 21 goals and was an integral part of the side that established Queen Park Rangers as a more than competent First Division outfit. Although Rangers finished runners-up in the First Division in 1976, pipped by Liverpool by one point, major domestic honours would not come the club's way. In June 1979 Dave was sold to Bolton Wanderers for £170,000 and spent a little over a year with the club, making 33 League appearances. He switched to Fulham in October 1980 and sent a year at Craven Cottage before making the journey across London to sign for Wimbledon, finishing his League career with nine appearances for the Dons. Aside from his five full caps for England Dave also represented the country at Youth level. In March 1982, suffering from depression, Dave took his own life.

Dave Clement

Brian Howard CLOUGH O.B.E.

Born: Middlesbrough, 21st March 1935
Died: Derby, 20th September 2004
Role: Centre-Forward
Career: Great Boughton, Middlesbrough, Sunderland
Debut: v Wales (a) 17-10-1959
Appearances: 2

Whilst Brian had a successful career as a player, he really made his mark in the game as a manager, one of the most successful in terms of trophies won since the Second World War. He was spotted by Middlesbrough whilst playing for Great Broughton and was offered amateur forms in November 1951, upgrading to the professional ranks in May 1953. He was a phenomenal goalscorer for Middlesbrough and later Sunderland, netting 251 goals in just 274 appearances for the two north east clubs. He had joined Sunderland in a £45,000 deal in July 1961 having already collected two full caps for England to go with his one B cap and three Under-23 appearances. He also represented the Football League on two occasions. He was forced to retire owing to a knee injury in November 1964 and joined the coaching staff at Sunderland for a spell before beginning his managerial career with Hartlepool United in October 1965. He was at the club for two years before accepting an invitation to take over at Derby County in July 1967. Having restored the club to the First Division in 1968 he led them to the League title in 1972, but a fall out with the board of directors led to him handing in his resignation in October 1973. Despite a concerted effort by the players and supporters of the club he refused to return, taking over at Brighton the following month. Less than a year later he joined Leeds United, replacing the England-bound

Brian Clough

Don Revie, but whereas the Derby players had been right behind him, those at Elland Road were not and 44 days later he was ousted. He returned to the East Midlands in January 1975, taking over at Nottingham Forest and set about building one of the most successful club sides of the era and a team to challenge Liverpool's domination of the domestic and European game. He won promotion to the First Division in 1977 and then led them to the League title the following year, the first manager to have taken two different clubs to the League title since Herbert Chapman in the 1930s. The same year Forest also won the League Cup. The following year there was even greater glory; the European Cup, the League Cup and runners-up in the League. In 1980 Forest retained the European Cup and reached the final of the League Cup for a third consecutive season. Whilst it was another nine years before another major trophy arrived at the club there were a number of near misses, including reaching the semi final of the UEFA Cup in 1984 against Anderlecht, although it was later found that the Belgian club had bribed the referee in order to ensure their passage into the final. In 1989 Forest again won the League Cup (as well as the minor Simod Cup) and retained the trophy the following year, Brian's eighth major trophy of his managerial career. The only trophy to elude him during his illustrious career was the FA Cup, although Forest reached the final in 1991. Victory in the Zenith Data Systems Cup in 1992 provided Brian with his final piece of silverware during his career and in 1993, with Forest having been relegated back into the Second Division, Brian resigned as manager. His abilities as a manager were never in question, his success almost unrivalled, and yet he never got a chance at the one job his career had been building towards; that of England manager. His abrasive style may have found favour at Forest and with the football fan at large but scared the FA to death! It has also to be said that he also tried for the position of national manager of Scotland, Northern Ireland and Wales, all without success, although he was offered the Welsh position on a part-time basis, the job to run concurrent with his Forest role; Forest's board vetoed the proposal. He won more Manager of the Month awards than anyone else; a total of 25. His son Nigel also played for Forest and England.

Nigel Howard CLOUGH

Born: Sunderland, 19th March 1966
Role: Forward
Career: Nottingham Forest, Liverpool, Manchester City, Nottingham Forest, Sheffield Wednesday
Debut: v Malaysia (a) 12-6-1991
Appearances: 14

The son of former England striker Brian Clough, Nigel began his career with non-League Heanor Town before signing with Nottingham Forest, where his father was manager, in September 1984. He went on to become a mainstay of the side for almost nine years, helping the club win two League Cups and two Full Members Cups as well as reaching the final of the FA Cup in 1991. He also made the breakthrough into the full England side having already collected 15 caps at Under-21 level and three appearances for the B side. In 1993, with Forest having been relegated into the First Division and his father having resigned his position, Nigel announced his desire to try fresh pastures and was on his way to Liverpool in a deal worth £2.275 million. After a bright start to his career at Anfield he began to lose out in the competition for places and in 1996 he was sold to Manchester City for £1.5 million. This move did not fully work out either and he was loaned back to Nottingham Forest in December 1996 where he rediscovered his form and confidence. He also spent a brief spell on loan to Sheffield Wednesday before returning to Maine Road to try and help the club restore themselves to former glories. At the end of the 1997-98 season he left Manchester City and went into the non-League game as manager of Burton Albion.

Nigel Clough

Ralph COATES

Born: Hetton-Le-Hole, County Durham, 26th April 1946
Role: Midfield
Career: Burnley, Tottenham Hotspur, Orient
Debut: v Northern Ireland (h) 21-4-1970
Appearances: 4

Having been passed over as a youngster Ralph took a job at the Eppleton Colliery and was subsequently spotted by Burnley whilst playing for the Colliery Welfare side. Signed as an amateur in October 1961 he was elevated to the professional ranks in June 1963, making his debut in December 1964. By this time Burnley's great side of the late 1950s and early 1960s had all but broken up, and Ralph's spell at Turf Moor was one of almost constant battling against relegation. A £190,000 move to Spurs followed in May 1971, and he was an important member of the team that won the UEFA Cup at the end of his first season at White Hart Lane. Although he was on the bench for the following season's League Cup final against Norwich, an injury to John Pratt gave Ralph an early opportunity to make a name for himself, scoring the only goal of the game. Ralph remained with Spurs until 1978 when he went to play in Australia, later returning to England and signing with Leyton Orient. After finishing his playing career Ralph became the manager of a leisure complex.

William Nevill COBBOLD

Born: Long Melford, Suffolk, 4th February 1863
Died: 8th April 1922
Role: Forward
Career: Cambridge University, Old Carthusians, Wratting Park, Corinthians
Debut: v Ireland (a) 24-2-1883 (scored twice)
Appearances: 9 (6 goals)

William Cobbold first excelled at rugby, playing the sport whilst at Cranbrook and only switched to association football upon arriving at Charterhouse. He then went on to Cambridge University and was awarded his Blue in 1883, 1884, 1885 and 1886, being made captain of the side in the final two years. He was also more than competent at tennis and cricket, representing the university at both sports and going on to play in one match for Kent at cricket. Upon leaving Cambridge he worked as a private tutor and played football for Old Carthusians and Corinthians, both leading amateur sides of the day. Having made his England debut whilst still at Cambridge University (he scored twice in England's 7-0 win over Ireland) he was something of a regular for the next four years, scoring a total of seven goals in his nine matches. To the spectators he was known as 'The Prince of Dribblers', recognition of his superb ball control and ability to take on and invariably beat opponents. His team-mates, however, used to call him 'Nuts' because, according to Charles Fry, 'he was all kernel and extremely hard to crack.'

John Gilbert COCK

Born: Hayle, Cornwall, 14th November 1893
Died: 19th April 1966
Role: Centre-Forward
Career: West Kensington United, Forest Gate, Old Kingstonians, Brentford, Huddersfield Town, Chelsea, Everton, Plymouth Argyle, Millwall, Folkestone, Walton FC
Debut: v Ireland (a) 25-10-1919 (scored once)
Appearances: 2 (2 goals) + 1 War appearance

John Cock

After playing junior football for West Kensington United, Forest Gate and Old Kingstonians Jack signed as an amateur with Brentford in March 1914. Less than four months later he joined Huddersfield Town, also as an amateur but was subsequently added to the professional ranks. With the outbreak of the First World War Jack enlisted in the Army and rose to the rank of Sergeant Major and won a Military Medal and the Distinguished Conduct Medal during the conflict. When the war was at an end he returned to Huddersfield Town and resumed his football career, earning his first call-up for England in the Victory International against Wales at Stoke in October 1919. A week later he was awarded his first full cap for his country, scoring after just 30 seconds to register the fastest debut goal for England. By the end of the month he had been transferred, costing Chelsea £2,650 for his signature. He remained at Chelsea until January 1923 when he was transferred to Everton and after two years moved on to Plymouth Argyle. He then joined Millwall in November 1927 and helped the club win the Third Division South championship in 1928. He finished his playing career in non-League circles with Folkestone and Walton, playing in the Surrey Senior League for the latter club. Jack later served Millwall as manager, taking over in 1944 and remaining in charge until August 1948. He also ran a public house at New Cross. In addition to his two full caps for England Jack represented the Football League twice.

Henry COCKBURN

Born: Ashton-under-Lyme, Lancashire, 14th September 1923
Died: 2nd February 2004
Role: Wing-Half
Career: Goslings FC, Manchester United, Bury, Peterborough United, Corby Town, Sankeys
Debut: v Northern Ireland (a) 28-9-1946
Appearances: 13

Henry played schoolboy football in Manchester before joining junior side Gosling and signed as an amateur with Manchester United in 1943, subsequently turning professional in August 1944. He was one of the mainstays of the first great side assembled by Matt Busby at Old Trafford, helping the club finish runners-up in the First Division four times in the first five seasons after the Second World War and adding the FA Cup in 1948 for good measure. United's consistency was rewarded when they finally landed the title, the third in their history, in 1951-52, but Busby was already planning his next team, one which would find a lasting place in the annals of history as the 'Busby Babes'. Unfortunately for Henry, his place in the United side came under threat from none other than Duncan Edwards and in October 1954 he was sold to Bury for £3,000, having made 243 League appearances for United and scoring four goals. He was at Gigg Lane less than two years, making 35 appearances for the club before switching to the non-League game in July 1956 with Peterborough United. He later played for Corby Town and Sankeys before retiring. He then turned to coaching and joined Oldham Athletic in February 1961 as assistant trainer, a post he held for over three years before accepting an invitation to join Huddersfield Town as assistant trainer and coach in September 1964. In 1969 he was appointed senior coach for the Leeds Road club, remaining in the position until the summer of 1975. Apart from his 13 full caps for England, which saw him part of the same half-back line-up with Neil Franklin and Billy Wright, Henry won one B cap and also represented the Football League on one occasion.

Henry Cockburn

George Reginald COHEN

Born: Kensington, London, 22nd October 1939
Role: Full-Back
Career: Fulham
Debut: v Uruguay (h) 6-5-1964
Appearances: 37

George represented West London and London at schools level and joined the ground staff at Fulham in 1955, signing amateur forms in 1955 and being upgraded to the professional ranks in October 1956. He was a regular in the same side as Johnny Haynes and went on to make 408 League appearances before injury forced his retirement in March 1969. He was unfortunate that Fulham seldom challenged for the game's top honours, constantly battling against relegation and making just one appearance in the FA Cup semi final during his time with the club. He did, however, figure in the greatest moment in English football history, helping the country win the world Cup in 1966 with a series of solid and reliable performances. After his retirement, for which Fulham received a then record compensation fee, he became youth team manager until June 1971 and then had a spell as manager of Tonbridge from March 1974. Away from the game he ran a sports shop until 1971 and then became a property developer. In 1998 his World Cup winners' medal was put up for auction but failed to meet its £75,000 reserve figure and subsequently withdrawn from sale. As well as 37 full caps for England George won eight caps for the Under-23 side and also represented the Football League on four occasions. In later life George has had to overcome cancer.

George Cohen

Andrew Alexander COLE

Born: Nottingham, 15th October 1971
Role: Striker
Career: Arsenal, Fulham, Bristol City, Newcastle United, Manchester United, Blackburn Rovers, Fulham, Manchester City
Debut: v Uruguay (h) (substitute) 29-3-1995
Appearances: 15 (1 goal)

Signed as a trainee by Arsenal, Andy made only one substitute appearance for the Highbury club before being loaned to Fulham and then Bristol City. His performances for City prompted a permanent transfer for £500,000 in March 1992, and after scoring 12 goals in 29 games he was then sold on to Newcastle United for £1.75 million. At St. James' Park they structured the team around his strengths and were rewarded when he scored 41 goals in the 1993-94 season, including 34 in the League. As the front line in an adventurous side selected by Kevin Keegan he seemed assured of a promising future, but then in January 1995 he was sensationally sold to Manchester United for £7 million, the fee being made up by £6 million in cash and Keith Gillespie moving in the opposite direction. He took a while to settle at Old Trafford, not least because he had to adapt himself to United's formation, but slowly but surely he started grabbing the goals he was bought to get. After helping United win numerous Premiership titles, the FA Cup and the European Champions League, he was allowed to move on to Blackburn Rovers during the 2001-02 season, going on to collect the one domestic honour that had eluded him at Old Trafford with a victory in the League Cup.

Andy Cole

Whilst he found goalscoring a relatively easy task at club level, netting just short of 200 League goals at the end of the 2002-03 season, it was considerably harder at international level and Andy's only goal for England came in his thirteenth appearance. He was named PFA Young Player of the Year in 1994. In the summer of 2004 he rejoined Fulham, this time on a permanent basis, but at the end of the season returned to Manchester, joining Manchester City on a free transfer.

Ashley COLE

Born: Stepney, London, 20th December 1980
Role: Defender
Career: Arsenal, Crystal Palace
Debut: v Albania (a) 28-3-2001
Appearances: 44

Ashley joined Arsenal as a trainee and was signed as a professional in 1998. After representing England at Youth level he was loaned to Crystal Palace during the 1999-2000 season to gain first team experience and made 14 appearances for the Selhurst Park club, scoring one goal. Upon his return to Highbury he was handed a Premiership debut against Newcastle United and the following season began to force his way into the Arsenal side on a regular basis. His performances at club level got him recognition at international level and, having played for the Under-21s, he was given a full England debut in a World Cup qualifier against Albania and would go on to replace Graeme Le Saux at left-back within the side on a regular basis. A knee ligament injury disrupted his 2001-02 season but he returned to fitness in time to feature in the England side for the 2002 World Cup. Whilst at Arsenal he has helped the club win two Premiership titles and the FA Cup three times, including the coveted double in 2001-02. An almost permanent fixture within both the Arsenal and England side, he had a very public fall out with Arsenal during the 2004-05 season when, in the middle of protracted contract negotiations, he attended a meeting with representatives of Chelsea in contravention of FA rules, for which he, Chelsea manager Jose Mourinho and Chelsea Football Club were heavily fined. On appeal Ashley's fine was reduced from £100,000 to £75,000, but Ashley continued to protest his innocence and appealed once again. After initially claiming that he would not sign a new contract with Arsenal in protest he re-signed with the club in July 2005.

Joseph John COLE

Born: Islington, London, 8th November 1981
Role: Midfield
Career: West Ham United, Chelsea
Debut: v Mexico (h) 25-5-2001
Appearances: 30 (5 goals)

A hugely talented midfield player, Joe excelled as a schoolboy and was courted by many clubs, finally joining West Ham United as a trainee. Upgraded to the professional ranks in 1998 he was an integral part of the side that won the FA Youth Cup with a 9-0 aggregate win over Coventry City in 1999. By then he had already made his first team debut for the Hammers and finished the season with eight League appearances. Over the next couple of years he developed into one of the best young midfield players in the country, alongside team-mates Frank Lampard, Glen Johnson and Michael Carrick. The departure of Lampard to Chelsea, a move Joe himself would make in 2003, saw him given extra responsibility at club level, but Joe rose to the challenge and in 2001 was given a full England cap when he replaced Steven Gerrard during the friendly against Mexico. Following West Ham's relegation from the Premiership in 2003 Joe joined Chelsea in a deal worth £7 million but struggled to command a regular place within the Chelsea team which duly affected his England career. After working on his all-round contribution and cutting out some of the selfish aspects of his game he began to feature more and more for Chelsea, helping them win the Premiership and League Cup in 2004-05. As a result he has once again broken into the England squad on a more regular basis. He has represented England at schoolboy, Youth, Under-21 and full level.

Ashley Cole

Joe Cole

Henry COLCLOUGH

Born: Meir, Staffordshire, 1891
Died: 1941
Role: Left-Back
Career: Crewe Alexandra, Crystal Palace
Debut: v Wales (a) 16-3-1914
Appearances: 1

After playing junior football in Staffordshire, Henry (who in other sources is sometimes referred to as Horace) was invited along to Crewe Alexandra, originally on trial and then offered professional forms in August 1910. After impressing with Crewe for the two seasons he was with the club he was transferred to Crystal Palace of the Southern League and quickly established himself as a regular within the side. He was selected for England on one occasion, proof that his performances in the Southern League were of sufficiently good quality that he represented the League on three occasions and he seemed set for a lengthy and rewarding career in the game. Unfortunately the outbreak of the First World War brought his League career to an end, for whilst playing for the Army during the hostilities he suffered the injury that was to bring his playing career to an end.

Ernest Herbert COLEMAN

Born: Steyning, Sussex, 19th October 1889
Died: 15th June 1958
Role: Goalkeeper
Career: Croydon Amateurs, Dulwich Hamlet
Debut: v Wales (a) 14-3-1921
Appearances: 1

Ernest Coleman was one of the most gifted amateurs of the day, beginning his career with Croydon but making his reputation with Dulwich Hamlet. He joined the South London club in 1912 and was their first choice goalkeeper until his retirement in 1925. By this time he had won an FA Amateur Cup winners' medal in 1920 and won four amateur caps for England. His selection for the full England side came at a time when a natural successor to Sam Hardy had yet to emerge and six different players were tried out in the position. Although Ernest Coleman was never likely to be anything more than a temporary measure he gave a good account of himself in the 0-0 draw. Upon his retirement as a player Ernest maintained his involvement with Dulwich, serving on the club's committee and as a member of the finance committee. He was later appointed honorary assistant treasurer, a position he held until ill health forced his retirement in 1956 and he was thereafter made a life member. As well as England Ernest also represented Surrey and London at amateur level during his playing career. By profession he was an accountant, hence his appointment as honorary assistant treasurer at Dulwich.

John George 'Tim' COLEMAN

Born: Kettering, 26th October 1881
Died: 20th November 1940
Role: Inside-Forward
Career: Kettering, Northampton Town, Woolwich Arsenal, Everton, Sunderland, Fulham, Nottingham Forest, Tunbridge Wells Rangers
Debut: v Ireland (h) 16-2-1907
Appearances: 1

Tim Coleman played for Kettering before joining Northampton Town of the Southern League during the summer of 1901. After barely a year he was persuaded to join Woolwich Arsenal, then of the Second Division of the Football League and he went on to help them win promotion into the First Division at the end of the 1903-04 season. His only cap for England came in 1907 against Ireland at Goodison Park, a prophetic ground since in February 1908 he joined Everton for £700 having made 196 first team appearances for the Gunners, scoring 84 goals. He was at Goodison Park for a little over two years, moving on to Sunderland in May 1910 and then joining Fulham in June 1911. He finished his League career with Nottingham Forest, joining the club in the summer of 1914 just before the outbreak of the First World War and subsequently retiring as a player during the hostilities, although in 1920 he was reported to be turning out on a regular basis for Tunbridge Wells Rangers. As well as his one cap for England Tim also represented the Football League on three occasions.

Stanley Victor COLLYMORE

Born: Cannock, 22nd January 1971
Role: Forward
Career: Wolverhampton Wanderers, Crystal Palace, Southend United, Nottingham Forest, Liverpool, Aston Villa, Fulham, Leicester City, Bradford City, Real Oviedo
Debut: v Japan (h) 3-6-1995
Appearances: 3

After failing to make the grade with Wolves Stan drifted into the non-League game with Stafford Rovers and subsequently came to the attentions of Crystal Palace, signing with the Selhurst Park club for £100,000 in 1991. He made 20 League appearances for the club, although 16 of these were as a substitute and was sold to Southend United for another £100,000 fee in November 1992. Here he averaged a goal every other game and alerted other clubs to his talents, prompting Nottingham Forest to pay £2 million for his signature in July 1993. His run of good form continued with Forest and he netted 41 League goals in 65 appearances, earning a call-up for the full England side in 1995. That summer he announced his desire to play for a bigger club, signing for Liverpool for £8.5 million and subsequently losing a court case after he had demanded part of the transfer fee from Forest. He never fully settled at Liverpool, refusing to move nearer the club's training ground and often being fined for turning up late for training and was sold to Aston Villa for £7 million in 1997. Here too he had his share of problems, including a highly-publicised argument with his then girlfriend, television presenter Ulrika Johnsson in France during the World Cup finals in 2002. This prompted Villa manager John Gregory to haul him in for extra training prior to the start of the new season and warn him that time was running out for him at Villa Park. He subsequently moved on to Leicester City and then Bradford City after a loan spell at Fulham, often infuriating his team-mates and management in equal doses and booking himself into a private clinic claiming to be suffering from depression. After a protracted transfer to Spain he announced he was retiring which prompted a further court case with his new club and, despite announcing in 2003 that he was contemplating a return to the game has remained retired.

Alfred COMMON

Born: Sunderland, 25th May 1880
Died: 3rd April 1946
Role: Centre-Forward
Career: Jarrow, Sunderland, Sheffield United, Middlesbrough, Woolwich Arsenal, Preston North End
Debut: v Wales (a) 29-2-1904 (scored once)
Appearances: 3 (2 goals)

Even if transfer fees have gone into orbit in recent years, Alf Common is assured a permanent place in the record books, for he was the first player to be transferred for £1,000. He was also the first player to be transferred for a sum in excess of £500, making him the early 1900s' Trevor Francis and Alan Shearer rolled into one. He began playing with Jarrow and signed with Sunderland in 1900 and spent eighteen months with the club before Sheffield United paid £325 to take him to Bramall Lane. At the end of his first season he had won an FA Cup winners' medal, scoring the opening goal in the first game against Southampton which was drawn 1-1 and laying on the winner in the replay as United won 2-1. During the summer of 1904 Sunderland paid a record fee of £520 to take the by now, England international back to Roker Park, but just seven months later

Stan Collymore

Alf Common

local rivals Middlesbrough almost doubled the fee, paying £1,000 to move him along the North East. Not surprisingly, the virtual doubling of the British transfer record in such a short space of time caused a sensation, but Alf managed to remain level headed and continued adding to his reputation. He spent five years at Middlesbrough before joining Woolwich Arsenal for a rather more modest £250 and just over two years later a similar fee took him to Preston North End where he finished his career in 1914. Alf, whose moves had cost his clubs £2,345, was known to be a powerful and aggressive player on the pitch but a warm hearted and humorous character off it. Once he retired from playing he became a licensee in Darlington. There is still considerable confusion as to how many goals Alf scored for England, for some sources credit his goal against Wales on his debut to George Davis and others credit one of his two goals against Ireland to the same George Davis! On the basis that at least three newspaper reports of the Ireland match credit him with both goals, we can safely assume he scored three goals for England during his career.

Leslie Harry COMPTON

Born: Woodford, Essex, 12th September 1912
Died: 27th December 1984
Role: Centre-Half
Career: Hampstead Town, Arsenal
Debut: v Wales (a) 15-11-1951
Appearances: 2 + 5 War appearances

The elder brother of fellow footballer and cricketer Denis Compton, Les played his schools football in Hendon and then joined Bell Lane Old Boys before signing with Hampstead Town at the age of 17. He was then spotted by Arsenal and persuaded to sign amateur forms in the summer of 1931, subsequently turning professional in February 1932. The presence of England half-backs George Male and Eddie Hapgood restricted Les's first team opportunities at Highbury and by the time the Second World War broke out in 1939 he had made just 67 appearances in seven seasons. He represented the Army during the hostilities and also went on to earn his first cap for England, albeit in an unofficial wartime international. He returned to Highbury at the end of the war and was a member of the side that won the League championship in 1948 and the FA Cup two years later, beating Liverpool 2-0 in the final at Wembley. Then, in 1951, he was surprisingly called up for England to face Wales. At the age of 38 years and 64 days, he is the oldest known player to make his debut for England. He did well enough in the 4-2 win to earn selection the following week against Yugoslavia at Highbury, but the second game was not as successful; Les put through his own net in the 2-2 draw! He remained a player at Highbury until July 1955, having made 253 League appearances and scored five goals, although in one London War Cup match in 1941 he scored 10 of Arsenal's goals in the 15-2 win over Orient. He then joined the coaching staff but left some eight months later and became a wine company representative. Like his brother Dennis, Les also combined a successful football career with playing cricket, playing in 272 matches for Middlesex as wicketkeeper between 1938 and 1956. Les also represented the Football League on one occasion during his football career.

Les Compton

James CONLIN

Born: Consett, County Durham, 6th July 1881
Died: Killed in action in Flanders, 23rd June 1917
Role: Left-Winger
Career: Colt's Rovers Cambuslang, Hibernian, Falkirk, Albion Rovers, Bradford City, Manchester City, Birmingham, Airdrieonians
Debut: v Scotland (a) 7-4-1906
Appearances: 1

Although he was born in County Durham Jimmy Conlin spent much of his early life in Scotland and began his professional career north of the border with Cambuslang. After turning out for Hibernian, Falkirk and Albion Rovers he was signed by Bradford City in the summer of 1904 and proved to be an extremely agile and athletic performer in the Football League, representing the League on two occasions and also getting called up for the full England side for the international against Scotland. After two years with Bradford City he was transferred to Manchester City and in 1910 helped them win the Second Division championship and promotion into the First Division. In September 1911 he was transferred to Birmingham and played out the rest of the season with the club before returning to Scotland and signing for Airdrieonians. At the outbreak of the First World War Jimmy enlisted with the 15th Highland Light Infantry and was killed whilst fighting in Flanders in Belgium in 1917.

John Connelly

John Michael CONNELLY

Born: St. Helens, Lancashire, 18th July 1938
Role: Right-Winger
Career: St. Helens Town, Burnley, Manchester United, Blackburn Rovers, Bury
Debut: v Wales (a) 17-10-1959
Appearances: 20 (7 goals)

John began his professional career with Burnley in 1956 and developed into one of the best wingers in the game, helping the Turf Moor side to the League title in 1960 and an appearance in the 1962 FA Cup final where they were beaten by Spurs. After 215 League appearances he was sold to Manchester United for £60,000 in April 1964 and won a second championship medal in his first full season at the club. He had first broken into the England side in

1959 and was a member of the World Cup squads for 1962 in Chile and 1966 in England, appearing in just one game, England's opener against Uruguay in 1966 and which turned out to be his last appearance for England as Alf Ramsey decided to dispense with wingers. In September 1966 he was sold to Blackburn Rovers for £40,000 having made 80 League appearances for the Old Trafford club. He was to remain at Ewood Park for just under four years before switching to Bury where he finished his playing career, having made 572 League appearances for his four clubs and scored 181 goals. After retiring from playing John concentrated on his fish and chip shop Connelly's Plaice at Brierfield near Burnley and also served as a magistrate. In addition to his eight full caps for England John also represented the country once at Under-23 level and the Football League on eight occasions.

Thomas Edwin Reed COOK

Born: Cuckfield, Sussex, 5th February 1901
Died: 15th January 1950
Role: Centre-Forward
Career: Cuckfield, Brighton & Hove Albion, Northfleet, Bristol Rovers
Debut: v Wales (a) 28-2-1925
Appearances: 1

Tommy Cook played junior football in Sussex and enlisted in the Royal Navy towards the end of the First World War, representing the force at football. At the end of the hostilities he joined Cuckfield FC and impressed enough to be offered terms by Brighton, joining the club in 1921. Within four years he had earned selection for England, even though Brighton were still a Third Division club. He remained with Brighton until the summer of 1929 when he went to South Africa in order to become a cricket coach and returned to England in September 1930 and joined Northfleet. He returned to League football with Bristol Rovers, joining the club in October 1931 and remained with them until his retirement in the summer of 1933. He was also well known as a cricketer, playing for Sussex between 1922 and 1937, at which point he took another coaching appointment in South Africa. With the outbreak of the Second World War Tommy enlisted in the South African Air Force and was seriously injured in an accident at an air school in 1943. He came back to England once again at the end of the war and served Brighton as manager until 1947. He then suffered a number of mishaps, with his wife leaving him and, physically and mentally ill, he committed suicide in January 1950.

Colin Terence COOPER

Born: Sedgefield, 28th February 1967
Role: Defender
Career: Middlesbrough, Millwall, Nottingham Forest
Debut: v Sweden (h) 8-6-1995
Appearances: 2

Colin began his career with Middlesbrough, joining the club as a trainee in 1984 and going on to make over 200 first team appearances before moving on to Millwall for £300,000 in 1991. Over the next two years he developed into a highly competent player, able to play at the back or in midfield and give a good account of himself wherever he was selected. That form prompted Nottingham Forest to pay £1.7 million for him in 1993 and he continued his development at the City Ground, subsequently earning the first of his two England caps in 1995. Following the departure of Stuart Pearce to Newcastle United, Colin took over as captain of Nottingham Forest and continued to lead by example as Forest won the First Division League title in 1998 and with it promotion to the Premier League. In addition to his two full caps he also represented the Under-21 side on eight occasions.

Colin Cooper

Norman Charles COOPER

Born: Norbiton, Surrey, 12th July 1870
Died: 30th July 1920
Role: Wing-Half
Career: Cambridge University, Corinthians, Old Brightonians, Sussex
Debut: v Ireland (h) 25-2-1893
Appearances: 1

Norman was educated at Brighton College and represented the college football side from 1887 to 1889, being made captain during his last year. He then went on to Cambridge University and was awarded his first Blue in 1891, subsequently earning additional Blues in 1892 and 1893. He was also captain of the side in 1893, the year he earned selection for England in the 6-1 win over Ireland at Perry Barr. Norman also played for Old Brightonians and the Corinthians between 1891 and 1895 when he seemingly retired. He was also a noted cricketer, turning out for Cambridge University between 1890 and 1893 and also being linked with Surrey, although he did not actually play for the county.

Terence COOPER

Born: Castleford, Yorkshire, 12th July 1944
Role: Left-Back
Career: Ferrybridge Amateurs, Leeds United, Middlesbrough, Bristol City, Bristol Rovers, Doncaster Rovers, Bristol City
Debut: v France (h) 12-3-1969
Appearances: 20

Terry was playing amateur football with Ferrybridge as a winger and working as an apprentice fitter in a coal mine when he was first spotted and offered trials by Wolverhampton Wanderers, but in May 1961 he was taken on as an apprentice by Leeds United. Upgraded to the professional ranks in July 1962 he made his League debut, still as a winger, in the final game of the 1963-64 season as Leeds United won promotion back to the First Division. Terry's experience as a winger served him in good stead when he was converted to full-back, with his overlapping runs a big feature of his game. He was a key part of the Leeds United side that was on the brink of dominating the domestic game and helped them win the League Cup in 1968, Inter-Cities Fairs Cup in 1968 and 1971 and the League championship in 1969, along with numerous runners-up placings in a variety of competitions. With considerable competition for the left-back position Terry had to wait until 1969 before making his England debut and his final tally of 20 caps would have been greater but for a badly broken leg that put him out of the game for a considerable time in 1972 and robbed him of a chance of an FA Cup winners' medal. In March 1975 he was sold to Middlesbrough for £50,000 and helped the club consolidate its First Division status. Three years later, in July 1978 he was sold to Bristol City for £20,000 but had less than a year at Ashton Gate before switching across the city to become player-coach at Bristol Rovers. The following year he became manager and remained in charge at Eastville until October 1981 when he joined Doncaster Rovers and former Leeds United team-mate Billy Bremner as a player. In May 1982 he was appointed player-manager of Bristol City, making his last appearance as a player in 1984, by which time he had become the first player-director. Victory in the 1986 Freight Rovers Trophy was the highlight of his managerial career at Bristol City and in 1988 he left to take over at Exeter City, a position he retained until 1991. He then took over at Birmingham City but rejoined Exeter City in January 1994. A little over a year later, in the summer of 1995, ill health forced him to quit the game for good.

Terry Cooper

Snowy Cooper

Thomas 'Snowy' COOPER

Born: Fenton, Staffordshire, 1904
Died: 25th June 1940
Role: Right-Back
Career: Trentham, Port Vale, Derby County, Liverpool
Debut: v Northern Ireland (a) 22-10-1927
Appearances: 15

Snowy Cooper came into the professional game relatively late, having starred for Trentham in the Cheshire League before Port Vale paid £20 in August 1924 to bring him into the professional game. Less than two years later he cost newly promoted Derby County £2,000 and he excelled in the highest division, earning the first of his England caps the following year. Considered to be a fine tackler and with good distribution, he was a regular feature at right-back for the next seven years until replaced by George Male. In December 1934 he joined Liverpool for £7,500, linking up with another England international Ernie Blenkinsop to create one of the meanest defences in the country. At the outbreak of the Second World War Snowy joined the Military Police and lost his life in a motorcycle accident whilst on duty in June 1940.

Steven James COPPELL

Born: Liverpool, 9th July 1955
Role: Winger
Career: Tranmere Rovers, Manchester United
Debut: v Italy (h) 16-11-1977 (WCQ)
Appearances: 42 (7 goals)

Steve had signed with Tranmere as a professional in 1974 and was soon being tipped for greater honours. Indeed, Bill Shankly, then helping out at Tranmere, recommended him to Liverpool but was turned down so in turn rang Tommy Docherty at Manchester United. United paid £60,000 to take him to Old Trafford in February 1975 and he lived up to his early promise. A member of the side that won the FA Cup in 1977 and reached the finals of 1976 and 1979, he broke into the England squad in 1977 and went on to win 42 caps. He retired from playing in October 1983 after sustaining a serious knee injury whilst playing for England and was appointed manager of Crystal Palace, the then youngest Football League manager and held the position for nine years. After a brief spell as manager at Manchester City he returned to Palace, initially as manager and later as director of football. He later had spells in charge at Brighton & Hove Albion and Reading. Steve is a former chairman of the Players Union and also graduated as a Bachelor of Science in Economics from Liverpool University.

Wilfred COPPING

Born: Barnsley, 17th August 1909
Died: June 1980
Role: Left-Half
Career: Middlecliffe Rovers, Leeds United, Arsenal, Leeds United
Debut: v Italy (a) 17-5-1933
Appearances: 20 + 1 War appearance

Wilf was working as a miner and playing non-League football for Middlecliffe Rovers when he was spotted by Leeds United and signed as an amateur in March 1929. He was upgraded to the professional ranks the following year and quickly became known as one of the original 'hard men' of the game, putting in crunching tackles and an equally impressive shoulder charge at a time when such attributes were allowed in the English game. First called up for the England side whilst with Leeds United, he made his debut for his country against Italy in Rome. This was the match where Arsenal manager Herbert Chapman made a brief tactical talk to the side prior to the kick off and a little over a year later the same manager paid £6,000 to bring the left-half to London. Wilf went on to help the club win the League championship in 1935 and 1938 and the FA Cup in 1936 and also represented the Football League on two occasions. In March 1939 Wilf returned to Leeds United and made his final appearance for the England side in May of that year against Romania in Bucharest as war clouds were beginning to grow over Europe. The outbreak of the Second World War effectively brought Wilf's playing career to an end, although he did make one further appearance for the national side in a friendly against Wales before retiring. At the war's end he headed off to the continent to coach in Belgium, returning to Britain in 1946 to take up the role of trainer at Southend United. He remained at Southend Stadium until July 1954 when he took up a similar position with Bristol City and in November 1956 moved on to Coventry City. He retired from the game in May 1959.

Bertram Oswald CORBETT

Born: Thame, Oxfordshire, 15th May 1875
Died: 30th November 1967
Role: Left-Winger
Career: Oxford University, Corinthians, Reading, Slough
Debut: v Wales (h) 18-3-1901
Appearances: 1

Bertie Corbett first played football for Thame Grammar School and was considered something of a young prodigy,

Steve Coppell

Bertie Corbett

being selected to represent Oxfordshire when aged just 15. He then went to Oxford University and won his Blue in 1896-97 before joining the leading amateur side of the day, Corinthians in 1897. A player for the club for the next nine years, Bertie also served as club secretary between 1902 and 1904 and edited the publication Annals Of The Corinthian Football Club in 1906. Having earned a BA at university he went on to teach at Brighton College and later in Derbyshire before taking over as proprietor of a Dorset preparatory school. Like many of his era Bertie was something of an all-round sportsman, playing cricket for Buckinghamshire and one first class match for Derbyshire in 1910. His brother Reg also represented England.

Reginald CORBETT

Born: Thame, Oxfordshire, 1879
Died: 2nd September 1967
Role: Inside-Left, Left-Winger
Career: Old Malvernians, Corinthians
Debut: v Wales (h) 2-3-1903
Appearances: 1

Brother of Bertie Corbett, Reg first represented Malvern College in 1898 and then went on to play for Old Malvernians and Corinthians, often turning out with his brother for the latter club and helping the former win the FA Amateur Cup in 1902. Better known as an outside-left, like his brother, he was also able to play as an inside-forward, and although his performances were often described as erratic he was able to get onto the scoresheet with regularity. He was also a teacher like his brother.

Walter Samuel CORBETT

Born: Wellington, Shropshire, 26th November 1880
Died: 1955
Role: Full-Back
Career: Asbury Richmond, Bournbrook, Aston Villa, Birmingham, Queens Park Rangers, Wellington Town
Debut: v Austria (a) 6-6-1908
Appearances: 3

Educated at the King Edward Grammar School, Walter Corbett was first capped for England at amateur level, earning the first of his amateur caps in 1907 and collected the first of his full caps the following year as part of the touring side that visited Central Europe during the summer. He returned home to take his place in the United Kingdom side that eventually won the gold medal at the London Olympics. The following year he joined Wellington Town where he effectively finished his career, having won 18 caps for England at amateur level and three at full level.

Joseph Thomas CORRIGAN

Born: Manchester, 18th November 1948
Role: Goalkeeper
Career: Sale FC, Manchester City, Seattle Sounders (USA), Brighton & Hove Albion, Norwich City, Stoke City
Debut: v Italy (substitute) (New York) 28-5-1976
Appearances: 9

Joe joined Manchester City as an amateur from Sale FC in September 1966 and was upgraded to the professional ranks the following January. He made his debut for the club in two League Cup ties in 1967-68, replacing the injured Ken Mulhearn and by 1969-70 was established as City's first choice goalkeeper, helping them win the European Cup Winners' Cup and League Cup in 1970. Although he briefly fell out of favour with manager Ron Saunders in 1974 and was transfer listed, he remained very much City's number one custodian until 1983, by which time he had made 476 League appearances for the club. First capped by England in 1976 he was unfortunate that the country were also served by Peter Shilton and Ray Clemence at the same time, thus restricting his opportunities. By the time he left City in March 1983, bound for America, he had collected a further winners' medal in the League Cup (in 1976) and a runners-up medal in the FA Cup in 1981. He cost Seattle Sounders £30,000 when he joined them for their summer season in 1983, returning to England to play for Brighton for a season, and after brief loan spells with Norwich City and Stoke City retired in February 1985 through injury.

Joe Corrigan

Anthony Richard COTTEE

Born: West Ham, 11th July 1965
Role: Forward
Career: West Ham United, Everton, West Ham United, Leicester City, Birmingham City
Debut: v Sweden (a) (substitute) 10-9-1987
Appearances: 7

Tony Cottee

Signed by West Ham as an apprentice in 1982 he broke into the first team whilst still a teenager and spent six years at Upton Park before a £2.3 million move to Everton in 1988. At 5' 8" tall he relied on his speed of thought to get into goalscoring positions and developed into a striker feared throughout the League, having plundered over 100 goals in under 250 first team appearances for the Hammers, and continued to terrorise defences whilst at Goodison Park, netting 99 goals in almost 250 appearances. He returned to Upton Park in 1994 and spent a further three years with his first club before moving on to Leicester City for £500,000 in August 1997. He spent a brief spell on loan to Birmingham City during his first season at Filbert Street but returned to resume the fight for a first team place by 1998-99. Tony was a substitute for six of his seven appearances for England; the one game he started he was substituted himself!

George Hugh COTTERILL

Born: Brighton, 4th April 1868
Died: 1st October 1950
Role: Centre-Forward
Career: Brighton College, Cambridge University, Old Brightonians, Weybridge, Burgess Hill, Surrey, Sussex, Corinthians
Debut: v Ireland (h) 7-3-1891
Appearances: 4 (2 goals) + 1 unofficial appearance (1 goal)

Although George Cotterill represented his country at football, this was not the only sport he excelled at, for he also played cricket for Cambridge University and Sussex, rugby for Richmond and Surrey and, during his university days, was also a member of the track, field and rowing teams. He began his football career with Brighton College in 1882, being made captain two years later, a position he held for two years before joining Cambridge University. Awarded his Blue in 1888, 1889, 1890 (in which he was captain) and 1891, this ultimately led to a call-up for the England team. George also played for the leading amateur side Corinthians between 1887 and 1898.

Joseph Richard COTTLE

Born: Bedminster, Bristol, 1886
Died: 3rd February 1958
Role: Left-Back
Career: Eclipse, Dolphin FC, Bristol City
Debut: v Ireland (h) 13-2-1909
Appearances: 1

A local Bristol lad Joe was discovered by Bristol City whilst playing in the Bristol & District League for Dolphin FC and joined the Ashton Gate club in 1904. A member of the side that were Second Division champions and FA Cup runners-up in 1909, the same year he won his only cap for England, Joe was regarded as a fearless defender. He retired at the relatively young age of 25 although the reasons for his retirement are not known, for he was not injured at the time he announced he was leaving the game. Joe then became a licensee in the Bristol area.

Samuel COWAN

Born: Chesterfield, 10th May 1901
Died: 4th October 1964
Role: Centre-Half
Career: Bullcroft Colliery, Denaby United, Doncaster Rovers, Manchester City, Bradford City, Mossley
Debut: v Belgium (a) 24-5-1926
Appearances: 3

Something of a late developer at football, for Sam did not start playing football until he was 17, he quickly made up for lost time, being snapped up by Doncaster Rovers in 1923. Eighteen months later he moved on to Manchester City, going on to help the club win the Second Division championship in 1928 and FA Cup in 1934. He also collected two runners-up medals in the same competition, in 1926 and 1933. After eleven years at Maine Road Sam was sold to Bradford City for £2,000 in October 1935 where he finished his League career. After a year playing non-League football Sam moved to Brighton & Hove Albion as coach in June 1938, subsequently returning to Manchester City as manager between November 1946 and June 1947. He later had a physiotherapy practice in Brighton and was masseur to the Sussex county cricket team as well as several MCC touring sides. He collapsed and died whilst refereeing a football match at Haywards Heath.

Sam Cowan

Gordon Cowans

Gordon Sidney COWANS

Born: Cornforth, County Durham, 27th October 1958
Role: Midfield
Career: Aston Villa, Bari (Italy), Italy, Blackburn Rovers, Aston Villa, Derby County, Wolverhampton Wanderers, Sheffield United, Bradford City, Stockport County, Burnley
Debut: v Wales (h) 23-2-1983
Appearances: 10 (2 goals)

After graduating through the ranks at Aston Villa he was handed a debut in 1976 and went on to help the club win the League Cup in 1977, the League in 1981 and the European Cup the following season, as well as collecting the first of his 10 caps for England. A broken leg in 1983 kept him out of the side throughout 1983-84 and in 1985 he was sold to Bari in Italy for £500,000. Three years later he returned to Villa for £250,000 and re-established himself in the side before being sold to Blackburn for £200,000 in 1991. He returned to Villa Park for a third time in 1993 and took his number of first team appearances to 527 before going to Derby for £80,000 in 1994. Gordon later played for Wolves, Sheffield United, Bradford City, Stockport County and Burnley, becoming reserve team coach at Turf Moor. In addition to his tally of 10 full caps he also represented England at Youth, Under-21 and B level.

Arthur COWELL

Born: Blackburn, 20th May 1886
Died: 12th February 1959
Role: Left-Back
Career: Nelson, Blackburn Rovers
Debut: v Ireland (a) 12-2-1910
Appearances: 1

Spotted playing for a Sunday school side Arthur began his career with Nelson in 1904 before being snapped up by Blackburn Rovers in May 1905. Arthur was to spend fifteen years at Ewood Park, helping the club win the League championship in 1912 and 1914 and proving the perfect defensive partner to Bob Crompton. Upon retiring in the summer of 1920 Arthur became trainer for the club, a position he held until May 1937 when he left, shortly before taking up a similarly position with Wrexham. He was appointed manager of Wrexham in August 1938 but left the club early in 1939. At the end of his football career Arthur worked as a newsagent in Kirkham and Darwen.

John COX

Born: Blackpool, 21st November 1877
Role: Left-Winger
Career: South Shore Standard, Blackpool, Liverpool, Blackpool
Debut: v Ireland (h) 9-3-1901
Appearances: 3 + 1 unofficial appearance

After playing non-League football in and around Blackpool John was signed by the senior club in the summer of 1897 and quickly established himself as a left-winger of some note, also able to play on the opposite flank or even in an inside-forward position. Liverpool paid £150 to take him to Anfield after barely seven months at Blackpool, so sure were they of his potential. John did not disappoint either, helping them win the First Division in 1901 and then the Second Division and First Division championship again in consecutive seasons, 1905 and 1906. Also called up to represent the Football League on three occasions, John returned to Blackpool in 1909, becoming player-manager and retired in 1911.

John Davies COX

Born: Spondon, Derbyshire, 1870
Died: June 1957
Role: Right-Half
Career: Spondon, Long Eaton Rangers, Derby County
Debut: v Ireland (a) 5-3-1892
Appearances: 1

He began his career with his local side before stepping up a level to Long Eaton Rangers before joining Derby County in 1891. An almost instant success, as his call-up for the full England side a year later would confirm, he was a member of the Derby County side that reached consecutive FA Cup finals in 1898 and 1899, although both were to end in defeat, the first against local rivals Nottingham Forest and the second against Sheffield United. The following year he retired from the game and emigrated to Canada, where he died in Toronto in 1957.

James William CRABTREE

Born: Burnley, 23rd December 1871
Died: Birmingham, 28th June 1908
Role: Full-Back, Left-Half
Career: Burnley Royal Swifts, Burnley Rossendale, Heywood Central, Burnley, Aston Villa, Oreston Rovers, Plymouth Argyle, Oreston Rovers
Debut: v Ireland (a) 1-3-1894
Appearances: 14

Jimmy Crabtree was a versatile player for both club and country, playing in all five defensive positions (bar that of goalkeeper) for England as the need arose. He began his

League career with Burnley as a full-back and was later successfully converted to left-half by Aston Villa, whom he joined in July 1895. Whilst at Villa he linked with Howard Spencer and made Villa one of the best defensive units in the game, helping them to four League titles and the FA Cup once, although this latter success completed the 'double' in 1897. In addition to his 14 caps for England (11 of them won whilst with Villa, indicative of his standing in the game at the time) he also represented the Football League on six occasions, finally leaving Aston Villa in the close season of 1902 for Oreston Rovers. Within a year he had moved on to Plymouth, but after only four games returned to Oreston in August 1904. He retired two years later and made his home in Birmingham but died at the comparatively young age of 36.

John Crawford

John Forsyth CRAWFORD

Born: South Shields, 26th September 1896
Died: Epsom, 27th July 1975
Role: Left-Winger
Career: Jarrow Celtic, Palmer's Works FC, Hull City, Chelsea, Queens Park Rangers
Debut: v Scotland (a) 28-3-1931
Appearances: 1

After serving in the Royal Navy during the First World War John joined Hull City in December 1919, having previously turned out for Jarrow Celtic and local works side Palmer's during the hostilities. Initially used as a left-winger he switched to the opposite flank when the club signed David Mercer, an England international. In May 1923 he was sold to Chelsea for £3,000 and used on the left wing again, returning to the right wing when Chelsea signed Alex Jackson. Despite this switching between the wings, John did show enough promise to be awarded a full England cap against Scotland in 1931, thus becoming the only England international in an all-international forward line at Stamford Bridge. He moved on to Queens Park Rangers in May 1934 where he finished his playing career in the summer of 1937, subsequently becoming coach at the club. He was a factory worker during the Second World War.

Raymond CRAWFORD

Born: Portsmouth, 13th July 1936
Role: Centre-Forward
Career: Portsmouth, Ipswich Town, Wolverhampton Wanderers, West Bromwich Albion, Ipswich Town, Charlton Athletic, Kettering Town, Colchester United, Durban City, Brighton & Hove Albion
Debut: v Northern Ireland (h) 22-11-1961
Appearances: 2 (1 goal)

Ray began his career with his local side Portsmouth and netted 12 goals in just 22 appearances before being sold to Ipswich Town for £6,000 in September 1958. The spearhead of the side that was assembled by future England manager Alf Ramsey, Ray helped the club to the Second Division championship in 1960-61 and the League title the following year, earning his first England cap during this spell. In September 1963 he was sold to Wolverhampton Wanderers for £42,000, a remarkable return on the fee Ipswich had originally paid for the player. He remained at Molineux until February 1965 when he was sold to West Bromwich Albion for £35,000, but a little over a year later returned to Ipswich for £15,000. His second spell at Portman Road was to last for three years, during which time he again helped them win the Second Division championship in 1968 before he was on his travels again, this time costing Charlton Athletic £12,500. A little over six months later he left the League game to turn out for Kettering Town but returned to League action with Colchester United in June 1970, his signature costing the club £3,000. Ray finished his playing career in South Africa with Durban City in 1971 and later had spells coaching at Brighton & Hove Albion, Eden FC in New Zealand and Portsmouth. In all Ray netted an impressive 289 goals in the League for his various clubs, including 203 for Ipswich Town where he is still their record goalscorer.

Ray Crawford

Thomas Henry CRAWSHAW

Born: Sheffield, 27th December 1872
Died: 25th November 1960
Role: Centre-Half
Career: Park Grange, Altercliffe, Heywood Central, Sheffield Wednesday, Chesterfield
Debut: v Ireland (h) 9-3-1895
Appearances: 10 (1 goal)

Spotted by Sheffield Wednesday whilst playing for the local Heywood Central club, Tom joined the Hillsborough club in 1894 and was an integral part of the first great side the club assembled. A member of the team that won the FA Cup in 1896 against Wolverhampton Wanderers, Tom then helped them win the Second Division championship in 1900. Three years later he helped them win the First Division championship and the following year retain the title. He added a second FA Cup winners' medal in 1907 after victory over Everton and served the club for another year before moving on for a brief spell with Chesterfield. As well as his 10 full caps Tom represented the Football League on eight occasions. After a spell as secretary of Glossop, FC Tom ran a newsagents in Sheffield.

William Crayston

William John CRAYSTON

Born: Grange-over-Sands, Lancashire, 9th October 1910
Died: 26th December 1992
Role: Right-Half
Career: Ulverston Town, Barrow, Bradford, Arsenal
Debut: v Germany (h) 4-12-1935
Appearances: 8 (1 goal)

After playing schoolboy football in Barrow-In-Furness and minor league football for Ulveston Town, Jack signed with Barrow in August 1928, subsequently moving on to

Bradford Park Avenue in May 1930. Four years later a £5,250 fee took him to Highbury where he helped Arsenal win the third of their three consecutive League titles in 1935, adding a second championship medal in 1938. He also won an FA Cup winners' medal in 1936 in the 1-0 victory over Sheffield United as well as an appearance for the Football League representative side. Injury brought his playing career to an end in 1943 and he joined the staff at Highbury, serving as assistant manager and then stepping up to become manager between December 1956 and May 1958. Jack left Highbury in 1958 and took up the position of manager at Doncaster Rovers, combining both this and the position of secretary from March 1959. He left the club in June 1965 and ran a newsagents near Birmingham.

Frederick Norman Smith CREEK M.B.E.

Born: Darlington, 12th January 1898
Died: 26th July 1980
Role: Centre-Forward
Career: Cambridge University, Corinthians, Darlington
Debut: v France (a) 10-5-1923 (scored once)
Appearances: 1 (1 goal)

Norman first played representative football for Darlington Grammar School before going on to win his first Blue at Cambridge University in 1920, adding a second in 1922 (he had been injured in 1921). He first began playing for the Corinthians in 1919 and remained associated with the club into the 1930s. He also signed amateur forms with Darlington and made two Football League appearances between 1922 and 1924. Aside from his one appearance for the full England side, Norman won five caps for the amateur side, scoring four goals on his debut. His association with the amateur side continued after his own retirement from playing, for he managed the international side and also the Olympic Games side during his time working for the Football Association, between January 1954 and October 1963. He was awarded the Military Cross during the First World War and an MBE in 1943 and also worked as a schoolmaster at Dauntsey's School in Wiltshire, during which time he turned out for the county at cricket. Norman was later a football writer for the Daily Telegraph for twenty years and the author of A History of Corinthians FC, published in 1933.

Warneford CRESSWELL

Born: South Shields, 5th November 1897
Died: South Shields, 20th October 1973
Role: Full-Back
Career: Hearts, Hibernian, South Shields, Sunderland, Everton
Debut: v Wales (a) 14-3-1921
Appearances: 7

Warney Cresswell represented South Shields Schools and England Schools as a youngster and also played junior football in the area, although he got his first taste of first class football in Scotland, playing for Morton, Hearts and Hibernian during the First World War (unlike England, the Scottish League continued for the duration of the war, thus giving Warney valuable experience). He later joined the Army and was captured and held as a prisoner of war before being repatriated at the end of hostilities. In the summer of 1919 he signed for South Shields and was initially used as a right-back. He was subsequently switched to left-back, a move which, in the opinion of Charles Buchan, turned him into 'the complete defender' and earned him his first cap for England in 1921. In March 1922 Sunderland paid a then record fee of £5,500 to take him to Roker Park where he won a further four caps for England. He spent five years with Sunderland before a £7,000 move to Everton in February 1927, and his arrival heralded an upturn in the Merseyside club's fortunes. He helped them win the League title in both 1928 and 1932, the Second Division championship in 1931 and the FA Cup in 1933. He remained with the club until May 1936 when he retired in order to become coach to Port Vale and later had a spell managing the Staffordshire club. He was then manager of Northampton Town between April 1937 and the outbreak of the Second World War in September 1939. After service during the war he became a licensee.

Warney Cresswell

Robert CROMPTON

Born: Blackburn, 26th September 1879
Died: Blackburn, 15th March 1941
Role: Right-Back
Career: Rose & Thistle, Blackburn Trinity, Blackburn Rovers
Debut: v Wales (a) 3-3-1902
Appearances: 41 + 1 unofficial appearance

Bob Crompton began his playing career in local schools football and was spotted by Blackburn Rovers whilst playing in a Sunday School League for Trinity. He was signed by Rovers in September 1896, making his debut at centre-half the following April in an end-of-season friendly against Darwen. Although Bob did well enough and played in the opening game of the 1897-98 season he did not become a regular until 1898-99 and by then had been converted to left-back. He switched to right-back the following season so that Allan Hardy could slot into the left-back position, and this pairing gave exceptional service to the club. Bob was first capped by England in 1902 and went on to register a then record number of caps for the country, a figure that was not overhauled until Billy Wright emerged after the Second World War. Bob helped Blackburn win the League title in 1912 and 1914 and continued to serve the club during the First World War, finally announcing his retirement as a player in May 1920. He was invited to join the board of directors and in December 1926, following the departure of Jack Carr, became 'honorary manager', a position he held for nearly five years. He guided the club to the FA Cup in 1928 (the one trophy to have eluded him as a player) but already the relationship between him and the rest of the club was beginning to become strained. His autocratic managerial style was often at odds with the rest of the board and following rumours of unrest among the players he stood down in February 1931, subsequently being voted off the board the following month. He then went on to manage Bournemouth & Boscombe Athletic for eight months before returning to the Blackburn area where he had interests in the plumbing and motor trades. Towards the end of the 1937-38 season Blackburn Rovers were involved in a desperate battle to avoid relegation to the Third Division (North) and a call went out to Bob Crompton to help his beloved club once again. He steered the club to safety in the closing weeks of the season, was appointed full time manager as a reward and then took the club to the Second Division title in 1938-39. The outbreak of the Second World War put paid to his future plans for the club although he remained at the helm during the hostilities. Indeed, it was shortly after watching the side beat Burnley at Ewood Park in March 1941 that he collapsed and died. In 1907 Bob had

Bob Crompton

Peter Crouch

caused something of a sensation at Ewood Park when he arrived at the ground in a motor car, a then almost unheard of luxury for players. Bob was also known to have been an inventor of gadgets!

Samuel Dickinson CROOKS

Born: Bearpark, County Durham, 16th January 1908
Died: 5th February 1981
Role: Right-Winger
Career: Tow Law Town, Durham City, Derby County, Retford Town, Shrewsbury Town
Debut: v Scotland (h) 5-4-1930
Appearances: 26 (7 goals)

After turning out for Bearpark Colliery at the age of 15, Sammy played for Brandon Juniors and Tow Law Town before signing as an amateur with Durham City in the summer of 1926, being upgraded to the professional ranks during the following season. He joined Derby County for £300 in April 1927 and remained associated with the club for the next twenty years, retiring as a player during the summer of 1947. Unfortunately he was unable to win any club honours during his time at the Baseball Ground (he missed the 1946 FA Cup final through injury), but his solid performances for his club were recognised at international level, collecting 26 full caps and also representing the Football League on five occasions. After a two year spell on the Derby County coaching staff Sammy moved on to Retford Town as manager in August 1949 but a few weeks later was appointed manager of Shrewsbury Town, guiding the club in to Division Three North of the Football League in 1950. He remained in charge at Gay Meadow until June 1954 before managing in non-League circles again. He later served Derby County as chief scout between 1960 and 1967 and then doing freelance scouting for the club.

Peter James CROUCH

Born: Macclesfield, 31st January 1981
Role: Striker
Career: Tottenham Hotspur, Queens Park Rangers, Portsmouth, Aston Villa, Norwich City, Southampton, Liverpool
Debut: v Columbia (USA) 31-5-2005
Appearances: 5 (1 goal)

Signed by Spurs as a trainee, Peter joined the professional ranks in July 1998 but was unable to make the grade at White Hart Lane, being sold to Queens Park Rangers for £60,000 in July 2000. A year later he cost Portsmouth £1.25 million and began to develop as a vital target man, not least because of his height. Aston Villa paid £4 million to sign him in March 2002 but a change in manager saw him drop down the pecking order and, after a spell on loan at Norwich City he was sold to Southampton for £2 million in July 2004. The arrival of Harry Redknapp as manager began to improve his fortunes, for he became something of a regular in the Southampton side, won the club's Player of the Year award and scored a number of vital goals for the club, even though they were eventually relegated to the First Division. In the summer of 2005, during which time he made his England debut, he was sold to Liverpool for £7 million.

Christopher CROWE

Born: Newcastle-upon-Tyne, 11th June 1939
Died: 2003
Role: Inside-Forward
Career: Leeds United, Blackburn Rovers, Wolverhampton Wanderers, Nottingham Forest, Bristol City, Auburn (Australia), Walsall, Bath City
Debut: v France (h) 3-10-1962 (EC)
Appearances: 1

Capped by Scotland at schoolboy level, having played for Edinburgh Schoolboys in his junior days, Chris was given a trial by Hearts before joining Leeds United as an amateur in October 1954. He turned professional in June 1956, having won eight England Youth caps, and spent a further two years at the club before moving on to Blackburn Rovers for £25,000. He spent nearly two years at Ewood Park before costing Wolverhampton Wanderers £30,000 in January 1962, winning his only England cap during his spell at Molineux. He cost Nottingham Forest £30,000 in August 1964 and three years later was signed by Bristol City for £15,000. After a spell playing with Auburn in Australia Chris finished his League career at Walsall. Upon leaving the game Chris worked variously as a newsagent, estate agent, shoe-shop owner and taxi driver until ill health forced his retirement.

Francis CUGGY

Born: Walker, Northumberland, 16th June 1889
Died: 27th March 1965
Role: Right-Half
Career: Willington Athletic, Sunderland, Wallsend
Debut: v Ireland (a) 15-2-1913
Appearances: 2

Spotted by Sunderland whilst playing non-League football for Willington Athletic, he joined the Roker Park club in March 1909 and quickly established an effective partnership with John Mordue and Charlie Buchan on the right wing for Sunderland. A member of the side that won the League championship in 1913, he narrowly missed out on the coveted double as Sunderland were beaten in the FA Cup final by the side that had finished runners-up behind them in the League, Aston Villa! Unfortunately the outbreak of the First World War robbed Sunderland of the chance to further dominate the domestic game and he left the club in May 1921 to become player-manager of Wallsend, In November 1923 he accepted a five year contract to coach in Spain and when his involvement in football came to an end he worked in the shipyards at Wearside.

Stanley CULLIS

Born: Ellesmere Port, Cheshire, 25th October 1915
Role: Centre-Half
Career: Ellesmere Port Wednesday, Wolverhampton Wanderers
Debut: v Northern Ireland (a) 23-10-1937
Appearances: 12 + 20 War appearances

Stan Cullis

James Cunliffe

Like Brian Clough, Stan Cullis ultimately became better known as a manager, guiding Wolves as surely and successfully as Clough would later do with Derby and Nottingham Forest. Stan had begun playing schools football in Ellesmere Port before signing for the local Wednesday club and was offered professional forms by Wolves in February 1934. Although he remained signed as a player for thirteen years the outbreak of the Second World War in 1939 brought his career to a temporary halt and when League football resumed in 1946 his playing career was almost at an end, although he could count three appearances for the Football League and a runners-up medal in the FA Cup in 1939 among his honours to go alongside his international caps. He retired in August 1947 and was immediately appointed assistant manager to Ted Vizard, subsequently becoming manager in June 1948. His appointment coincided with the emergence of Wolves as one of the most dominating sides of the 1950s, starting with victory in the FA Cup Final against Leicester City in 1949. Five years later he guided the club to their very first League title and repeated the success in 1958 and 1959. Wolves missed out by a single point on becoming only the third side to have achieved a hat-trick of League titles in 1960, although there was adequate compensation as the FA Cup was lifted against Blackburn Rovers. Stan remained at Wolves until September 1964 and took over at Birmingham City in December 1965, remaining in charge for almost five years before his retirement in 1970. He then became managing director of a photographic agency in Wolverhampton and was appointed to the Midland Sports Council in 1972.

Arthur CUNLIFFE

Born: Blackrod, Lancashire, 5th February 1909
Died: 28th August 1986
Role: Left-Winger
Career: Adlington, Chorley, Blackburn Rovers, Aston Villa, Middlesbrough, Burnley, Hull City, Rochdale
Debut: v Northern Ireland (h) 17-10-1932
Appearances: 2

After turning out for Adlington at the age of 14 and a brief spell at Chorley, Arthur was snapped up by Blackburn Rovers in January 1928 and spent over five years with the Ewood Park club, during which time he made his England debut. In May 1933 he joined Aston Villa for two and a half years before a move to Middlesbrough in December 1935. In April 1937 he returned to the North West, signing for Blackburn's bitter rivals Burnley, but a year later saw him joining Hull City. The outbreak of the Second World War effectively brought his playing career to an end, although he did sign for Rochdale in the summer of 1946 for a year. He was then appointed the club's trainer, a position he held for three years before switching to the south coast and joining Bournemouth in July 1950. He remained in this position for over twenty years, becoming the club's physiotherapist in 1971 until his retirement in 1974. His cousin Jimmy Cunliffe also represented England at full level.

Daniel CUNLIFFE

Born: Bolton, 1875
Died: 28th December 1937
Role: Inside-Right
Career: Little Lever, Middleton Borough, Oldham County, Liverpool, New Brighton Tower, Portsmouth, New Brighton Tower, Portsmouth, Millwall Athletic, Heywood, Rochdale
Debut: v Ireland (a) 17-3-1900
Appearances: 1

Something of a football nomad, being employed by clubs in both the north and south of the country, Danny was to win only one major honour with his various clubs, helping Portsmouth win the Southern League championship in 1902. He had also collected his only cap for England whilst at Fratton Park, a club he served twice during his time as a professional player. Danny also played for New Brighton Tower in two separate spells before finishing his career with Rochdale in 1914.

James Nathaniel CUNLIFFE

Born: Blackrod, Lancashire, 5th July 1912
Died: 21st November 1986
Role: Inside-Forward
Career: Adlington, Everton, Rochdale
Debut: v Belgium (a) 9-5-1936
Appearances: 1

He began his career with Adlington FC and joined Everton in 1930, breaking into the first team in 1932-33. He first broke into the side as a replacement for the injured Dixie Dean, but when Dean returned Cunliffe was moved to outside-right and provided countless chances for the legendary figure. Cunliffe could also be relied upon to weigh in with some vital goals of his own, scoring 76 for Everton in 187 first team appearances. He won only one cap for England whilst with the club and at the end of the Second World War joined Rochdale, making two League appearances for them before retiring. His cousin Arthur was also a noted professional footballer, playing for Blackburn, Aston Villa, Middlesbrough, Rochdale and England during his career.

Lawrence Paul CUNNINGHAM

Born: Archway, London, 8th March 1956
Died: Madrid, 15th July 1989
Role: Forward
Career: Orient, West Bromwich Albion, Real Madrid (Spain), Manchester United, Marseille (France), Leicester City, Charlerio (Belgium), Wimbledon, Real Madrid (Spain)
Debut: v Wales (h) 23-5-1979
Appearances: 6

Laurie represented Haringey and South-East Counties Schools before being taken on as an apprentice by Orient in August 1972. He was upgraded to the professional ranks in March 1974 and over the next three years developed in to an exceptionally talented wing player, usually operating on the left hand side of the field. He was sold to West Bromwich Albion for £110,000 in March 1977, the same year he became the first coloured player to be capped by England at Under-21 level. His form continued at such a pace he was coveted by clubs both domestic and overseas and in June 1979 Spanish giants Real Madrid paid £995,000 (then a record fee paid to Albion) to take him to the Bernabeu Stadium. A succession of injuries interrupted

Laurie Cunningham

his career in Spain and he spent loan spells with Manchester United, Olympique Marseille (France), Leicester City, Sporting Gijon (Spain), Charleroi (Belgium) and Wimbledon. Whilst in Spain he collected a runners-up medal in the European Cup (1981) and winners' medals in the Spanish League and Spanish Cup, both in 1980. Aside from his six full caps for England, Laurie also collected six caps at Under-21 level and also represented his country at B level and in 1988 collected his only major domestic medal, a winners' medal in the FA Cup when he came on as a substitute in Wimbledon's surprise win over Liverpool. He returned to Spain and Real Madrid to try and resurrect his career with the club but was killed in a car crash in 1989 whilst returning from a nightclub.

Keith Curle

Keith CURLE

Born: Bristol, 14th November 1963
Role: Defender
Career: Bristol Rovers, Torquay United, Bristol City, Reading, Wimbledon, Manchester City, Wolverhampton Wanderers
Debut: v CIS (a) (substitute) 29-4-1992
Appearances: 3

Keith began his career as an apprentice with Bristol Rovers but was sold to Torquay United for just £5,000 in 1983. Four months later his career took an upturn with a move to Bristol City which cost the Ashton Gate club £10,000. Here he helped the club win the Associate Members Cup in 1986 and was then sold on to Reading for £150,000 in 1987. A return trip to Wembley beckoned in the Full Members Cup as Reading beat Luton, with Keith's defensive qualities well in evidence. He then moved to Wimbledon and became part of the 'Crazy Gang' and became a much coveted defender, subsequently costing Manchester City £2.5 million when he was transferred in August 1991. At Maine Road he achieved his breakthrough into the full England side, making three appearances, and was a stalwart of the City defence for five years before leaving to join Wolves in August 1996. He was made captain at Molineux and proved to be a quality acquisition by the club.

Edward Samuel CURREY

Born: Lewes, Sussex, 28th January 1868
Died: 12th March 1920
Role: Inside-Forward
Career: Oxford University, Old Carthusians, Corinthians, Sussex
Debut: v Wales (a) 15-3-1890
Appearances: 2 (2 goals)

Educated at Charterhouse School, for whom he played football between 1885 and 1886 he later won his Blue at Oxford University in 1888, 1889 and 1890, captaining the side in 1890. He began his association with Corinthians in 1888 and went on to score 25 goals in just 30 matches and would also turn out for both Old Carthusians and Sussex. A solicitor by profession, having been admitted in 1895, he opened a practice in London.

Anthony William CURRIE

Born: Edgware, Middlesex, 1st January 1950
Role: Midfield
Career: Watford, Sheffield United, Leeds United, Queens Park Rangers, Torquay United
Debut: v Northern Ireland (h) 23-5-1972
Appearances: 17 (3 goals)

Despite having been associated with both Chelsea and Queens Park Rangers as a schoolboy, Tony left school and began working for a building company before being signed by Watford as an amateur in September 1965. He was then offered apprentice forms in February 1966 and upgraded to the professional ranks in May 1967, by which time he was an England Youth international. After just 17 appearances for the Vicarage Road club he was signed by Sheffield United for £26,500 in February 1968, going on to collect 13 caps for England at Under-23 level before collecting the first of his 17 full caps in 1972. Despite almost constant interest from bigger clubs, Tony remained at Bramwell Lane until June 1976 when Leeds United paid £240,000 to take him to Elland Road. Unfortunately, Leeds' great days were already behind them and Tony had little or nothing to show for his time with the club in terms of medals, although he continued to add to his tally of England caps. In August 1979 he joined Queens Park Rangers, costing the club £450,000 for a player they could have had considerably cheaper some twenty-four years previously! The highlight of his time at Loftus Road was an appearance in the 1982 FA Cup final, although Tony had to settle for a runners-up medal as QPR were beaten by Spurs in a replay, the only goal coming from a penalty awarded for a foul committed by Tony. After a spell in the non-League game with Chesham United, Tony returned briefly to League action with Torquay United before winding down his playing career with Hendon and Goole Town.

Arthur William CURSHAM

Born: Wilford, Nottinghamshire, 14th March 1853
Died: Florida, 24th December 1884
Role: Right-Winger
Career: Nottingham Law Club, Notts County, Sheffield FC
Debut: v Scotland (a) 4-3-1876
Appearances: 6 (2 goals)

A colliery owner in Ambergate, Derbyshire, Arthur played for Oakham School and Nottingham Law Club before signing with Notts County in 1875. He remained with the club until 1884, having collected six caps for his country and captained them on one occasion. He also played cricket for both Derbyshire and Nottinghamshire, the same kind of all-round sportsman as was his brother below. He emigrated to Florida during 1884 but died before the year was out from yellow fever.

Henry Alfred CURSHAM

Born: Wilford, Nottinghamshire, 27th November 1859
Died: 6th August 1941
Role: Winger
Career: Notts County, Corinthians, Grantham, Thursday Wanderers
Debut: v Wales (a) 15-3-1880
Appearances: 8 (5 goals)

The brother of Arthur Cursham, Henry was educated at Repton School and played football for the school before linking with Notts County in 1880, going on to appear in the side that played in the inaugural Football League season. Henry was also a player for Corinthians and served on that club's original committee between 1882 and 1886. He later played for both Grantham and Thursday Wanderers of Sheffield. An insurance broker by profession, Henry was also a noted cricketer, appearing twice for Notts County Cricket Club. What makes these appearances unique is that they were more than twenty years apart – he first played in 1880 and then again in 1904!

Tony Currie

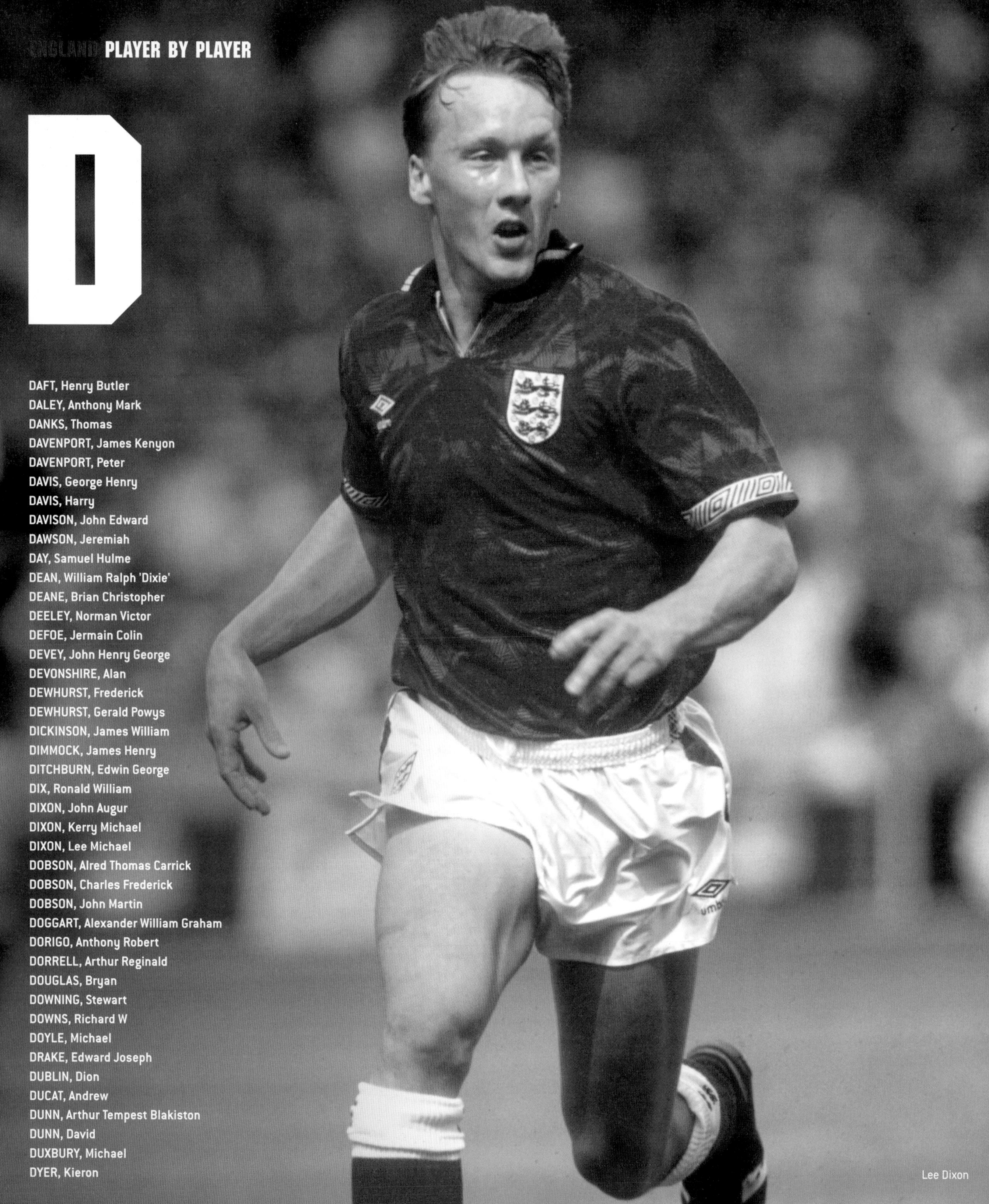

D

DAFT, Henry Butler
DALEY, Anthony Mark
DANKS, Thomas
DAVENPORT, James Kenyon
DAVENPORT, Peter
DAVIS, George Henry
DAVIS, Harry
DAVISON, John Edward
DAWSON, Jeremiah
DAY, Samuel Hulme
DEAN, William Ralph 'Dixie'
DEANE, Brian Christopher
DEELEY, Norman Victor
DEFOE, Jermain Colin
DEVEY, John Henry George
DEVONSHIRE, Alan
DEWHURST, Frederick
DEWHURST, Gerald Powys
DICKINSON, James William
DIMMOCK, James Henry
DITCHBURN, Edwin George
DIX, Ronald William
DIXON, John Augur
DIXON, Kerry Michael
DIXON, Lee Michael
DOBSON, Alred Thomas Carrick
DOBSON, Charles Frederick
DOBSON, John Martin
DOGGART, Alexander William Graham
DORIGO, Anthony Robert
DORRELL, Arthur Reginald
DOUGLAS, Bryan
DOWNING, Stewart
DOWNS, Richard W
DOYLE, Michael
DRAKE, Edward Joseph
DUBLIN, Dion
DUCAT, Andrew
DUNN, Arthur Tempest Blakiston
DUNN, David
DUXBURY, Michael
DYER, Kieron

Lee Dixon

Henry Butler DAFT

Born: Radcliffe-on-Trent, Nottinghamshire, 5th April 1866
Died: 12th January 1945
Role: Left-Winger
Career: Notts County, Nottingham Forest, Notts County, Newark, Corinthians
Debut: v Ireland (h) 2-3-1889
Appearances: 5 (3 goals)

Like many of his generation Henry was an all-round sportsman, being selected as a reserve for the England lacrosse team and to play for Notts at cricket. After attending Trent College he signed with Notts County and helped the club reach the FA Cup final in 1891, where they were beaten by Blackburn Rovers. Harry left in January 1893 to join local rivals Nottingham Forest but seven months later returned to Trent Bridge (then Notts County's ground) and would go on to help them win the FA Cup in 1894 with a 4-1 win over Bolton Wanderers, the only major trophy won by the oldest League club in the world. Harry left Notts County again in December 1894 to play for Newark. A player with Corinthians between 1887 and 1890, he also served on the FA Committee for a year. A cricketer with Notts between 1885 and 1899, appearing in 200 first class matches, he later umpired for Oxford University.

Anthony Mark DALEY

Born: Birmingham, 18th October 1967
Role: Winger
Career: Aston Villa, Wolverhampton Wanderers, Watford, Walsall
Debut: v Poland (substitute) (a) 13-11-1991 (ECQ)
Appearances: 7

Tony Daley

Tony joined Aston Villa straight from school and signed as a professional in May 1985, even though he had already made his debut for the club the previous month. His time with Villa was a mixture of disappointment, with relegation and a series of niggling injuries, and elation, including winning seven England caps during his time with the club. He did help Villa win the League Cup in 1994 shortly before a £1.25 million move to Wolves. He again suffered from injuries whilst at Molineux and took almost a year to register his debut for the club following his arrival from Villa. At the end of the 1997-98 season he was released by the club having made only 21 League appearances in four years and joined Watford on a free transfer. Having helped the club win promotion to the Premier League in 1999 he was released on a free transfer and joined Walsall.

Thomas DANKS

Born: Nottingham, 30th May 1863
Died: 27th April 1908
Role: Inside-Right
Career: Nottingham Forest, Notts County, Burslem Port Vale
Debut: v Scotland (h) 21-3-1885
Appearances: 1

After playing junior football in Nottingham he signed with Nottingham Forest in December 1882 and remained with the club for the next six and half years. During this period he made his only appearance for England against Scotland at Kennington Oval and did not enjoy the best of games, appearing to be 'somewhat outclassed' according to contemporary reports. He also turned out for Notts County and Burslem Port Vale during his time with Forest and after retiring from playing worked as an ironmonger in Nottingham.

James Kenyon DAVENPORT

Born: Bolton, 23rd March 1863
Died: 27th September 1908
Role: Forward
Career: Gilnow Rangers, Bolton Wanderers, Southport Central
Debut: v Wales (h) 14-3-1885
Appearances: 2 (2 goals)

Spotted by Bolton Wanderers whilst playing local football for Gilnow Rangers, Kenny linked with Wanderers in 1883 and played in a number of positions within the forward line for his club. Representative honours for Lancashire eventually led to a call-up for the full England side and he made his debut in the 1-1 draw with Wales in 1885, the first Bolton player to be capped for his country. He had to wait five years before earning his second and last cap but netted twice in the 9-1 victory over Ireland in Belfast. He moved on from Bolton in 1892, joining Southport Central where he finished his playing career. He later worked as a fitter.

Peter DAVENPORT

Born: Birkenhead, 24th March 1961
Role: Forward
Career: Cammell Laird, Nottingham Forest, Manchester United, Middlesbrough, Sunderland, Airdrieonians, St. Johnstone, Stockport County, Southport, Macclesfield Town
Debut: v Republic of Ireland (h) (substitute) 26-3-1985
Appearances: 1

Nottingham Forest signed Peter Davenport on a free transfer from non-League Cammell Laird in January 1982 and he soon developed into a feared striker and made his only appearance for England whilst with the club. Four years later Manchester United paid £750,000 for his signature but, like several others who have made the similar journey, he found life at Old Trafford difficult and two years later United recouped their money when selling him to Middlesbrough. The change of club revitalised his fortunes and he was an important team member for the next two years before moving on to fellow North East club Sunderland for £350,000. A spell in Scotland followed, turning out for Airdrie and St. Johnstone before he returned south of the border with Stockport County. That seemed to spell the end of his League career for he then joined Southport, but after failing in an attempt to get the manager's position he was released and joined Macclesfield Town. They ran away with the Vauxhall Conference in 1996-97 and he returned to League action in 1997-98 and even netted his 100th League goal, a feat achieved in the 3-1 win over Exeter City in the last League match of the season.

Peter Davenport

George Henry DAVIS

Born: Alfreton, Derbyshire, 5th June 1881
Died: 28th April 1969
Role: Outside-Left
Career: Alfreton Town, Derby County, Calgary Hillhurst FC (Canada)
Debut : v Wales (a) 29-2-1904
Appearances: 2 (1 goal)

Spotted whilst playing for Alfreton Town he signed with Derby County in December 1899 and helped the club reach the FA Cup final in 1903, although Derby were to suffer what remains the biggest ever cup final defeat in going down 6-0. He remained associated with Derby until 1909 when he emigrated to Canada and played a big part in helping establish the game in that country, even winning a Canadian cup-winners' medal in 1922 with Calgary Hillhurst and later coaching in Manitoba. Away from the game he became a very successful hotelier and returned to England during the 1950s where he retired in the Nottingham area. Although he is credited with having scored one goal for his country this goal is under some dispute.

Henry DAVIS

Born: Barnsley, 1880
Role: Right-Winger
Career: Barnsley, Sheffield Wednesday
Debut: v Ireland (h) 14-2-1903 (scored once)
Appearances: 3 (1 goal)

Harry began his playing career with non-League Ardsley Parish in 1895 before being signed by Barnsley in the summer of 1897. In January 1900 he cost Sheffield Wednesday £200 plus another player for his transfer and he quickly established himself as a vital part of the side that would win the Second Division championship at the end of the season. Harry and the Wednesday consolidated their position over the next two or so years before winning the League title in consecutive seasons, 1903 and 1904. Said to be the smallest forward playing in the top flight (he was only 5' 4" tall) Harry was unfortunate to break his leg during the 1906-07 season and his appearances thereafter greatly diminished, switching to the training staff as assistant trainer. When his football career came to an end he ran a newsagents in Sheffield.

John Edward DAVISON

Born: Gateshead, 2nd September 1887
Died: 1971
Role: Goalkeeper
Career: Gateshead St. Chad's, Sheffield Wednesday, Mansfield Town
Debut: v Wales (h) 13-3-1922
Appearances: 1

After a spell with Gateshead St. Chad's, Teddy signed with Sheffield Wednesday in April 1908 and would go on to give the club almost twenty years' service. Called into the England side for the match against Wales in 1922 that was won 1-0, Teddy is believed to be the smallest goalkeeper to represent his country, standing just 5' 7" tall. What he lacked in height he more than made up for with his agility and positional sense. He moved on to Mansfield Town in June 1926 as player-manager, but eighteen months later joined Chesterfield as secretary-manager. He returned to Sheffield, this time Sheffield United in June 1932 and spent twenty years assisting the Bramall Lane club, only leaving in August 1952 in order to take over the reins at Chesterfield a second time. This position lasted six years to May 1958 when he became the club's chief scout.

Jeremiah DAWSON

Born: Holme, Burnley, 18th March 1888
Died: 8th August 1970
Role: Goalkeeper
Career: Portsmouth Rovers, Holme, Burnley
Debut: v Ireland (a) 22-10-1921
Appearances: 2

Following spells in the non-League game with Portsmouth Rovers, Holme FC and Cliviger FC Jerry began his professional career with Burnley in February 1907. He was a virtual ever-present for the next twenty-two years, helping the club win the Football League championship in 1921. Jerry also helped the club reach the FA Cup final in 1914 where they beat Liverpool 1-0 but he missed the final owing to injury (the club did arrange for him to receive a winners' medal). He was equally unlucky that England were extremely well served by Sam Hardy in goal whilst Jerry was at his peak, meaning he only collected two caps for his country. After 530 League appearances for the Turf Moor club Jerry retired and later scouted for the club.

Samuel Hulme DAY

Born: Peckham Rye, London, 29th December 1878
Died: 21st February 1950
Role: Inside-Forward
Career: Cambridge University, Corinthians, Old Malvernians
Debut: v Ireland (a) 17-2-1906 (scored once)
Appearances: 3 (2 goals)

After playing football for Malvern College, Sam earned his Blue at Cambridge University in 1901. He played for Corinthians between 1902 and 1912 as well as Old Malvernians, with whom he won his three caps for England. He also helped Old Malvernians win the FA Amateur Cup in 1902 and collected five amateur caps for his country. Upon graduating from university he became a schoolteacher at Westminster, later becoming a headmaster of a preparatory school in Berkshire. Like many of his era he was an all-round sportsman, winning a Blue at university in four consecutive seasons and also playing for Kent between 1897 and 1919.

Sam Day

William Ralph 'Dixie' DEAN

Born: Birkenhead, 22nd January 1907
Died: Liverpool, 1st March 1980
Role: Centre-Forward
Career: Heswall, Pensby United, Tranmere Rovers, Everton, Notts County, Sligo Rovers
Debut: v Wales (a) 12-2-1927 (scored twice)
Appearances: 16 (18 goals)

One of the greatest goalscorers who ever played, Dean is perhaps best known for his exploits in one season - 1927-28. The previous season George Camsell had hit 59 goals for Middlesbrough in the Second Division, a record many said would never be beaten. On the last day of the 1927-28 season, with Dean on 57 goals, his Everton side were faced by Arsenal, but Dean managed to score a hat-trick (he scored his third goal some eight minutes before the end of the 3-3 draw) and take the record. He began his career with Tranmere before moving to Everton and won 16 England caps, although these all came in a spell of a little over five years and he scored only once in his final five matches. He scored a then record 379 goals in League games and won a League Champions medal and FA Cup winners' medal. He finished his League career with Notts County and went to Sligo Rovers just before the Second World War. He was captured and taken prisoner in the western desert and after the war ran a pub in Chester until forced to give up through ill health. Such was the regard with which he was held, 36,000 turned up at Everton for a testimonial held in 1964. Acknowledged throughout the game, a story is told of a chance meeting with Liverpool goalkeeper Elisha Scott. Dean nodded to acknowledge Scott, whereupon the goalkeeper dived across the pavement as though trying to save a header! A football man through and through, Dean died while watching a Liverpool and Everton derby match in 1980. He was known throughout his career as 'Dixie' in reference to his hair, but Dean hated the nickname.

'Dixie' Dean

Brian Christopher DEANE

Born: Leeds, 7th February 1968
Role: Forward
Career: Doncaster Rovers, Sheffield United, Leeds United, Sheffield United, Benfica (Portugal), Middlesbrough, Leicester City, West Ham United, Leeds United, Sunderland, Sheffield United
Debut: v New Zealand (a) (substitute) 3-6-1991
Appearances: 3

Brian joined Doncaster Rovers as a junior in 1985 and quickly became known as a feared striker in the lower Leagues. A £30,000 fee took him to Sheffield United in

Brian Deane

1988 where he became something of a folk hero at Bramall Lane as the club moved between the top two divisions with regularity. His move to Leeds United for £2.9 million in 1993 was not greeted with much pleasure by the Sheffield fans who believed their hero had been forced to leave in order to raise money for the club. Four years later he made a triumphant return home for £1.5 million and played as though he had not been away. In January 1998 Benfica of Portugal came in with an offer that proved too good to turn down and he was on his way to a warmer climate, although he had done sufficiently well enough at Bramall Lane between August and January to finish the season as top goalscorer. In October 1998 he returned home with Middlesbrough, costing the Teesside club over £3 million in the process. Three years later he moved on to Leicester City for £150,000 and subsequently had free transfers to West Ham United, Leeds United for a second spell, Sunderland and Sheffield United, his third spell at Bramall Lane. In addition to his three full caps Brian also won three caps at B level for England.

Norman Victor DEELEY

Born: Wednesbury, Staffordshire, 30th November 1933
Role: Right-Winger
Career: Wolverhampton Wanderers, Leyton Orient, Worcester City, Bromgrove Rovers, Darlaston
Debut: v Brazil (a) 13-5-1959
Appearances: 2

Despite standing only 5' 4? " tall, Norman never let his lack of height become a handicap, having already been the smallest player ever to represent England schoolboys (he was just 4' 4" in 1948). Educated at the Holyhead Road School in Wednesbury he joined Wolves straight from school, becoming a professional in November 1950. Initially used as a wing-half he was converted to the wing after being demobbed from the Army and in that position became a vital part of the Wolves side of the 1950s. He won two League championship medals and a winners' medal in the FA Cup and in 1959 was taken on England's tour of South America, making two appearances for the national side. He remained with Wolves until February 1962 when he left for Leyton Orient for £13,000 as Orient sought to strengthen their promotion-seeking side. He helped them into the First Division in 1962 and remained with Orient until July 1964 when he moved into non-League circles with Worcester City. He later played for Bromsgrove Rovers and Darlaston before retiring in 1974. He worked as manager of the Caldmore Community Programme Agency in Walsall and was also a steward in the VIP lounge at Fellows Park.

Norman Deeley

Jermain Colin DEFOE

Born: Beckton, London, 7th October 1982
Role: Striker
Career: Charlton Athletic, West Ham United, AFC Bournemouth, West Ham United, Tottenham Hotspur
Debut: v Sweden (a) 31-3-2004
Appearances: 16 (1 goal)

Widely tipped as one of the hottest goalscoring properties since Michael Owen, Jermain Defoe has managed to score goals at every level and for every club he has played for. Originally signed as a trainee by Charlton Athletic he moved on to West Ham United for £1.5 million in July 1999 despite having never played for the Charlton first team. Indeed, the deal was the subject of allegations of poaching by West Ham United, hence the transfer fee that was ordered to be paid (it has also assured Jermain of a hostile reception whenever he has visited The Valley ever since!). West Ham loaned him out to Bournemouth in October 2000 for the rest of the season and his goalscoring exploits, including a spell of scoring in 11 consecutive games, breaking the existing record, had the football world sit up and take notice. He returned to West Ham and linked up with Freddie Kanoute, but despite both players weighing in with more than their fair share of goals, West Ham were relegated from the Premiership at the end of the 2002-03 season. Almost as soon as he left the pitch in their final match Jermain handed in a transfer request (assuring him of a hostile reception from West Ham fans!), although this was later withdrawn and he set about scoring the goals that would hopefully return West Ham to the top flight. In February 2004 he moved across London to sign for Spurs in a deal worth an initial £6 million, with a further £1 million payable depending on 'specific performance criteria.' He linked up once again with Freddie Kanoute, who had moved to Spurs earlier the same season, and eventually was also reunited with Michael Carrick, who joined Spurs later the same year. He managed to score seven League goals in 14 games for Spurs during his first few months with the club and was taken to the England get-together prior to Sven Goran Eriksson announcing his squad for the 2004 European Championships. Although Jermain made his England debut during the warm-up games he was omitted from the final squad, but his continued goalscoring come the 2004-05 season saw him starting in the World Cup qualifying match against Poland and netting the opening goal. With Michael Owen and Michael Rooney also available for selection, Sven Goran Eriksson has an abundance of striking talent to choose from – time will tell who will be the odd man out.

Jermain Defoe

John Henry George DEVEY

Born: Birmingham, 26th December 1866
Died: Birmingham, 11th October 1940
Role: Inside-Right, Centre-Forward
Career: Excelsior, Aston Unity, Mitchell St. George's, Aston Villa
Debut: v Ireland (a) 5-3-1892
Appearances: 2 (1 goal)

One of the greatest names in Aston Villa's history was signed by the club after appearing for local sides Excelsior, Aston Unity, Mitchell St. George's and Aston Manor, joining Villa in March 1891. He made his League debut in the opening game of the following season and finished the campaign as top goalscorer with 29 goals to his credit, as well as helping Villa reach the FA Cup final. He subsequently became captain and guided the club to five League championships, two FA Cups and also won two caps for England. He was something of an all-round sportsman, for he also represented Warwickshire at cricket and scored over 6,500 runs. When he retired as a player he continued to serve Villa as a director, being appointed in 1902 and continuing in that capacity until 1934.

John Devey

Alan DEVONSHIRE

Born: Park Royal, London, 13th April, 1956
Role: Midfield
Career: Southall & Ealing Borough, West Ham United, Watford
Debut: v Northern Ireland (h) 20-5-1980
Appearances: 8

An extremely talented midfield player, Alan was linked with Crystal Palace as a schoolboy without being offered professional terms. Instead he worked as a forklift truck driver at Hoover's and played part time for Southall, where he was spotted by West Ham United who paid £5,000 to take him to Upton Park. He linked especially well with fellow midfield player Trevor Brooking and the pair helped the club win the 1980 FA Cup against Arsenal. The following season saw West Ham win the Second Division championship and reach the League Cup final, by which time Alan had picked up the first of his eight caps for England. A bad knee injury sustained in 1984 brought his career to a standstill for more than eighteen months, although he was back to his best in the 1986-87 season. The following season he snapped an Achilles' tendon and had to fight back to fitness all over again. After 446 games for West Ham he moved on to Watford where he finished his career.

Alan Devonshire

Frederick DEWHURST

Born: Preston, 16th December 1863
Died: 21st April 1895
Role: Inside-Forward
Career: Preston North End, Corinthians
Debut: v Ireland (a) 13-3-1886
Appearances: 9 (11 goals)

After playing local junior football in his native Preston he was signed by Preston North End in 1882, albeit as an amateur. Indeed he remained an amateur for his entire career, enabling him to also turn out for Corinthians whenever time allowed. Whilst with Preston he helped the club to the FA Cup final in 1888 and the following year, the first of the Football League, the double of League and Cup. In addition to his prolific goalscoring exploits for England he also netted 12 goals in his 28 Corinthian appearances. A master at the Preston Catholic Grammar School he died at the relatively young age of 31.

Gerald Powys DEWHURST

Born: London, 14th February 1872
Died: 29th March 1956
Role: Inside-Forward
Career: Cambridge University, Liverpool Ramblers, Corinthians
Debut: v Wales (h) 18-3-1895
Appearances: 1

Educated at Repton School for whom he played between 1889 and 1890, he attended Cambridge University and was awarded a Blue in 1892, 1893 and 1894. After graduating he became a cotton merchant based in Liverpool and became associated with Liverpool Ramblers, winning his only cap for England whilst with this club. He also played for the leading amateur side of the day, Corinthians, between 1892 and 1895, scoring 18 goals in his 32 appearances.

James William DICKINSON M.B.E.

Born: Alton, Hampshire, 24th April 1925
Died: Alton, 9th November 1982
Role: Left-Half
Career: Portsmouth
Debut: v Norway (a) 18-5-1949
Appearances: 48

Jimmy Dickinson was a model of consistency for both club and country; a dependable and reliable performer who preferred to do the simple things well rather than attempt the difficult and fail. It was a style of play that brought him 48 caps for his country and a record number of appearances for his club. First spotted as a schoolboy by Eddie Lever, a player and subsequent manager of Portsmouth, Jimmy was coached from the age of 8 and was therefore destined to sign for Portsmouth, signing as an amateur in 1943. In January 1944 he turned professional and made his debut for the club immediately following the Second World War and would remain a regular in the side until his retirement in April 1965. First capped for England in 1949 he was a regular for the next seven years, including one spell of 25 consecutive appearances. Whilst with Portsmouth he won two League titles (1949 and 1950), the Third Division championship in 1962 and also represented the England B side three times and the Football League on 11 occasions. When he finally retired as a player in April 1965 he had made 764 League appearances for the club, a record for a single club which has since been broken. He continued to serve Portsmouth in a number of capacities until 1979, including scout, public relations officer, secretary and manager between April 1977 and May 1979 when he was advised to retire on medical grounds. His devotion and service to Portsmouth was recognised in 1964 when he was awarded the MBE.

Jimmy Dickinson

James Henry DIMMOCK

Born: Edmonton, London, 5th December 1900
Died: Enfield, Middlesex, 23rd December 1972
Role: Left-Winger
Career: Park Avenue, Gothic Works, Clapton Orient, Edmonton Ramblers, Tottenham Hotspur, Thames - Clapton Orient, Ashford
Debut: v Scotland (a) 19-4-1921
Appearances: 3

Signed as an amateur in 1916, Jimmy Dimmock was promoted to the professional ranks in May 1919, signing for Spurs in the face of competition from Clapton (for whom he had guested during the First World War) and Arsenal. Seizing his place in the side following an injury to Jimmy Chipperfield, he made the left-wing berth his own and helped the side win the Second Division title at the end of his first season. The following year saw the FA Cup return to the White Hart Lane boardroom, placed there thanks to Jimmy's match-winning goal against Wolves at Stamford Bridge. He weighed in with a considerable number of goals for Spurs during his career, finishing with 100 in 400 League appearances. In 1931 he was allowed to leave the club, signing with Thames and switching to Clapton Orient when Thames folded at the end of the 1931-32 season. He finished his playing career with non-League Ashford and then worked in the road haulage business. Jimmy Dimmock was the first player known to be born in the twentieth century to win a cap for England.

Ted Ditchburn

Edwin George DITCHBURN

Born: Gillingham, Kent, 24th October 1921
Died: 26th December 2005
Role: Goalkeeper
Career: Northfleet, Tottenham Hotspur, Romford, Brentwood
Debut: v Switzerland (h) 1-12-1948
Appearances: 6 + 2 War appearances

The son of a professional boxer Ted Ditchburn joined Spurs in 1939 but lost seven years of League football to the Second World War, although by the time he left in 1959, he held the record for the most League appearances for Spurs, having made 419 if one abandoned match is taken into account. He made his debut for the club during the war in the Football League South and made a number of representative appearances for both the Royal Air Force and the FA XI as well as two wartime appearances for England. A safe and reliable goalkeeper he was the foundation upon which Spurs built their promotion and title winning sides of the early 1950s, especially as he missed only two matches in the seven seasons immediately following the Second World War and notched up 247 consecutive appearances. Unfortunately England was served by a plethora of quality goalkeepers during the same period and Ted made only six appearances for the full team. Having seen off almost all competition at Spurs until 1958, a back injury and a broken finger forced his retirement from first class football in April 1959, although he did continue to play non-League football until 1965. When his playing career finally came to an end he owned a sports outfitters shop in Romford in Essex.

Ronald William DIX

Born: Bristol, 5th September 1912
Role: Inside-Forward
Career: Bristol Rovers, Blackburn Rovers, Aston Villa, Derby County, Tottenham Hotspur, Reading
Debut: v Norway (h) 9-11-1938 (scored once)
Appearances: 1 (1 goal)

Discovered by Bristol Rovers he signed as a professional in 1929, by which time he had already made his League debut. Indeed, in scoring on his debut at the age of 15 years 180 days he became the youngest ever scorer. He joined Blackburn Rovers in 1932 and a year later Villa swooped to take him and his left-wing partner Arthur Cunliffe, making his debut in the last game of the 1932-33 season. He moved on to Derby where he won his only cap for England and in 1939 joined Spurs, finishing his career with Reading in 1949.

John Augur DIXON

Born: Grantham, 27th May 1861
Died: 8th June 1931
Role: Left-Wing
Career: Notts County, Corinthians
Debut: v Wales (h) 14-3-1885
Appearances: 1

Selected for all three of his schools during his education (Grantham Grammar, Nottingham High and Chigwell Grammar) he joined Notts County during the 1884-85 season and made such an impact that he was capped by England in March 1895. He also played for Corinthians the same season, but by 1886 he had been forced to retire on health grounds. This did not stop him partaking in sport, for he was a county cricketer for Notts between 1882 and 1905 and was captain from 1889. He later served on the committee of Notts CCC from 1895 to his death in 1931, and two years later memorial gates were erected at the main entrance of the Trent Bridge ground. A partner in a firm of clothes manufacturers, he was also a Justice of the Peace.

Kerry Michael DIXON

Born: Luton, Bedfordshire, 24th July 1961
Role: Forward
Career: Tottenham Hotspur, Dunstable Town, Reading, Chelsea, Southampton, Luton Town, Millwall, Watford, Doncaster Rovers, Borehamwood
Debut: v Mexico (a) (substitute) 9-6-1985
Appearances: 8 (4 goals)

After playing for non-League football for Cheshunt Kerry joined the ground staff as an apprentice at Spurs but failed to make the grade, subsequently returning to the non-League game with Dunstable Town. Here he found his goal touch once again, prompting a £20,000 transfer to Reading in July 1980. Over the next three years he netted with regularity in

Kerry Dixon

the lower divisions, which resulted in a £175,000 move to Chelsea in August 1983. He helped the club win the Second Division championship in 1984 and the following year collected the first of his eight caps for England. He added a second championship medal from the Second Division in 1989 but in 1992, having lost his club place to Tony Cascarino, was sold to Southampton for £575,000. A succession of injuries restricted his first team opportunities at The Dell and after a spell on loan with Luton Town the deal became permanent. He later played for Millwall and Watford before becoming player-manager at Doncaster Rovers, subsequently finishing his playing career with Borehamwood.

Lee Dixon

Lee Michael DIXON

Born: Manchester, 17th March 1964
Role: Full Back
Career: Burnley, Chester City, Bury, Stoke City, Arsenal
Debut: v Czechoslovakia (h) 25-4-1990
Appearances: 22 (1 goal)

Lee began his career with Burnley, signing as a junior in 1982 but failed to make the grade at Turf Moor, being released on a free transfer in 1984 and subsequently signing for Chester City. After less than eighteen months he was again released on a free, with Bury signing him in July 1985. He enjoyed a consistent and successful season with Bury, prompting Stoke to pay £40,000 for his services in July 1986. Here his career began to take off and Arsenal manager George Graham paid £400,000 to take him to Highbury in January 1988. For the next ten years he, David Seaman, Tony Adams, Steve Bould and Nigel Winterburn were in almost permanent residence in the Arsenal defence, and Lee collected winners' medals for three League titles, two FA Cups and the European Cup Winners' Cup. His form, despite his age, prompted Arsene Wenger to offer him an extension on his contract in 1998. In addition to his 21 caps for England at full level he has also represented England four times in the B side. In 1999 injuries to others in the England squad earned him a recall and a place in the side against France, his first cap in over five years.

Alfred Thomas Carrick DOBSON

Born: Basford, Nottingham, 1859
Died: 22nd October 1932
Role: Full-Back
Career: Notts County, Corinthians
Debut: v Ireland (a) 18-2-1882
Appearances: 4

Educated at Downside School, Alfred played for both Notts County and Corinthians during his career and collected four caps for his country, despite suffering from poor eyesight. Away from the game he and his brother Charles (below) were employed by the family's fabric company in their Nottingham hometown.

Charles Frederick DOBSON

Born: Basford, Nottingham, 9th September 1862
Died: 18th May 1939
Role: Half-Back
Career: Notts County, Corinthians
Debut: v Ireland (a) 13-3-1886
Appearances: 1

The brother of Alfred Dobson (above), Charles also played for Notts County and Corinthians during his career, although he was able to make only one League appearance for Notts County, against Aston Villa in December 1888 during the inaugural League season. He was also employed at the family fabric business in Nottingham.

John Martin DOBSON

Born: Blackburn, 14th February 1948
Role: Midfield
Career: Bolton Wanderers, Burnley, Everton, Burnley, Bury
Debut: v Portugal (a) 3-4-1974
Appearances: 5

Initially a centre-forward at Bolton Wanderers, Martin failed to impress and was subsequently released by the club in 1967. He was on the brink of giving up the game altogether when his father persuaded Burnley manager Harry Potts to have a second look at him and he was eventually signed by the Turf Moor club in August 1967. Switched to midfield he became a sensation, helping the club win the Second Division championship in 1973, subsequently prompting Everton to pay a then record £300,000 for him in August 1974, by which time he was a full England international. He remained at Goodison Park for five years and had collected a runners-up medal in the 1977 League Cup before returning to Turf Moor in August 1979 for £100,000. In his second spell at Turf Moor he collected a Division Three championship medal in 1982 and then in March 1984 moved on to Bury to become player-manager. He retired as a player in 1986 but continued as manager until March 1989. In addition to his five full caps Martin also represented the Under-23s and the Football League.

Martin Dobson

Alexander William Graham DOGGART

Born: Bishop Auckland, 2nd June 1897
Died: 7th June 1963
Role: Inside-Left
Career: Cambridge University, Corinthians, Darlington, Bishop Auckland
Debut: v Belgium (a) 1-11-1923
Appearances: 1

Educated at Darlington Grammar School and then Bishop's Stortford School, representing both, Alexander went to Cambridge University where he won his Blue in 1921 and 1922. He first linked with Corinthians in 1920 and remained associated with the amateur club until 1932, becoming the club's greatest goalscorer, having netted 160 goals in 170 matches. In between times he turned out for Darlington in two League matches during 1922 and later played for Bishop Auckland. At the end of his playing days in 1932 he was appointed to the FA Council, serving until 1950 when he was made vice-president. He served in this capacity until May 1961 when he was appointed president and remained in the position (as well as a brief period when he was also chairman) until he collapsed and died during the 1963 AGM. Aside from his football exploits, Alexander also earned a Blue at Cambridge for cricket in 1921 and 1922 and later played for both Durham and Middlesex. His son Hubert later played for England in two Test matches.

Anthony Robert DORIGO

Born: Melbourne, Australia, 31st December 1965
Role: Full-Back
Career: Aston Villa, Chelsea, Leeds United, Torino (Italy), Derby County – Stoke City
Debut: v Yugoslavia (substitute) (h) 13-12-1989
Appearances: 15

He arrived in England to sign as a schoolboy with Villa in January 1982 and made his debut at the end of the 1983-84 season. He soon became established as a regular within the side but could do little to help them in their battle against relegation from the First Division. Following relegation Aston Villa accepted a £475,000 offer to take Tony Dorigo to Stamford Bridge, but at the end of his first season with the club they too were relegated! He helped Chelsea regain their top flight status as Second Division champions after just one season and then scored the only goal as Chelsea won the Zenith Data Systems trophy in 1990. The following season he was sold to Leeds United for £1.3 million and helped them win the League title in 1992 (the last season before the Premier League came into being). A succession of injuries thereafter hampered his progress and in 1997 he left the club for Italy and Torino, subsequently returning to England to play for Derby County and finishing his career with Stoke City.

Tony Dorigo

Arthur Reginald DORRELL

Born: Small Heath, Birmingham, 30th March 1898
Died: 13th September 1942
Role: Left-Winger
Career: Carey Hall FC, Aston Villa, Port Vale
Debut: v Belgium (h) 8-12-1924
Appearances: 4 (1 goal)

The son of former Aston Villa player William Dorrell, Arthur began his playing career turning out in schools football in Leicester before lying about his age in order to enlist during the First World War. After playing representative football with the Army, Arthur signed for Aston Villa in May 1919 and would go on to help the club win the FA Cup against Huddersfield Town at the end of his first season at Villa Park. They returned to the cup final in 1924 at Wembley but this time lost out to Newcastle United. In June 1931 Arthur moved on to play for Port Vale, subsequently retiring in the summer of 1932. As well as his four full caps for England, Arthur represented the Football League on two occasions.

Bryan DOUGLAS

Born: Blackburn, 27th May 1934
Role: Forward
Career: Blackburn Rovers, Great Harwood
Debut: v Wales (a) 19-10-1957
Appearances: 36 (11 goals)

Bryan was born in Blackburn and played for Blackburn schools and youth and so there was always only ever going to be one team he signed for: Blackburn Rovers. He signed as an amateur in 1950 and was upgraded to the professional ranks in April 1952, making his debut for the first team in September 1954. It was only after completing his National Service that he became a regular in the side, beginning his run in September 1955. By the following year he had collected the first of his five Under-23 caps and in 1957 was awarded his first full cap for England. Initially he was used as a wing alternative to either Tom Finney or Stanley Matthews, both of whom were approaching the end of their international careers, but Bryan was invariably utilised as an inside-forward for Blackburn. He helped Rovers to the FA Cup Final in 1960 where they were beaten by Wolves, the closest he came to collecting domestic honours with his club. On the representative front, however, Bryan added four appearances for the Football League and an England B cap to go with his 36 full appearances. The appointment of Alf Ramsey as England manager effectively spelt the end of Bryan's international career, his final cap coming in 1963 against Switzerland, as Ramsey began doing away with wing players. Bryan remained an important part of the Blackburn side until June 1969 when he was released after seventeen years as a professional with the club. He then joined non-League Great Harwood where he finished his playing career.

Bryan Douglas

Stewart DOWNING

Born: Middlesbrough, 22nd July 1984
Role: Midfield
Career: Middlesbrough, Sunderland, Middlesbrough
Debut: v Holland (h) 9-2-2005
Appearances: 1

After serving as a trainee at the Riverside Stadium, Stewart signed professional forms with Middlesbrough in September 2001. Unable to break into the first team on a regular basis he was sent on loan to local rivals Sunderland and after 10 games for the Black Cats returned with his confidence restored. He then became an integral part of the side that lifted the first major honour in Middlesbrough's history, the Carling Cup in 2004, and was soon knocking on the door of the England side. Given his first cap in the friendly against Holland, he is still a fringe player for the first team but has time on his side to rectify that position.

Stewart Downing

Richard W. DOWNS

Born: Middridge, County Durham, 13th August 1886
Died: 24th March 1949
Role: Right-Back
Career: Crook, Shildon Athletic, Barnsley, Everton, Brighton & Hove Albion
Debut: v Ireland (h) 23-10-1920
Appearances: 1

Dicky Downs played non-League football for Crook and Shildon Athletic before being spotted by Barnsley, signing with the Yorkshire club in May 1908. Two years later he had made his first appearance in an FA Cup final, being a member of the side that lost 2-0 in a replay to Newcastle United. He received more than adequate compensation two years later, helping Barnsley overcome West Bromwich Albion 1-0 in extra time after a 1-1 draw in the first match. The outbreak of the First World War robbed Dicky of some five years of first class football, but he remained at Oakwell until March 1920 when he was sold to Everton for £2,500. Seven months later he won his only cap for England in the 2-1 defeat by Wales at Highbury. Dicky remained at Goodison for four years before moving on to Brighton in August 1924, but less than a year later was forced to retire owing to injury. He then coached extensively throughout Europe. In additional to his full cap Dicky represented the Football League on two occasions.

Michael DOYLE

Born: Manchester, 25th November 1946
Role: Defender
Career: Manchester City, Stoke City, Bolton Wanderers, Rochdale
Debut: v Wales (a) 24-3-1976
Appearances: 5 + 1 unofficial international

Mike was spotted by Manchester City playing schools football in Stockport and joined the Maine Road ground staff in

May 1962, subsequently signing professional forms in May 1964. Although City were languishing in the Second Division at the time he made his debut, he soon stood out as an exceptional defender and helped them win promotion back into the top flight in 1966. Thereafter he was a member of the side that won the League championship in 1968, the FA Cup in 1969, the European Cup Winners' Cup and League Cup in 1970, a further League Cup success in 1974 and a runners-up medal in the same competition in 1976. That year saw him win his first cap for England, even though he was approaching his 30th birthday, his no-nonsense defensive style much admired by manager Don Revie. Revie's subsequent departure brought an end to Mike's international career, but he had enjoyed his Indian summer. Injured during the 1977-78 season and having made over 500 first team appearances for Manchester City, he was allowed to move on to Stoke City for £50,000 and went on to register well over 100 appearances for the Potteries club. He later had spells with Bolton Wanderers and Rochdale before retiring in 1984. He now combines sports sales management with commentating on football for local radio.

Ted Drake

Edward Joseph DRAKE

Born: Southampton, 16th August 1912
Died: London, 30th May 1995
Role: Centre-Forward
Career: Winchester City, Southampton, Arsenal
Debut: v Italy (h) 14-11-1934 (scored once)
Appearances: 5 (6 goals)

Had Ted Drake not made it as a professional footballer he might well have remained a gas meter inspector, for during his time with Southampton he combined both roles! He had joined Southampton from Winchester City having played schools football in his hometown, but fortunately his performances at The Dell were of sufficient quality that he was able to give up his gas board job and concentrate full time on football. In March 1934 Arsenal paid £6,000 to take him to Highbury and eight months later had turned him into an England international. He won two League titles and the FA Cup once whilst with Arsenal and in 1934-35 he established a record number of League goals for the club in a single season, 42, which has yet to be broken. The following season he scored seven goals in one match at Villa Park against Aston Villa, a feat made all the more remarkable by the fact that he was carrying a serious injury at the time and his seven goals came from only eight attempts at goal; the one that missed hit the bar! Injury brought his career to an end in 1945 and he moved to Hendon to become manager, returning to the League in June 1947 when he took over the reins at Reading. He spent five years at Elm Park before accepting an invitation to take over at Chelsea in June 1952, setting up a youth policy that became known as 'Drake's Ducklings' (in deference to the 'Busby Babes') guiding the club to their first League title in 1955. Denied the chance to compete in the inaugural European Cup, Ted remained at Stamford Bridge until September 1961 when he was replaced by Tommy Docherty. He then spent spells as a bookmaker and salesman, returning to the game in 1970 when appointed assistant manager at Barcelona. He later scouted for Fulham, a position he maintained until the 1980s. Ted had also played cricket at county level for Hampshire between 1931 and 1936, and in 1963 was appointed to the pools panel. Ted Drake was the first man to both play for and manage a side to the League title.

Dion Dublin

Dion DUBLIN

Born: Leicester, 22nd April 1969
Role: Forward
Career: Norwich City, Cambridge United, Manchester United, Coventry City, Aston Villa, Millwall, Leicester City
Debut: v Chile (h) 11-2-1998
Appearances: 4

Dion joined Norwich City from non-League Oakham United in 1988 but was released five months later without having made a single appearance for the first team. He joined Cambridge United on a free transfer and picked up the pieces of his career, scoring over 70 goals in under 200 appearances before a £1 million move to Manchester United in 1992. He spent two years at Old Trafford but suffered from a broken leg soon after his arrival and in September 1994 he was sold to Coventry City for £2 million. At Highfield Road he became an adaptable player, equally at home leading the attack or marshalling the defence when selected to play in the back four. It was his form up front that earned him his initial selection for England and subsequently a move to Aston Villa in November 1998 in a deal worth £5.75 million. At Villa Park he was also used as something of an emergency defender as well as his more usual position leading the attack. Sent on loan to Millwall during the 2001-2 season, he was released in the summer of 2004 and promptly joined Leicester City on a free transfer.

Andrew DUCAT

Born: Brixton, London, 16th February 1886
Died: London, 23rd July 1942
Role: Right-Half
Career: Westcliff Athletic, Southend Athletic, Woolwich Arsenal, Aston Villa, Fulham, Casuals
Debut: v Ireland (a) 14-2-1910
Appearances: 6 (1 goal)

Andy played schoolboy football in Southend before joining Westcliff Athletic and then Southend Athletic, finally turning professional with Woolwich Arsenal in February 1905. He spent seven years at Arsenal before a £1,500 move to

Andrew Ducat

David Dunn

Aston Villa in June 1912 but broke his leg four games into the season and was forced to sit out as the club made the FA Cup Final at the end of the season. He had to wait seven years before fortune smiled on him; Jimmy Harrop was injured before the 1920 final and Andy Ducat captained the side at Stamford Bridge. He was one of the few players to have been capped by England at both football and cricket, and when he left Villa in 1921 it was to sign for Fulham so that he could be nearer to Surrey Cricket Club. He later managed Fulham for two years and also played as an amateur for the London Casuals. He retired from first class cricket in 1931 and was then coach at Eton for five years before becoming a sports journalist and later a hotel manager. He died whilst batting (29 not out) for Surrey Home Guard in their match against Sussex Home Guard at Lord's in July 1942 (apparently he is the only player to have died during a game at Lord's).

Arthur Tempest Blakiston DUNN

Born: Whitby, 12th August 1860
Died: 20th February 1902
Role: Centre-Forward
Career: Cambridge University, Old Etonians, Granta, Corinthians, Cambridgeshire
Debut: v Ireland (a) 24-2-1883
Appearances: 4 (2 goals)

Educated at Eton College, Arthur later played for Old Etonians and helped them reach successive FA Cup finals, collecting a winners' medal in 1882 and a runners-up medal the following year. A year later he won his first Blue at Cambridge University, adding a second a year later. Associated with the Corinthians between 1886 and 1892 he also represented Cambridgeshire and Norfolk. Away from the game Arthur founded Ludgrove School in New Barnet where he served as schoolmaster, the school subsequently having future England internationals William Oakley and Gilbert Smith as joint headmasters.

David DUNN

Born: Blackburn, 27th December 1979
Role: Midfield
Career: Blackburn Rovers, Birmingham City
Debut: v Portugal (h) 7-9-2002
Appearances: 1

Taken on as a trainee by his local club Blackburn Rovers, David was upgraded to the professional ranks in September 1997. After representing his country at Youth level David went on to win 20 caps at Under-21 level. He helped Blackburn return to the top flight in 2001 and the following year win the Worthington Cup. In September 2002 he won his first and so far only cap for the full England side, one of a number of fringe players within the squad. A £5.5 million fee took him to Birmingham City in July 2003 but a succession of injuries has hampered his progress at club level and therefore his chances of breaking back into the England squad.

Michael DUXBURY

Born: Blackburn, 1st September 1959
Role: Full-Back
Career: Manchester United, Blackburn Rovers, Bradford City
Debut: v Luxembourg (a) 16-11-1983 (ECQ)
Appearances: 10

Signed as an apprentice by Manchester United in 1975 he was upgraded to the professional ranks in October 1976 but struggled to make his first team breakthrough, languishing in the Central League side for almost five years. He was drafted into the first team in August 1980 but didn't fully establish himself as a regular until 1982. Thereafter he won FA Cup winners' medals in 1983 and 1985 and also helped the club reach the final of the Milk Cup in 1983. He went on to make 376 first team appearances for Manchester United before being allowed to leave on a free transfer to join Blackburn Rovers. He spent eighteen months at Ewood Park before moving on to Bradford City where he ended his playing career. As well as his 10 full caps Mike also represented his country at Under-21 level on seven occasions.

Michael Duxbury

Kieron Courtney DYER

Born: Ipswich, 29th December 1978
Role: Midfield
Career: Ipswich Town, Newcastle United
Debut: v Luxembourg (h) 4-9-1999
Appearances: 28

Discovered by Ipswich Town whilst playing junior football on their doorstep, Kieron was signed as a trainee and subsequently upgraded to the professional ranks in January 1997. He soon established himself as a player of real potential, representing his country at Youth, Under-21 and B level whilst at Portman Road. In July 1999 Newcastle United paid £6 million to take him to St. James' Park and he soon won his first full cap for England, subsequently going on to become something of a regular in the squad if not the team. His career at Newcastle has been blighted by injuries, including a stress fracture of the shin and foot. In 2005 he suffered a breakdown shortly after returning to first team action, the cause being unknown.

Kieron Dyer

D E F

E

EARLE, Stanley George James
EASTHAM, George Edward
EASTHAM, George Richard
ECKERSLEY, William
EDWARDS, Duncan
EDWARDS, John Hawley
EDWARDS, Willis
EHIOGU, Ugochuku
ELLERINGTON, William
ELLIOTT, George Washington
ELLIOTT, William Henry
EVANS, Robert Ernest
EWER, Frederick Harold

Ugo Ehiogu

Stanley George James EARLE

Born: Stratford, London, 6th September 1897
Died: 26th September 1971
Role: Inside-Right
Career: Clapton, Arsenal, West Ham United, Clapton Orient
Debut: v France (a) 17-5-1924
Appearances: 2

The son of Harry Earle, the former Millwall Athletic goalkeeper, Stanley played schools football in West Ham before signing with Clapton. As an amateur he was also able to sign for Arsenal and made four League appearances in three seasons. In August 1924 he was persuaded to sign as an amateur with West Ham United although he retained his connection with Clapton, helping them win the FA Amateur Cup in 1924. The following year he was finally persuaded to sign as a professional by West Ham, even though he was now nearly 28 years of age, and went on to give the club eight years of service. In May 1932 he signed for Clapton Orient (as a professional), retiring from playing the following year. He later had a spell as manager of Leyton Orient. As well as his two full caps, Stanley also represented his country at schoolboy and amateur level.

Stanley Earle

George Edward EASTHAM O.B.E.

Born: Blackpool, 23rd September 1936
Role: Inside-Forward
Career: Ards, Newcastle United, Arsenal, Stoke City, Hellenic (South Africa), Stoke City
Debut: v Brazil (h) 8-5-1963
Appearances: 19 (2 goals)

George junior followed his father into professional football, winning considerably more caps and achieving lasting notoriety for his court case against Newcastle United in 1963 that saw the end of the retain and transfer system. He began his career with Ards, where his father was manager (the pair even appeared in the same match), signing as an amateur and then turning professional in May 1956. A couple of weeks later he was transferred to Newcastle United for £9,000, making 124 League appearances for the club before indicating he wished to move on. Arsenal were willing to pay (and indeed did pay) £47,500 for his signature, but it was Newcastle's initial refusal to allow the transfer to go ahead that prompted George to instigate legal proceedings against the club. The case finally came before the courts in 1963, with the judge ruling in George's favour and thus ending the retain and transfer system after almost 100 years. Whilst at Arsenal George broke into the England side, thus enabling George senior and junior to become the first father and son to have represented England at full level. George junior remained with Arsenal until August 1966 when he was transferred to Stoke City for £30,000, remaining with the club for five years before going to play in South Africa with Hellenic. He returned to Stoke City in October 1971 and helped the club to the first major honour of their history, the League Cup in 1972. In December of the same year George was promoted to assistant manager, retiring from playing in February 1975. He was appointed manager at the Victoria Ground in May 1977 having been caretaker manager for three months and held the position until January 1978. He was awarded the OBE in 1973.

George Edward Eastham

George Richard EASTHAM

Born: Blackpool, 13th September 1913
Died: January 2000
Role: Inside-Forward
Career: South Shore Wednesday, Bolton Wanderers, Brentford, Blackpool, Swansea Town, Rochdale, Lincoln City, Hyde United, Ards
Debut: v Holland (a) 18-5-1935
Appearances: 1

George played junior football in Blackpool and worked in a bakery in the town before being signed by Bolton Wanderers in 1932. In June 1937 he was signed by Brentford but the following year returned to the North West, joining Blackpool in a deal worth £7,000. The outbreak of the Second World War robbed him of some seven years of League football, although he remained with the club until August 1947. He then moved on to Swansea Town for a year and finished his League career with Rochdale and then Lincoln City. After a brief spell playing with non-League Hyde United he became player-manager of Ards, retiring from playing in 1955 and continuing as manager until 1958. He was appointed Accrington Stanley manager in October 1958 but returned to Northern Ireland the following year to take over at Belfast Distillery and later Ards for a second spell. George senior then had a spell scouting for Stoke City before joining his son in South Africa at Hellenic FC, eventually replacing George junior as manager! George senior finished his involvement after a spell managing Glentoran. His style of play led some sections of the media to give him the nickname of Diddler.

William ECKERSLEY

Born: Southport, 16th July 1926
Died: Blackburn, 25th October 1982
Role: Left-Back
Career: High Park, Blackburn Rovers
Debut: v Spain (Rio de Janeiro) 2-7-1950 (WC)
Appearances: 17

Bill Eckersley was working as a lorry driver during the day and playing football at amateur level when he was spotted by Blackburn Rovers in November 1947, maintaining his daytime job and signing as an amateur the same month. His form for the reserves at Blackburn was sufficiently good enough for him to be offered professional forms in March 1948 and he made his League debut for the club in the final match of the season, with Blackburn already doomed to relegation. Despite the fact that Blackburn languished in the Second Division for the next ten years, Bill's performances were of such consistency that he was considered one of the

William Eckersley

best full-backs in the country and was taken with the England squad to the 1950 World Cup finals in Brazil, collecting his first cap in the final match against Spain. Whilst Blackburn battled to get out of the division Bill continued to give England great service, collecting 17 caps for his country at full level, three at B level and representing the Football League on six occasions. By the time Blackburn were restored to the First Division Bill's better days were already behind him and he therefore missed out on domestic honours, especially when the club reached the final of the FA Cup in 1960. The following year, in February 1961, his career was brought to an end by injury, although such was the esteem with which he was regarded in Blackburn that a crowd of 21,000 turned out for his testimonial match. After retirement as a player he ran a confectionery business that ultimately failed and he then worked as a taxi driver in the town before returning to lorry driving. Following his untimely death his ashes were scattered around the pitch at Ewood Park by his sons prior to a match.

Duncan EDWARDS

Born: Dudley, Worcestershire, 1st October 1936
Died: Munich, 21st February 1958
Role: Left-Half
Career: Manchester United
Debut: v Scotland (h) 2-4-1955
Appearances: 18 (5 goals)

Duncan joined Manchester United straight from school and made his debut in 1952, even before he had signed professional forms with the club. Indeed, Duncan was still eligible to play for the youth team and helped them win the FA Youth Cup in 1953, 1954 and 1955. He signed as a professional in October 1953 (Matt Busby made sure he signed for United by waiting inside his house until a minute after Duncan had reached the age of 16 and was therefore able to sign), by which time he was an established team member and one of the most gifted youngsters of his age. He became England's youngest ever cap when selected to play against Scotland having moved through the ranks of schoolboy (he won nine caps), Youth and Under-23 level (six caps). Despite a relatively short career, Duncan was capped 18 times for the full team, four times by the England B side and had won two League championship medals and a runners-up medal in the FA Cup. On the day of the Munich air disaster Duncan confidently expected that the entire team would remain in Munich overnight after two aborted attempts at take-off and sent a telegram to his landlady back in Manchester to this effect. By the time it was delivered the plane had crashed and Edwards was terribly injured, his kidneys having been crushed. After a two week battle Duncan died, some two days after Manchester United had returned to the football field. A stained glass window in his honour can be found at the St. Francis in the Priory church in Dudley, his hometown.

John Hawley EDWARDS

Born: Shrewsbury, 1850
Died: 14th January 1893
Role: Forward
Career: Shropshire Wanderers, Wanderers, Shrewsbury
Debut: v Scotland (a) 7-3-1874
Appearances: 1

By profession a qualified solicitor, being admitted in 1871, John Edwards was playing football for Shropshire Wanderers when he was called into the England side as a late replacement for John Wylie, another Shrewsbury born player. He later played for Wanderers and was also instrumental in helping set up the Welsh Football Association, serving as its first Treasurer. Indeed, in 1876 he helped Wanderers win the FA Cup against Old Etonians after a replay and the following week played for Wales against Scotland in Glasgow. John was also a more than useful cricketer, playing for Shropshire for a number of years and serving the club as secretary. He was later clerk to Shrewsbury magistrates for nineteen years until his death.

Willis EDWARDS

Born: Newton, Derbyshire, 28th April 1903
Died: 27th September 1988
Role: Right-Half
Career: Newton Rangers, Chesterfield, Leeds United
Debut: v Wales (h) 1-3-1926
Appearances: 16

After a spell playing for Newton Rangers, Willis was signed by Chesterfield during the summer of 1922 and soon established himself as a commanding right-half. Leeds United paid £1,500 to sign him in March 1925 and thus began an association with the club that was to last thirty-five years. He retired as a player during the Second World War but was retained by the club as trainer, a position he held virtually unbroken until June 1960 apart from nearly a year when he was manager (May 1947 through to April the following year). As well as his 16 full caps for England, achieved in just four years, Willis also represented the Football League on 11 occasions.

Ugochuku EHIOGU

Born: Hackney, London, 3rd November 1972
Role: Defender
Career: West Bromwich Albion, Aston Villa, Middlesbrough
Debut: v China (a) (substitute) 23-5-1996
Appearances: 4 (1 goal)

After beginning his career with West Bromwich Albion Ugo Ehiogu had made just two substitute appearances when Aston Villa paid £40,000 to take him to Villa Park in 1991. Here he has developed into one of the best defenders in the game, helping the club win the League Cup in 1996 and earning a full cap for England to go with one appearance for the B side and 15 Under-21 caps. He spent much of the

Duncan Edwards

Ugo Ehiogu

1997-98 season injured but recovered to take his place in the Villa defence, although a return to the England side proved beyond him. In October 2000 he was sold to Middlesbrough for £8 million, the move reviving his international career as he was called back into the England side in 2001 and scored in the match against Spain at Villa Park! Whilst at Middlesbrough he helped the club win the first major honour in their history, the Carling Cup in 2004, but he has again suffered a number of injury setbacks.

William ELLERINGTON

Born: Southampton, 30th June 1923
Role: Right-Back
Career: Southampton
Debut: v Norway (a) 18-5-1949
Appearances: 2

The son of a former Southampton, Middlesbrough and Sunderland professional, Bill Ellerington played schools football in Sunderland and represented England at that level and was associated with the local club as an amateur. However, he subsequently signed for his father's first club, Southampton, signing as an amateur in 1940, making his debut in the Southern Regional League and turning professional at the end of the Second World War, by which time he was something of a seasoned performer, having turned out more than 60 times for the first team. At first he competed with Alf Ramsey for the right-back position at Southampton, but just as he appeared to have made the role his, a bout of pneumonia, caught when Southampton played at Newcastle United, kept him out of the game for nearly a year. Indeed, there were fears he would be unable to resume his playing career, but Bill eventually recovered to battle once again for a regular slot in The Saints' side. By the time he returned, Alf Ramsey was also England's right-back, and with a surplus of talent in this position, Southampton decided to cash in on Ramsey's transfer value and placed their trust in Ellerington. He did not let them down either, going on to make a total of 237 appearances before he retired in the summer of 1961. By then Bill had won two caps for the full England side, one for the England B team and represented the Football League twice. At the end of his playing career Bill joined the coaching staff at The Dell under Ted Bates.

George Washington ELLIOTT

Born: Sunderland, 1889
Died: 27th November 1948
Role: Inside-Forward, Centre-Forward
Career: Redcar Crusaders, South Bank, Middlesbrough
Debut: v Ireland (a) 15-2-1913
Appearances: 3

After playing local football in the North East, George was signed by Middlesbrough in May 1909 and soon established himself as an exceptional centre-forward, representing the Football League on three occasions and collecting two full caps for England before the outbreak of the First World War. During the hostilities he guested for Celtic and returned to Middlesbrough after the war and earned his third and final England cap in 1920. He was moved to inside-forward in 1921 and retired from playing in 1925. He later worked as a cargo superintendent at Middlesbrough docks.

George Elliott

William Henry ELLIOTT

Born: Bradford, 20th March 1925
Role: Left-Winger, Left-Half, Left-Back
Career: Bradford Park Avenue, Burnley, Sunderland, Wisbech Town
Debut: v Italy (a) 18-5-1952
Appearances: 5 (3 goals)

Billy Elliott played schools and junior football in his native Bradford before being spotted by the local Park Avenue club, signing as an amateur just as the Second World War was breaking out and being elevated to the professional ranks in March 1942. A regular in the side that performed in the Second Division throughout the late 1940s, he was transferred to Burnley for £23,000, then a club record fee, in August 1951 and less than a year later had earned his first cap for England and made the first of his four appearances for the Football League. A firm favourite of the Turf Moor crowd, Billy may have struggled to score goals but created countless chances for his colleagues. His all-action displays were also to delight the crowds, although he did achieve the dubious honour of being the only player sent off for Burnley in more than twenty years after the Second World War! In June 1953 he was sold to Sunderland for £26,000, seemingly another piece of the expensive jigsaw being assembled by the so-called Millionaires team. Unfortunately, Sunderland were relegated from the First Division in 1958 without having challenged for honours, and a year later Billy left for non-League football with Wisbech Town, where he finished his playing career. Billy then became a coach and manager, serving as national coach in Libya between 1961 and 1963, scouting for Sheffield Wednesday and coaching in Germany and Brussels. He returned to Roker Park in January 1968 to take up the position of coach, which he held until December 1978 when he was appointed caretaker manager. He left Sunderland in May 1979 and the following month took over as manager of Darlington, spending four years in the position before his retirement from the game.

Robert Ernest EVANS

Born: Chester, 21st November 1885
Died: 28th November 1965
Role: Left-Winger
Career: Saltney Ferry, Wrexham, Aston Villa, Sheffield United
Debut: v Ireland (h) 11-2-1911 (scored once)
Appearances: 4 (1 goal)

Robert Evans was discovered by Wrexham playing for Saltney Ferry and signed with the Welsh club in the summer of 1905. It was here that he made his debut for the Welsh national side, appearing in the matches against England and Scotland. These performances attracted the interest of Aston Villa and he joined the club soon after. He continued to add to his tally of Welsh caps before a 1908 move to Sheffield United, and by 1910 he had 10 caps and two goals to his credit. Then it was discovered that whilst his parents were both Welsh, he had been born in Chester and was therefore qualified to play for England, prompting his selection for the match against Ireland in February 1911! Robert would go on to win four caps for England and helped Sheffield United win the FA Cup in 1915 in the so-called Khaki Final against Chelsea. He retired from playing during the First World War but later played for the Shell Mex oil company team in Ellesmere Port where he was employed.

Frederick Harold EWER

Born: West Ham, London, 30th September 1898
Died: 29th January 1971
Role: Wing-Half
Career: Casuals, Corinthians
Debut: v France (a) 17-5-1924
Appearances: 2

A member of the Stock Exchange by profession, he played amateur football for both the Casuals and Corinthians and was capped by England at amateur level on 14 occasions. His most successful period came between 1923 and 1930, when he won representative honours at both amateur and full level. He retired from playing after the 1931-32 season, by which time he had racked up well over 100 appearances for Corinthians.

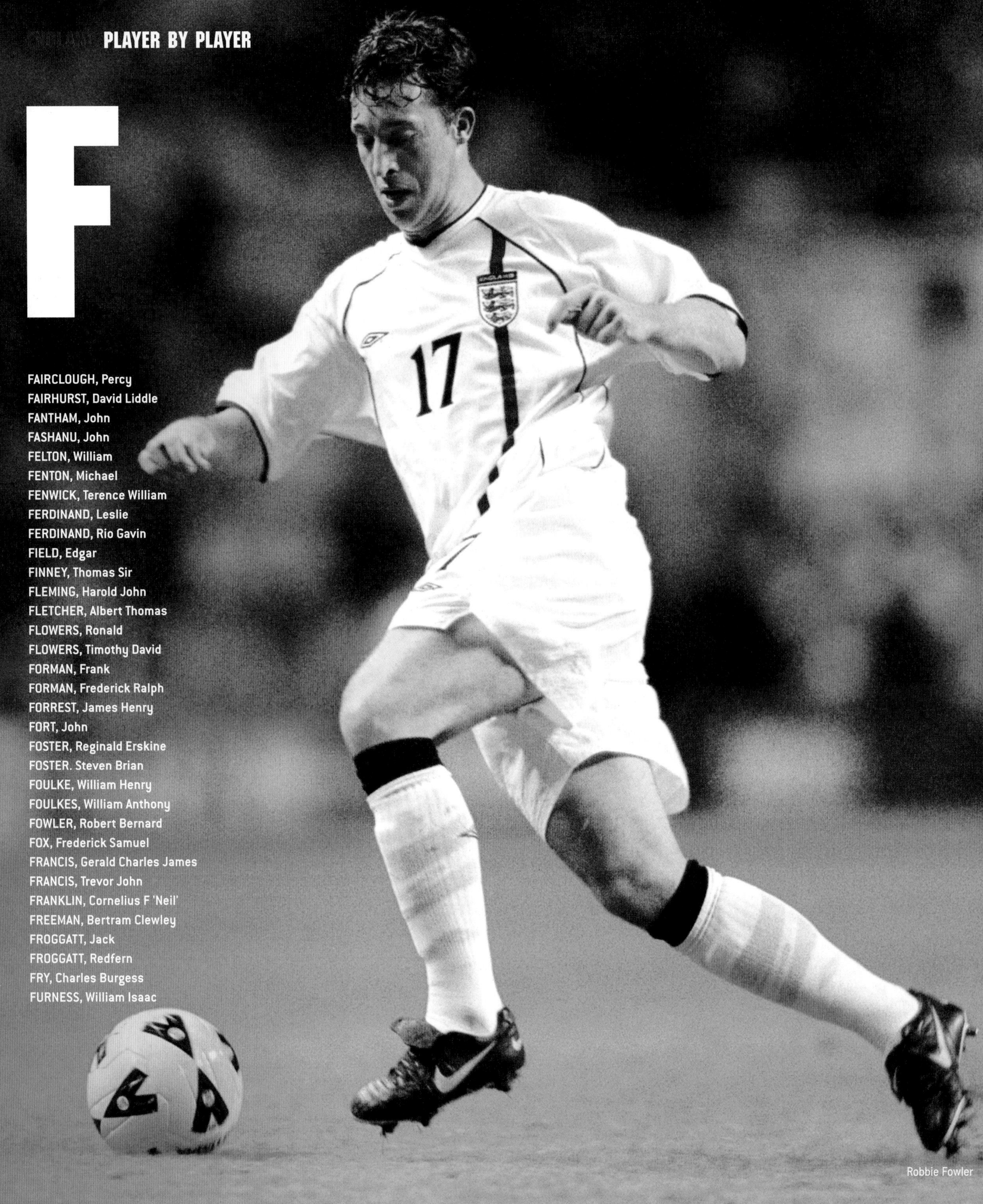

F

FAIRCLOUGH, Percy
FAIRHURST, David Liddle
FANTHAM, John
FASHANU, John
FELTON, William
FENTON, Michael
FENWICK, Terence William
FERDINAND, Leslie
FERDINAND, Rio Gavin
FIELD, Edgar
FINNEY, Thomas Sir
FLEMING, Harold John
FLETCHER, Albert Thomas
FLOWERS, Ronald
FLOWERS, Timothy David
FORMAN, Frank
FORMAN, Frederick Ralph
FORREST, James Henry
FORT, John
FOSTER, Reginald Erskine
FOSTER. Steven Brian
FOULKE, William Henry
FOULKES, William Anthony
FOWLER, Robert Bernard
FOX, Frederick Samuel
FRANCIS, Gerald Charles James
FRANCIS, Trevor John
FRANKLIN, Cornelius F 'Neil'
FREEMAN, Bertram Clewley
FROGGATT, Jack
FROGGATT, Redfern
FRY, Charles Burgess
FURNESS, William Isaac

Robbie Fowler

Percy FAIRCLOUGH

Born: London, 1st February 1858
Died: 22nd June 1947
Role: Forward
Career: Old Foresters, Corinthians, Essex
Debut: v Scotland (a) 2-3-1878
Appearances: 1

Educated at Forest School, playing for the school team he later played for both Old Foresters and Corinthians and won representative honours for Essex and London before his selection for the full England side to face Scotland in 1878. Unfortunately England lost the match 7-2 and Percy, described as a powerful if somewhat ungainly forward was not called upon again. A member of the Stock Exchange for forty years he was killed in a road accident.

David Liddle FAIRHURST

Born: Blyth, Northumberland, 20th July 1907
Died: 26th October 1972
Role: Left-Back
Career: New Delaval Villa, Blyth Spartans, Walsall, Newcastle United
Debut: v France (h) 6-12-1933
Appearances: 1

Hailing from a footballing family, David began his League career with Walsall in June 1927 and was signed by Newcastle United for £1,750 in March 1929. A member of the side that won the FA Cup in controversial circumstances in 1932 Percy was to enjoy 10 seasons of League football at St. James' Park and was a first choice regular in six of them. The outbreak of the Second World War effectively brought his playing career to an end although he did not announce his retirement until May 1946. After a spell as trainer at Birmingham City he worked in the shipyards and mines.

John FANTHAM

Born: Sheffield, 6th February 1939
Role: Inside-Forward
Career: Sheffield Wednesday, Rotherham United, Macclesfield
Debut: v Luxembourg (h) 28-9-1961 (WCQ)
Appearances: 1

The son of a former Rotherham United professional, John was spotted playing schools and junior football in Sheffield and signed amateur forms with Sheffield Wednesday in 1954, turning professional in October 1956. After struggling to establish himself at Hillsborough his opportunities for first team action improved following the departure of Albert Quixall for Manchester United and he made the most of his break. Over the course of his thirteen years at Hillsborough he helped the club win the Second Division championship in 1959 and reach the FA Cup final in 1966, as well as collecting representative honours for England at Under-23 and full level. He also represented the Football League on three occasions. Unfortunate that England were well served with inside-forwards during his career, he enjoyed an exceptional 1961-62 season, netting 24 goals for his club and collecting his only full England cap. He remained at Hillsborough until October 1969 when he was sold to Rotherham United for £5,000, finishing his playing career with Macclesfield. After his playing days were over he became a successful businessman.

John Fashanu

John FASHANU

Born: London, 18th September 1962
Role: Striker
Career: Cambridge United, Norwich City, Crystal Palace, Lincoln City, Millwall, Wimbledon, Aston Villa
Debut: v Chile (h) 23-5-1989
Appearances: 2

The younger brother of fellow footballer Justin Fashanu, John was an associated schoolboy with Cambridge United but signed professional forms with Norwich City. Unable to break into the first team with regularity at Carrow Road, John spent a spell on loan with Crystal Palace before signing full time with Lincoln City. Here he found his mark and was subsequently snapped up by Millwall in November 1984, going on to help the club win promotion to the Second Division. In March 1986 he was sold to Wimbledon for £125,000, scoring four goals that helped his new club win promotion into the First Division. One of the key players within the so-called 'Crazy Gang', John helped Wimbledon defy the odds to win the FA Cup in 1988 against Liverpool and the following year collected the first of his England caps. In the summer of 1994 he was sold to Aston Villa for £1.3 million, despite frantic efforts by Wimbledon chairman Sam Hammam to get him to stay. Unfortunately his time at Villa Park was blighted by injury and he eventually retired to concentrate on his business interests.

William FELTON

Born: Heworth, Gateshead, 1st August 1900
Died: Manchester, 22nd April 1977
Role: Left-Back
Career: Pelaw Albion, Pandon Temperance, Pelaw Albion, Wardley Colliery, Jarrow, Grimsby Town, Sheffield Wednesday, Manchester City, Tottenham Hotspur, Altrincham
Debut: v France (a) 21-5-1925
Appearances: 1

After playing non-League football in his native North East, Bill signed with Grimsby Town in January 1921 and soon became a regular within the first team. A £1,500 fee took him to Sheffield Wednesday two years later and he was a member of the side that won the Second Division championship in 1926. In March 1929 he moved on to Manchester City and spent three years at Maine Road before moving south to join Spurs. Captain of the side that won promotion to the First Division in 1933, he lost his place the following year and was allowed to join Altrincham where he finished his playing career.

Michael FENTON

Born: Stockton-on-Tees, 30th October 1913
Role: Centre-Forward
Career: South Bank East End, Middlesbrough
Debut: v Scotland (h) 9-4-1938
Appearances: 1 + 1 War appearance + 2 unofficial appearances (1 goal)

Micky was signed by local club Middlesbrough in March 1933 and thus began an association with the club that was to last more than thirty years. He was unfortunate to lose a considerable slice of his career to the Second World War and was appointed player-coach in January 1949, retiring as a player in 1951. He did, however, remain as club coach until 1966. As well as his full England cap, Micky toured with the FA side to South Africa in 1939. Outside of football he ran a newsagents in his home town of Stockton.

Terence William FENWICK

Born: Camden, London, 17th November 1959
Role: Defender
Career: Crystal Palace, Queens Park Rangers, Tottenham Hotspur, Leicester City, Swindon Town
Debut: v Wales (a) 2-5-1984
Appearances: 20

Taken on as an apprentice by Crystal Palace, Terry signed professional forms in December 1976 and went on to help the club win the Second Division championship in 1979 and collect three caps for England at Under-21 level. In December 1980 he was sold to Queens Park Rangers for £100,000, following former Palace manager Terry Venables. He added to his tally of Under-21 caps, taking his final total to 11, and helped the club to the final of the 1982 FA Cup and 1986 Milk Cup, although both of these were lost.

Terry Fenwick

DEF

An established full England player he linked up with Terry Venables for a third time in December 1987, joining Spurs for £550,000. Injuries blighted his time at White Hart Lane, including a broken leg and then a broken ankle, sustained in the warm up before a match with Portsmouth! After a loan spell with Leicester City, Terry finished his playing career with Swindon Town and later had a spell as manager of Portsmouth.

Leslie FERDINAND

Born: Acton, London, 8th December 1966
Role: Centre-Forward
Career: Hayes, Queens Park Rangers, Brentford, Besiktas (Turkey), Newcastle United, Tottenham Hotspur, West Ham United, Leicester City, Bolton Wanderers, Reading, Watford
Debut: v San Marino (h) 17-2-1993 (scored once) (WCQ)
Appearances: 17 (5 goals) + 1 unofficial appearance (1 goal)

After impressing in the non-League for Hayes, Les was signed by QPR for £15,000 in 1987, later being loaned to Turkish side Besiktas for whom he won a Turkish Cup medal in 1989. After gaining valuable experience with the Turkish club he returned to Loftus Road to resume his QPR career and became a feared striker for the club. In 1995 he was sold to Newcastle United for £6 million and continued a rich vein of goalscoring form, linking up at club level with Alan Shearer and repeating the pairing at international level. After two years on Tyneside he was reluctantly sold to Spurs for £6 million, although a series of injuries restricted his first team appearances at White Hart Lane. He recovered sufficiently to win his first domestic honour with victory in the 1999 Worthington Cup. Midway through the 2002-03 season he was allowed to join West Ham United on a free transfer to try and score the goals that would keep them in the Premiership. The club was to be relegated, however, and Les subsequently joined Leicester City on a free transfer. He later had spells with Bolton Wanderers, Reading and Watford. A qualified helicopter pilot, he also represented the country at B level and is the cousin of West Ham's Rio Ferdinand.

Les Ferdinand

Rio Ferdinand

Rio Gavin FERDINAND

Born: Peckham, London, 7th November 1978
Role: Defender
Career: West Ham United, Bournemouth, Leeds United, Manchester United
Debut: v Cameroon (h) (substitute) 15-11-1997
Appearances: 45 (1 goal)

Rio Ferdinand joined West Ham as a trainee in November 1995 and was loaned to Bournemouth in 1996 in order to gain first team experience. He returned to Upton Park and emerged as one of the brightest defensive talents in the game and with a composure that belied his relative youth. He might have earned more caps for England but for a drink-driving conviction that had manager Glenn Hoddle omitting him from the squad. He returned towards the end of the 1997-98 season with the slate wiped clean and was considered good enough to accompany the squad to France for the World Cup finals. Although he did not play during the tournament his performances at club level soon had him a permanent fixture in the England setup and attracted interest from other clubs. Midway through the 2000-01 season he was transferred to Leeds United for £18 million and helped the club reach the semi finals of the European Champions League. His performances for England during the 2002 World Cup in Japan and Korea earned him a reputation as one of the finest defenders in the world, and soon after returning from England duty he was transferred to Manchester United, this time costing his new club £31 million for his signature. He finished the season with a Premiership League medal to his name. In October 2003 he was dramatically omitted from the England squad after it was revealed he had missed a mandatory drug test after a United training session. He was later suspended for nine months, missing England's campaign to lift the 2004 European Championship (although a number of his Manchester United and England team-mates threatened to strike over the issue), although he made a triumphant return to both club and country in September of that year.

Edgar FIELD

Born: Wallingford, Berkshire, 29th July 1854
Died: 11th January 1934
Role: Full-Back
Career: Clapham Rovers, Reading, Berkshire/Buckinghamshire
Debut: v Scotland (a) 4-3-1876
Appearances: 2

Educated at Lancing College, playing for the college team, he made his name with Clapham Rovers, helping them reach successive FA Cup finals, losing to Old Etonians in 1879 and beating Oxford University the following year. He won the first of his two England caps in 1876 and had to wait five years before collecting his second. He also won representative honours with Berkshire/Buckinghamshire. By profession he was a chartered accountant.

Sir Thomas FINNEY O.B.E.

Born: Preston, 5th April 1922
Role: Right-Winger, Left-Winger
Career: Holme Slack, Preston North End, Distillery
Debut: v Northern Ireland (a) 28-9-1946 (scored once)
Appearances: 76 (30 goals) + 2 unofficial appearances (1 goal)

Tom Finney joined the local club in 1937 as an amateur and became a full professional in 1940 having completed his apprenticeship in plumbing (he was known as the 'Preston Plumber' thereafter). He spent his entire career with Preston who were seemingly cast as permanent runners-up during his time, finishing second in the League on two occasions and once in the FA Cup, being beaten by West Bromwich Albion 3-2 in 1954. Finney did win a Second Division championship medal and 76 England caps, forming

Tom Finney

a wing partnership with Stanley Matthews, as well as a cup winners' medal in 1941. Finney was also named Footballer of the Year on two occasions (1954, when his role in Preston's run to the FA Cup Final was honoured, and 1957, the first player to win the honour twice), awarded an OBE and after retiring returned to his job as a plumber. In 1963 he guested for Distillery in the European Cup match against Benfica. He was knighted in 1998 and still retains his affection for Preston, where he is club president. Although he did not win his first cap for England until 1946, he did represent the country twice in matches against Switzerland in 1945, both of which are considered unofficial England games. Such was his versatility on the wings, he won 40 of his England caps playing at outside-right, 33 playing outside-left and the remaining three at centre-forward in something of an emergency. His final tally of 30 goals therefore is an exceptional figure for a player who spent virtually his entire career playing out on the wing, but Tom Finney was an exceptional player.

Harry Fleming

Harold John FLEMING

Born: Downton, Wiltshire, 30th April 1887
Died: 23rd August 1955
Role: Inside-Right
Career: Swindon Town
Debut: v Scotland (h) 3-4-1909
Appearances: 11 (9 goals)

Spotted by Swindon playing local junior football, Harry signed with the club in October 1907 and went on to give the club seventeen years exceptional service. He began his career playing in the Southern League and was called up to represent the League on six occasions as well as helping Swindon on their various FA Cup runs prior to the First World War. At the same time his exploits attracted wider attention and he won his 11 caps for England between 1909 and 1914. He was also a member of the FA touring party on two occasions. In 1920 Swindon were admitted into the newly formed Third Division and thus Harry was able to play League football at a higher level. He retired as a player in 1924 and became a successful businessman in the Swindon area, including running a football boot factory in the town.

Albert Thomas FLETCHER

Born: Wolverhampton, 4th June 1867
Died: 1940
Role: Right-Half
Career: Willenhall Pickwick, Wolverhampton Wanderers
Debut: v Wales (h) 23-2-1889
Appearances: 2

Albert Fletcher was signed by Wolves in 1887 from Willenhall Pickwick and went on to become one of the most loyal servants the club has ever had. He remained a player until his retirement in 1891 and then joined the coaching staff, holding posts until 1920, having thus served the club for almost 35 years. As a player the highlight of his career was helping Wolves reach the final of the FA Cup in 1889 where they were beaten by Preston, although Albert collected the first of his two caps for England the same year. His playing career was brought to an end by a broken leg sustained in a match against Aston Villa at Perry Barr. He then became assistant trainer to Jack Lewis and in 1896 was promoted to chief trainer, a position he maintained until his retirement in 1920 at the age of 53 years.

Ronald FLOWERS

Born: Edlington, Doncaster, 28th July 1934
Role: Wing-Half
Career: Doncaster Rovers, Wath Wanderers, Wolverhampton Wanderers, Northampton Town, Telford United
Debut: v France (a) 15-5-1955
Appearances: 49 (10 goals)

Ron Flowers was spotted whilst playing for Edlington Grammar school and was linked to Doncaster Rovers junior side as well as representing Doncaster and Yorkshire Boys. He joined Wath Wanders, a nursery club for Wolverhampton Wanderers as an amateur in July 1950 and signed professional forms with Wolves in July 1952. He made his League debut the same year and went on to make well over 500 appearances for the first team. At club level he won three League championship medals and an FA Cup winners' medal during his time at Molineux. He also won two caps for England at Under-23 level and represented the Football League on 13 occasions. Although he played as a half-back it was a feature of his play that he loved to roam forward whenever the opportunity arose and he once scored in four consecutive games for England, a record for someone not found in the forward line. Ron remained with Wolves until September 1967 when he joined Northampton, subsequently becoming player-manager between May 1968 and May 1969. In July 1969 he left to become player-coach of Wellington Town (later to become Telford United) and he guided them to the final of the FA Trophy before resigning in October 1971 in order to concentrate on his sports shop business in Wolverhampton.

Ron Flowers

Tim Flowers

Timothy David FLOWERS

Born: Kenilworth, Warwickshire, 3rd February 1967
Role: Goalkeeper
Career: Wolverhampton Wanderers, Southampton, Swindon Town, Blackburn Rovers, Leicester City, Stockport County, Coventry City
Debut: v Brazil (Washington) 13-6-1993
Appearances: 11

Tim was taken on as an apprentice by Wolves in August 1984 and went on to make just over 70 appearances for the club before a £70,000 move to Southampton. After two brief loan spells with Swindon Town he returned to The Dell and emerged as one of the best young goalkeeping talents in the game and forced his way into the England setup, usually as understudy to David Seaman. Shortly after making his debut for England he was sold to Blackburn Rovers for £2.4 million where he linked up once again with striker Alan Shearer and helped the club win the Premier League title in 1995. He was a member of the squad for the 1998 World Cup finals in France although he had to be content with a permanent place on the bench, David Seaman holding the first team place. He later moved to Leicester City and had spells on loan with Stockport Country and Coventry City before being forced to give up playing owing to arthritic problems.

Frank Forman

Frank FORMAN

Born: Aston-on-Trent, Derbyshire, 23rd May 1875
Died: 4th December 1961
Role: Right-Half, Centre-Half
Career: Aston-on-Trent, Beeston, Derby County, Nottingham Forest
Debut: v Ireland (a) 5-3-1898
Appearances: 9 (1 goal) + 1 unofficial appearance

After playing local football Frank signed with Derby County as an amateur in 1894 but the following year linked with Nottingham Forest. He helped Forest win the FA Cup in 1898, ironically enough against Derby County, having earlier made his debut for England. He remained a player with Forest until his retirement in 1905 but served the club as a member of the committee between 1903 until his death in 1961. As well as his nine caps for England Frank also represented the Football League on two occasions. Away from the game he was a building contractor with his brother-in-law Henry Linacre, himself an England international, whilst his younger brother (below) also represented the country.

Frederick Ralph FORMAN

Born: Aston-on-Trent, Derbyshire, 8th November 1873
Died: 14th June 1910
Role: Inside-Forward, Left-Winger
Career: Beeston Town, Derby County, Nottingham Forest
Debut: v Ireland (h) 18-2-1899 (scored twice)
Appearances: 3 (3 goals)

Younger brother of Frank Forman (above) his career followed almost exactly the same path as his elder brother, playing for Beeston and having a brief spell associated with Derby County before linking with Nottingham Forest. Although he remained with Forest until his retirement in 1903, he did not get to play in the 1898 FA Cup final. Whilst his brother and brother-in-law concentrated on their building contractors business, he worked as a railway draughtsman.

James Henry FORREST

Born: Blackburn, 24th June 1864
Died: 30th December 1925
Role: Left-Half
Career: Imperial United, Witton, King's Own Blackburn, Blackburn Rovers, Darwen
Debut: v Wales (a) 17-3-1884
Appearances: 11

Jimmy Forrest began playing football at school and by the time he was 12 was captain of Imperial United. Blackburn Rovers took an interest in him after spotting him playing for Witton in 1880 and later King's Own and in January 1883 he was persuaded to sign for the club. Whilst he worked as a tape sizer in the cotton trade Jimmy made much more of an impact on the football field, helping Rovers become only the second side to have won the FA Cup three years in succession (Wanderers were the first), a feat achieved in 1884, 1885 and 1886. Jimmy scored in the first two of those finals, both of which were against Scottish side Queen's Park and won 2-1 and 2-0 respectively. His first FA Cup Final came twelve days after he had represented England for the first time at the tender age of just 19 years. The following year saw him achieve something of another first; he is believed to have been the very first professional player to have been selected by England, his status being confirmed in the match against Scotland on 21st March 1885, his fourth cap for England. The Scots objected to his inclusion in the England side since professionalism was not recognised north of the border until 1895, and Forrest was made to play in the match wearing a slightly different coloured jersey in order to differentiate him from the amateurs! At the time he was believed to be earning £1 a week from Rovers. A member of the Rovers side that were founder members of the Football League in 1888, Jimmy was still in the side when Rovers won the FA Cup again in 1890 and 1891, thus becoming one of only three players to have won as many as five winners' medals in the competition. Jimmy remained with Blackburn Rovers until October 1895 when there was an acrimonious parting of the ways; Forrest claimed the committee at Rovers had asked him to revert back to amateur status in order to save paying him a wage, a charge that was vigorously denied by the club. Jimmy Forrest went on to play for local rivals Darwen in the Second Division before retiring in 1896. He had already began making plans for his retirement from the game, becoming licensee of the Audley Arms Hotel in Blackburn but later joined a local firm of shuttle peg makers, joiners and mill furnishers. In 1906 he accepted an invitation to join the board of directors at Blackburn Rovers and during his spell on the board saw his son, also named James Henry, play for the club.

John FORT

Born: Leigh, Lancashire, 15th April 1889
Died: 23rd November 1965
Role: Right-Back
Career: Atherton, Exeter City, Millwall Athletic
Debut: v Belgium (a) 21-5-1921
Appearances: 1

Jack Fort began his professional career with Atherton in the Lancashire Combination in 1907 and switched to Exeter City in 1911. After three years he moved to London to join Millwall Athletic, thus beginning an association with the club that was to last for virtually the rest of his life. After service during the First World War, Jack returned to Millwall and won his only cap for England. Representative honours with the Southern League were followed by helping Millwall win the Third Division South championship in 1928. He finally retired as a player in 1930 and then assisted the club in a variety of capacities, including coach, groundsman, trainer and scout. Indeed, he was still working for the club up until a few days before his death.

Reginald Erskine FOSTER

Born: Malvern, Worcestershire, 16th April 1878
Died: 13th May 1914
Role: Inside-Forward
Career: Oxford University, Old Malvernians, Corinthians
Debut: v Wales (a) 26-3-1900
Appearances: 5 (3 goals)

Educated at Malvern College he won his Blue at Oxford University in 1898 and 1899 and played for both Old Malvernians and Corinthians between 1899 and 1902. He won an FA Amateur Cup winners' medal with Old Malvernians in 1902 but was equally adept as a cricketer, having won his first Blue in 1897 and going on to play for Worcestershire and eight Tests for England. He is the only man to have captained England at both sports and was named Wisden Cricketer of the Year in 1901, later serving on the MCC Committee between 1903 and 1907 and again from 1910 until his death. One of seven brothers who played for Worcestershire, the county was dubbed 'Fostershire' in some quarters. Known as 'Tip' during his various careers he worked as a stockbroker and died at an early age owing to diabetes.

Steven Brian FOSTER

Born: Portsmouth, 24th September 1957
Role: Centre-Back
Career: Portsmouth, Brighton & Hove Albion, Aston Villa, Luton Town, Oxford United, Brighton & Hove Albion
Debut: v Northern Ireland (h) 23-2-1982
Appearances: 3

After playing junior football, Steve was signed by Southampton as an apprentice but failed to make the grade as a centre-forward, being allowed to join Portsmouth in October 1975. Successfully converted to a defender, he became an integral part of the Fratton Park side before a £130,000 move to Brighton in July 1979. His form at the Goldstone Ground continued, leading to his eventual call-up for the full England side, and helping Brighton reach the FA Cup final in 1983, although Steve was suspended from the

Steve Foster

first match. He was eligible however for the replay, which Brighton lost 4-0! He was sold to Aston Villa for £150,000 and another player in March 1984 although by the end of the year he had been sold on to Luton Town for £70,000. Here he made up for earlier cup final disappointment, helping them win the Littlewoods Cup in 1988 with victory over Arsenal. In July 1989 he joined Oxford United and spent two years with the club before returning to Brighton where he finished his career in 1995.

Bill Foulke

William Henry FOULKE

Born: Dawley, Shropshire, 12th April 1874
Died: Blackpool, 1st May 1916
Role: Goalkeeper
Career: Alfreton, Blackwell Colliery, Sheffield United, Chelsea, Bradford City
Debut: v Wales (h) 29-3-1897
Appearances: 1

When Bill Foulke began his playing career in 1892 he stood 6' 2" and weighed 15 stone. By the end of the decade he had gained half an inch and 6 stone, earning him the ironic nickname Tiny although he was also known as Fatty, though not to his face! Despite his size he was an agile goalkeeper, although such was his size that forwards had to be extremely capable in order to put the ball past him. He joined Sheffield United during the summer of 1894 and made his name with the club, appearing in three FA Cup finals in four years. Two of these were won, in 1899 and 1902, and for good measure United also won the League championship in 1898. In May 1905 he was transferred to Chelsea (by which time his weight had increased still further to 22 stone), thus becoming their first League goalkeeper, although the following year he joined Bradford City where he finished his career in 1907. He also made four appearances for Derbyshire County cricket club during the 1900 season. His days after his retirement were not entirely happy, for he spent some time running a 'penny a go' show on Blackpool sands in which penalty takers were paid three pence if they could score past him. He died from pneumonia in a private nursing home in 1916.

William Anthony FOULKES

Born: St. Helens, Lancashire, 5th January 1932
Role: Right-Back
Career: Manchester United
Debut: v Northern Ireland (a) 2-11-1955
Appearances: 1

Bill Foulkes joined Manchester United in August 1951, signing from Whiston Boys Club and made his first team debut in 1952. By 1953 he was a regular and one of the renowned 'Busby Babes' who dominated English football during the mid-fifties. He survived the Munich air disaster of 1958 (although the experience put him off flying for life) and recovered sufficiently to captain United in their FA Cup Final appearance that same year against Bolton. He won a winners' medal in the same competition in 1963 and, five years later, was centre-half in the side that finally won the European Cup at Wembley. Indeed it was Foulkes' goal in the second leg of the semi final against Real Madrid that secured United's place in the final. Foulkes made 563 appearances for Manchester United, (a record since overtaken by Bobby Charlton), scoring six goals. He retired in 1969.

Bill Foulkes

Robert Bernard FOWLER

Born: Liverpool, 9th April 1975
Role: Striker
Career: Liverpool, Leeds United, Manchester City, Liverpool
Debut: v Bulgaria (h) (substitute) 27-3-1996
Appearances: 26 (7 goals) + 1 unofficial appearance

As Ian Rush approached the end of his illustrious Anfield career, Liverpool revealed his natural successor: Robbie Fowler. Quick in the penalty area and with a sharp eye for goal, Robbie scored 92 League goals in just 160 League appearances and repeated his phenomenal goalscoring rate in both domestic cup competitions and in Europe. Terry Venables gave him his first run out for England in 1996, although the stronger claims of Alan Shearer and Teddy Sheringham restricted his opportunities. In February 1998 he suffered an horrendous injury in a match against Everton which ruled him out for the rest of the season and ended his chances of accompanying the squad to France for the World Cup finals. In his absence Michael Owen had come to the fore, both for club and country. He returned to the Liverpool starting line-up early into the 1998-99 season

Robbie Fowler

and immediately linked up with Owen, forming a devastating partnership for the club that looked as though it would be repeated for the country. However, a loss of form for Liverpool prompted the Anfield club to sell him to Leeds United for £11 million in November 2001 where he began to rediscover his form. Leeds' growing financial problems saw them sell him on to Manchester City for a cut price £3 million in January 2003, although he returned to Liverpool on loan in January 2006. In addition to his seven full caps for England he has also earned one cap at B level, eight for the Under-21s and was a member of the youth side that won the UEFA Youth Cup in 1993.

Frederick Samuel FOX

Born: Highworth, Swindon, 22nd November 1898
Died: 1968
Role: Goalkeeper
Career: Swindon Town, Abertillery, Preston North End, Gillingham, Millwall Athletic, Halifax Town, Brentford
Debut: v France (a) 21-5-1925
Appearances: 1

Fred Fox won his only cap for England whilst playing for Gillingham in the Third Division South, the only player from that club to achieve full England honours. He had begun his career with Preston North End in the summer of 1921 and made three appearances for the club before being released to join Gillingham in July 1922. Almost three years later he joined Millwall Athletic and later had spells with Halifax Town and Brentford, having spent virtually his entire career plying his trade in the Third Division. He retired in 1931.

Gerald Charles James FRANCIS

Born: Chiswick, London, 6th December 1951
Role: Midfield
Career: Queens Park Rangers, Crystal Palace, Queens Park Rangers, Coventry City, Bristol Rovers
Debut: v Czechoslovakia (h) 30-10-1974 (ECQ)
Appearances: 12 (3 goals) + 1 unofficial international (1 goal)

Gerry was playing Sunday morning football in the Chiswick League when he was spotted by Queens Park Rangers and offered an apprenticeship in 1968, subsequently turning professional in June 1969. He spent some ten years at Loftus Road, helping turn QPR into a formidable First

Gerry Francis

Division outfit, and helping them finish runners-up in the League in 1975-76. After making six appearances for the England Under-23 side he was handed his first full cap in 1974 and was later appointed captain. He was on the way to establishing himself as a long term regular when he suffered a back injury playing for QPR. He remained at Loftus Road until June 1979 when he was sold to Crystal Palace for £462,000, returning to QPR in February 1981 for £150,000. A year later he had a month's trial with Coventry City and subsequently signed in a deal worth £150,000. Eighteen months later, in July 1983 he was appointed player-manager of Exeter City, although this position lasted less than a year before he was dismissed. He then spent brief spells as a player with Cardiff City, Swansea City, Portsmouth, Wimbledon and then Bristol Rovers, subsequently becoming manager of Rovers in July 1987 with a seat on the board. He returned to Loftus Road for a third time in 1991 as manager, holding the position until 1994 when he suddenly resigned, citing the board's decision to appoint Rodney Marsh into an executive role without consultation as his reason. He then took over at Spurs in place of Ossie Ardiles, holding the position until 1997 when he resigned. After a year away from the game he returned to QPR in October 1998 as manager for a second time. He later returned to Bristol Rovers before leaving the game to concentrate on his antiques business in Chertsey.

Trevor John FRANCIS

Born: Plymouth, 19th April 1954
Role: Forward
Career: Birmingham City, Nottingham Forest, Manchester City, Sampdoria (Italy), Glasgow Rangers, Queens Park Rangers, Sheffield Wednesday
Debut: v Holland (h) 9-2-1977
Appearances: 52 (12 goals)

Trevor broke into the Birmingham City first team at the age of 16 and went on to become one of the club's favourite sons. He had played schools football in Plymouth before being taken on as an apprentice at St. Andrews, turning professional in April 1971 by which time he had already featured in the first team. In February 1979 Brian Clough made him the first £1 million player when he signed him for Nottingham Forest (the actual fee was £1.15 million), and he helped the club win the European Cup at the end of his first season at the City Ground. The following season Forest retained the trophy, although Trevor was forced to sit out the final owing to injury; indeed, Clough banned Trevor from attending the final, believing the sight of him on crutches would distract his team. Trevor did play in the 1980 League Cup however, collecting a runners-up medal. He remained with Forest until September 1981 when another £1 million fee took him to Manchester City, but the transfer almost broke the club and he was sold to Sampdoria of Italy in July 1982 for £700,000. He was one of the British successes in Italy at the time (along with Ray Wilkins), going on to play for Atalanta in 1986 before returning home, this time north of the border with Glasgow Rangers. He collected a winners' medal in the Scottish League Cup in 1988 and then joined the other Rangers, Queens Park Rangers of London in March 1988. In December he became player-manager, although Brian Clough claimed he was too nice to be a manager. Whether this played on Trevor's mind and affected his judgement will never be known, but he had a number of run-ins with his players and was dismissed in 1989. He resumed his playing career with Sheffield Wednesday, subsequently becoming manager in 1991 when Ron Atkinson departed, and guided the club to the finals of both the FA Cup and League Cup in 1993. Unfortunately they were beaten in both competitions by Arsenal. He remained in charge until 1995 and then in May 1996 took over the reins at Birmingham City. He took them to the final of the League Cup in 2001 but was sacked later the same year, subsequently taking over at Crystal Palace for two years.

Trevor Francis

Cornelius 'Neil' FRANKLIN

Born: Stoke-on-Trent, 24th January 1922
Died: 9th February 1996
Role: Centre-Half
Career: Stoke City, Santa Fe (Columbia), Hull City, Crewe Alexandra, Stockport County, Wellington Town, Sankeys
Debut: v Northern Ireland (a) 28-9-1946
Appearances: 27 + 10 War appearances + 2 unofficial appearances

One of the most cultured centre-backs to have played since the Second World War, Neil was discovered playing schools football in Stoke and taken onto the ground staff at the Victoria Ground in 1936, turning professional in January 1939. The outbreak of the Second World War interrupted his career but his guest performances for Gainsborough Trinity and Stoke City were of such quality that he made 10 appearances for England in wartime internationals. With the resumption of normal League football Neil maintained his progress and was a regular in the England side, usually alongside Billy Wright, and the pair were largely responsible for England qualifying for the 1950 World Cup finals in Brazil. Before the squad departed for Brazil, however, Neil dropped a bombshell by announcing he was going to play in Colombia for the Santa Fe club, having secretly agreed a deal to join the club along with team-mate George Mountford. The move caused considerable controversy at the time, for with the maximum wage still set at £20 per week in the domestic game Neil's announcement that he had been offered £200 a week led many to the conclusion he was being greedy. With Colombia not a member of FIFA at the time there was little the football authorities could do to thwart the move. In the event the move turned into little short of a disaster, for the Santa Fe club did not pay salaries as promised and Neil's wife, expecting their second child, decided against giving birth in Bogota as originally planned and headed for home less than two months after arriving in Colombia. Neil accompanied her to New York as agreed but then found forwarding flights to England had not been booked. He and his wife then flew home together, the end of Neil's brief sojourn in Colombia. Whilst he did not expect to be greeted like a conquering hero on his return to Stoke, he certainly did not expect the club to be quite so vindictive in their actions, being suspended for breach of contract without pay until the following year. Stoke City also sought to offload him and his career never fully recovered, being sold to Second Division Hull City for £22,500 but never being selected for England again. He moved on to Crewe Alexandra for £1,250 in February 1956, finishing his League career with another £1,250 move to Stockport County in October 1957. He then joined Wellington Town as player-coach in July 1959 before moving on to Sankeys FC in July 1960. After a spell as player-manager during the 1960-61 season he retired from playing in December 1962 and flew out to Nicosia to become coach to Appoel FC in February 1963. He returned in November the same year to take over as manager of Colchester United, remaining in the position until May 1968. He then ran a public house in Oswaldtwistle.

Neil Franklin

Bertram Clewley FREEMAN
Born: Birmingham, October 1885
Died: 11th August 1955
Role: Centre-Forward
Career: Aston Manor, Aston Villa, Woolwich Arsenal, Everton, Burnley, Wigan Borough, Kettering Town
Debut: v Wales (h) 15-3-1909 (scored once)
Appearances: 5 (3 goals)
A much travelled centre-forward, Bert effectively made his name during his spells with Everton and Burnley. After playing schoolboy and junior football in Birmingham he was signed by Aston Villa in April 1904 and was signed by Woolwich Arsenal the following year. After two years he joined Everton and was finally recognised as one of the most prolific goalscorers of the day, netting 38 goals during the 1908-09 season. In April 1911 Burnley paid £800 and another player to take him to Turf Moor and despite losing a number of seasons through the First World War he scored many vital goals for the club, helping them win the League championship in 1914. He joined Wigan Borough in September 1921 and moved on to Kettering Town where he retired in 1924. As well as his five caps for England he also represented the Football League on four occasions.

Jack FROGGATT
Born: Sheffield, 17th November 1922
Died: 17th February 1993
Role: Centre-Half, Left-Winger
Career: Portsmouth, Leicester City, Kettering Town
Debut: v Northern Ireland (h) 16-11-1949 (WCQ) (scored once)
Appearances: 13 (2 goals)
Jack first came to the attention of the football world whilst serving in the Royal Air Force during the Second World War, representing the service on a number of occasions and then being offered a trial with Portsmouth in 1945. Signed immediately as an amateur, Jack joined the professional ranks in September 1945 and made his debut for the club at centre-half. He was later able to persuade manager Jack Tinn that he could play equally well at outside-left, scoring a hat-trick soon after in a match against Sheffield United. His ability to play equally well in either position was also utilised by the full England side, able to create and finish chances whilst playing in the forward line (as his debut proved) and later stopping the opposition from scoring whilst playing in the back line. A member of the Portsmouth side that won back to back League championships in 1949 and 1950, Jack remained at Fratton Park until March 1954 when Leicester City paid £15,000 to take him to Filbert Street. There he became captain and helped the club win the Second Division championship in 1957 and with it promotion back into the First Division. Jack had only three months back in the top flight however, for in November 1957 he was sold to non-League Kettering Town for £5,000, where he became player-coach and then, in January 1958, player-manager. After the club had been relegated and promoted in successive seasons, Jack opted to concentrate on playing only and remained on the club's books from September 1961, finally retiring in the summer of 1963. Jack then returned to Portsmouth where he ran a number of public houses in the area. As well as his 13 full caps Jack also represented the Football League on four occasions. Four of his England caps were won playing alongside his cousin Redfern Froggatt. His father was also a noted footballer, playing for Sheffield Wednesday, Notts County and Chesterfield during the 1920s.

Redfern FROGGATT
Born: Sheffield, 23rd August 1924
Died: 26th December 2003
Role: Inside-Forward
Career: Sheffield Wednesday, Stalybridge Celtic
Debut: v Wales (h) 12-11-1952
Appearances: 4 (2 goals)
The son of Jack Froggatt, captain of the Sheffield Wednesday side that won the Second Division championship in 1926, there was always only going to be one side that Redfern joined, and after being spotted turning out for Sheffield YMCA he duly signed with the Owls in July 1942. Redfern made 86 wartime appearances for the Hillsborough club before League football resumed in 1946 and quickly established himself as a regular, a position he was to enjoy for the next fourteen or so years. In that time he made 458 first team appearances, netting 149 goals, of which 140 were in the League and helped Sheffield Wednesday win the Second Division championship on three occasions as the club endured something of a yo-yo existence between the First and Second Divisions. He also emulated his father, captaining the side to the Second Division championship in 1958-59. His tally of goals for Wednesday is a post-war record. He made his final appearance for the club in the final League match of the 1959-60 season and had a brief spell playing for non-League Stalybridge Celtic before becoming a sales representative for an oil company. A cousin of Jack Froggatt, with whom he played at full England level, Redfern also won one cap for the England B side and turned out for the Football League once.

Charles Burgess FRY
Born: Croydon, Surrey, 25th April 1872
Died: London, 7th September 1956
Role: Right-Back
Career: Oxford University, Old Reptonians, Southampton, Portsmouth, Corinthians
Debut: v Ireland (h) 9-3-1901
Appearances: 1 + 1 unofficial appearance
Charles Burgess Fry was an all-round sportsman who excelled at any sporting activity he turned his hand to. Educated at Wadham College, where he gained first-class honours, he played county cricket for Surrey (where he was born) once and then for Sussex, being named one of Wisden's five Cricketers of the Year in 1895. He made his Test debut the same year against South Africa, going on to make 26 appearances for the national side. At football he was selected for England in the unofficial international against Canada in 1891 and made his only full appearance for the full side ten years later, as well as helping Southampton to the 1902 FA Cup Final. He also played rugby for the Barbarians and Blackheath and took an active interest in athletics, equalling the world record in the long jump in 1893 at 23 feet 6 _ inches. This jump would have been good enough to have won him the gold medal at the 1896 Olympics, at which Fry intended competing but forgot all about the games until he read about them in the morning papers! Away from sporting activities Fry had become a schoolmaster at Charterhouse after graduating from Oxford and also turned to journalism. He was named commander of the Merchant Navy ship HMS Mercury in 1908, a position he held until 1950. This prompted a move to Hampshire, for whom he also played county cricket. In 1922 he stood for election to the Houses of Parliament in the General Election at Brighton, but was beaten into third place by two Conservative candidates. The following year he stood at Banbury and failed by just 224 votes to Major Edmonson of the Unionist party. His final attempt came in 1924 when he stood at Oxford where he was again beaten by the Conservatives. After the First World War Fry served as adviser to Ranjitsinjhi, a member of the Indian delegation to the League of Nations. As Ranji was seldom in Geneva long enough to attend full meetings of the League, Fry was invariably a de facto Indian representative. He was also offered the kingdom of Albania in 1920, but whoever accepted the offer would have to spend some £10,000 per year in the country. As Fry had insufficient funds himself he turned to his friend Ranji, but Ranji was reluctant to lose the services of his advisor and refused, thus leaving the way clear for King Zog! Married to Beatrice Holme-Somner he had two children and wrote his autobiography in 1939 entitled A Life Worth Living.

William Isaac FURNESS
Born: Washington, County Durham, 8th June 1909
Died: 29th August 1980
Role: Inside-Forward
Career: Usworth Colliery, Leeds United, Norwich City
Debut: v Italy (a) 13-5-1933
Appearances: 1
Billy cost Leeds United £50 when they signed him from Usworth Colliery in August 1928 and over the next nine years got more than their money's worth. All he had to show for his club exploits however was a solitary cap for England. He was sold to Norwich City for £2,750 in June 1937, although his playing career was effectively brought to an end by the outbreak of the Second World War. Despite this he did not retire as a player until 1947, upon which he was appointed assistant trainer and subsequently head trainer, a position he held until 1955. He then continued to serve the club as physiotherapist for a further eight years.

D E F

G

Paul 'Gazza' Gascoigne

GALLEY, Thomas
GARDNER, Anthony
GARDNER, Thomas
GARFIELD, Ben Walter
GARRATTY, William
GARRETT, Thomas
GASCOIGNE, Paul John
GATES, Eric Lazenby
GAY, Leslie Hewitt
GEARY, Fred
GEAVES, Richard Lyon
GEE, Charles William
GELDARD, Albert
GEORGE, Charles Frederick
GEORGE, William
GERRARD, Steven
GIBBINS, William Vivian Talbot
GIDMAN, John
GILLARD, Ian Terry
GILLIAT, Reverend Walter Evelyn
GODDARD, Paul
GOODALL, Frederick Roy
GOODALL, John
GOODHART, Harry Chester
GOODWYN, Alfred George
GOODYER, Arthur Copeland
GOSLING, Robert Cunliffe
GOSNELL, Albert Arthur
GOUGH, Harold C
GOULDEN, Leonard Arthur
GRAHAM, Leonard
GRAHAM, Thomas
GRAINGER, Colin
GRAY, Andrew Arthur
GRAY, Michael
GREAVES, James Peter
GREEN, Frederick Thomas
GREEN, George Henry
GREEN, Robert Paul
GREENHALGH, Ernest Harwood
GREENHOFF, Brian
GREENWOOD, Doctor Haydock
GREGORY, John
GRIMSDELL, Arthur
GROSVENOR, Arthur Thomas
GUNN, William
GUPPY, Stephen
GURNEY, Robert

Tom Galley

Thomas GALLEY

Born: Hednesford, Staffordshire, 4th August 1915
Role: Right-Half, Inside-Right
Career: Cannock Town, Wolverhampton Wanderers,Grimsby Town,Kidderminster Harriers, Clacton Town
Debut: v Norway (a) 14-5-1937 (scored once)
Appearances: 2 (1 goal)

Tom Galley signed for Cannock Town after leaving school and was then offered amateur forms by Notts County. He subsequently turned professional with Wolverhampton Wanderers in April 1934 and went on to play for the club in seven different positions, including all three in the half-back line. He made over 300 appearances for the club, including wartime fixtures, and helped the club reach the FA Cup Final in 1939, although they were beaten by Portsmouth, and victory in the 1942 Wartime League (North) Cup Final against Sunderland. He remained at Molineux until November 1947 when he joined Grimsby Town, soon becoming captain of the club. His spell with Grimsby was brought to an end by injury and he was allowed to join Kidderminster Harriers in the summer of 1949 and remained with the club for a year. He then became player-coach of Clacton Town in May 1950, retiring in June 1960. His son John later played for Wolves, Rotherham, Bristol City, Nottingham Forest, Peterborough and Hereford.

Anthony GARDNER

Born: Stone, 19th September 1980
Role: Defender
Career: Port Vale, Tottenham Hotspur
Debut: v Sweden (a) 31-3-2004
Appearances: 1

Born in Stone in Staffordshire in 1980, Anthony joined Port Vale as a trainee straight from school and was upgraded to the professional ranks in July 1998. At 6' 5" he was always likely to win his duels in the air, but his accomplished ability with the ball when it was on the ground soon had bigger clubs tracking his progress. In January 2000 he was signed by Spurs for £1 million and put into the reserves in order to further learn his craft. Although not a regular within the Spurs side, he could always be relied upon whenever he received the first call and eventually his progress was noted by Sven Goran Eriksson and he was selected for the match against Sweden, in which the England manager tried out a number of fringe players. His ability to further add to his tally of caps will largely depend on whether he can form an effective club partnership with Ledley King.

Thomas GARDNER

Born: Huyton, Liverpool, 28th May 1910
Died: May 1970
Role: Right-Half
Career: Orell FC, Liverpool, Grimsby Town, Hull City, Aston Villa, Burnley, Wrexham, Wellington Town, Oswestry Town
Debut: v Czechoslovakia (a) 16-5-1934
Appearances: 2

He began his career with Liverpool, making his debut in 1930 but was transferred to Grimsby after only four games. A year later he joined Hull City and helped them win the Third Division North championship in 1933 and in February 1934 moved on again and joined Aston Villa for £4,500. His performances during the rest of the season earned him the first of two caps for England. He remained with the club until 1938 when he joined Burnley, remaining with the club until December 1945 although he guested for Blackpool during the Second World War. He wound down his playing career with Wellington Town and Oswestry Town, where he was also player-manager, later amending his duties to become player-coach. He later served Chester City as assistant trainer for thirteen years.

Ben Walter GARFIELD

Born: Burton-on-Trent, 4th April 1872
Died: 1942
Role: Left-Winger
Career: Burton Wanderers, West Bromwich Albion, Brighton & Hove Albion
Debut: v Ireland (a) 5-3-1898
Appearances: 1

Signed by West Bromwich Albion in May 1896, Ben became a popular figure in and around The Hawthorns, netting 39 goals in 115 appearances for the club, a healthy return for a winger. His form at club level was rewarded with a solitary cap for his country and in May 1902 he was allowed to join Brighton & Hove Albion. Here he helped his new club win the South League Second Division championship in 1903, the only club honour he collected before his retirement in 1905.

Anthony Gardner

William GARRATTY

Born: Saltley, Birmingham, 6th October 1878
Died: 6th May 1931
Role: Inside-Right
Career: Highfield Villa, Aston Shakespeare, Aston Villa, Leicester Fosse, West Bromwich Albion, Lincoln City
Debut: v Wales (h) 2-3-1903
Appearances: 1

Having played for Highfield Villa and Aston Shakespeare it was destined that Bill was to play for Aston Villa, joining the club in the summer of 1897, a time when Aston Villa was the dominant force in the game. He helped them win the League title in both 1899 and 1900 (he was the club's top goalscorer in this season), although he only made sufficient appearances in the latter to collect a medal, but more than made up for it with a winners' medal in the FA Cup in 1905. He remained at Villa Park until September 1908 when he joined Leicester Fosse, returning to the Birmingham area a month later when he signed with West Bromwich Albion. He remained at The Hawthorns for two years before finishing his career with Lincoln City, retiring in 1911. He later worked as a driver for a brewery company for twenty-three years until his death in 1931.

Thomas GARRETT

Born: Sunderland, 28th February 1927
Role: Full-Back
Career: Horden Colliery, Blackpool, Millwall, Fleetwood, Mayfield United (Australia)
Debut: v Scotland (a) 5-4-1952
Appearances: 3

Tommy Garrett was spotted by Blackpool whilst he was working as a miner at the Horden Colliery, turning out for the works side. Signed as an amateur in the summer of 1942, he was upgraded to the professional ranks in 1946 and made his League debut in March 1948. Initially an inside-forward when he joined the club, he was later successfully switched to full-back, so much so that he eventually forced his way into the England team, partnering Alf Ramsey. He remained at Blackpool for fifteen years, helping the club reach the FA Cup final in 1951 (where they lost) and 1953 (when they won), his devotion to the cause being proved when he played in the 1953 final with a broken nose sustained in a match the week previously. In May 1961 he was released and joined Millwall on a free transfer, having made over 300 appearances for the Seasiders. He spent only one season at Millwall, making just 12 appearances, but it was enough to help Millwall win the Fourth Division championship. Tommy then returned to the North West to sign for non-League Fleetwood and a year later went to Australia to play for Mayfield United.

Paul John GASCOIGNE

Born: Gateshead, 27th May 1967
Role: Midfield
Career: Newcastle United, Tottenham Hotspur, SS Lazio (Italy), Glasgow Rangers, Middlesbrough, Everton, Burnley
Debut: v Denmark (h) 10-9-1988
Appearances: 57 (10 goals)

He joined Newcastle United as a junior and made steady progress following his debut in 1985. Local hero Jackie Milburn claimed Paul was the brightest talent he'd ever seen in the game and in 1988 Spurs paid £2 million for his signature. He remained with Spurs until 1992 and having learned to curb his tendency for pure entertainment and upped his work rate, he was given a call-up for England in 1989 and was eventually selected for the 1990 World Cup squad. In Italy he grew in stature as the tournament progressed and ended up being acclaimed throughout the world. Back home he helped Spurs to the 1991 FA Cup final, scoring in virtually every round and then a moment of madness and a rash tackle put him out of the final and the game for nearly a year. When he recovered he was sold to SS Lazio for £5.5million, later returning to Britain to play for Scottish giants Rangers. In March 1998 he returned to England, signing for Middlesbrough in time to play in their Coca Cola Cup Final against Chelsea. On his day he was without doubt one of the most skilful midfield players ever produced, and his performances for England had seldom been less than excellent. Unfortunately, off the field distractions had caused a number of problems over the years and his omission from the squad for the 1998 World Cup finals in France brought criticism and praise in equal measure. A spell at Everton saw him a little more than a shadow of his former glories and, unable to cope with the pace of the Premiership game he moved down a division for a brief loan spell with Burnley. A much publicised spell with a Chinese Second Division club seemed to spell the end of Gascoigne's playing career, one that had promised much but delivered nowhere near its potential, but by October 2003 he was back in England and training with Wolverhampton Wanderers, looking to get himself fit enough for one last spell in the game. Although this ultimately failed, he attempted to remain in the game by coaching at Boston United and had an even briefer spell in charge at Kettering as manager before being sacked over his drinking.

Eric Lazenby GATES

Born: Ferryhill, County Durham, 28th June 1955
Role: Midfield
Career: Ipswich Town, Sunderland, Carlisle United
Debut: v Norway (h) 10-9-1980
Appearances: 2

Eric Gates

Taken on by Ipswich Town as an apprentice, Eric was upgraded to the professional ranks in October 1972. He made his debut the following year and went on to become an integral part of the exciting Ipswich side that challenged hard for the major honours in the game, helping them win the UEFA Cup in 1981 and twice finish as runners-up in the League. Injuries did not help his club or international career and in August 1985 he was sold to Sunderland for £150,000, making 181 League appearances for the Roker Park club before finishing his career with Carlisle United.

Leslie Hewitt GAY

Born: Brighton, 24th March 1871
Died: 1st November 1949
Role: Goalkeeper
Career: Cambridge University, Old Brightonians, Corinthians
Debut: v Scotland (h) 1-4-1893
Appearances: 3 + 1 unofficial appearance

Educated at Brighton College, playing for the college football team, he then went to Cambridge University and won Blue at both football and cricket in 1892. The following year he added a second Blue for cricket and collected the first of his three full caps for England at football. After graduating he played for Old Brightonians and Corinthians at football as well as cricket for Hampshire and Somerset and represented England in one Test, scoring 37 runs. For good measure he also turned out for Devon at golf! After a spell working in Ceylon as a coffee planter during the late 1890s he settled into a profession of land agent.

Fred GEARY

Born: Hyson Green, Nottinghamshire, 23rd January 1868
Died: 8th January 1955
Role: Centre-Forward
Career: Balmoral, Notts Rangers, Grimsby Town, Notts Rangers, Notts County, Notts Rangers, Everton, Liverpool
Debut: v Ireland (a) 15-3-1890
Appearances: 2 (3 goals)

Fred Geary made his reputation with Everton but had first been spotted by the club whilst playing for Notts Rangers. Everton finally landed him in 1888 and he went on to become as important to Everton in his era as Dixie Dean was some years later. He scored 86 goals in just 98 first team outings and helped the club to the League title in 1891. As well as his two caps he also collected a gold medal for representing the Football League against their Scottish counterparts in 1893. In 1894 he moved across Stanley Park to sign for Liverpool and although injury and loss of form restricted him to just 56 appearances in six seasons, he did collect a Second Division championship medal in 1896.

Richard Lyon GEAVES

Born: Mexico, 6th May 1854
Died: 21st March 1935
Role: Winger
Career: Cambridge University, Clapham Rovers
Debut: v Scotland (h) 6-3-1875
Appearances: 1

Educated at Harrow he won his Blue at Cambridge University in 1874 and later played for Clapham Rovers and Old Harrovians. His football career was effectively brought to an end in 1875 when he joined the 14th Buckinghamshire Prince of Wales regiment, retiring in 1881 having attained the rank of captain.

Charles William GEE

Born: Stockport, 6th April 1909
Died: 1981
Role: Half-Back
Career: Reddish Green Wesleyans, Stockport County, Everton
Debut: v Wales (h) 18-11-1931
Appearances: 3

He began his career with Stockport County before switching to Goodison Park in July 1930 for £3,000. Initially he was put into the Central League team but got his chance at first team action when called in for the injured Tommy Griffiths and made the position his own. Indeed, for his international debut his opposite number on the Welsh side was the same Tommy Griffiths! Whilst at Goodison he helped the club win successive League titles: the Second Division championship in 1931 and the First Division title in 1932. Unfortunately a cartilage operation later that year kept him out of the side that went on to win the FA Cup in 1933. He played his last game for the club in 1940.

Albert Geldard

Albert GELDARD

Born: Bradford, 11th April 1914
Role: Right-Winger
Career: Mannington Mills, Bradford, Everton, Bolton Wanderers, Darwen
Debut: v Italy (a) 13-5-1933
Appearances: 4

Regarded as a schoolboy prodigy, Albert was snapped up by Bradford as an amateur in 1928 and made his League debut before signing professional forms. Indeed, at 15 years and 156 days he was the then youngest ever League debutant. He signed professional forms with Bradford in 1930 and two years later moved on to join League champions Everton. In his first season at Goodison he helped the club win the FA Cup and collected the first of his four England caps. In June 1938 he was sold to Bolton Wanderers for £6,500 but saw his League career almost immediately curtailed by the outbreak of the Second World War. He retired during the summer of 1947 but was persuaded out in November 1949 to assist Darwen. As well as his four full caps for England Albert won three caps at schoolboy level and also represented the Football League once.

Charlie George

Charles Frederick GEORGE

Born: Islington, London, 10th October 1950
Role: Forward
Career: Arsenal, Derby County, Southampton, Nottingham Forest, Bulova FC (Hong Kong), AFC Bournemouth, Dundee United, Coventry City
Debut: v Republic of Ireland (h) 8-9-1976
Appearances: 1

Spotted by Arsenal whilst turning out for Islington Schools, Charlie was signed by The Gunners as an apprentice in May 1966, turning professional in February 1968. He made his debut at the start of the 1969-70 season and would go on to help the club win the Inter Cities Fairs Cup, their first major honour for seventeen years. The following season he played an even more significant part as Arsenal completed the double, scoring the winning goal in the FA Cup final against Liverpool. A mixture of injuries, loss of form and disciplinary problems restricted his club appearances for the next four years, finally brought to an end with his sale to Derby County for £80,000 in July 1975. Here he rediscovered his form and won his only cap for England before a then Southampton record fee of £400,000 took him to The Dell. A knee injury meant he made only 22 appearances for Southampton and he had a spell on loan with Nottingham Forest before going to try his luck in Hong Kong and America. He returned to the UK and played for Bournemouth and later had trials with Dundee United and Coventry City.

William GEORGE

Born: Shrewsbury, 29th June 1874
Died: 4th December 1933
Role: Goalkeeper
Career: Woolwich Ramblers, Royal Artillery, Trowbridge Town, Aston Villa
Debut: v Wales (a) 3-3-1902
Appearances: 3 + 1 unofficial appearance

Billy George made his debut in goal for Villa in a 1-1 draw with West Bromwich Albion. He had signed with the club after impressing in a trial friendly against the same opposition, a move which infringed an FA rule and earned Villa a £50 fine and Billy, along with Fred Rinder (the club's financial secretary) and George Ramsay a one month ban. Billy George recovered to become a regular for some 13 seasons, earned three caps for England, two League title medals and a winners' medal in the 1905 FA Cup final. He finished his career with Villa in 1911 and left to become a trainer at Birmingham City. He also played cricket for Warwickshire, Wiltshire and Shropshire and later worked at the Austin Motor Works at Longbridge.

Steven George GERRARD

Born: Huyton, 30th May 1980
Role: Midfield
Career: Liverpool
Debut: v Ukraine (h) 31-5-2000
Appearances: 40 (6 goals)

Initially signed by Liverpool as a trainee he was upgraded to the professional ranks in February 1998 and soon broke into the first team, alerting England manager Kevin Keegan as to his potential. Given his first cap aged 19 against the Ukraine, Steven then became a vital part of the Liverpool side that won a unique treble in 2001 of the League Cup, FA Cup and UEFA Cup and finished the season having won the PFA Young Player of the Year Award. He eventually became Liverpool captain and guided them to further success in the League cup in 2003 and two years later the ultimate prize, the UEFA Champions League. Indeed, it was this match that best epitomised Steven's worth to his club, for with Liverpool 3-0 down at half time, he scored the vital first goal in their historic comeback. This success proved that he could win the game's big honours with Liverpool and despite frequent overtures from Chelsea he remains a Liverpool player, if not the Liverpool player.

Steven Gerrard

William Vivian Talbot GIBBINS

Born: Forest Gate, London, 7th January 1903
Died: 21st November 1979
Role: Centre-Forward
Career: Clapton, West Ham United, Clapton, Brentford, Bristol Rovers, Southampton, Leyton
Debut: v France (a) 17-5-1924 (scored twice)
Appearances: 2 (3 goals)

Vivian signed as an amateur with Clapton in 1919 and retained his amateur status for his entire career, despite frequent requests to consider it by his numerous clubs. Combining his playing career with being a schoolmaster in East London, he was able to help Clapton win the FA Amateur Cup in 1924 and 1925, although by this time Vivian was also turning out for West Ham United, having first linked with The Hammers in 1923. He was to make 138 first team appearances for West Ham before signing with Brentford in February 1932. That same summer he joined Bristol Rovers for eighteen months, subsequently joining Southampton. Midway through the 1933-34 season he joined Leyton and helped them reach the FA Amateur Cup final at the end of the season, although this time he ended up with a runners-up medal. After assisting Catford Wanderers he ended his playing career in 1939 when the school he was teaching at was evacuated! By this time he had also notched up 12 caps for England at amateur level. He remained a schoolteacher until 1967.

John GIDMAN

Born: Garston, Liverpool, 10th January 1954
Role: Full-Back
Career: Liverpool, Aston Villa, Everton, Manchester United, Manchester City, Stoke City
Debut: v Luxembourg (h) 30-3-1977 (WCQ)
Appearances: 1

He joined Liverpool straight from school but failed to make the grade and subsequently moved to Aston Villa. Whilst at Villa Park he won a League Cup winners' tankard and a solitary England cap before a £600,000 transfer took him to Everton in 1979. Two years later he made the opposite move as Mickey Thomas moved from Old Trafford to Goodison Park, and although his career at Manchester United was interrupted by injury, he was a member of the side that won the FA Cup in 1985. He later played for Manchester City and Stoke City before becoming assistant manager at Darlington.

John Gidman

Ian Gillard

Ian Terry GILLARD

Born: Hammersmith, London, 9th October 1950
Role: Left-Back
Career: Queens Park Rangers, Aldershot
Debut: v West Germany (h) 12-3-1975
Appearances: 3

After playing representative football at schoolboy level for London Schools Ian signed schoolboy forms with Spurs but was taken on as an apprentice by Queens Park Rangers in March 1967, turning professional in October the following year. He formed an effective full-back partnership with Dave Clement and won five caps for England at Under-23 level. His only major club honour came in his very last season with the club as he helped QPR reach the FA Cup final where they were beaten by Spurs! He then moved to Aldershot, subsequently being appointed player-coach.

Reverend Walter Evelyn GILLIAT

Born: Stoke Poges, Buckinghamshire, 22nd July 1869
Died: Woking, 2nd January 1963
Role: Forward
Career: Oxford University, Old Carthusians, Woking
Debut: v Ireland (h) 25-2-1893 (scored three times)
Appearances: 1 (3 goals)

Educated at Charterhouse he represented the school for two years before moving on to Oxford University where he won his Blue in 1892. The following year he collected his only cap for England, netting a hat-trick in the 6-1 victory over Ireland. Despite this he never turned out for his country again, becoming one of only five players to have scored three goals in their only international appearance for England. Instead he was ordained in 1895 and served as curate at Woking and Tunbridge Wells, later becoming Vicar of Iver between 1901 and 1921 and then Rector of Sevenoaks between 1921 and 1929 before retiring to Woking.

Paul GODDARD

Born: Harlington, Middlesex, 12th October 1959
Role: Forward
Career: Queens Park Rangers, West Ham United, Newcastle United, Derby County, Millwall, Ipswich Town
Debut: v Iceland (substitute) (a) 2-6-1982 (scored once)
Appearances: 1 (1 goal)

After signing with Queens Park Rangers as both an associate schoolboy and apprentice, Paul signed professional terms with the Loftus Road club in July 1977. He made his breakthrough during the 1979-80 season, linking especially well with Clive Allen and prompting numerous offers before a £800,000 move took him to Upton Park in August 1980. He spent a little over six years with West Ham, helping them win the Second Division championship and reach the League Cup final in 1981. He moved on to Newcastle United for £432,000 in November 1986 although he and his family never fully settled in the North East and he was allowed to join Derby County for £425,000 in July 1988. He returned to London and Millwall in December 1989 but after 20 appearances moved on again, this time to Ipswich Town where he finished his career.

Frederick Roy GOODALL

Born: Dronfield, Yorkshire, 31st December 1902
Died: 19th January 1982
Role: Right-Back
Career: Dronfield Woodhouse, Huddersfield Town
Debut: v Scotland (h) 17-4-1926
Appearances: 25

Discovered by Huddersfield Town whilst playing local football he was signed by the Leeds Road club in January 1921. Playing on the opposite flank as Sam Wadsworth he became an integral part of the side that dominated the domestic game in the 1920s, winning the League title in three consecutive seasons (the first time this had been achieved) in 1924, 1925 and 1926. He did not have as much luck in the FA Cup, having to settle for runners-up medals in 1928 and 1930. He retired as a player in 1937 and was appointed trainer at Nottingham Forest, remaining with the club until 1944. He then had a four year spell as secretary-manager at Mansfield Town before accepting an invitation to return to Leeds Road in August 1949 as trainer. He served in this capacity until 1964 when he became assistant-trainer, finally leaving the club in July 1965. As well as his 25 full caps for England he also represented the Football League on eight occasions.

John GOODALL

Born: London, 19th June 1863
Died: 20th May 1942
Role: Inside-Right, Centre-Forward
Career: Great Lever, Preston North End, Derby County, New Brighton Tower, Glossop, Watford, Maerdy
Debut: v Wales (h) 4-2-1888
Appearances: 14 (12 goals)

One of the original greats of the game, John Goodall's reputation was effectively made during his success-laden spell with Preston North End. Born to Scottish parents he grew up in Scotland and began his playing career with

Paul Goddard

Kilmarnock Burns and then Kilmarnock Athletic before signing with Great Lever in 1883. He was signed by Preston during the 1885-86 season and in 1887 scored nine of their goals as they beat Hyde FC 26-0 in the FA Cup. Although Preston made it all the way to the final that season they had to settle for runners-up medals, although they returned the following year to add the FA Cup to the League championship that had already been won and so complete the first double. Although the defence gained most of the plaudits (the League was won without suffering a defeat, the cup without conceding a goal), it was John Goodall's goals that ultimately secured the trophies. He then left the club to sign for Derby County, helping them reach the FA Cup final in 1898 before switching to New Brighton Tower in the summer of 1899. A year later he joined Glossop and three years later was appointed player-manager of Watford where he subsequently opened a shop. John was also a noted cricketer, playing professionally for both Derbyshire and Hertfordshire.

Harry Chester GOODHART

Born: Wimbledon, 17th July 1858
Died: 21st April 1895
Role: Forward
Career: Cambridge University, Old Etonians
Debut: v Wales (h) 3-2-1883
Appearances: 3

Educated at Eton he played for Cambridge University but did not get awarded a Blue. Instead he played for Old Etonians and helped them reach the FA Cup final on four occasions, collecting two winners' medals in 1879 and 1882 and runners-up medals in 1881 and 1883. He returned to Cambridge University, this time as a lecturer between 1884 and 1890 and was later Professor of Humanities at Edinburgh University between 1890 and his death in 1895.

Alfred George GOODWYN

Born: India, c1849
Died: 14th March 1874
Role: Full-Back
Career: Royal Military Academy Woolwich, Royal Engineers
Debut: v Scotland (h) 8-3-1873
Appearances: 1

After service in the Royal Military Academy in Woolwich he was commissioned into the Royal Engineers as a Lieutenant and played for the regiment's football team, appearing in the very first FA Cup final in 1872 that ended in defeat at the hands of the Wanderers. The following year he won his only cap for England shortly before going with his regiment to the East Indies where he died in 1874.

Arthur Copeland GOODYER

Born: Nottingham, 1854
Died: America, 8th January 1932
Role: Winger
Career: Nottingham Forest
Debut: v Scotland (h) 5-4-1879
Appearances: 1 (1 goal)

After playing junior football in his Nottingham hometown he was signed by Nottingham Forest in 1877 but did not play his first match for the club until November 1878. He played his last in March 1880 but his impact was little short of tremendous, netting 10 goals in ten cup ties, even though he was a winger, and earning selection for his country. For some reason he gave up the game in 1880, perhaps in order to concentrate on his work in the lace trade. In 1888 he emigrated to the United States where he was killed in a car accident in 1932.

Robert Cunliffe GOSLING

Born: Hassiobury, 15th June 1868
Died: Hassiobury, 18th April 1922
Role: Inside-Forward
Career: Cambridge University, Old Etonians, Corinthians
Debut: v Wales (a) 5-3-1892
Appearances: 5 (2 goals)

Robert Gosling was one of three brothers who all excelled at sport and were to serve Essex in county affairs. Educated at Eton he represented Eton, Cambridge University and Essex at cricket and won a Blue at Oxford for football, later going on to win five caps for England. He was appointed High Sheriff of Essex in 1907, a position his middle brother William also attained in 1927. Although Robert was the only Gosling brother to earn a full cap for England, William was a member of the Upton Park side which won the Olympic Games tournament in France in 1900, although the chaotic organisation of the event meant that no one realised until many years later that the competition they had won was in fact the Olympic Games!

Albert Arthur GOSNELL

Born: Colchester, 10th February 1880
Died: Norwich, 6th January 1972
Role: Left-Winger
Career: The Albion, Colchester Town, Essex County, New Brompton, Chatham, Newcastle United, Tottenham Hotspur, Darlington, Port Vale
Debut: v Ireland (a) 17-2-1906
Appearances: 1

After an unspectacular start to his career, Albert finally started to receive recognition and reward after signing with Newcastle United in May 1904, although as he was ultimately to replace crowd favourite Bobby Templeton he never really received the acclaim at Newcastle that his abilities deserved. Despite this he was an important member of the side that won the League championship in 1905 and 1907 and reached the FA Cup final in 1905 and 1906, both of these ending in defeat. In July 1910 he was allowed to join Spurs and spent a year in the south before returning to the North East with Darlington in the summer of 1911. He finished his playing career with Port Vale before returning to Newcastle, where he was resident during the First World War. At the end of the hostilities he joined the staff at Newcastle United before his appointment as Norwich City manager in January 1921. He remained in this position until March 1926, later becoming coach to Colchester United. After he left the game he became a licensee.

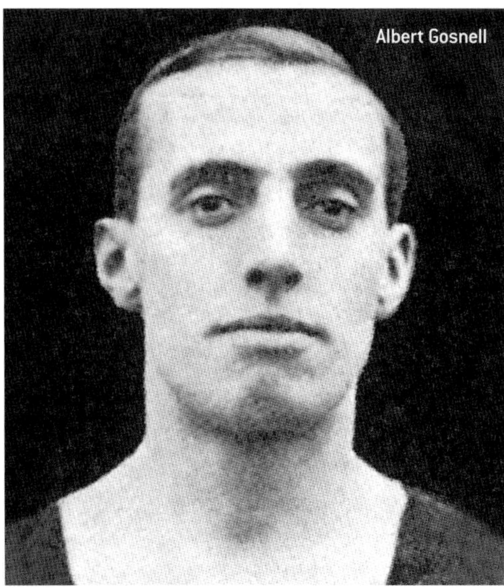
Albert Gosnell

Harold GOUGH

Born: Chesterfield, 31st December 1890
Died: 1970
Role: Goalkeeper
Career: Spital Olympic, Bradford, Castleford Town, Sheffield United, Castleford Town, Harrogate, Oldham Athletic, Bolton Wanderers, Torquay United
Debut: v Scotland (a) 19-4-1921
Appearances: 1

Harry spent three years playing non-League football before being signed by Sheffield United for £30 from Castleford Town in April 1913. He was a member of the side that won the FA Cup in 1915, the last major competition before professional football shut down for the duration of the First World War. He returned to Sheffield at the end of hostilities but was suspended by the club in the summer of 1924 for taking over a public house in Castleford in contravention of club rules. Suspended until December that year, he made plans to leave the club as soon as the suspension was lifted and promptly signed again for Castleford Town. The following year he joined Harrogate but was eventually lured back into League football with Bolton in December 1927, joining Torquay United in the summer of 1928. He retired through injury in 1930.

Len Goulden

Leonard Arthur GOULDEN
Born: West Ham, 16th July 1912
Died: 14th February 1995
Role: Inside-Left
Career: Chelmsford, Leyton, West Ham United, Chelsea
Debut: v Norway (a) 14-5-1937 (scored once)
Appearances: 14 (4 goals) + 6 War appearances (3 goals)
Len joined West Ham United as an amateur in 1931 and signed professional forms in April 1933. He remained with West Ham for the next twelve years, winning his 14 England caps during his spell with the club but unfortunately he lost half of this time through the outbreak of the Second World War. After guesting for Chelsea during the hostilities he signed with the Stamford Bridge club in December 1945 for £5,000, remaining on the playing staff until his retirement in 1950. He then spent two years on the ground staff before accepting an invitation to take over as manager at Watford, a position he held from November 1952 to July 1956. He had a second spell at Watford as coach between July 1959 and the summer of 1962 before coaching in Libya. He finished his involvement with football with a spell coaching Oxford United.

Leonard GRAHAM
Born: Leyton, 20th August 1901
Died: 21st December 1962
Role: Left-Half
Career: Capworth United, Leytonstone, Millwall
Debut: v Wales (a) 28-2-1925
Appearances: 2
After playing non-League football in and around East London, Len signed as an amateur with Millwall in the summer of 1923, subsequently turning professional in October the same year. Whilst with Millwall he developed into a commanding left-half, earning two caps for his country and helping his club win the League Division Three South championship in 1928. Unfortunately injury brought his playing career to an end in 1934, after which he was an FA coach and also coached on the Continent. He then returned to Britain and became a licensee in London before joining the Army for service during the Second World War. At the end of the hostilities he returned to his public house before going into business.

Thomas GRAHAM
Born: Hamsterley, 12th March 1905
Died: 29th March 1983
Role: Centre-Half
Career: Hamsterley Swifts, Consett Celtic, Nottingham Forest
Debut: v France (a) 14-5-1931
Appearances: 2
Tommy had a trial with Newcastle United before joining Nottingham Forest, initially on a two month trial period in May 1927 and would go on to give the club service in a variety of capacities for over fifty years. As well as his two full England caps Tommy represented the Football League twice. He retired as a player in 1944 and became club trainer, a position he retained until January 1961, subsequently becoming chief scout until March 1969. He then became a part-time scout for a little over a year, finally retiring in July 1970.

Colin GRAINGER
Born: Wakefield, 10th June 1933
Role: Left-Winger
Career: South Elmsall, Wrexham, Sheffield United, Sunderland, Leeds United, Port Vale, Doncaster Rovers, Macclesfield
Debut: v Brazil (h) 9-5-1956 (scored twice)
Appearances: 7 (3 goals)
Hailing from a footballing family, Colin became a professional with Wrexham in October 1950. He cost Sheffield United £2,500 and quickly developed into an outstanding winger with an eye for goal, earning the first of his seven full caps and also representing the Football League on three occasions. Having netted 26 goals in 88 games he attracted considerable interest from elsewhere and subsequently joined Sunderland for £7,000 and another player in February 1957. Although Sunderland were relegated from the First Division at the end of the 1957-58 season, Colin was widely regarded as having been one of their few consistent performers. He was on the move again in July 1960 for £13,000 but failed to find his form at Elland Road, being sold on to Port Vale for £6,000 a year later. After almost three years at Vale Park he finished his League career with Doncaster Rovers and also had a spell in the non-League game with Macclesfield. After football Colin was variously employed as a regional manager and sales representative as well as maintaining a career as a singer on the Northern pub and club circuit.

Andrew Arthur GRAY
Born: Lambeth, 22nd February 1964
Role: Midfield
Career: Crystal Palace, Aston Villa, Queens Park Rangers, Crystal Palace, Tottenham Hotspur, Swindon Town, Marbella (Spain), Falkirk, Bury, Millwall
Debut: v Poland (a) 13-11-1991 (ECQ)
Appearances: 1
Andy Gray began his career with non-League Dulwich Hamlet and cost Crystal Palace just £2,000 when he initially signed in November 1984. His performances in Palace's midfield earned considerable attention and he cost Aston Villa £150,000 when he signed in November 1987. A little over a year later he was back in London having signed for Queens Park Rangers for £425,000 but he remained at Loftus Road for only six months before going back to Crystal Palace. Here he rediscovered his form and helped the club to the 1990 FA Cup final (where they were beaten by Manchester United), victory in the Full Members Cup the following year and subsequently got called up by England, having previously represented his country twice at Under-21 level. In 1992 he was loaned to Spurs, the deal subsequently becoming permanent after they had paid £900,000 for his services. Unfortunately this move did not work out and after a spell on loan to Swindon he was allowed to join Marbella in Spain on a free transfer. He returned to Britain in 1995, turning out for Falkirk in the Scottish League and then came south of the border to play for Bury. A six match ban kept him out of the side for two months and when he returned he was unable to reproduce his earlier form, being allowed to join Millwall in January 1998.

Michael GRAY
Born: Sunderland, 3rd August 1974
Role: Defender
Career: Sunderland, Celtic, Blackburn Rovers, Leeds United
Debut: v Hungary (a) 28-4-1999
Appearances: 3

Michael Gray

Jimmy Greaves

Sunderland born and bred, Michael joined the local club as a trainee and was elevated to the professional ranks in July 1992. Although he scored on his debut later the same year it was to take him three years before he became a first team regular but he was an ever-present as Sunderland won the First Division championship in 1996. His club performances earned him a call-up to the Football League Under-21 representative side. In 1998 he had the misfortune to miss the vital penalty kick that denied Sunderland a place in the Premier League but the following season made amends as the club romped to the First Division title, also earning his first full cap for England. Over the next four years he was the club's most consistent player before he was loaned to Celtic in August 2003, although the move did not become permanent. Released on a free transfer in January 2004 he signed for Blackburn Rovers, subsequently spending a spell on loan to Leeds United the following year.

James Peter GREAVES

Born: East Ham, 20th February 1940
Role: Inside-Forward
Career: Chelsea, AC Milan (Italy), Tottenham Hotspur, West Ham United, Barnet
Debut: v Peru (a) 17-5-1959 (scored once)
Appearances: 57 (44 goals)

Perhaps the most prolific goalscorer of his era, Jimmy was a schoolboy phenomenon, scoring over 100 goals in a single season for Chelsea Juniors and a first team regular by the time he was 17, scoring on his debut against Spurs. Thereafter Greaves scored on every debut match; for England Youth, England Under-23, England full, AC Milan (whom he joined in 1960 for £80,000), Spurs (who paid £99,999 to bring him back home to England) and West Ham (joining in 1970). In all he scored 357 League goals, all of which were scored in the First Division, and 44 goals for England (he is England's third top goalscorer behind Bobby Charlton and Gary Lineker, although Greaves played only 57 matches), but it was Alf Ramsey's decision to leave him out of the 1966 World Cup final for which he is probably best remembered, a bout of hepatitis the season before the World Cup robbed him of a yard or two of pace and contributed to his grabbing only 15 League goals that season, his worst tally ever. After retiring as a player (although he made a brief comeback with non-League Barnet in the seventies) he slipped into a well-publicised alcoholic state before emerging with a successful career in journalism and broadcasting, forming a partnership with former Liverpool and Scotland striker Ian St. John.

Frederick Thomas GREEN

Born: 21st June 1851
Died: 6th July 1928
Role: Half-Back
Career: Oxford University, Wanderers, Middlesex
Debut: v Scotland (a) 4-3-1876
Appearances: 1

Educated at Winchester College he represented Oxford University and helped them win the FA Cup in 1874. He later played for Wanderers, where he won further FA Cup winners' medals in 1877 and 1878, the first of these against Oxford University! As well as his one full cap for England he also represented Middlesex. Called to the bar in 1877 he left the legal profession in 1880 and became an Inspector of Schools.

George Henry GREEN

Born: Leamington, 2nd May 1901
Died: 1980
Role: Left-Half
Career: Leamington Town, Nuneaton Borough, Sheffield United, Leamington Town
Debut: v France (a) 21-5-1925
Appearances: 8

After playing junior football in and around his native Leamington he first came to prominence whilst playing for Nuneaton Borough, being selected to play for the Birmingham FA against Scotland in a junior international and attracting the interest of a number of bigger clubs. He subsequently signed for Sheffield United in May 1923 and helped the club win the FA Cup in 1925 against Cardiff City. A permanent fixture in the United side for more than ten years, he returned to Leamington Town in July 1934 where he finished his playing career. He also represented the Football League on three occasions and after his retirement from playing returned to his earlier profession of turner and fitter.

Robert Paul GREEN

Born: Chertsey, 18th January 1980
Role: Goalkeeper
Career: Norwich City
Debut: v Colombia (USA) 31-5-2005
Appearances: 1

A product of the Norwich youth scheme, Robert rose through the club's ranks to become a professional in July 1997 and made his League debut during the 1998-99 season. He established himself as the regular 'keeper for his club in the 2001-02 season and was a vital member of the side that won the 2004 First Division championship. Although Norwich struggled in their only season in the

Robert Green

Premiership, Robert's performances earned him a regular call-up to the England squad and he was rewarded with his first cap during the summer tour of the United States in 2005.

Ernest Harwood GREENHALGH

Born: Mansfield, 1849
Role: Full-Back
Career: Notts County
Debut: v Scotland (a) 30-11-1872
Appearances: 2

Ernest was a player with Notts County between 1867 and 1883 and appeared in England's first two official international matches, thus being the club's first international representative. After retiring from playing he played an important part in the development of the game, being secretary to Greenhalgh's FC in Mansfield. He was also the proprietor of the Field Mill at Mansfield, which was the home of Mansfield Mechanics FC until becoming the new home of Mansfield Town FC in 1916.

Brian GREENHOFF

Born: Barnsley, 28th April 1953
Role: Defender
Career: Manchester United, Leeds United, Rochdale
Debut: v Wales (a) 8-5-1976
Appearances: 18 + 1 unofficial international

The younger brother of Jimmy Greenhoff, Brian began his career as an apprentice at Manchester United in August 1968 and was upgraded to the professional ranks in June 1970. He made his League debut in 1973 and went on to become a regular member of the side that won the Second Division championship in 1975 and then reached successive FA Cup finals, collecting a runners-up medal in 1976 and a winners' medal the following year. He was also a non-playing substitute in 1979 when United were again runners-up. He moved on to Leeds United for £350,000 in August 1979 but his time at Elland Road was blighted by injuries and in November 1983 he linked up with his brother again at Rochdale, where Jimmy was manager. As well as 18 full caps Brian also won 4 caps at Under-23 level. Brian retired in 1984 and later became a sales representative for a sports goods wholesaler.

Doctor Haydock GREENWOOD

Born: Blackburn, 31st October 1860
Died: 3rd November 1951
Role: Full-Back
Career: Blackburn Rovers, Corinthians
Debut: v Ireland (a) 18-2-1882
Appearances: 2

Educated at Malvern College and a member of the college team between 1878 and 1879, Doctor (his real name, not a medical qualification) went on to play for Blackburn Rovers and was a member of the Corinthians committee at the time of their formation in 1882.

John Charles GREGORY

Born: Scunthorpe, 11th May 1954
Role: Defender
Career: Northampton Town, Aston Villa, Brighton & Hove Albion, Queens Park Rangers, Derby County, Portsmouth, Plymouth Argyle, Bolton Wanderers
Debut: v Australia (a) 12-6-1983
Appearances: 6

A graduate from the Northampton Town youth scheme, John signed professional forms in January 1973 and quickly became established as a defender of great potential. He was sold to Aston Villa in June 1977 for £40,000 and then on to Brighton two years later for £250,000 where he helped the club maintain their First Division status. His career began to take off however following a £300,000 move to QPR in June 1981, helping the club reach the FA Cup the following season and the Second Division championship in 1983, the same year he won the first of his six caps for England. A £100,000 deal took him to Derby County in 1985 where he won a further Second Division championship medal in 1987. Appointed assistant coach at Portsmouth in 1988 he became player-manager in July 1989 although he left the club at the end of the year and had non-contract spells at Plymouth and Bolton. He later coached at Leicester City and Aston Villa before returning to management with Wycombe Wanderers before taking over at Aston Villa in 1998. He remained at Villa Park until 2002 and then had a spell in charge at another of his former clubs, Derby County.

Brian Greenhoff

John Gregory

Arthur GRIMSDELL

Born: Watford, 23rd March 1894
Died: Watford, 12th March 1963
Role: Left-Half
Career: Watford St. Stephens, Watford, Tottenham Hotspur, Clapton Orient
Debut: v Wales (h) 15-3-1920
Appearances: 6 + 2 War appearances (2 goals)

Arthur played his schools football at centre-forward and represented England at schoolboy level in this position in 1908. The following year he signed as an amateur with Watford, where they converted him to centre-half and offered him professional forms in November 1911. Less than four months later he was sold to Spurs for £350 and made his first few appearances at centre-half. Peter McWilliam, appointed manager in December 1912 realised that Arthur might be better suited for a more adventurous wing-half position and slotted him into the left side of the field. Arthur proved an instant success in this position and in 1913, still only aged 19 years, took part in an international trial match for England. The outbreak of the First World War saw him enlist almost immediately and play little football during the four years that followed, but upon his return in 1919 he was eager to make up for lost time. He helped Spurs win the Second Division title in 1919-20, scoring 14 goals from the wing-half position and also earning his first cap for England. The following year he captained Spurs to victory in the FA Cup Final (he collected the cup from the King, was photographed outside Stamford Bridge

Arthur Grimsdell

with the trophy and then got on a train back home to Watford!) and was widely reckoned to have been one of the most complete wing-halves the game has ever seen, perhaps only second to Duncan Edwards. In October 1925 he broke his leg, keeping him out of action until April 1927, but he was not the same player when he returned and in April 1929 was released to join Clapton Orient, later serving that club as secretary-manager. He held the post for a year before turning to coaching schoolboys. He later served both Orient and Watford as a director and ran a sports outfitters business in Romford. He was also a noted cricketer, playing for Hertfordshire between 1922 and 1947 and appearing in one first class match.

Arthur Thomas GROSVENOR

Born: Netherton, 22nd November 1908
Died: 31st October 1972
Role: Inside-Right
Career: Stourbridge, Birmingham, Sheffield Wednesday, Bolton Wanderers
Debut: v Northern Ireland (a) 14-10-1933 (scored once)
Appearances: 3 (2 goals)

The brother of fellow professional Percy Grosvenor, Tommy began his professional career with Birmingham in March 1928 and established a reputation as a valuable provider of goalscoring chances, even if he was not a prolific goalscorer himself. After winning three caps for England and representing the Football League on one occasion, Tommy was released to join Sheffield Wednesday in February 1936, spending a little over a year at Hillsborough before moving on to join Bolton in May 1937. He retired as a player during the Second World War.

William GUNN

Born: Nottingham, 4th December 1858
Died: 29th January 1921
Role: Forward
Career: Nottingham Forest, Notts County
Debut: v Scotland (a) 15-3-1884
Appearances: 2 (1 goal)

Billy made just one appearance for Nottingham Forest during 1881 and then signed for Notts County where he was a regular in the side for almost nine years. In 1890 he had his amateur status restored and then continued to give service to a number of clubs in the area. He also joined the board of directors at Notts County and remained on the board until his death, at which time he had become vice-president of the club. Billy was also an excellent cricketer, playing for Notts between 1880 and 1904 and representing England in 11 tests, scoring a total of 392 runs. Billy also became the first former professional to serve on a County committee, being elected to the Nottinghamshire committee soon after his retirement. He was also co-founder of the sports good firm Gunn & Moore in 1885 and was named Wisden Cricketer of the Year in 1890.

Stephen Andrew GUPPY

Born: Winchester, 29th March 1969
Role: Midfield
Career: Wycombe Wanderers, Newcastle United, Port Vale, Leicester City, Glasgow Celtic, Leicester City, Leeds United, Stoke City, Wycombe Wanderers
Debut: v Belgium (h) 10-10-1999
Appearances: 1

Signed by Wycombe Wanderers from local side Colden Common, Steve helped the club win the FA Trophy twice and the GM Vauxhall Conference before a £150,000 move took him to Newcastle United in August 1994. Unable to break into the first team he was sold on to Port Vale for £225,000 in November the same year and set about reviving his career. A £950,000 move saw him join Leicester City in February 1997 where he was switched from the left wing to a more midfield role. This new position saw his career reach even greater heights, helping the club win the League Cup in 2000 and him his only cap for England. Although a regular in the Leicester side under manager Martin O'Neill, he struggled to gain selection under Peter Taylor and in August 2001 linked up with O'Neill at Celtic in a deal worth £350,000. There he won a Scottish Premier Division championship medal in 2002 before being released on a free transfer in January 2004. A short spell at old club Leicester City was followed by even shorter spells with Leeds United and Stoke City before he returned to Wycombe Wanderers in November 2004.

Tommy Grosvenor

Steve Guppy

Robert GURNEY

Born: Silksworth, 13th October 1907
Role: Centre-Forward
Career: Bishop Auckland, Sunderland
Debut: v Scotland (a) 6-4-1935
Appearances: 1 + 1 unofficial appearance (1 goal)

After playing junior football in the North East he was signed by Sunderland in May 1925 and became one of the club's greatest ever goalscorers, netting 228 goals in 388 League and cup appearances and helping them win the First Division championship in 1936 and the FA Cup the following year. Despite this prowess at club level he won only one full England cap, injuries (he suffered two broken legs) and the likes of Ted Drake restricting his international opportunities. He retired in May 1946 and promptly joined the training staff at Roker Park, subsequently having a spell in charge at non-League Horden Colliery before taking over at Peterborough United in February 1950. He returned to the North East in March 1952 as manager of Darlington, a position he held until October 1957, and after scouting for Leeds United and a spell managing Horden Colliery for a second time, he finished his football career as manager of Hartlepool United, a position he held between April 1963 and January 1964.

H

Glenn Hoddle

HACKING, John
HADLEY, Harry
HAGAN, James
HAINES, John T W
HALL, Albert Edward
HALL, George William
HALL, Jeffrey James
HALSE, Harold James
HAMMOND, Henry Edward Denison
HAMPSON, James
HAMPTON, Harry
HANCOCKS, John
HAPGOOD, Edris Albert
HARDINGE, Harold Thomas Walter
HARDMAN, Harold Payne
HARDWICK, George Francis M
HARDY, Henry
HARDY, Samuel
HARFORD, Michael Gordon
HARGREAVES, Frederick William
HARGREAVES, John
HARGREAVES, Owen
HARPER, Edward Cashfield
HARRIS, Gordon
HARRIS, Peter Philip
HARRIS, Stanley Schute
HARRISON, Alban Hugh
HARRISON, George
HARROW, Jack Harry
HART, Ernest Arthur
HARTLEY, Frank
HARVEY, A
HARVEY, James Colin
HASSALL, Harold William
HATELEY, Mark Wayne
HAWKES, Robert Murray
HAWORTH, George
HAWTREY, John Purvis
HAYGARTH, Edward Brownlow
HAYNES, John Norman
HEALLESS, Henry
HECTOR, Kevin James
HEDLEY, George Albert
HEGAN, Kenneth Edward
HELLAWELL, Michael Stephen
HENDRIE, Lee
HENFREY, Arthur George
HENRY, Ronald Patrick
HERON, Charles Francis William
HERON, George Hubert Hugh
HESKEY, Emile
HIBBERT, William
HIBBS, Henry Edward
HILL, Frederick
HILL, Gordon Alec
HILL, John Henry
HILL, Richard Henry
HILL, Ricky Anthony
HILLMAN, John
HILLS, Arnold Frank
HILSDON, George Richard
HINCHCLIFFE, Andrew George
HINE, Ernest William
HINTON, Alan Thomas
HIRST, David Eric
HITCHENS, Gerald Archibald
HOBBIS, Harold Henry Frank
HODDLE, Glenn
HODGE, Stephen Brian
HODGETTS, Dennis
HODGKINSON, Alan
HODGSON, Gordon
HODKINSON, Joseph
HOGG, William
HOLDCROFT, George Henry
HOLDEN, Albert Douglas
HOLDEN, George Henry
HOLDEN-WHITE, Charles Henry
HOLFORD, Thomas
HOLLEY, George H
HOLLIDAY, Edwin
HOLLINS, John William
HOLMES, Robert
HOLT, John
HOPKINSON, Edward
HOSSACK, Anthony Henry
HOUGHTON, William Eric
HOULKER, Albert Edward 'Kelly'
HOWARTH, Robert Henry
HOWE, Donald
HOWE, John Robert
HOWELL, Leonard Sidgwick
HOWELL, Rabbi
HOWEY, Stephen Norman
HUDSON, Alan Anthony
HUDSON, John
HUDSPETH, Francis Carr
HUFTON, Arthur Edward
HUGHES, Emlyn Walter
HUGHES, Lawrence
HULME, Joseph Harold Anthony
HUMPHREYS, Percy
HUNT, George Samuel
HUNT, Rev. Kenneth Reginald Gunnery
HUNT, Roger
HUNT, Steven
HUNTER, John
HUNTER, Norman
HURST, Geoffrey Charles Sir M.B.E.

John HACKING

Born: Blackburn, 22nd December 1897
Died: Accrington, 1st June 1955
Role: Goalkeeper
Career: Blackpool, Fleetwood, Oldham Athletic, Manchester United, Accrington Stanley
Debut: v Northern Ireland (h) 22-10-1928
Appearances: 3

After playing local football in Blackburn he was signed by Blackpool in December 1919 but struggled to break into the first team, subsequently leaving the League game in the summer of 1925 in order to sign for non-League Fleetwood. Here he re-discovered his form and was promptly snapped up by Oldham Athletic in early 1926, going on to represent the Football League twice and win three caps for England. He remained at Boundary Park until March 1934 when he signed for Manchester United, spending a little over a year at Old Trafford before taking over as player-manager at Accrington Stanley in May 1935. He retired from playing in October the same year and later joined Barrow as secretary-manager in May 1949, a position he retained until his death.

Harold HADLEY

Born: West Bromwich, 1878
Role: Wing-Half
Career: Halesowen, West Bromwich Albion, Aston Villa, Nottingham Forest, Southampton
Debut: v Ireland (h) 14-2-1903
Appearances: 1

Spotted playing for Halesowen, Harry signed for West Bromwich Albion in February 1897 and went on to help the club win the Second Division championship in 1902. In February 1905 he moved across the city of Birmingham to sign for Aston Villa and spent a year at Villa Park before joining Nottingham Forest in April 1906. The following summer he moved south to join Southampton and later had a spell with Croydon Common before finishing his playing career back at Halesowen. He then moved into management, being in charge at Merthyr Town on four occasions and also Chesterfield, Abedare Athletic, Gillingham and Bangor City before retiring from the game in 1936.

James HAGAN

Born: Washington, County Durham, 21st January 1918
Died: 27th February 1998
Role: Inside-Forward
Career: Liverpool, Derby County, Sheffield United
Debut: v Denmark (a) 26-9-1948
Appearances: 1 + 16 War appearances (13 goals)

The son of former professional footballer Alf Hagan, who had played for Newcastle United, Cardiff City and Tranmere Rovers during the 1920s, Jimmy signed as an amateur with Liverpool in January 1932 after playing schools football in Washington and collecting two caps for England at schoolboy level. The following year he left for Derby County, signing again as an amateur during the 1933 close season and being upgraded to the professional ranks in 1936. Unable to settle at Derby he was sold to Sheffield United for £2,500 in November 1938. His arrival galvanised the Bramall Lane club, helping them win promotion to the First Division in 1939 (at the expense of city rivals Sheffield Wednesday) and on the verge of establishing themselves as a major force in the top flight when the

Jimmy Hagan

Second World War broke out. Jimmy Hagan's development and progress as an inside-forward can be gauged by the fact he was selected for his country on 16 occasions during the war, scoring 13 goals, one of which was netted after only 50 seconds against Scotland. When the Football League resumed in 1946 Jimmy was still a key member of the Sheffield United side and returned to the England side in 1948 for his only cap. In 1953 he helped Sheffield United win the Second Division title (they had been relegated back into the division at the end of the 1948-49 season), although they were subsequently relegated again in 1955-56. He retired from playing in 1958 having made over 400 appearances for Sheffield United and had also represented the Football League on three occasions. He took over as manager of Peterborough United, taking them into the Football League in 1960 and the Fourth Division title at the end of the first season, although Jimmy was dismissed in October 1962, subsequently taking over at West Bromwich Albion in April 1963. He remained in charge for four years, guiding them to the League Cup in 1965 and the final of the same competition two years later. He left Albion in May 1967 and spent a spell scouting for Manchester City before accepting an invitation to take over at Portuguese giants Benfica in March 1970, winning the League title three seasons on the trot and the double in 1972. He left Benfica in September 1973 and coached the Kuwaiti national side between 1974 and 1976, later returning to Portugal to take over at Sporting Lisbon and Oporto.

John Thomas William HAINES

Born: Wickhamford, 24th April 1920
Died: 19th March 1987
Role: Inside-Forward
Career: Evesham Town, Cheltenham Town, Liverpool, Swansea Town, Leicester City, West Bromwich Albion, Bradford Park Avenue, Rochdale, Chester, Wellington Town, Kidderminster Harriers, Evesham Town
Debut: v Switzerland (h) 1-12-1948 (scored twice)
Appearances: 1 (2 goals)

After playing schools football in his native Evesham, Jack signed with the then non-League Cheltenham Town before joining Liverpool during the 1937-38 season. Released before he had appeared for the club, Jack moved to Vetch Field to join Swansea Town during the summer of 1939. The outbreak of the Second World War would delay his League debut for the club until 1946, but during the war he guested for Bradford Park Avenue, Doncaster Rovers, Lincoln City, Notts County and Wrexham and also represented the Royal Air Force on a number of occasions. Upon the resumption of League football in 1946 Jack spent a season with Swansea before moving on to Leicester City, where manager Johnny Duncan was uncertain of his best position and tried him out in five in an attempt to work it out! In March 1948, having failed to make one position his own, he was transferred to West Bromwich Albion in a swap deal with Peter McKennan. As well as helping West Bromwich Albion win promotion to the First Division, Jack earned his only cap for England before setting off on his travels again in December 1949, Bradford Park Avenue paying £10,000 for his services. Bradford were to be relegated into the Third Division North during Jack's time with the club and in September 1953 he was sold to Rochdale for £2,000, remaining at Spotland a little under two years before finishing his League career with a move to Chester City in July 1955. Jack dropped out of League football in the summer of 1957, subsequently turning out for Wellington Town, Kidderminster Harriers and Evesham before retiring during the 1959-60 season. Despite his constant travels, Jack managed to rack up 340 League appearances for his various clubs, scoring 94 goals, figures that might have been greater had he not suffered from a number of injuries during his career.

Albert Edward HALL

Born: Wordsley, 1882
Died: 17th October 1957
Role: Left-Winger
Career: Stourbridge, Aston Villa, Millwall Athletic
Debut: v Ireland (a) 12-2-1910
Appearances: 1

Signed by Aston Villa in the summer of 1903 after being spotted whilst playing for Stourbridge, Albert formed an extremely effective left-wing partnership with fellow England international Joe Bache. Together they helped the club win the FA Cup in 1905 and the League championship in 1910, Albert remaining at Villa Park until 1913 when he moved south to join Millwall Athletic. He retired from playing during the First World War, subsequently enlisting in the 5th South Staffordshire Regiment and being badly gassed during the hostilities. At the end of the war he returned to Stourbridge and became an enamel ware manufacturer until ill health forced his retirement.

Willie Hall

George William HALL
Born: Newark, 12th March 1912
Died: Newark, 22nd May 1967
Role: Inside-Forward
Career: Notts County, Tottenham Hotspur
Debut: v France (h) 6-12-1933
Appearances: 10 (9 goals) + 2 War appearances

Willie Hall was spotted by Notts County whilst playing for a works side and joined the Meadow Lane club in November 1930, helping the club to the Third Division (South) title at the end of his first season at the club. His impact did not go unnoticed by bigger clubs and in December 1932 he was transferred to Spurs, although Notts County were so sure he was destined for an international career they inserted a clause in his contract which stipulated Spurs had to pay an additional £500 when and if he was capped. They had to wait a little over twelve months for their money, for Willie was subsequently capped by England against France in 1933. At Spurs he proved an instant success and more than made up for the loss of George Greenfield through a broken leg. Despite his early form however, further England honours did not come for another four years and he was slowly brought back to the side, first being selected for the Football League against their Irish counterparts in 1937. Willie Hall obviously had some affection for the Irish, for the following year, in October 1938, he scored five goals in the 7-0 win at Old Trafford, including a hat-trick within three and a half minutes. During the war he made a further two appearances for England before a serious leg disease forced him to retire in February 1944 and he subsequently had the lower parts of both legs amputated. Willie tried to make light of his disability, accepting an invitation to become coach at Clapton Orient in August 1945 and taking over as manager the following month, but two months later accepted that his ability to do the job properly was being hampered and resigned. He later had spells in charge of non-League clubs Chelmsford City and Chingford Town and was also a publican in East London for many years despite being affected by poor health.

Jeffrey James HALL
Born: Scunthorpe, 7th September 1929
Died: 4th April 1959
Role: Right-Back
Career: Wilsden Bank Top, Birmingham City
Debut: v Denmark (a) 2-10-1955
Appearances: 17

Jeff was an amateur winger on the books of Bradford Park Avenue before being taken on by Birmingham City in May 1950 and successfully converted to wing-half. After helping Birmingham City win the Second Division championship in 1955, Jeff collected the first of his 17 full caps for England later the same year and ended the season with an FA Cup runners-up medal. He went on to make 265 appearances for City, had represented the Football League on four occasions and won an England B cap when his life was cut tragically short after contracting polio and dying at the age of 29. A memorial scoreboard and clock were erected at St. Andrew's to commemorate his career.

Harold James HALSE
Born: Leytonstone, 1st January 1886
Died: April 1951
Role: Inside-Right
Career: Newportians, Wanstead, Barking Town, Clapton Orient, Southend United, Manchester United, Aston Villa, Chelsea, Charlton Athletic
Debut: v Austria (a) 1-6-1909 (scored twice)
Appearances: 1 (2 goals)

After a remarkable two seasons as a junior with Southend United, during which he scored 200 goals, Harold was snapped up by Manchester United for £350 in March 1908. Although he didn't score with the same regularity at Old Trafford, he was one of the most dangerous forwards of his age and would go on to score six goals in the FA Charity Shield match against Swindon. He won a League championship and FA Cup winners' medal whilst at United, and was sold to Aston Villa for £1,200 in 1912, adding a second FA Cup winners' medal at the end of his first season at Villa Park. His third appearance in the final came in 1915 when he was playing for Chelsea, although this time he had to settle for a runners-up medal. At the end of the First World War he returned to Chelsea, subsequently moving on to Charlton in 1921, retiring in 1923 and then scouting for the club for a further two years.

Henry Edward Denison HAMMOND
Born: Priston, 26th November 1866
Died: 16th June 1910
Role: Half-Back
Career: Oxford University, Corinthians
Debut: v Scotland (h) 13-4-1889
Appearances: 1

Educated at Lancing College and a member of the college team from 1883 to 1885, captaining the side in his final year, he went to Oxford University and excelled at virtually all sporting activities, collecting a Blue in athletics in 1886, 1887 and 1889. He also collected a Blue for football in 1888 and 1889 and later played for Lancing Old Boys and the Corinthians. A master at Blair House School in 1889 and then at Edinburgh Academy between 1890 and 1899 he became Director General of Education for Rhodesia in 1900. He was forced to leave the post after less than twelve months owing to ill health and was unable to undertake regular work for the rest of his life. His time, however, was taken up travelling around Somerset and Dorset collecting folk songs with his brother Robert on behalf of the Folk Song Society.

James HAMPSON
Born: Little Hulton, 23rd March 1906
Died: Fleetwood, 10th January 1938
Role: Centre-Forward
Career: Walkden Park, Little Hulton St. Johns, Nelson, Blackpool
Debut: v Northern Ireland (a) 20-10-1930 (scored once)
Appearances: 3 (5 goals)

After a trial with Manchester United, Jimmy signed with Nelson in the summer of 1925 and quickly became noted as a prolific goalscorer. Blackpool paid £1,250 to take him to Bloomfield Road in October 1927 and his goalscoring exploits continued, helping Blackpool win the Second Division championship in 1930 during which he scored 45 goals, still the club's record, and made the first of his four appearances for the Football League. Jimmy was to find the net on 246 occasions whilst in Blackpool's League colours, another club record, and would have continued to add to that tally but for an incident in which a yacht he was sailing collided with a trawler off the coast of Fleetwood which resulted in his drowning.

Harry HAMPTON
Born: Wellington, 21st April 1885
Died: Rhyl, 15th March 1963
Role: Centre-Forward
Career: Wellington Town, Aston Villa, Birmingham, Newport County, Wellington Town
Debut: v Wales (h) 17-3-1913 (scored once)
Appearances: 4 (2 goals)

Harry was taken on by Aston Villa in May 1904 and made an immediate impact with the club, helping them win the FA Cup in 1905. He later added to this tally with a second FA

Harry Hampton

Cup winners' medal in 1913 and also helped win the First Division championship in 1910 as well as making three appearances for the Football League. During the First World War he guested for Stoke and in February 1920 he joined Birmingham, helping them win the Second Division championship in 1921. The following year he joined Newport County, where he officially retired in the summer of 1923 but later returned to playing with Wellington Town. He later had a brief spell coaching at Preston North End and Birmingham before concentrating on his catering interests in Rhyl.

Johnny Hancocks

John HANCOCKS

Born: Oakengates, 30th April 1919
Died: 14th February 1994
Role: Right-Winger
Career: Oakengates Town, Walsall, Wolverhampton Wanderers, Wellington Town, Cambridge United, Oswestry, Sankeys
Debut: v Switzerland (h) 1-12-1948 (scored twice)
Appearances: 3 (2 goals)

Johnny Hancocks was only 15 years of age when he started playing with Oakengates, subsequently turning professional with Walsall in 1938. During the Second World War he represented the Army and at the end of the hostilities he was transferred to Wolves for £4,000. He was to spend eleven years with Wolves, helping the club win the FA Cup in 1949 and the League title in 1954, but Johnny's importance to the side can be revealed in his goalscoring record, 168 goals in 378 matches, a truly remarkable rate for a winger. He also scored twice for England on his debut against Switzerland at Highbury and later represented the Football League twice. He lost his first team place at Wolves to Harry Hooper and played for the reserve side before joining Wellington Town (later Telford United) in July 1957 as player-manager. He continued as a player only for a couple of months in 1959 and then joined Cambridge United in January 1960. He finished his career playing for Oswestry and then Sankeys in 1961. Johnny then worked at Maddock & Sons (Ironfounders) in Oakengates until his retirement in 1979.

Edris Albert HAPGOOD

Born: Bristol, 27th September 1909
Died: Leamington Spa, 20th April 1973
Role: Left-Back
Career: Bristol Rovers, Kettering Town, Arsenal
Debut: v Italy (a) 13-5-1933
Appearances: 30 + 13 War appearances + 1 unofficial appearance

Eddie played junior football in Bristol and was signed as an amateur by Bristol Rovers at the age of 18, although didn't make the grade and so joined non-League Kettering Town in 1927. A matter of months later Arsenal paid £750 to take him to Highbury and he went on to become a stalwart of the side that dominated the game during the 1930s. First capped by England in 1933 he made 13 of his appearances with his club colleague George Male at right-back, the club partnership being successfully transferred to the international stage. He won five League championship medals whilst with Arsenal (1931, 1933, 1934, 1935 and 1938), two FA Cup winners' medals (1930 and 1936) and also a runners-up medal in the same competition in 1932. He guested for Luton Town and Chelsea during the Second World War and announced his retirement from playing in 1944 and became manager of Blackburn Rovers. He remained in the position until February 1947 and was appointed player-coach of Shrewsbury Town and then manager of Watford. He subsequently had a spell as manager of Bath City between March 1950 and February 1956. He then became a tennis coach and later held a job as warden of a hostel for apprentices of the Atomic Energy Authority, losing this job when the hostel closed in 1970. His son, also named Edris, made a handful of League appearances for Burnley and Watford after the Second World War.

Eddie Hapgood

Harold Thomas Walter HARDINGE

Born: Greenwich, 25th February 1886
Died: 8th May 1965
Role: Inside-Left
Career: Maidstone United, Newcastle United, Sheffield United, Arsenal
Debut: v Scotland (a) 2-4-1910
Appearances: 1

Spotted by Newcastle United whilst playing for Maidstone United, Wally signed for the St. James' Park club in May

Wally Hardinge

1905 although he found it difficult to break into the first team on a regular basis. He was signed by Sheffield United in December 1907 where he made a breakthrough, culminating in winning his one cap for England. He was signed by Arsenal for £500 in May 1913 and retired during the summer of 1921, later having a spell as reserve team coach at Spurs. He was also a more than capable cricketer, playing for Kent between 1902 and 1933 and representing England in one Test against Australia in 1921. He was named Wisden Cricketer of the Year in 1915 and later went to work for the company as a sales representative, but in 1928 he asked the company if they would pay half his expenses to accompany the MCC touring team. Not only was this request rejected, the board voted 'that no leave of absence be granted.'

Harold Payne HARDMAN

Born: Manchester, 4th April 1882
Died: Sale, 9th June 1955
Role: Left-Winger
Career: Northern Nomads, Worlsey Wanderers, Chorlton-cum-Hardy, South Shore Choristers, Blackpool, Everton, Manchester United, Bradford City, Stoke
Debut: v Wales (h) 27-3-1905
Appearances: 4 (1 goal)

Harold spent his entire playing career as an amateur, but was still good enough to have collected an FA Cup winners' medal with Everton in 1906 (and a runners-up medal the following year), make four appearances for the full England team and win an Olympic Gold medal in the 1908 Games in London, where the United Kingdom amateurs overcame their Danish counterparts 2-0. He had two spells at Manchester United as a player and made only four first team appearances, but served the club for over fifty years as a director (he was appointed in November 1912) and was chairman of the club from 1951 to 1965. He also served on the Football Association, Lancashire FA and the Central League and was widely regarded as one of the finest administrators the game has ever seen. He won 10 caps for England at amateur level to go with his four at senior level. He qualified as a solicitor in 1907 and set up in business in Manchester.

George Hardwick

George Francis Moutry HARDWICK

Born: Saltburn, 2nd February 1920
Died: 19th April 2004
Role: Left-Back
Career: South Bank East End, Middlesbrough, Oldham Athletic
Debut: v Northern Ireland (a) 28-9-1946
Appearances: 13 + 17 War appearances + 2 unofficial appearances

After playing schools football in Cleveland, George played junior football for South Bank East End before signing amateur forms with Middlesbrough in October 1935. In April he was upgraded to the professional ranks and made his League debut for Middlesbrough in December 1937, although it was not an auspicious start as he scored an own goal in the 2-1 defeat by Bolton Wanderers! The outbreak of the Second World War brought a halt to George's professional career and he served in RAF Bomber Command during the war as well as turning out for the RAF in inter-service matches. First called up for England in April 1941 against Wales, George went on to make 17 wartime appearances for his country, all as captain as well as playing in one of England's unofficial matches against Switzerland in 1945 and against Scotland in the Bolton Disaster Fund Match against Scotland the following year. At the end of the war George returned to Middlesbrough and was virtually ever-present for the next five or so years, subsequently being selected for the full England side in September 1946. Captain for each of his 13 appearances for his country, George also captained the Great Britain side that played against the Rest of Europe in 1947 to celebrate the return of the four Home Countries into FIFA. In November 1950 George was transferred to Oldham Athletic for £15,000 to become player-manager of the Third Division club. He guided them to the Third Division North title (and thus his only first class medal, although he did appear in two wartime cup finals at Wembley whilst guesting for Chelsea during the Second World War) and promotion in 1952-53 but with financial restrictions at Boundary Park was unable to build a side to capitalise on their higher status and they were relegated after just one season. George continued in the post until April 1956 when he resigned as manager and retired as a player, going over to Germany to coach the US Army side and also having spells coaching at PSV Eindhoven before accepting the position of coach to the Dutch FA in June 1957. He remained in the position for two years before returning home, becoming Middlesbrough's youth team coach in August 1961, a position he held until November 1963. A year later he became manager of Sunderland but was at Roker Park for barely six months before leaving the club. His final job in football was as manager of former League side Gateshead, joining them in 1968 and remaining in charge until February 1970. In between football jobs George worked in both garage management and the steel industry. For all of his travels it is with Middlesbrough he will forever be associated and in 1983 the then Ayresome Park club granted him a joint testimonial with Wilf Mannion. When the club moved into the Cellnet Riverside Stadium in 1995 one of the hospitality suites was named after him in his honour and he was a regular at the ground right up until his death in April 2004.

Henry HARDY

Born: Stockport, 14th January 1895
Died: 17th February 1969
Role: Goalkeeper
Career: Stockport County, Everton, Bury
Debut: v Belgium (h) 8-12-1924
Appearances: 1

After playing junior football in Stockport, Harry signed for Stockport County in 1920 and established a reputation as one of the best goalkeepers outside the top flight, helping the club win the Third Division North championship in 1922 and collecting his one cap for England in 1924. He was signed by Everton in October 1925 for £2,350 and remained at Goodison Park for nearly four years before joining Bury in July 1929 where he finished his playing career. Harry also represented the Football League on two occasions and later became a professional musician.

Samuel Hardy

Samuel HARDY

Born: Newbold, Chesterfield, 26th August 1883
Died: Chesterfield, 24th October 1966
Role: Goalkeeper
Career: Newbold White Star, Chesterfield, Liverpool, Aston Villa, Nottingham Forest
Debut: v Ireland (h) 16-2-1907
Appearances: 21 + 3 War appearances

Considered by many to have been the greatest goalkeeper to have turned out for England, despite the later claims of the likes of Frank Swift, Gordon Banks and Peter Shilton, he joined Chesterfield from Newbold White Star in April 1903 and spent two years with the club before Liverpool paid £500 to take him to Anfield in the summer of 1905. He helped Liverpool win the League title in 1906 and earned a call-up to the England side the following year, seeing off the challenges from Horace Bailey and Tim Williamson to remain England's first choice until after the First World War. Despite his stature on the international scene, Liverpool surprisingly allowed him to join Aston Villa in May 1912 and at the end of his first season with the club had collected an FA Cup winners' medal. He guested for Nottingham Forest during the First World War, returning to Villa Park at the end of the hostilities and collected a second FA Cup winners' medal in 1920. He then joined Forest full time in August 1921, helping them win the Second Division title in 1922 and announced his retirement in 1925, having made 549 League appearances for his four clubs and represented the Football League on 10 occasions. Upon his retirement he owned and ran a hotel in Chesterfield.

Michael Gordon HARFORD

Born: Sunderland, 12th February 1959
Role: Forward
Career: Lincoln City, Newcastle United, Bristol City, Birmingham City, Luton Town, Derby County, Luton Town, Chelsea, Sunderland, Coventry City, Wimbledon
Debut: v Israel (a) 17-2-1988
Appearances: 2

Mick began his career with Lincoln City and proved to be an exceptional target man, prompting Newcastle United to pay

Mick Harford

£216,000 for his signature in December 1980, then a record for a Fourth Division player. He failed to settle at Newcastle, who sold him to Bristol City for £160,000 in August 1981, but with the Ashton Gate club on the verge of bankruptcy the fee was never paid in full, resulting in his registration being returned to Newcastle who then sold him to Birmingham City for £100,000 in March 1982. After helping Birmingham avoid relegation he was sold again, this time to Luton in December 1984 for £270,000. Here he found his mark, helping the club win the League Cup in 1988, the same year he made the first of his two appearances for England. In January 1990 he was allowed to join Derby County, returning to Luton in September the following year and then on to Chelsea in August 1992. He finished his playing career with spells at Sunderland, Coventry and Wimbledon where he has also had a spell as coach.

Frederick William HARGREAVES

Born: Blackburn, 16th August 1858
Died: 5th April 1897
Role: Half-Back
Career: Blackburn Rovers, Lancashire
Debut: v Wales (a) 15-3-1880
Appearances: 3

Educated at Malvern College, playing for the college team in 1877, Fred joined Blackburn Rovers and helped the club reach the FA Cup final in 1882 where they were beaten by Old Etonians. He was also a useful cricketer, playing for the East Lancashire Club in Blackburn and once for Lancashire, a county he also represented at football. He later studied as a law student and his younger brother John also played for Blackburn and England.

John HARGREAVES

Born: Blackburn, 13th December 1860
Died: 13th January 1903
Role: Left-Winger
Career: Blackburn Rovers
Debut: v Wales (h) 26-2-1881
Appearances: 2

Like his elder brother, John was educated at Malvern College and played for the college team in 1878 and 1879, signing with Blackburn Rovers in 1878. He collected a runners-up medal in the 1882 FA Cup final, alongside his brother, but went one better in 1884, helping Blackburn beat Queen's Park of Glasgow 2-1 in the final. He became a solicitor in 1884 and practiced in his native Blackburn until his early death in 1903.

Owen HARGREAVES

Born: Calgary, Canada, 20th January 1981
Role: Midfield
Career: Bayern Munich
Debut: v Holland (h) 15-8-2001
Appearances: 29

Owen Hargreaves is unique among England's many full international players, for he has never lived in the country for which he has won his caps! Born in Calgary in Canada, he showed considerable promise as a schoolboy to attract the attentions of German side Bayern Munich's Canadian scout and sent over to Germany for a trial. Impressing none other than German legend Franz Beckenbauer, Owen was taken on by the German side and made steady progress through the ranks. By the time he became a regular in the first team, interest had expanded to national level and he had the option of playing for no fewer than four countries; Wales (the birthplace of his mother), Canada, England or Germany (qualifying for the latter through the residency ruling). He eventually opted for England and was quickly given a debut against Holland in a friendly (albeit out of position) and then Germany, ironically, in a World Cup qualifier in order to secure his services for the future. An exciting and dependable midfield player, Owen has since gone on to become a regular fixture of the England side. His ambition is to at one time play for Bolton Wanderers, the side supported by his father.

Edward Cashfield HARPER

Born: Sheerness, 22nd August 1901
Died: Blackburn, 22nd July 1959
Role: Centre-Forward
Career: Sheppey United, Blackburn Rovers, Sheffield Wednesday, Tottenham Hotspur, Preston North End, Blackburn Rovers
Debut: v Scotland (h) 17-4-1926
Appearances: 1

Ted Harper did not begin playing football until he was 16 years of age but quickly set about making up for lost time, netting 102 goals in a single season in Kent junior football! He was spotted by Blackburn Rovers whilst playing for Sheppey United and signed in May 1923 and made his debut for the club in the opening game of the 1923-24 season. He made it a scoring debut too, netting the second as Rovers beat Chelsea 3-0 and went on to net 18 goals during the season, the best goalscoring return from a Rovers player since 1914-15. Unfortunately, however, other aspects of Ted's game left a lot to be desired and the general feeling was that if he wasn't scoring he wasn't contributing, and when the goals dried up in 1924-25 he was relegated to the reserves. He returned three games into the following season and hit five goals in the 7-1 win at Newcastle United. This was the start of a purple period for Ted, for he finished the season with 43 goals to his credit and a call-up to the England side. Not surprisingly, Ted's tally for the 1925-26 season remains Blackburn's record for a single season. In November 1927 he was sold to Sheffield Wednesday to help them in their battle against relegation, a battle ultimately won. Wednesday recovered from their struggles at the bottom of the table to win the League title in two successive seasons but Ted had already moved on by then, joining Spurs for £5,500 in March 1929. His reputation as a goalscorer often meant he was singled

Owen Hargreaves

out for some rough tackling and he made just 63 appearances during his two and a half years with the club, but he also scored 62 goals. In 1930-31 he netted 36 goals in just 30 League appearances. This tally of goals remained Spurs' record until Jimmy Greaves scored one more in 1962-63. Ted was sold to Preston in December 1931 for £5,000 and showed he could still find the net with regularity, hitting 43 goals in the 1932-33 season. Not surprisingly, this tally remains a record for the Deepdale club! He returned to Blackburn in November 1933 and retired from playing in May 1935. He then joined the training staff and held this position until May 1948 when he went to work for English Electric until his death in 1959.

Gordon HARRIS

Born: Worksop, 2nd June 1940
Role: Left-Winger
Career: Firbeck Colliery, Burnley, Sunderland, South Shields
Debut: v Poland (h) 5-1-1966
Appearances: 1

Gordon was working as a miner and playing for the works side when he was spotted by Burnley, subsequently signing with the Turf Moor club in January 1958. It was not until the 1960-61 season that he became a regular in the side, going on to represent the Football League for the first of two occasions in November 1961, collect the first of two caps for England at Under-23 level a week later and help Burnley reach the FA Cup final in 1962. He had to wait until 1966 to pick up his only full cap for England but was unable to break into what became the World Cup winning squad. He remained at Burnley until early 1968 when following disciplinary action culminating in his being dropped from the side he was transferred to Sunderland for £65,000. He was at Roker Park until July 1972 when he joined non-League South Shields where he finished his playing career.

Peter Philip HARRIS

Born: Portsmouth, 19th December 1925
Died: 17th December 2002
Role: Right-Winger
Career: Gosport Borough, Portsmouth
Debut: v Republic of Ireland (h) 21-9-1949
Appearances: 2

Peter Harris

Peter played schools football in Portsmouth and then junior and non-League football for the De Haviland works side, Havant Juniors and Gosport Borough before being spotted by Portsmouth, signing as an amateur in early 1944 and professional forms in November the same year after he had completed his apprenticeship as a woodworker. The previous month he had made his first team debut against Watford as an 18-year-old and by the 1947-48 season was established as a regular in the side. A member of the team that won back to back League championships (1949 and 1950), Peter was also called to represent the Football League on five occasions. In September 1949 he won the first of his two England caps, but as the match against the Republic of Ireland ended in a 2-0 defeat, England's first against overseas opposition, he was discarded by the selectors for a further five years. He was unfortunate to be recalled into the side for the 7-1 defeat against Hungary in 1954 and discarded once again, this time for good. Whilst he may have struggled to impose himself on the international scene, he was a vital member of the Portsmouth side of the 1950s, netting eight hat-tricks during his career and scoring 208 goals in 520 games, an astonishing return for a winger. In November 1959 a serious chest condition forced him into hospital for a considerable time and brought about the end of his playing career. When he hung up his boots he moved to Hayling Island where he opened a restaurant with Portsmouth team-mate Cyril Rutter.

Stan Harris

Stanley Schute HARRIS

Born: Clifton, 19th July 1881
Died: 4th May 1926
Role: Inside-Left
Career: Cambridge University, Old Westminsters, Casuals, Worthing, Portsmouth, Surrey, Corinthians
Debut: v Scotland (a) 9-4-1904
Appearances: 6 (2 goals)

Educated at Westminster School and played for the college team in 1900 and 1901, Stan collected a Blue at Cambridge University in 1902, 1903 and 1904. He left university in 1904 and became headmaster of a preparatory school in Worthing, a position he held until his death in 1926. In between time he also played football for a variety of clubs, including Portsmouth and the Corinthians and cricket for Surrey and Sussex, having previously played for Cambridge University and Gloucestershire. He also won one amateur cap for England at football.

Alban Harrison

Alban Hugh HARRISON

Born: Bredhurst, 30th November 1869
Died: 15th August 1943
Role: Full-Back
Career: Cambridge University, Old Westminsters, Corinthians
Debut: v Ireland (h) 25-2-1893
Appearances: 2

Another player educated at Westminster College and a member of the college team in 1887 and 1888, Alban attended Cambridge University and won his Blue in 1889 and 1891, captaining the side on the latter occasion. He later played for Old Westminsters and the Corinthians between 1891 and 1894, during which time he collected his two caps for England, the second coming in a 5-2 win over Scotland.

George HARRISON

Born: Church Gresley, 18th July 1892
Died: 12th March 1939
Role: Left-Winger
Career: Gresley Rovers, Leicester Fosse, Everton, Preston North End, Blackpool
Debut: v Belgium (a) 21-5-1921
Appearances: 2

Spotted by Leicester Fosse whilst turning out for Gresley Rovers, 'Jud' Harrison was said to have one of the hardest shots in the game. He was signed by Everton in April 1913 and helped them win the last First Division championship before the professional game shut down for the duration of the First World War in 1915. He returned once the hostilities were ended to collect the first of his two caps for England and remained at Goodison Park until November 1923 when he joined Preston North End. He gave Preston a further eight years' service before moving on to Blackpool, where he finished his playing career in 1932. He then returned to Preston to become a licensee.

Jack Harry HARROW

Born: Beddington, 8th October 1888
Died: 19th July 1958
Role: Left-Back
Career: Mill Green Rovers, Croydon Common, Chelsea
Debut: v Northern Ireland (h) 21-10-1922
Appearances: 2

Jack began his professional career with Croydon Common, having already made a number of appearances for the club as an amateur. He was then signed by Chelsea for £50 in April 1911 and went on to represent the Football League once and help Chelsea reach the FA Cup final in 1915. After the First World War shutdown Jack resumed his playing career with Chelsea and was a regular in the side until December 1924 when he was struck full on in the face by the ball and this affected his eyesight. He remained on the playing staff until he retired in the summer of 1926 but stayed at Chelsea on the backroom staff until 1938. He then went on to work for the Mitcham local authority until his retirement in 1956.

Ernest Arthur HART

Born: Overseal, 3rd January 1902
Died: 21st July 1954
Role: Centre-Half
Career: Woodlands FC, Leeds United, Mansfield Town, Coventry City, Tunbridge Wells Rangers
Debut: v Wales (a) 17-11-1928
Appearances: 8

Ernie was a 17-year-old playing local football in the Doncaster area when Leeds City were ordered to disband owing to financial regularities in October 1919 and a new club, Leeds United was formed the following month, with Ernie one of the first players taken on. After a season in the Midland League the club was admitted into Division Two of the Football League and Ernie's performances helped the club win the championship in 1924. He was also selected for the Football League on three occasions and was part of the FA touring side of South Africa in 1929. After nearly seventeen years with the Elland Road club, Ernie moved on to Mansfield Town in August 1936 where he finished his League career a season later. He later scouted for Coventry City and had a spell as player-manager of Tunbridge Wells before returning to the Doncaster area in order to concentrate on his haulage business.

Frank HARTLEY

Born: Shipton-under-Wychwood, 7th February 1896
Died: Shipton-under-Wychwood, 20th October 1965
Role: Inside-Forward
Career: Oxford City, Tottenham Hotspur, Corinthians, Tottenham Hotspur
Debut: v France (a) 10-5-1923
Appearances: 1

Signed by Spurs as an amateur, having already represented his country at that level whilst with Oxford City, he joined the White Hart Lane club in November 1922 and made his League debut the following April. At the end of the season he decided that the risk of injury in the game was too great for him and opted instead to play for Corinthians, despite having gained his only full cap for England. In February 1928 he was finally persuaded to pursue the professional game but made only six appearances over the next three seasons before being released. Frank was another all-round sportsman, playing cricket for Oxfordshire and also having trials for England at hockey.

A. HARVEY

Role: Full-Back
Career: Wednesbury Strollers, Staffordshire
Debut: v Wales (h) 26-2-1881
Appearances: 1

Very little is known about A. Harvey, other than a brief description written by Charles Alcock in his 1881 football annual which described him as 'A clever, hard-working back; dodges well.' So far as is known, he was probably the first player from a Black Country club to be capped by England. Another source claims his first name to have been Alf and that he was connected with Aston Villa, even mentioning that a photograph of the player exists in an old publication. No conclusive proof has yet been found, however.

Colin Harvey

James Colin HARVEY

Born: Liverpool, 16th November 1944
Role: Wing-Half
Career: Everton, Sheffield Wednesday
Debut: v Malta (a) 3-2-1971 (ECQ)
Appearances: 1 + 1 unofficial appearance

Colin Harvey played junior football in Liverpool but on leaving school worked as a clerk in the National Health Service, a playing career seemingly lost. He was then spotted by Everton and after a spell as an amateur with the club was upgraded to the professional ranks in October 1962, making his debut in the 1963-64 season in a European Cup tie. Eventually he linked to form the midfield triumvirate with Alan Ball and Howard Kendall, helping the club win the FA Cup in 1966 and the League championship in 1970 as well as finishing runners-up in the FA Cup in 1968. After collecting five caps for England at Under-23 level and representing the Football League on three occasions, he was awarded his only cap for the full England side in 1971. In September 1974 he was sold to Sheffield Wednesday for £70,000 although his career was ended by injury in 1976. He then returned to Goodison Park, serving the club as youth coach and rising through the ranks to become first reserve team coach and then first team coach under Howard Kendall. Following Kendall's departure for Spain in 1987 Colin was appointed manager but found the going particularly tough, being sacked in 1990. Six days later he was back at the club, appointed assistant to the returning Howard Kendall! When Kendall's second sojourn at Goodison came to an end Colin too moved on, serving as assistant to Andy King at Mansfield and later assistant to Graeme Sharp at Oldham Athletic.

Harold William HASSALL

Born: Astley, 4th March 1929
Role: Inside-Left
Career: Huddersfield Town, Bolton Wanderers
Debut: v Scotland (h) 14-4-1951 (scored once)
Appearances: 5 (4 goals)

Although Harold was born near Bolton and played for Astley & Tyldesley in the Bolton Combination League, he was offered professional forms by Huddersfield Town in September 1946. He made his League debut two years later and during his three years in the first team showed considerable form at club level to earn four caps for England. Harold also had the distinction of saving a penalty from Tom Finney, the incident occurring during a League match in which the regular Huddersfield goalkeeper was injured. In January 1952 Harold was transferred to his home town club Bolton Wanderers, subsequently winning his final cap for England whilst representing the Trotters. He also helped the club reach the FA Cup Final in 1953 where they were beaten by Blackpool. On New Year's Day 1955 Harold suffered a severe knee injury that brought his playing career to an immediate end. Harold then became a teacher, subsequently lecturing on physical training at Padgate College of Education and in 1958 he was appointed manager-coach of the England youth team. In 1966 he was invited by FIFA to join the panel of coaches and report on the World Cup taking place in England. Harold also had a brief spell as coach of the Malayan national team and scouted for Preston North End. In addition to his five caps Harold represented the Football League on three occasions.

Mark Wayne HATELEY

Born: Wallasey, 7th November 1961
Role: Centre-Forward
Career: Coventry City, Portsmouth, AC Milan (Italy), AS Monaco (France), Glasgow Rangers, Queens Park Rangers, Leeds United, Glasgow Rangers, Hull City
Debut: v USSR (h) (substitute) 2-6-1984
Appearances: 32 (9 goals)

Mark Hateley

The son of former professional footballer Tony Hateley (Notts County, Aston Villa, Chelsea, Liverpool, Coventry City, Birmingham City, Notts County and Oldham Athletic) Mark began his career with one of his father's former clubs, joining Coventry City as an apprentice in 1978. He remained at Highfield Road for five years, making over 100 appearances for the first team before moving on to Portsmouth for £220,000 in 1983. His impact at Fratton Park was little short of remarkable, for in the space of twelve months he had scored 22 League goals in just 32 appearances, earned the first of his 32 caps for England and been sold to AC Milan for £1 million. He had better luck with the Italian giants than another English centre-forward, Luther Blissett, and was given the nickname 'Atilla' by the fans. He then moved on to French club AS Monaco where he linked up with Glenn Hoddle and helped them win the French League before a move to Glasgow Rangers for £1 million in 1990. Whilst at Ibrox he helped the club win five consecutive League titles (they were to win nine in a row, thus equalling Celtic's record), two Scottish Cups and the League Cup on three occasions. He then joined the other Rangers, Queens Park Rangers of London in a £1.5 million move in November 1995 but struggled to win over the fans, prompting a loan move to Leeds United and then a shock return to Ibrox for £300,000 in March 1997. After four games and helping Rangers win the League once again he was released on a free transfer, taking over as player-manager at Hull City in August 1997.

Robert Hawkes

Robert Murray HAWKES

Born: Breachwood Green, 18th October 1880
Died: Luton, 12th September 1945
Role: Left-Half
Career: Luton Stanley, Luton Victoria, Luton Clarence, Herts County, Luton Town, Bedford Town
Debut: v Ireland (h) 16-2-1907
Appearances: 5

Educated at Luton Higher Grade School he began his playing career with local sides before joining Luton Town in 1901. He was appointed captain of the club in 1905-06 and in 1907 earned not only his first full cap for England but was also selected at amateur level. After making four appearances during the full England side's tour of Central Europe he was a member of the United Kingdom team that won the Olympic Games in London, beating Denmark 2-0 in the final. Although he was not selected for the full England side again he did win a total of 22 caps for the amateur side before becoming a professional in 1911, remaining with Luton Town until the end of the 1919-20 season when he joined Bedford Town. At the end of his playing career he set up in business in Luton as a straw-hat manufacturer.

George HAWORTH

Born: Accrington, 17th October 1864
Role: Right-Half, Centre-Half
Career: Accrington, Blackburn Rovers
Debut: v Ireland (h) 5-2-1887
Appearances: 5

George played for Christ Church FC from 1878 and linked with the Accrington club in 1883 and continued to play for the club until 1892. Somewhere along the way he was either loaned to Blackburn Rovers or temporarily transferred, for he helped Blackburn win the FA Cup in 1885 before returning to Accrington at the end of the season.

John Purvis HAWTREY

Born: Eton, 19th July 1850
Died: 17th August 1925
Role: Goalkeeper
Career: Old Etonians, Remnants, Berkshire-Buckinghamshire
Debut: v Wales (h) 26-2-1881
Appearances: 2

Although John was educated at Eton between 1857 and 1864 he did not play football during his time at the college, nor at his subsequent college Clifton, only taking up the game after his education was complete. He more than made up for lost time, helping Old Etonians win the FA Cup in 1879 and also representing London against Birmingham, earning selection for his country following his performance in the representative match. He later followed his brother into acting and also found considerable success as a playwright under the name John Trent-Hay. He also ran the publication Sporting World.

Edward Brownlow HAYGARTH

Born: Cirencester, 26th April 1854
Died: 14th April 1915
Role: Full-Back
Career: Wanderers, Swifts, Reading, Berkshire
Debut: v Scotland (h) 6-3-1875
Appearances: 1

Edward played for Lancing College during his youth and then went on to play for Wanderers, Swifts and Reading, appearing for the latter during their inaugural season and subsequently earning representative honours for Berkshire. He actually came from a cricketing family and played himself for Gloucestershire, Hampshire and Berkshire between 1875 and 1883, serving as a wicket-keeper and under-arm bowler! He qualified as a solicitor in 1876 and practiced in Cirencester.

John Norman HAYNES

Born: Kentish Town, London, 17th October 1934
Died: Edinburgh, 18th October 2005
Role: Inside-Forward
Career: Fulham, Feltham United, Wimbledon, Woodford Town, Fulham, Durban City
Debut: v Northern Ireland (a) 2-10-1954 (scored once)
Appearances: 56 (18 goals)

Johnny Haynes will forever be known as the first player to earn as much as £100 per week, five times his previous salary following the abolition of the maximum wage in 1960. He had represented Edmonton, Middlesex and London schools before being taken onto the Fulham ground staff in July 1950, although he was farmed out to local non-League sides to continue his football education. Fulham signed him as a professional in May 1952 and he had an immediate impact at Craven Cottage, subsequently collecting his first full cap for England before he was 20 years of age. He remained a permanent fixture in the national side for the next eight years, captaining the country on 22 occasions and scoring 18 goals. His greatest contribution came as a creator and instigator of attacks however, a role he also maintained for his club. He remained loyal to Fulham for his entire career, with the result that he won no major honours and sometimes managed to upset his team-mates; if a Fulham player failed to latch onto a defence-splitting pass from Johnny he could expect a blast from his captain, whilst Tommy Trinder's well-publicised offer of a £100 a week for the then England captain caused resentment among his lesser talented team-mates, all of whom expected a similar wage! Johnny was captain of England during the 1962 World Cup tournament in Chile, making his final appearance in the quarter final defeat against Brazil. The arrival of Alf Ramsey as manager and a car crash in which he broke his leg spelt the end of Johnny's international career at the age of 27, although there were numerous calls for his return over the next few years. He had a brief spell as caretaker manager of Fulham in 1968 but did not want the job on a full time basis, preferring to remain a player. He stayed at Craven Cottage until August 1970 when he headed off to South Africa to play for Durban City, finally collecting a winners' medal when they won their championship. After a brief spell with Wealdstone in England he returned to South Africa in 1972 where he finished his playing career. As well as his 56 full caps for England Johnny also represented the country at schoolboy, Youth, Under-23 and B level as well as turning out for the Football League on 13 occasions. Johnny died in hospital the day after another serious car accident in October 2005.

Johnny Haynes

Kevin Hector

Henry HEALLESS

Born: Blackburn, 10th February 1893
Died: 11th January 1972
Role: Half-Back
Career: Blackburn Athletic, Victoria Cross, Blackburn Trinity, Blackburn Rovers
Debut: v Northern Ireland (h) 22-10-1924
Appearances: 2

Harry Healless was spotted by Blackburn Rovers whilst playing local junior football and signed as an amateur in April 1915. The shutdown of League football at the end of that season meant that he continued his football education in junior football until signing professional forms with Rovers in May 1919. His early days at Ewood Park saw him struggle to hold down a regular place in the side, although in fairness he had yet to discover his best position, appearing at half-back, centre-forward and outside-right over the first two years with the club. By 1921-22 he had begun to form an effective half-back partnership with Frank Reilly and Jimmy McKinnell and he went on to become captain of the club and earn the first of his two caps for England. At club level he became the first Rovers captain to collect the FA Cup at Wembley, a feat achieved in 1928, the year he earned his second and last cap for England, and he remained an integral part of the Rovers side until his retirement as a professional in April 1933. He then joined the club's coaching staff before accepting an invitation to join Almelo of Holland as coach, a position he held between September 1935 and October 1937. He returned to England and was reinstated as an amateur and was playing for Haslingden Grange. Indeed, Harry was still playing junior football after World War II when well into his fifties! He rejoined the Ewood Park coaching staff in November 1951 and remained with the club until the appointment of Johnny Carey as manager in 1953.

Kevin James HECTOR

Born: Leeds, 2nd November 1944
Role: Forward
Career: Bradford Park Avenue, Derby County, Vancouver Whitecaps (Canada), Derby County
Debut: v Poland (h) 17-10-1973 (WCQ)
Appearances: 2

Discovered by Bradford Park Avenue whilst playing for South Leeds, Kevin was signed as a professional in July 1962 and became an instant success for the perennial strugglers, netting 113 goals in 178 appearances for the club. In September 1966 he was transferred to Derby County for £34,000, going on to help the club win the Second Division championship in 1969 and the First Division title in 1972 and 1975. In January 1978 he was sold to Canadian club Vancouver Whitecaps, although he spent the English seasons with Burton Albion and Boston United. He returned to England permanently in October 1980, re-signing with Derby County and taking his tally of League appearances with the Rams to 486, a record. He is also one of a select band of players who have scored more than 100 goals for two clubs, netting 155 for Derby County.

George Albert HEDLEY

Born: South Bank, 20th July 1876
Died: 16th August 1942
Role: Centre-Forward
Career: South Bank, Sheffield United, Southampton, Wolverhampton Wanderers
Debut: v Ireland (h) 9-3-1901
Appearances: 1

Originally signed by Sheffield United as an amateur during the 1897-98 season, George turned professional at the end of the season. He helped the club win the FA Cup in 1899 and 1902 and reach the final in 1901 before moving on to Southampton in May 1903. A year later he had helped his new club win the Southern League and in May 1906 returned to the Football League with Wolverhampton Wanderers. In 1908 he collected his third FA Cup winners' medal as Wolves beat Newcastle United and remained at Molineux until 1913 when he left to become manager of Bristol City. He remained in charge until the end of the First World War upon which he became a licensee in the city, returning to Wolverhampton in 1941 where he took over a boarding house.

George Hedley

Kenneth Edward HEGAN O.B.E.

Born: Coventry, 24th January 1901
Role: Winger
Career: RMC Sandhurst, Army, Corinthians
Debut: v Belgium (h) 19-3-1923 (scored twice)
Appearances: 4 (4 goals)

After attending Bablake School he attended the Royal Military College at Sandhurst, going on to represent both the college and the Army whilst serving with the 1st Dublin Fusiliers. He also played for the Corinthians and whilst with that club would win 23 caps for England at amateur level. He also earned four full caps for his country, proving his worth as a winger when weighing in with four goals. This followed 37 goals in 138 matches for Corinthians. Having being awarded an OBE during the Second World War, he retired from the Army in July 1949 having attained the rank of Lieutenant Colonel.

Michael Stephen HELLAWELL

Born: Keighley, 30th June 1938
Role: Winger
Career: Salts, Huddersfield Town, Queens Park Rangers, Birmingham City, Sunderland, Huddersfield Town, Peterborough United, Bromsgrove Rovers
Debut: v France (h) 3-10-1962 (EC)
Appearances: 2

After a spell with Huddersfield Town as an amateur, Mike joined the professional ranks with Queens Park Rangers in August 1955, earning his first representative honour when called up for the Third Division South side against their Northern counterparts. His speed and abilities demanded an outing at a higher level and in May 1957 he was transferred to Birmingham City. He took a while to settle into the side but by 1959-60, following the departure of Harry Hooper, he got an extended run in the side. He was a member of the side that finished runners-up in the Fairs Cup in 1961 and the following year won his two caps for England, replacing the injured Bryan Douglas. In 1963 he won his only major honour in the game, a winners' medal in the League Cup. He remained at St. Andrews until January 1965 when he was sold to Sunderland for £27,599 but returned to Huddersfield Town in September the same year for £15,000. Mike finished his League career with Peterborough United, joining the London Road side in November 1968 for £4,000. He was also a useful cricketer, making one appearance for Warwickshire in 1962.

Lee Andrew HENDRIE

Born: Birmingham, 18th May 1977
Role: Midfield
Career: Aston Villa
Debut: v Czech Republic (h) (substitute) 18-11-1998
Appearances: 1

Lee Hendrie was born into a footballing family, being the son of former Birmingham City player Paul and cousin of Barnsley's John Hendrie. Despite training with Birmingham City as a youngster (all of his family were City supporters) he signed with Aston Villa as a trainee and progressed through the ranks to become a professional in 1994. He was initially used somewhat sparingly by the then manager Brian Little and it appeared that he might have to leave the club in order to get a regular run at first team football, but the subsequent appointment of John Gregory proved the making of Lee. He was given an extended run in the Villa

Lee Hendrie

first team and responded with some inspirational performances as Villa charged up the table towards the end of the 1997-98 season, qualifying for Europe. He continued his form into the 1998-99 season, prompting a call-up for the full England side. Although his cousin and father had represented Scotland at numerous levels and Lee also qualified for Scotland, he chose to represent England and represented the country at Youth, Under-21 and B level before making his full debut.

Arthur George HENFREY

Born: Finedon, 19th December 1867
Died: Finedon, 17th October 1929
Role: Half-Back
Career: Cambridge University, Finedon, Corinthians, Northamptonshire
Debut: v Ireland (h) 7-3-1891
Appearances: 5 (2 goals) + 1 unofficial appearance (1 goal)

After attending Wellingborough Grammar School, Arthur studied at Cambridge University and won his Blue at football in 1890 and 1891, winning his first England cap in March 1891. He was associated with the Corinthians between 1890 and 1903 and also represented Northamptonshire. He was also a useful cricketer, playing for Cambridge University and later Northants between 1886 and 1899, serving as captain in 1893 and 1894.

Ronald Patrick HENRY

Born: Shoreditch, 17th August 1934
Role: Left-Back
Career: Luton Town, Harpenden Town, Redbourne, Tottenham Hotspur
Debut: v France (a) 27-2-1963 (EC)
Appearances: 1

Ron first signed with Spurs in March 1953 as an amateur, upgrading to professional status in January 1955. He made his debut at centre-back at Huddersfield Town in April 1955 but was later converted successfully to full-back. A solid and reliable performer in this position, he was rewarded with an England cap in 1963 against France, Alf Ramsey's first match in charge of England. A 5-1 defeat coupled with the outstanding performances of Ray Wilson meant Ron never won another cap for England, but he did of course collect a League championship, two FA Cup and a European Cup Winners' Cup winners' medals with Spurs. A cartilage injury and the emergence of Cyril Knowles effectively ended his first team career at Spurs in the summer of 1965, although he did not retire until May 1969. He then became coach of Spurs juniors, a position he held for many years until leaving to concentrate on his nursery business.

Ron Henry

Charles Francis William HERON

Born: Uxbridge, 1853
Died: 23rd October 1914
Role: Forward
Career: Uxbridge, Swifts, Wanderers, Windsor
Debut: v Scotland (a) 4-3-1876
Appearances: 1

The younger brother of Hubert Heron (below), he was educated at Mill Hill School and later played for Uxbridge, the Swifts, Wanderers and Windsor. His only cap for England came in a 3-0 defeat against Scotland in which he lined up alongside his brother. He also partnered his brother in the 1876 FA Cup final as Wanderers beat Old Etonians 3-0 in a replay. An amateur as a player, he earned his living as a wine merchant.

George Hubert Hugh HERON

Born: Uxbridge 30th January 1852
Died: 5th June 1914
Role: Wing-Forward
Career: Uxbridge, Wanderers, Swifts, Middlesex
Debut: v Scotland (h) 8-3-1872
Appearances: 5

Hubert Heron was the older of the two brothers who won England honours and also played for exactly the same clubs during his career. Whilst Francis' career stalled at one cap and one FA Cup winners' medal, Hubert managed to appear for England on five occasions in six seasons (all against Scotland) and won FA Cup winners' medals in three consecutive seasons – 1876 (alongside his brother), 1877 and 1878. Hubert also served on the FA Committee between 1873 and 1876 and like his brother worked as a wine merchant in Bournemouth.

Emile William Ivanhoe HESKEY

Born: Leicester, 11th January 1978
Role: Forward
Career: Leicester City, Liverpool, Birmingham City
Debut: v Hungary (a) 28-4-1999
Appearances: 43 (5 goals)

A product of the Leicester City youth scheme, Emile signed professional forms with the Filbert Street club in October 1995. An England youth international Emile developed under manager Martin O'Neill into a strong and purposeful target man and helped the club win the League Cup in 1997 and win representative honours for the Under-21 side. His debut for the full side came in 1999 and the following year he added another League Cup winners' medal. He was sold to Liverpool for £11 million in March 2000 and at the end of the 2000-01 season had collected a third League Cup winners' medal and similar gongs from the FA Cup and UEFA Cup. He remained at Anfield until July 2004 when a £3.5 million deal took him to Birmingham City, still on the fringes of the England squad.

Emile Heskey

William HIBBERT
Born: Golborne, 21st September 1884
Died: Blackpool 16th March 1949
Role: Inside-Right
Career: Newton Le Willows, Brynn Central, Bury, Newcastle United, Bradford City, Oldham Athletic
Debut: v Scotland (a) 2-4-1910
Appearances: 1

Billy played in the Lancashire Combination League at the age of 16 with Newton Le Willows and had a season with Brynn Central before signing with Bury in May 1906. A little over five years later Newcastle United paid a then record £1,950 to take him to St. James' Park, by which time he had picked up his only cap for England. He did get to represent the Football League on three occasions however and guested for Leeds City during the First World War. In May 1920 he was sold to Bradford City for £700 and finished his League career with Oldham Athletic. He then had spells coaching in the United States and Spain before joining Wigan Borough as trainer in 1929.

Henry Edward HIBBS
Born: Wilnecote, Staffordshire, 27th May 1905
Died: Hatfield, Hertfordshire, 23rd April 1984
Role: Goalkeeper
Career: Wilnecote Holy Trinity, Tamworth Castle, Birmingham
Debut: v Wales (h) 20-11-1929
Appearances: 25 + 1 unofficial appearance

In the nine years after Sam Hardy's last appearance for England in 1920, the selection committee tried no fewer than 21 different goalkeepers in the 46 internationals before Harry Hibbs made his debut in 1929. Harry was almost a carbon copy of Hardy; unspectacular but highly reliable, preferring to do everything in as simple a manner as possible, a style that was to see him become England's most capped goalkeeper up to that time. After playing junior football for Wilnecote Holy Trinity and Tamworth Castle he was signed by Birmingham in May 1924 and remained with the club for the next sixteen years until his retirement in April 1940. He represented the Football League on three occasions and was part of the FA's touring party to South Africa in 1929, appearing against the national side and performing well enough to earn a call-up for the full England side a few months later. The closest he came to major honours with Birmingham came in the FA Cup in 1931, although Birmingham were beaten in the final by local rivals West Bromwich Albion. Four years after his retirement he took over as manager of Walsall, a post he held until June 1951 and later played non-League football for a season as well as coaching Ware FC of the Delphian League in the early 1960s. He had originally been a plumber's apprentice.

Frederick HILL
Born: Sheffield, 17th January 1940
Role: Inside-Forward
Career: Bolton Wanderers, Halifax Town, Manchester City, Peterborough United
Debut: v Northern Ireland (a) 20-10-1962
Appearances: 2

Despite playing schools football in Sheffield, Freddie turned down a chance to sign for Sheffield Wednesday, preferring to take his chances with Bolton Wanderers, joining the Trotters in March 1957. He made his debut in April 1958 and soon became a regular in the side, earning a call-up for the England Under-23 side (for whom he won 10 caps) and the following year a full England cap against Northern Ireland. Freddie remained with Bolton until July 1969 when he was sold to Halifax for £5,000 although the following May he returned to the top flight with Manchester City, joining them in a £13,000 deal. He was at Maine Road for three years before moving on to Peterborough United for £5,000 and helped the side win the Fourth Division championship in 1974. He finished his playing career with Droylsden in 1976.

Gordon Alec HILL
Born: Sunbury, 1st April 1954
Role: Forward
Career: Southall, Millwall, Manchester United, Derby County, Queens Park Rangers
Debut: v Italy (New York) 28-5-1976
Appearances: 6

He began his career with Millwall in 1973 and soon established a reputation of being a tricky winger, with Manchester United paying £70,000 in November 1975, with a further £10,000 being payable in the event he won full England honours, he did so within six months. At United he linked with Steve Coppell and helped the club to successive FA Cup finals in 1976 and 1977, and although he was substituted in both finals collected a winners' medal in 1977 as United overcame Liverpool. A disagreement with the management at Old Trafford prompted a reunion with Tommy Docherty at Derby for £250,000 in 1978. He did not settle at the Baseball Ground and in November 1979 was sold to QPR for £175,000, the buying manager being Tommy Docherty for the third time! In 1981 he went to play in America and later in Europe before returning home for non-League football.

Gordon Hill

John Henry HILL
Born: Hetton-le-Hole, 2nd March 1897
Died: April 1972
Role: Centre-Half
Career: Durham City, Plymouth Argyle, Burnley, Newcastle United, Bradford City, Hull City
Debut: v Wales (a) 28-2-1925
Appearances: 11

After playing junior football in and around Durham he briefly signed with Durham City before switching to Plymouth Argyle in September 1920. In May 1923 he was sold to Burnley for £5,450 and made his England breakthrough as well as representing the Football League on three occasions. He was transferred to Newcastle United for £8,100 in October 1928 and continued to add to his tally of England caps, finally collecting 11. In June 1931 he was sold to Bradford City for £600 but less than three months later was swapped with another player and joined Hull City. Here he helped the club win the Third Division North championship in 1933 before retiring as a player in 1934 and taking over as manager. He retained this position until January 1936 but returned to the club after the Second World War, serving as club scout between 1948 and 1955.

Richard Henry HILL
Born: Mapperley, 26th November 1893
Died: April 1971
Role: Left-Back
Career: Millwall Athletic, Torquay United
Debut: v Belgium (a) 24-5-1926
Appearances: 1

After serving in the Grenadier Guards during the First World War and representing the Army at football in that time, he joined Millwall Athletic in the summer of 1919 and spent more than eleven years at the club. As well as his one cap for England he also helped the club win the Third Division South championship in 1928. In July 1930 he left for Torquay United and spent a year with the club before finishing his playing career with Newark Town. He then served Mansfield Town as trainer until 1935 before taking up a similar position with Coventry City, a post he held until 1950 when he returned to Torquay United as trainer.

Ricky Anthony HILL
Born: London, 5th March 1959
Role: Midfield
Career: Luton Town, Le Havre, Leicester City
Debut: v Denmark (substitute) (a) 22-9-1982
Appearances: 3

A graduate of the Luton Town youth scheme, Ricky joined the club as a schoolboy and then as an apprentice, finally signing professional forms in May 1976 by which time he had become an England youth international. He was a Luton first team regular for some twelve seasons, helping them win the Second Division championship in 1982 and the League cup in 1988, as well as collecting three full caps for England. He made 429 League appearances for the Hatters before moving to Le Havre, returning to England to join Leicester City in August 1990. A year later he was on his travels again, playing for Tampa Bay Rowdies in the United States and returned home again to finish his playing career with Hitchin Town. Ricky later had an unsuccessful spell as manager of Luton Town.

Jack Hillman

John HILLMAN

Born: Tavistock, 1871
Died: 1st August 1955
Role: Goalkeeper
Career: Burnley, Everton, Dundee, Burnley, Manchester City, Millwall
Debut: v Ireland (h) 18-2-1899
Appearances: 1

Jack Hillman had played junior football in Devon before signing with Burnley in 1891 and went on to become one of the major characters in the game, especially as he stood 6' 4" tall and weighed over 16 stone. Known throughout his career as Happy Jack he spent four years at Turf Moor before being sold to Everton for £150 in February 1895. He was unable to settle at Goodison Park and in June 1896 was on the move again, this time signing for Dundee. His time in Scotland was not a success either, for midway through the 1897-98 season he was suspended by the club for supposedly 'not trying', although it was known that the club was bankrupt and unable to afford his wages. He returned to England in March 1898, costing his former club Burnley £225 for his signature. His second spell at Turf Moor was both successful and disastrous, for in addition to earning his one cap for England he was charged with attempted bribery. At the end of the 1899-1900 season and with Burnley desperately battling against relegation to the Second Division for the first time in their history, Jack was reported to have twice attempted to bribe the Nottingham Forest captain before the game and again at half time. McPherson, the Forest captain refused, Forest won the game 4-0 thus relegating Burnley and after the game the Forest secretary wrote to the FA to complain about Jack Hillman's activities. Hillman was summoned to a joint FA - Football League commission in Manchester. His defence, such as it was, was that the approach had all been a joke, inspired by the fact Forest were themselves the subject of suspicion surrounding their 8-0 defeat a few weeks previously against West Bromwich Albion; Hillman claimed he was only asking for a similar favour. The FA failed to see the funny side however, banning Jack for one season and announcing that but for his previous good conduct he would have been thrown out of the game for good. Jack Hillman lost a year's wages and a promised benefit of £300 but was at least able to resume his career. In January 1902 he was sold to Manchester City, helping his new club win the Second Division championship in 1903 and the FA Cup the following season, although once again he became embroiled in controversy and bribery allegations. Towards the end of the 1904-05 season, with City challenging for the First Division title, they were involved in two particularly violent clashes against Aston Villa and Everton. A joint commission was set up to look into matters and whilst the watching world expected suspensions to arise for violent conduct, the subsequent announcement that a number of players were to be suspended because of bribery attempts caused a furore. That Billy Meredith was one of those named was a sensation, and when he was later reported to the football authorities for attempting to claim his wages, yet another investigation into matters at Manchester City was promised. This time the authorities found evidence of wholesale disregard for the maximum wage and bonus rulings and ordered City to sell a total of 17 players, including Jack Hillman. Jack was one of the last to be sold, joining Millwall Athletic in January 1907, although his playing career came to an end soon after with an elbow injury. Jack retired from the game in order to concentrate on his confectionery shop in Burnley, although after the First World War he did return to Turf Moor, serving the club as trainer for a year. In addition to his one England cap he also represented the Football League on one occasion.

Arnold Frank HILLS

Born: London, 12th March 1857
Died: 7th March 1927
Role: Winger
Career: Oxford University, Old Harrovians
Debut: v Scotland (h) 5-4-1879
Appearances: 1

Educated at Harrow and captain of the football team in 1876, Arnold attended Oxford University and was exceptional as a footballer, winning his Blue in 1877 and 1878 and in athletics, for which he won a Blue for four consecutive years. In his first year at Oxford he helped the side reach the FA Cup final and the same year he won his only cap for England and was crowned AAA mile champion. He later became managing director of Thames Ironworks and founded the works football team, which eventually became West Ham United.

George Richard HILSDON

Born: London, 10th August 1885
Died: 10th September 1941
Role: Centre-Forward
Career: South West Ham, Clapton Orient, Luton Town, West Ham United, Chelsea, West Ham United, Chatham
Debut: v Ireland (h) 16-2-1907
Appearances: 8 (14 goals)

George was briefly connected with Clapton Orient before signing with Luton Town in the summer of 1902 but returned to his native London the following year upon signing with West Ham. In May 1906 he was signed by Chelsea to spearhead their challenge for promotion to the First Division, a feat achieved at the end of his first season at the club. Nicknamed 'Gatling Gun' on account of his shooting abilities with both feet, he broke into the England side the same season and amassed his eight caps between 1907 and 1910. In the summer of 1912 he returned to West Ham although on the outbreak of the First World War he enlisted in the Army and was badly gassed serving in France. At the end of the war he signed with Chatham where he finished his playing career. He was later reported to be a member of Fred Karno's company during the 1920s.

Andrew George HINCHCLIFFE

Born: Manchester, 5th February 1969
Role: Defender
Career: Manchester City, Everton, Sheffield Wednesday
Debut: v Moldova (a) 1-9-1996 (WCQ)
Appearances: 7

A product of the Manchester City youth scheme he signed as an apprentice in February 1986 and made over 100 appearances for the club before an £800,000 move to Everton in 1990. He then became a permanent fixture in the defence, winning an FA Cup winners' medal in 1995 and also broke into the England side, winning three caps. He then had a difference of opinion with Everton manager Howard Kendall and was placed on the transfer list, with Spurs being the first club to show an interest in him. Unfortunately he failed a medical examination and therefore returned to Goodison Park, subsequently joining Sheffield Wednesday for £2.85 million in January 1998. He recovered sufficiently enough to reclaim his place in the England side, thus becoming the first Wednesday player to be capped for England in over five years, but was eventually forced to retire with an Achilles heel injury.

Andy Hinchcliffe

Ernest William HINE

Born: Smithy Cross, 9th April 1901
Died: Huddersfield, 1974
Role: Inside-Forward
Career: Barnsley, Leicester City, Huddersfield Town, Manchester United, Barnsley
Debut: v Northern Ireland (h) 22-10-1928
Appearances: 6 (4 goals)

Born in Smithy Cross, near Barnsley, Ernie joined his local club as an amateur in April 1921 and turned professional the following January. He was sold to Leicester City for £3,000 in January 1926 and developed into a fearsome striker, breaking into the England side in 1928 and also representing the Football League on five occasions. He joined Huddersfield Town in May 1932 but in February 1933 moved on to Manchester United where his luck and form deserted him and in 53 appearances he was to find the net only 12 times. In December 1934 he was sold back to Barnsley where he finished his career, having netted 287 goals in just over 600 League appearances for his various clubs.

Alan Hinton

Alan Thomas HINTON

Born: Wednesbury, 6th October 1942
Role: Left-Winger
Career: Wolverhampton Wanderers, Nottingham Forest, Derby County
Debut: v France (h) 3-10-1962 (EC)
Appearances: 3 (1 goal)

Alan played for South-East Staffordshire and Birmingham County at schoolboy level and joined Wolves after leaving school in 1958, turning professional in October 1959. He played 78 senior matches for Wolves and whilst with the club represented England at Youth, Under-23 and full level before joining Nottingham Forest. Three years later he made the short journey to Derby Country and went on to help them win the Second Division in 1969 and the League title in 1972. He remained at the Baseball Ground until 1976 when he left for America. He was coach at Tulsa Roughnecks and later Seattle Sounders, winning the NASL Coach of the Year award in 1980.

David Eric HIRST

Born: Cudworth, 7th December 1967
Role: Striker
Career: Barnsley, Sheffield Wednesday, Southampton
Debut: v Australia (a) 1-6-1991
Appearances: 3 (1 goal)

David Hirst began his career with Barnsley and signed as an apprentice in November 1985, subsequently going on to make 29 appearances for the side before a £200,000 move to Sheffield Wednesday in August 1986. At Hillsborough he developed into a versatile player, best used as a striker but also able to use his knowledge in the art of defence when an injury crisis robbed the club of most of its central defenders. It was as a striker, however, that he first earned his call-up to the England squad. In October 1997 Southampton paid their then record fee of £2 million to take him to The Dell, and after overcoming a number of injuries he began to show the form that had prompted their approach in the first place. Unfortunately he suffered a fall in training at the end of his first season at Southampton that subsequently forced his retirement owing to a badly damaged knee.

Gerald Archibald HITCHENS

Born: Rawnsley, 8th October 1934
Died: 13th April 1983
Role: Centre-Forward
Career: Kidderminster Harriers, Cardiff City, Aston Villa, AC Milan (Italy), Torino (Italy), Atalanta (Italy), Cagliari (Italy), Worcester City
Debut: v Mexico (h) 10-5-1961 (scored once)
Appearances: 7 (5 goals)

Gerry began his career with non-League Kidderminster Harriers and was signed by Cardiff City in 1953. Over the next four years he developed into one of the great talents in the game and was snapped up by Villa in December 1957 for £22,500. He spent four years with Villa, his goals helping them to the Second Division title and then reach the final of the League Cup in 1960-61, although by the time the final was played at the beginning of the following season he had gone, sold to Inter Milan for £85,000. He went on to become one of the few British successes in Italian football, along with John Charles, and after giving Inter Milan great service went on to play for Torino, Atalanta and Cagliari during the course of eight years in the country. Capped seven times by England he returned to these shores in 1969 and played non-League football for Worcester City and Merthyr Tydfil before retiring.

Harold Henry Frank HOBBIS

Born: Dartford, 9th March 1913
Role: Left-Winger
Career: Bromley, Charlton Athletic, Tonbridge
Debut: v Austria (a) 6-5-1936
Appearances: 2 (1 goal)

After playing local football in Kent, Harry joined Charlton as an amateur in February 1931 and turned professional in March the same year. He quickly established himself a vital member of the side that won the Third Division South in 1935 and finished runners-up in the Second Division and then First Division in successive seasons, one of the quickest ascents to the top flight. He remained at Charlton until November 1948 when he left to become player-manager of Tonbridge where he finished his career.

David Hirst

Glenn HODDLE

Born: Hayes, 27th October 1957
Role: Midfield
Career: Tottenham Hotspur, Monaco (France), Swindon Town, Chelsea
Debut: v Bulgaria (h) 22-11-1979 (ECQ) (scored once)
Appearances: 53 (8 goals)

One of the most naturally gifted players of his generation, he signed with Spurs as a youngster after a recommendation from Martin Chivers. He made his League debut in 1975 and was an established first team player by the end of the following year. He made his England debut in 1979 against Bulgaria at Wembley and marked the occasion by scoring. He remained with Spurs until 1987, during which time he won two FA Cup winners' medals and 44 England caps, although it was felt by some that his work rate was insufficient and he was not capped as often as his talent dictated. He joined AS Monaco in 1987 and won a League championship medal in his first season in France but was then troubled by injuries. Upon returning to England in 1990 he trained with Chelsea but then accepted an offer to become player-manager at Swindon, guiding them into the Premier Division in 1993. He then left to hold a similar position with Chelsea and was subsequently appointed England manager in 1996. Ill-considered comments regarding the disabled led to him being relieved of the position in 1999,

Glenn Hoddle

although he was brought back to club management with Southampton and then returned to White Hart Lane the following year. Although he took over the club a little over a week before they were due to appear in the FA Cup semi final and later guided them to the final of the Worthington Cup, his return to Spurs was not as successful as had been anticipated, and five games into the 2003-04 season he was dismissed. Almost a year to the day later he was appointed manager of Wolverhampton Wanderers.

Stephen Brian HODGE

Born: Nottingham, 25th October 1962
Role: Midfield
Career: Nottingham Forest, Aston Villa, Tottenham Hotspur, Nottingham Forest, Leeds United, Derby County, Queens Park Rangers, Watford, Hong Kong, Leyton Orient
Debut: v USSR (a) (substitute) 26-3-1986
Appearances: 24

A graduate of the youth scheme at Nottingham Forest, Steve was taken on as an apprentice in October 1980 and broke into the team at the end of the 1981-82 season. He was also selected for the England Under-21 side in 1983 and had collected five caps before a move to Aston Villa in August 1985 for £450,000. He was unable to settle at Villa, despite having collected his first full cap for England and joined Spurs for £650,000 in December 1986, slotting into a five man midfield. A member of the squad that went to Mexico for the 1986 World Cup finals he expressed a desire to return home to Nottingham Forest and was sold for £550,000 in 1988, subsequently helping Forest to the League Cup in 1989 and 1990 and the FA Cup final the following year. In 1991 he moved on again, this time to Leeds United for £900,000 but was unable to hold a regular place in the side, spending a spell on loan to Derby County before joining Queens Park Rangers for £300,000. A little over a year later he joined Watford but made only two appearances before being released less than a month later. After a spell playing in Hong Kong he returned to the Football League after an eighteen month absence to play for Leyton Orient.

Dennis HODGETTS

Born: Birmingham, 28th November 1863
Died: 26th March 1945
Role: Inside-Left, Left-Winger
Career: Birmingham St. George's, Great Lever, Birmingham St. George's, Aston Villa, Small Heath
Debut: v Wales (h) 4-2-1888
Appearances: 6 (1 goal)

One of the most prestigious names in Aston Villa's history, Dennis signed with the club in 1886 having played for a number of clubs in the area. He helped Aston Villa win the FA Cup at the end of his first season and would reach two further finals during his time at Villa Park, collecting a runners-up medal in 1892 and a winners' medal in 1895. He also helped them win the League championship in 1894 and 1896 and represented the Football League on one occasion. Soon after the start of the 1896-97 season, which would see Aston Villa win the coveted double, Dennis moved on to sign for Small Heath (later Birmingham City) where he finished his playing career in 1898. A licensee in the area when his playing career ended he retained his connection with Aston Villa, being appointed a vice president at the club in 1930.

Steve Hodge

Alan HODGKINSON

Born: Sheffield, 16th August 1936
Role: Goalkeeper
Career: Worksop Town, Sheffield United
Debut: v Scotland (h) 6-4-1957
Appearances: 5

Alan signed with Sheffield United as an amateur in January 1953, thus beginning an association with the club that was to last more than twenty years. He was upgraded to the professional ranks the following August and after representing the Army during his national service returned to Bramall Lane to become a first team regular. As well as his five full caps he also collected 7 caps at Under-23 level and represented the Football League once. Alan made 576 appearances for the club before his retirement in 1971, having already been appointed assistant trainer at the club in January 1971. He left the club in November 1975 to become assistant manager at Gillingham and later was appointed specialist goalkeeping coach at Coventry City and for the Scottish national squad!

Gordon HODGSON

Born: Johannesburg, South Africa, 18th April 1904
Died: 14th June 1951
Role: Inside-Right
Career: Transvaal, Liverpool, Aston Villa, Leeds United
Debut: v Northern Ireland (a) 20-10-1930
Appearances: 3 (1 goal)

Gordon played for Transvaal and was capped by South Africa at amateur level when he was selected to accompany a South African FA touring party in 1924-25. His performances, together with those of goalkeeper Arthur Riley, prompted Liverpool to sign the pair, with Gordon finally joining the club in December 1925. He remained at Anfield for the next eleven years, scoring 241 goals in 377 games, representing the Football League once and also collecting three full England caps, before he was sold to Aston Villa for £3,000 in January 1936. Less than a year later he was on the move again, this time signing for Leeds United, retiring from playing during the Second World War and becoming club coach. In October 1946 he was appointed manager of Port Vale, a position he held for four years. Gordon was also a useful cricketer, playing for Lancashire and Forfarshire during his career. At the end of the 1950-51 season he was admitted to hospital where he died a few weeks later.

Joseph HODKINSON

Born: Lancaster, 1889
Died: 18th June 1954
Role: Left-Winger
Career: Lancaster Town, Glossop, Blackburn Rovers, Lancaster Town
Debut: v Wales (h) 17-3-1913
Appearances: 3 + 1 War appearance

After playing local football in Lancaster, Joe began his professional career with Glossop in the summer of 1909 and was soon being marked out as an exceptional talent, prompting a £1,000 move to Blackburn Rovers in January 1913. Two months later he collected his first cap for England and the following year helped Rovers win the First Division championship. He remained at Ewood Park for ten years, returning to former club Lancaster Town in April 1923 and retiring from playing in January 1925. He later became a licensee in his native Lancaster.

William HOGG

Born: Newcastle-upon-Tyne, 29th May 1879
Died: 30th January 1937
Role: Right-Winger
Career: Willington Athletic, Sunderland, Glasgow Rangers, Dundee, Raith Rovers
Debut: v Wales (a) 3-3-1902
Appearances: 3 + 1 unofficial appearance

Bill started his professional career with Sunderland, joining the club in October 1899 and helped the club win the First Division championship in 1902. He made his England debut in 1902, his unofficial appearance coming in that season's match against Scotland at Ibrox that was expunged from the records after the collapse of a stand left twenty-five dead. After playing in the re-arranged fixture, Bill did not appear in the England side again. He remained at Roker Park until May 1909 when he returned to Ibrox, this time signing for Rangers for £100 and helping them win the Scottish League in three consecutive seasons, 1911, 1912 and 1913. Four years later he joined Dundee for a season before accepting the position of player manager of Raith Rovers, returning to the Sunderland area at the outbreak of the First World War to work in an engineering works. After the war he became a local licensee.

George Henry HOLDCROFT

Born: Norton-le-Moor, 23rd January 1909
Died: 17th April 1983
Role: Goalkeeper
Career: Biddulph, Norton Druids, Whitfield Colliery, Port Vale, Darlington, Everton, Preston North End, Barnsley, Morecambe, Chorley
Debut: v Wales (a) 17-10-1936
Appearances: 2

After spells with Port Vale, Darlington and Everton, Harry's career finally took off following a £1,500 transfer to Preston North End in December 1932, where he quickly became the first team goalkeeper. A broken finger kept him out of the side that reached the FA Cup final in 1937 which was lost to Sunderland but he returned the following year and was in fine form as Preston beat Huddersfield Town 1-0 after extra time. He remained at Deepdale until August 1945, having made 289 League and Cup appearances for the side, before joining Barnsley, but retiring from injury soon after. Harry also represented the Football League once during his career.

Albert Douglas HOLDEN

Born: Manchester, 28th September 1930
Role: Winger
Career: Bolton Wanders, Preston North End, Hakoah (Australia)
Debut: v Wales (h) 26-11-1958
Appearances: 5

Discovered playing schoolboy football in Manchester, Doug signed with Bolton Wanderers as an amateur in 1948, being upgraded to the professional ranks in May 1949. An England youth international by the time he made his League debut in 1951, Doug was a member of the Bolton side that lost the 1953 FA Cup final to the Stanley Matthews-inspired Blackpool side but made amends five years later with victory over Manchester United. That same year he won the first of his five caps for England and remained at Burnden Park until November 1962 when he was transferred to Preston for £8,000. He collected a second runners-up medal in the FA Cup in 1964 and remained at Deepdale until the summer of 1965 when he emigrated to Australia. He continued playing with Hakoah of Sydney until 1968 and was then coach at the club, later moving to Auburn of Sydney to take over in a similar capacity. He returned to England in 1970 and had a spell on Grimsby Town's coaching staff.

George Henry HOLDEN

Born: West Bromwich, 6th October 1859
Died: 1920s
Role: Right-Winger
Career: Wednesbury Old Park, Wednesbury St. James, Wednesbury Old Athletic, West Bromwich Albion, Wednesbury Old Athletic, Derby Midland, Staffordshire
Debut: v Scotland (h) 12-3-1881
Appearances: 4

Playing at a time when there were no organised Leagues and the only football was friendly fixtures and representative matches, George Holden established a reputation for being an extremely fast winger with exceptional dribbling skills. His caps were won during his first spell with Wednesbury Old Athletic, which subsequently attracted the attention of West Bromwich Albion, whom he joined in May 1886 for a single season. He also represented Birmingham FA and Staffordshire during his career.

Charles Henry HOLDEN-WHITE

Born: 1869
Died: 14th July 1948
Role: Half-Back
Career: Swifts, Clapham Rovers, Corinthians
Debut: v Wales (h) 4-2-1888
Appearances: 2

Educated at Brentwood School, Charles played for Clapham Rovers before joining the Corinthians in 1882, having the distinction of being the club's first captain and serving on the committee. A business man in the City of London by trade, he remained a player with Corinthians until 1891 and also served on the FA Committee between 1883 and 1885.

Thomas HOLFORD

Born: Hanley, 28th January 1878
Died: 6th April 1964
Role: Centre-Half
Career: Colbridge, Stoke, Manchester City, Stoke, Port Vale
Debut: v Ireland (h) 14-2-1903
Appearances: 1

Tommy joined Stoke in the summer of 1898 and remained with the club until they resigned from the Football League in 1908, upon which he joined Manchester City. He helped them win the Second Division championship in 1910 and after six years at Hyde Road (City's then ground) he accepted an invitation to become player-manager of Port Vale. During the First World War he guested for Nottingham Forest, returning to Port Vale at the end of the hostilities and made his final League appearance for the club during the 1923-24 season, when he was already in his mid-forties. He later served the club as trainer, manager again between the summer of 1933 and September 1935 and scout until his retirement in 1950.

George H. HOLLEY

Born: Seaham Harbour, 25th November 1885
Died: 27th August 1942
Role: Inside-Forward
Career: Seaham Athletic, Seaham Villa, Seaham White Star, Sunderland, Brighton & Hove Albion
Debut: v Wales (h) 15-3-1909 (scored once)
Appearances: 10 (8 goals)

George played local football in Sunderland before signing for the senior club in November 1904, going on to represent the Football League on five occasions during his time at Roker Park. Also a member of the FA touring party of South Africa in 1910, he helped Sunderland win the League championship in 1913 and narrowly miss out on the coveted double, being beaten by Aston Villa in the FA Cup final. In July 1919 he moved on to Brighton but retired the following year, subsequently returning to Sunderland to become coach. He later had spells coaching at Wolves for ten years and then Barnsley. His son Tom later played for Leeds United.

Edwin HOLLIDAY

Born: Barnsley, 7th June 1939
Role: Left-Winger
Career: Middlesbrough, Sheffield Wednesday, Middlesbrough, Hereford United, Workington, Peterborough United
Debut: v Wales (a) 17-10-1959
Appearances: 3

Signed by Middlesbrough as an amateur in 1955 he turned professional the following year and by 1957 was an established first team player, creating and providing chances for the likes of Brian Clough and Alan Peacock. Awarded a cap at Under-23 level in September 1959, the following month he made the step up to the full side. After five Under-23 and three full caps for his country, Edwin was transferred to Sheffield Wednesday for £27,000 in March 1962. Never able to settle at Hillsborough, he returned to Middlesbrough in June 1965 and a further season. After a spell with non-League Hereford United he returned to League action with Workington in February 1968 and joined Peterborough in July 1969. A broken leg brought his career to an end and he retired in September 1970.

John Hollins

John William HOLLINS

Born: Guildford, 16th July 1946
Role: Midfield
Career: Chelsea, Queens Park Rangers, Arsenal
Debut: v Spain (h) 24-5-1967
Appearances: 1

Born into a footballing family (his father played for Stoke and Wolves whilst his brother was with Newcastle and Mansfield) he signed professional forms with Chelsea in July 1963 and quickly established himself as the human dynamo of the side with his non-stop running. He helped the club win the FA Cup in 1970, the League Cup in 1965 and the European Cup Winners' Cup in 1971. John's first spell at Stamford Bridge was to last until June 1975 when he was transferred to Queens Park Rangers after 436 League appearances for the club (he scored 47 goals). John remained at Loftus Road for four years before moving to North London and signing for Arsenal, supposedly in the twilight of his career, but he went on to top the one hundred mark for League appearances for the third time (he made 151 appearances for QPR) over the next three years, racking up 127 appearances for the Gunners and helped them reach the final of the European Cup Winners' Cup in 1980. Even then John's career was not at an end, for in June 1983, at the age of 37, he returned to Stamford Bridge a second time to finish out his playing days, helping them win the Second Division championship in 1984. After 29 turnouts John finally called it a day and moved into coaching. When John Neal was moved from manager to director in 1985, John stepped into the manager's role and served in that capacity for three years. Had John not left Stamford Bridge in 1975 it is quite conceivable that he would have registered the club's greatest tally of appearances. Although he won numerous caps at Youth, Under-23 and B level, John was unfortunate to have been picked for the full England side on only one occasion, but in so doing he created something of a record that may never be beaten; his brother had previously been capped for Wales!

Robert HOLMES

Born: Preston, 23rd June 1867
Died: 17th November 1955
Role: Full-Back
Career: Preston Olympic, Preston North End
Debut: v Ireland (a) 31-3-1888
Appearances: 7

After playing for Preston Olympic, Robert joined Preston North End in 1884 and was an integral part in their early domination of the domestic game, helping them reach the FA Cup final in 1888 where they were beaten by West Bromwich Albion. The following season, the first of the Football League, they won the double, collecting the League without losing a match and winning the cup without conceding a goal. They won the League again in 1890 and finished runners-up in 1891, 1892 and 1893. Robert remained a Preston player until 1901 when he was reinstated as an amateur and placed on the Football League referees list. He later coached at Bradford City and Blackburn Rovers.

John HOLT

Born: Blackburn, 10th April 1865
Role: Centre-Half
Career: King's Own Blackburn, Blackpool St. John's, Bootle, Everton, Reading
Debut: v Wales (a) 15-3-1890
Appearances: 10

Johnny Holt joined Everton in 1888 in time for the opening season of the Football League and quickly became established as one of the best defensive markers in the game. His ability to read the game meant he was often in the right place at the right time to make last-ditch tackles, although he also developed a reputation as 'an artist in the perpetuation of clever minor fouls. When they were appealed for, his shocked look of innocence was side-splitting.' He spent ten years at Everton, helping the club to the League title in 1891 and reaching two FA Cup finals as well as earning nine of his tally of caps for England. He left for Reading in 1898 and was still considered good enough to earn his final cap for England in 1900. He retired from playing in 1902 and was elected to the board of Reading that year, although he was unable to take up his appointment as the FA refused to reinstate him to amateur status. Instead he returned to Liverpool in order to scout for Reading in the area, a position he held until 1914. As well as his 10 caps for England he represented the Football League on two occasions.

Edward HOPKINSON

Born: Royton, 29th October 1935
Died: 25th April 2004
Role: Goalkeeper
Career: Oldham Athletic, Bolton Wanderers
Debut: v Wales (a) 19-10-1957
Appearances: 14

A brief spell as an amateur with Oldham Athletic was followed by similar status at Bolton, Eddie finally signing professional forms with the Trotters in November 1952. He was

Eddie Hopkinson

to remain on the club's books for the next eighteen years, collecting an FA Cup winners' medal in 1958 and also picking up caps for England at Under-23 and full level and representing the Football League twice. He made 519 League appearances for the club between 1956, when he made his debut, and the summer of 1970, when he announced his retirement, a club record. He then joined the coaching staff at Burnden Park although he later spent a brief spell as assistant and acting manager at Stockport County during the 1970s.

Anthony Henry HOSSACK

Born: Walsall, 2nd May 1867
Died: Torquay, 24th January 1925
Role: Wing-Half
Career: Cambridge University, Corinthians
Debut: v Wales (a) 5-3-1892
Appearances: 2

Educated at Chigwell School, playing for the school's side between 1882 and 1886 (he was captain in his final year) he attended Cambridge University and collected a Blue in 1890. He also played cricket for the university and Essex and later played football for Corinthians. He qualified as a solicitor in 1897 and practised at Dawlish in Devonshire.

William Eric HOUGHTON

Born: Billingborough, 29th June 1910
Died: 1st May 1996
Role: Left-Winger
Career: Donnington GS, Boston Town, Billingborough, Aston Villa, Notts County
Debut: v Northern Ireland (a) 20-10-1930 (scored once)
Appearances: 7 (5 goals)

Eric Houghton spent over fifty years associated with Aston Villa, serving the club as a player, manager and director during that time. He was educated at Donnington Grammar School and was spotted by Villa whilst playing for Billingborough, signing amateur forms in August 1927 and turning professional a year later. His playing career at Villa Park coincided with something of a downturn in the club's fortunes, culminating in their relegation into the Second Division for the first time in their history in 1936. Despite this lack of success at club level, Eric was rightly regarded as one of the best left-wingers of the age and collected seven full caps for England and represented the Football League on four occasions. Eric was part of the Villa side that won the Second Division championship in 1938, his only major honour at club level. He remained at Villa Park until 1946, making 361 appearances and scoring 160 goals (72 of these came from only 79 penalty attempts, a phenomenal record) before leaving to join Notts County in December 1946. He finished his playing career in May 1949 and was immediately appointed manager of the Meadow Lane club, remaining in charge for four years before accepting an invitation to return to Villa Park. He guided the club to the FA Cup in 1957, their first success in the competition since 1920. A poor start to the 1958-59 campaign cost him his job in November 1958 and he next resurfaced as chief scout for Nottingham Forest in July 1959, a position he held for a little over a year before becoming manager of non-League club Rugby Town. He scouted for Walsall in 1965 and later joined the board of directors at the club, although in September 1972 he was invited to join the board at his beloved Villa Park. He served on the board until 1979 when he returned to Walsall, serving as general secretary into the following decade. He had also been a noted cricketer earlier in his career, representing Warwickshire and Lincolnshire and in 1971 was awarded the MCC's advanced coaching certificate.

Albert Edward 'Kelly' HOULKER

Born: Blackburn, 27th April 1872
Died: 27th May 1962
Role: Left-Half
Career: Blackburn Hornets, Oswaldthistle Rovers, Cob Wall, Park Road Blackburn, Blackburn Rovers, Portsmouth, Southampton, Blackburn Rovers, Colne
Debut: v Scotland (h) 3-5-1902
Appearances: 5 + 1 unofficial appearance

He played local football in and around the Blackburn area before signing with Blackburn Rovers during the 1893-94 season, going on to represent the Football League once and won the first of his five caps for England. He moved south to Portsmouth in May 1902 where he won a further two caps and journeyed along the coast to join Southampton a year later, winning his final two caps and also helping the club win the Southern League championship in 1904. He returned to Blackburn Rovers in the summer of 1906, officially retiring the following year but later turning out for Colne FC in October 1909. In 1918 he made an emergency appearance for Blackburn in a wartime fixture, being 45 years of age at the time. Upon leaving football he worked at a mill and then ran a coal and haulage business up to his retirement in 1947.

Robert Henry HOWARTH

Born: Preston, 20th June 1865
Died: 20th August 1938
Role: Right-Back
Career: Preston North End, Everton, Preston North End
Debut: v Ireland (h) 5-2-1887
Appearances: 5

Robert Howarth was working as a lawyer's clerk and studying to qualify as a solicitor as well as playing junior football in Preston when he was persuaded to sign for Preston North End in 1884. He helped the club reach the FA Cup final in 1888 where they were beaten by West Bromwich Albion but recovered to dominate the game for the next few years, winning the League and Cup double in 1889 and retain the League title in 1890. He left to join Everton in November 1891, collecting a second runners-up medal in the FA Cup in 1893 before returning to Preston in 1894 and finishing his playing career the following year. He qualified as a solicitor in 1908 and practised in his hometown.

Robert Howarth

Don Howe

Donald HOWE

Born: Wolverhampton, 12th October 1935
Role: Right-Back
Career: West Bromwich Albion, Arsenal
Debut: v Wales (a) 19-10-1957
Appearances: 23

Don signed amateur forms with West Bromwich Albion in December 1950, turning professional in November 1952. He had to wait almost three years before making his first team debut but became a regular in the side soon after, going on to win caps for England at Under-23 and B level before being capped at full level in 1957. After 342 League appearances for the club he was sold to Arsenal for £45,000 in April 1964, but a broken leg sustained in March 1966 forced his retirement. He then joined the coaching staff at Highbury, becoming chief coach in 1967 and assistant manager (to Bertie Mee) in March 1969. He left in July 1971 to return to West Bromwich Albion as manager, remaining in charge for almost four years. After spells at Galatasaray in Turkey and Leeds United he returned to Highbury as coach in August 1977 and then had spells as caretaker manager and manager, a position he held between April 1984 and March 1986. He later had spells coaching Wimbledon and Queens Park Rangers and was also England coach under the likes of Bobby Robson.

John Robert HOWE

Born: West Hartlepool, 7th October 1915
Died: 5th April 1987
Role: Left-Back
Career: Hartlepool United, Derby County, Huddersfield Town, Kings Lynn, Long Sutton, Wisbech Town
Debut: v Italy (a) 16-5-1948
Appearances: 3

After starring in junior football in his native Hartlepool, Jack signed with Hartlepool United in June 1934 and quickly

GHI

established himself as a player with a promising future. In March 1936 he was signed to Derby County by manager George Jobey and stepped almost immediately into the first team. Although he was more usually found at left-back, the fact that he was equally adept with either foot made him a versatile player and he made numerous appearances at right-back. Widely tipped for international honours, the outbreak of the Second World War meant he had to wait considerably longer than many predicted before finally achieving the honour. During the war he served with the Cameron Highlanders and guested for Aberdeen, Falkirk, Hearts and St. Mirren as well as appearing for the Scottish League against the British Army. Unlike club colleague Tim Ward, Jack was demobbed after service in India in time to play an integral part in the side that won the FA Cup in the first season after the war, helping Derby County overcome Birmingham City in the semi final 4-0 in a replay (where he played at centre-half) and Charlton Athletic 4-1 in the final (where he was employed in the right-back position). Following the departure of Raich Carter, Jack took over as captain at Derby, but in October 1949 he was allowed to move to Huddersfield Town where he finished his professional career at the end of the 1950-51 season. He then had spells as player-manager at Kings Lynn and Long Sutton before taking over as manager of Wisbech Town. He is also one of the first known players to have played wearing contact lenses.

Leonard Sidgwick HOWELL

Born: Dulwich, 6th August 1848
Died: Lausanne, Switzerland, 7th September 1895
Role: Full-Back
Career: Wanderers, Surrey
Debut: v Scotland (h) 8-3-1873
Appearances: 1

Educated at Winchester College he played for Wanderers at the time of winning his only cap for England and also helped that club retain the FA Cup in 1873. He also represented Surrey at football and cricket, a member of the cricket team between 1869 and 1890 and appearing in 19 first class matches. Unfortunately his football career appears to have been brought to a halt owing to an injury sustained some time during the 1873-74 season.

Rabbi HOWELL

Born: Wincobank, 12th October 1869
Died: 1937
Role: Right-Back
Career: Ecclesfield, Rotherham Swifts, Sheffield United, Liverpool, Preston North End
Debut: v Ireland (h) 9-3-1895
Appearances: 2 (1 goal)

After playing amateur football for Ecclesfield, Rabbi (whose name is sometimes listed as Raby) signed professional forms for Rotherham Swifts in 1889 and spent one season with the club before joining Sheffield United. Whilst at Bramall Lane he helped the club win the League title in 1898, having already collected two caps for England. He was sold to Liverpool for £200 in April 1898 and spent three seasons with the Anfield club before switching to Preston North End in the close season of 1901. A broken leg sustained in September 1903 brought his playing career to an end. Rabbi was a gypsy and born in a caravan and is thus believed to have been the only gypsy to have represented England at full international level. His nephew Colin Myers enjoyed a professional career during the 1920s.

Stephen Norman HOWEY

Born: Sunderland, 26th October 1971
Role: Centre-Back
Career: Newcastle United, Manchester City, Leicester City, Bolton Wanderers, Hartlepool United
Debut: v Nigeria (h) 16-11-1994
Appearances: 4 + 1 unofficial appearance

Originally a trainee at St. James' Park, Steve signed professional forms in December 1989, at which time he was playing as a striker. He was successfully converted to centre-back by manager Ossie Ardiles and helped the club win the First Division championship in 1993. A £2 million deal took him to Manchester City in August 2000, by which time he was an England international, and he formed a particularly effective defensive partnership with Richard Dunn at Maine Road, helping the club win the First Division title in 2002. In July 2003 he was sold on to Leicester City for £300,000 but was unable to settle, moving on to Bolton in January 2004 on a free transfer. After a spell playing in America for New England Revolution, he returned to England in March 2005 and signed for Hartlepool United.

Steve Howey

Alan Anthony HUDSON

Born: London, 21st June 1951
Role: Midfield
Career: Chelsea, Stoke City, Arsenal, Chelsea, Stoke City
Debut: v West Germany (h) 12-3-1975
Appearances: 2

Born just around the corner from Stamford Bridge, Alan signed schoolboy forms with Chelsea before being taken on as an apprentice in 1966. Upgraded to the professional ranks in June 1968, he quickly established a reputation as an exciting, flair player and was seemingly on his way to writing a large part in the Chelsea history book for himself. Troubled by injuries throughout his career, he was forced to sit it out as Chelsea won the FA Cup in 1970 but was an integral part of the side that lifted the European Cup Winners' Cup the following season. His undoubted abilities on the pitch were frequently rocked by revelations and upsets off it and in January 1974 he was sold to Stoke City for

Alan Hudson

£240,000. His arrival coincided with an upturn in fortunes for the Potteries club, but in December 1976, having fallen out with the manager and with the club in desperate need of money, he was sold back to London, this time to Arsenal, for £180,000. A runners-up medal in the 1978 FA Cup was the highlight of his brief stay at Highbury and in October 1978 he was on his way again, heading over the Atlantic to join Seattle Sounders for £100,000. He was to enjoy the less intense atmosphere of North American football for almost five years before returning to Stamford Bridge in August 1983, but failed to make the first team and moved back to Stoke City. Made club captain, Alan made 39 appearances for Stoke during his second spell with the club before calling time on his career owing to injury at the age of 34.

John HUDSON

Born: Sheffield, 1860
Died: November 1941
Role: Full-Back
Career: Sheffield Heeley, Sheffield, Sheffield Wednesday, Blackburn Olympic, Sheffield United
Debut: v Ireland (a) 24-2-1883
Appearances: 1

He played for a number of clubs in and around the Sheffield area, winning his only cap for England whilst associated with the Sheffield club, the oldest football club in the world having been formed in 1850. He later joined Sheffield Wednesday, where he was briefly club secretary, had a spell with Blackburn Olympic and returned to the Sheffield area to sign for Sheffield United, playing in that club's very first match. Injury brought his playing career to an end and he worked as an engraver in the city.

Francis Carr HUDSPETH

Born: Percy Main, 20th April 1890
Died: 8th February 1963
Role: Left-Back
Career: Scotswood, Newburn, Clare Vale, North Shields Athletic, Newcastle United, Stockport County
Debut: v Northern Ireland (a) 24-10-1925
Appearances: 1 + 1 War appearance

After playing local football in the North East he was signed by Newcastle United in March 1910, costing £100 to transfer

Francis Hudspeth

his registration from North Shields Athletic. The outbreak of the First World War severely disrupted his playing career, although he did take part in one Victory International in 1919 against Wales at Stoke. After the war he became captain of Newcastle United and guided them to victory in the FA Cup in 1924 and the following year was finally rewarded with a full cap for England against Northern Ireland. In 1927 there was further domestic success as Newcastle won the League title, with Hudspeth still captain and an ever-present at the age of 37.

Arthur Edward HUFTON

Born: Southwell, 25th November 1892
Died: 2nd February 1967
Role: Goalkeeper
Career: Atlas & Norfolk Works, Sheffield United, West Ham United, Watford
Debut: v Belgium (a) 1-11-1923
Appearances: 6

Ted Hufton played works football in Sheffield prior to signing for Sheffield United in the summer of 1912. He made his name and reputation however at West Ham, guesting for the club during the First World War and signing for them as soon as normal football resumed in 1919. He was the club's goalkeeper in the first FA Cup final staged at Wembley, although this ended in a 2-0 defeat to Bolton Wanderers. Despite suffering a number of injuries during his career, including a broken arm sustained whilst playing for England, Ted remained at Upton Park until June 1932 when he joined Watford for a season. At the end of his playing career he worked in the motor trade but could still be seen at Upton Park where he worked as a press steward after the Second World War.

Emlyn Walter HUGHES O.B.E.

Born: Barrow, 28th August 1947
Died: 9th November 2004
Role: Defender, Midfield
Career: Roose FC, Blackpool, Liverpool, Wolverhampton Wanderers, Rotherham United, Hull City, Mansfield Town, Swansea City
Debut: v Holland (a) 5-11-1969
Appearances: 62 (1 goal)

After playing for North Lancashire Schools and Roose FC, Emlyn was signed by Blackpool in September 1964. Over the next two years or so he developed into a highly prized midfield player, attracting interest from a number of bigger clubs. It was Blackpool's fate to lose two key players during the 1966-67 season, with Alan Ball joining Everton and Emlyn heading for their rivals across Stanley Park, costing the Anfield club £65,000 when signed in February 1967. Indeed, legend has it that as Bill Shankly and Emlyn Hughes returned to Liverpool following the transfer, Shankly's car was pulled up by the police following a minor traffic offence. "Do you know who is in the car?" asked Shankly, "The future captain of England." Shankly's prediction came true, for Emlyn's all-action performances in the red shirt of Liverpool soon earned him selection for the white shirt of England. Whilst with Liverpool Emlyn won two European Cups, two UEFA Cups, four League titles and the FA Cup as well as runners-up medals from the FA Cup twice and the League Cup. Emlyn also won eight caps for England at Under-23 level and represented the Football League on four occasions. Although Emlyn was a member of the England squad for the 1970 World Cup finals in Mexico he was not picked during the tournament and thus missed out on appearing in the finals, for when England next qualified in 1982 his England career was at an end. In August 1979 he was sold to Wolves for £90,000 and at the end of his first season with the club had collected a winners' medal in the one domestic competition to have previously eluded him, the League Cup. He remained at Molineux until July 1981 when he joined Rotherham United as player-manager, although his brief spell in charge was not a success and he finished his playing career with spells at Hull City, Mansfield Town and Swansea City. He also served on the board of Hull City for a time before leaving the game altogether in order to concentrate on a media career, serving as one of the captains on A Question of Sport for a time.

Emlyn Hughes

Lawrence HUGHES

Born: Liverpool, 2nd March 1924
Role: Centre-Half
Career: Tranmere Rovers, Liverpool
Debut: v Chile (Rio de Janeiro) 25-6-1950 (WC)
Appearances: 3

Laurie played schools and junior football in Liverpool before signing as an amateur with Tranmere Rovers in 1942. The following February he signed professional forms with Liverpool, although without having a settled position and was used in a variety of positions during wartime games. At the end of the Second World War and with the resumption of League football, Laurie slotted into the centre-half position and was an integral part of the side that won the First Division championship in 1946-47. In 1950 he helped Liverpool reach the FA Cup final, where they were beaten by Arsenal 2-0, and that summer was drafted into the England squad for the World Cup campaign in Brazil. He replaced club mate Bill Jones, who in turn had been brought into the side to replace Neil Franklin, but a disastrous World Cup, which saw England beaten by the United States and Spain, meant Laurie's international career was brought to an abrupt end. Despite missing almost two seasons through injury, Laurie continued to give Liverpool exceptional service, making over 300 appearances for the first team before he retired in the summer of 1960. In addition to his three full caps, Laurie was capped by England at B level on one occasion.

Joseph Harold Anthony HULME

Born: Stafford, 26th August 1904
Died: Winchmore Hill, 26th September 1991
Role: Right-Winger
Career: York City, Blackburn Rovers, Arsenal, Huddersfield Town
Debut: v Scotland (a) 2-4-1927
Appearances: 9 (4 goals)

Joe Hulme was reputed to be the fastest winger of his era and joined York City in 1923 after playing for Stafford YMCA. He cost Blackburn Rovers £250 when he signed in February 1924 and two years later Arsenal paid £3,500 to take him to Highbury in February 1926. There he linked especially well with Alex James and helped Arsenal win five League titles, although he only qualified for a medal in 1931, 1933 and 1935. He also won winners' medals in the FA Cup in 1930 and 1936 and appeared in the final in 1927 and 1932. He left Arsenal for Huddersfield Town in January 1938 and made it to the final of the FA Cup at the end of his first season, a record fifth appearance at Wembley in the competition, although once again he had to settle for a runners-up medal as Preston North End won 1-0 with a penalty in the last minute of extra time. He retired from playing at the end of the season having scored 113 goals in 414 League appearances. He then joined Spurs as assistant secretary and replaced Peter McWilliam as manager in

Joe Hulme

1944, a position he held until 1949. He guided them to the FA Cup semi final in 1948 and assembled most of the side that would later win the League title, but by then Joe had gone into sports journalism, a profession he maintained until his retirement in 1965. He was also a noted cricketer, playing for Middlesex between 1929 and 1939 and scored over 8,103 runs, including over 1,000 runs in a season three times, his undoubted speed between the wickets a contributing factor.

Percy HUMPHREYS

Born: Cambridge, 3rd December 1880
Died: London, 13th April 1959
Role: Inside-Right
Career: Cambridge St. Mary's, Queens Park Rangers, Notts County, Leicester Fosse, Chelsea, Tottenham Hotspur, Leicester Fosse, Hartlepool United
Debut: v Scotland (h) 14-4-1903
Appearances: 1

Percy was a renowned centre-forward for QPR, Notts County, Leicester Fosse and Chelsea before signing for Spurs in December 1909, having lost his place at Stamford Bridge to Vivian Woodward. Although Percy made only 45 appearances in the League for Spurs and scored 24 goals, none were as vital as the one he scored in the game against Chelsea in the final match of 1909-10 season, for it ensured Chelsea were relegated instead of Spurs into the Second Division! Thereafter he struggled to command a regular place in the side and was transferred back to Leicester in October 1911, later becoming player-manager of Hartlepool United.

George Samuel HUNT

Born: Barnsley, 22nd February 1910
Died: 29th September 1996
Role: Centre-Forward
Career: Chesterfield, Tottenham Hotspur, Arsenal, Bolton Wanderers, Sheffield Wednesday
Debut: v Scotland (a) 1-4-1933 (scored once)
Appearances: 3 (1 goal) + 1 unofficial appearance

After unsuccessful trials with Barnsley, Sheffield United and Port Vale, George was signed by Chesterfield in September 1929 and quickly became known as a good quality goalscorer, earning the nickname 'The Chesterfield Tough'. His exploits at Chesterfield had several clubs anxious to acquire his services, and whilst Herbert Chapman at Arsenal was known to be keen, he preferred to let George mature a little while longer before making his move. Chapman's hesitancy let in Percy Smith at Spurs and in June 1930 George was bound for White Hart Lane. After making his debut in September 1930 George was allowed to continue his education in the reserves, being brought into the first team usually when Ted Harper was injured. George became a regular in 1932-33, helping the club win promotion to the First Division and collecting his first England cap at the end of the season, scoring in the 2-1 defeat by Scotland. He scored an astonishing 125 goals in just 185 League appearances for Spurs and it was therefore a surprise when he was allowed to make the short move across North London to join Arsenal in October 1937. He was initially signed as replacement for Ted Drake and during his brief six month stay at Highbury helped the club win the League title. He then joined Bolton Wanderers in March 1938 and played for the Trotters during the Second World War, finishing his playing career with Sheffield Wednesday in May 1948. He then returned to Bolton and spent twenty years on the ground staff, serving as coach, scout and assistant trainer until his retirement in September 1968.

Reverend Kenneth Reginald Gunnery HUNT

Born: Oxford, 24th February 1884
Died: Heathfield, 28th April 1949
Role: Wing-Half
Career: Oxford University, Corinthians, Leyton, Crystal Palace, Wolverhampton Wanderers, Oxford City
Debut: v Wales (h) 13-3-1911
Appearances: 2

Educated at Trent College and Queen's College, Oxford, Kenneth Hunt spent his entire career as an amateur and along with Vivian Woodward was considered one of the leading players of the age. Four weeks after playing his final match for Oxford against Cambridge he was a member of the Wolverhampton Wanderers side that won the 1908 FA Cup Final against Newcastle United, scoring one of the goals in the 3-1 victory. A few months later he was a member of the United Kingdom side that won the gold medal against Denmark in the Olympic Games. The same year he was made assistant master at Highgate School, a position which meant he was not always available for Wolves, although he continued to make sporadic League appearances for them and Leyton in the Southern League. Indeed, when he earned his first full cap for England he was credited with being a Leyton player. He also found time to turn out for Oxford City, helping them to the final of the FA Amateur Cup in 1913 (and thus narrowly missed out on becoming only the third man to win winners' medals in both the FA Cup and the FA Amateur Cup) and Crystal Palace. During the First World War he also made a single appearance for Spurs in a match that was abandoned after 15 minutes owing to fog, but after Crystal Palace discovered he had taken part they complained to the FA that Spurs had used their player without permission. Spurs were to successfully plead that as Hunt had not appeared for Palace in over two years they were unaware he was registered with them. After the war he made a further League appearance for Wolves and was also a member of the 1920 United Kingdom side that competed in the Olympic Games at Antwerp (he missed out on the successful side of 1912) and finished his playing career with three years with the Corinthians. In addition to his two full appearances for England he also won 20 amateur caps between 1907 and 1921, his last coming when he was 37 years of age. He retired from teaching in 1945 having spent 37 years at Highgate School.

Roger HUNT

Born: Golborne, 20th July 1938
Role: Inside-Forward
Career: Stockton Heath, Liverpool, Bolton Wanderers
Debut: v Austria (h) 4-4-1962 (scored once)
Appearances: 34 (18 goals)

Roger played schools and youth football in Lancashire and was spotted by Liverpool in 1958, signing amateur forms the same year. He was upgraded to the professional ranks in July 1959 and broke into the side soon after, going on to become a feared goalscorer for the club. He was first capped by England in the same season as helping Liverpool win the Second Division title, with his 41 goals in a season setting a new club record. He then went on to set a new aggregate record, netting 245 goals for the club between 1959 and 1969. During that time he helped Liverpool win the League title in 1964 and 1966 and the FA Cup in 1965 as well as being part of the England side that won the World Cup in 1966. Although he scored in the group matches it was believed he was the player most under threat from the recovered Jimmy Greaves for the final itself, but Roger held his place and played his part in the 4-2 extra time win over West Germany. He left Liverpool in December 1969 for Bolton Wanderers, costing the club £31,000 and spent two and a half years at Burnden Park before retiring in the summer of 1972. As well as his 34 full appearances for England he also represented the Football League on five occasions and the Army whilst doing his national service. After retiring from the game he concentrated on the family haulage business.

Roger Hunt

Stephen Kenneth HUNT

Born: Birmingham, 4th August 1956
Role: Forward
Career: Aston Villa, New York Cosmos (USA), Coventry City, West Bromwich Albion, Aston Villa, Sheffield Wednesday, Aston Villa
Debut: v Scotland (a) (substitute) 26-5-1984
Appearances: 2

His first spell at Villa Park was not a success and he left to join New York Cosmos for £50,000, helping them win the NASL Championships in 1977 and 1978, returning to England with Coventry in September the same year. An £80,000 transfer took him to West Bromwich Albion in 1984 and he won two caps for England during his time at The Hawthorns. He returned to Villa in a £90,000 plus Darren Bradley deal and he finished his career with the club when injury forced his retirement in 1987.

John HUNTER

Born: Sheffield, 1852
Died: 13th April 1903
Role: Half-Back
Career: Sheffield Heeley, Providence, Sheffield Albion, Sheffield Wednesday, Blackburn Olympic, Blackburn Rovers
Debut: v Scotland (a) 2-3-1878
Appearances: 7

Jack Hunter worked as a butcher and silver cutler in Sheffield whilst playing for a number of clubs in the area, winning all of his England caps whilst assisting Sheffield Heeley, a club he joined in 1870. He joined Blackburn Olympic in 1882 and won an FA Cup winners' medal in 1883, remaining with the club until 1887 when he moved across the town to sign for Blackburn Rovers for a short spell. He then became assistant trainer and groundsman at Ewood Park as well as working as a licensee in the town.

Norman HUNTER

Born: Middlesbrough, 29th October 1943
Role: Half-Back
Career: Leeds United, Bristol City, Barnsley
Debut: v Spain (a) 8-12-1965
Appearances: 28 (2 goals)

A tough-tackling defensive midfield player, Norman acquired the nickname 'Bite Yer Legs' during his career but was much more skilful than he was given credit for. Signed by Leeds United in November 1960 he won just about every honour within the game, including the Second Division championship (1964), two League titles (1969 and 1974), the FA Cup (1972), the League Cup (1968) and two Inter Cities Fairs Cups (1968 and 1971) as well as countless runners-up medals from both the European and domestic game during his time at Elland Road. He left for Bristol City for £40,000 in October 1976 and returned to Yorkshire with Barnsley in June 1979, remaining on the playing staff until 1983 but taking over as manager in September 1980. After a spell as assistant manager at West Bromwich Albion he became manager of Rotherham United, later returning to the coaching staff at Elland Road. He then had a spell assisting Terry Yorath at Bradford City before becoming a pundit on BBC Radio Leeds. Norman holds the distinction of being the first official substitute for England when he replaced Joe Baker during the match against Spain in 1965.

Norman Hunter

Sir Geoffrey Charles HURST M.B.E.

Born: Ashton, 8th December 1941
Role: Centre-Forward
Career: West Ham United, Stoke City, West Bromwich Albion
Debut: v West Germany (h) 23-3-1966
Appearances: 49 (24 goals)

Geoff Hurst made 49 appearances for England and scored 24 goals, yet he will forever be remembered for one match and a hat-trick; against West Germany in the 1966 World Cup Final. He represented Chelmsford and Essex schools before being taken onto the West Ham ground staff in 1958, turning professional in April 1959. After breaking into the first team he helped West Ham to the most successful spell of their history, winning the FA Cup in 1964, the European Cup Winners' Cup in 1965 and reaching the final of the League Cup in 1966. There was a bigger prize to come in 1966, of course, and Geoff broke into the squad just before Alf Ramsey named his 22 for the World Cup finals. An injury to Jimmy Greaves gave Geoff his chance in the quarter final against Argentina and he headed home the only goal of the game. Although Greaves was fit by the time of the final, Alf Ramsey decided to keep the side intact. It has always been claimed that Geoff Hurst kept Jimmy Greaves out of the World Cup final, although the player most at risk was in fact Roger Hunt. Regardless of the circumstances surrounding his selection Geoff made the most of the day, equalising in the first half and then scoring twice in extra time to ensure England won the cup. His second goal is still surrounded in controversy; did it or did it not cross the line? We may never know, but in the final seconds of the match Geoff latched on to a clearance from club mate Bobby Moore and raced through to put the result beyond doubt. In so doing he became the first and still only player to have scored a hat-trick in a World Cup Final. After that, his club career, indeed his international career, were unlikely to reach such heights again, although he remained an England regular until April 1972 - his last opponents were the same as his first; West Germany! In August 1972 he left West Ham to sign for Stoke City in an £80,000 deal having made 409 League appearances for the Hammers and scored 180 goals. He made a further 100 League appearances for Stoke before moving on to West Bromwich Albion in August 1975 for £20,000, although a little over six months later he left for Cork Celtic. He was player-manager at Telford United and had a spell as assistant coach to England before joining the coaching staff at Stamford Bridge, stepping up to become caretaker manager in September 1979 and accepted the position on a permanent basis the following month. He was in charge at Chelsea until April 1981 when he was sacked and has gone on to work in the insurance business, alongside his fellow goalscorer from 1966, Martin Peters. He was knighted in 1998.

Geoff Hurst

I-J

INCE, Paul Emerson Carlyle
IREMONGER, James

JACK, David Nightingale Bone
JACKSON, Elphinstone
JAMES, David Benjamin
JARRETT, Reverend Beaumont Griffith
JEFFERIS, Frank
JEFFERS, Francis
JENAS, Jermaine
JEZZARD, Bedford A G
JOHNSON, Andy
JOHNSON, David Edward
JOHNSON, Edward
JOHNSON, Glen
JOHNSON, Joseph Alfred
JOHNSON, Seth Art Maurice
JOHNSON, Thomas Clark Fisher
JOHNSON, William Harrison
JOHNSTON, Henry
JONES, Alfred
JONES, Harry
JONES, Herbert
JONES, Michael David
JONES, Robert Marc
JONES, William
JONES, William Henry
JOY, Bernard

Paul Ince

Paul Emerson Carlyle INCE

Born: Ilford, 21st October 1967
Role: Midfield
Career: West Ham United, Manchester United, Internazionale (Italy), Liverpool, Middlesbrough, Wolverhampton Wanderers
Debut: v Spain (a) 9-9-1992
Appearances: 53 (2 goals) + 1 unofficial appearance

Paul signed apprentice forms with West Ham United in July 1985 and quickly established himself as a combative type of midfield player. After four years at Upton Park, during which time he had made nearly 100 first team appearances he was sold to Manchester United for £1 million, although he hardly endeared himself to West Ham fans by being photographed in Manchester United kit before the deal had gone through. At Manchester United he helped the club win the FA Cup in 1990, the European Cup Winners' Cup in 1991, the League Cup in 1992, the League title in 1993 and the domestic double in 1994, narrowly missing out on a second double in 1995 when United were runners-up in both the League and FA Cup. Although United did accomplish a second double in 1996, Paul had already left, bound for Internazionale of Milan for £8 million in July 1995. He spent two years with the Italian club before returning home with Liverpool in a deal worth £4.2 million. An England regular since 1992 he was one of the country's best performers against Italy in 1997 when England qualified for the World Cup finals and then gave assured performances out in France, although he had the misfortune to miss one of England's penalties when they were eliminated after a shoot out against Argentina in the second round. His next appearance for England was hardly better, for he was sent off in the match against Sweden and was handed a three match ban by UEFA. In August 1999 he moved on to Middlesbrough for £1 million and spent three years with the club before being released on a free transfer and signing for Wolverhampton Wanderers. He is a cousin to former boxer Nigel Benn.

James IREMONGER

Born: Norton, 5th March 1876
Died: 25th March 1956
Role: Full-Back
Career: Wilford, Nottingham Jardine, Nottingham Forest
Debut: v Scotland (h) 30-3-1901
Appearances: 2

Jimmy came from a sporting family, with his brother Albert serving as Notts County's goalkeeper between 1904 and 1926. Jimmy signed with Nottingham Forest in 1896 and went on to represent the Football League on four occasions as well as collecting his four full caps for England during his spell with the club. He retired in 1910 and effectively concentrated on his other sporting interest, cricket, playing for the county side 334 times between 1899 and 1914 and the MCC touring side of Australia in 1911-12. The following year (1913) he was named Wisden's Cricketer of the Year. He coached the Notts County Cricket Club between 1921 and 1938 and was also trainer at Notts County football club between 1919 and 1927.

David Bone Nightingale JACK

Born: Bolton, 3rd April 1899
Died: London, 10th September 1958
Role: Inside-Right
Career: Plymouth Presbyterians, Royal Navy, Plymouth Argyle, Bolton Wanderers, Arsenal
Debut: v Wales (h) 3-3-1924
Appearances: 9 (3 goals)

David Jack played schools football in Southend and after playing junior football in Plymouth signed for Plymouth Argyle, where his father was manager in 1919, having guested for Chelsea during the First World War. After just one season he returned to his hometown, costing Bolton £3,000 in the process. He appeared in two FA Cup Finals for Bolton, scoring the very first goal ever at Wembley in the 1923 final and the only goal of the game in 1926 before being sold to Arsenal for £10,890 in October 1928. This was the first five figure transfer fee and almost double the previous record, and although eyebrows were raised at Arsenal paying so much for a player who was already 30 years of age, David made just as much an impact at Highbury as he had at Burnden Park. He collected a third winners' medal in the FA Cup in 1930 and a runners-up medal in 1932 as well as three League titles, in 1931, 1933 and 1934. He retired as a player in the summer of 1934 having scored nearly 300 League goals in some 500 appearances and became secretary-manager of Southend United, a position he held until August 1940. He was then manager of Sunderland greyhound stadium until returning to the game when appointed manager of Middlesbrough in September 1944, holding this position until April 1952. He then went to Ireland where he was manager of Shelbourne between August 1953 and April 1955. His father Bob had two spells as manager of Plymouth, between 1905 and 1906 and then 1910 until 1938, whilst his son David was a football journalist in England and Australia.

David Jack

Elphinstone JACKSON

Born: Calcutta, India, 9th October 1868
Died: December 1945
Role: Full-Back
Career: Oxford University, Corinthians
Debut: v Wales (h) 7-3-1891
Appearances: 1

Educated at Lancing College and captain of the college team in 1887 he then attended Oxford University, earning his Blue in 1890 and 1891. He also played for Corinthians in 1890 and 1891 and after finishing university he returned to India where he helped form the Indian FA in 1893.

David Benjamin JAMES

Born: Welwyn Garden City, 1st August 1970
Role: Goalkeeper
Career: Watford, Liverpool, Aston Villa, West Ham United, Manchester City
Debut: v Mexico (h) 27-3-1997
Appearances: 33

Taken on by Watford as a trainee in 1988 he spent four years at Vicarage Road, becoming recognised as one of the best goalkeepers outside the top division and regularly being watched by scouts from other clubs. A £1 million transfer took him to Anfield in July 1992, with the intention being that he would eventually replace Bruce Grobbelaar, although he took a while to break into the first team. When he finally did he appeared nervous and unsure of the step up through the divisions, prompting a spell in the reserves. He returned to first team duty, re-discovering some of his form and earned a call-up for the full England side, but further hesitant performances led to Liverpool swooping onto the transfer market again, this time landing American Brad Friedel, albeit after a number of wrangles with the Department of Employment over securing a work permit. David then left Anfield and joined Aston Villa and, away from the intense glare of publicity, finally began showing his old promise. By the time he moved on to West Ham United he was established as the replacement for David Seaman and made the goalkeeper's berth his own for England. Having replaced David Seaman at England level, David James then did the same at club level, moving to Manchester City after Seaman had announced his retirement following an injury. David seemed set for an extended run in the England side,

David James

but a couple of hesitant performances, culminating in a 2-2 draw against Austria in the first qualifying match for the 2006 World Cup in which David was at fault for at least one of the goals saw him relegated to the bench for England's next match away in Poland. The assured performances of his replacement Paul Robinson meant he had to be content with a place on the bench, but further poor performances during a tour of the United States in 2005 and a friendly against Denmark in August the same year saw him dropped from the squad altogether. Off the field David is an accomplished artist, with his drawings having appeared regularly in the Watford programme during his time with the club.

Reverend Beaumont Griffith JARRETT

Born: London, 18th July 1855
Died: 11th April 1905
Role: Half-Back
Career: Cambridge University, Old Harrovians
Debut: v Scotland (a) 4-3-1876
Appearances: 3

Educated at Harrow he attended Cambridge University and won a Blue in three consecutive years, 1876, 1887 and 1888, serving as captain of the side in 1877. After university he played for both Old Harrovians and Grantham FC and served on the FA Council between 1876 and 1878. He was ordained in 1878 and then worked in Lancashire for the rest of his life.

Frank JEFFERIS

Born: Fordingbridge, 3rd July 1884
Died: 21st May 1938
Role: Inside-Right
Career: Fordingbridge Turks, Southampton, Everton, Preston North End, Southport
Debut: v Wales (a) 11-3-1912
Appearances: 2

Taken on as a professional by Southampton in 1905, he performed well in the Southern League, prompting a move to Everton in March 1911 for £750. In 1915 he helped Everton win the last League championship before organised football shut down for the duration of the First World War but retained his place when football resumed. He was sold to Preston in January 1920, helping the club reach the FA Cup final in 1922 and the following year joined Southport as player-coach, a position he retained until his retirement in the summer of 1925. He was taken on by Southport again as trainer/coach in 1926 but actually played two League matches during the 1926-27 season in an emergency. He joined Millwall Athletic as coach in May 1936 and collapsed and died at the ground in May 1938.

Francis JEFFERS

Born: Liverpool, 25th January 1981
Role: Forward
Career: Everton, Arsenal, Everton, Charlton Athletic, Rangers
Debut: v Australia (h) 12-2-2003
Appearances: 1

A graduate of Everton's youth scheme, Francis made his League debut whilst still a 16-year old in 1997 and did not become a professional with the club until the following February. Two months later he helped the club win the FA Youth Cup and the following season was given an extended run in the side, becoming a scorer of considerable potential. By the time of his transfer to Arsenal in June 2001 for £8 million, he was an established member of the Under-21 side (he has 16 caps to his name) and although he struggled to break into the Arsenal side with regularity, did earn a full England cap in 2003. A spell on loan back with Everton prompted rumours he was on his way back to Goodison Park on a permanent basis, but in August 2004 he was sold to Charlton for £2.6 million. He had a spell on loan to Rangers during the 2005-06 season.

Francis Jeffers

Jermaine Anthony JENAS

Born: Nottingham, 18-2-1983
Role: Midfield
Career: Nottingham Forest, Newcastle United, Tottenham Hotspur
Debut: v Australia (h) 12-2-2003
Appearances: 14

Taken on as a trainee by his hometown club Nottingham Forest, Jermaine signed professional forms in February 2000 having already represented his country at Youth level. Consistent performances for his club earned a call-up to the Under-21 side (he has won nine caps) and a £5 million move to Newcastle United in February 2002. The higher profile led to his winning his first full cap for his country a year later as well as selection as the PFA Young Player of the Year, but by the summer of 2005 he was claiming that he was unsettled in Newcastle and wished to move away from the area. He was promptly sold to Spurs for £7 million.

Jermaine Jenas

Bedford Alfred George JEZZARD

Born: Clerkenwell, 19th October 1927
Died: 21st May 2005
Role: Centre-Forward
Career: Fulham
Debut: v Hungary (a) 23-5-1954
Appearances: 2

Bedford had briefly been signed to Watford as an amateur but was working at Old Merchant Taylor's sport ground when he was invited to join Fulham, signing amateur forms in the summer of 1948 and being upgraded to the professional ranks in October. He helped them win the Second Division championship in 1949 and made appearances for England at B level and the Football League before earning his first full cap for his country in the 7-1 defeat by Hungary. He was on tour with the FA XI in South Africa in 1957 when he sustained the ankle injury that brought his playing career to an end, having netted 154 goals in 306 games for Fulham. He was appointed to the coaching staff at Craven Cottage later in 1957, becoming manager in June 1958, remaining in the post until October 1964 when he became general manager. He left the club in December the same year and became a licensee in Hammersmith.

Andrew JOHNSON

Born: Bedford, 10th February 1981
Role: Striker
Career: Birmingham City, Crystal Palace
Debut: v Holland (h) 9-2-2005
Appearances: 2

Taken on as a junior by Birmingham City, Andy was upgraded to professional in March 1998 but was unable to become a regular within the side at St. Andrews, prompting a £750,000 move to Crystal Palace in August 2002. Here he discovered a rich vein of goalscoring form, helping the club reach the Premiership in 2004. His first season in the top flight saw him net 21 goals for a struggling Palace side, earning a number of call-ups to the England squad and his first cap in the friendly against Holland in February 2005. Although Palace were relegated at the end of the 2004-05 season, Andy signed a new long term contract with the club.

Andy Johnson

David Edward JOHNSON

Born: Liverpool, 23rd October 1951
Role: Centre-Forward
Career: Everton, Ipswich Town, Liverpool, Everton, Barnsley, Manchester City, Tulsa Roughnecks (USA), Preston North End
Debut: v Wales (h) 21-5-1975 (scored twice)
Appearances: 8 (6 goals)

A former Everton apprentice, David was taken on as a professional in April 1969 but struggled to make the grade at Goodison Park, being swapped for another player from Ipswich Town in October 1976. He proved an almost immediate success at Portman Road, earning the first of his eight caps for England. He was transferred to Liverpool in August 1976 for £200,000, going on to collect a runners-up medal in the FA Cup, three League titles and a winners' medal in the 1981 European Cup. He returned to Everton for £100,000 in August 1982 but could not reproduce his earlier form, spending a month on loan with Barnsley before moving on to Manchester City in March 1984. After a spell with Tulsa Roughnecks he finished his playing career with Preston North End.

Edward JOHNSON

Born: Stoke-on-Trent, 1860
Died: 30th June 1901
Role: Winger
Career: Stoke, Birmingham FA, Staffordshire
Debut: v Wales (a) 15-3-1880
Appearances: 2 (2 goals)

Educated at Saltley College and a member of the college team when he won his first cap for England, he joined Stoke in 1880 and won his second cap four years later, also scoring twice in the 8-1 win over Ireland in Belfast. An injury sustained in a fall from a horse-drawn carriage forced his retirement as a player, although he served the Staffordshire FA as a member for a number of years before ill health brought about his resignation in 1898.

Glen McLeod JOHNSON

Born: London, 23rd August 1984
Role: Defender
Career: West Ham United, Chelsea
Debut: v Denmark (h) 16-11-2003
Appearances: 5

Signed by the Hammers from school, Glen was promoted to the professional ranks in 2001. He made just 15 League appearances for the Upton Park outfit and had a spell out on loan at Millwall before moving on to Chelsea, signed by Claudio Ranieri for £6 million in 2003. Whilst Joe Cole and Frank Lampard were already seasoned and experienced professionals by the time they arrived at Stamford Bridge, the acquisition of Glen Johnson was seen by many as one for the future, although he did manage to make 19 League appearances for the club during the 2003-04 season. The arrival of Paulo Ferreira, further competition for the full-back berth, meant restricted outings during the following season, although restricted club appearances do not appear to have harmed his international chances, for he was capped by England in November 2003 against Denmark and has since added to his tally of caps.

Glen Johnson

Joe Johnson

Joseph Alfred JOHNSON

Born: Grimsby, 4th April 1911
Died: 8th August 1983
Role: Left-Winger
Career: Scunthorpe United, Bristol City, Stoke City, West Bromwich Albion, Northwich Victoria, Hereford United
Debut: v Northern Ireland (h) 18-11-1936
Appearances: 5 (2 goals)

After playing schools football in Grimsby and being briefly associated with Scunthorpe United, Joe signed with Bristol City in May 1931. After only seven appearances for the club he was sold to Stoke City for £150 in April 1932 and helped the club win the Second Division championship in 1933, playing on the opposite wing to Stanley Matthews. Joe was signed by West Bromwich Albion in November 1937, remaining with the club until the end of the Second World War and signing with Northwich Victoria in August 1946. He finished his playing career with Hereford United in 1948.

Seth Art Maurice JOHNSON

Born: Birmingham, 12th March 1979
Role: Midfield
Career: Crewe Alexandra, Derby County, Leeds United, Derby County
Debut: v Italy (h) 15-11-2000
Appearances: 1

A graduate of the Crewe Alexandra youth scheme, Seth signed professional forms in July 1996 and quickly became noted as a midfield player of considerable promise. A £3 million move took him to Derby County in May 1999, by which time he was an England Youth and Under-21 international. His progress continued at Derby, culminating in a full England cap in November 2000 and the following year, in October 2001 a £7 million move to Leeds United. His time at Elland Road was rocked by a succession of injuries, with him being released on a free transfer in the summer of 2005. After training and proving his fitness with Derby County, he signed on with the club a second time.

Seth Johnson

Thomas Clark Fisher JOHNSON

Born: Dalton-in-Furnace, 19th August 1900
Died: 28th January 1973
Role: Inside-Left
Career: Dalton Casuals, Manchester City, Everton, Liverpool, Darwen
Debut: v Belgium (a) 24-5-1926 (scored once)
Appearances: 5 (5 goals)

After a spell as an amateur with Manchester City, Tommy Johnson signed professional forms in February 1919 and became renowned as a feared goalscorer, netting 158 goals for the club before moving on in 1930, including 38 in the 1928-29 season, both tallies still being club records. Having helped the club win the Second Division championship in 1928 and reach the FA Cup final in 1926, he was sold to Everton for £6,000 in March 1930. At Goodison Park he collected championship medals from the Second and First Divisions in successive seasons, 1931 and 1932 and an FA Cup winners' medal in 1933. He moved across the city to sign for Liverpool in March 1934 before finishing his playing career with Darwen.

William Harrison JOHNSON

Born: Ecclesfield, 4th January 1876
Died: 17th July 1940
Role: Right-Half
Career: Sheffield United
Debut: v Ireland (a) 17-3-1900 (scored once)
Appearances: 6 (1 goal)

Originally a centre-half whilst playing for Ecclesfield Church, he joined Sheffield United in 1895 and was successfully converted to wing-half, helping the club win the FA Cup in 1899 and 1902 and reach the final in 1901. He retired through injury in the summer of 1909 and was subsequently appointed assistant trainer at Bramall Lane, a position he retained until the mid 1930s. His two sons, Harry and Tom also played for Sheffield United.

Henry JOHNSTON

Born: Manchester, 26th September 1919
Died: 12th October 1973
Role: Half-Back
Career: Droylsden Athletic, Blackpool
Debut: v Holland (h) 27-11-1946
Appearances: 10

Harry was born in the Droylsden area of Manchester and played for the local side before signing as an amateur with Blackpool in June 1935, being upgraded to the professional ranks the following year. The outbreak of the Second World War cost him six years of his career, but he was widely regarded as being at his best immediately after the hostilities ended, collecting his first cap for England in 1946. He helped Blackpool reach the FA Cup Final on three occasions, collecting runners-up medals in 1948 and 1951 and then playing a major part in the success of 1953, the final that has since become known as the Matthews Final, collecting the trophy as captain of the side. Harry was named Footballer of the Year in 1951 and remained with Blackpool despite overtures from several other clubs until his retirement in November 1955 when he became manager of Reading. He remained in charge at Elm Park until January 1963 and later returned to Blackpool as chief scout and caretaker manager before leaving the club in 1972. He also had spells as a sports journalist and ran a newsagents in Blackpool. In addition to his 10 full caps, Harry also represented the Football League on four occasions.

Harry Johnston

Alfred JONES

Born: Walsall, 1861
Role: Full-Back
Career: Walsall Town Swifts, Great Lever, Walsall Town Swifts, Aston Villa
Debut: v Scotland (a) 11-3-1882
Appearances: 3

Alf played junior football in and around Walsall before signing with Walsall Town Swifts, going on to become the club's first player to gain international recognition. After a spell with Great Lever, during which he collected his final cap for England, he returned to Walsall in the summer of 1883. Two years later he joined Aston Villa where he finished his career.

Harry Jones

Harry JONES

Born: Blackwell, May 1891
Role: Left-Back
Career: Wesley Guild, Blackwell Colliery, Nottingham Forest, Sutton Town
Debut: v France (a) 10-5-1923
Appearances: 1

Harry joined Nottingham Forest from Blackwell Colliery in the summer of 1911 and proved to be a solid and reliable defender for the club, helping them win the Second Division championship in 1922. His club performances earned him representative honours from the Football League and a place in the England side that beat France 4-1 in Paris in 1923. His chance of winning further honours was brought to a halt by serious injury that prompted him to retire in the summer of 1924, although he later played a number of games for Sutton Town.

Herbert JONES

Born: Blackpool, 3rd September 1896
Died: 11th September 1973
Role: Left-Back
Career: South Shore Strollers, Fleetwood, Blackpool, Blackburn Rovers, Brighton & Hove Albion, Fleetwood
Debut: v Scotland (a) 2-4-1927
Appearances: 6

After playing for the Army during the First World War he signed for Fleetwood in 1920 and soon came to the attention of the local professional club, Blackpool. He signed in the summer of 1922 and spent three and a half years at Bloomfield Road before a £3,850 move to Blackburn Rovers in December 1925. He helped the club win the FA Cup in 1928, by which time he was a full England international, before moving on to Brighton in June 1934. After a season with Brighton he returned to Fleetwood where he finished his playing career. As well as six full caps for England, Taffy, as he was known, also represented the Football League on three occasions.

Michael David JONES

Born: Workspop, 24th April 1940
Role: Centre-Forward
Career: Sheffield United, Leeds United
Debut: v West Germany (a) 12-5-1965
Appearances: 3

Mick worked in a cycle factory before being taken on by Sheffield United as an apprentice, turning professional in November 1962. An aggressive and courageous centre-forward he formed a particularly effective partnership with Alan Birchenall and earned nine caps for England at Under-23 level before being selected for the full side in successive friendlies against West Germany and Sweden in 1965. A £100,000 move took him to Elland Road in 1967 and he won a succession of honours with the club, including the League title in 1969 and 1974, the FA Cup in 1972 and the Inter Cities Fairs Cup in 1968 and 1971 as well as various runners-up medals. Recalled into the England side for the friendly against Holland in 1970, it proved to be his last appearance for his country. Injuries had interrupted his career during his time at Elland Road and he was forced to retire in August 1975.

Mick jones

Robert Marc JONES

Born: Wrexham, 5th November 1971
Role: Right-Back
Career: Crewe Alexandra, Liverpool
Debut: v France (h) 19-2-1992
Appearances: 8

Rob was born in Wales and represented that country as a schoolboy but opted to play for England at Youth level. He was snapped up by Crewe Alexandra straight from school, signing as a trainee in December 1988. Guided by manager Dario Gradi he became one of the best full-backs in the lower divisions, prompting a swoop by Liverpool to take him to Anfield for £300,000 in 1991. For the next couple of years Rob's career continued its upward march, winning his first full cap for England and the FA Cup with Liverpool in 1992 and the League Cup, again with Liverpool, in 1995. Thereafter things started to go wrong, with a succession of injuries halting his run in the side for both club and country. He had to undergo a hernia operation at the end of the 1997-98 season and sat out the entire following season before retiring from the game.

Rob Jones

William JONES

Born: Brighton, 6th March 1876
Died: 1908
Role: Inside-Left
Career: Heaton Rovers, Willington Athletic, Loughborough Town, Bristol City, Tottenham Hotspur, Swindon Town
Debut: v Ireland (h) 9-3-1901
Appearances: 1

Billy Jones began his career as an inside-forward with Heaton Rovers, Willington Athletic, Loughborough Town and Bristol City, arriving at City in 1897. During his nine years with the club he was successfully converted to half-back and earned his sole cap for England, but by 1906 was considered to be surplus to requirements at Ashton Gate, even though he had recently helped them to the Second Division title. He was snapped up by Spurs, despite his 30 years of age, and gave the club adequate service for the year he spent at White Hart Lane. During his time at Spurs he was named Bristol Jones in order to distinguish him from J. L. Jones, a Welsh international player also at the club at the time. He then joined Swindon Town in May 1907 but spent only one year with the Wiltshire club before retiring. Sadly he died from typhoid soon after.

William Henry JONES

Born: Whalley, 13th May 1921
Role: Half-Back
Career: Hayfield St. Matthews, Liverpool, Ellesmere Port Town
Debut: v Portugal (a) 14-5-1950
Appearances: 2

Bill played for Hayfield St. Matthews in Derbyshire before being spotted by Liverpool and signed with the Anfield club in September 1938. The outbreak of the Second World War put his Liverpool debut on hold for more than seven years but he returned at the end of the hostilities, during which he won the Military Medal, desperate to make up for lost time. An adaptable player, Bill played in six different positions for the club during the 1946-47 season, which saw Liverpool crowned League champions, although he was usually to be found at either centre-forward or centre-half. It was in this latter position that he won his two caps for England, drafted into the side after the defection of Neil Franklin to Colombia. Although England won both matches, Bill was not used again by his country. He subsequently switched to left-half when Liverpool reached the FA Cup final in 1950. Unfortunate that England were well served in most of the positions Bill favoured, he did represent the Football League on one occasion and also collected an England B cap. In May 1954 Bill left Liverpool to become player-manager at Ellesmere Port Town, having made 257 League appearances for the Anfield club. At the end of his playing career Bill went into business but continued to scout for Liverpool during the 1960s and 70s.

Bernard JOY

Born: Fulham, 29th October 1911
Died: 18th July 1984
Role: Centre-Back
Career: London University, Casuals, Corinthians, Southend United, Fulham, Arsenal, Casuals
Debut: v Belgium (a) 9-5-1936
Appearances: 1 + 1 War appearance

The last amateur player to represent England at full level, Bernard attended London University and played for the Casuals before signing with Southend and then Fulham as an amateur, making one League appearance for the Craven Cottage side during the 1933-34 season. He was working as a schoolmaster when he linked up with Arsenal in May 1935, going on to win an FA Amateur Cup winners' medal with Casuals in 1936 and then a League championship medal with Arsenal in 1938. He remained signed to Arsenal until the summer of 1947, by which time he had become a sports journalist, when he returned to Casuals, finally retiring as a player in the summer of 1948. Best known for his writing in the London newspapers The Star and Evening Standard he retired in 1976. As well as his two appearances for the England side (one of which came in a wartime fixture) he also won 12 caps for England at amateur level.

Bernard Joy

K

KAIL, Edgar Isaac Lewis
KAY, Anthony Herbert
KEAN, Frederick William
KEEGAN, Joseph Kevin
KEEN, Errington Ridley Liddell
KELLY, Robert
KENNEDY, Alan Philip
KENNEDY, Raymond
KENYON-SLANEY, Right Hon William Stanley
KEOWN, Martin Raymond
KEVAN, Derek Tennyson
KIDD, Brian
KING, Canon Robert Stuart
KING, Ledley
KINGSFORD, Robert Kennett
KINGSLEY, Matthew
KINSEY, George
KIRCHEN, Alfred John
KIRKE-SMITH, Reverend Arnold
KIRTON, William John
KNIGHT, Arthur Egerton
KNIGHT, Zat
KNOWLES, Cyril Barry
KONCHESKY, Paul

Kevin Keegan

Edgar Isaac Lewis KAIL

Born: London, 26th November 1900
Died: 1976
Role: Inside-Right
Career: Dulwich Hamlet, Surrey County
Debut: v France (a) 9-5-1929 (scored twice)
Appearances: 3 (2 goals)

An amateur throughout his career, Edgar won just about every honour available with Dulwich Hamlet, the club he joined in 1915 and remained with as a player until 1934, apart from a very brief spell with Chelsea in 1930, although he did not appear in a single match for the Stamford Bridge club. He represented England at schoolboy level on two occasions, collected 21 caps at amateur level and helped Dulwich Hamlet win the FA Amateur Cup in 1920 and 1932. He also represented the Ishmian League, in which Dulwich Hamlet competed, on 24 occasions. He was employed as a travelling sales representative for a wine and spirit company before retiring in 1966.

Anthony Herbert KAY

Born: Sheffield, 13th May 1937
Role: Wing-Half
Career: Sheffield Wednesday, Everton
Debut: v Switzerland (a) 5-6-1963 (scored once)
Appearances: 1 (1 goal)

Tony spent nine years with local club Sheffield Wednesday and had developed into one of the best wing-halves in the game during his time at Hillsborough. In December 1962 he was transferred to Everton for £55,000, helping the club win the title at the end of his first season at Goodison. He also won one cap for England and seemed on the verge of greatness when he was embroiled in the greatest scandal to hit football since 1915. In April 1964 the Sunday People accused him, Peter Swan and David Layne, all of whom had been team-mates at Sheffield Wednesday, of having been bribed to throw the match against Ipswich Town on December 1st 1962 (Ipswich won 2-0 at Portman Road, although Kay was named man of the match!). Before even the FA could react to the accusations the three players, along with others involved in what transpired to be a betting syndicate, were brought before the courts and given prison sentences ranging from four months to four years. All were then banned for life from the game by the Football Association, although one of the players concerned, Brian Phillips, successfully appealed against the ban in 1971. For Tony Kay, however, it was the end of his career, for he was not interested in trying to return to playing or management. When Kay had served his sentence he remained in Liverpool for a while and even became a bookmaker before emigrating to Spain.

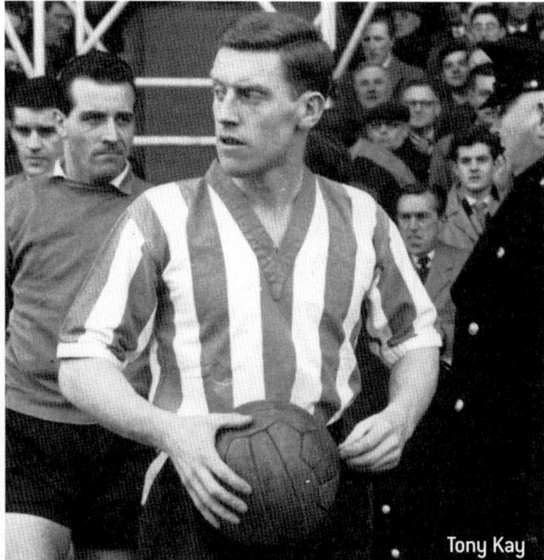
Tony Kay

Fred Kean

Frederick William KEAN

Born: Sheffield, 3rd April 1897
Died: 28th October 1973
Role: Right-Half, Centre-Half
Career: Hallam, Portsmouth, Sheffield Wednesday, Bolton Wanderers, Luton Town, Sutton Town
Debut: v Belgium (h) 19-3-1923
Appearances: 9

Although born in Sheffield and a player for the local Hallam side, Fred began his career with Portsmouth in 1919 before returning to his native Sheffield to sign for Wednesday in the summer of 1920. He helped the club win the Second Division championship in 1926 and had won seven caps for England before a £5,500 move to Bolton Wanderers in September 1928. By the end of the season he had helped his new side win the FA Cup and collected the last of his caps in the European tour against France and Spain. He joined Luton in June 1931 and remained with the club until moving onto Sutton as player-coach in November 1935.

Joseph Kevin KEEGAN O.B.E.

Born: Doncaster, 14th February 1951
Role: Midfield, Forward
Career: Scunthorpe United, Liverpool, SV Hamburg (West Germany), Southampton, Newcastle United
Debut: v Wales (a) 15-11-1972 (ECQ)
Appearances: 63 (21 goals) + 1 unofficial international (2 goals)

Whilst Kevin may not have been the most naturally of gifted player to have represented England, he was certainly one of the hardest working. He played school and junior football in Doncaster before being taken on as an apprentice by Scunthorpe United in December 1967 and was upgraded to the professional ranks in December 1968. In May 1971 Bill Shankly returned to Scunthorpe (he had previously bought Ray Clemence from the same club) to take the former right winger to Anfield, paying £33,000 for his signature. His rise at Liverpool was little short of phenomenal, for a little over a year later he had broken into the England side and had began collecting an impressive array of medals. During his time at Anfield he won winners medals in the European Cup (1977), UEFA Cup (1973 and 1976) and three League titles (1973, 1976 and 1977) and was named Footballer of the Year in 1976. He surprisingly elected to leave Liverpool in June 1977, signing for SV Hamburg in a deal worth £500,000, although the move had little effect on his standing within the game, for in 1978 and 1979 he was named European Player of the Year, also collecting the German Player of the Year award in 1978. He helped Hamburg win the Bundesliga championship in 1979 and the following was inspirational as they reached the European Cup final, although they were beaten in that final by Nottingham Forest. He returned to England in July 1980, linking with Lawrie McMenemy at Southampton for £400,000, and whilst domestic honours eluded the Saints Kevin was again named Footballer of the Year in 1982. He was suffering from injury shortly before the 1982 World Cup finals in Spain, finally coming on for the final ten minutes of the match against the host nation as England desperately sought the two goals that would take them through to the semi finals. A fully fit Keegan (and Trevor Brooking for that matter) might well have scored the required goals, but England's two late chances fell to the two players still struggling for fitness and the nation went out of the competition. New manager Bobby Robson left him out of the very next squad, with Kevin learning of his omission from the media, a fact that did not go down too well with the player. He left Southampton the same year in order to galvanise Newcastle United's promotion push, costing the club £100,000 but repaying the fee when promotion was secured in 1984. He then announced his retirement from the game and spent much of the next few years doing little other than play golf in Spain. In 1992, after eight years out of football and with his golf well up to par he came back into the fore by accepting the position of manager of Newcastle United. his impact at St James' Park matched that he had achieved as a player, guiding the club to the First Division championship and promotion into the Premier League. They then became chief rivals to Manchester United for the League title, although had to be content with a runners up spot. In January 1997 he sensationally resigned, with the club's impending flotation on the stock exchange and need to tie their manager down to a lengthy contract cited as the reason. Once again, Kevin was replaced by Kenny as Dalglish took over at Newcastle. After a brief spell spent as a television pundit Kevin returned to the game with Fulham, accepting an invitation to become Director of Football. He appointed long time friend Ray Wilkins as manager, but at the end of the 1997-98 season, with Fulham in the middle of the play-offs, he dismissed Wilkins and took over team matters himself. He ultimately set them on the road to the Premiership, but by the time they arrived, Keegan was already elsewhere. Following the departure of departure of Glenn Hoddle from the England manager's position Keegan was seen by many as the ideal replacement and initially Keegan intended doing the job on a part-time basis. Eventually he was persuaded to take over the England role on a more permanent basis and guided the team to the finals of the 2000 European Championships. Despite finally beating the Germans in the group stages, England progressed no further. Germany was to loom large again a few months later, for in England's opening game of the 2002 World Cup qualifying campaign, the Germans won 1-0 in the last game played at Wembley before the over 75 year old stadium was pulled down. Keegan tendered his resignation immediately following the game, saying he had taken the team as far as he could. After a few months out of the game, Kevin Keegan returned once again, this time in charge of Manchester City. In 2005, with his contract due to expire at the end of the season, he announced that we would not be renewing it, intending to see out the 2004-05 season and then retire. A couple of months before the end of the season, however, it was agreed that he should leave the club.

Errington Ridley Liddell KEEN

Born: Walker-on-Tyne, 1910
Died: July 1984
Role: Left-Half
Career: Nun's Moor, Newcastle Swifts, Newcastle United, Derby County, Chelmsford City, Hereford United, Leeds United, Bacup Borough
Debut: v Austria (h) 7-12-1932
Appearances: 4

Ike Keen was spotted by Newcastle United whilst playing local football for Newcastle Swifts and signed with the St. James' Park club in September 1927. He made only one appearance for the club in three years before being swapped with Derby County's Harry Bedford in December 1930. He went on to become a regular at Derby, representing the Football League and won four caps for England between 1932 and 1936 before moving on to Chelmsford City in May 1938. After serving Hereford United as player-manager for the duration of the Second World War, Ike signed with Leeds United in December 1945 and finished his playing career with Bacup Borough before going on to coach in Hong Kong.

Robert KELLY

Born: Ashton-in-Makerfield, 16th November 1893
Died: Fylde, Lancashire, 22nd September 1969
Role: Right-Winger, Inside-Right
Career: Ashton White Star, Ashton Central, Earlestown, St. Helens Town, Burnley, Sunderland, Huddersfield Town, Preston North End, Carlisle United
Debut: v Scotland (h) 10-4-1920 (scored twice)
Appearances: 14 (8 goals)

Bob Kelly cost Burnley £275 when he signed from St. Helens Town in November 1913 and proved equally at home as an inside or outside-right for both club and country. He helped Burnley win the League title in 1921 having already broken into the England side. He remained at Turf Moor until December 1925 when he cost Sunderland a then record fee of £6,550, although he was to stay at Roker Park a little over a year before switching to Huddersfield Town for £3,500 in February 1927. He helped Huddersfield reach the final of the FA Cup in 1928 and 1930, although he had to settle for runners-up medals on both occasions. He then joined Preston North end in July 1932 and was appointed player-manager of Carlisle United in March 1935. He retired from playing in early 1936 and then became manager of Stockport County in March 1936, remaining in charge until March 1939. After the Second World War he was a trainer for Sporting Club de Portugal and was manager of Barry Town from December 1960. In addition to his 14 full caps for England Bob also represented the Football League on seven occasions.

Alan Philip KENNEDY

Born: Sunderland, 31st August 1954
Role: Defender
Career: Newcastle United, Liverpool, Sunderland, Hartlepool United, Beerschot (Belgium), Wigan Athletic, Wrexham
Debut: v Northern Ireland (h) 4-4-1984
Appearances: 2

Alan was signed as an apprentice by Newcastle United in July 1971 and upgraded to the professional ranks in September 1972. He helped the club reach the finals of the FA Cup in 1974 and League Cup in 1976, although both finals ended in defeat. Having collected six caps at Under-23 level and one appearance in the B team, full honours seemed a certainty and he was selected for the side in 1975 but had to pull out owing to a knee injury. A £330,000 move took him to Liverpool in August 1978 and he won a host of medals with the club, including five League championships, four League Cups and two European Cups. He also got recalled into the England side in 1984 and earned caps in the Home International Championship against Wales and Northern Ireland. Alan was sold to Sunderland for £100,000 in September 1985 before moving on to Hartlepool United in the summer of 1987, but after a few months moved to Belgium to join Beerschot. He returned to England with Wigan Athletic in December 1987 and finished his League career with Wrexham.

Alan Kennedy

Raymond KENNEDY

Born: Seaton Delavel, 28th July 1951
Role: Midfield
Career: Arsenal, Liverpool, Swansea City, Hartlepool United
Debut: v Wales (24-3-1976 (scored once)
Appearances: 17 (3 goals)

Ray was turned down by Port Vale before signing as an apprentice with Arsenal in May 1968, turning professional in November the same year. He made his League debut as a forward in February 1970 and ended the season with a winners' medal from the Inter Cities Fairs Cup, scoring one of the goals in the 4-3 aggregate win against Ajax. The following season he helped the club win the double, scoring the goal that clinched the League title and in 1971-72 he helped them reach the FA Cup final again. He was sold to Liverpool for £180,000 in July 1974, the last signing made by manager Bill Shankly and converted into a midfield player, helping the club win the European Cup three times, the UEFA Cup once, five League titles and the League Cup once as well as runners-up medals in the FA Cup and League Cup. In January 1982 he was sold to Swansea City for £160,000, helping them win the Welsh Cup in 1982 and 1983 before finishing his playing career with Hartlepool United. After a spell as a licensee in his native North East it was revealed he was suffering from Parkinson's Disease.

Ray Kennedy

Right Hon. William Stanley KENYON-SLANEY

Born: Rajkot, India, 24th August 1847
Died: 24th April 1908
Role: Forward
Career: Oxford University, Old Etonians, Wanderers
Debut: v Scotland (h) 8-3-1873
Appearances: 1 (2 goals)

Educated at Eton and a player for Oxford University prior to the annual 'Varsity' match, he played for Wanderers in the 1873 FA Cup final against Oxford University, helping Wanderers win 2-0. He then played for Old Etonians, helping them reach the finals of 1875 (he appeared in the first drawn match but not the replay) and 1876, the latter of which was lost against Wanderers. He served in the Grenadier Guards between 1867 and 1888, becoming a colonel, was elected Member of Parliament for Newport in 1886 and served that constituency until his death in 1908, also being a Privy Councillor from 1904. He was also a useful cricketer, playing for the MCC between 1869 and 1880 and serving on the MCC Committee for eight years. He was born William Slaney but changed his name in 1862. According to contemporary reports, both of his goals for England were scored direct from throw-ins and his first, in the first minute, was the first goal England ever scored in international matches.

Martin Raymond KEOWN

Born: Oxford, 24th July 1966
Role: Defender
Career: Arsenal, Brighton & Hove Albion, Aston Villa, Everton, Arsenal, Leicester City, Reading
Debut: v France (h) 19-2-1992
Appearances: 43 (2 goals)

Signed by Arsenal as an apprentice in February 1984, Martin spent a spell on loan to Brighton & Hove Albion in order to gain experience before being pitched into the Arsenal first team. He was unable to claim a regular place in the side and requested a transfer, subsequently being sold to Aston Villa for £200,000 in 1986. He made over 100 appearances for Villa before switching to Everton in a £750,000 deal in August 1989. Whilst at Goodison Park he broke into the England squad and developed into one of the best central defenders in the game, prompting fresh inquiries from Arsenal as to his availability. In February 1993 he became the first player to re-sign for Arsenal since the Second World War, costing the Highbury club £2 million. Initially used as a squad player he eventually replaced Steve Bould as one of the first choice central defenders and helped Arsenal to the double in 1998. A member of the England squad for the World Cup finals in France he was not called upon to play but became a regular in the side from 1999. He remained at Arsenal until the summer of 2004, helping the club win three League titles and the FA Cup three times, joining Leicester City on a free transfer. He moved on to Reading the following January.

Martin Keown

Derek Kevan

Derek Tennyson KEVAN

Born: Ripon, 6th March 1935
Role: Inside-Forward
Career: Bradford, West Bromwich Albion, Chelsea, Manchester City, Crystal Palace, Peterborough United, Luton Town, Stockport County, Macclesfield, Boston United, Stourbridge
Debut: v Scotland (h) 6-4-1957 (scored once)
Appearances: 14 (8 goals)

After a failed trial with Sheffield United, Derek joined Bradford Park Avenue in October 1952 and quickly gained a reputation as a hugely effective forward, prompting a £3,000 move to West Bromwich Albion in July 1953. He was to spend almost ten years at The Hawthorns, netting 173 goals in 291 appearances for the first team and making one appearance for the Football League alongside his 14 full caps. He was sold to Chelsea for £45,000 in March 1963 but five months later moved on to Manchester City for £40,000, spending two years at Maine Road before returning to London with Crystal Palace in July 1965. He then had spells at Peterborough and Luton before picking up his only domestic honour in the game, a Fourth Division championship medal with Stockport County in 1967. He finished his playing career with a number of non-League clubs before his retirement in 1969. He then worked for a brewery for a number of years before returning to The Hawthorns to assist the commercial office in 1982.

Brian KIDD

Born: Manchester, 29th May 1949
Role: Forward
Career: Manchester United, Arsenal, Manchester City, Everton, Bolton Wanderers
Debut: v Northern Ireland (h) 21-4-1970
Appearances: 2 (1 goal)

After playing for Manchester Schools he was offered an apprenticeship at Old Trafford in August 1964, subsequently turning professional in June 1966. Two years later, on his 19th birthday, he helped United win the European Cup, scoring in the 4-1 extra time win over Benfica. That turned out to be the only major medal Brian won during his career! He remained with Manchester United until July 1974 when he was sold to Arsenal for £110,000, his departure coming at a time when United's European Cup winning side was being dismantled; Charlton and Law had retired officially, Best unofficially. He made 77 League appearances for Arsenal, scoring 30 goals before returning to Manchester, this time with City, for £100,000 in July 1976. Despite his earlier allegiance he was well received at Maine Road and made nearly 100 League appearances for the club, scoring 44 goals. He was sold to Everton in March 1979 for £150,000 and had mixed fortunes at Goodison Park, being sent off in an FA Cup semi final the following year. After just 40 appearances for Everton he was on the move again, this time joining Bolton Wanderers for £110,000 in May 1980. Two years later he went to play in America, turning out for Atlanta Chiefs, Fort Lauderdale Strikers and Minnesota Kicks before retiring from playing. Aside from his two full caps Brian also represented England at Youth and Under-23 level as well as playing for the Football League on one occasion. Brian had been a member of the original squad named for the World Cup finals in Mexico but was omitted from the final squad of 22; he scored his only goal for England in the last warm up match before he returned home to England! After retiring as a player Brian entered coaching and management, taking charge at Barrow, having spells as assistant manager at Swindon and Preston and then taking over briefly at Deepdale. The odds were stacked against him at Preston and he left soon after, subsequently becoming assistant manager at Manchester United under Alex Ferguson in 1991. Over the next seven years he helped the club win the League title four times, the FA Cup twice, the European Cup Winners' Cup and the League Cup, including two domestic doubles (in 1994 and 1996). During this time he rejected the overtures of a number of clubs who wished to make him their manager, including Manchester City and Everton, but in December 1998 he finally accepted another offer, taking over at Ewood Park as manager of Blackburn Rovers in succession to Roy Hodgson. Unfortunately his time in charge was not a success, culminating in relegation from the Premier League and he was subsequently sacked, returning to coaching with a variety of clubs.

Brian Kidd

Canon Robert Stuart KING

Born: Leigh-on-Sea, 4th April 1862
Died: Leigh-on-Sea, 4th March 1950
Role: Half-Back
Career: Oxford University, Upton Park, Grimsby Town, Essex
Debut: v Ireland (a) 18-2-1882
Appearances: 1

Educated at Felsted School and a member of the school team between 1878 and 1880, captaining the side in his final year, he attended Oxford University and won a Blue in four consecutive years, 1882 through to 1885, also being captain in 1885. He then played for Upton Park and Grimsby Town and represented Essex before being ordained in 1887, serving as Rector of Leigh-on-Sea until his death, a period of more than 58 years.

Ledley Brenton KING

Born: Bow, 12th October 1980
Role: Defender
Career: Tottenham Hotspur
Debut: v Italy (h) 15-11-2002
Appearances: 16 (1 goal)

Taken on by Spurs as a trainee, Ledley was upgraded to become a professional in July 1998 and made his League debut the following May against Liverpool. Already an England youth international, he collected his first cap at Under-21 level in 2000 and formed an effective club partnership with Sol Campbell. Following Campbell's switch to Arsenal, Ledley became the vital component in the Spurs defence and in November 2002 collected his first full cap for England, replacing Sol Campbell! During the 2003-04 season he was used as a midfield player by Spurs, although his preferred position is in central defence, but this versatility proved useful when he was moved into midfield by England.

Ledley King

Robert Kennett KINGSFORD

Born: Sydenham Hill, 23rd December 1849
Died: Adelaide, Australia, 14th October 1895
Role: Forward
Career: Wanderers, Surrey
Debut: v Scotland (a) 7-3-1874 (scored once)
Appearances: 1 (1 goal)

Educated at Marlborough College he played for both the college and Old Malburians teams as well as Wanderers, winning an FA Cup winners' medal with Wanderers in 1873. He also represented Surrey at football and cricket for the county and succeeded Charles Alcock as secretary of Wanderers in 1874. A one time law student, he emigrated to Australia where he died in 1895.

Matthew KINGSLEY

Born: Turton, 1875
Died: 27th March 1960
Role: Goalkeeper
Career: Turton, Darwen, Newcastle United, West Ham United, Queens Park Rangers, Rochdale
Debut: v Wales (h) 18-3-1901
Appearances: 1

After playing for Darwen, Matthew signed for Newcastle United in April 1898 and went on to earn the distinction of becoming the first Newcastle player to win international honours. He also represented the Football League on three occasions before signing for West Ham in May 1904, spending a season with the club before switching across London to join Queens Park Rangers. He retired after a year at the club but was coaxed back into the game by Rochdale in October 1907, also turning out occasionally for Barrow.

George KINSEY

Born: Burton-on-Trent, 20th June 1866
Died: January 1911
Role: Left-Half
Career: Burton Crusaders, Burton Swifts, Mitchells St. George, Wolverhampton Wanderers, Aston Villa, Derby County, Notts County, Eastville Rovers
Debut: v Wales (a) 5-3-1892
Appearances: 4

An early career spent playing junior football saw George signed by Wolverhampton Wanderers in the summer of 1891 and quickly establish himself as a regular within the side, helping Wolves win the FA Cup in 1893. In June the following year he joined Aston Villa but spent only a year at Villa Park before moving on to Derby County where he remained until March 1897 and signing for Notts County. Barely months later he was on the move again, signing for Bristol Eastville Rovers where he spent three years before retiring from the professional game in 1900. Four years later he was reinstated as an amateur.

Alfred John KIRCHEN

Born: Shouldham, 26th April 1913
Role: Right-Winger
Career: Shouldham, Norwich City, Arsenal
Debut: v Norway (a) 14-5-1937 (scored once)
Appearances: 3 (2 goals) + 3 War appearances

Alf represented King's Lynn Schools and played for the Old Boys side before joining junior side Shouldham, in whose colours he was spotted by Norwich City and signed as an amateur in October 1933. The following month he was

Alf Kirchen

upgraded to professional and turned in impressive displays, prompting a move to Arsenal in March 1935 for £6,000. A member of the side that won the League championship in 1938, Alf remained at Highbury until injury forced his retirement in 1943. He then returned to Norfolk and became a farmer, later being appointed a director of Norwich City.

Reverend Arnold KIRKE-SMITH

Born: Ecclesfield, 23rd April 1850
Died: Boxworth, 8th October 1927
Role: Forward
Career: Oxford University, Sheffield FC
Debut: v Scotland (a) 30-11-1872
Appearances: 1

Educated at Cheltenham College and Oxford University, Arnold was made captain of the Oxford University side in 1872, although the annual match against Cambridge University had yet to be introduced. He was known to be a powerful and quick attacker and was selected to play for England in the very first international match, against Scotland in 1872. He was ordained in 1875 and held curacies at Biggleswade for two years and later at East Socon in Bedfordshire between 1877 and 1881 and Somersham in Cambridgeshire in 1881, becoming Vicar of the parish in 1883. In 1889 he became vicar of Boxworth, a position he held until his death in 1927. In 1998 the knitted woollen jersey he wore in the first international match sold for £21,275 at auction in Scotland.

William John KIRTON

Born: Newcastle-upon-Tyne, 2nd December 1896
Died: 27th September 1970
Role: Inside-Right
Career: North Shields, Pandon Temperance, Leeds City, Aston Villa, Coventry City, Kidderminster Harriers, Leamington Town
Debut: v Ireland (a) 22-10-1921 (scored once)
Appearances: 1 (1 goal)

Billy played for North Shields before the outbreak of the First World War and Pandon Temperance during it before signing with Leeds City in May 1919. He made just one appearance for the club before it was ordered to disband by the FA for financial irregularities with Billy being snapped up by Aston Villa for a cut-price £400. He helped Aston Villa reach the FA Cup final in both 1920 and 1924, scoring the winning goal in the first match when a corner kick hit him on the back of the neck and flew into the goal! He remained at Villa Park until September 1928 when he joined Coventry City, spending two years at Highfield Road before finishing his career with non-League Kidderminster Harriers and Leamington Town.

Arthur Egerton KNIGHT

Born: Godalming, 7th September 1887
Died: Milton, 10th March 1956
Role: Left-Back
Career: Portsmouth, Corinthians, Surrey
Debut: v Ireland (a) 25-10-1919
Appearances: 1 + 1 War appearance

Arthur Knight was educated at King Edward VI Grammar School in Guildford and represented Surrey at the age of 17 before moving to Portsmouth in 1909. He was immediately signed by the Fratton Park club and spent a year in the reserves before breaking into the first team, going on to play regularly until the outbreak of the First World War. By then Arthur had already earned international recognition at amateur level and had been a member of the United Kingdom side that retained the Olympic gold medal in Stockholm in 1912. With the outbreak of the First World War, Arthur enlisted as a private with the Hampshire Regiment and saw service in India and Egypt and was later commissioned into the Border Regiment and was elevated to the rank of captain after service in France. He returned to Fratton Park when the hostilities were at an end and resumed his playing career, turning out for England in a Victory International before earning his first full cap in 1919. At the end of the same season he helped Portsmouth to the Southern League title and then went to Antwerp as a member of the United Kingdom side in the Olympic Games which was surprisingly beaten by Norway in the first round. After collecting 30 caps for England at amateur level he finished his playing career with the Corinthians, where he was later given the distinction of becoming an honorary life member. He also made four appearances for Hampshire at cricket between 1913 and 1923 and spent his working life in the insurance business, managing an office in Portsmouth. During the Second World War he served as a squadron leader with the RAF.

Zatyiah KNIGHT

Born: Solihull, 2nd May 1980
Role: Defender
Career: Fulham, Peterborough United
Debut: v USA (a) 28-5-2005
Appearances: 2

Zat was spotted by Fulham whilst playing for Rushall Olympic and signed as a professional in February 1999. A year later he was sent on loan to Peterborough United to gain first team experience and made eight appearances for the London Road club during this spell. He returned to Fulham and continued his progress, winning four caps for England at Under-21 level. An almost ever-present in the Fulham side of 2004-05, he earned a call-up to the full England squad for the tour of America in 2005 and made his debut against the United States.

Zat Knight

Cyril Barry KNOWLES

Born: Fitzwilliam, 13th July 1944
Died: Middlesbrough, 31st August 1991
Role: Full-Back
Career: Monckton Colliery, Middlesbrough, Tottenham Hotspur
Debut: v USSR (h) 6-12-1967
Appearances: 4

Cyril began his career as a winger and had an unsuccessful spell with Manchester United and a trial with Blackpool before being taken on by Middlesbrough who converted him to full-back. He found his true vocation in this position, making his debut in April 1963 and being spotted by Spurs manager Bill Nicholson. After just 39 appearances for the Ayresome Park outfit he was transferred to Spurs for £45,000 and almost immediately made the right-back spot his own. After twelve months in the role he was switched to left-back and was one of the most solid and dependable players in the League in this position. He used his previous experience as a winger to good effect, overlapping whenever the opportunity presented itself and seldom being afraid to have a shot at goal. A member of the Spurs teams that won the FA Cup in 1967, the League Cup in 1971 and 1973 and the UEFA Cup in 1972, the success of a television advert for bread led to the catchphrase 'Nice One Cyril' being taken on by Spurs followers and then turned into a hit record! In 1976 Cyril was forced to retire owing to a serious knee injury sustained in December 1973 and moved into management. Although his managerial career was confined to the football basement, Cyril proved adept at working with limited budgets but unlimited success, taking a succession of clubs to promotion until, in February 1991 he was forced once again to retire, this time owing to a serious brain illness. In June 1991 Hartlepool (where he had been manager) reluctantly announced the cancellation of his contract and in August 1991 he sadly died in Middlesbrough. Both Spurs and Hartlepool staged memorial matches for his dependents and as an opportunity to pay tribute to one of the finest players ever to have graced the football field. His brother Peter was a professional with Wolves and also tipped for international honours, although he retired in order to become a Jehovah's Witness.

Paul Martyn KONCHESKY

Born: Barking, 15th May 1981
Role: Defender
Career: Charlton Athletic, Tottenham Hotspur, Charlton Athletic, West Ham United
Debut: v Australia (h) 12-2-2003
Appearances: 2

Paul was taken on as a trainee by Charlton Athletic and signed professional forms in May 1998, having already represented England at Youth level. He went on to collect 15 caps for England at Under-21 level and was seen as a defender with a promising future, going on to earn his first full cap for England when replacing Ashley Cole. He joined Spurs on loan in September 2003 and made 15 appearances for the club but was recalled by Charlton when they hit an injury crisis. He remained at Charlton until the summer of 2005 when he asked for a transfer, subsequently joining West Ham United in a cut-price £2 million deal. He rediscovered his form at Upton Park and forced his way back into the England squad, collecting his second cap in the friendly against Argentina.

Paul Konchesky

L

LABONE, Brian Leslie
LAMPARD, Frank James
LAMPARD, Frank R G
LANGLEY, Ernest James
LANGTON, Robert
LATCHFORD, Robert D
LATHERON, Edwin Gladstone
LAWLER, Christopher
LAWTON, Thomas
LE SAUX, Graeme Pierre
LE TISSIER, Matthew Paul
LEACH, Thomas
LEAKE, Alexander
LEE, Ernest Albert
LEE, Francis Henry
LEE, John
LEE, Robert Martin
LEE, Samuel
LEIGHTON, John Edward
LILLEY, Henry E
LINACRE, Henry James
LINDLEY, Tinsley
LINDSAY, Alec
LINDSAY, William
LINEKER, Gary Winston O.B.E.
LINTOTT, Evelyn Henry
LIPSHAM, Herbert Broughall
LITTLE, Brian
LLOYD, Larry Valentine
LOCKETT, Arthur
LODGE, Lewis Vaughn
LOFTHOUSE, Joseph Morris
LOFTHOUSE, Nathaniel
LONGWORTH, Ephraim
LOWDER, Arthur
LOWE, Edward
LUCAS, Thomas
LUNTLEY, Edwin
LYTTELTON, Hon. Alfred
LYTTELTON, Reverend the Hon. Edward

Gary Lineker

Brian Leslie LABONE

Born: Liverpool, 23rd January 1940
Role: Centre-Half
Career: Everton
Debut: v Northern Ireland (a) 20-10-1962
Appearances: 26

One of the greatest players to have played for Everton, he spent his entire career at Goodison Park, making over 500 appearances for the first team during his time. He was signed as a junior and joined the professional ranks in July 1957, making his debut in the 1957-58 seasons. By 1959-60 he was a regular in the side and helped them win the League title in 1963 and 1970 and the FA Cup in 1966, also playing in the FA Cup Final in 1968. Although initially selected for the squad for the 1966 World Cup, he asked not to be included in order to concentrate on his wedding! He then stunned the football world with the announcement of his retirement in 1967, although he subsequently changed his mind and went on to play in the 1970 World Cup finals in Mexico. He might have gone on to better Ted Sagar's record for the number of League appearances for Everton but for an injury which forced him to retire in June 1972.

Brian Labone

Frank James LAMPARD

Born: Romford, 21st June 1978
Role: Midfield
Career: West Ham United, Chelsea
Debut: v Belgium (h) 10-10-1999
Appearances: 38 (10 goals)

Frank joined West Ham United straight from school and gradually rose through the ranks. That he should have joined West Ham was no surprise; his father, Frank Sr. was a former player and assistant manager, whilst his uncle Harry Redknapp was manager. He signed professional forms with West Ham in 1994 but had to wait until the 1995-96 season before making his League debut. He also had a spell on loan at Swansea City before becoming a regular fixture of the West Ham midfield. Everything seemed set for a comfortable career at Upton Park, but the news that the club had sold Rio Ferdinand to Leeds United for £17 million in November 2000 started a period of unrest at the club, culminating in the sacking of Harry Redknapp and subsequent departure of Frank Lampard Sr. in May 2001. Announcing he would never play for West Ham again prompted a number of clubs to make enquiries for Frank Jr. and he was subsequently snapped up by Chelsea for £11.5 million. Although he initially struggled to fit into the side he eventually won over the fans with his powerhouse displays and consistency; he has broken both Chelsea's consecutive Premiership and League records, overtaking John Hollins' record of 135 games. It was also his goals that made him such a vital component in the side that won both the FA Premiership and League Cup and reached the semi finals of the UEFA Champions League in 2004-05. He has also become a regular fixture in the England side, repeating his club form at international level.

Frank Lampard Jnr

Frank Richard George LAMPARD

Born: West Ham, 20th September 1948
Role: Defender
Career: West Ham United, Southend United
Debut: v Yugoslavia (h) 11-10-1972
Appearances: 2

Frank represented East London at schoolboy and England at Youth level, joining West Ham as an apprentice in July 1964 and being upgraded to professional in September 1965. He made his debut for the club during the 1967-68 season but broke a leg a matter of months later that kept him out of action for a considerable time. He returned and forced his way back into the West Ham side, subsequently earning a call-up for the England Under-23 side, going on to win four caps at this level. After collecting his first full cap for England under Alf Ramsey, Frank helped West Ham to a number of honours during his time with the club, including the FA Cup in 1975 and the final of the European Cup Winners' Cup the following season. Here, against Anderlecht, Frank suffered the second major injury scare of his career, but recovered to earn a second FA Cup winners' medal in 1980, got a recall into the England side and won a Second Division championship medal and League Cup runners-up medal in 1981. He remained at West Ham until 1985 and made 660 first team appearances when he left to join Southend United, where former West Ham player Bobby Moore was manager, finally retiring from playing in 1986. He returned to West Ham and was assistant manager to Harry Redknapp until 2001 when the pair left the club. His son Frank junior also played for West Ham and England.

Frank Lampard

Ernest James LANGLEY

Born: Kilburn, 7th February 1929
Role: Left-Back
Career: Yiewsley, Hounslow Town, Uxbridge, Hayes, Guildford City, Leeds United, Brighton & Hove Albion, Fulham, Queens Park Rangers, Hillingdon Borough
Debut: v Scotland (a) 19-4-1958
Appearances: 3

Jim played for a number of clubs as an amateur before signing with Leeds United in June 1952 and made a handful of appearances at left-wing. He was transferred to Brighton in July 1953 for £1,500 and successfully converted to left-back, subsequently getting selected to represent the Football League and earn three caps for England at B level.

Jim Langley

In February 1957 he was sold to Fulham for £12,000 and became noted as a dependable defender with an ability to join the attack when needed, which brought him 57 goals during the course of his career and three full caps for England. An extremely popular member of the Fulham side for eight seasons, he moved on to Queens Park Rangers for £4,000 in June 1965 and helped the club win the Third Division championship and the League Cup in 1967. In September that year he moved to Hillingdon Borough as player-manager, a position he held until May 1971. After a brief spell as coach at Crystal Palace, Jim returned to Hillingdon as manager later the same year.

Robert LANGTON

Born: Burscough, 8th September 1918
Died: 15th November 1996
Role: Left-Winger
Career: Burscough Victoria, Blackburn Rovers, Preston North End, Bolton Wanderers, Blackburn Rovers, Ards, Wisbech Town, Kidderminster Harriers, Wisbech Town, Colwyn Bay
Debut: v Northern Ireland (a) 28-9-1946 (scored once)
Appearances: 11 (1 goal)

Bobby Langton was spotted by Blackburn Rovers whilst playing at amateur level for Burscough Victoria and signed as an amateur to the Ewood Park club in September 1937. He showed enough potential to be offered professional terms within two months and made his debut for the side in September 1938, remaining in the side for the rest of the season and collecting a championship medal as Blackburn won the Second Division title. The outbreak of the Second World War saw him in Army service in India, although he did represent the forces side and play for Glentoran during the hostilities. He returned to Ewood Park at the end of the war and earned his first cap for England in the first official international since 1939. Unfortunately, his club career was not as successful this time and following Blackburn's relegation at the end of the 1947-48 season he elected to join Preston North End. A little over a year later he was on the move again, costing Bolton Wanderers £22,500 in November 1949 and going on to help the club to the FA Cup Final in 1953. The exploits of the opposition winger Stanley Matthews ensured Bobby collected a runners-up medal that year and in September 1953 he returned to Blackburn for a second spell, costing the Ewood Park club £2,500 in the process. He was to remain with the club for almost three years before going back to Ireland, this time with Ards and when he returned to England in 1957 he both played and coached in non-League circles. In addition to his 11 full caps for England he represented the country at B level on four occasions, the Football League nine times and also collected a runners-up medal in the Irish Cup in 1945 with Glentoran. He later became a publican in Wisbech.

Bob Latchford

Robert Dennis LATCHFORD

Born: Birmingham, 18th January 1951
Role: Forward
Career: Birmingham City, Everton, Swansea City, NAC Breda (Holland), Coventry City, Lincoln City, Newport County, Merthyr Tydfil
Debut: v Italy (h) 16-11-1977 (WCQ)
Appearances: 12 (5 goals)

Along with his brother Dave he began his career as an apprentice with Birmingham City, turning professional in August 1968. After making over 150 League appearances for the St. Andrews club he was sold to Everton for £350,000 in February 1974. He was top goalscorer in each of his first four full seasons at Goodison and in 1977-78 becoming the first player in six years to reach 30 League goals in a season, having helped them win the League Cup the previous season. In 1981 he was transferred to Swansea for £125,000, helping the club win the Welsh Cup in 1982 and 1983 before moving on to NAC Breda in Holland in February 1984. He returned to England in the summer the same year to sign for Coventry City and spent a year at Highfield Road before moving on to Lincoln City. Six months later he moved to Newport County for six months and finished his playing career with Merthyr Tydfil where he won another Welsh Cup winners' medal in 1987.

Edwin Gladstone LATHERON

Born: Grangetown, 1887
Died: 14th October 1917
Role: Inside-Left
Career: Grangetown, Blackburn Rovers
Debut: v Wales (h) 17-3-1913 (scored once)
Appearances: 2 (1 goal)

Known as Pinky because of his complexion and red hair, he played for his hometown club before being spotted by Blackburn Rovers and signed with the Ewood Park club in March 1906 for £25. He represented the Football League on two occasions and helped Blackburn win the League title in 1912 and 1914. Following the outbreak of the First World War he joined the Royal Field Artillery and lost his life in action in October 1917.

Christopher LAWLER

Born: Liverpool, 20th October 1943
Role: Defender
Career: Liverpool, Portsmouth, Stockport County, Bangor City
Debut: v Malta (h) 12-5-1971 (scored once) (ECQ)
Appearances: 4 (1 goal)

After representing Liverpool Schools, Chris signed with Liverpool as an amateur in May 1959 and turned professional the following October. Known as the Silent Knight, he

Chris Lawler

began his career as a centre-half but was converted to full-back during 1964-65 and helped Liverpool win the FA Cup at the end of the season. He also won two League titles, in 1966 and 1973, the UEFA Cup in 1973 and collected runners-up medals in the European Cup Winners' Cup in 1967 and the FA Cup in 1971. Chris represented England at Youth, Under 23 and full level and also twice represented the Football League. He remained at Anfield until October 1975 when he left to join Portsmouth, finishing his League career with Stockport County before joining Bangor City. After coaching in Norway and serving as assistant manager at Wigan Athletic, Chris returned to Anfield to join the coaching staff, remaining with the club until the appointment of Kenny Dalglish as manager.

Tommy Lawton

Thomas LAWTON

Born: Bolton, 6th October 1919
Died: 6th November 1996
Role: Centre-Forward
Career: Rossendale United, Burnley, Everton, Chelsea, Notts County, Brentford, Arsenal, Kettering Town, Notts County
Debut: v Wales (a) 22-10-1938 (scored once)
Appearances: 23 (22 goals) + 23 War appearances (24 goals) + 2 unofficial appearances

Tommy Lawton played schools football in Bolton and represented Lancashire Schoolboys before playing junior football for Hayes Athletic and Rossendale United at the age of 15, subsequently being invited to sign amateur forms with Bolton Wanderers and Sheffield Wednesday. He signed similar forms with Burnley in May 1935 and was upgraded to the professional ranks in October 1936 and quickly established himself as one of the most lethal goalscorers in the game. Everton swooped to sign him in January 1937, with Tommy joining the Goodison Park club in a deal worth £6,500. Initially seen as an eventual replacement for Dixie Dean he won a League championship medal in 1939 and spent the Second World War guesting for Aldershot, Chelsea, Tranmere Rovers and Morton. At the end of the war and before the resumption of League football he was sold to Chelsea for £11,500, remaining at Stamford Bridge for two years before he was surprisingly sold to Third Division Notts County in a then record deal worth £20,000. Despite slipping down the League, Tommy was still a regular for the England side, having collected his first cap in 1938. He helped Notts County win their divisional title in 1950 and in 1952 returned to the capital, signing for Brentford for £12,000. He subsequently became player-manager in January 1953 but by September had moved back into the top flight, arranging his own transfer to Arsenal for £10,000. He spent three years at Highbury before going into the non-League game with Kettering Town. He had a second spell with Notts County, serving as manager between May 1957 and July 1958 and later returned to Kettering Town as manager and then director. He also served Notts County a third time as coach and chief scout between October 1968 and April 1970. He was believed to have been the youngest player to have scored a League hat-trick, a feat achieved four days after his 17th birthday, scored 212 goals during the Second World War and 150 post-war League goals for his various clubs. Tommy was unfortunate to have spent his entire playing career at a time when the maximum wage was in force and this was to cause him numerous problems in later years, although a number of benefit matches in his honour helped alleviate some of his financial hardship.

Graeme Pierre LE SAUX

Born: Jersey, 17th October 1968
Role: Defender
Career: Chelsea, Blackburn Rovers, Chelsea, Southampton
Debut: v Denmark (h) 9-3-1994
Appearances: 36 (1 goal)

Chelsea signed Graeme Le Saux on a free transfer from St. Paul's club in Jersey in December 1987 and he made over 100 appearances during his first spell with the club. His desire for regular first team football led him to request a transfer and in March 1993 he was sold to Blackburn Rovers for £650,000. Whilst at Ewood Park he developed into one of the best attacking full-backs in the game and helped his new club win the League title in 1995. The following season he and team-mate David Batty had a fall out during a European Cup tie, the first indication that Graeme had not entirely settled in the north. At the beginning of the 1997-98 season Chelsea found themselves without adequate cover at left wing-back and, despite competition from the likes of Arsenal, Juventus and Barcelona, swooped to bring him back to Stamford Bridge. It cost them £5 million to re-sign the player but he proved a vital acquisition for the club, helping them to the League Cup and the final of the European Cup Winners' Cup in his first season back. Unfortunately he suffered an injury, ironically against Blackburn Rovers, that forced him to sit out the European Cup Winners' Cup Final, which Chelsea won, but returned to full fitness in time to claim a place in the squad for the 1998 World Cup finals in France. He played in all four of England's games and proved the ideal man for the left wing-back position within the national side. He joined Southampton in the summer of 2003 and announced his retirement two years later, going on to become a television pundit.

Graeme Le Saux

Matthew Paul LE TISSIER

Born: Guernsey, 14th October 1968
Role: Midfield
Career: Southampton
Debut: v Denmark (h) (substitute) 9-3-1994
Appearances: 8

Signed by Southampton as an apprentice in October 1986 he soon broke into the side and showed himself to be an exceptional midfield talent able to weigh in with vital goals, most of which tended to be spectacular shots rather than simple tap ins. Despite it being rumoured that he had once been sold to Spurs and promptly allowed to return to Southampton as his wife disliked the thought of living in London, he remained faithful to Southampton and for almost a decade he was the most vital member of the side and the first name to be put on the team sheet. His call-up

Matt Le Tissier

for England was inevitable, but just like Glenn Hoddle there were those who questioned his work rate. Whilst this may have limited his use as an international player, his devotion to Southampton was never in question and he remained with the club until 2001 when he retired. Scorer of many special goals, he had the honour of scoring Southampton's last at their old ground The Dell.

Thomas LEACH

Born: Wincobank, 23rd September 1903
Died: 1970
Role: Wing-Half
Career: Wath Athletic, Sheffield Wednesday, Newcastle United, Stockport County, Carlisle United, Lincoln City
Debut: v Northern Ireland (a) 20-10-1930
Appearances: 2

Tony joined Sheffield Wednesday from non-League Wath Athletic in 1926 as a forward and was successfully converted to half-back whilst at Hillsborough. Indeed, all three of Wednesday's half-backs in their 1929 championship winning side, Leach, Alf Strange and Bill Marsden were converted forwards! Tony helped Wednesday retain the championship in 1930 and remained with the club until being sold to Newcastle United for £1,100 in June 1934, going on to captain the side. Two years later he joined Stockport County for £300 and helped them win the Third Division North championship in 1937, although Tony had left the club by the time the trophy was lifted, having signed for Carlisle in February that year. The following September he joined Lincoln City and retired from playing in the summer of 1939.

Alexander LEAKE

Born: Small Heath, 11th July 1872
Died: 29th March 1938
Role: Centre-Half, Left-Half
Career: Hoskin & Sewell, King's Heath, Old Hill Wanderers, Small Heath, Aston Villa, Burnley, Wednesbury Old Athletic, Crystal Palace
Debut: v Ireland (a) 12-3-1904
Appearances: 5

Alec began his professional career with Small Heath and made 199 appearances and was captain of the club before switching to Aston Villa in the summer of 1902. He went on to become an important member of the side that won the FA Cup in 1905 and won five caps for England during his time with the club. He made 141 first team appearances before leaving for Burnley in 1907, later playing for Crystal Palace in 1912. Even though he was by now 40 years of age, he was still selected for England, although he did not play. He then became coach at Crystal Palace until 1915 and after the First World War was trainer at Merthyr Town for a period. Aside from a little coaching Alec then concentrated on his career as a blacksmith.

Ernest Albert LEE

Born: Bridport, 1879
Died: 14th January 1958
Role: Right-Half
Career: Poole, Southampton, Dundee, Southampton
Debut: v Wales (a) 29-2-1904
Appearances: 1

Spotted by Southampton whilst playing for Poole, Bert joined the Southern League club in the summer of 1900 and helped them win the divisional championship in 1901, 1903 and 1904. He also helped them reach the FA Cup final in 1902 although they were soundly beaten by Bury. In May 1906 he joined Dundee, collecting a Scottish FA Cup winners' medal in 1910 and returned to Southampton in the summer of 1911. Appointed player-trainer in 1913, he retired from playing during the First World War and remained on the staff at The Dell until 1935.

Francis Henry LEE

Born: West Houghton, 29th April 1944
Role: Winger
Career: Bolton Wanderers, Manchester City, Derby County
Debut: v France (h) 12-3-1969 (scored once)
Appearances: 27 (10 goals)

After playing for Lancashire Schools, Francis Lee was signed by Bolton as an amateur in July 1959 and was just 16 years of age when he made his League debut, against Manchester City. He signed professional forms in May 1961 and in October 1967 was sold to Manchester City for £60,000. He was an integral part of the City side of the late 1960s and early 1970s that challenged for the game's top honours, winning the League in 1968, the FA Cup in 1969 and the League Cup and European Cup Winners' Cup in 1970. At international level he represented England at Youth level but was overlooked for an Under-23 cap, having to wait until he was 24 and his first appearance for the senior side. He remained with City until August 1974 when he was sold to Derby County for £110,000 and collected a second championship medal in 1975. He announced his retirement in May 1976 and left the game in order to concentrate on various business ventures, including a waste paper company and later became a racecourse trainer, holding a National Hunt licence from 1984 and the flat from 1987. He did later return to football, becoming chairman of Manchester City.

Franny Lee

John LEE

Born: Sileby, 4th November 1920
Died: Rugby, 15th January 1995
Role: Centre-Forward
Career: Quorn Methodists, Leicester City, Derby County, Coventry City
Debut: v Northern Ireland (a) 7-10-1950 (scored once)
Appearances: 1 (1 goal)

Jack Lee was spotted playing for Quorn Methodists in the Leicestershire Senior League and snapped up by Leicester City in February 1941. Service in the RAF in India restricted his playing opportunities at home but he returned at the end of the hostilities to establish himself as a quality striker. After making a scoring debut for Leicester City, Jack was a member of the side that went on to reach the FA Cup final in 1949, but at Wembley against Wolverhampton Wanderers he was switched to inside-right and the club lacked a more direct centre-forward – Leicester lost 3-1. He was restored to his more usual position in the very next Leicester game against Cardiff where he scored the equalising goal as Leicester got the point they needed to avoid relegation into the Third Division. In June 1950 Leicester accepted a Derby County bid of £18,500 for his transfer, much to the disgust of the Filbert Street fans, who then saw their prize asset become the second highest goal scorer in the First Division the following season. Jack remained at the Baseball Ground until November 1954 when he was sold to Coventry City for £5,000, but injuries, which had plagued him throughout his career, finally saw him calling it a day in the summer of 1955. Jack was also a noted cricketer and played for Leicestershire during the 1947 season.

Rob Lee

Robert Martin LEE

Born: West Ham, 1st February 1966
Role: Midfield
Career: Charlton Athletic, Newcastle United, Derby County, West Ham United, Oldham Athletic, Wycombe Wanderers
Debut: v Romania (h) 12-10-1994 (scored once)
Appearances: 21 (2 goals)

Robert Lee began his career with non-League Hornchurch before being signed by Charlton Athletic in July 1983. He spent nine years with the club, making over 300 appearances and being regarded as one of the brightest midfield prospects in the game. In September 1992 he was sold to Newcastle United for £700,000 and within two years had broken into the England side, thus confirming his potential. A member of the side that won the First Division championship in 1993 and thus restored the club to the top flight, Rob went on to become a vital part of the side as they attempted to bring major silverware back to the North East. He was a member of the England squad for the 1998 World Cup finals, making one brief substitute appearance against Colombia in the group stages. When Kevin Keegan bought him for Newcastle he described him as the best midfielder in the country, whilst his team-mates referred to him as 'Lurker', for he was invariably to be found hanging around the opponents' penalty area! He was sold to Derby County for £250,000 in February 2002, remaining at the club until released on a free transfer in August the following year and joining West Ham. Freed during the 2004 summer, he had a break from the game before making one appearance with Oldham Athletic and then joined Wycombe in March 2005.

Sammy Lee

Samuel LEE

Born: Liverpool, 7th February 1959
Role: Midfield
Career: Liverpool, Queens Park Rangers, Osasuna (Spain), Southampton, Bolton Wanderers
Debut: v Greece (a) 17-11-1982 (scored once) (ECQ)
Appearances: 14 (2 goals)

Sammy played schoolboy football in his hometown before signing with Liverpool as an apprentice in 1975, turning professional in April 1976. He broke into the first team on a regular basis in 1980 and went on to help the club win the League title in 1982, 1983 and 1984, the League Cup in 1981, 1982, 1983 and 1984 and the European Cup in 1981. He remained at Anfield until August 1986 when he joined QPR for £200,000 and a year later moved to Spain to play for Osasuna. He returned to England to sign for Southampton but found injuries hampered his progress, prompting a switch to Bolton Wanderers where he finished his playing career. Sammy, who also represented England at Youth and Under-21 level, then went into coaching, returning initially to Anfield and then Bolton and also being part of the England coaching staff.

John Edward LEIGHTON

Born: Nottingham, 26th March 1865
Died: Nottingham, 15th April 1944
Role: Left-Winger
Career: Nottingham Forest, Corinthians
Debut: v Ireland (a) 13-3-1886
Appearances: 1

After playing schoolboy and junior football in his Nottingham hometown John joined Nottingham Forest in 1884 and spent four years with the club. An amateur throughout his career, earning his living as a wholesale stationer and paper merchant within Nottingham he also played for the Corinthians between 1885 and 1889 before retiring as a player. He was then a regular at the City Ground as a fan, watching any Forest match that might be played, irrespective of the level, and actually collapsed and died at the City Ground in April 1944.

Henry E. LILLEY

Born: Staveley, 1873
Role: Left-Back
Career: Staveley, Sheffield United, Gainsborough Trinity
Debut: v Wales (a) 5-3-1892
Appearances: 1

Signed by Sheffield United during the summer of 1890, Henry formed an extremely effective full-back partnership at club level with Michael Witham, so much so that both were selected for England on 5th of March 1892. Henry Lilley played against the Welsh at Wrexham, whilst his partner played in Belfast against Ireland, albeit at left-half! Henry helped England to a 2-0 win and was said to have had a solid game in what enabled him and Witham to become the first United players to earn international honours. He finished his career with Gainsborough Trinity, joining them in 1894.

James Henry LINACRE

Born: Aston-on-Trent, 1880
Died: 11th May 1957
Role: Goalkeeper
Career: Aston-on-Trent, Draycott Mills, Derby County, Nottingham Forest
Debut: v Wales (h) 27-3-1905
Appearances: 2

Educated at Loughborough Grammar School, Henry played football for a number of sides before signing with Derby

Henry Linacre

County in December 1898 and switched to local rivals Nottingham Forest in August 1899. Here he helped the club win the Second Division championship in 1907 and was a first team regular for more than a decade, making over 330 appearances for the club in League and cup matches and also representing the Football League once before his retirement from playing in 1909. A brother-in-law of the Forman brothers who also played for England, he formed a building contractors company with Frank Forman.

Tinsley LINDLEY O.B.E.

Born: Nottingham, 27th October 1865
Died: 31st March 1940
Role: Centre-Forward
Career: Cambridge University, Corinthians, Casuals, Notts County, Crusaders, Swifts, Preston North End, Nottingham Forest
Debut: v Ireland (a) 13-3-1886
Appearances: 13 (14 goals)

After early education at Nottingham High School, Tinsley attended Cambridge University and won a Blue at football in 1885, 1886, 1887 and 1888, captaining the side in this final year. He also represented the university at cricket and his college, Caius, at rugby. He had begun his association with Nottingham Forest in 1883 and remained with the club until 1892, later playing for Casuals, Notts County, Crusaders and Swifts and also making one appearance for Preston in 1892. He was also a player for Corinthians between 1885 and 1894 and played cricket for Nottinghamshire between 1885 and 1893. Called to the Bar in 1889 he lectured on law at Nottingham University as well as becoming a County Court judge. He was awarded an OBE in 1918 in recognition of his work as chief officer of the Nottingham Special Constabulary.

Tinsley Lindley

Alec LINDSAY

Born: Bury, 27th February 1948
Role: Defender
Career: Bury, Liverpool, Stoke City, Oakland (USA), Toronto Blizzard (Canada)
Debut: v Argentina (h) 22-5-1974
Appearances: 4

Alec was signed by Bury as a professional in March 1965 after a spell as an apprentice and was used by the club as

Alec Lindsay

a wing-half and inside-forward. This experience as a forward player served him in good stead following his transfer to Liverpool for £67,000 in March 1969, for they converted him to full-back although with a license to press forward. A member of the side that won the League title in 1973, Alec also helped Liverpool win the UEFA Cup in 1973 and the FA Cup the following year. He went on loan to Stoke City in August 1977, with the deal becoming permanent the following month for £20,000 and in March 1978 he went to the United States to play for Oakland, later playing for Toronto Blizzard in Canada. He finished his playing career with Newton FC in minor League football.

William LINDSAY

Born: India, 3rd August 1847
Died: Rochester, Kent, 15th February 1923
Role: Full-Back, Forward
Career: Old Wykehamists, Wanderers, Surrey
Debut: v Scotland (h) 3-4-1877
Appearances: 1

Educated at Winchester College, William played for the Old Boys side and also linked with Wanderers, being a member of the side that won the FA Cup in three consecutive seasons, 1876, 1877 and 1878. He also represented Surrey at both football and cricket, playing 33 matches in the latter sport between 1876 and 1882. He worked in the Indian Office between 1865 and 1900.

Gary Winston LINEKER O.B.E.

Born: Leicester, 30th November 1960
Role: Forward
Career: Leicester City, Everton, Barcelona (Spain), Tottenham Hotspur, Grampus 8 (Japan)
Debut: v Scotland (a) (substitute) 26-5-1984
Appearances: 80 (48 goals)

He joined Leicester City as an apprentice and after being upgraded to the professional ranks made his League debut in 1979. He won a Second Division championship medal with Leicester and in 1985 was transferred to Everton for £800,000. He spent just one season with the Merseysiders, scoring 40 goals but missing out on both the League and FA Cup honours to Liverpool, although he did win Footballer of the Year award from both the writers' and players' associations. He then went to Mexico with the England squad and won the 'Golden Boot' for finishing the competition's top goalscorer, which alerted Europe's top clubs as to his talents. A £2,750,000 deal took him to Barcelona where he won domestic and European honours, the latter in the European Cup Winners' Cup. He moved back to Britain in 1989, linking up with former Barcelona manager Terry Venables at Spurs and two years later won his first major honour in the domestic game, an FA Cup winners' medal (despite becoming only the second player to miss a penalty in an FA Cup final at Wembley). He won his first England cap in 1984 and finished his England career with 80 caps and 48 goals, one goal agonisingly short of Bobby Charlton's record, which he might have equalled but for an uncharacteristic penalty miss against Brazil. At the end of the 1991-92 season he moved on from Spurs to Japan to help launch the Japanese League, although a niggling toe injury later forced him to retire from playing. He is a superb ambassador for the game, where he was never booked, and his country, being awarded the OBE in 1992. He is now a television presenter for the BBC.

Gary Lineker

Evelyn Henry LINTOTT

Born: Godalming, 2nd November 1883
Died: Somme, France, 1st July 1916
Role: Left-Half
Career: Exeter, Woking, Surrey County, Plymouth Argyle, Queens Park Rangers, Bradford City, Leeds City
Debut: v Ireland (a) 15-2-1908
Appearances: 7

Evelyn attended St. Luke's Training College where he qualified as a teacher, playing football in his spare time and as an amateur for Exeter and Woking, earning his first representative honour when selected to play for Surrey. After a spell with Plymouth Argyle he joined QPR as an amateur in September 1907, by which time he had won five caps for England at amateur level. He helped the club win the Southern League championship in 1908 and turned professional with QPR in May the same year. He then joined Bradford City in November 1908 and became an important figure within the Players Union, serving as chairman for a spell until January 1911. He finished his playing career with Leeds City, joining the club in June 1912 and leaving in order to enlist in the 1st Yorkshire Regiment at the outbreak of the First World War. He was killed in action at the Somme in July 1916.

Herbert Broughall LIPSHAM

Born: Chester, 29th April 1878
Died: Canada, 1932
Role: Left-Winger
Career: Chester, Crewe Alexandra, Sheffield United, Fulham, Millwall
Debut: v Wales (a) 3-3-1902
Appearances: 1

Educated at King's School in Chester, Bert played for the local side and a number of minor League clubs before linking with Crewe Alexandra in the summer of 1898. In February 1900 he moved on to Sheffield United and helped the club reach successive FA Cup finals, collecting a runners-up medal in 1901 and a winners' medal the following year. In 1907-08 he joined Fulham, newly admitted into the Second Division that season, and remained at Craven Cottage until 1910 when he joined Southern League side Millwall Athletic, going on to add representative honours for the Southern League to those of the Football League he had won whilst with Sheffield United. He was appointed player-manager of Millwall in 1913 and after the First World War had spells coaching at West Norwood and managing Northfleet before emigrating to Canada in 1923. Employed in a sawmill, Bert had the misfortune to lose a hand in an accident at the mill. He was killed in a train accident sometime during 1932.

Bert Lipsham

Brian Little

Brian LITTLE

Born: Durham, 25th November 1953
Role: Forward
Career: Aston Villa
Debut: v Wales (substitute) (h) 21-5-1975
Appearances: 1

Signed by Aston Villa as an apprentice, Brian turned professional in 1971 and made his debut the same year against Blackburn Rovers. He went on to make 301 first team appearances, helping the club win the League Cup in 1975 and 1977, as well as promotion to the First Division. In 1979 a proposed move to Birmingham for £160,000 fell through on medical grounds and he was forced to give up the game at the end of the 1980-81 season. He then switched to management, with Wolves, Darlington (who went out of the Football League but returned a year later as GM Vauxhall Conference champions) and Leicester City before accepting an offer to take over at Villa Park in November 1994. Midway through the 1997-98 season he announced his decision to resign, despite having guided the club to the League Cup in 1996. He subsequently became manager of Stoke City in 1998 and later had spells in charge of Hull City and Tranmere Rovers. Brian's only appearance for England saw him replace Mick Channon for the final 19 minutes of the match against Wales in 1975, the sixth shortest England career on record.

Laurence Valentine LLOYD

Born: Bristol, 6th October 1948
Role: Centre-Half
Career: Bristol Rovers, Liverpool, Coventry City, Nottingham Forest, Wigan Athletic, Notts County
Debut: v Wales (h) 19-5-1971
Appearances: 4

After playing schools and junior football in his hometown, Larry joined Bristol Rovers as an amateur, turning professional in July 1967. A tall and commanding centre-half his performances soon attracted the attention of bigger clubs, with Liverpool and Bill Shankly paying £50,000 to take him to Anfield in April 1969. He helped the club reach the final of the FA Cup in 1971 and win the League title and UEFA Cup in 1973, but following the appointment of Bob Paisley as manager he was allowed to move to Coventry City for £225,000 in August 1974. He was unable to settle at Highfield Road and went on loan to Nottingham Forest in October 1976, the deal becoming permanent the following month for a fee of £60,000. Larry was to enjoy an Indian summer at the City Ground, helping the club win the League title in 1978, the League Cup in 1978 and 1979 and the European Cup in 1979 and 1980. This in turn led to a surprise recall into the England side, with his last cap in 1980 coming nine years after he had collected his first three. He left Forest in March 1981 to become player-manager of Wigan Athletic, subsequently becoming team manager of Notts County in July 1983, a position he retained until October 1984.

Larry Lloyd

Arthur LOCKETT

Born: Alsagers Bank, 1875
Died: 1957
Role: Left-Winger
Career: Crewe Alexandra, Stoke, Aston Villa, Preston North End, Watford
Debut: v Ireland (h) 14-2-1903
Appearances: 1

Arthur played for Alsagers Bank FC before signing with Crewe Alexandra, subsequently joining Stoke in May 1900. Almost three years later Aston Villa paid the then princely sum of £400 to take him to Villa Park, where he spent two and a half years before moving on again to Preston North End. Three years later he joined Watford where he finished his playing career in 1912, having also represented the Football League on one occasion to go with his solitary cap.

Lewis Vaughn LODGE

Born: Aycliffe, 21st December 1872
Died: Burbage, Derbyshire, 21st October 1916
Role: Full-Back
Career: Cambridge University, Casuals, Corinthians
Debut: v Wales (a) 12-3-1894
Appearances: 5

Educated at Durham School, Lewis attended Cambridge University and won a Blue in 1893, 1894 and 1895, being acting captain in 1895. He linked with both the leading amateur clubs of the day in Corinthians (where he played between 1894 and 1898) and Casuals, helping the Casuals win the FA Amateur Cup in 1894. He was also a useful cricketer playing for Durham and Hampshire during his career (he made three first class appearances for the latter county, scoring just six runs). After leaving Cambridge University he became a schoolteacher at a Newbury school.

Nat Lofthouse

Joseph Morris LOFTHOUSE

Born: Blackburn, 14th April 1865
Died: 10th June 1919
Role: Right-Winger
Career: King's Own Blackburn, Blackburn Rovers, Accrington, Blackburn Rovers, Darwen, Walsall
Debut: v Ireland (h) 28-2-1885
Appearances: 7 (3 goals)

Joe played schoolboy football in his hometown and joined Blackburn Rovers in 1882, going on to help the club win the FA Cup in 1884 and 1885. He moved on to Accrington in 1887 and remained with the club for two years before returning to Ewood Park in the summer of 1889. He again helped Blackburn win the FA Cup in consecutive seasons, collecting winners' medals in 1890 and 1891 and left the club for good for Darwen in 1892. He finished his playing career with Walsall and later had a short spell coaching in Hungary with the Magyar Athletic Club. He returned to England to coach New Brompton during the 1902-03 season and the following year took up a similar position with Everton.

Nathaniel LOFTHOUSE

Born: Bolton, 27th August 1925
Role: Centre-Forward
Career: Bolton Wanderers
Debut: v Yugoslavia (h) 22-11-1950 (scored twice)
Appearances: 33 (30 goals)

Nat Lofthouse was, along with the likes of Tom Finney, one of the most loyal players in the game, remaining with Bolton Wanderers for his entire career. He had first come to the club's attention whilst playing schools football in the town and was taken on as an amateur in September 1939, turning professional during the Second World War. He made his League debut in 1946 and was to remain a regular in the side until his eventual retirement in 1961, having made 452 League appearances and scored 255 goals, Bolton's record goalscorer. During his time with the club he appeared in two FA Cup Finals, collecting a runners-up medal in 1953 as England team-mate Stanley Matthews rescued Blackpool, and a winners' medal in 1958 against Manchester United. Nat was credited with scoring both of Bolton's goals in the 2-0 win, although his second remains one of the most controversial ever scored at Wembley, for Nat charged both the goalkeeper and the ball into the goal. A story was told, perhaps apocryphal, of Nat and Eddie Hopkinson (Bolton's goalkeeper) going out for a drink in Manchester shortly after the final. The barman refused to take any money from Hopkinson, looking directly at Nat Lofthouse and uttering the statement 'We don't charge goalkeepers in here!' Nat's reputation had effectively been made with a stirring performance for England in Austria in 1952, scoring two goals in the 3-2 win and surviving some robust tackling from the opposition to earn the nickname 'The Lion of Vienna', which remained with him for the rest of his career. Although Nat retired from playing in 1961 he continued to serve Bolton in a number of positions, including reserve team trainer, chief coach, caretaker manager, manager, general manager and chief scout. He was also in charge of the executive club at Burnden Park, returned briefly as manager in 1985 and, by the time Bolton moved to the new Reebok Stadium, was president of the club. His only involvement with any club apart from Bolton was in 1973 when he served as Arsenal's Lancashire scout. Nat is one of only four England players to have scored in every round of the FA Cup in a single season, a feat he achieved in 1953.

Ephraim LONGWORTH

Born: Halliwell, 2nd October 1887
Died: 7th January 1968
Role: Right-Back
Career: Bolton St. Luke's, Hyde St. George, Bolton Wanderers, Leyton, Liverpool
Debut: v Scotland (h) 10-4-1920
Appearances: 5 + 2 War appearances

Ephraim played for Bolton St. Luke's in the Lancashire Combination League before starting his professional career with Hyde St. George's and moving on to Bolton Wanderers in June 1907. Later the following year he joined Leyton before moving to Liverpool in May 1910. A member of the side that reached the FA Cup final in 1914, Ephraim was a permanent member of the side after the First World War and helped them win the League title in 1922 and 1923, earned representative honours with the Football League

Ephraim Longworth

and toured with the FA party to South Africa in 1920. He retired in the summer of 1928 and joined the coaching staff at Anfield, a position he held for some time.

Arthur LOWDER

Born: Wolverhampton, 1863
Died: Taunton, 4th January 1926
Role: Left-Half
Career: Wolverhampton Wanderers
Debut: v Wales (h) 23-2-1889
Appearances: 1

Arthur Lowder was another pupil of St. Luke's School in Blakenhall who went on to play for Wolverhampton Wanderers, following in the footsteps of the likes of Jack Brodie and Dickie Baugh. He linked with Wolves in 1882 and remained with them until October 1891, during which time he helped them reach the FA Cup Final in 1889, where they lost to Preston, and played in their very first League match. Upon his retirement he turned to coaching and was one of the very first English coaches to work extensively in Europe, coaching in France, Norway and Germany. He later returned to England and served as Chairman of Brewood Parish Council.

Edward LOWE

Born: Hawne, 11th July 1925
Role: Left-Half
Career: Finchley, Aston Villa, Fulham
Debut: v France (h) 3-5-1947
Appearances: 3

Signed by Aston Villa in the summer of 1945 he made 104 appearances for the League side, winning three caps for England (he was the first Villa player to be so honoured after the Second World War) before switching to Fulham in 1950 for £15,000. He then made 511 appearances for the Craven Cottage club, helping them win promotion from the Second Division into the First Division in 1958-59 before retiring as a player at the end of the 1962-63 season. He then took over as manager of Notts County but had a disastrous season in charge which saw the club relegated to the Fourth Division, and the following season saw him turn out as a player once again in an attempt to turn the tide. Unfortunately it did not work out and he was sacked in April 1965. His brother Reg was also on Villa's books at one point (as was their goalkeeper father) but left for Fulham without having played for the Villa first team as part of the same deal that took Eddie to Craven Cottage. After leaving football, Eddie became a purchasing manager for an international boiler company whilst also scouting for Plymouth Argyle in the Midlands.

Eddie Lowe

Thomas LUCAS

Born: St. Helens, 20th September 1895
Died: 11th December 1953
Role: Right-Back
Career: Sherdley Villa, Sutton Commercial, Heywood United, Peasley Cross, Eccles Borough, Liverpool, Clapton Orient
Debut: v Ireland (a) 22-10-1921
Appearances: 3

Tommy played for a number of junior sides and had a trial with Manchester United before linking with Liverpool in the summer of 1916. At the end of the First World War he became an integral part of Liverpool's defence, helping them win the League title in 1922 and made over 340 League appearances for the club before moving on to Clapton Orient in July 1933. He retired as a player the following year and had a spell in charge of the Orient's nursery club Ashford. He later became a licensee in Stoke Mandeville in Buckinghamshire for 18 years prior to his death.

Edwin LUNTLEY

Born: Croydon, 1857
Died: 1st August 1921
Role: Right-Back
Career: Nottingham Castle, Nottingham Forest
Debut: v Scotland (a) 13-3-1880
Appearances: 2

One of three brothers who played for Nottingham Forest in the club's early years, Edwin was the only one to go on to win international honours for his country. He had joined Forest in 1878 and remained with the club until 1883, leaving to concentrate on his lace manufacturing business. He was also a founder member of Chilwell Manor Golf Club.

Hon. Alfred LYTTELTON

Born: Hagley, 7th February 1857
Died: 5th July 1913
Role: Forward
Career: Cambridge University, Old Etonians, Hagley
Debut: v Scotland (h) 3-3-1877
Appearances: 1 (1 goal)

The younger of the two Lyttelton brothers to represent England, Alfred attended Eton College and played for the school team, being captain in 1875. He then attended Cambridge University, winning his Blue in football in 1876, 1877 and 1878 and also a Blue in cricket in 1876, 1877, 1878 and 1879. In 1876 he helped Old Etonians reach the FA Cup final where they lost to Wanderers after a replay. Although he represented England at football on one occasion, he probably made more of an impact at cricket, playing for Worcestershire, Middlesex and England (he appeared in four Tests) and was president of the MCC in 1898. This all around sportsman also represented Cambridge University at athletics, rackets and tennis, was Member of Parliament for Warwick between 1895 and 1906 and then the constituency of St. George's Hanover Square from 1906 until his death. He was a barrister and Knight Commander and served as Secretary of the Colonies between 1902 and 1905.

Reverend the Hon. Edward LYTTELTON

Born: London, 23rd July 1855
Died: 26th January 1942
Role: Full-Back
Career: Cambridge University, Old Etonians, Hagley
Debut: v Scotland (a) 2-3-1878
Appearances: 1

Like his younger brother, Edward attended Eton College and Cambridge University, although he did not win a Blue at football. Instead his prowess was shown in cricket, earning a Blue in 1875, 1876, 1877 and 1878 and going on to play for Middlesex, Hertfordshire and Worcestershire. Also like his brother he was a member of the Old Etonians side that reached the FA Cup final in 1876 and he later played for Hagley in Worcestershire. A master at Wellington College between 1880 and 1882 he then returned to Eton to become a master, a position he held for seven years before his appointment as Headmaster of Haileybury in 1890. He remained here until 1905 when he was appointed Headmaster of Eton, holding this position until 1916, subsequently holding a number of clerical positions up until his death in 1942. Six of the Lyttelton brothers played what is considered first class cricket, Alfred, Charles, George, Arthur, Robert and Edward, as did their father George and nephews John and Charles Lyttelton.

M-N

Bobby Moore

MABBUTT, Gary Vincent M.B.E.
McCALL, Joseph
McCANN, Gavin Peter
MACAULEY, Reginald Herbert
McDERMOTT, Terry
McDONALD, Colin Agnew
MACDONALD, Malcolm
McFARLAND, Roy Leslie
McGARRY, William Harry
McGUINNESS, Wilfred
McINROY, Albert
McMAHON, Stephen
McMANAMAN, Steven
McNAB, Robert
McNEAL, Robert
McNEIL, Michael
MACRAE, Stuart
MADDISON, Frederick Brunning
MADELEY, Paul Edward
MAGEE, Thomas Patrick
MAKEPEACE, Joseph William Harold
MALE, Charles George
MANNION, Wilfred J
MARINER, Paul
MARSDEN, Joseph Thomas
MARSDEN, William
MARSH, Rodney William
MARSHALL, Thomas
MARTIN, Alvin Edward
MARTIN, Henry
MARTYN, Anthony Nigel
MARWOOD, Brian
MASKREY, Harry Mart
MASON, Charles
MATTHEWS, Reginald D
MATTHEWS, Stanley Sir
MATTHEWS, Vincent
MAYNARD, William John
MEADOWS, James
MEDLEY, Leslie Dennis
MEEHAN, Thomas

MELIA, James
MERCER, David William
MERCER, Joseph O.B.E.
MERRICK, Gilbert Harold
MERSON, Paul Charles
METCALFE, Victor
MEW, John William
MIDDLEDITCH, Bernard
MILBURN, John Edward Thompson 'Jackie'
MILLER, Brian George
MILLER, Harold Sydney
MILLS, Daniel John
MILLS, George Robert
MILLS, Michael Denis
MILNE, Gordon
MILTON, Clement Arthur
MILWARD, Arthur Weatherell
MITCHELL, Clement
MITCHELL, James Frederick
MOFFAT, Hugh

MOLYNEUX, George
MOON, William Robert
MOORE, Henry Thomas
MOORE, James
MOORE, Robert Frederick O.B.E.
MOORE, William Gray Bruce
MORDUE, John
MORICE, Charles John
MORLEY, Anthony William
MORLEY, Herbert
MORREN, Thomas
MORRIS, Frederick
MORRIS, John
MORRIS, William Walter
MORSE, Harold
MORT, Thomas
MORTEN, Alexander
MORTENSEN, Stanley Harding
MORTON, John R
MOSFORTH, William

MOSS, Frank junior
MOSS, Frank senior
MOSSCROP, Edwin
MOZLEY, Bertram
MULLEN, James
MULLERY, Alan Patrick M.B.E.
MURPHY, Daniel John

NEAL, Philip George
NEEDHAM, Ernest
NEVILLE, Gary Alexander
NEVILLE, Philip John
NEWTON, Keith Robert
NICHOLLS, John
NICHOLSON, William Edward O.B.E.
NISH, David John
NORMAN, Maurice
NUTTALL, Henry

Gary Vincent MABBUTT M.B.E.

Born: Bristol, 23rd August 1961
Role: Midfield
Career: Bristol Rovers, Tottenham Hotspur
Debut: v Greece (a) 17-11-1982 (ECQ)
Appearances: 16 (1 goal)

The son of Ray Mabbutt, a former forward with Bristol Rovers and Newport and brother of Kevin, who played for Crystal Palace, Gary signed with Bristol Rovers as a professional in January 1979 and played in every outfield position in his four years at Eastville. He was capped by England at Under-21 level in March 1982 and was snapped up by Spurs for £120,000 in the summer of the same year. With injuries having decimated the Spurs side he made his first senior appearance in the FA Charity Shield at Wembley against Liverpool and quickly settled into the side. In October 1982 he was capped by England at full level, playing at right-back. He won a winners' medal for Spurs playing in the 1984 UEFA Cup (he replaced captain Steve Perryman in the second leg) and was then successfully converted to centre-back by manager David Pleat. He collected a runners-up medal in the 1987 FA Cup final, having the misfortune to score for both sides, but received more than adequate compensation in 1991 when as captain he led the team to victory over Nottingham Forest. He was recalled to the England team for the final qualifying games of the European Championship. Early in his football career he was diagnosed as suffering from diabetes, but has been an inspiration to all other sufferers by continuing to play at the highest level in the game. He was awarded the MBE in 1994 and was released by Spurs on a free transfer at the end of the 1997-98 season having made 619 first team appearances.

Gary Mabbutt

Joseph McCALL

Born: Kirkham, 6th July 1886
Died: 3rd February 1965
Role: Centre-Half
Career: Kirkham FC, Preston North End
Debut: v Wales (h) 17-3-1913 (scored once)
Appearances: 5 (1 goal) + 2 War appearances

Joe was spotted by Preston North End whilst playing for Kirkham and first linked with the club as an amateur during the 1905-06 season, turning professional in July 1906. He quickly established himself as a key member of the side, helping them win the Second Division championship in 1913, the year he made his England debut. After appearances for England in two Victory Internationals and having also represented the Football League twice, Joe helped Preston reach the FA Cup final in 1922 and retired in 1925. He was also a cricket professional for a number of sides in Lancashire and coached in the sport at Stoneyhurst College. After retiring from football he became a poultry farmer near Kirkham.

Gavin Peter McCANN

Born: Blackpool, 10th January 1978
Role: Midfield
Career: Everton, Sunderland, Aston Villa
Debut: v Spain (h) 28-2-2001
Appearances: 1

A graduate from Everton's trainee scheme, Gavin struggled to make a first team breakthrough at Goodison Park, making just 11 appearances in four seasons. A £500,000 fee took him to Sunderland in November 1998 and he quickly established himself as a regular within the Sunderland side, helping them regain their Premiership place at the end of the 1998-99 season as First Division champions. A cruciate knee ligament injury sustained in February 2000 caused him to miss the rest of the season, but he returned the following season with a series of commanding performances that had him earmarked out as a fine prospect. Called into Sven Goran Eriksson's first England squad for the friendly against Spain in February 2001, Gavin replaced Nicky Butt midway through the match to earn his first England cap. Although he soon fell out of reckoning for future England appearances, he was a central figure in the Sunderland side and would make 116 League appearances for the side in his five seasons with the club. Following Sunderland's relegation back into the First Division at the end of the 2002-03 season he was transferred to Aston Villa, becoming new manager David O'Leary's first signing for a fee of £2.25 million.

Reginald Herbert MACAULEY

Born: Hodnet, 24th August 1858
Died: 15th December 1937
Role: Forward
Career: Cambridge University, Old Etonians
Debut: v Scotland (h) 12-3-1881
Appearances: 1

Educated at Eton College, Reginald played for the college team in 1878 and attended Cambridge University where he won a Blue in 1881 and 1882. He had already proved his worth as an athlete whilst at the university, representing them between 1879 and 1882, winning the high jump in both 1879 and 1880 and the quarter mile in 1880, 1881 and 1882. He was also the Amateur Athletics Association high jump champion in 1879. Reginald continued to play football for Old Etonians, helping them reach three successive FA Cup finals and collecting a winners' medal in 1882 and runners-up medals either side of this. He then went to work in India, returning to England in 1901 and subsequently becoming a merchant in London.

Terry McDERMOTT

Born: Kirkby, 8th December 1951
Role: Midfield
Career: Bury, Newcastle United, Liverpool, Newcastle United
Debut: v Switzerland (h) 7-9-1977
Appearances: 25 (3 goals)

Although Terry played schoolboy football in Liverpool, Bury were the first club to show any real interest in him, offering him an apprenticeship and subsequently upgrading him to the professional ranks in October 1969. After 90 League appearances in a little over three years he was sold to Newcastle United for £22,000 in February 1973. He appeared in the 1974 FA Cup Final against Liverpool and was one of the few United players to emerge from the game with any credit, so much so that in November 1974 he was bought by Liverpool for £170,000. In the space of eight years he won three European Cup winners' medals (he scored Liverpool's first goal in their first final), four League championships, two League Cups and runners-up medals from both the FA Cup and League Cup as well as breaking into the England side and being named Player of the Year by both the Football Writers Association and PFA in 1980. In September 1982 he returned to Newcastle United for £100,000, later linking up with former Liverpool team-mate Kevin Keegan and helping the club win promotion to the top flight in 1984. In the space of four months Newcastle lost both players; Keegan retired at the end of the season and Terry moved on to Cork City in September for five games, later playing in Cyprus with Apoel FC. He then went into coaching, serving both Kevin Keegan and Kenny Dalglish during their spells in charge at St. James' Park.

Terry McDermott

Colin Agnew McDONALD

Born: Tottington, 15th October 1930
Role: Goalkeeper
Career: Burnley, Headington United, Altrincham
Debut: v USSR (a) 18-5-1958
Appearances: 8

Colin signed with Burnley as an amateur in August 1948, becoming a part-time professional in October the same year. After playing for Headington United on loan whilst doing his national service, he returned to Turf Moor and became a full professional in July 1952. He made his League debut for the club in 1954 and became a permanent fixture in the side, earning representative honours with the Football League. In May 1958 he replaced Eddie Hopkinson as England's goalkeeper after a 5-0 defeat in their previous game and held his position during that year's World Cup competition. He seemed set for an extended run as England's first choice until March 1959 when on Football League duty again, he broke a leg in three places and never played again at the top level, finally retiring in the summer of 1961. He then had spells as a coach at Wycombe Wanderers and scouted for Bury before briefly coming out of retirement to play for Altrincham. He subsequently scouted again for Bury and Bolton and coached the youngsters at Oldham Athletic and Tranmere Rovers.

Malcolm McDonald

Malcolm Ian MACDONALD

Born: Fulham, 7th January 1950
Role: Centre-Forward
Career: Tonbridge, Fulham, Luton Town, Newcastle United, Arsenal
Debut: v Wales (a) 20-5-1972
Appearances: 14 (6 goals)

Malcolm began his career as a full-back with Tonbridge and was signed by Fulham in August 1968. Manager Bobby Robson first converted him to centre-forward, but when Robson left the club Malcolm fell out of favour and was sold to Luton Town for £17,500 in July 1969. In the space of two years he became noted as one of the best goalscorers in the lower Leagues, prompting a £180,000 move to Newcastle United in May 1971. He quickly established a rapport with the Newcastle fans, becoming known as 'Supermac' and scoring goals with regularity. He helped Newcastle reach the FA Cup final in 1974 but, like many of his team-mates, suffered an off day as Liverpool ran out 3-0 winners. Two years later he fared little better in the League Cup final before stunning Tyneside with a £333,333 move to Arsenal in July 1976. He helped the Gunners reach the FA Cup final in 1978 but again had to settle for a runners-up medal. Four games into the following season he suffered a leg injury that was to bring his playing career to an end in August 1979 and he went on to become commercial manager and later manager of Fulham. His connection with football ended with a spell as manager of Huddersfield Town between 1987 and 1988, after which he became a licensee. Five of Malcolm's six goals for England came in one match against Cyprus in 1975, equalling the individual scoring record.

Roy Leslie McFARLAND

Born: Liverpool, 5th April 1948
Role: Centre-Half
Career: Tranmere Rovers, Derby County, Bradford City, Derby County
Debut: v Malta (a) 3-2-1971 (ECQ)
Appearances: 28

After playing for Edge Hill Boys Club, Roy signed with Tranmere Rovers in July 1966 and soon attracted the interest of bigger clubs, signing for Derby County for £24,000 in August 1967. Roy became an integral part of the side assembled by Brian Clough, winning a Second Division championship medal in 1969 and captaining the side to the League title in 1972, by which time he had also made his international breakthrough. A number of niggling injuries then began to punctuate his career, with an Achilles tendon injury picked up whilst playing for England keeping him out of the Derby side that won the League title in 1975. Roy remained at the Baseball Ground until May 1981 when he joined Bradford City as player-manager, returning to Derby in November 1982 as team manager and also making a further eight appearances as a player. Roy became assistant manager following the arrival of Arthur Cox in June 1984. He became manager again in 1993, remaining in charge until June 1995 when he took over at Bolton Wanderers. A year later he moved on to become manager of Cambridge United, a position he held until 2001 and later took over at Chesterfield.

Roy McFarland

William Harry McGARRY

Born: Stoke, 10th June 1927
Role: Right-Half
Career: Port Vale, Huddersfield Town, Bournemouth & Boscombe Athletic
Debut: v Switzerland (Berne) 20-6-1954 (WC)
Appearances: 4

Bill joined Port Vale from Northwood Mission in Hanley and spent five years at Vale Park before moving to Huddersfield Town for £10,000 in March 1951. He enjoyed ten years with Huddersfield, earning representative honours from the Football League and England at B and full level before joining Bournemouth as player-manager in March 1961. This was the start of a hugely successful career in management, taking in Watford from June 1963, Ipswich between September 1964 and November 1968 and then Wolverhampton Wanderers, where he was in charge until May 1976. He then had a spell as national coach in Saudi Arabia and returned to England to take over as manager of Newcastle United in November 1977. He left the club in August 1980 and scouted for Brighton and coached in Africa before returning to Wolves for 61 days in 1985, after which he returned to Africa.

Wilfred McGUINNESS

Born: Manchester, 25th October 1937
Role: Left-Half
Career: Manchester United
Debut: v Northern Ireland (a) 4-10-1958
Appearances: 2

Wilf joined Manchester United straight from school as an apprentice in June 1953, turning professional in November 1954. He was one of the original 'Busby Babes', collecting three winners' medals from the FA Youth Cup and making his League debut in October 1955. He was originally understudy to the great Duncan Edwards and did not become a regular in the side until after Edwards lost his life in the Munich air disaster. Unfortunately, Stan Crowther was preferred at left-half in the FA Cup final at the end of the 1958 season, although Wilf did enough to earn selection for England in October 1958 and again the following May in Mexico. A badly broken leg sustained in a reserve match for United in December 1959 brought his playing career to an end although he did not announce his retirement until December 1961, and in 1966-67 attempted a comeback that failed. Instead he returned to United as youth team coach and rose through the ranks, becoming chief coach in June 1969 and team manager in August 1970, replacing Sir Matt Busby. In December 1970 he was relieved of his position, with Busby returning as manager and Wilf becoming reserve team manager and coach. He later managed Greek clubs Aris Salonika and Panaraiki before returning to England and management with York City, later assisting Hull City and Bury in a number of positions.

Albert McINROY

Born: Walton-le-dale, 23rd April 1901
Died: 7th January 1985
Role: Goalkeeper
Career: Upper Walton FC, Coppull Central, Leyland, Sunderland, Newcastle United, Sunderland, Leeds United, Gateshead
Debut: v Northern Ireland (h) 20-10-1926
Appearances: 1

Having played as a left-winger as a schoolboy and after a brief spell with Preston as an amateur, Albert began his professional career with Sunderland in May 1923. He made one appearance for England four years later and in October 1929 was surprisingly sold to local rivals Newcastle United for £2,750. After helping Newcastle win the FA Cup in 1932, Albert returned to Sunderland in June 1934, remaining at Roker Park for eleven months before moving on to Leeds United. In June 1937 he joined Gateshead and retired during the Second World War, subsequently becoming a licensee in the North East.

Steve McMohon

Stephen McMAHON

Born: Liverpool, 20th August 1961
Role: Midfield
Career: Everton, Aston Villa, Liverpool, Manchester City, Swindon Town
Debut: v Israel (a) 17-2-1988
Appearances: 17

Signed by Everton as an apprentice in August 1979 he made exactly 100 League appearances for the club before being sold to Aston Villa for £175,000 in May 1983. He spent just over two years at Villa Park before returning to the city of Liverpool, this time to play for the club the other side of Stanley Park, for £375,000 in September 1985. Whilst at Liverpool he helped the club win two League titles and two FA Cups, including the domestic double in 1986. His firebrand style of midfield play was also rewarded with 17 full caps for England, Steve having already collected two caps at B level and six appearances for the Under-21 side. In December 1991 he was sold to Manchester City for £900,000 and spent three years at Maine Road before being sold to Swindon for £100,000 where he was appointed player-manager. Although he continued playing, albeit sporadically, into the 1997-98 season, a persistent back problem brought his playing career to an end and he could then concentrate on management, although he left the club in September 1998. He later managed Blackpool where his son was a player.

Steven McMANAMAN

Born: Bootle, 11th February 1972
Role: Midfield
Career: Liverpool, Real Madrid (Spain), Manchester City
Debut: v Nigeria (h) (substitute) 16-11-1994
Appearances: 37 (3 goals) + 1 unofficial appearance

Steve joined Liverpool as a trainee in February 1990 and within two years had helped the club win the FA Cup. He was a last minute choice to replace the injured John Barnes in the final against Sunderland and made the most of his selection, creating the goal for Michael Thomas that set Liverpool on the road to victory. His ability to take men on was reminiscent of an old-style winger and he was responsible for creating a succession of chances for the likes of Ian Rush, Robbie Fowler and then Michael Owen in the Liverpool attack. He could also be relied upon to score a fair few himself, making him a dangerous proposition for any defence and he was named Man of the Match in the 1995 League Cup final, which Liverpool won. First called up to the England side in 1994 he was a member of the England squad for the 1998 World Cup finals in France, making a single substitute appearance in the match against Colombia. In July 1999 he left Liverpool on a free transfer and signed for Spanish giants Real Madrid, helping them win the European Champions League during his time with the club. He returned to England in August 2003 on a free transfer, joining Manchester City, but a succession of injuries has hampered his career.

Steve McManaman

Bob McNab

Robert McNAB

Born: Huddersfield, 20th July 1943
Role: Left-Back
Career: Huddersfield Town, Arsenal, Wolverhampton Wanderers, Barnet
Debut: v Rumania (a) 6-11-1968
Appearances: 4 + 1 unofficial appearance

Bob joined Huddersfield as an amateur in 1961, turning professional in April 1962 and quickly became a first team regular. He was signed by Arsenal for £50,000 in October 1966, a then record fee for a full-back. Whilst at Highbury, Bob helped Arsenal reach the final of the League Cup in 1968 and 1969, win the Inter Cities Fairs Cup in 1970 and the following season the League and FA Cup double. He also collected a runners-up medal in the 1972 FA Cup final. Injuries and loss of form saw him replaced by Sammy Nelson and in July 1975 he moved on to Wolverhampton Wanderers, but after only one season and a brief spell playing for non-League Barnet, Bob headed to America where he finished his career. After a spell coaching Vancouver Whitecaps in Canada he moved to California.

Robert McNEAL

Born: Hobson, 15th January 1891
Died: West Bromwich, 15th May 1956
Role: Left-Half
Career: Hobson Wanderers, West Bromwich Albion
Debut: v Wales (a) 16-3-1914
Appearances: 2

Bob was spotted by West Bromwich Albion whilst playing for Hobson Wanderers and joined The Hawthorns side in June 1910. He helped the club win the Second Division championship in 1911 and reach the FA Cup final the following year and during the First World War he guested for Port Vale and Middlesbrough. He returned to West Bromwich at the end of the hostilities and won a League championship medal in 1920. Injury brought about his retirement in May 1926 and he became a licensee in the area as well as continuing to assist West Bromwich on a part time basis as a coach.

Mick McNeil

Michael McNEIL
Born: Middlesbrough, 7th February 1940
Role: Left-Back
Career: Middlesbrough, Ipswich Town, Cambridge City
Debut: v Northern Ireland (a) 8-10-1960
Appearances: 9
Mick played junior and schools football in his hometown before signing for Middlesbrough as an amateur in June 1954, turning professional in February 1957. Initially a left-half he subsequently switched to left-back and proved such a natural at the position he was capped by England at Under-23 level on nine occasions, going on to represent the full team and the Football League. In June 1964 he was sold to Ipswich Town and finished his playing career with non-League Cambridge City. Mick then concentrated on his growing empire of sports shops in East Anglia.

Stuart MACRAE
Born: Port Bennatyne, Scotland, 1856
Died: 27th January 1927
Role: Wing-Half
Career: Notts County, Newark, Corinthians
Debut: v Wales (h) 3-2-1883
Appearances: 5
Stuart attended Edinburgh Academy and played rugby for them between 1872 and 1873, being captain of the side in the latter year. He then moved south of the border to play football for Notts County and Newark as well as serving the Corinthians between 1883 and 1890. He was later employed by a Newark company as a maltster.

Frederick Brunning MADDISON
Born: 1850
Died: 25th September 1907
Role: Full-Back, Forward
Career: Oxford University, Wanderers, Crystal Palace
Debut: v Scotland (a) 30-11-1872
Appearances: 1
Educated at Marlborough Grammar School he was originally called Frederick Patey Chappell and assumed his new name in 1873. Although he played for Oxford University he did not win a Blue, instead he collected a winners' medal from the FA Cup final in 1874 having previously received a runners-up medal the year before. He went on to play for Wanderers, collecting a second winners' medal in the FA Cup in 1876. That same year he became a barrister and was called to the Bar but was disbarred in 1884 at his own request in order to become a solicitor.

Paul Edward MADELEY
Born: Leeds, 20th September 1944
Role: Defender
Career: Farsley Celtic, Leeds United
Debut: v Northern Ireland (a) 15-5-1971
Appearances: 24
Paul spent his entire professional career with Leeds United and proved himself to be one of the most valuable assets during almost twenty years with the club. Signed in May 1962 and seen initially as a successor to centre-half Jackie Charlton, Paul went on to play for the club in every position bar that of goalkeeper! He helped Leeds win the League title in 1969 and 1974, the FA Cup in 1972, the Inter Cities Fairs Cup in 1968 and 1971 and the League Cup in 1968 as well as numerous runners-up medals in various competitions. He might have made his England breakthrough earlier, for he was given a call to join the England squad for the 1970 World Cup finals in Mexico as a replacement for his club team-mate Paul Reaney but declined the offer! He retired in May 1981 and initially concentrated on a sports shop he had opened in the city in 1980 but later switched to the family chain of DIY retail outlets.

Paul Madeley

Thomas Patrick MAGEE
Born: Widnes, 12th May 1898
Died: 4th May 1974
Role: Right-Half
Career: Appleton Hornets, Widnes Athletic, West Bromwich Albion, Crystal Palace, Runcorn
Debut: v Wales (a) 5-3-1923
Appearances: 5 + 1 unofficial appearance
Tommy originally played Rugby League before switching to football, although he only played local and junior football before the outbreak of the First World War. He joined the Army and was spotted playing representative football, being recommended to West Bromwich Albion who signed him as an amateur in January 1919 and upgraded him to the professional ranks in May 1920. By then Tommy had already collected his first honour in the game, helping Albion win the League title in 1920. Although small for a half-back (he was only 5' 3") he more than made up for his lack of inches with his tenacity and accurate passing. He helped win the FA Cup in 1931 and remained at Albion until May 1934 when he joined Crystal Palace as player-coach. The following year he joined Runcorn as player-manager, retiring as a player in the summer of 1937 and remaining with the club as manager and coach until 1947.

Joseph William Henry MAKEPEACE
Born: Middlesbrough, 22nd August 1881
Died: Bebington, 19th December 1952
Role: Left-Half
Career: Everton
Debut: v Scotland (a) 7-4-1906
Appearances: 4
Harry Makepeace's family moved to Merseyside when he was 10 and he began his playing career with Bootle Amateurs, being snapped up by Everton in 1902. A regular member of the side for much of the period up to the First World War, which caused the abandonment of League football and the effective end of his career, he made over 300 first team appearances for the club and helped them win the FA Cup in 1906, finish runners-up in the same competition the following year and win the League title in 1915. Capped by England at both football and cricket (he appeared in four Test matches), like team-mate Jack Sharp, he became coach at Goodison at the end of his playing career. He also coached in Holland for a spell before returning to England to coach the amateur side Marine Crosby. He also coached cricket with Lancashire from 1931 to 1951, becoming an honorary life member upon his retirement.

George Male

George Charles MALE
Born: West Ham, 8th May 1910
Died: 20th February 1998
Role: Right-Back
Career: Clapton, Arsenal
Debut: v Italy (h) 14-11-1934
Appearances: 19 + 1 unofficial appearance
George joined Arsenal as an amateur in November 1929 and worked as a bank messenger before he turned professional in May 1930. Originally a left-half, he helped the club reach the FA Cup final in 1932 before being switched to right-back

at the start of the following season. This proved to be the launch of Arsenal's domination of the domestic game, winning the League title in 1933, 1934, 1935 and 1938 and also winning the FA Cup in 1936. George remained at Highbury as a player until the summer of 1948 when he announced his retirement and had a spell as coach before being appointed chief scout.

Wilf Mannion

Wilfred James MANNION
Born: South Bank, 16th May 1918
Role: Inside-Forward
Career: South Bank St. Peters, Middlesbrough, Hull City, Poole Town, Cambridge United, Kings Lynn, Haverhill Rovers, Earlestown
Debut: v Northern Ireland (a) 28-9-1946 (scored three times)
Appearances: 26 (11 goals) + 4 War appearances + 1 unofficial appearance

Wilf Mannion was dubbed the 'Golden Boy of Soccer', a moniker that reflected both his play on the field and film star looks off it. He had played local football in Middlesbrough before being taken on as an amateur by the Ayresome Park club in September 1936, being upgraded to the professional ranks in January 1937. He broke into the Middlesbrough first team prior to the outbreak of the Second World War and played for the Army during the hostilities (he served with the Green Howards and was one of those evacuated from Dunkirk in 1940, later serving in the Middle East and Italy before being invalided out of the army after suffering from shell shock), earning a call-up for the England side against Scotland in the unofficial international of 1941. He made a total of four appearances for his country during the war and retained his place once proper international matches resumed in 1946. Thus he is credited with scoring a hat-trick on his England debut in the 7-2 win over Northern Ireland. At the end of the war he had returned to Middlesbrough and seemed set to spend his entire career with the club, although he refused to play for the club for six months following a wage dispute in 1948. He announced his retirement in June 1954 having made 368 appearances for the Middlesbrough League side and scoring 110 goals. Six months later he returned to League football, signing for Hull City (Hull were obliged to pay Middlesbrough £5,000 as a result) and making 16 appearances and scoring just one goal. His time at Hull was not a success and he left again in September 1955 having made allegations of illegal payments. Wilf then drifted into non-League football, playing for Poole Town, Cambridge United, King's Lynn, Haverhill Rovers and Earlestown, becoming player-manager of the latter club in October 1962. In between his last two clubs Wilf had worked at the Vauxhall Motors plant in Luton and when he left Earlestown he returned to the Teeside area to live. Wilf's 26 appearances for England included the embarrassing 1-0 defeat inflicted by the United States in the 1950 World Cup tournament. "Bloody ridiculous," he said after the game. "Can't we play them again tomorrow?"

Paul MARINER
Born: Bolton, 22nd May 1953
Role: Centre-Forward
Career: Chorley, Plymouth Argyle, Ipswich Town, Arsenal, Portsmouth
Debut: v Luxembourg (h) (substitute) 30-3-1977 (WCQ)
Appearances: 35 (13 goals)

Paul played for non-League Chorley before being signed by Plymouth for £5,000 in May 1973 and helped the club win promotion to the Second Division in 1976, his goalscoring exploits attracting the attention of a number of First Division sides. He was subsequently sold to Ipswich Town for £130,000 in October 1976 and less than six months later he had picked up his first cap for England. He helped Ipswich win the FA Cup in 1978 and the UEFA Cup in 1981 before a £150,000 move to Arsenal in February 1984, although a little over two years later he moved on to Portsmouth where he finished his playing career. After a spell as commercial manager of Colchester United he went to the United States to coach.

Paul Mariner

Joseph Thomas MARSDEN
Born: Darwen, 1868
Died: 18th January 1897
Role: Right-Back
Career: Darwen, Everton
Debut: v Ireland (h) 7-3-1891
Appearances: 1

Joe Marsden joined Darwen from junior football and developed into a highly dependable right-back, earning selection for England towards the end of the 1890-91 season, the last Darwen player to earn selection for England. His form for both club and country was sufficient to attract the interest of Everton and he was transferred during the close season. He appeared in Everton's opening game of the campaign on 5th September 1891, against West Bromwich Albion, but was injured during the match and never played again.

William MARSDEN
Born: Silksworth, 10th November 1901
Died: 1983
Role: Inside-Right
Career: Sunderland, Sheffield Wednesday
Debut: v Wales (h) 20-11-1929
Appearances: 3

Bill worked as a miner at the Silksworth Colliery before being spotted playing for the works side by Sunderland, signing with the Roker Park club in October 1920. In May 1924 he joined Sheffield Wednesday and helped them win the Second Division championship in 1926. Over the next four years Bill played a vital part in helping the club win further honours, including the League title in 1929 and 1930 and also represented the Football League during this period. He seemed set for a lengthy spell in the England side when he suffered a serious spinal injury against Germany in Berlin in 1930. This brought an end to his playing career and he joined Gateshead as trainer, subsequently becoming assistant coach to the Dutch FA before the Second World War broke out. He then served Doncaster Rovers as manager between April 1944 and January 1946 and was later in charge at Worksop Town.

Rodney William MARSH
Born: Hatfield, 11th October 1944
Role: Forward
Career: West Ham United, Fulham, Queens Park Rangers, Manchester City, Tampa Bay Rowdies (USA), Fulham
Debut: v Switzerland (h) (substitute) 10-11-1971 (ECQ)
Appearances: 9 (1 goal)

Rodney Marsh was one of the most talented players of his era and a supreme entertainer, but his sometimes irreverent attitude probably cost him a lengthy England career. After playing for Hackney Schools he signed with West Ham United as an amateur, subsequently joining the professional ranks with Fulham in October 1962. After 66 League appearances for the Craven Cottage side (and having gone

Rodney Marsh

deaf in one ear after heading home a goal!) he was sold to Third Division Queens Park Rangers, costing the Loftus Road outfit £15,000 in March 1966. The following season he proved inspirational as QPR won the Third Division title and upset the form book with a League Cup Final victory over holders West Bromwich Albion at Wembley, with Rodney scoring one of Rangers' goals in the 3-2 win. He was made captain of QPR in 1970 and shaved his beard off in order to appear more dignified, won his first cap for England in 1971 and was then the subject of intense transfer speculation as a result. Manchester City paid £200,000 to take him to Maine Road in March 1972 as they looked to strengthen a side that was challenging for the League title. Unfortunately, the closest Rodney came to collecting honours at City came in the 1974 League Cup final, but Wolves won 2-1 at Wembley and Rodney refused to applaud the opposition or collect his runners-up medal. He remained with City until January 1976 when he was sold to Tampa Bay Rowdies for £45,000, although he came back to England to play for Fulham between August 1976 and February 1977, linking him with George Best. He returned to America and finally retired as a player in 1979, although he continued to manage the club. He later returned to England once again and had an after-dinner act with George Best. It was believed a flippant remark made to Alf Ramsey cost him his England career, a remark that Rodney himself does not deny.

Thomas MARSHALL

Born: Withnell, 12th September 1858
Died: 29th April 1917
Role: Right-Winger
Career: Darwen, Blackburn Olympic
Debut: v Wales (a) 15-3-1880
Appearances: 2

Tommy played junior football in Lancashire before signing with Darwen in 1878, becoming known as a speedy winger with an accurate passing ability. This earned him two caps for his country, both against Wales and the second of which saw him alongside his Darwen team-mate Tot Rostron. Tommy remained with Darwen until 1886 when he joined Blackburn Olympic but retired from playing soon after and went to work in a cotton mill.

Alvin Martin

Alvin Edward MARTIN

Born: Bootle, 29th July 1958
Role: Centre-Back
Career: West Ham United, Leyton Orient
Debut: v Brazil (h) 12-5-1981
Appearances: 17

Alvin played schoolboy football on his native Merseyside but was turned down by Everton, subsequently joining West Ham as an apprentice in 1974 and being upgraded to the professional ranks in July 1976. A member of the side that lost in the FA Youth Cup in 1975, Alvin had to wait until March 1978 to make his first team debut but became a regular the following season, going on to help the club win the FA Cup in 1980 and the Second Division championship the following season as well as reach the final of the League Cup in 1981. He remained at Upton Park for over twenty years, moving on in the summer of 1996 after 596 games in the claret and blue of West Ham to join Leyton Orient. Continuing injury problems, which had hampered his last few years at West Ham, forced his retirement after just 17 appearances for Orient.

Henry MARTIN

Born: Selston, 5th December 1891
Role: Left-Winger
Career: Sutton Junction, Sunderland, Nottingham Forest, Rochdale
Debut: v Ireland (h) 14-2-1914
Appearances: 1 + 2 War appearances

Henry was a player of considerable potential who lost some of the best years of his career to the First World War. He signed with Sunderland in January 1912 and made rapid progress for the club, helping them win the League title and finish runners-up in the FA Cup in 1913, agonisingly close to the first double of the twentieth century. The following year he made his debut for England, having already represented the Football League (he would finish his career with three appearances to his name) and seemed set to add to his tally of caps but for the outbreak of the First World War which brought organised football to an end. He guested for Nottingham Forest during the hostilities and took part in the first two Victory Internationals in 1919 but was unable to break back into the full England side. He joined Nottingham Forest on a permanent basis in May 1922 and remained with the club for three years before moving on to Rochdale. He was appointed club trainer at Spotland in 1929, although he made one final appearance for the club during the 1930-31 season. In December 1933 he became manager of Mansfield Town, a position he held until March 1935, joining Swindon Town as trainer the following year and holding the position into the 1950s.

Nigel Martyn

Anthony Nigel MARTYN

Born: St. Austell, 11th August 1966
Role: Goalkeeper
Career: Bristol Rovers, Crystal Palace, Leeds United, Everton
Debut: v CIS (a) (substitute) 29-4-1992
Appearances: 9

Bristol Rovers signed Nigel Martyn from St. Blazey in August 1987 and he quickly established himself as a goalkeeper with great potential with a string of superb performances for the West Country club. Crystal Palace paid a then record fee for a goalkeeper, £1 million to take him to Selhurst Park in November 1989 and he continued his progress, making his first appearance for England in 1992. The continued good form of David Seaman in the England goal and competition from the likes of Ian Walker and Tim Flowers restricted his chances of breaking into the side on a regular basis but he seldom let anyone down when called upon. His transfer to a club with a bigger profile, Leeds United, for £2.25 million in 1996, helped add to his tally of caps, but in 2003 he came under pressure from the blossoming Paul Robinson, prompting a move to Everton.

Brian MARWOOD

Born: Seaham Harbour, 5th February 1960
Role: Midfield
Career: Hull City, Sheffield Wednesday, Arsenal, Sheffield United, Middlesbrough, Swindon Town, Barnet
Debut: v Saudi Arabia (substitute) (a) 16-11-1988
Appearances: 1

Brian joined Hull City as an apprentice and was upgraded to the professional ranks in February 1978, going on to become a winger with a good goalscoring knack. This prompted a move to Sheffield Wednesday for £115,000 in August 1984 and in his second season at Hillsborough, he finished as the club's top goalscorer. Injury during the 1986-87 season affected his confidence and in March 1988 he was sold to Arsenal for £600,000, going on to recover his form and help the club win the League championship in 1989. The arrival of Anders Limpar cost him his club place and he was sold to Sheffield United in October 1991 but made only 22 appearances for the club. After a brief loan spell with Middlesbrough, Brian was released and joined Swindon, making only a handful of appearances for them before finishing his playing career with Barnet.

Harry Mart MASKREY

Born: Dronfield, 8th October 1880
Died: 21st April 1927
Role: Goalkeeper
Career: Ripley Athletic, Derby County, Bradford City, Ripley Town, Burton All Saints, Derby County, Burton All Saints
Debut: v Ireland (a) 15-2-1908
Appearances: 1

Harry was working as a miner when he joined Derby County in 1902 and went on to make over 200 League and cup appearances during his first spell with the club, also representing the Football League once and collecting his only cap for England. He moved on to Bradford City in October 1909 and spent two years at Valley Parade before leaving League football and signing for Ripley Town in the summer of 1911. Harry then joined Burton All Saints during the First World War and returned to the Baseball Ground in September 1920, making a further five appearances for the club before rejoining Burton All Saints where he finished his career in 1922. Harry then went into business in Derby where he died five years later.

Charles MASON

Born: Wolverhampton, 1st April 1863
Died: Wolverhampton, 3rd February 1941
Role: Left-Back
Career: Wolverhampton Wanderers
Debut: v Ireland (h) 5-2-1887
Appearances: 3

Charlie Mason was a pupil of St. Luke's School in Blakenhall and helped establish a football side in 1877, this subsequently amalgamating with Blakenhall Wanderers Cricket Club to form Wolverhampton Wanderers. Thus, along with John Brodie, Charlie Mason can truly be said to have been a founding father of Wolves. He remained a player with the club until 1892 and made over 300 appearances for Wolves, a remarkable figure given that regular League football did not commence until 1888. The closest Charlie came to collecting a domestic honour was in the FA Cup in 1889, for Wolves reached the final only to be beaten by Preston. Two years earlier Charlie had achieved the distinction of becoming the first Wolves player to earn international honours when selected for a match against Ireland. In May 1888 he guested for West Bromwich Albion against Scottish side Renton in a match billed as the 'Championship of the World', as both sides had won their respective FA Cups.

Reg Matthews

Reginald Derrick MATTHEWS

Born: Coventry, 20th December 1933
Role: Goalkeeper
Career: Coventry City, Chelsea, Derby County, Rugby Town
Debut: v Scotland (a) 14-4-1956
Appearances: 5

Reg played schools football in his hometown and was taken on to the ground staff in 1947 when aged just 14. He turned professional in May 1950 and soon made the goalkeeping berth at Highfield Road his own, going on to earn selection for England at Under-23 and B level, although it was thought unlikely that a Third Division player would gain selection for the full side. Reg confounded those doubters, for all five of his caps came whilst he was playing his League football in the Third Division (South), the first player since the Second World War to be capped for England whilst playing outside the top two divisions of the Football League. Despite denials from Coventry City that he would be sold, a fee of £22,500 took him to Chelsea in November 1956. It is unlikely that Reg himself wanted the move, for he continued to live in Coventry and was unable to train with his new team-mates, and although he made 135 League appearances for the club, he was unable to reclaim his England place. In October 1961 he was sold to Derby County for £10,000 and went on to make 225 appearances for the Rams, a then record for a goalkeeper before leaving to become player-manager of Rugby Town in August 1968.

Sir Stanley MATTHEWS C.B.E.

Born: Hanley, 1st February 1915
Died: 23rd February 2000
Role: Right-Winger
Career: Stoke St. Peters, Stoke City, Blackpool, Stoke City
Debut: v Wales (a) 29-9-1934 (scored once)
Appearances: 54 (11 goals) + 29 War appearances (2 goals) + 1 unofficial appearance

The son of a professional boxer, he joined local side Stoke City as a brilliant schoolboy prodigy when aged 17 and made his debut soon after, going on to help Stoke win the Second Division championship in 1933. Within two years he had made the first of 54 full appearances for England and established himself as a regular in the side. During the Second World War he guested for Morton, Rangers and Blackpool and at the end of the hostilities rejoined Stoke but was sensationally transferred to Blackpool in 1947 for the comparatively small fee of £11,500. The following season he helped Blackpool to the FA Cup final where they were beaten 4-2 by Manchester United, but Matthews' performances throughout the season earned him the accolade of Footballer of the Year from the Football Writers' Association, the first player thus honoured. He helped Blackpool again reach the cup final in 1951 (beaten by Newcastle) and 1953, where for much of the game it seemed as if he would be returning home with a third runners-up medal - with 20 minutes to go Bolton led 3-1. The remaining 20 minutes have since passed into folklore, for Matthews, known as the 'Wizard of the Dribble' took control of the game and carved opening after opening for his forwards, in particular Stan Mortensen, who grabbed a hat-trick, the first Wembley cup final hat-trick. With barely seconds remaining Blackpool grabbed their fourth goal and Stanley Matthews had his winners' medal. Such was his contribution to the game it has remained known as 'The Matthews Final'. Although Matthews was now 38 years old, he showed little sign of losing either his appetite or enthusiasm for the game, winning the last of his England caps in 1957 (aged 42) and turning out for Blackpool for a further five years after that. Then he went back to Stoke in 1962 and incredibly helped them win the Second Division title again, thirty years after first collecting a championship medal. Stan was also named Footballer of the Year for a second time, 15 years after first collecting the accolade. He carried on playing at the top level past his fiftieth birthday, the only player ever to have appeared in the First Division over such an age. After retiring he tried his hand at management with Port Vale but was caught up in the financial irregularities scandal that rocked the club and left soon after. He then coached around the world, the perfect ambassador for the game. He was awarded the CBE in 1957 and in 1965 became the first footballing knight, a first to go alongside the accolade of European Footballer of the Year, which he collected in 1956, again the first player so honoured. He was awarded an honorary degree from Keele University in 1987. His son, also named Stanley, won the Wimbledon Boys singles title in 1962 and represented the country in

Sir Stanley Matthews

the Davis Cup in 1971. Among the many records held by Sir Stanley is one that must surely stand for all time; his international career covered 22 years and 228 days, with only Peter Shilton's mere 19 years 224 days coming anywhere near it for longevity.

Vincent MATTHEWS

Born: Aylesbury, 15th January 1896
Died: Oxford 15th November 1950
Role: Centre-Back
Career: St. Frideswide FC, Oxford City, Bournemouth & Boscombe Athletic, Bolton Wanderers, Tranmere Rovers, Sheffield United, Shamrock Rovers, Shrewsbury Town, Oswestry Town
Debut: v France (a) 17-5-1928
Appearances: 2 (1 goal)

Vincent Matthews was something of a late developer at football, playing non-League football before a move to Bolton Wanderers in January 1923 for £1,000 from Bournemouth and making his League debut when aged 27. His spell at Bolton didn't really work out and he was released in the summer of 1925 and signed for Tranmere Rovers, spending two years with the club before moving on to Sheffield United in the summer of 1927. Here he found his true form and by the end of his first season at Bramall Lane had won his first cap for England at the age of 32. He remained with the club for four years before heading over to Ireland to play for Shamrock Rovers, collecting winners' medals from the FAI Cup in 1932 and 1933, returning home to sign for Shrewsbury Town as player-manager in June 1935 where he finished his career. Vincent moved to Oxford to work at Morris Motors in 1944 and coached the works side from 1948 until his death two years later.

William John MAYNARD

Born: London, 18th March 1853
Died: Durham 2nd September 1921
Role: Goalkeeper, Winger
Career: 1st Surrey Rifles, Wanderers, Surrey
Debut: v Scotland (a) 30-11-1872
Appearances: 2

William Maynard first came to prominence as a forward, playing on the wing for 1st Surrey Rifles and was selected to the squad for the very first international, between Scotland and England in 1872. Alex Morten had originally been selected to play in goal for England but was unavailable on the day, with the result that Robert Barker played the first half in goal and was replaced by Maynard for the second period. Despite playing in an unfamiliar position (a charge that could also be levelled at Barker) he did well enough to help England to a goalless draw. He returned to the England side four years later, this time as a winger, in a game England lost 3-0. In 1877 he represented Surrey and later spent a year with Wanderers. After retiring as a player he served as District Registrar of Durham from 1903 until his death eighteen years later. His son, Alfred Frederick Maynard, represented England at Rugby Union and lost his life in the First World War.

James MEADOWS

Born: Bolton, 21st July 1931
Died: January 1994
Role: Right-Back
Career: Southport, Manchester City
Debut: v Scotland (h) 2-4-1955
Appearances: 1

Jimmy Meadows began his career as a winger but was successfully converted to full-back and made 60 League appearances for the Haig Avenue outfit before switching to Maine Road in March 1951. He quickly became established as a permanent fixture in the City defence and helped the club to the FA Cup Final in 1955 where they were beaten by Newcastle United. He had also broken into the England side that same year but any chance he had of adding to his collection of caps or medals was wrecked the following season when his playing career was brought to a premature end after an injury sustained in a cup-tie. He joined the City training staff and remained for almost a decade before joining Stockport County, eventually becoming manager and guiding them to the Fourth Division title in 1967. Two years later he went to Bury as assistant manager to Les Shannon and a year later followed Les to Blackpool. He subsequently had spells in sole charge at Bolton Wanderers and Southport, taking the latter club to the Fourth Division title in 1973, and later returned to both Stockport (in 1974) and Blackpool (1978). He finished his career with coaching appointments in Kuwait and Sweden.

Leslie Dennis MEDLEY

Born: Edmonton, 3rd September 1920
Role: Left-Winger
Career: Northfleet, Tottenham Hotspur, Greenbacks (Canada), Ulster United (Canada), Tottenham Hotspur, Randfontein (South Africa)
Debut: v Wales (h) 15-11-1950
Appearances: 6 (1 goal)

After playing for local school sides and Tottenham Juniors, Les Medley joined Spurs as an amateur in 1935 and then joined the professional ranks in February 1939. He joined the Royal Air Force and was posted to Canada, where he met his future wife and on the cessation of hostilities returned to Spurs. He made his full debut in the cup-tie against Brentford in 1946, although he had to wait for his League debut - his wife was homesick for Canada and in November 1946 the Medleys sailed across the Atlantic to begin a new life. After less than two years Les announced he was homesick and the Medleys came home again! Les took time to readjust to English football and it was not until April 1949 he was able to firmly establish himself in the team. Of course, this was just prior to the 'push and run' side that was to dominate domestic football for two or three seasons and Les Medley certainly played a vital role. Operating from the wing he was both creator and taker of goals and in November 1950 was awarded the first of his six full England caps, against Wales. At the end of the 1952-53 season he announced his retirement, having made 150 League appearances and scored 45 goals. Once again the Medleys emigrated to Canada, although Les did have a spell coaching in South Africa from 1958 to 1961.

Tommy Meehan

Thomas MEEHAN

Born: Manchester 1896
Died: London, 18th August 1924
Role: Left-Half
Career: Newtown, Walkden Central, Rochdale, Manchester United, Chelsea
Debut: v Ireland (a) 20-10-1923
Appearances: 1

Tommy Meehan joined Manchester United from Rochdale in June 1917 although he had to wait until the end of the First World War before making his League debut. He remained at United until December 1920 when Chelsea paid £3,300 to take him south. He seemed set for a lengthy career for both Chelsea and England but in August 1924 suffered a bout of sleeping sickness and was taken to St. George's Hospital in London where he later died. Such was his popularity that over 2,000 mourners turned out for his funeral in Wandsworth, and a fund set up to assist his widow and four children raised £1,580.

James MELIA

Born: Liverpool, 1st November 1937
Role: Inside Forward
Career: Liverpool, Wolverhampton Wanderers, Southampton, Aldershot, Crewe Alexandra
Debut: v Scotland (h) 6-4-1963
Appearances: 2 (1 goal)

Jimmy played schools football for his hometown and joined the Liverpool ground staff in 1953, turning professional the following November having been capped for England at schoolboy and Youth level. He went on to make 269 League appearances for the club, scoring 76 goals, a more than useful return as he helped the club win the Second Division championship in 1962 and the League title itself in 1964. By then Jimmy had already moved on, having lost his club place and been transferred to Wolves for £55,000 in March 1964. Jimmy made just 24 appearances for the club before being sold on to Southampton in December 1964 for £30,000 and helping them win promotion to the First Division in 1965-66. After 139 appearances Jimmy moved down the league again to sign for Aldershot for £9,000 as player-coach, racking up another 135 appearances for the club and becoming player-manager in April 1969. He held this position until January 1972 when he left the club, later joining Crewe Alexandra as player-manager between May 1972 and December 1974. After finishing his playing career Jimmy then turned to management and coaching, taking over as Southport manager in July 1975 but ending the year coaching in the Middle East. Jimmy later joined Brighton as a coach and in March 1983 took over as manager from Mike Bailey, helping guide the club to the FA Cup final at the end of the season. He remained in charge until October 1983, subsequently managing in Portugal and also having a spell in charge at Stockport County.

David Mercer

David William MERCER

Born: St. Helens, 20th March 1893
Died: 4th June 1950
Role: Right-Winger
Career: Prescot Athletic, Skelmersdale, Hull City, Sheffield United, Shirebrook, Torquay United
Debut: v Northern Ireland (h) 21-10-1922
Appearances: 2 (1 goal)

After playing non-League football with Prescot Athletic and Skelmersdale, David signed with Hull City in January 1914. Whilst the outbreak of the First World War a few months later eventually brought organised League football to a halt in 1915, David had an unbroken run of 200 games for the club in wartime fixtures and it was his performances here that alerted bigger clubs as to his abilities. He was bought by Sheffield United in December 1920 for £4,500, then a record fee, and here played alongside his brother Arthur. A member of the side that won the FA Cup in 1925, he remained at Bramall Lane until November 1928 when he signed for Shirebrook. He returned to League action with Torquay United, joining the club in June 1929 and retiring a year later. His son Arthur later played for Torquay after the Second World War.

Joe Mercer

Joseph MERCER O.B.E.

Born: Ellesmere Port, 9th August 1914
Died: Merseyside, 9th August 1990
Role: Wing-Half
Career: Chester, Runcorn, Blackburn Rovers, Ellesmere Port Town, Everton, Arsenal
Debut: v Northern Ireland (h) 16-11-1938
Appearances: 5 + 27 War appearances (1 goal) + 2 unofficial appearances

Joe Mercer joined Everton as a 15-year-old and soon became established as a regular in the side, helping them to the League title in the last season before the outbreak of the Second World War. After the hostilities were ended he was surprisingly sold to Arsenal for £7,000 in November 1946, Everton believing they had perhaps got the best out of him. Despite a series of leg injuries Joe enjoyed a new lease of life at Highbury, although it has to be said that he only ever saw his new team-mates on match days; Arsenal manager Tom Whittaker allowed him to remain living in the North West and train with Everton during the week! Despite this arrangement Joe was as popular in the Arsenal dressing room as he had been at Everton, not least because his occupation of grocer gave him access to a number of goods that were rationed in the immediate aftermath of the war, most of which he brought with him when he came down to London for matches! On the field Joe proved the guiding light behind a side that was to win two League titles and the one medal Joe treasured more than any other, the FA Cup in 1950, the same year he was named the Football Writers' Footballer of the Year. He was still playing beyond his 40th birthday, but a broken leg sustained in 1954 brought his playing career to an end. He then went into management, first with Sheffield United and in 1958 with Aston Villa. His arrival at Villa Park immediately restored the club to its former glories, winning promotion back into the First Division and winning the League Cup, the first such winners, in 1961. By 1964 the strain of being manager was becoming too great and he was advised to retire. After a year's rest and recuperation he returned to management with another fallen giant, Manchester City, and in tandem with Malcolm Allison won the League title in 1967-68, the FA Cup in 1969 (thus becoming the first man to have captained and managed an FA Cup winning team at Wembley) and the European Cup Winners' Cup and League Cup in 1970. He became general manager in 1971 before retiring in 1972, although he was briefly caretaker manager of England following the departure of Don Revie. Indeed, when he turned up at Lancaster Gate, the home of the Football Association, to take over he was asked by the doorman if he had an appointment. "Yes", he replied, "for seven matches!"

Gilbert Harold MERRICK

Born: Birmingham, 26th January 1922
Role: Goalkeeper
Career: Solihull Town, Birmingham City
Debut: v Northern Ireland (h) 14-11-1951
Appearances: 23

Effectively a one-club man, Gil Merrick played non-League and junior football in the Birmingham area before signing amateur forms with Solihull Town in August 1939. The ink on that contract was barely dry when Gil was snapped up by Birmingham City the same month, thus beginning a relationship with the club that was to last more than twenty-four years. Gil modelled his goalkeeping style on former Birmingham and England player Harry Hibbs, who ended his own connection with Birmingham in 1940. Gil forced his way into the first team during the wartime matches, making 172 appearances before League football resumed in 1946. Over the next fourteen years Gil was an almost ever-present, helping the club win the Second Division championship in 1947-48 and 1954-55 and reach the FA Cup Final in 1956. There they were beaten 3-1 by Manchester City, but it was the exploits of the opposite goalkeeper, Bert Trautmann, who captured the headlines, playing on with a broken neck. Despite this disappointment, Gil was rightly regarded as a solid and reliable goalkeeper, a reputation he earned during the course of 485 League appearances for Birmingham (he made 551 appearances in all competitions) and 23 appearances for his country, in which only five were lost. Gil also represented the Football League on 11 occasions. He retired as a player in May 1960 and was then appointed manager of the club, with the then Inter-Cities Fairs Cup Final against Barcelona virtually his first match in charge. Although the final was lost, Gil would be responsible for bringing the club their first major piece of silverware, the League Cup in 1963, a victory made even sweeter by victory over local rivals Aston Villa in the final. Gil remained in charge at St. Andrews until April 1964 when he left football to become personnel manager for a local stores group, although he did have spells managing both Bromsgrove Rovers and Atherstone Town on a part-time basis over the next few years.

Gil Merrick

Paul Charles MERSON

Born: Harlesden, 20th March 1968
Role: Midfield
Career: Arsenal, Brentford, Middlesbrough, Aston Villa, Walsall
Debut: v Germany (h) (substitute) 11-9-1991
Appearances: 21 (3 goals)

Paul Merson joined Arsenal as an apprentice in 1985 and after a loan spell at Brentford fought his way into the first team, going on to become an exciting midfield player. Whilst at Arsenal he helped the club win two League titles, the League Cup, FA Cup and European Cup Winners' Cup, but his career almost became blighted by off-the-field activities. He publicly admitted to being an alcoholic, gambler and suffering from drug dependency and was banned from the game for a time, although he overcame these problems and returned to the Arsenal first team. During the summer of 1997 he was surprisingly sold to First Division side Middlesbrough for £4.5 million but helped them gain promotion back into the Premier League and to the final of the League Cup in his first season, with his England career suffering little whilst he was out of the top flight. Indeed, after captaining the England B side he was included in the squad for the World Cup finals in France, playing in the match against Argentina. At the beginning of the 1997-98 season he announced he was unhappy at Middlesbrough and wished to move away from the club, subsequently being bought by Aston Villa for over £6 million three games into the season. He later moved onto Walsall as player-manager.

Paul Merson

Victor METCALFE

Born: Barrow, 3rd February 1922
Died: 6th April 2003
Role: Left-Winger
Career: Ravensthorpe Albion, Huddersfield Town, Hull City
Debut: v Argentina (h) 9-5-1951
Appearances: 2

The son of a former Barrow rugby player, Vic Metcalfe played schools football in the West Riding area before linking with Ravensthorpe Albion and then signing as an amateur with Huddersfield Town in January 1940. During the Second World War, Vic served as an RAF radio operator and at the end of hostilities looked to resume his football career, signing as a professional with Huddersfield Town in December 1945. He was a virtual ever-present for the next twelve seasons, making 434 League appearances for the first team, weighing in with 87 goals in the process. His performances during the early 1950s did not go unnoticed by the various selectors either, for he won two full caps for England and represented the Football League on two occasions during this period. Although Huddersfield Town were relegated at the end of the 1951-52 season, they bounced straight back the following season as runners-up, with Vic being one of seven ever-present players in their squad. Their First Division status was preserved until 1956 when they were again relegated, although this time there was to be no immediate return. By 1958, with the club looking to reduce the average age of the playing staff, they allowed Vic to move on to Hull City in June of that year. Vic made only six appearances for the club before retiring in February 1960, although he did score three goals in that time. He then rejoined Huddersfield as youth team coach, remaining in this position until October 1964. Vic moved on to Halifax Town, serving them initially as coach and scout before taking over as manager in June 1966 and leaving the club, and football, in November 1967.

John William MEW

Born: Sunderland, 30th March 1889
Died: 1963
Role: Goalkeeper
Career: Blaydon United, Marley Hill Colliery, Manchester United, Barrow
Debut: v Ireland (h) 23-10-1920
Appearances: 1

Signed by Manchester United as an amateur in July 1912, Jack Mew was upgraded to the professional ranks in September the same year. Although he made his League debut in March 1913 the First World War cut right across his playing career and the bulk of his appearances were made when League football resumed in 1919. He remained at United until September 1926 when he joined Barrow, by which time he had made 199 appearances for the first team, won an England cap and received two benefits from the club. He later coached in Belgium and South America before returning to England to work in a factory in Manchester. He later went into partnership with Cecil Parkin, the Lancashire and England cricketer.

Bernard MIDDLEDITCH

Born: Highgate, 1871
Died: 3rd October 1949
Role: Right-Half
Career: Cambridge University, Corinthians
Debut: v Ireland (h) 20-2-1897
Appearances: 1

Bernard was educated privately before attending Cambridge University, earning a Blue at football in 1895. He began his involvement with the Corinthians the same year, going on to make 82 appearances for the club over the next ten years. After qualifying as a schoolteacher, he worked at University School in Hastings between 1895 and 1900, and then accepted a position at the public school at Malvern. After three years he moved on to another public school, Harrow, serving there from 1903 until his retirement in 1932.

John Edward Thompson 'Jackie' MILBURN

Born: Ashington, 11th May 1924
Died: Ashington, 8th October 1988
Role: Forward
Career: Ashington, Newcastle United, Linfield, Yiewsley
Debut: v Northern Ireland (a) 9-10-1948 (scored once)
Appearances: 13 (10 goals)

Jackie Milburn is probably one of the finest footballers ever produced by the North East and was known as 'Wor Jackie' for his entire career. He first linked with Newcastle United in August 1943 and went on to make his League debut in 1946, eventually making 354 League appearances for the club and scoring 177 goals, an aggregate record for the club. He is perhaps best remembered for his FA Cup exploits; he scored in every round of the 1951 competition as United beat Blackpool in the final, where he netted both goals in the 2-0 victory, helped them retain the cup the following year and also scored in the first minute in their 1955 success against Manchester City. He remained with Newcastle until 1957 when he joined Linfield as player-manager and added an Irish FA Cup winners' medal to his tally in 1960, having been a finalist in the same competition in 1958. He became player-manager with Yiewsley in 1960 but subsequently returned to League football, serving Reading as part-time coach from 1962 and was appointed manager of Ipswich Town as replacement for the England-bound Alf Ramsey in January 1963. He was also manager of Gateshead from November 1965. He then became a journalist, writing for the News of the World. Four of his cousins, George, Jack, Jim and Stanley also played League football whilst a fifth, Cissie, was the mother of Bobby and Jackie Charlton. The Milburns, therefore, are probably the greatest football dynasty the country has ever known. In addition to his 12 caps for England Jackie also represented the Football League on three occasions. Following his death from cancer in 1988 the entire city turned out to join in with the mourning at the passing of such a hero, and his ashes were scattered on the pitch at St. James' Park.

Jackie Milburn

Brian George MILLER

Born: Hapton, 19th January 1937
Role: Wing-Half
Career: Burnley
Debut: v Austria (a) 27-5-1961
Appearances: 1

Brian represented Blackburn Schools in his junior days and initially signed with Burnley on a part-time basis whilst serving an apprenticeship as a marine engineer. He signed professional forms with Burnley in February 1954, making his debut two years later. The following season he became a regular in the side, going on to help Burnley win the League title in 1959-60 and reach the FA Cup two years later. Having earned three caps for England at Under-23 level Brian was called into the full side in 1961 against Austria but was played out of position as England lost 3-1. He made 455 games for Burnley, the last coming against Aston Villa and resulting in a knee injury that brought his career to an end, although he joined the coaching staff at Turf Moor soon after. Promoted to first team trainer in 1969, he had ten years in the role before stepping up to become manager in October 1979, leading the club to the Third Division championship in 1982. The following January he was sacked, but he returned as manager a second time in July 1986 and held the position until January 1989 when he was appointed chief scout.

Harold Sydney MILLER

Born: Watford, 20th May 1902
Role: Inside-Left
Career: St. Albans City, Charlton Athletic, Chelsea, Northampton Town
Debut: v Sweden (a) 24-5-1923 (scored once)
Appearances: 1 (1 goal)

Harry was born in Watford and joined local side St. Albans City before being lured to Charlton Athletic, signing as an amateur in January 1922 and turning professional in December the same year. Barely six months later he joined Chelsea having already been capped for England at full level, but his career never hit the same heights again. He remained at Stamford Bridge until the summer of 1939 when he joined Northampton Town, retiring from playing during the Second World War.

Daniel John MILLS

Born: Norwich, 10th May 1977
Role: Defender
Career: Norwich City, Charlton Athletic, Leeds United, Middlesbrough, Manchester City
Debut: v Mexico (h) 25-5-2001
Appearances: 19

Danny joined local side Norwich City as a trainee and signed professional forms in November 1994, going on to make his debut during the 1995-96 season. The following season he was awarded the first of his 14 caps for England at Under-21 level, his performances for both club and country alerting several other clubs as to his abilities. He eventually signed with Charlton Athletic in a £350,000 deal in March 1998 but a little over a year later cost £4 million when Leeds United took him to Yorkshire. The Elland Road club's financial problems eventually saw him sent on loan to Middlesbrough in August 2003 and he helped the club win the first piece of silverware in their history, the League Cup, in 2004. After his contract with Leeds was settled in the summer of 2005 he joined Manchester City on a free transfer.

Danny Mills

M N O

George Robert MILLS

Born: Deptford, 29th December 1908
Died: 15th July 1970
Role: Centre-Forward
Career: Emerald Athletic, Bromley, Chelsea
Debut: v Northern Ireland (a) 23-10-1937 (scored three times)
Appearances: 3 (3 goals)

George played representative football for South East London schools and junior football for Emerald Athletic and Bromley before signing amateur forms with Chelsea in November 1929, going on to join the professional ranks the following February. Although never a regular within the Chelsea side, making just 239 appearances for the club in League and cup matches, he did score 123 goals, a more than useful return. He also netted a hat-trick on his England debut but failed to find the net in either of his two other appearances. George remained a player at Chelsea until retiring midway through the Second World War, subsequently being appointed coach to the A team at Stamford Bridge. He later worked in the City for a printing company.

Mick Mills

Michael Denis MILLS M.B.E.

Born: Godalming, 4th January 1949
Role: Defender
Career: Portsmouth, Ipswich Town, Southampton, Stoke City
Debut: v Yugoslavia (h) 11-10-1972
Appearances: 42 + 1 unofficial international

Mick Mills was signed by Portsmouth as a youngster but subsequently released when they abandoned their youth policy. He therefore joined the Ipswich Town ground staff, signing as an amateur in 1965, being offered an apprenticeship later that year and in February 1966 being upgraded to the professional ranks. He was to remain with the club until 1982, making 591 League appearances, a record for the club that still stands, and leading them to victory in the 1978 FA Cup and 1981 UEFA Cup. First capped by England in 1972 his international career lasted almost ten years and he captained the side on eight occasions. He left Ipswich in November 1982 for Southampton, costing the south coast club £50,000 and spent three years at The Dell before accepting an invitation to take over as player-manager of Stoke City in July 1985. He remained in charge at the Victoria Ground until 1989. He later managed Colchester United and had a spell as assistant manager at Coventry City. In addition to his 42 full caps Mick also represented his country at Youth and Under-23 level and twice turned out for the Football League. He was awarded the MBE in 1984.

Gordon MILNE

Born: Preston, 29th March 1937
Role: Wing-Half
Career: Preston North End, Morecambe, Preston North End, Liverpool, Blackpool, Wigan Athletic
Debut: v Brazil (h) 8-5-1963
Appearances: 14

Gordon played amateur football in Preston and Morecambe before signing with Preston North End in January 1956, the same club his father Jimmy had been a player with. He replaced Tommy Docherty in the side and seemed set for a lengthy career at Deepdale until the club accepted an offer of £16,000 from Liverpool in August 1960. Gordon became one of the key players in the first great Liverpool sides assembled by Bill Shankly, helping them win the Second Division title in 1962 and the First Division in both 1964 and 1966. In between the two League titles Liverpool won the FA Cup, but Gordon was sidelined by injury, the same fate that had befallen his father with Preston in 1938! Gordon did help Liverpool reach the final of the European Cup Winners' Cup final in 1966 and was a member of the England squad for the World Cup finals the same year, although he made his final appearance for his country in a friendly against Belgium in 1964. He remained at Anfield until May 1967 when he was sold to Blackpool for £30,000, spending three years with the club before accepting the position of player-manager at Wigan Athletic in January 1970. In 1972 he became manager of Coventry City, later going on to manage Leicester City and Besiktas of Turkey.

Gordon Milne

Clement Arthur MILTON

Born: Bristol, 10th March 1928
Role: Right-Winger
Career: Arsenal, Bristol City
Debut: v Austria (h) 28-11-1951
Appearances: 1

After playing schools football in his Bristol hometown, Arthur Milton was offered amateur forms by Arsenal, which he duly signed in April 1945. A little over a year later he was upgraded to the professional ranks, but any thoughts of breaking into the Arsenal first team were to be put on hold when he was called up to do his National Service, prompting a two year break from the game. He finally made his debut for the Highbury club in March 1951 and eight months later, having played only 12 games for Arsenal, earned his one and only cap for England, at least as far as football was concerned. Another of the players at Highbury who excelled at both the winter (football) and summer (cricket) sports, Arthur played for Gloucestershire between 1948 and 1974, appearing in a total of 585 matches and scoring over 30,000 runs. His return from football was considerably lower, however, making just 75 appearances for Arsenal between his debut and his eventual departure on a transfer to Bristol City in February 1955. He did, however, help the League championship trophy come to Highbury in 1952-53. He cost Bristol City £4,000 for his signature, but when he announced his retirement the following July, aged just 27 and having made only 14 appearances for the Ashton Gate club, half of this was refunded! It was his abilities at the summer sport that had influenced his decision to retire from football, and as he appeared in six tests for England, scoring a century in his very first innings, he could well have been vindicated. At the end of his cricket career he became a postman, apparently maintaining his fitness by jumping on and off his bicycle whilst doing his round!

Arthur Weatherell MILWARD

Born: Great Marlow, 12th September 1870
Died: June 1941
Role: Left-Winger
Career: Old Borlasians, Marlow, Everton, New Brighton Tower, Southampton, New Brompton
Debut: v Wales (h) 7-3-1891
Appearances: 4 (3 goals)

He first made his name with Old Borlasians and Marlow and joined Everton in 1888, spending nine seasons with the club, making 224 appearances and scoring 96 goals. Whilst with the club he helped them to the League title in 1891 and the FA Cup final in 1893 and 1897. A more than able goalscorer in his own right, he linked especially well with Edgar Chadwick and went on to collect four caps for England. He left Everton to join New Brighton Tower in 1897 and subsequently switched to Southampton (where he teamed up again with Edgar Chadwick), earning a Southern League championship medal and a further runners-up medal in the FA Cup before finishing his career with New Brompton.

Clement MITCHELL

Born: Cambridge, 20th February 1862
Died: 6th October 1937
Role: Centre-Forward
Career: Upton Park, Essex, Corinthians
Debut: v Wales (a) 15-3-1880
Appearances: 5 (5 goals)

Educated at Felsted School, Clement played for the school side between 1877 and 1879, captaining the side in his final year. He then played regular football for Upton Park and earned representative honours with London, Essex and eventually England and also turned out for the Corinthians. Early in the 1880s he went to India where he played cricket for Calcutta, later returning to England and playing eight matches for Kent County Cricket Club between 1890 and 1892.

James Frederick MITCHELL

Born: Manchester, 18th November 1897
Died: 30th May 1975
Role: Goalkeeper
Career: Blackpool, Northern Nomads, Manchester University, Preston North End, Manchester City, Leicester City
Debut: v Northern Ireland (h) 22-10-1924
Appearances: 1

Jimmy attended Arnold Grammar School in Blackpool and signed with the local club during the 1914-15 season, the last before organised football shut down for the duration of the First World War. He played for Northern Nomads and Manchester University during the war and in 1920, after representing the United Kingdom at the Olympic Games in Antwerp at the high jump, he joined Preston North End. He remained at Deepdale until May 1922 when shortly after appearing in the FA Cup final (they lost to Huddersfield Town) he moved on to Manchester City. Having already collected six caps for England at amateur level, Jimmy earned a full cap in 1924 and finished his playing career with Leicester City during the 1926-27 season. A one-time schoolmaster at Arnold Grammar School, he later joined the footwear company Stead & Simpson. Jimmy was especially known for wearing spectacles during his playing career.

Hugh MOFFAT

Born: Congleton, January 1885
Died: 14th November 1952
Role: Right-Half
Career: Burnley, Oldham Athletic, Chesterfield Municipal
Debut: v Wales (h) 17-3-1913
Appearances: 1

Hugh played junior football in an around his hometown before being signed by Burnley in 1903. He remained at Turf Moor until 1910 when he joined Oldham Athletic. He had played as a left-half at Burnley but was switched to the opposite flank at Oldham, where he formed an effective partnership with David Wilson. Hugh also made two representative appearances for the Football League during his career.

George MOLYNEUX

Born: Liverpool, 1875
Died: 14th April 1942
Role: Left-Back
Career: Third Grenadiers, South Shore, Wigan County, Stoke, Everton, Southampton, Portsmouth, Southend United, Colchester Town
Debut: v Scotland (h) 3-5-1902
Appearances: 4 + 1 unofficial appearance

George played non-League football with a number of clubs before stepping into League action with Stoke in 1897-98. At the end of the season he moved on to Everton and spent two years at Goodison Park before joining Southern League side Southampton in the summer of 1900. He helped his new club win the Southern League championship in 1901, 1903 and 1904 and also reach the FA Cup final in 1902, although they were beaten by Sheffield United after a replay. In May 1905 George moved along the coast to join Portsmouth, spending a year with the club before moving on to Southend United. He finished his playing career with Colchester Town.

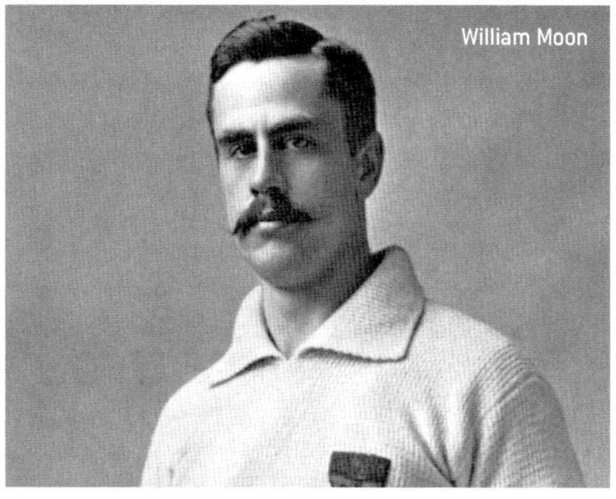
William Moon

William Robert MOON

Born: London, 7th June 1868
Died: 9th January 1943
Role: Goalkeeper
Career: Old Westminsters, Corinthians
Debut: v Wales (h) 4-2-1888
Appearances: 7

William played for Westminster School XI in 1884 and 1885, going on to represent the Old Boys side after he had left. He also played for Corinthians and earned representative honours with London as well as England. He was also a notable cricketer, playing twice for Middlesex in 1891 and scoring 17 runs as well as wicketkeeping. He qualified as a solicitor in 1891 and became a partner in a firm practising in Bloomsbury.

Henry Thomas MOORE

Born: Nottingham, 27th June 1861
Died: 24th September 1939
Role: Full-Back
Career: Notts County
Debut: v Ireland (a) 24-2-1883
Appearances: 2

Henry played junior football in his hometown before linking with Notts County in 1881, remaining with the club for the next seven years. Away from the game he owned an off-licence in the city and eventually moved to Sunbury in Middlesex when he retired.

James MOORE

Born: Birmingham, 11th May 1889
Role: Inside-Left
Career: Quebec Albion, Glossop, Derby County, Chesterfield, Mansfield Town
Debut: v Sweden (a) 21-5-1923 (scored once)
Appearances: 1 (1 goal)

Jimmy began his professional career with Glossop, joining the club in the summer of 1911 from Quebec Albion, a team from Handsworth in Birmingham despite the quaint name. In October 1913 he was sold to Derby County for £1,500 and helped the club win the Second Division championship in 1915. He had to wait until the 1919-20 season, however, before he could make his First Division debut, the First World War having brought organised football to a halt in 1915. Jimmy remained with Derby until March 1926 when he joined Chesterfield and retired a year later. He came out of retirement to make a number of appearances for Mansfield Town from November 1927 and finally finished his playing career with a spell at Worcester City.

Robert Frederick Chelsea MOORE O.B.E.

Born: Barking, 12th April 1941
Died: London, 24th February 1993
Role: Left-Half
Career: West Ham United, Fulham
Debut: v Peru (a) 20-5-1962
Appearances: 108 (2 goals) + 1 unofficial appearance

Bobby Moore was probably the most influential captain ever to have served club and country and his death through cancer was mourned nationwide, irrespective of club allegiances. After starring as a schoolboy, Bobby signed for his local West Ham club as a professional in June 1958 and represented England at Youth level the following season. His assured and polished performances soon made him a regular at half-back in the West Ham side and he quickly became captain. In a three-year spell during the 1960s he collected three of the game's greatest prizes, all at Wembley. In 1964 he inspired West Ham to overcome plucky Preston in the FA Cup Final (the same year as he was named Footballer of the Year), twelve months later to the European Cup Winners' Cup against TSV Munich and then, in 1966, was captain as England won the World Cup. His performances during the 1966 tournament were exceptional; four years later he had become perhaps the best defensive half-back in the world, as the 1970 tournament was to prove. The campaign hardly began with an auspicious start, for he was arrested in Colombia and falsely accused with stealing a gold bracelet from a jewellers in the city of Bogota, but after a spell under house-arrest at the British Embassy rejoined his team-mates in Mexico preparing for the World Cup. Moore quickly demonstrated that the fuss had not unsettled him, and his performance against future world champions Brazil was perhaps the most accomplished ever seen on the world stage, a fact acknowledged by Pele who made immediate tracks for Moore at the final whistle to warmly shake his hand. Alf Ramsey kept faith with Moore until 1973, handing him a then record haul of 108 caps for England, and in 1973 Bobby moved across London to join Fulham after 544 League appearances for West Ham. Two years later Moore inspired Fulham to their first ever FA Cup Final, ironically against West Ham at Wembley. There the fairytale ended, with West Ham winning 2-0. Bobby was widely expected to move into management at the end of his playing career,

Bobby Moore

but apart from brief spells with non-League Oxford City and later Southend United did not get a chance to realise his potential. It is pure speculation, of course, but the success enjoyed by the likes of West Germany who appointed Franz Beckenbauer with little or no managerial experience but still emerged as world champions inevitably lead to the conclusion that England should perhaps have taken a chance, especially after the barren years following Alf Ramsey's departure. As it was Bobby Moore was lost to the game he had graced for so long other than as a journalist, a role he held right up to his death. Memories and stories of Bobby Moore are legendary; from the way he thoughtfully wiped his hand on his shirt before collecting the World Cup from Queen Elizabeth II, his speed of thought to blow the referee's whistle after the official had been knocked unconscious during a match at Upton Park in 1970, the time he was forced to go in goal during a League Cup semi final and saved a penalty but, more than anything, the calm, authoritative way he went about playing his game. In addition to the 108 caps Bobby won playing for England, he also made one appearance against them, turning out for Team America in an unofficial friendly in Philadelphia in 1976.

William Grey Bruce MOORE

Born: Newcastle-upon-Tyne, 6th October 1894
Died: 26th September 1968
Role: Inside-Left
Career: Seaton Delaval, Sunderland, West Ham United
Debut: v Sweden (a) 24-5-1923 (scored twice)
Appearances: 1 (2 goals)

Billy joined Sunderland as an amateur in November 1912 and went on to win four caps for England at amateur level before joining the professional ranks at Sunderland during the First World War. In May 1922 Billy joined West Ham United, thus beginning an association with the club that was to last nearly forty years. He was a member of the side that reached the very first FA Cup final at Wembley, where West Ham lost 2-0 to Bolton Wanderers, but the following month he accompanied the England team on their tour of Sweden and made his debut in the second match, scoring twice. Despite this the England sides selected to play Sweden were largely experimental and neither Billy nor his namesake Jimmy Moore (above) were selected again. Billy remained a player on West Ham's books until he retired in 1929, subsequently being appointed assistant trainer. He was promoted to head trainer in 1932 and held the position until his retirement in May 1960.

John MORDUE

Born: Edmondsley, 1887
Died: 14th December 1957
Role: Winger
Career: Sacriston, Spennymoor United, Barnsley, Woolwich Arsenal, Sunderland, Middlesbrough, Hartlepool United, Durham City
Debut: v Ireland (a) 10-2-1912
Appearances: 2

Jackie Mordue was spotted by Barnsley whilst playing for Spennymoor United and joined the Oakwell club in October 1906. In April the following year he was sold to Woolwich Arsenal for £450 but after one season he was sold to Sunderland. Here he eventually formed an extremely effective right-wing partnership with Charlie Buchan and Frank Cuggy, helping the club win the League championship and finish FA Cup runners-up in 1913. Jackie, who also represented the Football League on three occasions, was sold on to Middlesbrough in May 1920, spending three years at Ayresome Park before accepting the position of player-manager of Durham City in February 1923, a post he held for twelve months.

Charles John MORICE

Born: London, 27th May 1850
Died: 17th June 1932
Role: Forward
Career: Harrow Chequers, Barnes
Debut: v Scotland (a) 30-11-1872
Appearances: 1

Educated at Harrow School, Charles represented the school at football and later played for Harrow Chequers and Barnes. A member of the Stock Exchange, he served on the Football Association Committee between 1873 and 1877 and played in the very first official England international.

Anthony William MORLEY

Born: Ormskirk, 26th August 1954
Role: Forward
Career: Preston North End, Burnley, Aston Villa, West Bromwich Albion, FC Seiko (Hong Kong), West Bromwich Albion, Birmingham City, Burnley, Den Haag (Holland)
Debut: v Hungary (substitute) (h) 18-11-1981
Appearances: 6

Tony played junior football in his hometown before joining the ground staff at Preston North End as an apprentice, turning professional in September 1972. He proved his worth in the Third Division, subsequently earning selection for England at Under-23 level and prompting a move to Turf Moor for £100,000 in February 1976 where Burnley were involved in a desperate struggle to avoid relegation to the Second Division. The struggle was ultimately lost and Tony was still plying his trade in the Second Division when Aston Villa stepped in with a £200,000 offer in June 1979. Chances created by Gordon Cowans were eagerly put away by Peter Withe and Tony Morley, turning all three players into England internationals and Aston Villa into League and European champions in successive seasons, 1981 and 1982. In December 1983 Tony moved on again, joining local rivals West Bromwich Albion for £70,000 where he made 33 appearances before moving to Hong Kong for a spell playing for FC Seiko. Tony returned to West Bromwich Albion but was loaned out to Birmingham City and Burnley before finishing his career in Holland with Den Haag.

Tony Morley

Fred Morris

Herbert MORLEY

Born: Sheffield, October 1882
Died: 15th July 1957
Role: Right-Back
Career: Kiveton Park, Grimsby Town, Notts County
Debut: v Ireland (a) 12-2-1910
Appearances: 1

Herbert began his League career with Grimsby Town, joining the club in August 1904. In March 1907 he joined First Division outfit Notts County, and although the club were relegated in 1913 they bounced straight back, winning the Second Division championship in 1914. Unfortunately there was to be only one more season of First Division football for Herbert before organised football shut down for the duration of the First World War, with Herbert retiring during the hostilities. He retained his association with Notts County however, scouting for the club for a number of years after.

Thomas MORREN

Born: Middlesbrough, 1875
Died: 31st January 1929
Role: Centre-Half
Career: Middlesbrough Victoria, Middlesbrough Ironopolis, Middlesbrough, Barnsley St. Peters, Sheffield United
Debut: v Ireland (a) 5-3-1898 (scored once)
Appearances: 1 (1 goal)

Tommy played for three Middlesbrough clubs, helping Middlesbrough FC win the FA Amateur Cup in 1895. His performances did not go unnoticed by a number of League clubs, being snapped up by Sheffield United via Barnsley St. Peters soon after New Year 1896. Tommy proved to be a solid and reliable performer at the heart of the United defence, helping them win the League championship in 1898 and win the FA Cup final the following season. Tommy returned to Crystal Palace (venue for the FA Cup final between 1895 and 1914) in 1901, although the match against Spurs was drawn and Sheffield United lost the replay at Burnden Park, Bolton. Tommy retired from playing in the summer of 1904 and ran a newsagents in the city until his death.

Frederick MORRIS

Born: Tipton, 27th August 1893
Died: 4th July 1962
Role: Inside-Left
Career: Redditch, West Bromwich Albion, Coventry City, Oakengates Town
Debut: v Scotland (h) 10-4-1920 (scored once)
Appearances: 2 (1 goal)

Fred played schoolboy football in Staffordshire and junior football for a number of clubs before signing with West Bromwich Albion in May 1911, just as the club were being crowned Second Division champions. During the First World War, Fred made guest appearances for Fulham and Watford but returned to West Bromwich Albion at the end of the hostilities to become an integral part of the side that went on to win the League championship in the first season after the war. Fred was a vital goalscorer for the side, netting a then club record of 37 goals in their championship winning season, also representing the Football League and collecting his first full cap for England. He remained at The Hawthorns until August 1924 when he stepped down the League to play for Coventry City but spent only a year with the club before joining non-League Oakengates Town. Fred finished his playing career five years later, in 1930, before returning to his Tipton hometown where he worked for the rest of his life.

John MORRIS

Born: Radcliffe, 27th September 1924
Role: Inside-Left
Career: Radcliffe, Manchester United, Derby County, Leicester City, Corby Town, Kettering Town
Debut: v Norway (a) 18-5-1949 (scored once)
Appearances: 3 (3 goals)

After being spotted playing schools football in Manchester by Louis Roca, Johnny Morris was signed by Manchester United at the age of 15 and made his debut for the club, albeit in a wartime fixture, before he had turned 17. During the war he also made guest appearances for Bolton Wanderers, Charlton Athletic and Wrexham and at the end of the hostilities signed professional forms with United. He was a key member of the first great United side Matt Busby built after the war, helping the club win the FA Cup in 1948 and seemingly set for a lengthy career at Old Trafford. Unfortunately he disagreed with Busby over tactics and the manager moved swiftly to transfer him away from the club, with Derby County paying a then record fee of £23,850 to take him to the Baseball Ground in March 1949. Less than two months later he had won the first of his three England caps. He moved on again for £20,000 to Leicester City in October 1952, eventually helping the club win the Second Division championship in 1954 and again in 1957. At the start of the following season the always volatile Johnny Morris was sent off in a practice match for insulting the referee, and at the end of the season he left the club to become player-manager of Corby Town. He later managed Kettering Town, Great Harwood and Oswestry Town before leaving the game. Johnny also won one cap for the England B side and represented the Football League on five occasions. After coming out of football he worked as a tyre salesman.

Johnny Morris

William Walter MORRIS

Born: Handsworth, 20th August 1915
Role: Right-Back
Career: West Bromwich Albion, Halesowen Town, Wolverhampton Wanderers
Debut: v Northern Ireland (h) 16-11-1938
Appearances: 3

Bill was born close to West Bromwich Albion's Hawthorns ground and attended and played for Handsworth New Road and Nineveh Road schools. He then played for Hansworth Old Boys and was associated with West Bromwich Albion Colts and then Halesowen Town before signing professional forms with Wolverhampton Wanderers in May 1933. He remained with the club until his retirement in 1947, by which time he had made over 250 appearances and collected a winners' medal in the FA Cup in 1939. But for the Second World War Bill would have almost doubled his tally of appearances for his club and perhaps country, and after leaving Wolves he spent two seasons playing for Dudley Town in the Birmingham Combination. In fact, his two seasons with Dudley found him appearing at centre-forward, the position he had first occupied when he signed for Wolves in 1933!

Harold MORSE

Role: Full-Back
Career: Notts County, Notts Rangers
Debut: v Scotland (h) 5-4-1879
Appearances: 1

Very little is known about Harold Morse, other than he had previously played rugby for Derby Wanderers before switching codes and playing for Notts County and Notts Rangers. Capped for England at full-back, he spent the 1879-80 season at centre-forward but did not prove a success, prompting a return to defence.

Thomas MORT

Born: Kearsley, 1st December 1897
Died: 6th June 1967
Role: Left-Back
Career: Newton Lads, Altrincham, Rochdale, Aston Villa
Debut: v Wales (h) 3-3-1924
Appearances: 3

Tommy played junior football for a number of clubs before the outbreak of the First World War, upon which he enlisted in the Lancashire Fusiliers and represented his battalion at football. After the war he signed for non-League Altrincham and then Rochdale, joining the latter in the summer of 1919. In 1921 Rochdale were elected to Division Three North and Tommy's performances during their first season attracted considerable interest, prompting a move to Aston Villa in April 1922. Two years later Tommy helped Villa reach the final of the FA Cup and collected his first cap for England, winning his final cap in 1926. Tommy remained on Villa's books until his retirement in 1935.

Alexander MORTEN

Role: Goalkeeper
Career: Crystal Palace, Middlesex
Debut: v Scotland (h) 8-3-1873
Appearances: 1

Alex Morten played for the No Name club of Kilburn between 1863 and 1866 and then switched to Crystal Palace (the original club formed in 1861) for some nine years. He is also known to have played for Wanderers on a number of occasions between 1865 and 1872 and represented both London and Middlesex during his career. He had originally been selected for the squad for the very first England and Scotland match in 1872 but was unavailable on the day with the result that William Maynard was forced to go in goal, even though he was more usually found on the wing. Alex did play the following year, but was approaching the end of his career. It is believed that he was born in Middlesex in 1831 or 1832, making him the oldest debutant to have been capped by England. If he is indeed this Alex Morten, then he worked in the Stock Exchange as a broker and died on February 24th 1900 at Earl's Court in London. It is known that Morten served on the FA Committee from 1874 and continued to appear on the football field as an umpire, the forerunners to today's referees.

Stan Mortensen

Stanley Harding MORTENSEN

Born: South Shields, 26th May 1921
Died: Blackpool, 22nd May 1991
Role: Forward
Career: Blackpool, Hull City, Southport, Bath City, Leicester City
Debut: v Portugal (a) 27-5-1947 (scored four times)
Appearances: 25 (23 goals) + 3 War appearances (3 goals)

Stan Mortensen scored a hat-trick in the 1953 FA Cup Final but saw his efforts almost entirely overshadowed by the exploits of Stanley Matthews as Blackpool beat Bolton 4-3. He joined Blackpool in April 1937 and guested for Aberdeen during the Second World War, although it was thought at one stage that his career was at an end when the bomber plane in which he was a passenger crashed, killing two crew members. Fortunately he recovered and went on to become one of the most feared strikers in the immediate post war period. With Stanley Matthews supplying the crosses and Stan Mortensen the goals, Blackpool reached the FA Cup Final on three occasions; in 1948, when beaten by Manchester United 4-2, 1951 when Newcastle triumphed 2-0 and 1953 against Bolton. If the 1953 final has since entered folklore as the 'Matthews Final' then the role played by Stan Mortensen cannot be understated, for he was a willing front runner and got on to the end of three chances for Blackpool. Stan remained at Bloomfield Road until November 1955 when Hull City paid £2,000 for his signature, and he joined Southport in February 1957 where he finished his League career. By the time he joined non-League Bath City in July 1958 he had made 395 League appearances for his three clubs, scoring 225 goals. He later played for Lancaster City before finally retiring from playing in March 1962. He was manager of Blackpool between February 1967 and April 1969 and then went into the entertainment business in Blackpool. As well as his 25 full caps for England, Stan made one appearance for the B side and turned out twice for the Football League, and during the Second World War actually made a substitute's appearance for Wales against England following an injury to left-half Ivor Powell that forced him to leave the field. Although there was no provision for substitutes at this time, England told Mortensen to play for the Welsh in a match England eventually won 8-3.

John R. MORTON

Born: Sheffield, 26th February 1914
Died: 8th March 1986
Role: Left-Winger
Career: Woodhouse Alliance FC, Gainsborough Trinity, West Ham United
Debut: v Czechoslovakia (h) 1-12-1937 (scored once)
Appearances: 1 (1 goal) + 1 unofficial appearance

John played schoolboy football in his hometown before setting off on the path to become a professional footballer, starting his career with Gainsborough Trinity, then in the Midland League. After barely a handful of appearances he was spotted by West Ham United and moved to Upton Park for £600. Although his first official cap for England came in the friendly against Czechoslovakia at White Hart Lane, he had played for his country two years earlier in the Jubilee International played against Scotland at Hampden Park. John also represented the Football League once and retired from playing during the Second World War. He remained in the East End of London, working as a bookmaker.

William MOSFORTH

Born: Sheffield, 1858
Died: 11th July 1929
Role: Left-Winger
Career: Ecclesfield, Sheffield Wednesday, Sheffield Albion, Hallam, Heeley, Providence, Sheffield United
Debut: v Scotland (h) 3-3-1877
Appearances: 9 (3 goals)

Billy spent his entire playing career in Sheffield, assisting minor clubs Hallam, Heeley, Providence and Ecclesfield before joining Sheffield Wednesday where he won his first cap for England. Billy also represented the Sheffield FA and switched to Sheffield Albion in 1878, where he was also capped, before returning to Wednesday in 1880. He spent nine years at the club before switching across the city to sign for the newly formed Sheffield United, playing in that club's very first fixture.

Frank Moss

Frank MOSS

Born: Aston, 17th April 1895
Died: 15th September 1965
Role: Wing-Half
Career: Walsall, Aston Villa, Cardiff City, Worcester City
Debut: v Ireland (a) 22-10-1921
Appearances: 5

Frank Moss had begun his professional career with Walsall and was transferred to Aston Villa for £250 in February 1914. He made only two appearances before the outbreak of the First World War and enlisted with the 4th Lincolnshire Regiment, seeing action in France. He was severely wounded in the knee and sent home where he became a PE instructor. By the end of the war he had recovered from his wound and so resumed his playing career, going on to win five caps for England and appearing in 283 games for Villa, helping them reach the FA Cup final in 1920 and 1924 and collecting a winners' medal in the former year. He was signed by Cardiff City in January 1929, playing two seasons for the club before joining Worcester City where he finished his playing career. His two sons, Frank junior and Amos also served the club with distinction.

Frank MOSS

Born: Leyland, 5th November 1909
Died: Preston, 7th February 1970
Role: Goalkeeper
Career: Preston North End, Oldham Athletic, Arsenal
Debut: v Scotland (h) 14-4-1934
Appearances: 4

Not the son of the player above, this Frank played local football in Leyland before starting work at Leyland Motors as a driller and playing for the works team when he was invited to sign for Preston North End as an amateur in October 1927. He was promoted to the professional ranks in February the following year but was sold to Oldham Athletic in May 1929. Here he found his form and put in performances that prompted Arsenal to sign him in November 1931 for £3,000. At the end of the season Frank had collected his first medal, helping the club reach the FA Cup final at Wembley where they were beaten in controversial circumstances by Newcastle United. Frank and Arsenal found consistency over the next few seasons however, winning the League championship in three successive seasons, 1933, 1934 and 1935. A serious shoulder injury sustained during the 1935-36 ultimately forced him to retire in the summer of 1936, with Frank returning to football as manager of Heart of Midlothian in 1937, retaining the position until called up for war work in 1940. After the war Frank became a licensee.

Edwin MOSSCROP

Born: Southport, 16th June 1892
Died: 14th March 1980
Role: Left-Winger
Career: Blowick, Shepherds Bush, Middlesex County, Southport YMCA, Southport Central, Burnley
Debut: v Wales (a) 16-3-1914
Appearances: 2

Edwin played local football in Southport before journeying south and turning out for Shepherds Bush, also representing Middlesex during this time. He returned to local football in Southport and signed with Burnley as an amateur in the summer of 1912 and professional forms a couple of months later. The 1913-14 season was one of his most successful as he collected a winners' medal in the FA Cup final and

Jimmy Mullen

made two appearances for England, against Wales and Scotland in the final internationals of the season. With the outbreak of the First World War these turned out to be the last internationals for five years, and by the time international football resumed in 1919, Edwin was overlooked. He continued to be a vital player for Burnley however, helping them win the League title in 1921. Edwin, who had guested for Reading during the war and also represented the Football League, retired on health grounds in November 1922 and returned to being a schoolteacher, his original profession.

Bertram MOZLEY

Born: Derby, 23rd September 1923
Role: Right-Back
Career: Shelton United, Nottingham Forest, Derby County
Debut: v Republic of Ireland (h) 21-9-1949
Appearances: 3

After representing Derby Schools as a junior, Bert joined non-League side Shelton United before signing amateur forms with Nottingham Forest in early 1944, during the Second World War. In March 1945, however, he joined local rivals Derby County, being upgraded to the professional ranks the following June. Bert became a permanent fixture in the Derby side for the next nine years and was widely reckoned to be one of the quickest full-backs in the country. After earning representative honours with the Football League, Bert won the first of his three full England caps in 1949 and the following year was part of the FA touring party that visited and played representative matches in Canada. After nearly 300 appearances for Derby, Bert emigrated to Canada in January 1955.

James MULLEN

Born: Newcastle-upon-Tyne, 6th January 1923
Died: Wolverhampton, 2nd October 1987
Role: Left-Winger
Career: Wolverhampton Wanderers
Debut: v Scotland (h) 12-4-1947
Appearances: 12 (6 goals) + 3 War appearances

Jimmy Mullen was an extremely fast and tricky winger despite his size and more than capable of cutting inside in order to try a shot at goal. He was educated in Newcastle and represented Newcastle Schools, joining the Wolves ground staff at the age of 14 in July 1937. That same year he represented England at schoolboy level and in February 1939 made his League debut for Wolves at the tender age of just 16 years. He was upgraded to the professional ranks in January 1940 and made his first appearance for England, albeit in a wartime international, in 1942, the same year he helped Wolves win the Wartime League Cup. Having served in the Army during the Second World War (attaining the rank of corporal) he resumed his football career in earnest in 1946, being awarded his first full cap in 1947 and helping Wolves win the FA Cup in 1949. The following year Jimmy became the very first England substitute, replacing the injured Jackie Milburn 10 minutes into the match against Belgium in Brussels. He also scored in the 4-1 win. He went on to win three League championship medals whilst with Wolves, in 1954, 1958 and 1959 and made 486 appearances for the first team, scoring 112 goals. In addition to his full caps for England Jimmy also represented the B side on three occasions and the Football League once. He retired in 1960 after 23 years association with Wolves and became a proprietor of a sports shop in Wolverhampton.

Alan Patrick MULLERY M.B.E.

Born: Notting Hill, 23rd November 1941
Role: Wing-Half
Career: Fulham, Tottenham Hotspur, Fulham, Tottenham Hotspur, Fulham
Debut: v Holland (a) 9-12-1964
Appearances: 35 (1 goal) + 1 unofficial appearance

Signed by Fulham as a professional at the age of 17, he was drafted into the first team and soon established himself alongside such stars as Johnny Haynes and George Cohen. In March 1964, with Spurs looking for replacements for Danny Blanchflower and Dave Mackay, he was transferred for a fee of £72,500. Although he took time to settle at White Hart Lane he gradually became an integral part of the midfield and when Dave Mackay left in 1968 became club captain. He won an FA Cup medal in 1967, the League Cup in 1971 and the UEFA Cup the following year, being recalled by Spurs from a loan spell at Fulham. In the summer of 1972 he was transferred back to Fulham permanently and along with Bobby Moore guided them to the 1975 FA Cup, although they were beaten by West Ham at the last hurdle. He retired as a player in May 1976 and then went into management, taking over the reigns at Brighton, Charlton, Crystal Palace, QPR and a second spell with Brighton. Alan had been expected to make his England debut during the South American tour of 1964 but on the morning the squad was due to report at the airport, he ricked his back whilst shaving! He made his debut later the same year and in 1968 became the first England player to be sent off, a fate that befell him in the European Championship clash with Yugoslavia. He recovered from the blow and was a member of the squad for the 1970 World Cup finals in Mexico, appearing in all four of England's matches. He now earns a living as a journalist and television pundit.

Alan Mullery

Danny Murphy

Daniel Benjamin MURPHY

Born: Chester, 18-3-1977
Role: Defender
Career: Crewe Alexandra, Liverpool, Crewe Athletic, Charlton Athletic, Tottenham Hotspur
Debut: v Sweden (h) 10-11-2001
Appearances: 9 (1 goal)

Danny joined Crewe Alexandra as a trainee and was upgraded to the professional ranks in March 1994. The following season he was captain of the youth side and made a number of appearances for the first team, testament to the progress he was making. His performances at Gresty Road, where he helped the club win promotion to the First Division in 1997 attracted outside interest and he was sold to Liverpool for £1.5 million in July of that year. Although he broke into the England Under-23 side (he already had schoolboy and youth caps) he found it more difficult to get into the Liverpool side and he was loaned back to Crewe in February 1999. He returned to Anfield with his confidence restored and forced his way into the side, collecting winners' medals in the League, FA and UEFA Cups in 2001. Later the same year he won his first cap for England and in 2003 added another winners' League Cup medal. He was surprisingly sold to Charlton Athletic in August 2004 for £2.5 million and has since gone on to force his way back to the fringes of the England squad. On transfer deadline day in January 2006 he was sold to Spurs for £2 million.

Phil Neal

Philip George NEAL
Born: Irchester, 20th February 1951
Role: Full-Back
Career: Northampton Town, Liverpool, Bolton Wanderers
Debut: v Wales (a) 24-3-1976
Appearances: 50 (5 goals)
Phil Neal began his career as a striker and was invited along to Spurs as a schoolboy for a trial. Although he successfully came through the trial and was offered a contract, he decided to continue with his education. Upon leaving school he signed with the local Northampton Town club as an apprentice and was upgraded to the professional ranks in December 1968. He was subsequently converted to full-back and did well enough in the lower divisions to have a host of scouts watching his progress, finally joining Liverpool for £60,000 in October 1974. As a ready made replacement for Tommy Smith in the left-back position, Phil later switched to right-back, but as he had played in all eleven positions at Northampton (he once played as an emergency goalkeeper) he could slot into the side in any position. A key feature of his time at Anfield was his reliability, going through ten seasons having missed only one League match. During his eleven years at Anfield he helped the club win seven League championships, four European Cups, four League Cups and the UEFA Cup once. The only major domestic honour to elude him was the FA Cup, having to settle for a runners-up medal in 1977. He collected his first cap for England in 1976 and went on to represent his country on 50 occasions. He joined Bolton Wanderers as player-manager in December 1985 and took them to the Freight Rover Trophy final at the end of his first season in charge, although he lost his job in 1992. He then joined Coventry City as coach, stepping up to become manager following the departure of Bobby Gould, and later assisted Graham Taylor in the England setup.

Ernest NEEDHAM
Born: Newbold Moor, 21st January 1873
Died: Chesterfield, 8th March 1936
Role: Left-Half
Career: Waverley FC, Staveley Wanderers, Staveley Town, Sheffield United
Debut: v Scotland (a) 7-4-1894
Appearances: 16 (3 goals)
One of the greatest names in Sheffield United's history, if not the game as a whole, Ernest 'Nudger' Needham played non-League football for Waverley (in Staveley!), Staveley Wanderers and Staveley Town before linking with Sheffield United in April 1891. Although the club had only been formed two years previously, in 1889, it was admitted into the Second Division in 1892 and won promotion to the First Division at the end of its first season as a League club. By 1898 it had won the League title, adding the FA Cup the following year. He helped the club reach successive FA Cup finals in the new century, having to settle for a runners-up medal in 1901 but adding a second winners' medal in 1902. Nudger, who represented the Football League 10 times during his career retired from playing in the summer of 1913, his place in Sheffield folklore assured. He was also a more than useful cricketer, playing for Derbyshire between 1901 and 1912. He remained living in Sheffield where he found employment in a steel works.

Gary Alexander NEVILLE
Born: Bury, 18th February 1975
Role: Full-Back
Career: Manchester United
Debut: v Japan (h) 3-6-1995
Appearances: 78
Signed by Manchester United as an apprentice in 1991 and after helping United win the FA Youth Cup in 1992 he was upgraded to the professional ranks in January 1993 and made his League debut in May 1994. He quickly became a permanent member of the side, able to play in almost any of the defensive positions, and would go on to help the club win six Premiership titles, the FA Cup three times and the European Champions League in 1999. A former England youth international, he also helped England win the Under-18 European Championship in 1993. He and his younger brother Phil became the first brothers to be capped for England in the same side since the celebrated Charltons. As both Gary and Phil were on Manchester United's books at the time, they also became the first pair of brothers from the same club to represent England since 1899.

Gary Neville

Phil Neville

Philip John NEVILLE
Born: Bury, 21st January 1977
Role: Full-Back
Career: Manchester United, Everton
Debut: v China (a) 23-5-1996
Appearances: 52 + 1 unofficial appearance
The younger brother of fellow Manchester United player Gary, Phil was a good all-round sportsman as a youngster, representing England Schoolboys at both football and cricket. Indeed, he was offered a professional contract with Lancashire as a cricketer but chose instead to concentrate on football and joined Manchester United. Captain of the Youth side that won the FA Youth Cup in 1994-95 he made his full League debut the same season. He became a first team regular the following season and has since won six Premiership medals, three FA Cup winners' medals and a European Champions League winners' medal. He has represented England at School, Youth, Under-21 and full levels, and in May 1996 against China he and Gary became the first brothers to represent England since the Charltons, 23 years previously. He was sold to Everton for £3 million during the summer of 2005.

Keith Robert NEWTON
Born: Manchester, 23rd June 1941
Died: June 1998
Role: Full-Back
Career: Bolton Wanderers, Blackburn Rovers, Everton, Burnley
Debut: v West Germany (h) 23-3-1966
Appearances: 27
Keith joined Blackburn Rovers as a junior and signed professional forms in October 1958. A member of the side that won the FA Youth Cup in 1959 he went on to register more than 300 appearances for the first team and had been capped for England on 19 occasions before being sold to Everton for £80,000 in December 1969. At the end of the season he had helped them win the First Division title and he went on to add a further eight caps for England before being sold to Burnley in 1972, helping them win the Second Division title in 1973. A member of the squad for the 1970

World Cup finals in Mexico he appeared in three of England's four games during the tournament. He retired in May 1978 but played in non-League football for a spell thereafter.

John NICHOLLS

Born: Wolverhampton, 3rd April 1931
Died: 1st April 1995
Role: Inside-Right
Career: Heath Town United, Wolverhampton Wanderers, West Bromwich Albion, Cardiff City, Exeter City, Worcester City, Wellington Town, Oswestry, Sankeys
Debut: v Scotland (a) 3-4-1954 (WCQ) (scored once)
Appearances: 2 (1 goal)

Johnny had a brief spell associated with Wolverhampton Wanderers as an amateur before joining West Bromwich Albion, also an amateur in August 1950. He signed professional forms a year later and quickly formed a particularly effective club partnership with Ronnie Allen, with the pair plundering the goals that took the club to the FA Cup final in 1954 against Preston North End, which was won, and second spot in the First Division. The pair also lined up alongside each other when Johnny made his England debut, Ronnie having collected his first cap two years previously. Johnny remained at The Hawthorns until May 1957 when, having made 131 League appearances and scored 58 goals he suffered an ankle injury and was sold to Cardiff City. He failed to settle at Ninian Park, making just five appearances for the club before being sold on to Exeter City for £4,000 in November 1957. He added a further 23 goals for the Grecians in his 55 appearances before dropping out of the League and playing for a number of non-League sides. He retained his affection for West Bromwich Albion, where he enjoyed the best part of his career, and died from a heart attack whilst returning home from watching them play Middlesbrough in April 1995.

William Edward NICHOLSON O.B.E.

Born: Scarbrough, 26th January 1919
Died: 23rd October 2004
Role: Right-Half
Career: Tottenham Hotspur, Northfleet
Debut: v Portugal (h) 19-5-1951 (scored once)
Appearances: 1 (1 goal)

Bill began his playing career with Spurs nursery side Northfleet before signing professional forms with Spurs in August 1938 and made his debut for the club in October 1938. Like many of his generation his best playing days were lost to the Second World War but, on the resumption of League action, he was a stalwart of the Spurs side that won the Second and First Divisions in the consecutive seasons of 1949-50 and 1950-51. That same year he won his only cap for England, netting with his first touch after 19 seconds to register the fastest ever debut goal by an England player. Although Bill was a regular member of the England squad and named as reserve on a record 22 occasions (at a time when there were no substitutions), the continued good form of Billy Wright prevented him adding to his tally of appearances. Upon his retirement as a player in 1955 he was appointed coach at Spurs and held this position until October 1958 (he also served as coach to the England squad for the 1958 World Cup in Sweden), when he accepted an offer to take over as manager from Jimmy Anderson. During his sixteen years in charge Spurs won the League and FA Cup double in 1961, the first side to accomplish the

Bill Nicholson

feat in the twentieth century, the FA Cup in 1962 and 1967, the European Cup Winners' Cup in 1963, the first British side to win a major European honour, the League Cup in 1971 and 1973 and the UEFA Cup in 1972. It had been Nicholson's intention to step down as manager following the UEFA Cup final in 1974, which Spurs lost against a backdrop of crowd violence, but the following season found him still holding the reins. After four matches of the new season, all of which were lost, and in dispute with a number of his players, Nicholson announced his retirement, to take effect as soon as Spurs had appointed a replacement. With no alternative role within the club, Nicholson spent some eighteen months at West Ham United as scout, until in July 1976 he accepted an invitation from Keith Burkinshaw to return to White Hart Lane as consultant and then chief scout. He continued in this role until 1991, when he was made club president. He was awarded the OBE for his services to football in 1975.

David John NISH

Born: Burton, 26th September 1947
Role: Full-Back
Career: Measham Imperial, Leicester City, Derby County, Tulsa Rednecks (USA), Seattle Sounders (USA)
Debut: v Northern Ireland (a, Goodison) 12-5-1973
Appearances: 5

Discovered by Leicester City on their doorstep, David signed with the club in July 1966 and was considered such a prodigy he was named as a substitute for the first team even though he was still studying at school! He became a regular in the side almost as soon as selected and went on to represent England at Youth and Under-23 level. Despite his youth, David was a commanding figure in the heart of Leicester's defence and was appointed club captain in 1969, guiding the club to the FA Cup final, becoming the youngest FA Cup captain of all time. In August 1972 he was sold to Derby County for £225,000, then a record fee, and although he suffered a number of niggling injuries that hampered his career at the Baseball Ground, he did win a League championship medal in 1975. He moved on to America to join Tulsa Rednecks in February 1979 for £10,000 and the following year joined Seattle Sounders. After returning to England he played for a number of non-League clubs before turning to coaching. A spell at Middlesbrough as youth team coach was followed by a return to Filbert Street as Youth Development officer.

Maurice NORMAN

Born: Mulbarton, 8th May 1934
Role: Centre-Half
Career: Wymondham Minors FC, Mulbarton, Norwich City, Tottenham Hotspur
Debut: v Peru (a) 20-5-1962
Appearances: 23

Maurice joined Norwich City in September 1952 and made his debut in February 1955, and after only 35 games for the Canaries was the subject of a bid from Spurs to take him to White Hart Lane. He was wanted to replace Alf Ramsey at full-back, and with winger Johnny Gavin returning to Carrow Road as part of the deal, Maurice became a Spurs player in November 1955. An injury sustained in September 1956 kept him out of the side for half a dozen games, and upon recovering found Peter Baker had taken the full-back slot. Maurice was therefore moved to the centre-half position, a role he took to immediately. A member of the double winning side in 1961, the FA Cup winning team in 1962 and the European Cup Winners' Cup the following season, his career came to an end following a horrific broken leg sustained in a friendly match against a Hungarian Select XI in 1965, and despite a number of operations never played again, retiring in the summer of 1967.

Maurice Norman

Henry NUTTALL

Born: Bolton, 9th November 1897
Died: April 1969
Role: Wing-Half
Career: Bolton St. Marks, Fleetwood, Bolton Wanderers, Rochdale, Nelson
Debut: v Northern Ireland (a) 22-10-1927
Appearances: 3

Harry played local football in his hometown before signing with Bolton Wanderers in December 1920, a club where his father Jack had once been trainer. He soon forced his way into the first team and was a regular for some twelve years, helping the club win the FA Cup in 1923 (the first at Wembley), 1926 and 1929. In May 1932 he finally left Burnden Park (he was actually born in a cottage owned by and located near the club) for Rochdale, spending a little over a year at the club before moving on to Nelson where he finished his playing career in 1935. Almost immediately Harry was back at Burnden Park, being appointed to the ground staff and serving in a number of capacities until his eventual retirement in 1964.

O

OAKLEY, William John
O'DOWD, James Peter
OGILVIE, Robert Andrew Muter Macindoe
O'GRADY, Michael
OLIVER, Leonard Frederick
OLNEY, Benjamin Albert
OSBORNE, Frank Raymond
OSBORNE, Reginald
OSGOOD, Peter Lesley
OSMAN, Russell Charles
OTTAWAY, Cuthbert John
OWEN, Michael James
OWEN, Reverend John Robert Blayney
OWEN, Sidney William

Michael Owen

William Oakley

William John OAKLEY

Born: Shrewsbury, 27th April 1873
Died: 20th September 1934
Role: Full-Back
Career: Oxford University, Corinthians
Debut: v Wales (h) 18-3-1895
Appearances: 16

William Oakley was an all-round sportsman, displaying exceptional talent at just about every sport he turned his hand to. Educated at Shrewsbury he represented the school at football between 1887 and 1892, being captain in his final year. He then attended Oxford University and won his Blue at the same sport in 1893, 1894, 1895 and 1896. He was president of the university's Athletics Club in 1895, representing them from 1893 through to 1896 and won the Amateur Athletics Association long jump in 1894, representing England in an athletics match against the USA at this sport and hurdles in 1895. A football player for Corinthians between 1894 and 1903, he was co-secretary of the club from 1898 to 1902. After graduating from Oxford University he became a schoolteacher, subsequently becoming joint headmaster of Ludgrove Preparatory School with fellow England international Gilbert Oswald Smith, with whom he wrote one of the earliest books on the sport of football. William was killed in a motor accident in 1934.

James Peter O'DOWD

Born: Halifax, 22nd February 1908
Died: 8th May 1964
Role: Centre-Half
Career: St. Bees GS, Apperley Bridge, Selby Town, Blackburn Rovers, Burnley, Chelsea, Valenciennes (France), Torquay United
Debut: v Scotland (h) 9-4-1932
Appearances: 3

Peter grew up in Bradford and played schools football in the area and had a spell on the books of Bradford Park Avenue as an amateur before signing with Blackburn Rovers as a professional in December 1926. A move to local rivals Burnley for £3,000 followed in March 1930 where he became noted as one of the most promising centre-halves in the game, prompting Chelsea to pay a then record fee of £5,250 to bring him to Stamford Bridge in November 1931. It proved to be money well spent, for Peter made his England debut five months later and also represented the Football League. He remained at Chelsea until September 1935 when French club Valenciennes paid £3,000 to take him across the English Channel, although Peter was to spend only eighteen months in France before returning to the English game with Torquay United in March 1937. A broken leg sustained in a trial match soon after brought his playing career to an end, after which he concentrated on the drapery business he had established before his move to France.

Robert Andrew Muter Macindoe OGILVIE

Born: London, 1853
Died: 7th March 1938
Role: Full-Back
Career: Upton Park, Clapham Rovers
Debut: v Scotland (a) 7-3-1874
Appearances: 1

Robert attended and played for Brentwood School before linking up with Upton Park in 1871, spending two years with the club before joining Clapham Rovers in 1873. Whilst with Clapham he helped them reach the FA Cup final in successive seasons, winning a winners' medal in 1880 after having collected a runners-up medal the previous year. He also served on the FA Committee for two spells, between 1874 and 1881 and then again from 1884 to 1886. Away from the game Robert was a member of Lloyds, becoming chairman of the Institute of Lloyds Underwriters from 1910 to 1911 and an underwriter of the Alliance Assurance Company to 1914. This experience was put to good use during the First World War, serving with the War Risks department from 1914 until it was disbanded in 1919.

Michael O'GRADY

Born: Leeds, 11th October 1942
Role: Left-Winger
Career: Huddersfield Town, Leeds United, Wolverhampton Wanderers, Birmingham City, Rotherham United
Debut: v Northern Ireland (a) 20-10-1962 (scored twice)
Appearances: 2 (3 goals)

Mike O'Grady

Although Mike was born in Leeds and played schoolboy football in the city, it was Huddersfield Town that first offered him terms, signing as a professional in October 1959. He made his League debut for the club the same season and within two years had broken into the England Under-23 side, going on to win three caps at this level. In 1962 he won his first full cap for England, netting twice in the 3-1 win over Northern Ireland, but despite this promising start he was overlooked thereafter. In October 1965 he was transferred to Leeds United and, although injuries restricted his chance of a regular place in the side, he did help the club win the Inter-Cities Fairs Cup in 1968 having been runners-up the year previously and win the League championship in 1969. That same season saw him recalled to the England side and he marked the occasion with a goal in the 5-0 win over France. In September 1969 he was sold to Wolverhampton Wanderers for £80,000 but injuries again blighted his career, with Mike losing over a year through a tendon injury. A spell out on loan to Birmingham City failed to reignite his career and he was sold to Rotherham United for £5,000 in November 1972, retiring in 1974 through a culmination of his injury problems.

Leonard Frederick OLIVER

Born: Fulham, 1st August 1905
Died: August 1967
Role: Right-Half
Career: Alma Athletic, Tufnell Park, Fulham
Debut: v Belgium (a) 11-5-1929
Appearances: 1

A local Fulham lad, Len played representative schools football and was working as a clerk in a London store when he was invited to join Fulham, signing amateur forms in the summer of 1924 and taking the plunge into professionalism a year later. Len spent eleven seasons at Craven Cottage, helping the club win the Division Three South championship in 1932 and was captain of the side for the last seven seasons. In 1937 he retired from playing and moved to Belfast to become coach to Cliftonville, although he returned to England at the outbreak of the Second World War and served as an Army PTI during the hostilities.

Benjamin Albert OLNEY

Born: Holborn, 30th March 1899
Died: September 1943
Role: Goalkeeper
Career: Fairleys Athletic, Aston Park Rangers, Stourbridge, Derby County, Aston Villa, Bilston United, Walsall, Shrewsbury Town
Debut: v France (a) 17-5-1928
Appearances: 2

Ben Olney made his debut for Derby in the last game of the 1920-21 season having impressed whilst representing the Birmingham FA and was a permanent fixture of the side for the next six years until he lost his place to Harry Wilkes. By chance, Villa were in desperate need of an experienced goalkeeper, and after suffering successive defeats over the Christmas period Villa signed Ben in December 1927. Five months later he was in the England team, collecting two caps. He remained with Villa until July 1930 when he moved into the non-League game with Bilston United, later returning to League football with Walsall and Shrewsbury.

Frank Osborne

Frank Raymond OSBORNE

Born: Wynberg, South Africa, 14th October 1896
Died: Epsom, 8th March 1988
Role: Right-Winger, Centre-Forward
Career: Bromley, Fulham, Tottenham Hotspur, Southampton
Debut: v Northern Ireland (h) 21-10-1922
Appearances: 4 (3 goals)

When his family returned home to England (Frank's father had been a colonel in the Royal Army Medical Corp serving in South Africa) Frank signed for Bromley as an amateur before joining the professional ranks with Fulham in 1921. He was transferred to Spurs in January 1924, his £1,500 fee reflecting the fact he was already an England international player. Able to play almost anywhere in the Spurs forward line he remained at White Hart Lane until June 1931 when he was sold to Southampton for £450. He retired as a player in 1933 and was appointed a director at Fulham in 1935. In September 1948 he resigned from the board in order to take over as manager, becoming general manager two years later, a position he held until 1964 when he retired. He is the elder brother of Reg Osborne (below), also an England international.

Reginald OSBORNE

Born: Wynberg, South Africa, 23rd July 1899
Died: 1977
Role: Left-Back
Career: Leicester City, Folkestone
Debut: v Wales (h) 28-11-1927
Appearances: 1

The younger brother of Frank Osborne, Reg joined the Army as a boy and served in the same unit as his father had done, the Royal Army Medical Corp, throughout the First World War. It was whilst representing the Army that he first attracted attention, earning two caps for England at amateur level. He eventually followed his brother into the professional game, joining Leicester City in February 1923. A member of the side that won the Second Division championship in 1925, Reg won his only cap for England at full level in 1927, a year after his elder brother had made his final appearance for his country. Reg remained at Filbert Street until the summer of 1933 when he announced his retirement but subsequently came out of retirement to assist non-League club Folkestone the following November.

Peter Lesley OSGOOD

Born: Windsor, 20th February 1947
Died: Slough, 1st March 2006
Role: Centre-Forward
Career: Windsor Corinthians, Chelsea, Southampton, Norwich City, Philadelphia Fury (USA), Chelsea
Debut: v Belgium (a) 25-2-1970
Appearances: 4

Initially signed as a junior, Peter was upgraded to the professional ranks in September 1964 and made his debut the same season, scoring twice in a League Cup tie as Chelsea progressed to win the tournament. Initially seen as the ideal cover for Barry Bridges, Peter made a proper breakthrough during the 1965-66 season until a broken leg brought his career to a temporary halt. He recovered and emerged to lead the line in his own right, scoring in every round as Chelsea won the FA Cup in 1970, one of only nine men to have achieved the feat. He netted in both the final and replay of the European Cup Winners' Cup the following season, enabling Chelsea to add a further trophy to their record. For good measure, Peter scored in a final for the third consecutive season in 1971-72, but this time Chelsea lost the League Cup 2-1 to Stoke City. Peter remained at Stamford Bridge until March 1974 when he moved on to Southampton for £240,000, having made 279 League appearances for the Blues and scored 103 goals. He remained at The Dell until 1977, apart from a brief period on loan to Norwich City, and left the club with another FA Cup winners' medal in his pocket after Southampton had surprisingly beaten Manchester United in 1976. After a brief spell in America with Philadelphia, Peter returned to Stamford Bridge to finish his playing career, registering a further 10 appearances and two goals. A member of the England 1970 World Cup squad, Peter won four full caps having already represented the country at Youth and Under-23 level. He later worked at Stamford Bridge as one of the greeting legends at home matches. He collapsed and died at a family funeral on 1st March 2006.

Peter Osgood

Russell Osman

Russell Charles OSMAN

Born: Repton, 14th February 1959
Role: Centre-Back
Career: Ipswich Town, Leicester City, Southampton, Bristol City, Brighton & Hove Albion, Cardiff City
Debut: v Australia (a) 31-5-1980
Appearances: 11

Educated at Burton-On-Trent Grammar School, Russell captained England Schoolboys at rugby before switching codes and joining Ipswich Town as an apprentice in 1974. The following year he helped the club win the FA Youth Cup and was upgraded to the full professional ranks in March 1976, making his League debut in September 1977. Once he was established as a first team regular he established a particularly strong partnership with Terry Butcher, helping Ipswich win the UEFA Cup in 1981 having already won his first full cap for England. Russell remained at Portman Road until July 1985 when, having made 384 appearances for the club, he was sold to Leicester City for £225,000. After 108 appearances for Leicester he was on his travels again, joining Southampton for £325,000 in June 1988. Russell made over 100 appearances for the Saints before joining Bristol City, later becoming caretaker manager and then manager. He was sacked in 1994, returned to playing with Sudbury and had a spell on loan with Plymouth, although he didn't play before returning to League action with Brighton & Hove Albion in September 1995. He then joined Cardiff City in February 1996 and was appointed manager in November 1996 but lost his job midway through the following season.

Cuthbert John OTTAWAY

Born: Dover, 19th July 1850
Died: 2nd April 1878
Role: Forward
Career: Oxford University, Old Etonians
Debut: v Scotland (a) 30-11-1872
Appearances: 2

Educated at Eton College, Cuthbert was another of the Victorian all-round sportsmen, winning the Public Schools rackets doubles in 1868 and 1869. He then attended Oxford University, winning a Blue at football in 1874 as captain, having already collected a Blue in cricket in 1870, 1871, 1872 and 1873 (he later played cricket for Kent and Middlesex and toured North America in 1872). In 1873 he helped Oxford University reach the FA Cup final where they were beaten by Wanderers, although Oxford University and Cuthbert returned the following year to win the cup, beating Royal Engineers 2-0 in the final. A year later Cuthbert appeared in his third consecutive final, although this time playing for Old Etonians, appearing in the first drawn match with Royal Engineers but not the replay which resulted in a 2-0 defeat for the Old Etonians. Cuthbert also excelled at real tennis and athletics, representing Oxford University at both. After graduating with a First degree he became a barrister, being called to the bar in 1873 but was to sadly die five years later after catching a chill at a dance. Cuthbert played in the very first England international match, against Scotland, but earned additional distinction in that he was captain on the day and therefore holds the honour of being England's very first captain.

Michael James OWEN

Born: Chester, 14th December 1979
Role: Striker
Career: Liverpool, Real Madrid, Newcastle United
Debut: v Chile (h) 11-2-1998
Appearances: 75 (35 goals)

One of the brightest talents to have emerged in the English game in many a year, Michael signed with Liverpool as a junior, despite being an Everton fan as a youngster. He made an immediate impact at Liverpool, scoring on his debut when called off the bench away at Wimbledon and quickly established himself in the side following Robbie Fowler's long term injury. His phenomenal pace and eye for goal demanded a call-up for the full England side and on 11th February he was selected for the match against Chile, thus becoming England's youngest international player this century; at 18 years and 59 days he beat Duncan Edwards' record by 124 days. He was part of the squad for the 1998 World Cup finals, scoring against Romania after coming on as a substitute and netting a breathtaking goal in the clash with Argentina in the second round. He quickly added further goals and seemed on course to seriously challenge the likes of Gary Lineker and Bobby Charlton as England's top goalscorer, netting 30 goals for his country in just 60 appearances. In the summer of 2004 however he refused to sign an extension to his Liverpool contract, citing his unhappiness at Liverpool not mounting a serious title challenge. Rather than let him eventually leave on a free transfer Liverpool sold him to Spanish giants Real Madrid for a cut-price £8 million. He spent much of his first season at the Bernabeu Stadium sitting on the bench but was invariably introduced at some stage during games and made his point by netting 14 goals for the club. Ultimately, Real Madrid ended the season empty handed as Barcelona won the Spanish League and Liverpool the Champions League! The arrival of additional strikers to the club seemed to spell the end of Michael's time with Real Madrid, and although overtures were made to Liverpool about signing him back and late bids from boyhood favourites Everton, he eventually moved to Newcastle United for £17 million on transfer deadline day, 31st August 2005.

Michael Owen

Reverend John Robert Blayney OWEN

Born: Reading, 1849
Died: 13th June 1921
Role: Forward
Career: Oxford University, Sheffield FC, Sheffield FA, Nottinghamshire, Maldon, Essex
Debut: v Scotland (a) 7-3-1874
Appearances: 1

John played for Queen's College, Oxford and also represented the university before regular 'Varsity matches with Cambridge were introduced. He later played for the Sheffield Club and Maldon FC as well as earning representative honours with the Sheffield FA and Essex. He was ordained in 1876 and became second master of Trent College between 1972 and 1881, master of Hawkshead Grammar School between 1881 and 1883 and then returned to Trent College to become headmaster in 1883, a position he held until 1890. He then left teaching and became vicar of Toftrees in Norfolk until 1905, finally serving as rector of Bradwell-on-Sea in Essex until his death in 1921.

Sidney William OWEN

Born: Birmingham, 29th September 1922
Died: 16th January 1999
Role: Centre-Half
Career: Birmingham City, Luton Town
Debut: v Yugoslavia (a) 23-5-1954
Appearances: 3

Sid played junior football in his Birmingham hometown and signed with Birmingham City in October 1945, just as the game was gearing up for the resumption of League football the following year. Severe competition for the left-half position, which Sid then occupied, meant his chances of regular first team football were extremely limited and after just five League appearances in Birmingham's colours he was sold to Luton Town for £1,500 in June 1947. Soon after his arrival at Kenilworth Road he was switched to centre-half, a position he subsequently excelled in. A member of numerous FA touring parties and twice a representative of the Football League, Sid broke into the full England side in 1954, even though Luton were a Second Division side at the time. Manager Dally Duncan effectively built a side around Sid Owen, who was made captain, with the result Luton earned promotion to the First Division in 1955. During the same summer Sid was named player-coach, working alongside Dally Duncan as the team attempted to consolidate its First Division status. In October 1957 Duncan left the club for Blackburn Rovers and the Luton board turned to Sid Owen for leadership, although he was not named manager at this time. He did, however, guide the club to Wembley for their first appearance in the FA Cup Final, and on a personal level was named Footballer of the Year. Sadly for Sid there was not to be a fairytale end at Wembley, his 413th and last match for the Hatters; Nottingham Forest won 2-1. However, Sid's galvanising abilities had not gone unnoticed by the Luton board and he was named manager shortly before the FA Cup final. His year in charge at Kenilworth Road was troubled, with Sid frequently clashing with the board over player signings, and in April 1960, having suffered relegation to the Second Division, Sid resigned and linked up with Don Revie at Leeds United as coach. During his fifteen years at Elland Road, he helped the club win the League championship twice (they were runners-up a further five times), the FA Cup once (they were runners-up three times), the Football League Cup once and the Inter-Cities Fairs Cup twice (they were European runners-up three times, once in each competition). In October 1975 Sid accepted an offer to become assistant manager to Willie Bell at Birmingham City, a position he held for two years before moving on to Hull City as first team coach under former Leeds United player Bobby Collins. Sid finished his involvement with football with spells as youth coach and scout at Manchester United.

Sid Owen

P-Q

Stuart Pearce

PAGE, Louis Antonia
PAINE, Terence Lionel
PALLISTER, Gary Andrew
PALMER, Carlton Lloyd
PANTLING, Harry Harold
PARAVACINI, Percy John de
PARKER, Paul Andrew
PARKER, Scott
PARKER, Thomas Robert
PARKES, Philip B
PARKINSON, John
PARLOUR, Raymond
PARR, Percival Chase
PARRY, Edward Hagarty
PARRY, Raymond Alan

PATCHITT, Basil Clement Anderson
PAWSON, Reverend Francis William
PAYNE, Joseph
PEACOCK, Alan
PEACOCK, Joseph
PEARCE, Stuart
PEARSON, Harold Frederick
PEARSON, James Stuart
PEARSON, John Hargreaves
PEARSON, Stanley C
PEASE, William Harold
PEGG, David
PEJIC, Michael
PELLY, Frederick Raymond
PENNINGTON, Jesse

PENTLAND, Frederick Beaconsfield
PERRY, Charles
PERRY, Thomas
PERRY, William
PERRYMAN, Stephen John M.B.E.
PETERS, Martin Stanford M.B.E.
PHELAN, Mike C
PHILLIPS, Kevin Mark
PHILLIPS, Leonard H
PICKERING, Frederick
PICKERING, John
PICKERING, Nicholas
PIKE, Thetwell Mather
PILKINGTON, Brian
PLANT, John

PLATT, David Andrew
PLUM, Seth Lewis
POINTER, Raymond
PORTEOUS, Thomas Stoddard
POWELL, Christopher George Robin
PRIEST, Alfred Ernest
PRINSEP, James Frederick McLeod
PUDDEFOOT, Sydney Charles
PYE, Jesse
PYM, Richard Henry

QUANTRILL, Alfred Edward
QUIXALL, Albert

Louis Antonio PAGE

Born: Kirkdale, 27th March 1899
Died: 12th October 1959
Role: Left-Winger
Career: South Liverpool, Stoke, Northampton Town, Burnley, Manchester United, Port Vale, Yeovil Town
Debut: v Wales (a) 12-2-1927
Appearances: 7 (1 goal)

Louis played schools football in Liverpool and for Sudley Juniors before linking with Stoke in the summer of 1919. Three years later he moved on to Northampton Town but failed to make a real impact, eventually being swapped in May 1925 with former England international Jack Tresarden who was wanted by Northampton to become their player-manager. Whilst the circumstances behind his transfer may not have been to Louis's liking, he made the most of his chance at Turf Moor – almost a year after he was transferred he was tried out as a centre-forward and netted six goals against Birmingham City, three in each half! Despite his obvious prowess as a centre-forward, the move did not become permanent, although the renewed confidence it gave Louis culminated in a call-up for the full England side in 1927 and an outing representing the Football League. In March 1932 he was sold to Manchester United but only seven months later joined Port Vale. The following summer he joined Yeovil as player-manager, a position he held until the summer of 1935 when he retired from playing and took up the post of manager at Newport County. Louis later coached Glentoran and had spells as manager at Swindon Town and Chester City before becoming a scout for Leicester City.

Terry Paine

Terence Lionel PAINE M.B.E.

Born: Winchester, 23rd March 1939
Role: Midfield
Career: Winchester Corinthians, Winchester City, Southampton, Hereford United
Debut: v Czechoslovakia (a) 20-5-1963
Appearances: 19 (7 goals)

Terry had trials with Arsenal and Portsmouth without being taken on, subsequently joining his hometown club Winchester City. His performances for the club prompted manager Harry Osman, a former Southampton player, to alert the then Saints manager Ted Bates as to Terry's potential and he was taken on as an amateur in August 1956, turning professional the following February. Terry soon became a regular in the side, helping Southampton win the Third Division championship in 1960, earn four caps for England at Under-23 level and make five representative appearances for the Football League. Capped by the full England side for the first time in 1963 Terry won 19 caps for England and was a member of the 1966 World Cup squad, although he was injured in the 2-0 win over Mexico and never played for his country again. Even so, the fact that all 19 of his caps had been won whilst playing Second Division football was proof that the right player would be spotted regardless of the League he played in. Terry did get to play in the top flight, helping Southampton win promotion to the First Division at the end of the 1965-66 season. He remained at The Dell until July 1974, having made 713 League appearances for the club, before accepting the position of player-manager of Hereford United. He guided them to the Third Division championship in 1976 and went on to make 111 League appearances for the club before he retired in 1977. He then managed Cheltenham Town for two years before going to South Africa to coach. He was awarded the MBE for his services to football and at one time was a town councillor for Southampton.

Gary Andrew PALLISTER

Born: Ramsgate, 30th June 1965
Role: Defender
Career: Middlesbrough, Darlington, Manchester United, Middlesbrough
Debut: v Hungary (a) 27-4-1988
Appearances: 22

Gary began his career with Middlesbrough in 1984 and was loaned to Darlington the following year, although a permanent move fell through after Darlington were unable to raise the £4,000. Upon returning to Ayresome Park he claimed a first team place and helped them to promotion in two successive seasons to reclaim their place in the First Division. In August 1989 a £2.3 million fee took him to Manchester United and he was almost ever present in the heart of the defence for the next nine years. He won four League titles, three FA Cups, the League Cup and the European Cup Winners' Cup and was named PFA Player of the Year in 1992, recognition for his consistent performances for United. In 1998 he returned to Middlesbrough, costing the club pretty much the £2 million they sold him for previously, and retired at the end of the 2000-01 season. He later became a television pundit.

Gary Pallister

Carlton Palmer

Carlton Lloyd PALMER

Born: Rowley Regis, 5th December 1965
Role: Midfield
Career: West Bromwich Albion, Sheffield Wednesday, Leeds United, Southampton, Nottingham Forest, Coventry City, Watford, Sheffield Wednesday, Stockport County, Dublin City
Debut: v CIS (a) 29-4-1992
Appearances: 18 (1 goal)

A much travelled midfield player, Carlton began his playing career as an apprentice with West Bromwich Albion and was upgraded to the professional ranks in December 1984. He made his first team debut in September 1985 and went on to make 121 League appearances for the club before being sold to Sheffield Wednesday for £750,000 in February 1989. A member of the side that won promotion to the First Division in 1991, Carlton was unfortunate to miss the club winning the League Cup that season through injury. He had racked up 205 League appearances for the club when he was sold to Leeds United for £2.6 million in June 1994 and subsequently had £1 million moves to Southampton and Nottingham Forest before joining Coventry City. He was loaned out to both Watford and Sheffield Wednesday before accepting the position of player-manager of Stockport County in November 2001, retiring from playing later that season in order to concentrate on full time management. However he was sacked in 2003 and returned to playing with Dublin City. He later returned to coaching and also had a spell as caretaker manager of Mansfield Town. Carlton's 18 England caps were won over an eighteen month period; the only games he missed for England in the run were against Germany and Poland.

Harry Harold PANTLING

Born: Leighton Buzzard, 1891
Died: 21st December 1952
Role: Right-Half
Career: Watford, Sheffield United, Rotherham United, Heanor Town
Debut: v Ireland (a) 20-10-1923
Appearances: 1

Harry played junior football in Bedfordshire before linking with Watford as an amateur in 1908, turning professional in

Paul Parker

the summer of 1911. His performances in the Third Division South alerted several other clubs to his abilities and he was transferred to Sheffield United in March 1914. Unfortunately Harry had only one full season of League football before it shut down for the duration of the First World War but returned to Bramall Lane at the end of the hostilities and continued his progress. A member of the side that won the FA Cup in 1925, Harry remained with United until the summer of 1926 when he returned to the Third Division, this time the North section, in joining Rotherham United. Harry finished his playing career with Heanor Town and then became a licensee in Sheffield.

Percy John de PARAVACINI

Born: London, 15th July 1862
Died: Pangbourne, 11th October 1921
Role: Full-Back
Career: Eton, Cambridge University, Old Etonians, Windsor, Berkshire-Buckinghamshire, Corinthians
Debut: v Wales (h) 3-2-1883
Appearances: 3

Percy was something of a rarity in Victorian football in that he was able to kick the ball equally well with either foot. This meant he was able to operate on either flank, an ability that was well utilised by both his club and national side. Educated at Eton, Percy was a member of the college team in 1880 and 1881 and then attended Cambridge University, earning his Blue in 1883. By then he was also playing for Old Etonians, helping them win the FA Cup in 1882 and reach the final the following year. Percy also played for Corinthians during the 1884-85 season and served on the FA Committee in 1885. He was also an exceptional cricketer, earning a Blue at Cambridge every year from 1882 to 1885 and playing 121 matches for Middlesex between 1881 and 1892. He was created a Member of the Victorian Order (MVO) in 1908 and became a CVO in 1921.

Paul Andrew PARKER

Born: West Ham, 4th April 1964
Role: Full-Back
Career: Fulham, Queens Park Rangers, Manchester United, Derby County, Sheffield United, Fulham, Chelsea
Debut: v Albania (substitute) (h) 26-4-1989 (WCQ)
Appearances: 19

Paul began his career as an apprentice with Fulham, making his first team debut in 1981. He was sold to QPR in the same deal that took Dean Coney to Loftus Road and was soon not only a regular in the QPR side but broke into the England setup as well. A £1.7 million transfer took him to Manchester United in August 1991 where he won two Premiership titles and an FA Cup winners' medal as well as further adding to his tally of England caps. He was released on a free transfer in August 1996 and promptly signed for Derby, later joining Sheffield United, Fulham and Chelsea in fairly quick succession before retiring in the summer of 1997.

Scott Matthew PARKER

Born: Lambeth, London, 13th October 1980
Role: Midfield
Career: Charlton Athletic, Norwich City, Charlton Athletic, Chelsea, Newcastle United
Debut: v Denmark (h) 16-11-2003
Appearances: 2

A graduate from the FA School of Excellence at Lilleshall, Scott signed for Charlton Athletic and made his first team debut in August 1997, two months before he became a fully-fledged professional. Although capped by England at Under-21 level, he was loaned to Norwich City in 2000 in order to gain first team experience and on his return to The Valley was called in to replace the injured Mark Kinsella. His performances for Charlton led to a cap for England against Denmark and speculation that he might be on the move, finally joining Chelsea in a £10 million deal in January 2004. Considerable competition for places coupled with a broken metatarsal bone hampered his progress at the club and eventually prompted a move to Newcastle United for £6.5 million in June 2005.

Thomas Robert PARKER

Born: Woolston, 19th November 1897
Died: Southampton, 5th November 1987
Role: Right-Back
Career: Shotley Rangers, Shotley Athletic, Southampton, Arsenal
Debut: v France (a) 21-5-1925
Appearances: 1

Tom joined Southampton at the end of the First World War and won a Third Division South championship medal in 1922, helping the club reach the Second Division for the first time in their history. Three years later he won his only cap for England, prompting a transfer to Arsenal in March 1926. A year later he collected an FA Cup runners-up medal, going on to help Arsenal win the FA Cup in 1930, the League championship in 1931 and finish runners-up again in the FA Cup in 1932. Tom retired from playing in March 1933 and almost immediately took over as manager at Norwich City, guiding them to the Third Division South championship at the end of his first season in charge. Tom returned to Southampton as manager in February 1937 and remained manager until May 1943. He had a second spell in charge at Norwich between April 1955 and March 1957 but was unable to lift them out of the Third Division South during his time in charge. After leaving Norwich he returned once again to Southampton where he served as chief scout.

Tom Parker

Philip Benjamin Neil Frederick PARKES

Born: Sedgley, 8th August 1950
Role: Goalkeeper
Career: Walsall, Queens Park Rangers, West Ham United
Debut: v Portugal (a) 3-4-1974
Appearances: 1

Phil played schools football in the West Midlands and joined Walsall as a professional in January 1968. His performances in the Third Division attracted considerable attention elsewhere, with Phil joining Queens Park Rangers for £18,500 in June 1970. He developed into one of the brightest goalkeeping talents in the game, winning six caps for England at Under-23 level, one appearance for the England B team and in 1974 his only full cap for his country. In February 1979 he was bought by West Ham United for a then world record fee for a goalkeeper, £560,000, going on to win an FA Cup winners' medal in 1980 and a Second Division championship and a League Cup runners-up medal the following season. In August 1990 he joined Ipswich Town but after only three games for the club announced his retirement. Having made 52 League appearances for Walsall, Phil made 344 appearances for Queens Park Rangers and West Ham United, an uncanny occurrence. His tally for England would undoubtedly have been much greater had it not been for the presence of both Ray Clemence and Peter Shilton at the same time.

John PARKINSON

Born: Bootle, September 1883
Died: 13th September 1942
Role: Centre-Forward
Career: Hertford Albion, Valkyrie, Liverpool, Bury
Debut: v Wales (a) 14-3-1910
Appearances: 2

Although Jack won two caps for England, his career was almost constantly blighted by injury, costing him the chance of further club and international honours. He signed with Liverpool as an amateur midway through the 1901-02 season and turned professional in 1903, going on to represent the Football League on three occasions and collect a Second Division champions medal in 1905. Although Liverpool went on to win the First Division championship the following season, Jack did not play enough games to qualify for a medal, injury having decimated his season. He was similarly out of luck during his final season with the club, 1913-14, when Liverpool made it through to the FA Cup final, for he was forced to watch from the sidelines as Liverpool went down 1-0 to Burnley. That summer Jack left the club and joined Bury but the outbreak of the First World War brought his career to a halt, with Jack calling it a day from playing during the hostilities. After the war he concentrated on his two newsagent and tobacconist shops in the city.

John Parkinson

Ray Parlour

Raymond PARLOUR

Born: Romford, Essex, 7th March 1973
Role: Midfield
Career: Arsenal, Middlesbrough
Debut: v Poland (h) (substitute) 27-3-1999
Appearances: 10

Ray joined Arsenal as a trainee in 1991 and soon emerged as a midfield player of considerable talent, earning selection for the England Under-21 side and collecting 12 caps at this level. Unfortunately, he too often showed an inclination to self-destruct, leading to an infamous incident during a club end-of-season tour to Hong Kong that saw him arrested and charged with assault. He worked hard to curb his off-the-field problems and was one of Arsenal's most improved players during the 1997-98 season, which saw Ray turn down an offer of a transfer to West Ham, preferring to battle for his place at Highbury. He went on to help the Gunners win the League and FA Cup double for the second time in their history and earned selection for the England squad, although he was not one of the 22 players that went to France for the World Cup finals. Following Glenn Hoddle's departure as England manager it was revealed that a less than respectful comment aimed at Eileen Drewery, Hoddle's faith healing confident, may well have been behind his omission. The subsequent appointment of Kevin Keegan earned Ray a call-up for the squad for the European Championship clash with Poland and his first cap midway through the match. At the end of the 2003-04 season he was granted a free transfer by Arsenal and subsequently signed with Middlesbrough (it was later revealed that although he had qualified for a testimonial match from Arsenal, having been with the club for more than ten years, he had turned down the honour as he would have had to have given his ex-wife virtually all the proceeds!).

Percival Chase PARR

Born: Bickley, 2nd December 1859
Died: Bromley, 3rd September 1912
Role: Forward
Career: Oxford University, West Kent
Debut: v Wales (a) 13-3-1882
Appearances: 1

Educated at Winchester College, Percival played for the college team in 1877 and then attended Oxford University, winning a Blue in 1880, 1881 and 1882, being captain of the side in the latter year. He later represented both West Kent and Kent at football and also played cricket for the Gentlemen of Kent in 1880. He qualified as a barrister and was called to the bar in 1885, also serving as a director of publishers W.H. Allen & Co. and editing two journals, National Observer and Ladies Field.

Edward Hagarty PARRY

Born: Toronto, Canada, 24th April 1855
Died: 19th July 1931
Role: Forward
Career: Oxford University, Old Carthusians, Swifts, Remnants, Stoke Poges, Windsor, Berkshire-Buckinghamshire
Debut: v Wales (h) 18-1-1879
Appearances: 3 (1 goal)

Edward was educated at Charterhouse and served as Gownboy of the school from 1868 to 1874, for which he was awarded the Talbot Scholarship Medal. He also represented the school football team from 1872 through 1874, captaining the team in 1873 and 1874. He then attended Oxford University, winning a Blue in 1875, 1876 and 1877, captaining this side in 1877. Upon leaving university he played for a number of sides, including Swifts, Remnants, Stoke Poges and Windsor and also represented the Berks & Bucks FA but enjoyed his greatest success playing for Old Carthusians. He made his first appearance in the FA Cup final in 1877 when he was a member of the Oxford University side that lost 2-1 to Wanderers after extra time and returned four years later, this time with Old Carthusians and enjoyed a much easier 3-0 win over Old Etonians for which he was captain and received the trophy. He qualified as a schoolmaster and taught at Felsted between 1879 and 1880 and Stoke House School in Slough from 1881 to 1892, upon which he was appointed headmaster and continued at the school until his retirement in 1918. Until the emergence of Owen Hargreaves more than 100 years later, Edward was the only Canadian-born player to have represented England.

Raymond Alan PARRY

Born: Derby, 19th January 1936
Died: 23rd May 2003
Role: Inside-Forward
Career: Bolton Wanderers, Blackpool, Bury
Debut: v Northern Ireland (h) 18-11-1959 (scored once)
Appearances: 2 (1 goal)

Ray joined Bolton as an amateur in September 1950 and made his League debut for the side before he had signed professional forms, turning out for the Trotters away at Wolves in October 1951, becoming the youngest ever First

Division player at the age of 15 years and 267 days. He finally signed professional forms with the club in January 1953 and seemed to have a glittering career ahead of him, but it took time for him to live up to his potential. He represented England at schoolboy, Youth and Under-23 level but had to wait until 1959 before making his full debut, by which time he had won his only major honour in the game, an FA Cup winners' medal from 1958. He was transferred to Blackpool for £20,000 in October 1960, having made 270 League appearances and scored 68 goals for Bolton and went on to net 27 goals in his 128 appearances for Blackpool. In October 1964 he was sold to Bury for £6,000, being appointed player-coach in 1970 and carrying on playing until 1972.

Ray Parry

Basil Clement Anderson PATCHITT

Born: 12th August 1900
Role: Centre-Half, Wing-Half
Career: Cambridge University, Corinthians, Castleford Town
Debut: v Sweden (a) 21-5-1923
Appearances: 2

Basil attended Charterhouse School and played for the school team between 1917 and 1919, being captain in his final year. He then went to Cambridge University, earning a Blue in 1922 and was later to play for leading amateur side Corinthians between 1921 and 1923. Despite this and the fact that he was capped for England at full level, he was never selected for England at amateur level. Basil also played for Castleford Town before he emigrated to South Africa, where he lived in Johannesburg.

Reverend Francis William PAWSON

Born: Sheffield, 6th April 1861
Died: Ecclesfield, Sheffield, 4th July 1921
Role: Forward
Career: Cambridge University, Swifts, Sheffield FC, Casuals, Surrey, Corinthians
Debut: v Ireland (a) 24-2-1883 (scored once)
Appearances: 2 (1 goal)

Francis first played for the Sheffield Collegiate School and then attended Cambridge University, earning a Blue in consecutive years between 1882 and 1884 and captaining the side in this final year. It was whilst attending Cambridge University that he won his England caps, collecting his second cap also against Ireland in 1885. After graduating he assisted a number of clubs but became most closely associated with Corinthians, for whom he played between 1885 and 1889. Indeed, he broke a leg whilst on duty for Corinthians against Cambridge University in 1886 but recovered to resume his career. Ordained in 1886 he served as curate of Battersea between 1886 and 1890, curate of Bexhill from 1890 to 1899, Rector of Lewes from 1900 to 1903 and then Vicar of Ecclesfield from 1903 until his death.

Joseph PAYNE

Born: Brinington Common, 17th January 1914
Died: 22nd April 1975
Role: Centre-Forward
Career: Bolsover Colliery, Biggleswade Town, Luton Town, Chelsea, West Ham United, Millwall, Worcester City
Debut: v Finland (a) 20-5-1937 (scored twice)
Appearances: 1 (2 goals)

No matter whatever else he achieved in his career, including winning a full cap for England, Joe Payne is forever remembered for netting 10 goals for Luton Town in the match against Bristol Rovers in April 1936, a record for a League match. Joe had joined Luton in the summer of 1934 and was a wing-half struggling to hold a regular place in the first team. He was switched to centre-forward in an emergency for that match against Bristol Rovers and his career began to progress almost immediately after his goalscoring prowess became appreciated. Joe helped Luton win the Third Division championship in 1937 and remained with the club until March 1938, having netted 82 goals in 72 matches, a phenomenal return that was rewarded with a full cap for England in 1937; true to form Joe scored twice. A £5,000 deal took him to Chelsea in March 1938 but the outbreak of the Second World War eighteen months later totally decimated his career and although he stayed at Stamford Bridge until December 1946, he made only 36 appearances for the club, still managing to score 21 goals. He was then transferred to West Ham United, making only 10 appearances (six goals) before joining Millwall in September 1947, but injury meant he did not make any appearances for the club before he retired a few months later. After five years Joe made a brief return with non-League Worcester City.

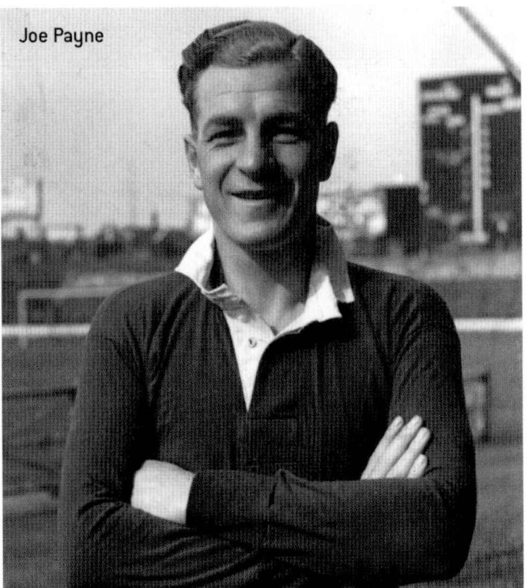
Joe Payne

Alan Peacock

Alan PEACOCK

Born: Middlesbrough, 29th October 1937
Role: Centre-Forward
Career: Middlesbrough, Leeds United, Plymouth Argyle
Debut: v Argentina (Rancagua) 2-6-1962 (WC)
Appearances: 6 (3 goals)

Alan joined his hometown club Middlesbrough as an amateur and signed professional forms in November 1954. Capped for England at Youth level, he finally broke into the Middlesbrough side on a regular basis during the 1957-58 season and linked especially well with fellow striker Brian Clough. Following Clough's transfer to Sunderland, Alan became the focal point of the Middlesbrough attack and responded by scoring 24 goals during the 1961-62 season. This earned him a place in the World Cup finals squad in Chile that summer and he appeared in the group matches against Argentina and Bulgaria as a replacement for Gerry Hitchens. In February 1964 he was bought for £60,000 by a Leeds United side in need of his goalscoring abilities to ensure they won the Second Division title, with Alan duly collecting a championship medal that May. The following season Alan appeared in the FA Cup final, although Leeds lost to Liverpool and in October 1967 he was sold to Plymouth Argyle, injuries forcing him to announce his retirement the following March having netted 153 League goals in his 284 appearances for his three clubs. He then returned to Middlesbrough where he ran a newsagents.

John PEACOCK

Born: Wigan, 15th March 1897
Died: 4th March 1979
Role: Right-Winger
Career: Atherton, Everton, Middlesbrough, Sheffield Wednesday, Clapton Orient
Debut: v France (a) 9-5-1929
Appearances: 3

Known as Joe throughout his career, he joined Everton from non-League Atherton in the summer of 1919 and went on to make 161 appearances for the club, scoring 12 goals during his eight seasons at Goodison Park. He left for Middlesbrough in 1927 and helped them to the Second Division championship in 1928-29 as well as earning international recognition, collecting three caps for England. Joe moved on to Sheffield Wednesday in May 1930 and stayed a year at Hillsborough before moving on to Clapton Orient where he made more than 50 appearances for the club before retiring. He then turned to coaching, having a spell in Sweden before returning to these shores to take up the post of trainer at Wrexham in July 1939.

Stuart Pearce

Stuart PEARCE M.B.E.

Born: Hammersmith, 24th April 1962
Role: Full-Back
Career: Wealdstone, Coventry City, Nottingham Forest, Newcastle United, West Ham United, Manchester City
Debut: v Brazil (h) 19-5-1987
Appearances: 78 (5 goals) + 1 unofficial appearance

One of the most feared full-backs in the game, Stuart was a late developer as far as professional football was concerned, beginning his career with non-League Wealdstone whilst working as an electrician. Coventry City signed him in October 1983 for £25,000 and he spent two years at Highfield Road before a £450,000 move to Nottingham Forest in June 1985. Guided by manager Brian Clough, Stuart developed into one of the most accomplished defenders in the game, with his ability to hit a dead ball almost harder than anyone else in the game an important part in Forest's armoury. He became captain at Forest following the departure of Johnny Metgod and helped the club win the League Cup in 1989 and 1990 and the final of the FA Cup in 1991, although he had to settle for a runners-up medal in the latter competition, despite scoring Forest's goal. In 1996 he became player-manager at Forest although he was unable to prevent the club being relegated into the First Division and in 1997 was released on a free transfer, subsequently joining Newcastle United. He helped his new club reach the final of the 1998 FA Cup Final, again finishing on the losing side. In 1990, during the World Cup finals, he was one of the England players who missed in the penalty shoot-out against Germany in the semi final, but he showed the incident had not affected his composure during the 1996 European Championships, twice taking (and scoring) as England again had to undertake penalty shootouts. In 1998 he was involved in a serious car accident but emerged virtually unscathed; there seems to be very little that fazed Stuart Pearce, on and off the field. From Newcastle United he joined West Ham United and finished his playing career with Manchester City. On the very last day of the 2003-04 season he was given an opportunity to score the 100th goal of his league career – he missed from the penalty spot in the final minute, even though the opposition goalkeeper Dave Beasant had promised not to try and save it! He was awarded an MBE for his services to football in the 1999 New Year's Honours List.

Harry Pearson

Harold Frederick PEARSON

Born: Tamworth, 7th May 1908
Died: 2nd November 1994
Role: Goalkeeper
Career: Glascote United Methodists, Belgrave Working Men's Club, Tamworth Castle, West Bromwich Albion, Millwall
Debut: v Scotland (h) 9-4-1932
Appearances: 1

Harry followed in the footsteps of his father Hubert, signing for West Bromwich Albion as an amateur in April 1925 and turning professional the following month. A member of the side that won the FA Cup in 1931, Harry also collected a runners-up medal in 1935. He was transferred to Millwall in August 1927 and helped his new club win the Third Division South championship in his first season before retiring during the Second World War. His one cap for England enabled him to go one better than his father, who was picked to play for England against France in 1923 but was injured before the game and never selected again.

James Stuart PEARSON

Born: Hull, 21st June 1949
Role: Centre-Forward
Career: Hull City, Manchester United, West Ham United
Debut: v Wales (a) 8-5-1976
Appearances: 15 (5 goals) + 1 unofficial international

Stuart joined his local club Hull City on amateur forms in May 1966 and was elevated to the professional ranks in July 1968. He went on to prove himself a regular goalscorer in the Hull side, netting 44 goals in 129 League appearances before being targeted by Manchester United as the spearhead for their attempts to return to top flight football in May 1974. Tommy Docherty paid £170,000 to take Stuart to Old Trafford and Stuart would repay him with 55 goals in his 139 appearances, helping them win the Second Division championship in 1975 and reach successive FA Cup finals, in 1976 and 1977, collecting a winners' medal in 1977. He was sold to West Ham United for £220,000 in August 1979 and collected a second winners' medal in the FA Cup in 1980 and was a substitute the following year when West Ham reached the League Cup final. He was released by West Ham in the summer of 1982 and went on the rebel tour of South Africa, later playing in North America before retiring through injury. He later managed Northwich Victoria and had spells coaching West Bromwich Albion and as assistant manager at Bradford City.

John Hargreaves PEARSON

Born: Crewe, 25th January 1868
Died: 22nd June 1931
Role: Inside-Right
Career: Crewe Alexandra
Debut: v Ireland (a) 5-3-1892
Appearances: 1

He joined Crewe Alexandra at the age of thirteen and a half and spent his entire playing career with the club, being forced to retire through injury soon after making his only appearance for England. He remained in football, however, qualifying as a referee and was on the Football League list until 1914, being given the honour of officiating the 1911 FA Cup final between Bradford City and Newcastle United. Away from the game he worked for the London & North Western Railways (later the LMS) until he retired in 1930.

Stanley Clare PEARSON

Born: Salford, 11th January 1919
Died: 20th February 1997
Role: Inside-Forward
Career: Manchester United, Bury, Chester
Debut: v Scotland (a) 10-4-1948
Appearances: 8 (5 goals) + 1 War appearance

Stan joined Manchester United from Adelphi Lads Club of the Manchester & District Amateur League, making his debut in November 1937 against Chesterfield and was beginning to break into the side with greater regularity when the Football League was suspended indefinitely owing to the Second World War. Like many of his era he lost a considerable part of his career to the war but scored a hat-trick in the 1948 FA Cup semi final against Derby and one of United's four in the final against Blackpool to ensure their trophy win. He was also a member of the 1952 League championship winning side, but Matt Busby's later introduction of a succession of youngsters into the first team signalled the end of Stan's United career. Even so he had netted 128 League goals in only 315 appearances, and 149 goals in all competitions from 345 appearances, a remarkable return. In February 1954 he moved on to Bury, remaining with the club a little over three years before moving on again to join Chester in October 1957. During his time he helped the club reach the Welsh Cup final in 1958 and was appointed player-manager of the club in April 1959, subsequently retiring from playing in order to concentrate on management full time. Unfortunately Stan found management somewhat difficult and stepped down in November 1961, after which he ran a newsagents business in Prestbury and coached a side in the local East Cheshire League. In addition to his eight full caps, Stan also turned out for the England B side on one occasion.

Stan Pearson

William Harold PEASE

Born: Leeds, 30th September 1899
Died: 2nd October 1955
Role: Right-Winger
Career: Leeds City, Northampton Town, Middlesbrough, Luton Town
Debut: v Wales (a) 12-2-1927
Appearances: 1

Billy played rugby at school and only took up football whilst serving in the Northumberland Fusiliers during the First World War. At the end of the hostilities he signed amateur forms with Leeds City but, as the club were forced to disband in October 1919 because of financial irregularities, he moved to Northampton Town where he was installed as a professional. He remained at Northampton until May 1926 when he was bought by Middlesbrough and helped his new club win the Second Division championship in his first season, his performances at club level also earning him recognition at international level. He won a second Division Two championship medal in 1929 and remained with the club until June 1933 when he moved to Luton Town. Injury forced him to retire in January 1935 and he returned to Middlesbrough to become a licensee.

David Pegg

David PEGG

Born: Doncaster, 20th September 1935
Died: Munich, 6th February 1958
Role: Left-Winger
Career: Manchester United
Debut: v Republic of Ireland (a) 19-5-1957 (WCQ)
Appearances: 1

David joined United straight from school and was an integral part of the youth side that won the FA Youth Cup in 1953 and 1954. He broke into the first team in 1955-56 and went on to win successive League title medals as well as a runners-up medal in the 1957 FA Cup final, the same year he made his debut for England and was viewed as a long term successor to Tom Finney in the left-wing position. A loss of form in 1957-58 saw his place in the United side being taken by Albert Scanlon, but David travelled with the squad to the ill-fated European Cup tie with Red Star Belgrade and lost his life in the crash at Munich, the youngest player killed.

Michael PEJIC

Born: Chesterton, 25th January 1950
Role: Full-Back
Career: Stoke City, Everton, Aston Villa
Debut: v Portugal (a) 3-4-1974
Appearances: 4

Born in Stoke, the son of a Yugoslavian immigrant, Mike joined his local club as an apprentice and was upgraded to the professional ranks in January 1968. He soon broke into the first team and was an integral part of the side that won Stoke City's only major honour, the League cup in 1972. His performances at club level earned him England recognition in 1974, with Mike appearing in four consecutive matches, having previously won eight caps at Under-23 level. He was sold to Everton for £135,000 in February 1977 but was unable to reclaim his England place, subsequently being sold to Aston Villa for £250,000 in September 1979. He made just 10 appearances for Villa before being forced to retire owing to a pelvic disorder, subsequently trying a number of different trades and professions, including farming and a spell as a greengrocer. He later returned to the game, coaching and managing Northwich Victoria before a short spell in charge at Chester City.

Frederick Raymond PELLY

Born: Upminster, 11th August 1868
Died: 16th October 1940
Role: Left-Back
Career: Old Foresters, Essex, Casuals, Corinthians
Debut: v Ireland (h) 25-2-1893
Appearances: 3 + 1 unofficial appearance

Educated at Forest School he played for the school team between 1882 and 1886 and then for Old Foresters as well as Casuals and Corinthians, the two leading amateur sides of the day, being captain of Casuals for much of his time associated with the club. He also earned representative honours with the London FA and Essex and was captain of the Essex side for five years.

Jesse PENNINGTON

Born: West Bromwich, 23rd August 1883
Died: Kidderminster, 5th September 1970
Role: Left-Back
Career: Summit Star, Smethwick Centaur, Langley Villa, Dudley, West Bromwich Albion
Debut: v Wales (h) 18-3-1907
Appearances: 25

Jesse played schoolboy football in Smethwick and then helped found junior side Summit Star. He then played for Smethwick Centaur, Langley Villa and Dudley Town before signing with West Bromwich Albion in April 1903, even though he had previously been associated with Aston Villa as an amateur. Jesse was an amateur with Albion during his early career but later became professional and remained with the club until August 1922. He helped them win the Second Division championship in 1911 and reach the FA Cup Final the following year, although Albion were beaten by Barnsley after a replay. He collected 23 of his

Jesse Pennington

England caps before the First World War and the final two after the end of the hostilities, although surprisingly did not appear in any of the Victory Internationals. He did win a League championship medal in 1920 and also represented the Football League on nine occasions during his career. After retiring as a player in 1922 Jesse served as a coach at The Hawthorns for a season and then went to Kidderminster Harriers to coach, a position he held until 1925. He then went back to West Bromwich Albion and scouted for the club until 1960 and was later made a life member of the club. His number of appearances for Albion, 494 in both the League and the FA Cup, was a club record until overhauled by Tony Brown in 1978.

Frederick Beaconsfield PENTLAND

Born: Small Heath, 1883
Died: 16th March 1962
Role: Right-Winger
Career: Small Heath, Blackpool, Blackburn Rovers, Brentford, Queens Park Rangers, Middlesbrough, Halifax Town
Debut: v Wales (h) 15-3-1909
Appearances: 5

He played junior football in the Birmingham area before signing with Small Heath in August 1900 and spent three years with the club before moving on to Blackpool. His stay at Bloomfield Road was a short one, however, for he was soon sold to Blackburn Rovers and spent a little over two years with the club before moving on again to London to sign for Brentford in May 1906. A year later he moved across the city to play for Queens Park Rangers, helping them win the Southern League championship in 1908 before moving on to Middlesbrough, where he finally received his England call-up. He was appointed player-manager of Halifax Town in the summer of 1912 but spent only a couple of months at the club before joining Stoke where he finished his playing career. Frederick then became a coach in Europe, although he was interned for the duration of the First World War, and at the end of the hostilities moved to Spain. He coached a number of sides in that country, including the Real Racing Club of Santander and Athletic Bilbao, guiding the latter club to five League titles in seven seasons. He also had a spell as national coach before returning to England in 1936 and joining Brentford. He finished his involvement with football with a spell as manager of Barrow.

Charles PERRY

Born: West Bromwich, January 1866
Died: 2nd July 1927
Role: Centre-Half
Career: West Bromwich Albion
Debut: v Ireland (a) 15-3-1890
Appearances: 3

One of five brothers who played for West Bromwich Albion, Charlie joined the club in June 1884 and won two FA Cup winners' medals, in 1888 and 1892. He also helped the club reach the final in 1886 and 1887 and represented the Football League once before injury forced his retirement from playing in May 1896. Charlie continued his association with the club, however, being appointed to the board in 1898, a position he held for four years. He also worked for a brewery, subsequently being appointed to the board of that company too.

Charles Perry

Thomas PERRY

Born: West Bromwich, 1871
Died: 18th July 1927
Role: Half-Back
Career: Christchurch West Bromwich, Stourbridge, West Bromwich Albion, Aston Villa
Debut: v Ireland (a) 5-3-1898
Appearances: 1

Brother of fellow England international Charlie Perry (above), Tom joined West Bromwich Albion in July 1890 and helped the club reach the FA Cup final in 1895. He also represented the Football League on three occasions and remained at The Hawthorns until October 1901 when he moved across the city to sign for Aston Villa. He retired from playing in the summer of 1903.

William PERRY

Born: Johannesburg, South Africa, 10th September 1930
Role: Left-Winger
Career: Johannesburg Rangers (South Africa), Blackpool, Southport, Hereford United, South Coast United (Australia), Holyhead Town
Debut: v Northern Ireland (h) 2-11-1955
Appearances: 3 (2 goals)

Although Bill was born in South Africa, he eventually qualified to play for England by virtue of his father. Bill began his playing career in South Africa and was recommended to Blackpool by former Bolton star Billy Butler, manager of Johannesburg Rangers, even though Bill had already turned down an approach by Charlton Athletic. Bill arrived in England in October 1949 and signed with the Seasiders immediately, going on to help them reach the FA Cup final in 1951 where they were beaten by Newcastle United. Blackpool and Bill returned two years later and, whilst Stan Mortensen's hat-trick and Stanley Matthews contribution have attracted all the attention, it was Bill Perry's goal that actually won the cup for Blackpool in their 4-3 win over Bolton Wanderers. Bill remained at Blackpool until June 1962, making 394 League appearances and scoring 119 goals, before moving on to Southport. After a year with the club he joined Hereford United where he spent a further twelve months and then had a brief spell in Australia before finishing his playing career with Holyhead Town. Bill later served Fleetwood as a director for five years.

Stephen John PERRYMAN M.B.E.

Born: Ealing, 21st December 1951
Role: Midfield
Career: Tottenham Hotspur, Oxford United, Brentford
Debut: v Iceland (a) 2-6-1982
Appearances: 1

Having represented London and England Schools as a youngster, Steve had the pick of the clubs to join, finally choosing Spurs and joining as an apprentice in July 1967. He was upgraded to the professional ranks in January 1969 and made his League debut in September the same year, appearing in the game against Sunderland. He collected winners' medals from the League Cup in 1971 and 1973, the FA Cup in 1981 and 1982 and the UEFA Cup in 1972, was named Footballer of the Year in 1982 by the Writers' Association and was capped by England the same year. By the time he left Spurs in 1986 he had amassed 656 League appearances, a club record. Not surprisingly, he has also made more appearances than any other Spurs player in the FA Cup, League Cup and European competition. After leaving Spurs he joined Oxford and in November 1986 joined Brentford as a player, later becoming player-manager. In 1990 he resigned, later becoming manager of Watford, but when Ossie Ardiles took over at White Hart Lane in 1993 Steve came with him as his assistant. When the pair were dismissed they continued their partnership in Japan for a spell. Steve later became director of football at Exeter City.

Martin Stanford PETERS M.B.E.

Born: Plaistow, 8th November 1943
Role: Midfield
Career: West Ham United, Tottenham Hotspur, Norwich City, Sheffield United
Debut: v Yugoslavia (h) 4-5-1966
Appearances: 67 (20 goals) + 1 unofficial appearance

Signed by West Ham as an apprentice in 1959 he became a professional in November 1960 and made his debut for the club in April 1962. A member of the side that won the

Martin Peters

European Cup Winners' Cup in 1965, Martin won his first cap for England in May 1966, just in time to be considered for the squad for the forthcoming World Cup finals. In fact, he was rather more than just a squad member, for West Ham supplied the winning captain in Bobby Moore and both of England's goalscorers in the final; Martin Peters and Geoff Hurst with a hat-trick. The exploits of both Moore and Hurst tended to overshadow Martin's own achievements, and coupled with the Alf Ramsey comment that he was 'ten years ahead of his time' led to him becoming unsettled with West Ham. He was transferred to Spurs in 1970 for a then British record fee of £200,000, with Jimmy Greaves making the opposite journey. Whilst at White Hart Lane Martin showed just why Sir Alf Ramsey had made his famous statement; his ability to ghost into positions few other players would have contemplated, his all round skill and vision meant he was a player who would have fitted into any era. Whilst with Spurs he helped the club win the League Cup in 1971 and 1973 (for which he was captain) and the UEFA Cup in 1972. He was surprisingly sold to Norwich City in March 1975 for £60,000 and after five years at Carrow Road joined Sheffield United as player-coach, later becoming player-manager and retiring in June 1981 following his dismissal after Sheffield United had been relegated. He was appointed to the board of directors at Spurs in 1998.

Michael Christopher PHELAN

Born: Nelson, 24th September 1962
Role: Defender
Career: Burnley, Norwich City, Manchester United, West Bromwich Albion
Debut: v Italy (substitute) (h) 15-11-1989
Appearances: 1

Mike joined Burnley as an apprentice and made his League debut for the club in February 1981, collecting his first youth cap for his country the same week. A member of the side that won the Third Division championship in 1982, Mike made 168 League appearances for the club before a £60,000 move to Norwich City in June 1985. He won a Second Division championship medal in 1986 and was a virtual ever-present during his four years with the club. He was sold to Manchester United in July 1989 and went on to help United win the FA Cup in 1990 and 1994, the League Cup in 1992, the European Cup Winners' Cup in 1991 and the Premier League in 1993 and 1994. He was given a free transfer in the summer of 1994 and joined West Bromwich Albion where he finished his playing career at the end of the 1994-95 season. Mike then went into coaching and has since served both Norwich City and Manchester United in this capacity.

Kevin Mark PHILLIPS

Born: Hitchin, 25th July 1973
Role: Forward
Career: Watford, Sunderland, Southampton, Aston Villa
Debut: v Hungary (a) 28-4-1999
Appearances: 8

Kevin began his playing career with non-League Baldock Town and cost Watford £10,000 when they signed him in December 1994. A broken foot sustained midway through his first season with the club hindered his progress but once recovered he proved himself to be a consistent goalscorer. Sunderland paid £325,000 to take him to Roker Park in July 1997 and he forged an effective club partnership with Niall Quinn, subsequently earning a call-up into the full England side. Following Sunderland's relegation from the Premier League in 2003 Kevin was sold to Southampton for £3.25 million where he was expected to link up with Peter Crouch, but injuries again caused disruption to his career. When Southampton were relegated in 2005 he was sold to Aston Villa.

Kevin Philips

Leonard Horace PHILLIPS

Born: Hackney, 11th September 1922
Role: Inside-Left
Career: Portsmouth, Poole Town, Chelmsford City, Bath City
Debut: v Northern Ireland (h) 14-11-1951
Appearances: 3

Len Phillips had played for Hillside Youth Club prior to the outbreak of the Second World War and joined the Royal Marines, for whom he played representative football during the war. After taking part in the D-Day landings, Len signed as an amateur with Portsmouth, subsequently becoming a professional in February 1946 after he had been demobbed. Although he appeared for the club a month later in a wartime fixture and made his League debut in December the same year, it was not until the 1948-49 season was well under way that he became a regular in the side. His timing was impeccable, however, for he was then a regular in the side that won successive First Division championships, in 1948-49 and 1949-50. His performances for the Fratton Park club soon had him tipped for representative honours and after turning out for the Football League twice, Len was called into the full England side in November 1951. He was a regular in the side for almost eight years, making 245 League appearances, until he tore a ligament in a cup tie against Grimsby Town. At the end of the 1955-56 season he was advised by doctors to retire from playing, which he duly did, but Len later turned out in non-League football, playing for Poole Town, Chelmsford City and Bath City before finally retiring in May 1963. At the end of his playing career Len was a machine operator for a local engineering company.

Frederick PICKERING

Born: Blackburn, 19th January 1941
Role: Centre-Forward
Career: Blackburn Rovers, Everton, Birmingham City, Blackpool, Blackburn Rovers, Brighton & Hove Albion
Debut: v USA (a) 27-5-1964 (scored three times)
Appearances: 3 (5 goals)

After playing local junior football in Blackburn, Fred was signed by Blackburn Rovers as an amateur before turning professional in January 1958. He began his career as a left-back and helped the youth side win the FA Youth Cup in May 1959 and broke into the first team the same October, although his performances over the next year or so were adequate rather than exceptional and he drifted back into reserve team football. Here he was tried out at centre-forward and proved an immediate hit, so much so that he was restored to the first team in March 1961 and scored twice in the 4-1 win over Manchester City. Over the next three years he saw off a number of challengers for the number nine shirt at Rovers and attracted the attention of a number of other clubs, finally earning an £82,000 move to Everton in March 1964. Two months later he accompanied England on tour and made his debut in the match against America in New York, scoring a hat-trick, the last occasion a debutant has scored as many as three goals in a game. He proved as deadly at Everton as he had been at Blackburn, but his Goodison Park career never fully recovered after he was surprisingly left out of the side for the 1966 FA Cup Final, his place going to Mike Trebilcock. That Trebilcock scored twice to help Everton come from behind to win the cup 3-2 against Sheffield Wednesday may have vindicated Harry Catterick's decision, but a year later Fred was on his way, signing for Birmingham City for £50,000. He spent two years at Birmingham before joining Blackpool for £45,000 in June 1969 and even returned to Blackburn in a £10,000 deal in March 1971 as his hometown club was desperately battling against relegation to the Third Division. With the battle lost and a new manager appointed, Fred's time at Rovers was rapidly coming to an end and his contract was cancelled in February 1972. He spent an unsuccessful two months on trial with Brighton before drifting out of the game.

John PICKERING

Born: High Green, 18th December 1908
Died: 10th May 1977
Role: Inside-Left
Career: Mortomley St. Saviours, Sheffield United
Debut: v Scotland (a) 1-4-1933
Appearances: 1

Jack attended Barnsley Grammar School and signed with Sheffield United in May 1925, thus beginning an association with the club that was to last twenty-three years. A member of the side that won the FA Cup in 1936, Jack also represented the Football League once during his career. He made 344 League appearances for the club before his retirement in 1948, a United record that was finally overtaken in 1966. Of course, both this and his tally of 103 goals would have been considerably higher but for the Second World War which robbed Jack of seven seasons of League action. After retiring from playing, Jack, who was an accountant by profession, became manager and coach at Poole Town.

John Pickering

Nicholas PICKERING

Born: Newcastle, 4th August 1963
Role: Defender
Career: Sunderland, Coventry City, Derby County, Darlington, Burnley
Debut: v Australia (a) 19-6-1983
Appearances: 1

Nick played junior football in North Shields before signing with Sunderland as an apprentice, turning professional in August 1981. He made his debut for the club soon after and in September 1982 was called into the England Under-21 side, going on to win 15 caps at this level. He was 19 years of age when he won his only full cap for England and in 1985 became the youngest captain to lead a side at Wembley when Sunderland played Norwich City in the League Cup final. Nick was sold to Coventry City for £120,000 in January 1986 and returned to Wembley in May 1987 as part of the FA Cup winning side. He remained at Coventry until August 1988 when he was sold to Derby County for £250,000 but his first team opportunities at the Baseball Ground were sporadic, with Nick joining Darlington in October 1991, finishing his playing career with Burnley.

Thetwell Mather PIKE

Born: 17th November 1866
Died: 21st July 1957
Role: Left-Winger
Career: Cambridge University, Old Malvernians, Crusaders, Brentwood, Swifts, Thanet Wanderers, Corinthians
Debut: v Ireland (a) 13-3-1886
Appearances: 1

Educated at Malvern School, Thetwell played for the school team in 1884 and 1885 before attending Cambridge University and earning a Blue in 1886 and 1888. After university he assisted various clubs, being most closely associated with Corinthians, for whom he played between 1886 and 1891. He was also a noted cricketer, playing for Worcestershire between 1886 and 1895. He was headmaster of Weybridge Preparatory School between 1897 and 1906 and then moved to Thanet School in Margate where he remained until his retirement.

Brian PILKINGTON

Born: Leyland, 12th February 1933
Role: Left-Winger
Career: Burnley, Bolton Wanderers, Bury, Barrow, Chorley
Debut: v Northern Ireland (a) 2-10-1954
Appearances: 1

Brian was serving an apprenticeship at Leyland Motors as a coach painter and playing for the works side when he was spotted by Burnley, signing with the Lancashire club in April 1951. He was to spend almost ten years at Turf Moor, helping the club win the League championship in 1960 and represented the Football League and England at B level during his time with the club. He was sold to Bolton in February 1961 for £25,000, remaining with the club for three years before a £5,000 move to Bury on February 1964. In January 1965 he was sold to Barrow where he finished his League career, later playing at non-League level with Chorley before injury forced his retirement. He returned to Leyland Motors in 1969, this time to manage the works side and later qualified as a magistrate.

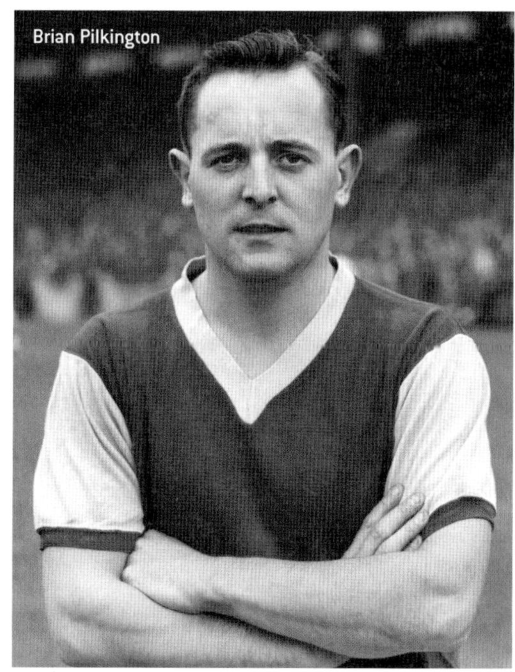
Brian Pilkington

John PLANT

Born: Bollington, 1871
Role: Left-Winger
Career: Denton, Bollington, Bury, Reading, Bury
Debut: v Scotland (a) 7-4-1900
Appearances: 1

After playing for Denton and Bollington, John joined Bury in April 1890 and was a member of the side that was elected to the Football League in 1894. This spelled the start of a boom period for the club, with Bury winning the Second Division championship in 1895, and although he left the club for Reading in the summer of 1898 he returned a year later and helped the club win the FA Cup in 1900 and 1903. He retired in 1907 having made 319 League appearances for the Shakers in his two spells at Gigg Lane.

Davd Platt

David Andrew PLATT

Born: Chadderton, 10th June 1966
Role: Midfield
Career: Manchester United, Crewe Alexandra, Aston Villa, Bari (Italy), Juventus (Italy), Sampdoria (Italy), Arsenal
Debut: v Italy (h) (substitute) 15-11-1989
Appearances: 62 (27 goals) + 1 unofficial appearance

After being shown the door by Manchester United he joined Crewe Alexandra and developed into a workmanlike midfielder and was snapped up by Aston Villa in 1988. He made his England debut in 1990, just in time to stake a place in the World Cup squad, where his performances grew with each successive game, not least his appearance off the substitutes' bench against Belgium to score the winner in the last minute of extra time. In 1991 he was signed by Bari for £5.5 million and a year later moved on for a similar fee to Juventus. After a further move within Italy (to Sampdoria) he returned to England with Arsenal in 1995, retiring from the game in the summer of 1998. He later had spells as manager of Nottingham Forest and the England Under-21 side.

Seth Lewis PLUM

Born: Edmonton, 15th July 1899
Died: 29th November 1969
Role: Wing-Half
Career: Midway Athletic, Tottenham Park Avondale, Barnet, Charlton Athletic, Chelsea, Southend United
Debut: v France (a) 10-5-1923
Appearances: 1

Seth played junior football in the Tottenham area before joining Charlton Athletic as an amateur in the summer of 1922, turning professional in August 1923. Thus his only appearance for England came as an amateur, but despite this he was not capped for England at this level. Seth remained at Charlton until March 1924 when he was sold to Chelsea but could not command a regular place at Stamford Bridge, moving on to Southend United in the summer of 1927 for one season before retiring. He then returned to live and work in North London.

Raymond POINTER

Born: Cramlington, 10th October 1936
Role: Centre-Forward
Career: Burnley, Bury, Coventry City, Portsmouth
Debut: v Luxembourg (h) 28-9-1961 (scored once)
Appearances: 3 (2 goals)

Ray played local and junior football and represented his unit whilst undertaking national service, subsequently signing for Burnley in August 1957. He won a League championship medal in 1960 and an FA Cup runners-up medal in 1962 and scored both of his goals for England in World Cup qualifying matches, but despite this prowess at international level did not make the squad for the 1962 finals in Chile. Ray remained at Turf Moor until August 1965 when, after a season decimated by injury, he was sold to Bury for £8,000. He made just 19 appearances at the club (scoring 17 goals) before moving on to Coventry City in December 1965 for £20,000. In January 1967 he moved to Portsmouth where he later became player-coach and retired from playing in 1972. He became youth coach at Blackpool in August 1973, a post he held until May 1976 and ended his involvement in the game with a spell as manager of Burnley youth team.

Thomas Stoddard PORTEOUS

Born: Newcastle-upon-Tyne, 1865
Died: 23rd February 1919
Role: Right-Back
Career: Hearts, Kilmarnock, Sunderland, Rotherham United, Manchester City
Debut: v Wales (h) 7-3-1891
Appearances: 1

Although Tom was born in Newcastle he began his playing career north of the border with Heart of Midlothian before joining Kilmarnock in 1884. He returned to England to join Sunderland in the summer of 1889 and won League championship medals in 1892 and 1893, an integral part of the side billed as 'The team of all talents.' Tom remained at Sunderland until June 1894 when he joined Rotherham United but a year later moved on to Manchester City where he ended his playing career.

Chris Powell

Christopher George Robin POWELL

Born: Lambeth, 8th September 1969
Role: Defender
Career: Crystal Palace, Aldershot, Southend United, Derby County, Charlton Athletic, West Ham United, Charlton Athletic
Debut: v Spain (h) 28-2-2001
Appearances: 5

Chris signed professional forms with Crystal Palace in December 1987 but was unable to command a regular place in the side, being sent on loan to Aldershot and then released on a free transfer in August 1990. He was snapped up by Southend United and set about resurrecting his career, making 290 appearances for the club before Derby stepped in with a £750,000 offer in January 1996. In July 1998 Charlton Athletic paid their then record fee of £825,000 to take him to The Valley and he helped the club win the First Division title in 2000. The appointment of Sven Goran Eriksson as England manager and his initial policy of watching all available players saw Chris one of the main beneficiaries, collecting his first cap in 2001 in the match against Spain. Chris remained at Charlton until September 2004 when he was released on a free transfer and promptly joined West Ham United, helping them earn promotion to the Premier League the following May.

Alfred Ernest PRIEST

Born: Guisborough, 1875
Died: Hartlepool, 5th May 1922
Role: Left-Winger
Career: Darlington, South Bank, Sheffield United, Middlesbrough
Debut: v Ireland (a) 17-3-1900
Appearances: 1

Fred played for Darlington and South Bank before linking with Sheffield United in the summer of 1896. He won a League championship medal in 1898 and an FA Cup winners' medal the following year whilst playing on the left wing. Following the arrival of Bert Lipsham in February 1900 Fred moved to inside-forward, with the pair forming an effective partnership at club level, reaching the FA Cup final in 1901 and 1902, and winning the cup in the latter year. Fred remained at Bramall Lane until the summer of 1906 when he accepted an offer to become assistant trainer and player at Middlesbrough. Two years later he became player-manager of Hartlepool United and when his footballing career ended remained in the town where he was a licensee until his death.

James Frederick McLeod PRINSEP

Born: India, 27th July 1861
Died: 22nd November 1895
Role: Half-Back
Career: Clapham Rovers, Surrey, Old Carthusians
Debut: v Scotland (h) 5-4-1879
Appearances: 1

James was educated at Charterhouse and played for the school team in 1877 and 1878. He enlisted in the Essex Regiment after school and assisted a number of clubs, including Clapham Rovers, with whom he made his first appearance in the FA Cup final in 1879 in the 1-0 defeat by Old Etonians. He returned to the final in 1881, this time with Old Carthusians and this time collected a winners' medal after the 3-0 win over Old Etonians. He saw action in the Sudanese campaign in 1884 and 1885 and later served the Egyptian Army from 1885 to 1890 before being transferred to the Egyptian Coastguard Service, subsequently becoming Sub-Inspector General. He was awarded the Albert Medal in 1884 after saving a man in his regiment from drowning.

Sydney Charles PUDDEFOOT

Born: West Ham, 17th October 1894
Died: 2nd October 1972
Role: Inside-Right
Career: Conder Athletic, Limehouse Town, West Ham United, Falkirk, Blackburn Rovers, West Ham United
Debut: v Northern Ireland (a) 24-10-1925
Appearances: 2 + 3 War appearances (4 goals)

Syd played schoolboy football in East London before joining West Ham United as an amateur in 1912, turning professional the following year. During the First World War he made a number of guest appearances for Falkirk, which was to prompt them to make an offer for Syd in 1922. Although quoted £5,000, then a record fee for a player, Falkirk secured the funds and ultimately the player in February 1922. Syd spent three years north of the border before returning to England, joining Blackburn Rovers for £4,000 in February 1925. He was a member of the team that won the FA Cup in 1928 and rejoined West Ham United in February 1932 and retired the following summer. He then turned to coaching, having spells with Fenerbahce and Galatia Seray in Turkey before accepting the position of manager of Northampton Town in March 1935. After two years he left the club and returned to Turkey, where he coached in Istanbul until 1940. He then returned to England again and became a civil servant until his retirement in 1963.

Jesse Pye

Jesse PYE

Born: Treeton, near Rotherham, 22nd December 1919
Died: 20th February 1984
Role: Centre-Forward
Career: Catliffe, Treeton, Sheffield United, Notts County, Wolverhampton Wanderers, Luton Town, Derby County, Wisbech Town
Debut: v Republic of Ireland (h) 21-9-1949
Appearances: 1 + 1 War Appearance (1 goal)

Jesse played for Catliffe Boys Club in Yorkshire and then the village side Treeton before signing as an amateur with Sheffield United in 1938, later becoming a part-time professional. After service in the Second World War with the Royal Engineers, Jesse resumed his football career, signing as a professional with Notts County in August 1945. Less than twelve months later he cost Wolves a then record fee of £12,000 to take him to Molineux, with a host of top clubs having battled for his signature. He was a member of the side that won the FA Cup in 1949, winning his only cap for England later the same year (all the more surprising since he had represented England in the 1946 wartime international against Belgium, scoring one of England's goals in the 2-0 win), although he did represent the B side on three occasions and the Football League once. He lost his way somewhat during the 1950-51 season, unable to reproduce the form that had made him a feared striker, although he was almost back to his best in 1951-52. He was sold to Luton Town in July 1952 for some £9,000 and two years later cost Derby County £5,000. He scored 145 goals in 309 League appearances for his three clubs, a satisfactory return. He finished his League career in July 1957 when he joined Wisbech Town, later becoming player-manager in March 1960. He resigned in 1966 and went on to become the proprietor of a private hotel in Blackpool.

Richard Henry PYM

Born: Topsham, 2nd February 1893
Died: 29th September 1988
Role: Goalkeeper
Career: Topsham St. Margarets, Exeter City, Bolton Wanderers, Yeovil Town
Debut: v Wales (a) 28-2-1925
Appearances: 3

Known as 'Pincher' he played schoolboy and junior football in Devon before signing with Exeter City in February 1911, initially as an amateur and working as a deep sea fisherman! He quickly became known as a dependable and consistent goalkeeper and in June 1921 was sold to Bolton Wanderers for £2,000, going on to collect a winners' medal in the FA Cup in 1923, the first at Wembley, 1926 and 1929. He returned to Devon in May 1931 upon signing with Yeovil and switched to coaching with Topsham in 1934. He later had spells as assistant trainer at Exeter City and scouting for Bolton.

Richard 'Pincher' Pym

Alfred Edward QUANTRILL

Born: Punjab, India, 22nd January 1897
Died: 19th April 1968
Role: Left-Winger
Career: Boston Swifts, Derby County, Preston North End, Chorley, Bradford, Nottingham Forest
Debut: v Wales (h) 15-3-1920
Appearances: 4 (1 goal)

Alf was spotted by Derby County whilst playing for Boston Swifts and signed for The Rams in August 1914. His performances in the first season after football resumed following the First World War earned him a call-up to the England side and he appeared in all three Home International matches and the following season's match against Wales. In June 1921 he was sold to Preston North End for £4,000 and spent three years with the club before dropping outof League football to join Chorley. He returned to League action with Bradford Park Avenue a month later and in May 1930 joined Nottingham Forest where he finished his career in the summer of 1932. He was the son-in-law of Steve Bloomer, the former Derby County and England player.

Albert Quixall

Albert QUIXALL

Born: Sheffield, 9th August 1933
Role: Inside-Forward
Career: Sheffield Wednesday, Manchester United, Oldham Athletic, Stockport County, Altrincham
Debut: v Wales (a) 10-10-1953 (WCQ)
Appearances: 5

Signed by Sheffield Wednesday in May 1948 he was taken on as a professional in August 1950, making his League debut at the age of 17 and winning his first England cap three years later. During his eight year spell as a professional at Hillsborough he helped the club win the Second Division championship twice, in 1952 and 1956, and reach the FA Cup semi final in 1954. Although not a prolific goalscorer whilst at Hillsborough, his tally of 65 goals in 260 games was often crucial and he finished the club's top goalscorer in the 1956-57 season. In September 1958 he was sold to Manchester United for a then record fee of £45,000, his experience being vital to Old Trafford in the wake of the Munich disaster. Although he struggled to establish himself at the club for a year or two, he eventually became an integral part of the side, netting 56 goals in 183 games and he won an FA Cup winners' medal in 1963. In September 1964 he was sold to Oldham Athletic for £7,000 and remained at Boundary Park until July 1966 when he was released on a free transfer and joined Stockport County. Injury forced his early retirement in February 1967, although he did subsequently turn out for non-League Altrincham later the same year. As well as five full caps for England, Albert represented his country at schoolboy, Under-23 and B level and also made four appearances for the Football League. When his playing career came to an end Albert went into the scrap metal business in Manchester.

RADFORD, John
RAIKES, Reverend George Berkeley
RAMSEY, Alfred Ernest Sir
RAWLINGS, Archibald
RAWLINGS, William Ernest
RAWLINSON, John Frederick Peel
RAWSON, Herbert Edward
RAWSON, William Stepney
READ, Albert
READER, Joe
REANEY, Paul
REDKNAPP, Jamie Frank
REEVES, Kevin Philip
REGIS, Cyrille
REID, Peter
REVIE, Donald George
REYNOLDS, John
RICHARDS, Charles Henry
RICHARDS, George Henry
RICHARDS, John Peter
RICHARDSON, James Robert
RICHARDSON, Kevin
RICHARDSON, Kieran
RICHARDSON, William 'Ginger'
RICKABY, Stanley
RICKETTS, Michael Barrington
RIGBY, Arthur
RIMMER, Ellis James
RIMMER, James
RIPLEY, Stuart Edward
RIX, Graham
ROBB, George
ROBERTS, Charles
ROBERTS, Frank
ROBERTS, Graham Paul
ROBERTS, Henry
ROBERTS, Herbert
ROBERTS, Robert John
ROBERTS, Wlliam Thomas
ROBINSON, John
ROBINSON, John William
ROBINSON, Paul
ROBSON, Bryan O.B.E.
ROBSON, Robert William
ROCASTLE, David Carlyle
ROONEY, Wayne
ROSE, William Crispin
ROSTRON, Thurston
ROWE, Arthur Sydney
ROWLEY, John Frederick
ROWLEY, William
ROYLE, Joseph
RUDDLESDIN, Herod
RUDDOCK, Neil
RUFFELL, James William
RUSSELL, Bruce Bremner
RUTHERFORD, John 'Jock'

Wayne Rooney

John Radford

John RADFORD

Born: Pontefract, 22nd February 1947
Role: Centre-Forward
Career: Arsenal, West Ham United, Blackburn Rovers
Debut: v Rumania (h) 15-1-1969
Appearances: 2

After playing schools and youth football in Yorkshire, John was invited to join the Arsenal ground staff in October 1962, signing for the Gunners just 24 hours after he had signed amateur forms with Bradford City, subsequently turning professional in February 1964. He made one League appearance before the end of the season and then went on to establish himself as the first choice centre-forward for the club. His elevation coincided with a change in the club's fortunes, and after finishing on the losing side in two League Cup finals in the1960s, he helped them win the Inter-Cities Fairs Cup and then the domestic double of League title and FA Cup in 1971. He linked especially well with fellow striker Ray Kennedy, with Ray's youthful enthusiasm being coupled with John's experience to form a potent strike force. After collecting four caps for England at Under-23 level and representing the Football League twice, John collected his first cap for the full England side in 1969 and then had to wait until 1972 before making his second and final appearance. That same year saw him collect a runners-up medal in the FA Cup, the last chance of success for an Arsenal side already in transition. John was then coupled with Brian Kidd in the Arsenal frontline, although the subsequent arrival of Frank Stapleton spelt the end of John's Highbury career. He was sold to West Ham for £80,000 in December 1976 but the move was not a success, subsequently joining Blackburn for £20,000 in February 1978. He finished his playing career with non-League Bishop's Stortford, later taking over as manager and combining this with a licensee's career in Essex.

Reverend George Berkeley RAIKES

Born: Wymondham, 14th March 1873
Died: Shepton Mallet, 18th December 1966
Role: Goalkeeper
Career: Oxford University, Wymondham, Norfolk, Corinthians
Debut: v Wales (h) 18-3-1895
Appearances: 4

Educated at Shrewsbury School, George kept goal for the school side between 1890 and 1892 before going on to further his education at Oxford University. He won a Blue in 1893, 1895, 1895 and 1896 and later played for Corinthians between 1893 and 1896 and Wymondham FC in Norfolk as well as earning representative honours for Norfolk. He was also a noted cricketer, earning a Blue at university in 1894 and 1895 and played nine matches for Hampshire between 1900 and 1902. Ordained in 1897 he served as curate of Portsea between 1897 and 1905, chaplain to the Duke of Portland from 1905 to 1920 and rector of Bergh Apton from 1920 to 1936.

Sir Alfred Ernest RAMSEY

Born: Dagenham, 22nd January 1920
Died: Ipswich, 28th April 1999
Role: Right-Back
Career: Southampton, Tottenham Hotspur
Debut: v Switzerland (h) 1-12-1948
Appearances: 32 (3 goals)

A grocer's lad, Alf was spotted by Portsmouth and signed as an amateur in 1940. With the Second World War in full swing, however, he never got to play for Portsmouth, being snapped up by their great rivals Southampton whilst playing against them for the Army. He therefore signed as an amateur to Southampton in 1943 and was upgraded to professional level the following year. In 1949 he signed for Spurs for a then record fee for a full-back of £21,000. A member of the 'push and run' side that won the Second and First Division championships in consecutive seasons, Ramsey won a total of 32 England caps (including one in the infamous 1-0 defeat against the USA in the 1950 World Cup - 'Did you play?' asked an inquisitive journalist a few years later. 'Yes' replied Ramsey, 'And I was the only bloody one who did!') before retiring to become part-time manager of Elton Manor. He was appointed full-time manager of Ipswich Town in 1955, steering the club from the Third Division South (champions in 1957), through the Second Division (champions in 1961) and into the First Division for the first time in their history. Astonishingly, Ramsey then led them to the League title in 1962, ostensibly because no one had played Ipswich before and didn't know what to expect and because Ramsey was the master tactician, able to take little more than average players and fashion them into an effective working unit. His achievements at Portman Road did not go unnoticed and he was appointed England manager in October 1962. His 'wingless wonders' won the World Cup at Wembley in 1966 and might have retained the title in Mexico in 1970 with a little more luck. England's reign as World Champions was perhaps ended as much by the substitution of Bobby Charlton too early into the quarter final against West Germany as by the mysterious illness which kept Gordon Banks out of the side. Sir Alf (he was knighted following the 1966 World Cup win) turned his attentions to the 1974 World Cup in West Germany and came close to qualifying, drawing at Wembley against Poland when they needed to win, with the Polish goalkeeper performing heroics. The Football Association relieved him of the manager's position in May 1974. His next involvement with football came in January 1976, when he became a director of Birmingham City, subsequently taking over the reigns as caretaker manager between September 1977 and March 1978. He suffered a stroke in 1998 and was admitted to a Suffolk nursing home where he subsequently died in April 1999 from prostate cancer.

Alf Ramsey

Archibald RAWLINGS

Born: Leicester, 2nd October 1891
Died: 11th June 1952
Role: Right-Winger
Career: Wombwell, Shirebrook, Northampton Town, Barnsley, Rochdale, Shirebrook, Dundee, Preston North End, Liverpool, Walsall, Bradford, Southport, Burton Town
Debut: v Belgium (a) 21-5-1921
Appearances: 1

Archibald began his professional career with Northampton Town in 1908 and spent three years with the club before moving on to Barnsley. Two years later he moved again, this time joining Rochdale, and during the First World War turned out for Shirebrook. He moved to Scotland to sign for Dundee in the summer of 1919 but returned to England with Preston for £1,500 in June 1920. He helped the club reach the FA Cup final in 1922 and in March 1924 moved to Anfield and Liverpool. In June 1926 Archibald signed for Walsall, later turning out for Bradford Park Avenue and Southport before leaving League football, having spells with Dick Kerr's FC and Burton Town before retiring. He later coached at Preston and his son Syd Rawlings became a professional player, most notably with Millwall.

William Rawlings

William Ernest RAWLINGS
Born: Andover, 3rd January 1896
Died: 25th September 1972
Role: Centre-Forward
Career: Andover, Southampton, Manchester United, Port Vale
Debut: v Wales (h) 13-3-1922
Appearances: 2
He played for Andover and representative football in the Army during the First World War before signing with Southampton in 1918, initially as an amateur and being upgraded to the professional ranks in May 1919. Southampton were elected to the newly formed Third Division in 1920 and in 1922 won the championship of the Third Division South, with William an integral part of the side, his performances at club level earning him the first of his England caps in March 1922. In March 1928 he was transferred to Manchester United and spent eighteen months at Old Trafford before moving on to Port Vale where he finished his career in the summer of 1930.

John Frederick Peel RAWLINSON
Born: New Alresford, 21st December 1860
Died: 14th January 1926
Role: Goalkeeper
Career: Cambridge University, Old Etonians, Corinthians
Debut: v Ireland (a) 18-2-1881
Appearances: 1
Educated at and a player for Eton, John then attended Cambridge University where he won a Blue in 1882 and 1883. He was also assisting the Old Etonians at this time and made three successive appearances in the FA Cup final, 1881 to 1883, collecting a winners' medal in 1882. That same year he became a member of the committee of Corinthians and later served on the FA Committee, from 1885 to 1886. He qualified as a barrister and was called to the bar in 1884, becoming a QC in 1897. He was also Recorder of Cambridge from 1896 and Member of Parliament for Cambridge University from 1906, holding both posts until his death in 1926. He was appointed a Privy Counsellor in 1923.

Herbert Edward RAWSON
Born: Port Louis, Mauritius, 3rd September 1852
Died: London, 18th October 1924
Role: Forward
Career: Royal Engineers, Royal Military Academy Woolwich, Kent
Debut: v Scotland (h) 6-3-1875
Appearances: 1
The older of the two Rawson brothers to represent England, Herbert was educated at Westminster School and played for the school team between 1869 and 1871, captaining the side in his final year. He then joined the Royal Engineers and appeared in two FA Cup finals, collecting a runners-up medal in 1874 and a winners' medal a year later. He was also a notable cricketer, making one appearance for Kent as wicketkeeper in 1873, although he failed to score a single run in either of his two innings!

William Stepney RAWSON
Born: Cape Town, South Africa, 14th October 1854
Died: 4th November 1932
Role: Half-Back
Career: Oxford University, Old Westminsters, Wanderers
Debut: v Scotland (h) 6-3-1875
Appearances: 2
Like his elder brother, William attended Westminster School and represented the school side in 1872 and 1873, being captain in his final year. He then went to Oxford University, winning a Blue in four consecutive years, 1874 to 1877 and being captain of the side in 1876. He was a member of the Oxford University side that won the FA Cup in 1874, beating his brother's side Royal Engineers, and collected a runners-up medal in 1877. William served on the FA Committee from 1876 to 1877 and again in 1879. He was also good at other sports, earning representative honours at lacrosse.

Albert READ
Born: Ealing 1899
Role: Centre-Half
Career: Tufnell Park, Queens Park Rangers, Reading
Debut: v Belgium (a) 21-5-1921
Appearances: 1
Albert was one of the best known amateur players of the immediate post-war period, winning two caps for England at this level and helping Tufnell Park reach the FA Amateur cup final in 1920. He also got a call-up into the full England side, which prompted Queens Park Rangers to offer him professional forms in May 1921. He spent a year with the club before moving on to Reading in July 1922, but only three games into the new season he suffered a bad knee injury and did not play for the first team again, although he made a number of appearances with the reserves in April 1923. Since it was obvious that he would never be the same player again, his contract was cancelled in the summer of that year.

Josiah READER
Born: West Bromwich, 27th February 1866
Died: 8th March 1954
Role: Goalkeeper
Career: West Bromwich Albion
Debut: v Ireland (a) 1-3-1894
Appearances: 1
Joe played schools football in West Bromwich and joined the professional club from Carters Green in January 1885. A member of the side that won the FA Cup in 1892 against Aston Villa, he also collected a runners-up medal in 1895 (also against Aston Villa) and made three appearances for the Football League. He was forced to retire from playing on the grounds of ill health in 1901 but continued to assist West Bromwich Albion in a variety of posts, including both trainer and coach and then was a steward at The Hawthorns, taking his service to the club beyond 65 years. It is said that he once turned out for his club with his arm in a sling!

Joe Reader

Paul REANEY
Born: London, 22nd October 1944
Role: Right-Back
Career: South Leeds, Leeds United, Bradford City, Newcastle (Australia)
Debut: v Bulgaria (h) (substitute) 11-12-1968
Appearances: 3
Although born in London, Paul was raised in Leeds and was serving an apprenticeship as a car mechanic when offered professional forms with Leeds United in October 1961. He made his debut the following year and went on to become a key fixture of the side that won the Second Division in 1964, the League championship in 1969 and 1974, the FA Cup in 1972, the League Cup in 1968 and the Inter-Cities Fairs Cup in 1968 and 1971. There were also assorted runners-up medals in all three major European competitions and the FA Cup, although a broken leg meant Paul missed Leeds' 1970 defeat by Chelsea. Unfortunately, it also kept him out of the World Cup squad for Mexico the same year and he made only one appearance for his country after recovering from the injury. He remained at Elland Road until June 1978 when he moved down the road to Bradford City, later going to Australia to play for Newcastle where he was named Player of the Year.

Jamie Frank REDKNAPP

Born: Barton-on Sea, 25th June 1973
Role: Midfield
Career: Bournemouth, Liverpool, Tottenham Hotspur, Southampton
Debut: v Colombia (h) 6-9-1995
Appearances: 17 (1 goal)

The son of former player and current manager of Portsmouth, Harry Redknapp, Jamie began his career with Bournemouth where his father was also manager. It was Jamie's refusal to sign a lengthy contract with the south coast club that ultimately cost his father his job at Dean Court, but with Jamie signing for Liverpool and Harry landing on his feet at Upton Park, one could argue that the decision worked out for the best for the pair of them. Jamie cost Liverpool £350,000 in 1990, going on to become one of the brightest midfield talents in the game and a certainty for the England side. Unfortunately a succession of injuries interrupted his career for both club and country, including a broken ankle sustained whilst playing for England against South Africa in 1997 and other niggling pulls and strains, but on his day he was as talented a player as has pulled on the white shirt. In April 2002 he was released on a free transfer and signed for Spurs, although injuries continued to interrupt his career. He was released on a free in January 2005 in order to sign for Southampton, where his father was manager, although he retired from playing at the end of the season. Jamie married pop singer Louise, formerly of Eternal in 1998.

Jamie Redknapp

Kevin Reeves

Kevin Philip REEVES

Born: Burley, 20th October 1957
Role: Forward
Career: Bournemouth, Norwich City, Manchester City, Burnley
Debut: v Bulgaria (h) 22-11-1979 (ECQ)
Appearances: 2

Kevin was associated with Bournemouth as a schoolboy, subsequently joining the club as an apprentice and signing professional forms in July 1975. His finished his first season of League action as top goalscorer and in February 1977 he was bought for £50,000 by Norwich City, where former Bournemouth manager John Bond was now in charge. Here his career began to blossom, with Kevin making a total of 10 appearances for England at Under-21 level and collecting his first cap at full level. In March 1980 he was sold to Manchester City for £1.25 million, where John Bond was soon to become manager, with Kevin collecting his second cap and helping the club to the FA Cup final in 1981 during his time at Maine Road. In July 1983 he was sold to Burnley for a cut-price £125,000, where John Bond was manager, but sadly Kevin had to retire owing to an arthritic hip in the summer of 1985. He later turned to coaching, having spells at Burnley and Birmingham City and was later assistant manager at Wrexham and Swansea City.

Cyrille REGIS

Born: Maripiasoula, French Guyana, 9th February 1958
Role: Centre-Forward
Career: Hayes, West Bromwich Albion, Coventry City, Aston Villa, Wolverhampton Wanderers, Wycombe Wanderers, Chester City
Debut: v Northern Ireland (h) (substitute) 23-2-1982
Appearances: 5

Cyrille had trials with Chelsea as a youngster but failed to impress and was seemingly lost to the professional game, turning out on a part-time basis for Hayes. It was former England player Ronnie Allen, then chief scout for West Bromwich Albion, who was convinced enough of his potential to recommend Cyrille was worth the £5,000 Hayes were asking and he duly signed for Albion in July 1977. Six months later Ronnie Allen was manager and handed Cyrille his League debut, with Cyrille responding by netting in the match against Rotherham. His progress at The Hawthorns was exceptional, with Cyrille going on to collect six caps for England at Under-21 level and collecting the first of his full caps in 1982. In October 1984 he was sold to Coventry City for £300,000 having made 237 appearances for Albion, netting 82 goals. Whilst at Coventry Cyrille helped the club win its first major honour, the FA Cup in 1987, and would go on to net 47 goals in his 237 appearances for the Sky Blues. In July 1991 he moved on to Aston Villa and made 52 appearances for the club, later having short spells with Wolves, Wycombe and Chester before hanging up his boots in 1996.

Cyrille Regis

Peter REID

Born: Huyton, 20th June 1956
Role: Midfield
Career: Bolton Wanders, Everton, Queens Park Rangers, Manchester City, Southampton, Notts County, Bury
Debut: v Mexico (a) 9-6-1985
Appearances: 13

The tough tackling midfield player was first introduced to League football by Bolton Wanderers and cost Everton £60,000 in December 1982. He was to become the engine room of the side that won the FA Cup, two League titles and the European Cup Winners' Cup and also earned him a call-up for England, collecting 13 caps. He later linked up again with Howard Kendall at Manchester City, initially as a player and then becoming manager, remaining in charge for three years. He then moved to Sunderland, guiding them into the Premiership twice and twice finishing just outside the

PQR

Peter Reid

European qualification spot during his seven and a half years at the helm. After a poor start to the 2002-03 season he was sacked in October 2002. He resurfaced later on that season at Leeds United with an eight match brief to save the club from relegation from the Premiership, he accomplished the feat in seven and subsequently earned the job on a full time basis. However, in October 2003, after just 20 games in charge at Elland Road, he was sacked with Leeds United bottom of the Premiership once again. He then had a brief spell in charge of Coventry City. He was named the Professional Footballer's Association Player of the Year in 1985.

Donald George REVIE C.B.E.

Born: Middlesbrough, 10th July 1927
Died: Edinburgh, 26th May 1989
Role: Centre-Forward, Inside-Forward
Career: Middlesbrough Swifts, Leicester City, Hull City, Manchester City, Sunderland, Leeds United
Debut: v Northern Ireland (a) 2-10-1954 (scored once)
Appearances: 6 (4 goals)

Don Revie played schools and junior football in Middlesbrough and was highly regarded during the Second World War by numerous clubs, finally signing with Leicester City in August 1944. Initially he was used as a traditional centre and inside-forward; leading the line and looking to get into goalscoring positions. In 1949 he helped Leicester reach the FA Cup Final, although he was forced to miss the final itself, recovering in hospital from a particularly bad nose haemorrhage. In November the same year he was sold to Hull City for £20,000, but in October 1951 moved on to Manchester City for £13,000 plus another player. The tactical innovations employed by the Hungarians in their 1953 beatings of England did not go unnoticed, not least by Don Revie, who believed that much the same ploy could be used at club level as they had been at international level. Thus, with Revie playing in a deeper position, Manchester City's fortunes took a turn for the better. They reached the FA Cup Final in 1955 and were beaten by Newcastle United but returned twelve months later to beat Birmingham City (although Revie only made the side owing to an injury to Billy Spurdle). Don was named Footballer of the Year in 1955 and won all his England caps between 1954 and 1956. In November 1956 he was on the move again, joining Sunderland for £23,000 and spent two years at Roker Park before switching to Elland Road and Leeds United for £14,000. It is doubtful whether Leeds ever spent a better fee, for in March 1961 he was appointed player-manager. After surviving a relegation battle in 1962 when Leeds came close to losing their Second Division status, he set about reviving the club's fortunes. He retired from playing in 1963 and then concentrated exclusively on management. Second Division champions in 1963-64, they nearly won the double the following season, finishing second in the League behind Manchester United on goal average and runners-up in the FA Cup to Liverpool after extra time. He guided them to the League title in 1968-69 and 1973-74, the FA Cup in 1972, the League Cup in 1968 and the Inter-Cities Fairs Cup in 1968 and 1971. His period in charge at Elland Road is equally remembered for the number of times they finished runners-up in the various competitions; five times in the League, three times in the FA Cup and twice in European competitions. He remained in charge until April 1974 in order to take over as manager of England, holding the position until his sudden resignation in July 1977. It has been said that Don's lack of success as England manager was largely due to his inability to recreate the same kind of atmosphere at national level as he had at club level, but perhaps he, like others since, found it easier to deal and work with players on a daily basis, a luxury not given to national managers. He coached in the United Arab Emirates from July 1977 until May 1980. He was awarded the OBE in 1970.

Don Revie

Jack Reynolds

John REYNOLDS

Born: Blackburn, 21st February 1869
Died: Sheffield, 12th March 1917
Role: Right-Half
Career: Park Road, Distillery, Ulster, West Bromwich Albion, Aston Villa, Celtic, Southampton, Bristol St. George, Stockport County
Debut: v Scotland (a) 2-4-1892
Appearances: 8 (3 goals)

Jack Reynolds had originally been capped for Ireland whilst playing for Distillery, collecting five caps between 1890 and 1891. When he arrived in England to play for West Bromwich Albion, it was discovered he had in fact been born in England and was therefore eligible to play for them! He and another Aston Villa player, Robert Evans, are the only players to have played on both sides of an annual British fixture. Reynolds, known as Baldy throughout his career began playing with Distillery and then Ulster before signing with West Bromwich Albion in March 1892 and scored one of their goals in their 3-0 FA Cup Final win over Villa in the same year. He joined Villa in May 1893 and won two further FA Cup winners' medals as well as two League titles, finishing his career at the club the end of the double year of 1897 and then going on to play for Celtic. In fact, because of his lack of hair the committee at Parkhead nearly turned him down, believing him to be much older than he was. He then spent spells with Southampton St. Mary's and Bristol St. George before coaching in New Zealand and returned to England in 1903 to resume his playing career with Stockport County. After coaching Cardiff City for a year he moved to Yorkshire where he worked in the coalfields.

Charles Henry RICHARDS

Born: Burton, 9th August 1875
Role: Inside-Right
Career: Gresley Rovers, Notts County, Nottingham Forest, Grimsby Town, Leicester Fosse, Newton Heath
Debut: v Ireland (a) 5-3-1898
Appearances: 1

Charlie started his playing career with Gresley Rovers and joined Notts County in 1895 but spent less than a year with the club before moving across the city to sign for Nottingham Forest in January 1896. A member of the side that won the FA Cup in 1898, Charlie left Forest in December 1898 to sign for Grimsby Town where he won a Second Division championship medal in 1901. A few months after receiving his medal he was off to Leicester Fosse but spent only a matter of months with the club before joining Newton Heath where he finished his career in 1903.

George Henry RICHARDS

Born: Castle Donington, 10th May 1880
Died: 1st November 1959
Role: Left-Half
Career: Whitwick White Cross, Derby County
Debut: v Austria (a) 1-6-1909
Appearances: 1

George was an inside left-forward when he began his career with Derby County in April 1902 and played in this position in the following year's FA Cup final where Derby went down 6-0 to Bury. He was switched to left-half during the 1907-08 season, a move that worked sufficiently well for George who got called up for the England side in 1909 for the match against Austria, having been a reserve for the match against Scotland earlier that year. He also toured with the FA party in South Africa in 1910 and helped Derby win the Second Division championship in 1912. He retired during the First World War having logged up over 300 first class appearances for Derby County during his time with the club.

John Richards

John Peter RICHARDS

Born: Warrington, 9th November 1950
Role: Centre-Forward
Career: Wolverhampton Wanderers, Maritomo (Portugal)
Debut: v Northern Ireland (a - Goodison) 12-5-1973
Appearances: 1

One of the most loyal servants Wolves have ever had, he joined the ground staff upon leaving school in July 1967 and was upgraded to the professional ranks two years later. He made his debut in the 1960-70 season and went on to make nearly 400 first team appearances, netting 146 goals in the League and 24 in the FA Cup. Whilst with the club he helped them reach the final of the UEFA Cup in 1972, win the Second Division title in 1977 and lift the League Cup in both 1974 and 1980, netting one of the goals in the 2-1 success over Manchester City in 1974. He represented England at B, Under-21, Under-23 and full level and also turned out once for the Football League. He was allowed to join Derby County on loan during the 1982-83 season and subsequently released by Wolves in order to join Maritimo FC of Portugal in August 1983. After his playing days were at an end he became Wolverhampton local authorities' sport and recreation officer and is currently managing director of Wolverhampton Wanderers.

Jimmy Richardson

James Robert RICHARDSON

Born: Ashington, 8th February 1911
Died: 28th August 1964
Role: Inside-Right
Career: Blyth Spartans, Newcastle United, Huddersfield Town, Newcastle United, Millwall, Leyton Orient
Debut: v Italy (a) 13-5-1933
Appearances: 2 (2 goals) + 1 War appearance

Jimmy began his playing career with non-League Blyth Spartans whilst aged just 15 and was playing part-time whilst training to be a car mechanic. His performances for Blyth Spartans attracted the attentions of Newcastle United who paid £200 to take him to St. James' Park in April 1928. A member of the side that won the FA Cup in 1932, Charlie moved on to Huddersfield Town in October 1934 for £4,000 but returned to Newcastle three years later, his value having increased to £4,500. His second sojourn at St. James' Park lasted less than six months, however, for in March 1938 he was sold to Millwall for £4,000. He remained with Millwall throughout the Second World War and finally moved in January 1948 to become player-coach at Leyton Orient. Charlie later served the club as assistant trainer and was trainer between June 1951 and June 1955. He returned to Millwall in November 1956 as assistant trainer but had to retire shortly after through ill health.

Kevin RICHARDSON

Born: Newcastle, 4th December 1962
Role: Midfield
Career: Everton, Watford, Arsenal, Real Sociedad (Spain), Aston Villa, Coventry City, Southampton, Barnsley, Blackpool
Debut: v Greece 17-5-1994
Appearances: 1

Kevin came through the ranks at Everton and was a member of the side that won the FA Cup in 1984, the League in 1985 and the European Cup Winners' Cup the same year before being sold to Watford for £225,000 in 1986. He returned to the top flight with Arsenal in 1987 following a £200,000 transfer, earning a second League championship medal in 1989. He then went to Real Sociedad for £750,000 in 1990 and returned in 1991 to Aston Villa for £450,000 and completed his set of domestic medals with the League Cup in 1994. The following year he moved on to Coventry for £300,000 and spent two years with the club before joining Southampton. After one season with the Saints he joined Barnsley, being appointed club captain, and made 30 appearances for the club. A loan spell to Blackpool was subsequently made permanent but he retired in 1999 having made 20 appearances for the Seasiders.

Kevin Richardson

Kieran RICHARDSON

Born: Greenwich, 21st October 1984
Role: Midfield
Career: Manchester United, West Bromwich Albion, Manchester United
Debut: v USA (a) 28-5-2005 (scored twice)
Appearances: 4 (2 goals)

Kieran originally trained with Arsenal and West Ham United before being signed by Manchester United, being placed in the club's academy and going on to make his first team debut in a League Cup tie in 2002. Lack of regular action saw him sent out on loan to West Bromwich Albion in

P Q R

Kieran Richardson

January 2005 and he played a key part in that club avoiding relegation from the Premiership that season. His performances earned him a call-up into the full England side for the tour of America, having already represented his country at Under-21 level. Although Albion wished to extend his loan period into the 2005-06 season, Kieran opted to remain at Old Trafford and battle for a place in United's side.

William 'Ginger' RICHARDSON

Born: Framwellgate Moor, 29th May 1909
Died: West Bromwich, 29th March 1959
Role: Centre-Forward
Career: Horden Wednesday, Hartlepool United, West Bromwich Albion, Shrewsbury Town
Debut: v Holland (a) 18-5-1935
Appearances: 1

Bill started his professional career with Hartlepool United in 1928 having previously been associated with the club as an amateur. He made an almost instant impact as a goalscorer, prompting West Bromwich Albion to pay £1,000 for him in June 1929. By coincidence, Albion already had a William Richardson on their books, and Bill was given the added initial G, for Ginger after his hair colour, to differentiate him! Whilst the other William was concerned with stopping goals, as a centre-half, Ginger was prolific at the other end, netting 217 in some 350 League appearances. He helped Albion win the FA Cup in 1931 and reach the final again in 1935 and remained on their books throughout the Second World War. He left League football in November 1945 to sign for Shrewsbury Town where he finished his playing career. He later returned to The Hawthorns, becoming assistant trainer and holding a number of other positions within the club right up until his death in 1959.

Stanley RICKABY

Born: Stockton-on-Tees, 12th March 1924
Role: Right-Back
Career: Middlesbrough, West Bromwich Albion, Poole Town, Weymouth, New Abbot Spurs
Debut: v Northern Ireland (h) 11-11-1953 (WCQ)
Appearances: 1

After playing schools football in Stockton, Stan was signed by Middlesbrough in 1941 but struggled to make a breakthrough at Ayresome Park, making just 10 appearances for the first team before he was transferred to West Bromwich Albion for £7,500 in February 1950. He had better luck at The Hawthorns, developing into a solid and reliable defender and an integral part of the Albion side that was soon challenging for honours. Stan played a key part in helping Albion reach the FA Cup semi final in 1954 but was badly injured in the match against Port Vale, which Albion eventually won 2-1. His injury was bad enough to keep him out of the final, but his absence also had the effect of knocking Albion out of their stride in the League, for at the time there were hopes Albion might achieve a League and cup double. They eventually won the FA Cup and had to settle for runners-up spot in the League, but the injury sustained by Stan was enough to bring an end to his first class professional career. After spells in the non-League game with Poole Town, Weymouth and New Abbot Spurs, Stan worked for a life insurance firm in Birmingham and emigrated to Australia in 1969. As well as his full cap for England, Stan represented the Football League on one occasion.

Stan Rickaby

Michael Barrington RICKETTS

Born: Birmingham, 4th December 1978
Role: Forward
Career: Walsall, Bolton Wanderers, Middlesbrough, Leeds United, Stoke City, Cardiff City, Burnley
Debut: v Holland (a) 13-2-2002
Appearances: 1

Michael began his career with Walsall, joining the club in 1996 and scored 15 goals in his 90 League appearances for the club before a £500,000 transfer to Bolton in July 2000. He was a key member of the side that won promotion to the Premiership via the play-offs in 2001, netting 24 goals. He continued his goalscoring in the top flight, hitting

Michael Ricketts

15 in the first half of the season and getting called into the full England team. Unfortunately he then fell out with the management at Bolton, which was eventually resolved when he was sold to Middlesbrough for £3.5 million in January 2003. His time at Middlesbrough was not a success, however, and although he helped the club win the League Cup in 2004 he was released on a free transfer at the end of the season. He then signed for Leeds United but has had spells on loan with Stoke City, Cardiff City and Burnley to try and resurrect his career.

Arthur RIGBY

Born: Manchester, 7th June 1900
Died: 25th March 1960
Role: Inside-Left
Career: Stockport County, Crewe Alexandra, Bradford City, Blackburn Rovers, Everton, Middlesbrough, Clapton Orient, Crewe Alexandra
Debut: v Scotland (a) 2-4-1927
Appearances: 5 (3 goals)

Arthur played schools football as a goalkeeper but had switched outfield by the time he began his professional career, being briefly associated with Stockport before joining Crewe Alexandra for the first time in 1919. In February 1921 he joined Bradford City and had just over four years at Valley Parade before being sold to Blackburn Rovers for £2,500 in April 1925. It was here that Arthur's career really took off, with representative honours for the Football League being followed by a winners' medal in the FA Cup in 1928 and a call-up for the full England side. Arthur had been a left-winger for Blackburn but was played out wide by his country, although the fact that he took to the role can be gauged by his return of three goals in his five matches, scoring twice against Belgium and once against France. He moved on to Everton in November 1929 for £2,000 and helped them win the Second Division championship in 1931 after relegation the previous season. In May 1932 he joined Middlesbrough, spending a year at Ayresome Park and then Clapton Orient before returning to Crewe in August 1935. The following year he won a winners' medal in the Welsh FA Cup and retired in the summer of 1937.

Ellis James RIMMER

Born: Birkenhead, 2nd January 1907
Died: 16th March 1965
Role: Left-Winger
Career: Parkside FC, Northern Nomads, Whitchurch, Tranmere Rovers, Sheffield Wednesday, Ipswich Town
Debut: v Scotland (h) 5-4-1930 (scored twice)
Appearances: 4 (2 goals)

Ellis played schoolboy and junior football in and around his hometown, being briefly associated with Everton before signing with Tranmere Rovers in 1924. Although a winger he could be relied upon to grab more than his fair share of goals. It was this ability that caused a desperate Sheffield Wednesday, battling against relegation from the First Division, to sign him for £3,000 in February 1928. With Ellis's help and inspired by Jimmy Seed, Wednesday picked up 17 points out of 20 and avoided relegation. From this springboard they maintained this form and won successive League titles, with Ellis weighing in with 17 goals in their first championship winning season. That year they also reached the semi final of the FA Cup, prompting hopes that the double might be on, but it is Ellis's achievements in another season, 1935, that ensure his place in Wednesday's hall of fame, for he scored in every round and added two in the final four minutes of the final against West Bromwich Albion to give Wednesday a 4-2 victory. He remained at Hillsborough until August 1938 when he signed for Ipswich Town, newly elected to the Football League, but Ellis retired in February 1939. A talented pianist it was said he could have pursued a professional career in music, but after leaving the game he became a licensee.

John James RIMMER

Born: Southport, 10th February 1948
Role: Goalkeeper
Career: Manchester United, Swansea City, Arsenal, Aston Villa, Swansea City
Debut: v Italy (New York) 28-5-1976
Appearances: 1

Signed by Manchester United as an amateur in May 1963, Jimmy was upgraded to the professional ranks in May 1965 having helped them win the FA Youth Cup a year previously. He was a member of the squad for the 1968 European Cup final, collecting a winners' medal even though he did not play, and was sold to Arsenal in 1974 for £40,000 after a spell on loan to Swansea City. Here he won an England cap, but the subsequent arrival of Pat Jennings as first choice goalkeeper prompted a move to Aston Villa in 1977. He won a League championship medal in 1981 and helped the club to the European Cup final the following season, although after only eight minutes was forced to leave the field with an injury, although he once again collected a winners' medal. The form of his replacement in that match, Nigel Spink, restricted Jimmy's first team opportunities and in July 1983 he was sold to Swansea City for £35,000. He made 66 appearances in his second spell with the Vetch Field club before linking with Luton Town but retired before he appeared in their side.

Stuart Ripley

Stuart Edward RIPLEY

Born: Middlesbrough, 20th November 1967
Role: Midfield
Career: Middlesbrough, Bolton Wanderers, Blackburn Rovers, Southampton, Barnsley, Sheffield Wednesday
Debut: v San Marino (a) 17-11-1993 (WCQ)
Appearances: 2

Stuart played for Middlesbrough Boys before joining his local side as an apprentice, being upgraded to the professional ranks in December 1985. By then he had already made his debut for the first team and in 1986 had a spell on loan with Bolton Wanderers, netting in his first game for that club. He returned to Middlesbrough and would help them rise from the Third Division to the First Division and back into the top flight after relegation, all inside five years. In July 1992 he was sold to Blackburn Rovers for £1.3 million and played an integral part in the club winning the Premier League title in 1995 as well as winning two caps for England, the second coming four years after his first. Unfortunately he suffered from a number of injuries and was sold to Southampton for £1.5 million in the summer of 1998, although injuries continued to halt his progress and he had spells out on loan to Barnsley and Sheffield Wednesday. He retired from playing at the end of the 2001-02 season.

Graham RIX

Born: Doncaster, 23rd October 1957
Role: Midfield
Career: Arsenal, Brentford, SM Caen (France), Le Havre (France), Chelsea
Debut: v Norway (h) 10-9-1980
Appearances: 17

Graham was playing for Askern Schools when he was invited along for trials by Leeds United, although Arsenal stepped in first to offer him an apprenticeship in 1974. He was upgraded to the professional ranks in January 1975, finally making his first team debut during the 1976-77 season. His arrival in the first team on a regular basis coincided with the emergence of Liam Brady in the same side, giving Arsenal one of the most creative midfields of the era. First selected for England by Ron Greenwood in 1979 he went on to collect 17 caps for his country, having already won seven Under-21 caps and an appearance for the B side. He helped Arsenal win the FA Cup in 1978, and the following season to the finals of both the FA Cup and European Cup Winners' Cup, although both were to end in defeat, with Graham one of the guilty players who missed in the penalty shoot-out in the latter competition (Liam Brady was the other!). He had previously helped Arsenal reach the final of the FA Cup in 1978, this also ending in defeat. Injured during the 1983-84 season he saw the emergence of Paul Davis and David Rocastle in the midfield and struggled to hold down a regular place in the side, spending a brief spell on loan to Brentford before being released by Arsenal on a free transfer in 1988. He went to France to play for Caen and Le Havre before returning to England to link up with Glenn Hoddle at Chelsea. Although the intention was for Graham to concentrate on coaching, the three-foreigners rule then in place meant he was used in a number of European games during the 1994-95 season. He subsequently assisted Ruud Gullit and then Gianluca Vialli at Stamford Bridge as the club won the FA Cup in 1997 and the League and European Cup Winners' Cups in 1998. His career came to a sudden halt when he was sent to prison for six months for a sexual offence, but this would be a temporary measure as Chelsea agreed to hold his position open for his eventual return. Following Vialli's dismissal at Stamford Bridge, Graham found himself similarly surplus to requirements, although he subsequently became manager of Portsmouth for a brief spell and later Oxford United and Heart of Midlothian.

Graham Rix

George Robb

George ROBB

Born: Finsbury Park, 1st June 1926
Role: Left-Winger
Career: Finchley, Tottenham Hotspur
Debut: v Hungary (h) 25-11-1953
Appearances: 1

After playing for Islington Schools and Finchley, George was offered amateur forms by Spurs in 1944. When Spurs did not offer full professional terms he continued playing for Finchley as an amateur and became a schoolmaster until in December 1951 Spurs again approached him with a view to signing him on amateur forms. He duly signed and made his League debut against Charlton on Christmas Day 1951, scoring once in the 3-0 win. When Les Medley left the club at the end of 1952-53, George was persuaded to sign full professional forms and went on to give a further seven years service. During this time he won his only England full international cap (he had previously won 11 amateur caps for his country) - he played in the 6-3 home defeat by Hungary! Although he played as a winger he was a more than capable goalscorer, returning 53 goals in only 182 appearances in the League. A serious injury sustained in the 1957-58 season finally ended his playing career in May 1960, upon which he returned to being a schoolmaster at Christ's College, Finchley. He later taught English at Ardingly public school.

Charles ROBERTS

Born: Darlington, 6th April 1883
Died: Manchester, 7th August 1939
Role: Centre-Half
Career: Darlington St. Augustines, Bishop Auckland, Grimsby Town, Manchester United, Oldham Athletic
Debut: v Ireland (h) 25-2-1905
Appearances: 3

Charlie played local football in the North East before being taken on by Grimsby Town in May 1903 and establishing himself as a commanding centre-half. A fee of £600 took him to Bank Street in Clayton, the then home of Manchester United, in April 1904 and he was soon installed as club captain. As such he guided the side to their greatest moments before the First World War, the League title in 1908 and 1911 and the FA Cup in 1909. Inspirational on the field, Charlie was equally involved off it, helping to form the Players Union and serving as its chairman until 1921, often instrumental in the numerous clashes between the union and the game's rulers. Indeed, this has often been cited as the reason he did not win more caps for his country, with the selection committees getting their own back on the player they saw as a thorn in their side! Charlie remained at United, who moved to Old Trafford in 1910, until August 1913 and was then sold to Oldham Athletic for £1,300. He retired from playing in January 1919 and initially left the game, although he was lured back to Oldham in July 1921 as manager, resigning the following December and stating that nothing could beat the excitement of playing. Charlie then became a wholesale tobacconist.

Frank ROBERTS

Born: Sandbach, 3rd April 1893
Died: 23rd May 1961
Role: Centre-Forward
Career: Sandbach Villa, Sandbach Ramblers, Crewe Alexandra, Bolton Wanderers, Manchester City, Manchester Central, Horwich RMI
Debut: v Belgium (h) 8-12-1924
Appearances: 4 (2 goals)

Frank played for a number of minor League sides in Cheshire before joining Crewe Alexandra, but his association with the club was brief, switching to Bolton Wanderers in August 1914. When League football resumed after the First World War, Frank became a vital member of the Bolton side but soon found himself at loggerheads with the management of the club, for he wished to become the licensee of a hotel in the town, in contravention of club rules. Frank persisted in his requests, finally prompting Bolton to reluctantly sell him to Manchester City for £3,400 in October 1922. Here Frank concentrated on his football, collecting a runners-up medal in the FA Cup in 1926 and a Second Division championship medal in 1928. Having netted 195 goals in his 373 appearances for his two clubs he left the League game in June 1929 and signed for Manchester Central, finishing his playing career with Horwich RMI. He then became a licensee!

Frank Roberts

Graham Roberts

Graham Paul ROBERTS

Born: Southampton, 3rd July 1959
Role: Defender
Career: Southampton, Sholing, Bournemouth, Portsmouth, Dorchester Town, Weymouth, Tottenham Hotspur, Glasgow Rangers, Chelsea, West Bromwich Albion
Debut: v Northern Ireland (a) 28-5-1983
Appearances: 6

A classic case of a late developer as a player, Graham had been on the books of Bournemouth and Portsmouth as an apprentice as a youngster but broke an ankle just before Portsmouth were to offer professional terms. After he recovered he joined Dorchester Town and then Weymouth. His performances at Weymouth received rave reviews and he signed for Spurs for £35,000 in 1980. Graham made his Spurs debut in October 1980, coming on as substitute at Stoke and earning a regular place in the defence from December onwards. By the end of the season the former fitter's mate turned defender had picked up a winners' medal in the FA Cup final (having previously only visited Wembley as a ballboy!). The following season he proved to be something of an all-rounder, slotting in well in midfield and providing some much needed bite to that area of the field. In 1986 manager David Pleat sold him to Rangers where he helped them win the Scottish Premier title and in 1988 the Skol Cup. He fell out with manager Graeme Souness and was transferred to Chelsea and made captain, leading them to the Second Division title in 1989 and then being appointed player-coach. A public row with chairman Ken Bates followed and he was transfer listed and subsequently sold to West Bromwich Albion in November 1990. He then drifted back into the non-League game, taking over as player-manager of Enfield in August 1992, and later appointments included Yeovil, Chesham United and Slough.

Henry ROBERTS

Born: Barrow-in-Furness, 1st September 1907
Died: October 1984
Role: Inside-Right
Career: Barrow, Chesterfield, Lincoln City, Port Vale, Millwall, Sheffield Wednesday
Debut: v Belgium (a) 16-5-1931 (scored once)
Appearances: 1 (1 goal)

Harry represented Lancashire Schools and played local football in Barrow before joining his local club in December 1925. Six months later he was signed by Chesterfield and spent a little over two years with the club before moving on to Lincoln City in August 1928. A £100 transfer took him to Port Vale in June 1930 and the following April he joined Millwall, winning his only England cap a month after arriving. Harry remained with Millwall until the summer of 1935 and then had a trial with Sheffield Wednesday in October the same year, although he was not offered a contract and subsequently retired. Virtually all of Harry's career was spent playing in the Third Division, then the basement of the Football League, so his achievement in winning selection for England showed that he could have played at a higher level.

Herbert ROBERTS

Born: Oswestry, 19th February 1905
Died: 19th June 1944
Role: Centre-Half
Career: Oswestry Town, Arsenal
Debut: v Scotland (a) 28-3-1931
Appearances: 1

Herbie Roberts was spotted by Arsenal whilst playing part-time for Oswestry Town (and working as a gunsmith, perhaps the ultimate irony) and cost £200 when signed in December 1926. His signing, perhaps more than any other made by Herbert Chapman, turned Arsenal into a force to be reckoned with, for Chapman used Herbie to combat the change in the offside rule and made the player something of a stopper centre-half, earning him the nickname 'The Policeman'. He helped the club win the League title on four occasions, 1931, 1933, 1934 and 1935, the FA Cup in 1936 and reach the final in 1932. Despite this club success he was only capped by England on one occasion, his entirely defensive displays for his club being viewed unattractive to watch and not what the national side needed. Injury brought Herbie's playing career to an end during the 1937-38 season and he went to Margate to act as trainer. He returned to Highbury during the summer of 1938 to serve on the coaching staff and enlisted in the Royal Fusiliers at the outbreak of the Second World War. He died from erysipelas while serving in the Royal Fusiliers during the war, the illness believed to have caused his retirement from football earlier.

Herbie Roberts

Robert John ROBERTS

Born: West Bromwich, April 1859
Died: 28th October 1929
Role: Goalkeeper
Career: West Bromwich Albion, Sunderland Albion, West Bromwich Albion, Aston Villa, West Bromwich Albion, Sunderland Albion
Debut: v Scotland (h) 19-3-1887
Appearances: 3

Robert played schoolboy football in West Bromwich in a variety of outfield positions before being converted to goalkeeper, where his height (he stood 6' 4") made him an imposing sight in goal. He was signed by West Bromwich Albion in September 1879 and helped the club reach the FA Cup final in three consecutive seasons, 1886, 1887 and 1888, finally collecting a winners' medal in 1888. He also holds the honour of being the first Albion player to earn international recognition, a feat he achieved in 1887. In May 1890 he joined Sunderland Albion but returned to West Bromwich a year later, spending a season at The Hawthorns before switching across the city to join Aston Villa where he retired in 1893. He then returned to Sunderland where he worked as a plasterer.

William Thomas ROBERTS

Born: Handsworth, 29th November 1898
Died: Preston, 13th October 1965
Role: Centre-Forward
Career: Kentish Rovers, Boyce Engineers, Lord Street, Soho Villa, Leicester Fosse, Southport Vulcan, Preston North End, Tottenham Hotspur, Dick Kerr's FC, Chorley
Debut: v Belgium (a) 1-11-1923 (scored once)
Appearances: 2 (2 goals)

Tommy assisted a number of local Birmingham sides before the First World War and was briefly on the books of Leicester Fosse, although he had not played for the club when war broke out. Tommy guested for Southport Vulcan during the hostilities and it was his performances for them that alerted other clubs to his talents, with Preston North End signing him for £400 in May 1919. Leicester's loss was most definitely Preston's gain, for Tommy scored regularly whilst at Deepdale, earning a place in the Football League side in October 1922 and his first full cap for England the following November. He was sold to Burnley for £4,600 in October 1924 but broke his pelvis, restricting his appearances at Turf Moor and he returned to Preston for £1,500 in July 1926. Nearly two years later he was sold to Spurs for £1,000 but made only four appearances for the club, his earlier broken pelvis proving problematic. Tommy then left the League game to play for Dick Kerr's FC and then Chorley before retiring as a player. He then spent thirty years working as a licensee in Preston.

John Allan ROBINSON

Born: Shiremoor, 10th August 1917
Died: 1979
Role: Inside-Right
Career: Shiremoor, Sheffield Wednesday, Sunderland, Lincoln City
Debut: v Finland (a) 20-5-1937 (scored once)
Appearances: 4 (3 goals)

Jackie played junior football in Northumberland before linking with Sheffield Wednesday in 1935 and was a regular first team player whilst still in his teens. The outbreak of the Second World War and loss of seven full seasons of League football meant he made only 108 League appearances for the club and scored 34 goals by the time he left for Sunderland in October 1946, costing the Roker Park club £5,000. In three years he made 82 appearances and netted 32 goals before moving on to Lincoln City in October 1949, but a broken leg sustained in his eighth game brought his playing career to an end. Aside from his four full caps, Jackie also represented the Football League once.

John William ROBINSON

Born: Derby, 22nd April 1870
Died: Turnditch, 28th October 1931
Role: Goalkeeper
Career: Derby Midland, Lincoln City, Derby County, New Brighton Tower, Southampton, Plymouth Argyle, Exeter City, Millwall Athletic, Green Waves, Exeter City, Stoke
Debut: v Ireland (h) 20-2-1897
Appearances: 11

John was one of the leading goalkeepers of the tail end of the nineteenth and early twentieth centuries, vying with Bill Foulke for the mantle of the greatest. John began his career with Derby County in the summer of 1891 and collected his first two caps for his country whilst with the club (they came in three matches, with Foulke earning his only cap for England in between John's appearances!) before moving on to New Brighton Tower in August 1897. He earned a further two caps before moving on again to Southampton in May 1898 and was an integral part of the side that was seen as one of the best teams outside the Football League, collecting championship medals from the Southern League in 1899, 1901 and 1903 and finishing runners-up in the FA Cup in 1900 and 1902 as well as his final seven full caps. John joined Plymouth in May 1903 but never scaled such heights again, having spells with Exeter twice, Millwall and Stoke before retiring in 1912. In October of that year he emigrated to the United States but returned shortly before his death to live at Turnditch near Derby.

Paul Robinson

Paul William ROBINSON

Born: Beverley, 15th October 1979
Role: Goalkeeper
Career: Leeds United, Tottenham Hotspur
Debut: v Australia (h) 12-2-2003
Appearances: 19

After attending Beverley Grammar School in Yorkshire, Paul joined the staff at Leeds United and showed exceptional ability at the club, forcing his way into the first team ahead of England goalkeeper Nigel Martyn. Following Martyn's departure to Everton, Paul became first choice and even managed to score for the club, coming up-field late in the game against Swindon in the League Cup, scoring the equalizer that ultimately led to penalties, during which Paul saved two to earn Leeds progress into the next round. Following Leeds' relegation from the Premiership in 2004, Paul was sold to Spurs for £1.5 million, a figure now seen as one of the bargains of all time given his abilities and potential. Having seen off the challenge of Nigel Martyn at club level, Paul ultimately did the same to David James at international level.

Bryan ROBSON O.B.E.

Born: Witton Gilbert, 11th January 1957
Role: Midfield
Career: West Bromwich Albion, Manchester United, Middlesbrough
Debut: v Republic of Ireland (h) 6-2-1980
Appearances: 90 (26 goals)

A former England Youth international, he signed with West Bromwich Albion as an apprentice and rose through the ranks to make his full League debut in 1974. After 197 League appearances for West Bromwich, during which time he had been capped for England at Under-21 and full level (13 caps) he was transferred to Manchester United for a then record fee of £1,500,000 in 1981. Over the next twelve years he won just about every honour the game has to offer - three winners' medals in the FA Cup, a winners' medal in the European Cup Winners' Cup, a total of 90 England caps and, during his final two years at Manchester United, winners' medals in the Premier League. He might have won another winners' medal in the FA Cup in 1994, but United manager Alex Ferguson preferred Brian McClair to the by now 37-year old Robson. Robson was given a free transfer at the end of the season and immediately appointed player-manager of Middlesbrough with a brief to revive football in the area, in much the same way Kevin Keegan had done a few miles further north at Newcastle, and return the club to the top flight, which he ultimately did. At the end of his first season in charge he guided them to the First Division championship and in 1997 took them to the finals of both the Coca Cola and FA Cups, although they were subsequently beaten in both and relegated during the same season! They returned to the Coca Cola Cup Final the following season but were once again beaten by Chelsea, who had won the FA Cup Final clash in 1997 between the two sides! At the end of 1997-98 however he had restored Middlesbrough to the Premiership. His tenure at Middlesbrough came to an end after seven years in 2001 and he spent two years out of the game before returning for a brief spell in charge at Bradford City. Midway through the 2004-05 season he was appointed manager of West Bromwich Albion. On a personal level he was awarded an OBE for his services to football. In the World Cup match against France on 16th June 1982, Bryan scored England's fastest ever recorded goal in a competitive match after just 27 seconds.

Bryan Robson

Sir Robert William ROBSON C.B.E.

Born: Langley Park, County Durham, 18th February 1933
Role: Inside-Right, Right-Half
Career: Langley Park, Fulham, West Bromwich Albion, Fulham, Vancouver Royals
Debut: v France (h) 27-11-1957 (scored twice)
Appearances: 20 (4 goals)

Sir Bobby Robson

Yet another product of the North East, Bobby joined Fulham in May 1950 and went on to make over 150 League appearances for the Craven Cottage side before a £25,000 move to West Bromwich Albion in March 1956. Here he developed into a skilful right-sided player, able to play either up front or at half-back and broke into the England side, winning 20 caps for the full side, having already represented England at Under-23 level on one occasion and the Football League five times. He returned to Fulham in August 1962, costing the club £20,000 and making another 193 League appearances before going off to play in Canada as player-coach to Vancouver Royals. He became manager at Fulham in January 1968 but was sacked less than a year later, subsequently re-emerging as manager of Ipswich Town in January 1969. Just as Alf Ramsey had revived Ipswich's fortunes in the 1950s, so Bobby Robson revived them in the 1970s, taking them to the FA Cup in 1978 and close to the League title on a number of occasions. In 1981 he guided them to the UEFA Cup and then in July 1982, following the World Cup in Spain, accepted an invitation to take over as manager of England. He held the post for eight years, qualifying for the finals of both the 1986 and 1990 World Cup finals and taking England to the semi finals in the latter competition. He was replaced in 1990 and took over as coach to PSV Eindhoven in Holland, guiding them to successive League titles and then coached in Portugal at both Sporting Lisbon and Porto. After further domestic success he moved on to Spain and Barcelona, winning the European Cup Winners' Cup during his spell in charge and later returned to PSV for a second spell. He returned to English football with Newcastle United in September 1999 and took them into European competition in each of his seasons in charge, but six games into the 2004-05 season was relieved of his post. He was awarded the CBE in 1991 and knighted in 2002. In January 2006 he was appointed international football consultant to the Republic of Ireland, assisting Steve Staunton following his appointment as national manager.

David Carlyle ROCASTLE

Born: Lewisham, 2nd May 1967
Died: 31st March 2001
Role: Midfield
Career: Arsenal, Leeds United, Manchester City, Chelsea, Norwich City, Hull City, Selangor (Malaysia)
Debut: v Denmark (h) 14-9-1988
Appearances: 14

David Rocastle

Known as Rocky, he joined Arsenal straight from school as an apprentice and spent two years in the youth team before signing a professional contract in 1985. He soon became a regular in the first team and helped the club win the League Cup in 1987 and the League title in 1989 and 1991, although a knee injury kept him out of the side for long periods during this latter season. He was sold to Leeds United for £2 million in the summer of 1992 but injuries had started to disrupt his career and he made only a handful of appearances before a £2 million move to Manchester City in December 1993. He barely had time to settle at the club, being sold on to Chelsea for £1.25 million in the summer of 1994 and he helped the club reach the semi finals of the European Cup Winners' Cup in his first season at Stamford Bridge. Then he was hit by injuries again, spending time out on loan with Norwich City and Hull City before his contract with Chelsea expired in 1998. After one season with Selangor in Malaysia, Rocky announced his retirement in 1999. In February 2001 it was announced that he had non-Hodgkin's lymphoma and he died the following month.

Wayne Rooney

Wayne Mark ROONEY

Born: Liverpool, 24th October 1985
Role: Forward
Career: Everton, Manchester United
Debut: v Australia (h) 12-2-2003
Appearances: 30 (11 goals)

One of the most exciting talents to have emerged in the English game for some considerable time, Wayne grew up an Everton supporter and joined the club as a trainee, signing professional forms at the age of 17. By then he had already broken into the first team, becoming the youngest goalscorer in the Premiership when netting against Arsenal in October 2002 at the age of 16 years and 360 days, although this record has since been broken. Four months later he was awarded his first cap for England, becoming the youngest player to represent his country at 17 years 111 days. One hundred and six days later, against Macedonia in a European Championship qualifier, he became the youngest player to score for his country. His performances in the European Championship finals in Portugal, where he became the youngest goalscorer in the competition (it was subsequently beaten four days later) sparked intense speculation that he would be on the move after the competition. Although Everton originally stated that they would hold out for £50 million for his transfer, they eventually settled for £22 million plus as much as £5 million on top depending on appearances and success for his new club and country.

William Crispin ROSE

Born: St. Pancras, London, 3rd April 1861
Died: Birmingham, 4th February 1937
Role: Goalkeeper
Career: Small Heath, Swifts, Preston North End, Stoke, Wolverhampton Wanderers, Loughborough Town, Wolverhampton Wanderers
Debut: v Ireland (a) 24-2-1883
Appearances: 5

Billy Rose began his playing career in Birmingham with Small Heath (forerunners to the current Birmingham City club) but made his name playing in the capital for the Swifts, linking with them in 1878 and remaining seven years. He was widely regarded as one of the best goalkeepers of his era, at a time when being a specialist goalkeeper was still something of a novelty. He joined Preston North End in February 1885 for a season and then Stoke in August 1886, remaining in the Potteries until January 1889 when he joined Wolverhampton Wanderers. During his five years with Wolves he helped the club win the FA Cup in 1893, with newspaper reports of the final against Everton commenting 'Rose did not have a great deal to do, but he often showed great nerve, especially in the first half.' In July 1894 he had something of a disagreement with the committee at Molineux and was 'sacked', joining Loughborough Town for a season. The disagreement was later forgotten for in August 1895 he returned to Wolves and helped the club reach the FA Cup Final again in 1896, although he was forced to miss the final through injury. He retired during the 1896 close season and became a licensee in Birmingham and Wolverhampton and also ran a tobacconist shop in Bordesley Green, close to the home of Birmingham City. In October 1893 Billy Rose had issued a circular letter to other players that was to be instrumental in the formation of the Players Union and it is believed that this was the main reason for his sacking, although the club also dismissed fellow international players Dickie Baugh, Harry Allen and George Kinsey and George Swift at the same time.

Thurston ROSTRON

Born: Darwen, 21st April 1863
Died: Darwen, 3rd July 1891
Role: Inside-Right
Career: Helmshore FC, Old Wanderers, Darwen, Great Lever, Darwen, Blackburn Rovers
Debut: v Wales (h) 26-2-1881
Appearances: 2

Known as 'Tot' on account of his size (he was 5' 5"), he began his career with Helmshore FC and the Old Wanderers and represented Lancashire at both football and athletics. He was still a teenager when he began playing for Darwen and was the youngest member of the side that reached the FA Cup semi final in 1881. The same year he became the second youngest player to represent England at the age of 17 years and 312 days (behind James Prinsep, with both being beaten in 2003 by Wayne Rooney). Although England lost the match against Wales at Blackburn, Tot did well enough to keep his place for the next match a fortnight later against Scotland at Kennington Oval, which was also lost, 6-1. Tot left Darwen during the 1883-84 season for Great Lever but returned to his hometown club at some point in 1884. The following year he played for Blackburn Rovers in an FA Cup tie in January and a friendly the following month before seemingly drifting out of the game. Originally a weaver, Tot became a bowling green keeper but died aged just 29 in 1891.

Arthur Sydney ROWE

Born: London, 1st September 1906
Died: London, 8th November 1993
Role: Centre-Half
Career: Northfleet, Tottenham Hotspur
Debut: v France (h) 6-12-1933
Appearances: 1

Arthur signed with Spurs as an amateur in 1923, being farmed out to the nursery clubs Cheshunt and Northfleet before returning and signing as a professional in May 1929. Although he appeared in the side for a London FA Charity Cup match in 1930 his League debut didn't materialise until the following year, but once he got in the side he was there to stay. A serious knee injury in 1934 kept him out of the side long enough for the team to slip back into the Second Division. That knee injury seemed to be the start of a series of injuries that put him in and out of the side, and in April 1939 he was made available for free transfer, choosing instead to retire from playing and pursue a coaching career. He took a position in Hungary, but the sudden outbreak of the Second World War hastened his departure back to England, and he spent much of the war coaching the Army team. At the end of hostilities he accepted the position of manager at Chelmsford City and guided them to the Southern League title at the end of his first season in charge. In May 1949 he accepted the one post his career had been building towards; manager of Spurs. Although most of the team that would eventually win the Second and First Division titles in consecutive titles was in place (the only major purchase Arthur made was the acquisition of Alf Ramsey from Southampton), it was Arthur who gave them a style that became known simply as 'push and run'. After suffering a nervous breakdown in 1954 he was forced to resign. After rest and recuperation he returned to football in 1957, scouting for West Bromwich Albion, later becoming assistant manager at Crystal Palace and then in 1960 taking over at Selhurst Park. He took the club out of the Fourth Division at the end of his first season in charge, but once again found the pressures too great to bear and resigned in December 1962, returning to the backroom staff. He later served both Orient and Millwall as a consultant.

John Frederick ROWLEY

Born: Wolverhampton, 7th October 1920
Died: 28th June 1998
Role: Forward
Career: Wolverhampton Wanderers, Cradley Heath, Bournemouth & Boscombe Athletic, Manchester United, Plymouth Argyle
Debut: v Switzerland (h) 1-12-1948 (scored once)
Appearances: 6 (6 goals) + 1 War appearance

After starring for Dudley Old Boys, Jack signed with Wolverhampton Wanderers in November 1935 and was loaned to Cradley Heath and then Bournemouth in order to gain experience. His performances for the Dean Court club attracted considerable attention and in October 1937 he was sold to Manchester United for £3,500 and thus began a seventeen year association with the club. During the Second World War he guested for Aldershot, Wolves (he scored two of the goals which won the club the 1942 War League Cup), Distillery and Spurs (he was top goalscorer for Spurs when they won the Football League South in 1944) and also made his debut for England against Wales in 1944. He returned to Manchester United at the end of the hostilities and continued his rich vein of goalscoring, netting twice when United won the FA Cup in 1948 against Blackpool and was top goalscorer when they won the League in 1952. After earning selection for the England B side and Football League in 1948, Jack was selected for the full England side at the end of the year, scoring in the match against Switzerland. He netted four of England's nine goals in the 9-2 win over Northern Ireland in 1949 and later the same month scored one of the two goals that saw off Italy 2-0 at White Hart Lane. By the time he left Manchester United in February 1955 he had made 317 League appearances and scored 163 goals and he was to net a further 14 for Plymouth where he was appointed player-manager. He retired as a player in 1957 and took the club back into the Second Division in 1959, remaining as manager until March 1960, taking over at Oldham Athletic in July the same year. He was in charge at Boundary Park for three years and then headed to Holland to become coach to Ajax. He held this position for a year and resurfaced in 1966 as manager of Wrexham, later serving Bradford and finishing his career with a second spell in charge at Oldham. Known as 'The Gunner' in recognition of his goalscoring achievements, Jack played in four of the five forward positions for England. His brother Arthur holds the record for the highest number of goals scored in the League, a total of 434 goals in 619 appearances.

Jack Rowley

William ROWLEY

Born: Hanley
Role: Goalkeeper
Career: Hanley Orion, Stoke, Burslem Port Vale, Stoke
Debut: v Ireland (h) 2-3-1889
Appearances: 2

A brave and cool goalkeeper, he played for Hanley Orion and Stoke's reserve side before joining Burslem Port Vale. He returned to Stoke in the summer of 1887 and was a member of the side that was a founder member of the Football League in 1888. The club failed to gain re-election in 1890 and joined the Football Alliance, winning the championship in their first season and being re-elected into the First Division. He remained a Stoke player until 1896 when he switched to club secretary, a position he held for two years. He left in August 1898 to take up a similar position at Leicester Fosse but there was obviously some kind of objection, possibly by Stoke, for the FA would not accept his registration and he was suspended in October 1898. As a player he suffered a number of serious injuries, including a broken breastbone but usually recovered, representing Staffordshire on numerous occasions.

Joseph ROYLE

Born: Liverpool, 8th April 1949
Role: Centre-Forward
Career: Everton, Manchester City, Bristol City, Norwich City
Debut: v Malta (a) 3-2-1970 (ECQ)
Appearances: 6 (2 goals)

Joe represented Liverpool Schools and signed apprentice forms with Everton in July 1964, turning professional in

Joe Royle

August 1966 by which time he had already made his first team debut. He went on to make 272 appearances for the club, winning a League championship medal in 1970 and an FA Cup runners-up medal in 1968. In December 1974 he was sold to Manchester City for £200,000 and helped them win the League Cup in 1976, although injuries began to affect his game. After a spell out on loan to Bristol City in December 1977 he was sold to Norwich City for £60,000 in August 1980 where he retired through injury in April 1982. He was then appointed manager of Oldham Athletic, a post he would hold for twelve years, rejecting overtures from a number of clubs including Everton during that time. He finally returned to Goodison Park in 1994, guiding the club to an FA Cup final victory in 1995 but resigned in 1997 following a number of disagreements with the board. He then had a spell as manager of Manchester City until 2001 and later took over at Ipswich Town.

Herod RUDDLESDIN

Born: Birdwell, 1st January 1876
Died: 26th March 1910
Role: Wing-Half
Career: Birdwell, Sheffield Wednesday
Debut: v Wales (a) 29-2-1904
Appearances: 3

Herod joined Sheffield Wednesday from part-time local side Birdwell in the summer of 1898, initially combining his playing career with working as a collier, and slotted in well into the half-back line, being able to play equally well on either flank. He helped the club win the Second Division championship in 1900 and after three seasons consolidating their position, went on to win successive League titles in 1903 and 1904. Unfortunately Herod's health deteriorated soon after and he was forced to retire from the game in December 1906. He made an attempted comeback two years later with Northampton Town but it soon became apparent he was no longer up to the rigours of full time football.

Neil Ruddock

Neil RUDDOCK

Born: Wandsworth, 9th May 1968
Role: Defender
Career: Millwall, Tottenham Hotspur, Millwall, Southampton, Tottenham Hotspur, Liverpool, Queens Park Rangers, West Ham United, Crystal Palace, Swindon Town
Debut: v Nigeria (h) 16-11-1994
Appearances: 1

Neil joined Millwall as an apprentice and signed professional forms with the club in March 1986, yet a month later joined Spurs without having made a single appearance for the Lions! He made only nine for Spurs before a £100,000 fee took him back to Millwall, where he made two substitute appearances before joining Southampton! Here Neil finally got a chance to establish himself within the side, going on to make 107 League appearances before being lured back to White Hart Lane! Neil later fell out with the management at Spurs and was sold to Liverpool for £2.5 million in July 1993. He helped the club win the League Cup in 1995 having already represented his country before moving on again to join QPR on loan in March 1998. A permanent move to West Ham United followed in July of that year, spending two years at Upton Park before moving across the city to join Crystal Palace. Neil then joined Swindon as player-coach in August 2001 but had an acrimonious parting of the ways with the club the following year.

Jimmy Ruffell

James William RUFFELL

Born: Doncaster, 8th August 1900
Died: 5th September 1989
Role: Left-Winger
Career: Fullers FC, Chadwell Heath United, Manor Park Albion, East Ham, Wall End Albion, West Ham United, Aldershot
Debut: v Scotland (h) 17-4-1926
Appearances: 6

Although born in Barnsley, Jimmy's family moved to London whilst he was still a child and he began his playing career in local and junior football in the East and West Ham areas of the city. He joined West Ham United as a professional in March 1920 and would go on to give the club some eighteen years of service, helping them reach the first FA Cup final to be held at Wembley in 1923 and represent the Football League on three occasions. He left West Ham for Aldershot in June 1938 having made 548 appearances for the club (a record finally beaten by Bobby Moore in 1973) and received four benefits but suffered a serious injury during his first season with Aldershot and was forced to retire soon after. He then moved to Essex where he was a licensee until his retirement in 1966.

Bruce Bremner RUSSELL

Born: London, 25th August 1859
Died: 13th May 1942
Role: Left-Back
Career: Royal Military College Woolwich, Royal Engineers
Debut: v Wales (h) 3-2-1883
Appearances: 1

Educated at Cheltenham public school where he played rugby, Bruce represented the Royal Military College at football and then the Royal Engineers, whom he joined in 1878. He remained in service with the Royal Engineers until 1907, by which time he had attained the rank of colonel, although he rejoined at the outbreak of the First World War and remained in service for the duration of the hostilities.

John RUTHERFORD

Born: Percy Main, 12th October 1884
Died: 21st April 1963
Role: Right-Winger
Career: Willington Athletic, Newcastle United, Arsenal, Clapton Orient
Debut: v Scotland (a) 9-4-1904
Appearances: 11 (3 goals)

Born in Northumberland, Jock began his career with Newcastle United and made his debut for the club in 1902, scoring twice in the match against West Bromwich Albion. He soon earned the nickname 'The Newcastle Flyer', helping the club reach five FA Cup finals, although only one of these ended in victory. Indeed, Jock played a vital part in the 1910 win, equalizing in the last minute of normal time to send the final to a replay, which Newcastle won 2-1 against Barnsley. He had greater success in the League, helping Newcastle win the title in 1905, 1907 and 1909, but he fell out with the management at Newcastle in 1913 over his wages and was sold to Arsenal, then in the Second Division. Although Jock lost four seasons of football to the First World War, he was still good enough to continue playing in their side after the war. In April 1923 he left to become manager of Stoke City but four months later returned to Highbury, even though he was then 39 years old. He retired in the summer of 1925 but in January 1926 found he missed football so much he signed for Arsenal a third time, making his final appearance in March 1926 and becoming the oldest player to have turned out for the club at 41 years and 159 days. Jock left Arsenal in the summer of 1926 and spent a season with Clapton Orient, taking his total number of first class appearances to almost 600. He then went to live in Neasden where he ran an off-licence. Jock had two brothers who were professional players and his son, John James Rutherford, also became a professional, making his League debut before Jock had played his last!

S

David Seaman

SADLER, David
SAGAR, Charles
SAGAR, Edward
SALAKO, John Akin
SANDFORD, Edward A
SANDILANDS, Rupert Renorden
SANDS, John
SANSOM, Kenneth Graham
SAUNDERS, Frank Etheridge
SAVAGE, A H
SAYER, James
SCALES, John Robert
SCATTERGOOD, Ernald Oak
SCHOFIELD, Joseph Alfred
SCHOLES, Paul
SCOTT, Lawrence
SCOTT, William Reed
SEAMAN, David Andrew
SEDDON, James
SEED, James Marshall
SETTLE, James
SEWELL, John
SEWELL, Walter Ronald
SHACKLETON, Leonard Francis
SHARP, John
SHARPE, Lee Stuart
SHAW, George Edward
SHAW, Graham L
SHEA, Daniel
SHEARER, Alan
SHELLITO, Kenneth J
SHELTON, Alfred
SHELTON, Charles
SHEPHERD, Albert
SHERINGHAM, Edward Paul
SHERWOOD, Timothy Alan
SHILTON, Peter Leslie

SHIMWELL, Edmund
SHUTT, George
SILCOCK, John
SILLETT, Richard Peter
SIMMS, Ernest
SIMPSON, John
SINCLAIR, Trevor
SINTON, Andrew
SLATER, William John
SMALLEY, Tom
SMART, Thomas
SMITH, Alan
SMITH, Alan M
SMITH, Albert
SMITH, Bertram
SMITH, Charles Eastlake
SMITH, Gilbert Oswald
SMITH, Herbert
SMITH, James Christopher Reginald
SMITH, John William
SMITH, Joseph
SMITH, Joseph
SMITH, Leslie George Frederick
SMITH, Lionel
SMITH, Robert Alfred
SMITH, Septimus Charles
SMITH, Stephen
SMITH, Thomas
SMITH, Trevor
SMITH, William Henry
SORBY, Thomas Heathcote
SOUTHGATE, Gareth
SOUTHWORTH, John
SPARKS, Francis John
SPENCE, Joseph Walter
SPENCE, Richard
SPENCER, Charles William

SPENCER, Howard
SPIKSLEY, Frederick
SPILSBURY, Benjamin Ward
SPINK, Nigel Philip
SPOUNCER, William Alfred
SPRINGETT, Ronald D G
SPROSTON, Bert
SQUIRE, Ralph Tyndall
STANBROUGH, Morris Hugh
STANIFORTH, Ronald
STARLING, Ronald William
STATHAM, Derek James
STEELE, Frederick Charles
STEIN, Brian
STEPHENSON, Clement
STEPHENSON, George Ternant
STEPHENSON, Joseph Eric
STEPNEY, Alex Cyril
STERLAND, Mel
STEVEN, Trevor McGregor
STEVENS, Gary Andrew
STEVENS, Michael Gary
STEWART, James
STEWART, Paul Andrew
STILES, Norbert Peter
STOKER, Lewis J
STONE, Steven Brian
STORER, Harry
STOREY, Peter Edwin
STOREY-MOORE, Ian
STRANGE, Alfred Henry
STRATFORD, Alfred Hugh
STRETEN, Bernard R
STURGESS, Albert
SUMMERBEE, Michael George
SUNDERLAND, Alan
SUTCLIFFE, John William
SUTTON, Christopher Roy
SWAN, Peter
SWEPSTONE, Harry Albermarle
SWIFT, Frank Victor

David Sadler

David SADLER

Born: Yalding, 5th February 1946
Role: Centre-Half
Career: Maidstone United, Manchester United, Preston North End
Debut: v Northern Ireland (h) 22-11-1967 (ECQ)
Appearances: 4

Spotted by Manchester United whilst playing for Maidstone United, he was signed as an amateur in November 1962 and upgraded to the professional ranks in February 1963, by which time he had won two caps for England at amateur level. Initially used as a forward he won a medal from the FA Youth Cup winning side in 1964, but found greater first team opportunities when converted to a defensive role. In this position he won a championship medal in 1967 and a European Cup winners' medal the following year, as well as four caps for England. After loan periods in the United States he left Old Trafford in November 1973 to link up with Bobby Charlton at Preston for £20,000, but was forced to retire owing to injury in May 1977. He later worked as a branch manager for a building society.

Charles SAGAR

Born: Edgworth, 28th March 1878
Died: 4th December 1919
Role: Centre-Forward, Inside-Forward
Career: Edgworth Rovers, Turton, Bury, Manchester United, Haslingden
Debut: v Ireland (a) 17-3-1900 (scored once)
Appearances: 2 (1 goal)

Charlie began his playing career turning out for a Sunday School side before linking with non-League Edgworth Rovers and Turton. He then joined Bury in the summer of 1898 and proved more than capable of stepping up a level, representing the Football League on four occasions and helping Bury win the FA Cup in 1900 and 1903. He remained with the club until the summer of 1905 when he joined Manchester United, spending two years at Bank Street before leaving the Football League in 1907. Two years later he returned to playing with Haslingden, another non-League side.

Edward SAGAR

Born: Moorends, Doncaster, 7th February 1910
Died: 16th October 1986
Role: Goalkeeper
Career: Thorne Colliery, Everton
Debut: v Northern Ireland (a) 19-10-1935
Appearances: 4

Although initially spotted by Hull City and given a trial at Boothferry Park, Everton nipped in to offer him professional forms first. He signed in 1929 and went on to remain with the club for an astonishing 24 years and one month, the longest spell any player has spent with one club and a record unlikely to be broken. In that time he made 495 appearances for the first team, a figure that would have been much higher but for the Second World War. He helped them win the League title in both 1932 and 1939 and also collected a winners' medal in the FA Cup in 1933. In 1939 he missed only one game all season; Everton lost 7-0! Although he did not play much during the Second World War he returned to Goodison upon the resumption of League football and was still a regular in the side until 1949-50, finishing his League career with a single appearance in 1952-53, although he helped the club win the Lancashire Senior Cup in his final match of the season.

John Akin SALAKO

Born: Lagos, Nigeria, 11th February 1969
Role: Winger
Career: Crystal Palace, Swansea City, Coventry City, Bolton Wanderers, Fulham, Charlton Athletic, Reading, Brentford
Debut: v Australia (a) (substitute) 1-6-1991
Appearances: 5

John joined Crystal Palace as an apprentice and signed professional forms in November 1986 and had a spell out on loan to Swansea City as he tried to establish himself within the Palace side. Often used as a substitute, he eventually became a regular in the 1990-91 season and broke into the England side during the end of season tour of Australia. He won a First Division championship medal in 1994 but the following season left for Coventry City, costing the Highfield Road club £1.5 million for his transfer. He was unable to re-establish himself at Coventry, being released on a free transfer in March 1998, subsequently having spells with Bolton and Fulham before a £150,000 fee took him to Charlton in August 1999. Here he was used even more frequently as a substitute, making 37 appearances from the bench and only 10 starts during his time with the club, although he did help them win the First Division championship in 2000. John joined Reading for £75,000 in November 2001 and finished his career with Brentford at the end of the 2004-05 season.

John Salako

Edward A. SANDFORD

Born: Handsworth, 22nd October 1910
Role: Inside-Left
Career: Tantany Athletic, Overend Wesley, Birmingham Carriage Works, Smethwick Highfield, West Bromwich Albion, Sheffield United
Debut: v Wales (a) 16-11-1932
Appearances: 1

Teddy played schoolboy and junior football in the Birmingham area, turning out for Tantany Athletic, Overend Wesley, Birmingham Carriage Works and Smethwick Highfield before signing amateur forms with West Bromwich Albion in October 1929. Having spent most of his early career as a half-back he was converted to inside-left whilst at The Hawthorns, signing as a professional in May 1930 and quickly establishing himself in the first team. A member of the side that won the FA Cup in 1931 (at the age of 20, one of the youngest players to represent the club in a cup final) he made his only appearance for England in 1932 but returned to Wembley in 1935, again with West Bromwich Albion as they were beaten 4-2 by Sheffield Wednesday in one of the great finals. He remained with Albion until March 1939 and made 317 League appearances before being sold to Sheffield United, although the outbreak of the Second World War six months later brought his League career to an end. He continued to guest for Sheffield United during the war, reverting back to his original half-back position, and retired in 1943. He returned to Albion at the end of the war and was a scout for the club as well as running a café close to the ground.

Rupert Renorden SANDILANDS

Born: Thrapston, 7th August 1868
Died: 20th April 1946
Role: Left-Winger
Career: Old Westminsters, Corinthians, Casuals
Debut: v Wales (a) 5-3-1892 (scored once)
Appearances: 5 (3 goals)

Educated at Westminster School and a member of the school team from 1885 to 1887, Rupert played for Old Westminsters, the Casuals and the Corinthians thereafter and also represented London and Kent as well as making five appearances for England. Away from the game he worked for the Bank of England.

John SANDS

Born: 4th March 1859
Died: 29th February 1924
Role: Goalkeeper
Career: Nottingham Forest
Debut: v Wales (a) 15-3-1880
Appearances: 1

John played junior football in Nottingham and joined Nottingham Forest in 1878, making his debut for the club during that year. He remained with the club until 1883, playing his last match in January of that year and seemingly retired from the game.

Kenneth Graham SANSOM

Born: Camberwell, 26th September 1958
Role: Left-Back
Career: Crystal Palace, Arsenal, Newcastle United, Coventry City, Watford
Debut: v Wales (h) 23-5-1979
Appearances: 86 (1 goal)

Kenny was playing schools football in London when he was invited to join the ground staff at Crystal Palace, signing professional forms at Selhurst Park in December 1975. He made 172 League appearances for the club and had broken into the England setup when he was sensationally transferred to Arsenal in August 1980. Arsenal had recently bought striker Clive Allen, played him in a few pre-season friendlies but decided that their problems lay in defence and offered Allen in a swap deal for Kenny, with goalkeeper Paul Barron also part of the deal. Kenny made an immediate impact at Highbury, subsequently becoming captain and helping the club to the League Cup in 1987. The following year saw the end of both his England and Arsenal career, for a fall out with his club manager led to him being sold to Newcastle United for £300,000 in December 1988. This move did not work out for him and he was soon on his travels, playing for Queens Park Rangers, Coventry, Everton, Brentford and non-League Chertsey, although he did briefly resurface at Watford. He represented England at schoolboy, Youth, Under-23 and B level in addition to his 86 full caps. During his time at Highbury he was known to his team-mates as Norman in recognition of his impersonations of comic Norman Wisdom!

Kenny Sansom

Frank Saunders

Frank Etheridge SAUNDERS

Born: Brighton, 26th August 1864
Died: Fricksburg, Orange River Colony, South Africa, 14th May 1905
Role: Half-Back
Career: Cambridge University, Swifts, Corinthians, St. Thomas's Hospital, Sussex
Debut: v Wales (h) 4-2-1888
Appearances: 1

Frank was educated at Repton School and played for the school team in 1882 and 1883. He then attended Cambridge University, earning a Blue in 1885, 1886 and 1887 and also assisted the Swifts and the Corinthians, the latter club between 1885 and 1891. He also played for St. Thomas's Hospital and earned representative honours with Sussex. A member of the Worshipful Society of Apothecaries of London he emigrated to South Africa where he died in 1905.

A. H. SAVAGE

Role: Goalkeeper
Career: Crystal Palace, Surrey
Debut: v Scotland (a) 4-3-1876
Appearances: 1

Discovering the true identity of A. H. Savage has proved to be one of the most difficult of all the thousand plus players to have represented England, with three possibilities existing for the player who took part in the game against Scotland in 1876. These are an Alfred Henry Savage (born in Reading in 1854), Arthur Harold Savage (who died in Penang on 4th August 1930) and Arthur Henry Patrick Savage, whose credentials seem the best as some match reports of the game referred to the player as A. H. P. Savage. If this is the case, then he was born in Sydney on 18th October 1850 and died in Bayswater on 15th August 1905. In any event, the goalkeeper on the day was described as having a terrific kick that was well used to set up attacks but defensively was prone to being in the wrong place at the wrong time - England lost 3-0 on his only appearance for his country. In recent years most researchers of the England football team have given him credit for appearance in this fixture.

James SAYER

Born: Mexborough, 1862
Died: 1st February 1922
Role: Right-Winger
Career: Mexborough, Sheffield Heeley, Sheffield Wednesday, Sheffield FA, Stoke
Debut: v Ireland (h) 5-2-1887
Appearances: 1

James played for his hometown club Mexborough before going on to join Sheffield Heeley and then Sheffield Wednesday, earning representative honours with the Sheffield FA during this time. He then moved to Stoke, where he worked as a secretary for a pottery company as well as playing for the local side. A favourite of the Stoke crowd, who dubbed him 'The Greyhound' because of his speed, James continued working for the pottery company after his playing career came to an end, eventually becoming a director.

John Robert SCALES

Born: Harrogate, 4th July 1966
Role: Defender
Career: Bristol Rovers, Wimbledon, Liverpool, Tottenham Hotspur, Ipswich Town
Debut: v Japan (h) 3-6-1995
Appearances: 3

John joined Leeds United on a YTS scheme in the summer of 1984 but was released the following year and promptly signed for Bristol Rovers. He spent two years at the club, making 72 League appearances and was one of the first players former manager Bobby Gould swooped on when he was installed as manager of Wimbledon. John won an FA Cup winners' medal in 1988 and, following his switch from full-back to central defender, became one of the brightest defenders in the game. A £3.5 million transfer took him to Liverpool (the side Wimbledon had beaten in 1988) in September 1994 and John made another appearance in the FA Cup final in 1996, although Liverpool were beaten by Manchester United. In December of that year he joined Spurs but was hit by a succession of injuries and in July 2000 was given a free transfer, subsequently signing for Ipswich Town. John made just two appearances for the club before injury forced him to retire from playing.

Ernald Oak SCATTERGOOD

Born: Riddings, 29th May 1887
Died: 2nd July 1932
Role: Goalkeeper
Career: Ripley Athletic, Derby County, Bradford
Debut: v Wales (h) 17-3-1913
Appearances: 1

Ernald played junior football for Alfreton before joining Ripley Athletic, a club that already had a good pedigree in grooming goalkeepers, with Harry Maskrey subsequently going on to represent England. Ernald followed Harry to Derby as well, joining the Rams in 1907 (the transfer fee was just £11!) and spending two years in Harry's shadow. With Harry's departure in 1909, Ernald became first choice and, despite his lack of height (he was 5' 8", somewhat small for a goalkeeper) more than made up for it with his agility and safe handling. A member of the side that won the Second Division championship in 1912, Ernald won his only cap for England the following year and in October 1914 left Derby to sign for Bradford. Although the First World War

Paul Scholes

robbed him of four seasons of League football, he remained on the club's books until his retirement in the summer of 1925. His son Ken later became a professional goalkeeper for Derby and Stoke.

Joseph Alfred SCHOFIELD

Born: Hanley, 1st January 1871
Died: 29th September 1929
Role: Left-Winger
Career: Stoke
Debut: v Wales (a) 5-3-1892
Appearances: 3 (1 goal)

Joe had a relatively short career, playing junior football in and around Stoke before linking with the professional club in 1891 and being forced to retire through injury in 1899. During that time, however, he managed to win three caps for England and represent the Football League twice. After finishing playing, Joe had a number of jobs, being at times a schoolteacher and Poor Law officer and also working in the office at Stoke before becoming secretary-manager of Port Vale in February 1920, a position he retained until his death in 1929.

Paul SCHOLES

Born: Oldham, 16th November 1974
Role: Striker, Midfield
Career: Manchester United
Debut: v South Africa (h) (substitute) 24-5-1997
Appearances: 66 (14 goals)

Paul joined Manchester United as a trainee straight from school in 1991 and at the end of his first season had helped the club win the FA Youth Cup. He made his first team debut in a Coca Cola Cup tie in September 1994, scoring twice. He was a fringe player in the 1995-96 season but won a medal as the side won the Premiership title, and also collected a winners' medal in the FA Cup Final when he replaced Andy Cole. The summer arrival of many foreign imports threatened his chances of a regular place, but his ability to play in midfield or up front proved beneficial and by 1997-98 he was a regular in the side, with his current medal tally comprising six Premiership titles, three FA Cups and the European Champions League. He became a regular in the England side from 1997 and went on to register 66 appearances for his country, playing at the 1998 and 2002 World Cup finals and 2000 and 2004 European Championships. He announced his retirement from international football immediately after the 2004 championships in Portugal, preferring to concentrate on his club career and refused to reconsider his decision despite appeals from the manager.

Lawrence SCOTT

Born: Sheffield, 23rd April 1917
Died: 7th July 1999
Role: Right-Back
Career: Bradford City, Arsenal, Crystal Palace
Debut: v Ireland (a) 28-9-1946
Appearances: 17 + 16 War appearances + 2 unofficial appearances

Laurie represented Sheffield Schools and played for Edgar Allen's FC in Sheffield before signing with Bradford City as an amateur in 1931 although he was only 14 years of age at the time. He signed as a professional in May 1935 and quickly established himself as a full-back with a great future in the game, with a number of bigger clubs eagerly watching his development. In February 1937 he followed former team-mate George Swindin to Arsenal in a deal that saw Ernest Tuckett make the reverse move. Unfortunately the outbreak of the Second World War halted his progress at Highbury and during the hostilities he served as a PT instructor in the RAF and also turned out for the Royal Air Force in a number of matches. His performances in the services earned a call-up for the England side during the war, collecting the first of his 16 appearances in the 1-0 defeat by Wales in Cardiff in May 1942. At the end of the war Laurie returned to Highbury and became a regular in the side, helping the club win the League championship in 1948 and the FA Cup two years later against Liverpool. Having missed only three games during Arsenal's championship winning year, Laurie was unfortunate to suffer a succession of injuries thereafter that hindered both his club and international career, with a serious knee injury sustained in a match against Wales in November 1948 bringing a halt to his international career. In October 1951 he was transferred to Crystal Palace where he was appointed player-manager, retiring from playing in August 1953 and continuing as manager until September 1954. He then moved into non-League football, serving as manager of Hendon and then Hitchin Town before leaving football for good and working as a sales representative for a hardware firm before retiring.

William Reed SCOTT

Born: Willington Quay, 6th December 1907
Died: 18th October 1969
Role: Inside-Right
Career: Middlesbrough, Brentford, Aldershot, Dover
Debut: v Wales (a) 17-10-1936
Appearances: 1

Billy was spotted playing for Howden British Legion by Middlesbrough and joined the club in the summer of 1927, although he had to wait until 1930 before he made his first team debut. Never a regular at Ayresome Park, making only 26 appearances for the club, he was sold to Brentford in May 1932 for £1,500 and with two other players making the opposite journey. Here Billy found his mark, helping the club win the Third Division South championship in 1933 and the Second Division championship in 1935. The following season, Brentford's first in the top flight, saw them finish a very respectable fifth in the table and the following October

Billy was called into the England side. He remained at Griffin Park until August 1947, making a then record 273 League appearances for the club before joining Aldershot. Billy spent a year at Aldershot, making 21 appearances and then joined Dover where he finished his playing career.

David Andrew SEAMAN

Born: Rotherham, 19th September 1963
Role: Goalkeeper
Career: Leeds United, Peterborough United, Birmingham City, Queens Park Rangers, Arsenal, Manchester City
Debut: v Denmark (a) (substitute) 7-6-1989
Appearances: 75 + 1 unofficial appearance

David signed with Leeds United in 1981 but was unable to break into the first team and so was sold to Peterborough United for £4,000 in August 1982. After over one hundred appearances for the club he was sold to Birmingham City for £100,000 in October 1984 and spent a little under two years at St. Andrews before a £225,000 move to Queens Park Rangers in August 1986. Four years later and having broken into the England squad he cost Arsenal a then record fee for a goalkeeper, £1.3 million, when moving across London in May 1990. At Highbury he developed into one of the best goalkeepers in the country, helped in no small way by the specialist coaching he received from former Arsenal and Scotland goalkeeper Bob Wilson. David particularly worked on his penalty technique, studying all possible opponents so that he was seldom caught out. The ploy worked to perfection when Arsenal were on their way to the European Cup Winners' Cup final in 1994 and for England in the 1996 European Championship matches against Scotland and Spain. Whilst with Arsenal David won four League titles, the FA Cup four times, the League Cup and the European Cup Winners' Cup, as well as a runners-up place in the European Cup Winners' Cup Final in 1995, the UEFA Cup in 1999 and the FA Cup in 2001. In 2003 he rejected overtures from Arsenal manager Arsene Wenger to retire and become goalkeeping coach at Highbury, preferring one final season in the Premiership with Manchester City. Midway through that final season, however, he was injured and accepted that his playing days were behind him, retiring and returning to Highbury to join the coaching staff.

David Seaman

James SEDDON

Born: Bolton, 20th May 1895
Died: 21st October 1971
Role: Centre-Half
Career: Hamilton Central, Bolton Wanderers, Dordrecht (Holland)
Debut: v France (a) 10-5-1923
Appearances: 6 + 1 unofficial appearance

Jimmy played schools football in Bolton and played in the West Lancashire League with Chorley before signing with Bolton Wanderers on amateur forms during the 1912-13 season. The outbreak of the First World War put his career on hold until June 1919 when, with League football about to resume, he signed a professional contract. He soon became a key member of the defence, helping Bolton win the FA Cup in 1923, 1926 and 1929, serving as captain in this last victory. Jimmy remained a Bolton player until the summer of 1932 when he retired from playing and then headed for Holland to coach Dordrecht. He spent three years in the country before returning to England, becoming trainer at Altrincham for a year and then Southport. Whilst in Southport, Jimmy became assistant manager of a hotel and after the Second World War also had a spell on the training staff at Liverpool where his son Kenneth was briefly on the books.

James Marshall SEED

Born: Blackhill, County Durham, 25th March 1895
Died: Farnborough, 16th July 1966
Role: Inside-Right
Career: Whitburn, Sunderland, Mid Rhondda, Tottenham Hotspur, Sheffield Wednesday
Debut: v Belgium (a) 21-5-1921
Appearances: 5 (1 goal)

Jimmy Seed had been signed by Sunderland in April 1914 but enlisted in the Army and suffered from a gas attack during the First World War. When he reported back to Roker Park in 1919 it was felt he would be unable to fully recover from the effects and he was allowed to leave, his playing career seemingly ended. He was snapped up by Mid Rhondda almost immediately, although Sunderland still held his registration whilst he negotiated a free transfer. The forms came through just before he was spotted by Spurs, who were impressed whilst on a scouting mission to see another player, 'Darkie' Lowdell of Ton Pentre. Seed's transfer to Spurs caused a sensation at the time and Jimmy was soon established in the Spurs side, making his debut against Wolves in April 1920. The following season he was a member of the team that won the FA Cup, scoring five goals along the way. In late 1926 Jimmy suffered a bad ankle injury that kept him out of the side for a considerable time, Taffy O'Callaghan proving a more than adequate replacement. Jimmy was unable to reclaim his place once fully fit, and although the team should have been structured around both Seed and O'Callaghan, manager Billy Minter astonishingly allowed Seed to leave for Sheffield Wednesday, with 'Darkie' Lowdell making the reverse journey and at last joining Spurs. The transfer of Seed was to have catastrophic effects, for at the time Seed joined Wednesday they were bottom of the First Division and seemingly doomed, whilst

Jimmy Seed

Spurs were hovering around mid-table. Inspired by Seed, Wednesday picked up 17 points in 10 games and saved themselves, at the expense of Spurs, who finished bottom! Whilst Spurs languished in the Second Division, Seed inspired Sheffield Wednesday to two consecutive championships before retiring as a player in May 1931 and accepting an invitation from Arsenal manager Herbert Chapman to take over the reins at Clapton Orient. Arsenal had designs on making Orient their nursery club, but after the Football League blocked the move Arsenal took all their players out of Orient, leaving Seed with a two year struggle. He then took over at Charlton, taking the club from the Third to the First Division in consecutive seasons before the Second World War and consecutive FA Cup finals after it, winning in 1947. He was sacked in September 1956, having held the position for 23 years and became adviser and then caretaker-manager at Bristol City. He became manager of Millwall in January 1958, stepping down eighteen months later, being appointed to the board in January 1960 and holding the position until his death.

James SETTLE

Born: Millom, 1875
Role: Inside-Left, Outside Left
Career: Bolton Wanderers, Halliwell, Bury, Everton, Stockport County
Debut: v Ireland (h) 18-2-1899 (scored 3 goals)
Appearances: 6 (6 goals) + 1 unofficial appearance

Jimmy played schoolboy football in Bolton and joined Bolton Wanderers in the summer of 1894 but failed to make the grade, being released a year later and joining Halliwell Rovers. After two years with the club he returned to League action with Bury, going on to make four appearances for the Football League and collecting the first of his England caps, netting a hat-trick into the bargain. By the time he was transferred to Everton for £400 in April 1899 he had three caps to his name and was to collect a further three with the Goodison Park club. Jimmy made 269 appearances for Everton, scoring 97 goals (he was the League's joint top scorer in 1901-02 with 18 goals) and won medals in the FA Cup finals of 1906 and 1907, collecting a winners' medal in the first. In May 1908 he joined Stockport County where he finished his career a year later.

John SEWELL

Born: Whitehaven, 24th January 1927
Role: Inside-Forward
Career: Whitehaven Town, Notts County, Sheffield Wednesday, Aston Villa, Hull City
Debut: v Northern Ireland (h) 14-11-1951
Appearances: 6 (3 goals)

Jackie played for Whitehaven Schools and later Whitehaven Town, guesting for Workington and Carlisle during the Second World War before he was invited to sign as an amateur with Notts County in 1942. He was upgraded to the professional ranks in October 1944 and when League football resumed at the end of hostilities became a regular in the side, usually alongside Tommy Lawton, who joined the club in November 1947. Whilst there was considerable speculation that Lawton would soon be on the move back into the First Division (which he ultimately did in 1953, joining Arsenal via Brentford), Jackie had caught the eye of many a top flight club scout and in March 1951 he was sold to Sheffield Wednesday for a then record fee of £34,500, having helped Notts County win the Third Division (South) championship in 1950. Wednesday were relegated into the Second Division a month or two later, although Jackie more than played his part in helping them win the Second Division championship at the first time of asking in 1951-52, netting 23 goals. He also won the first of his six England caps during this spell. In December 1955, having netted 92 goals in 175 games, Jackie was sold to Aston Villa for £18,000, although he had made enough appearances for Wednesday that term to collect a second Division Two championship medal which Wednesday won at the end of the 1955-56 season. Although Jackie was not as prolific at Villa Park as he had been at Hillsborough and Meadow Lane, he did help the club reach the FA Cup Final in 1957 and collected a winners' medal as they overcame Manchester United. Jackie remained at Villa Park until October 1959 when he was sold to Hull City for £5,000. He retired from playing in 1960, having made 510 League appearances and netted 227 goals for his various clubs. Jackie then had spells playing and coaching in Zambia with Lusaka City before taking over as Zambian national coach, a position he held until May 1973.

Jackie Sewell

Walter Ronald SEWELL

Born: Middlesbrough, 19th July 1890
Died: Lincoln, 4th February 1945
Role: Goalkeeper
Career: Wingate Albion, Gainsborough Trinity, Burnley, Blackburn Rovers
Debut: v Wales (h) 3-3-1924
Appearances: 1

Ronnie played for Wingate Albion in the North Eastern League before joining Gainsborough Trinity in the summer of 1911. In 1913 he and his two full-backs impressed enough in an FA Cup tie against Burnley (which Burnley won 4-1) for the Turf Moor club to pay £1,800 to take all three players, the move causing a sensation in Gainsborough at the time. Ronnie did not become an automatic choice, being unable to displace Jerry Dawson (a future England goalkeeper), but Ronnie did step into the side for the 1914 FA Cup final when Dawson was injured and played a large part in the 1-0 win over Liverpool. Jimmy left Burnley for Blackburn Rovers in February 1920 and enjoyed a more settled time in the side, winning his cap for England a year after Dawson had collected his first. In September 1927 Jimmy returned to Gainsborough Trinity where he finished his playing career, subsequently becoming a licensee in Lincoln.

Leonard Francis SHACKLETON

Born: Bradford, 3rd May 1922
Died: 28th November 2000
Role: Inside-Forward
Career: Kippax United, Arsenal, London Paper Mills, Enfield, Bradford Park Avenue, Newcastle United, Sunderland
Debut: v Denmark (a) 26-9-1948
Appearances: 5 (1 goals) + 1 War appearance

One of the greatest characters of the post Second World War era, Len was known as 'The Clown Prince of Soccer' because of the irreverent way he went about the game. He was signed to Arsenal's ground staff in 1938 and spent loan spells with London Paper Mills and Enfield but went back home to Bradford at the outbreak of the war, subsequently signing as a professional with the local Bradford Park Avenue club in 1940, although he also guested for rivals Bradford City during the hostilities. In October 1946 he was sold to Newcastle United for £13,000 (then the third highest fee ever paid for a single player) and got off to a flying start, scoring six of United's goals in the 13-0 hammering of Newport County. 'And they were lucky to get nil' was his comment after the match. He remained at Newcastle for a little over a year before switching to North East rivals Sunderland for £20,050 in February 1948. Here he developed into an England international and a player seldom afraid to take on the game's hierarchy, although he was much appreciated by the spectators. He was forced to retire owing to an ankle injury in September 1957 but still had plenty to say about the game. In his autobiography, entitled The Clown Prince of Soccer, one page was devoted to 'what the average director knows about football' and was left blank! Upon retiring, Len became a sports journalist based in the North East and later had a spell as a director of Fulham, perhaps to bring on board someone who did know something about the game! Len was also qualified as a boxing referee.

Len Shackleton

John SHARP

Born: Hereford, 15th February 1878
Died: Liverpool, 28th January 1938
Role: Right-Winger
Career: Hereford Thistle, Aston Villa, Everton
Debut: v Ireland (h) 14-2-1903 (scored once)
Appearances: 2 (1 goal)

Jack Sharp began his League career with Aston Villa in 1897, joining them from Hereford Thistle. He struggled to hold a regular place in the Villa side, making just 23 appearances before being released and joining Everton in 1899, but at Goodison he went on to make 300 League appearances and helped them to successive FA Cup Finals (a winners' medal in 1906 and runners-up medal the following year) before retiring in 1910 to concentrate on his other passion, cricket, although he maintained his connection with Everton, serving the club as a director. Having won two caps for England at football (and represented the Football League on three occasions), he was then awarded three at the summer sport, going on to become an England selector in 1924. His brother Bert was also a notable player (and indeed played for Hereford Thistle, Aston Villa and Everton!) whilst his son was a director of Everton at one time. Jack Sharp opened his own sports goods shop in the Liverpool district of Whitechapel, a shop that was later run by his son.

Lee Sharpe

Lee Stuart SHARPE

Born: Halesowen, 27th May 1971
Role: Winger
Career: Torquay United, Manchester United, Leeds United, Bradford City, Exeter City
Debut: v Republic of Ireland (h) 27-3-1991 (ECQ)
Appearances: 8

Lee was signed by Torquay United as a trainee and under the direction of manager Cyril Knowles developed into one of the best wing prospects in the lower divisions. Indeed, after a handful of appearances for Torquay there was intense speculation that he was being targeted by the bigger clubs, signing for Manchester United for £185,000 in June 1988 after just 19 first team outings. He continued his progress at Old Trafford, complementing Ryan Giggs on the other flank as United swept to a succession of trophies and honours. Whilst with the club, Lee won three League titles, two FA Cups, the League Cup and the European Cup Winners' Cup as well one FA Charity Shield. Having represented England eight times at Under-21 level and once for the B side, Lee made his senior debut in 1991, going on to make eight appearances. Competition for places at Old Trafford saw him sold to Leeds United for £4.5 million in August 1996, although his time at Elland Road saw him struggling against injury. He moved onto Bradford City and then returned to the West Country, turning out for Torquay's rivals Exeter City.

George Edward SHAW

Born: Swinton, 13th October 1899
Died: March 1973
Role: Right-Back
Career: Gillingham, Rossington Main Colliery, Doncaster Rovers, Huddersfield Town, West Bromwich Albion, Stalybridge Celtic, Worcester City
Debut: v Scotland (h) 9-4-1932
Appearances: 1

George played schools and junior football in Yorkshire but began his professional career with Gillingham, joining the club during the 1920-21 season. Later the same season he assisted Rossington Main Colliery but returned to League football with Doncaster Rovers in the summer of 1922. Two years later he joined Huddersfield Town, then on their way to winning their first of three consecutive League championships, but George was unable to break into the first team on a regular basis. His performances were always solid, however, prompting West Bromwich Albion their then record fee of £4,100 to take him to The Hawthorns in December 1926. George settled well into the side, helping them win the FA Cup in 1931 and reach the final four years later as well as making one appearance for the Football League. He joined Stalybridge Celtic in May 1938 and almost a year later was appointed player-manager of Worcester City although the outbreak of the Second World War brought his career to an end. At the end of the hostilities he had a spell coaching in Malta until 1951.

Graham Laurence SHAW

Born: Sheffield, 9th July 1934
Role: Left-Back
Career: Oaks Fold, Sheffield United, Doncaster Rovers, Scarborough
Debut: v USSR (h) 22-10-1958
Appearances: 5

Graham was a talented boxer as a schoolboy, being good enough to be crowned an ABA champion but decided upon a career in football, joining the ground staff at Bramall Lane in 1951. He made his League debut in January 1952 and would go on to make 439 League appearances during his sixteen years associated with the club, scoring 14 goals. A former England Under-23 international, with five caps to his name, Graham also represented the Football League on five occasions. The only club honour he won however was a Second Division championship medal in 1953. Graham left Sheffield United for Doncaster Rovers in September 1967 and made a further 22 appearances before joining non-League Scarborough as player-manager in March 1968, subsequently retiring in January the following year.

Daniel SHEA

Born: Wapping, 6th November 1887
Died: 25th December 1960
Role: Inside-Right
Career: Manor Park Albion, West Ham United, Blackburn Rovers, West Ham United, Fulham, Coventry City, Clapton Orient, Sheppey United
Debut: v Ireland (h) 14-2-1914
Appearances: 2 + 2 War appearances

Danny began his career with West Ham United in 1907, playing in the Southern League and going on to represent the League on three occasions as well as netting 111 goals in just 179 League appearances. By January 1913 he was reported to have been unsettled at the club and this prompted an enquiry from Blackburn Rovers, looking to revive their League title aspirations. It cost the Ewood Park club a then record fee of £2,000 to take Danny Shea to Blackburn, and the recently changed transfer regulations meant that £550 of the fee went directly to the player. Whilst he struggled to make an impact during the rest of the season, by 1913-14 he had linked with Jock Simpson on the right wing and the pair were the focal point of that season's League title success. Danny Shea scored an impressive 28 goals in 36 League appearances that season but was also the creator of numerous chances for others as Rovers swept all before them. A call-up to the full England side soon followed and he also went on to represent the Football League twice before the season's end. At the outbreak of the First World War and the temporary halt to League football, Danny returned to London to guest for West Ham, as well as a number of appearances for Nottingham Forest. He returned to Blackburn at the end of the war and made two appearances for England in victory internationals but was not the same effective force he had been prior to 1915. In May 1920 therefore, Rovers sold him back to West Ham for £1,000, half his original fee. Unable to settle at West Ham a third time he left for Fulham in November 1920 and later made League appearances for Coventry City and Clapton Orient before finishing his playing career with Sheppey United. He then ran a sub-post office in West Ham.

Alan SHEARER O.B.E.

Born: Newcastle, 13th August 1970
Role: Striker
Career: Southampton, Blackburn Rovers, Newcastle United
Debut: v France (h) 19-2-1992 (scored once)
Appearances: 63 (30 goals) + 1 unofficial appearance

Although Alan was born in Newcastle he began his career with Southampton, one of the clubs furthest away from his

Alan Shearer

hometown! He joined the Saints as a trainee and was upgraded to the professional ranks in April 1988, making an explosive start to his career and going on to become the youngest player to score a hat-trick in the (old) First Division. After 118 League appearances for Southampton and having netted 23 goals he was sold to Blackburn Rovers for £3.6 million in July 1992, and it was at Ewood Park that he developed into a highly polished and accomplished striker. He became the first player to net as many as 30 goals in three consecutive seasons since Jimmy Greaves in the 1960s, the first player to net as many as 100 goals in the Premier League, and helped Blackburn Rovers to the Premier League title in 1995. His form at club level was repeated at international level, finishing the 1996 European Championship finals as the top scorer with five goals to his credit. Shortly after helping England reach the semi finals of the European Championship he was sold to Newcastle, costing his hometown club a British record fee of £15 million. Although he announced his retirement from international football after the 2000 European Championships, he continued to score with regularity at St. James' Park, eventually equalling Jackie Milburn's record of 200 goals for the club and subsequently beating it in February 2006. He was awarded an OBE in the 2001 New Year's Honours List having previously been named PFA Player of the Year in 1995 and 1997 and the Football Writers Association Footballer of the Year in 1994.

Kenneth John SHELLITO

Born: East Ham, 18th April 1940
Role: Right-Back
Career: Chelsea
Debut: v Czechoslovakia (a) 20-5-1963
Appearances: 1

Ken represented Essex and London schools before joining Chelsea as an amateur in May 1956, turning professional the following April. He made his League debut in 1959 but did not establish himself as a regular in the first team until 1961, in the meantime continuing to learn his craft in the reserves. He helped Chelsea win promotion to the First Division at the end of the 1962-63 season and, seen as one of the brightest full-back prospects in the game, was taken on the European tour that summer, winning a full cap against Czechoslovakia. That October he severely damaged his knee in a League fixture against Sheffield Wednesday and spent the next three years battling to recover. Although he made a number of appearances for the first team again in 1965, it was obvious that he would never get back to full fitness and was forced to retire. Ken then went into coaching, having spells at Chelsea (where he was also manager between July 1977 and December 1978), Queens Park Rangers, Crystal Palace, Preston North End and Crystal Palace as well as manager of Cambridge United.

Ken Shellito

Alfred SHELTON

Born: Nottingham, 11th September 1865
Died: Nottingham, 24th July 1923
Role: Left-Half
Career: Notts Rangers, Notts County, Loughborough Town, Heanor Town, Ilkeston
Debut: v Ireland (h) 2-3-1889
Appearances: 6 (1 goal)

Alf and his brother Charles (below) were both playing for Notts Rangers when they were spotted by Notts County and invited to join the club in the summer of 1888. Of the two, Alf enjoyed the greater success, being part of the County side that reached the final of the FA Cup in 1891 and won the competition three years later. Alf remained at Notts County until the summer of 1896 when he joined Loughborough Town, spending a year with the club before moving on again to Heanor Town. A year later Alf applied to be reinstated as an amateur and played for Ilkeston. He was later employed at shipbuilders Cammell Laird's works and was killed in a crane accident in 1923.

Charles SHELTON

Born: Nottingham, 22nd January 1864
Died: 1899
Role: Left-Half
Career: Notts Rangers, Notts County
Debut: v Ireland (a) 31-3-1888
Appearances: 1

The elder brother of Alf (above), Charles was a member of the Notts Rangers side that reached the fourth round of the FA Cup and were invited to join Notts County in the summer of 1888, by which time Charles had collected his only cap for England. Both Charles and Alf played at left-half, but Alf was usually first choice for the first team, with the result Charles slipped out of the game at the end of the 1891-92 season.

Albert SHEPHERD

Born: Great Lever, 10th December 1885
Died: 8th November 1929
Role: Centre-Forward
Career: Bolton Temperance, Bolton Wanderers, Blackburn Rovers, Bolton Wanderers, Newcastle United, Bradford City
Debut: v Scotland (a) 7-4-1906 (scored once)
Appearances: 2 (2 goals)

Albert had spells on the books of both Bolton Wanderers and Blackburn Rovers as an amateur before finally signing professional forms with Bolton in the summer of 1904. His fast all action style saw him sold to Newcastle United for £850 in November 1908 and he made an already good side (if not great, for Newcastle were in the middle of a period of domination of the domestic game) even better, helping them win the League championship at the end of his first season. The following season, 1909-10, he collected an FA Cup winners' medal and appeared to be on his way to collecting another a year later before an injury halted his progress – Newcastle reached the final but missed his presence on the day and finished runners-up. Although Albert returned to the side the following season it was felt he was not the same player again and he was sold to Bradford City in July 1914 for £1,500 but retired midway through the First World War. He later became a licensee in Bolton.

Teddy Sheringham

Edward Paul SHERINGHAM

Born: Highams Park, 2nd April 1966
Role: Striker
Career: Millwall, Aldershot, Nottingham Forest, Tottenham Hotspur, Manchester United, Tottenham Hotspur, Portsmouth, West Ham United
Debut: v Poland (a) 29-5-1993 (WCQ)
Appearances: 51 (11 goals) + 1 unofficial appearance

After unsuccessful trials with Spurs and Leyton Orient and a spell training with Crystal Palace, Teddy Sheringham was signed as an apprentice by Millwall and upgraded to the professional ranks in January 1984. He was briefly loaned to Aldershot before breaking into the Millwall side on a regular basis, going on to score 93 goals in 220 League appearances and winning a Second Division championship medal in 1988. That prompted interest from a number of other clubs, with Nottingham Forest paying £2 million to take him to the City Ground in July 1991, and he helped the club win the Simod Cup in 1992 and reach the final of the League Cup the same season. After a handful of games into the 1992-93 season he was surprisingly sold to Spurs for £2.1 million, although following the transfer it was claimed that there had been an under the counter payment made to a number of personnel involved. At Spurs, Teddy became one of the best strikers in the top flight, making up for his lack of genuine pace with his positional sense and quick footballing brain. This earned him a call-up for the England squad and he has since proved his ability to be able to link with almost any striker and form a devastating partnership, perhaps best revealed during the 1996 European Championship against Holland when he and Alan Shearer demolished the Dutch with a four goal display. In July 1997 he announced his desire to leave Spurs and Manchester United paid £3.5 million to take him to Old Trafford. After a barren first season he helped the club win the League title three years in succession as well as the FA Cup and European Cup in 1999 (he scored in both finals). He returned to White Hart Lane in 2001 and had two seasons with the club before joining Portsmouth on a free transfer in 2003. At the beginning of the 2004-05 season he joined his boyhood idols West Ham United. Apparently, only two people have ever called him Edward; his mother and Brian Clough!

Timothy Alan SHERWOOD

Born: St. Albans, 6th February 1969
Role: Midfield
Career: Watford, Norwich City, Blackburn Rovers, Tottenham Hotspur, Portsmouth
Debut: v Poland (h) 27-3-1999
Appearances: 3

Tim joined Watford, the closest professional League club to his hometown of St. Albans, as a trainee in 1987 and went on to make just over 50 appearances for the club before a £175,000 move to Norwich City during the close-season of 1989. At Carrow Road he developed into a hugely talented midfield player and was called into the England Under-21 side, making four appearances at this level for his country. In February 1992 Blackburn Rovers paid £500,000 to take him to Ewood Park and he soon established himself as captain of the club, with the high spot of his career lifting the Premier League trophy in 1995. Despite success at club level, international honours proved somewhat more elusive and he collected just a single cap at B level. At the beginning of the 1998-99 season he expressed his disillusionment with Blackburn and was seeking a transfer to Spurs, although this seemed to have collapsed and he was told he was staying put. He subsequently became one of George Graham's first signings for Spurs following his appointment as manager and was soon turning in commanding performances that brought him a call-up to the England side for the European Championship qualifier against Poland. He did not get on so well with new Spurs manager Glenn Hoddle, however and was eventually allowed to leave the club, subsequently joining Portsmouth and helping them win the First Division title and promotion to the Premiership in 2003.

Tim Sherwood

Peter Shilton

Peter Leslie SHILTON M.B.E., O.B.E.

Born: Leicester, 18th September 1949
Role: Goalkeeper
Career: Leicester City, Stoke City, Nottingham Forest, Southampton, Derby County, Plymouth Argyle, Wimbledon, Bolton Wanderers, Coventry City, West Ham United, Leyton Orient
Debut: v East Germany (h) 21-11-1970
Appearances: 125 + 1 unofficial appearance

He signed for Leicester in September 1966 and made his debut shortly after, displacing the great Gordon Banks. Indeed, it was the potential of Peter Shilton that enabled Leicester to offload Banks to Stoke City. He picked up a runners-up medal in the FA Cup with Leicester in 1969 (his only appearance in the FA Cup Final) before his transfer to Stoke, ironically following Banks, in November 1974. After three years he was signed by Nottingham Forest and formed the backbone of the side that won the League championship and two European Cups in successive seasons as well as the League Cup in 1979 and a runners-up medal the following year. After 202 appearances for Forest he moved to Southampton and made a further 188 appearances for the Saints before joining Derby County and racking up another 175 appearances. First capped for England in 1971 against East Germany, he won a total of 125 caps to become England's most capped player, a figure that might have been even greater were it not for Ron Greenwood playing Shilton and Clemence in alternate games since he couldn't decide who was the better keeper. He bowed out of international football after the 3rd and 4th place play-off in the 1990 World Cup and then joined Plymouth as player-manager, although he went into semi-retirement as a player in order to concentrate on management. When he lost his job in 1995 he resumed his playing career, going on to become the first player to appear in 1000 League matches, a figure achieved whilst playing for Leyton Orient. In addition to his 125 full caps Peter also represented his country at schoolboy, Youth and Under-23 level, collecting three caps at the latter level.

Edmund SHIMWELL

Born: Winksworth, 27th February 1920
Died: 2nd October 1988
Role: Right-Back
Career: Winksworth, Sheffield United, Blackpool, Oldham Athletic, Burton Albion
Debut: v Sweden (a) 13-5-1949
Appearances: 1

After turning out for the local Winksworth FC, Eddie was signed by Sheffield United in 1939 and played for the club throughout the Second World War. At the end of hostilities Eddie was widely expected to be one of the cornerstones upon which the club would build a side to challenge for honours, but after falling out with the board after they refused him permission to run a public house in the city, he asked for a transfer and was sold to Blackpool for £7,500 in December 1946. He would have gone straight into the first team but for unfortunate circumstances prior to the match against Charlton Athletic – his train from his Chesterfield home was held up owing to snow and he failed to arrive at The Valley until half-time! After making a delayed debut for the club on Christmas Day 1946, he became a permanent fixture in the side for the next nine seasons, helping the club reach three FA Cup finals, in 1948, 1951 and the memorable win in 1953. Although he finished on the losing side in 1948 he did set something of a record, becoming the first full-back to score in a Wembley final when he gave Blackpool the lead after 12 minutes from the penalty spot. A dislocated shoulder brought his Blackpool career to an end in May 1957 and he moved down the League to join Oldham Athletic. In July 1958 he left League football to become player-manager at Burton Albion, but less than six months later he retired from football and became a licensee in Matlock.

George SHUTT

Born: Stoke-on-Trent, 1861
Died: 1936
Role: Centre-Half
Career: Stoke
Debut: v Ireland (a) 13-3-1886
Appearances: 1

George was one of the first professional players taken on by Stoke following their adoption of professionalism in August 1885, being paid half a crown a week, although there was a threat of a strike when the club wished to introduce different pay levels and they were all given a rise to five shillings. George remained with the club until 1889 and then qualified as a referee in 1891, becoming one of the youngest referees on the Football League list. He later became the proprietor of the Borough Exchange Hotel in Stoke.

Jack Silcock

John SILCOCK

Born: Wigan, 15th January 1898
Died: Ashton-under-Lyme, 26th June 1966
Role: Left-Back
Career: Atherton, Manchester United, Oldham Athletic
Debut: v Wales (a) 14-3-1921
Appearances: 3 + 1 unofficial appearance

Jack joined United in April 1916 as an amateur, becoming a professional the following year. He made his debut in 1919 against Derby and went on to make 449 appearances for the first team over the next 17 years, with three England caps the only honour he won whilst with the club. He joined Oldham in 1934 on trial but less than a year later dropped into the non-League game with Droylsden United. Having originally been a miner before taking up professional football, he became a publican in the Manchester area following his retirement from the game.

Richard Peter SILLETT

Born: Southampton, 1st February 1933
Died: 14th March 1998
Role: Right-Back
Career: Normansland, Southampton, Chelsea, Guildford City, Ashford
Debut: v France (a) 15-5-1955
Appearances: 3

Peter had played schools football in Salisbury and was playing local football in the city when he was offered professional forms by Southampton in June 1950. He made 60 League appearances for the Saints and had been capped by England at Youth and Under-23 level when Chelsea paid £10,000 to take him to Stamford Bridge in May 1953, with the transfer deal also stipulating that a further £1,000 was payable in the event he won a full England cap. Two years later Chelsea won the League title for the first and so far only time and the following month Peter was rewarded with his first cap for the full England side. He remained at Stamford Bridge until June 1962 when he joined non-League Guildford City, later serving Ashford Town as player-manager. In addition to his three full caps for England, Peter was also awarded one cap at B level and also represented the Football League on one occasion. His brother John also played for Chelsea and later managed Coventry City to their success in the FA Cup in 1987, whilst their father Charlie had played for Southampton in the 1930s.

Ernest SIMMS

Born: South Shields. 23rd July 1891
Died: 1971
Role: Centre-Forward
Career: Munton Colliery, Barnsley, Luton Town, South Shields, Stockport County, Scunthorpe United, York City
Debut: v Ireland (a) 22-10-1921
Appearances: 1

Ernie joined Luton in the summer of 1913 having previously played non-League and junior football for South Shields Adelaide, Murton Colliery and Barnsley. He remained with the club throughout the First World War, proving himself to be a reliable goalscorer in the London Combination League and was first called into the England squad in 1920, although he was a non-playing reserve. He finally won a cap in October 1921 against Ireland and at the end of the season returned to South Shields, later joining Stockport County in January 1924. Ernie spent two and a half years at the club before moving on to Scunthorpe United and eighteen months later to York City. He then returned to the Luton area to live, working at Vauxhall Motors and assisting the works side.

John SIMPSON

Born: Pendelton, 25th December 1885
Died: 4th January 1959
Role: Right-Winger
Career: Falkirk, Blackburn Rovers
Debut: v Ireland (h) 11-2-1911
Appearances: 8 (1 goal)

Jock was born near Manchester to Scottish parents and taken to Scotland when aged six weeks. He played schoolboy football in the Falkirk area and played for a number of junior sides after leaving school, as well as working initially as an iron moulder and then training to be a bus driver. He was given a trial by Rangers during 1906-07 but subsequently signed for Falkirk the same season, going on to make one appearance for the Scottish League. In January 1911 he was sold to Blackburn Rovers for a then record fee of £1,800 and, when his birthplace was revealed, won his first England cap the following month. Jock also made five appearances for the Football League and would go on to win the League championship with Rovers in 1912 and 1914. Injury brought about his retirement during the First World War and he later returned to Falkirk where he became a licensee.

Trevor Lloyd SINCLAIR

Born: Dulwich, 2nd March 1973
Role: Midfield
Career: Blackpool, Queens Park Rangers, West Ham United, Manchester City
Debut: v Sweden (h) 10-11-2001
Appearances: 12

Trevor joined Blackpool as a trainee and was upgraded to the professional ranks in August 1990 and won representative honours for England at Youth level. He was not a regular in the Blackpool side until the 1991-92 season but soon impressed with his wing play, prompting a £600,000 transfer to Queens Park Rangers in August 1993. Here Trevor continued his progress, going on to win the first of his 14 caps for England at Under-21 level and attracting considerable interest, especially when QPR suffered relegation from the Premier League. He was sold to West Ham United for £2.3 million in January 1998 and was a regular in the side until a knee injury forced him to sit out for a lengthy period. He returned during the 2001-02 season and forced his way into the England setup, appearing in the 2002 World Cup finals. Following West Ham's relegation he was sold to Manchester City for £2.5 million in July 2003 before making his final appearance for England.

Trevor Sinclair

Andrew SINTON

Born: Newcastle, 19th March 1966
Role: Midfield
Career: Cambridge United, Brentford, Queens Park Rangers, Sheffield Wednesday, Tottenham Hotspur, Wolverhampton Wanderers
Debut: v Poland (a) 13-11-1991 (ECQ)
Appearances: 12

Andy began his career with Cambridge United, signing as an apprentice in 1982 and upgrading to the professional ranks the following year. A fee of £25,000 took him to Brentford in 1985, but he made his reputation with QPR whom he joined in 1989 for £350,000. Capped whilst at Loftus Road, he was sold to Sheffield Wednesday for £2.75 million in 1993, but struggled to command a regular place in the side. He returned to the capital with Spurs in 1996 for £1.5 million and soon rediscovered his form, returning to the fringes of the England squad. He was sold on to Wolverhampton Wanderers in 1999 and finished his playing career with Burton Albion before becoming manager of Fleet Town.

Bill Slater

William John SLATER O.B.E.

Born: Clitheroe, 29th April 1927
Role: Half-Back, Inside-Left
Career: Blackpool, Brentford, Wolverhampton Wanderers, Brentford, Northern Nomads
Debut: v Wales (h) 10-11-1954
Appearances: 12

Bill Slater was educated at Clitheroe Grammar School and played junior football in Lancashire, signing amateur forms with Blackpool in 1944. He also turned out for Yorkshire Amateurs and Leeds University from time to time. In 1951 Bill was a member of the Blackpool side that reached the FA Cup Final where they were beaten by Newcastle United and six months later joined Brentford, again as an amateur. He joined Wolverhampton Wanderers in August 1952, still an amateur, although he was persuaded to turn semi-professional in February 1954, winning his first full cap for England near the end of the year. Whilst with Wolves he won three League championship medals, in 1954, 1958 and 1959 and collected a winners' medal in the FA Cup in 1960. In fact, 1960 turned out to be an exceptional year for Bill, for he qualified as a Bachelor of Science and was also named Footballer of the Year, even though he began the season in the reserves! He returned to Brentford in May 1963 and spent one season with the club before winding down his playing career, although he made the occasional appearance for Northern Nomads. He then became deputy director of the Crystal Palace Sports Centre, was director of Physical Education at Liverpool University from November 1964 and later held a similar post at Birmingham University. From 1984 to mid-1989 he was director of National Services and in July 1989 elected president of the British Gymnastics Association. He was awarded an OBE in 1982 for his services to sport. In addition to his 12 full caps for England, Bill also represented his country 21 times at amateur level. During Bill's amateur days with Wolves, the club would often arrange a chartered plane to take him from Birmingham University to wherever they happened to be playing. On the flight to one evening match in Sheffield, the pilot lost his way and landed at RAF Worksop, with the unannounced flight immediately being surrounded by fire tenders, ambulances and several irate servicemen. That was not the end of Bill's problems, either, for he was still hitchhiking to the ground when Wolves kicked off!

Thomas SMALLEY

Born: Kingsley, 13th January 1912
Died: Wolverhampton, 1st April 1984
Role: Right-Half
Career: South Kirby Colliery, Wolverhampton Wanderers, Norwich City, Northampton Town
Debut: v Wales (a) 17-10-1936
Appearances: 1

Tom was playing for South Kirkby Colliery when he was spotted by Wolverhampton Wanderers, signing for the Molineux club in May 1931. He spent seven years with the club, making nearly 200 first team appearances but was unfortunate that the club were unable to challenge for the game's top honours. His never-say-die attitude for his club did not go unnoticed by the England selectors however and in 1936 he was awarded his only cap for England. In August 1938 he was sold to Norwich City for £4,500 and remained with the club throughout the Second World War, signing for Northampton Town in October 1945. He was still playing for the club in 1951, by which time he was over 40 years of age and had made 421 League appearances for his three clubs. Later that year he became player-coach of Lower Gornal where he finished his career.

Thomas SMART

Born: Blackheath, 20th September 1897
Died: June 1968
Role: Right-Back
Career: Blackheath Town, Halesowen, Aston Villa, Brierley Hill Alliance
Debut: v Scotland (a) 19-4-1921
Appearances: 5

Tom was playing non-League football when the First World War broke out and like many of his generation enlisted, serving in the South Staffordshire Regiment and Field Artillery during the hostilities. He represented both units at football during the war and at the end of the hostilities joined Halesowen, where he was eventually spotted by Aston Villa. He moved to Villa Park in January 1920 for £300 and was put into the first team almost immediately, with the result he won an FA Cup winners' medal only three months after joining the club. The following year Tom picked up the first of his five England caps and would go on to represent the Football League and make another appearance in the FA Cup final in 1924, this time finishing up on the losing side. Tom was a regular in the Aston Villa side for some twelve seasons and was still at the top of the game at the end of the decade, picking up his final cap for England in November 1929, four years after his previous appearance. Tom eventually retired from the top class game in the summer of 1934 but later turned out for Brierley Hill Alliance.

Alan SMITH

Born: Leeds, 28th October 1980
Role: Forward
Career: Leeds United, Manchester United
Debut: v Mexico (h) 25-5-2001
Appearances: 15 (1 goal)

Alan first linked with Leeds as a schoolboy, subsequently joining their School of Excellence and signing professional forms in March 1998. He made his debut for the club against Liverpool soon after, scoring with his first touch and eventually formed an effective club partnership with Jimmy Floyd Hasselbaink. Having earned caps for his country at Youth and Under-21 level, he was handed his first full cap in 2001, the same year he helped Leeds reach the semi finals of the Champions League, although Alan was sent off as Leeds slipped out of the competition. Following relegation from the Premiership in 2004, Alan was sold to rivals Manchester United for £7 million where he was later switched to a more midfield role.

Alan Smith

Alan Martin SMITH

Born: Birmingham, 21st November 1962
Role: Striker
Career: Leicester City, Arsenal
Debut: v Saudi Arabia (substitute) (a) 16-11-1988
Appearances: 13 (2 goals)

Alan began his playing career with non-League Alvechurch before being offered professional forms with Leicester City in June 1982. He formed an extremely effective partnership with Gary Lineker and scored 13 goals as Leicester

Alan M Smith

won promotion to the First Division. He spent five seasons at Filbert Street before a £850,000 transfer took him to Arsenal in 1987, going on to help the club win the League title in 1989 and 1991, the FA Cup and League Cup in 1993 and the European Cup Winners' Cup in 1994. The following season saw him hit by injuries and in the summer of 1995 he retired from the game having netted 115 goals in 345 matches for Arsenal. He is now a television pundit.

Albert SMITH

Born: Nottingham, 23rd July 1869
Died: 18th April 1921
Role: Right-Half
Career: Notts Rangers, Long Eaton Rangers, Derby County, Nottingham Forest, Notts County, Nottingham Forest, Blackburn Rovers, Nottingham Forest
Debut: v Wales (h) 7-3-1891
Appearances: 3

Aside from a few months with Blackburn Rovers, Albert spent his entire football career in and around the Nottingham area. He joined Nottingham Forest for the first time in February 1889, spending a year with the club before crossing the city to sign for Notts County. He returned to Forest later in 1890 and enjoyed a second year with the club before joining Blackburn Rovers in November 1891 but this move did not work out and Albert returned to Forest for a third spell, helping them win the Football Alliance in 1892 and election to the First Division. Albert remained with Forest until his retirement in 1894 and then concentrated on his business as a boot factor.

Bertram SMITH

Born: Higham, 7th March 1892
Died: Biggleswade, September 1969
Role: Right-Half
Career: Vanbrugh Park, Crawford United, Metrogas, Huddersfield Town, Tottenham Hotspur, Northfleet, Young Boys (Switzerland)
Debut: v Scotland (a) 19-4-1921
Appearances: 2

Bert began his professional career with Huddersfield Town, signing in 1913, although during the First World War he made a number of guest appearances for Spurs, usually in his normal inside-forward role, but later switched to half-back. When the war finished, Spurs manager Peter McWilliam contacted Huddersfield Town and arranged the transfer of Town's reserve inside-forward Smith and converted him into Spurs first team half-back! Indeed, so successful was the conversion that Bert was a regular in the side for the next eight years, winning a Second Division championship medal in 1919-20 and an FA Cup winners' medal the following season. He was also capped for England against Scotland in April 1921, a match that saw no fewer than four Spurs players line up for England (the other three being Grimsdell, Dimmock and Bliss). Bert finished his career at Spurs in 1930 and went on to coach Northfleet and then worked in Switzerland before becoming Hitchin Town's trainer, coach and groundsman from 1937 until his retirement in 1966.

Charles Eastlake SMITH

Born: Colombo, Ceylon, 1850
Died: 10th January 1917
Role: Forward
Career: Crystal Palace, Wanderers, Surrey
Debut: v Scotland (a) 4-3-1876
Appearances: 1

The cousin of Gilbert Oswald Smith (below), Charles was educated at Rossall School and played for the school team in 1869 and 1870, captaining the side in the latter year. He then assisted Crystal Palace (not the current club) and Wanderers and earned representative honours with Surrey. He also served on the FA Committee between 1875 and 1876.

Gilbert Oswald SMITH

Born: Croydon, 25th November 1872
Died: Lymington, Hampshire, 6th December 1943
Role: Centre-Forward
Career: Oxford University, Old Carthusians, Corinthians, Surrey, Hertfordshire
Debut: v Ireland (h) 25-2-1893
Appearances: 20 (11 goals)

Gilbert Oswald Smith is considered by many to have been the greatest centre-forward to have pulled on an England shirt, his exploits made all the greater by his amateur status. Educated at Charterhouse School, Gilbert played for the school eleven between 1889 and 1892, being made captain in 1890. He then went on to Oxford University and won his first blue in 1893, retaining his place in 1894, 1895 and 1896 and being made captain for the 1896 clash with Cambridge. He was awarded his first full cap for England whilst at Oxford University and went on to collect 20 full caps, as well as representing England at amateur level. As a member of the Old Carthusians he reached the FA Amateur Cup Final in 1895, collecting a runners-up medal, and again in 1897 when he finished on the winning side. Gilbert was also a member of the Corinthians between 1892 and 1903, serving as joint secretary between 1898 and 1902. Additionally, he was the first player to collect as many as 20 caps for England, the first to play in 10 consecutive games and the first to captain England 10 games in a row. As impressive as these figures are, they are made all the more extraordinary when one considers that he suffered from asthma for his entire life and that the Scottish, against whom he appeared seven times, did not rate him at all, citing his one goal against them as a reason! He graduated from Oxford with a Master of Arts degree and became joint head of the Ludgrove Preparatory School with William John Oakley, with whom he also shared the secretarial duties of the Corinthians club. The pair were also joint authors of the book Association Football. Gilbert was also an exceptional cricketer, winning his blue at Oxford and scoring a century against Cambridge in 1896 and representing Hertfordshire and Surrey during his career. His cousin Charles Smith (above) also represented England at football.

Gilbert Smith

Herbert Smith

Herbert SMITH

Born: Witney, 22nd November 1879
Died: Witney, 6th January 1951
Role: Left-Back
Career: Witney Town FC, Reading, Oxford City, Witney, Richmond, Stoke, Derby County, Oxfordshire
Debut: v Wales (h) 27-3-1905
Appearances: 4

Educated at Oxford County School and Beccles School he began his career with Witney Town and helped them win the Oxfordshire Senior Cup three times during the 1890s. After moving through a number of clubs he joined Oxford City and helped them to the final of the FA Amateur Cup in 1903 and two years later won the first of his four full caps for England. Once his full England career was over he won the first of 17 caps for the country at amateur level and was also selected for the United Kingdom side at the 1908 Olympic Games in London, collecting a gold medal as the United Kingdom won 2-0 against Denmark in the final. He joined the council of the Oxfordshire FA and was appointed president in 1919, holding the post until his death in 1951.

James Christopher Reginald SMITH

Born: London, 20th January 1912
Role: Left-Winger
Career: Hitchin Town, Tottenham Hotspur, Millwall, Dundee, Corby Town
Debut: v Norway (h) 9-11-1938 (scored twice)
Appearances: 2 (2 goals) + 3 War appearances

Reg was actually born with the surname Schmidt, his father being a South African rugby international who toured Britain with the Springboks and decided to stay. Reg initially played for Hitchin Town and won representative honours with Hertfordshire and the Spartan League before linking with Spurs as an amateur in the summer of 1932. He eventually turned professional with Millwall in August 1935 and helped them win the Third Division South championship in 1938, making his England debut later the same year. Reg remained on the books of Millwall until March 1946 when he joined Dundee, spending two years with the club before moving on to Corby Town to become player-manager. He returned to Dundee early in 1949 to take up the position of trainer and coach and in September 1954 moved across the city to become manager of Dundee United. In January 1957 he accepted the post of manager of Falkirk, a role that he held until May 1959. Two months later he became manager of Millwall for eighteen months, then coached in South Africa before returning to England and taking up positions as manager of Bedford Town and Stevenage.

John William SMITH

Born: Whitburn, 28th October 1898
Died: 19th January 1977
Role: Inside-Right
Career: Whitburn, North Shields Athletic, South Shields, Portsmouth, Bournemouth & Boscombe Athletic, Clapton Orient
Debut: v Northern Ireland (h) 17-10-1931 (scored once)
Appearances: 3 (4 goals)

Born in County Durham, Jack began his professional career with South Shields, joining the club in the summer of 1919. He moved to Portsmouth in December 1927, following former South Shields manager Jack Tinn to the club, and went on to appear in the FA Cup final in 1929 and 1934, although both ended in defeat. Jack represented the Football League once and made three consecutive appearances for the full England side, scoring in each of his games. Despite this record, he was not called upon again. He remained at Portsmouth until May 1935 when he moved along the south coast to sign for Bournemouth, joining Clapton Orient eighteen months later where he finished his career in February 1937 having made 570 League appearances for his various clubs. From a footballing family, Jack had three brothers that pursued a professional career, with Septimus also earning international honours with England. After retiring Jack became a licensee.

Joseph SMITH

Born: Dudley Port, 25th June 1889
Died: 11th August 1971
Role: Inside-Left
Career: Newcastle St. Luke's, Bolton Wanderers, Stockport County, Darwen, Manchester Central, Hyde United
Debut: v Ireland (a) 15-2-1913
Appearances: 5 (1 goal) + 3 War appearances (1 goal)

Joe Smith cost Bolton Wanderers just £10 when they signed him from Newcastle St. Luke's in May 1908, probably the best 'tenner' they ever spent! He guested for Chelsea during the First World War but returned to Bolton at the end of the hostilities and eventually became club captain, skippering the side to FA Cup final victories in 1923 and 1926, as well as representing England either side of the conflict. Aside from his influence on the field, Bolton benefited from his exceptional prowess as a goalscorer that would see him net 277 in 492 appearances for the club. He was sold to Stockport County for £1,000 in March 1927, spending just over two years with the club before joining Darwen and then finishing his playing career with Manchester Central and Hyde United. Joe then turned to management, taking over at Reading in July 1931 for four years before joining Blackpool in a similar capacity in August 1935. Joe enjoyed some degree of success on both sides of the Second World War, earning promotion to the First Division in 1937 and finishing League runners-up in 1956, still the highest position attained by the club. In between times came the greatest moment in Blackpool's history; having been FA Cup runners-up in 1948 and 1951, they finally got to lift the trophy in 1953, the year of 'The Matthews Final'. Joe remained manager until his retirement in April 1958, his place in the history of both Bolton and Blackpool assured.

Joseph SMITH

Born: Darby End, 10th April 1890
Died: 9th June 1956
Role: Right-Back
Career: Cradley St. Lukes, West Bromwich Albion, Birmingham, Worcester City
Debut: v Ireland (a) 25-10-1919
Appearances: 2 + 1 War appearance

Joe joined West Bromwich Albion in May 1910 and became an almost instant regular in the side, helping them win the second Division championship in 1911. He appeared in the last of the Victory Internationals in 1919 against Wales and retained his position for the first full international for five years a week later (the other Joe Smith, as above, also appeared in both these matches). A member of the side that won the League championship in the first season after the war, Joe collected his second and final cap for England in 1922. He remained at The Hawthorns until May 1926, having missed only five League games for Albion since League football resumed, and joined Birmingham City. After three years he moved to Worcester City to become player-manager, ending his involvement with football in 1932.

Les Smith

Leslie George Frederick SMITH

Born: Ealing, 13th March 1918
Died: Lichfield, 20th May 1995
Role: Left-Winger
Career: Petersham, Brentford, Wimbledon, Hayes, Brentford, Aston Villa, Brentford, Kidderminster Harriers
Debut: v Romania (a) 24-5-1939
Appearances: 1 + 12 War appearances (3 goals) + 2 unofficial appearances

Les Smith began his career as an amateur and helped Wimbledon reach the FA Amateur Cup Final in 1935, becoming one of the youngest ever finalists at the age of 17, although Bishop Auckland won on the day. He joined Hayes during the same summer, although Brentford, where he had worked in the club's office for two years, also offered him amateur forms at the same time. He was subsequently offered professional terms with Brentford in March 1936 and made his League debut at the age of 18. His progress was such that he was awarded his first full cap for England in 1939, replacing the injured Stanley Matthews for the match against Romania. The outbreak of the Second World War brought a halt to his League career, although Matthews' ability to play on either wing for the national side meant Les added a further 12 appearances for England during wartime. Les guested for Brentford (he scored twice in the London War Cup Final against Portsmouth at Wembley) and Chelsea during the war and at the end of the hostilities was sold to Aston Villa for £7,500 in October 1945. He spent seven years at Villa Park and made 181 League appearances for the club even if he was unable to break back into the full England side and returned to Brentford for a second spell in June 1952, costing the Griffin Park club £3,000. He was at Brentford for only a year before returning to the Midlands, becoming player-manager of Kidderminster Harriers in August 1953. After a single season with the Harriers he retired from playing, becoming part of the scouting setup with Wolverhampton Wanderers in 1954 and remaining with the club for two years. He later ran a radio and television business in Aston in Birmingham.

Lionel Smith

Lionel SMITH

Born: Mexborough, 23rd August 1920
Died: 15th November 1980
Role: Left-Back
Career: Arsenal, Watford, Gravesend & Northfleet
Debut: v Wales (a) 15-11-1951
Appearances: 6

After playing junior football for Mexborough Albion and Denaby United, Lionel was spotted by Arsenal turning out for Yorkshire Tar Distillers and signed as an amateur in August 1939. The outbreak of the Second World War the following month brought his career to an abrupt halt. During the war he served as a sapper, suffering injury in a crane accident, and returned to Arsenal at the end of the war. A regular in the reserve side, he was drafted into the first team at the very end of the 1947-48 season to replace Leslie Compton, away on cricket duties. Initially a centre-half, Lionel was successfully converted to left-back, switching to this position following injury to Laurie Scott which required Wally Barnes becoming the permanent right-back. Lionel made the most of this switch, becoming recognised as one of the best left-backs in the country, earning three appearances for the Football League side and in 1951 a call-up for the England side. A member of the side that reached the 1952 FA Cup final, where Arsenal were beaten by Newcastle United, compensation was received the following season when the club won the First Division championship. Lionel remained at Highbury until June 1954 when he joined Watford on a free transfer. After a season at Vicarage Road, Lionel joined Gravesend & Northfleet as player-manager in May 1955 where he finished his football career in April 1960.

Robert Alfred SMITH

Born: Langdale, 22nd February 1933
Role: Centre-Forward
Career: Redcar United, Chelsea, Tottenham Hotspur, Brighton & Hove Albion, Hastings United
Debut: v Northern Ireland (a) 8-10-1960 (scored once)
Appearances: 15 (13 goals)

Bobby joined Chelsea as an amateur in 1948 and was upgraded to the professional ranks in May 1950. He made his debut at the age of 17 and hit 30 goals in 86 games for the first team but was seldom a regular for the centre-forward slot, that honour being held by Roy Bentley. In December 1955 Spurs paid £16,000 to take him to White Hart Lane (Bobby originally refused to go but changed his mind!) where the club were engaged in a desperate battle against relegation. It was largely his goals that enabled them to build a side good enough to win the double in 1961, retain the FA Cup the following year and then win the European Cup Winners' Cup a year later. Only 5' 10", Bobby used every ounce of his 12st 11lbs weight to intimidate opponents, not only for his own benefit but also to create space and chances for his team-mates, with Jimmy Greaves in particular capitalising at both club and international level. In May 1964 Bobby was transferred to Brighton for £5,000 and scored 18 goals to help them win the Fourth Division championship in 1965 but was sacked before the start of the following season because of a series of newspaper comments. He then played for Hastings before retiring from the game, undertaking a variety of jobs thereafter.

Septimus Charles SMITH

Born: Whitburn, 13th March 1912
Role: Right-Half
Career: Whitburn, Leicester City
Debut: v Northern Ireland (a) 19-10-1935
Appearances: 1

The youngest of four brothers who played League football (with Jack Smith also representing England during his career), Sep played for Sunderland Schools and earned representative honours for England at that level before joining Leicester City in March 1929. He was to spend twenty years on the club's books as a player, although seven seasons were lost owing to the Second World War. Despite this he still managed to make 350 appearances for the club, helping them win the Second Division championship in 1937. Unfortunately, by the time Leicester made the FA Cup final in 1949, Sep was no longer a first team regular, although as Leicester had to take to the final without Don Revie, perhaps his steadying influence might have been worth a gamble. As it was, Leicester lost to Wolves and Sep left the game a month later. Sep then had three years on the Leicester coaching staff before leaving in 1950 and working as a fitter.

Stephen SMITH

Born: Hednesford, 14th January 1874
Died: 19th May 1935
Role: Left-Winger
Career: Cannock Town, Rugeley, Ceal FC, Aston Villa, Portsmouth, New Brompton
Debut: v Scotland (h) 6-4-1895 (scored once)
Appearances: 1 (1 goal)

Steve Smith was snapped up by Aston Villa in 1893 and made a bright start to his career, scoring on his debut in the 4-0 win over Burnley. At the end of his first season he had helped the club win the League title and went on to collect a further five League championship medals and a winners' medal in the FA Cup in 1895. Unfortunately, however, his career was littered by a succession of niggling injuries and he was forced to sit out the FA Cup Final in 1897 when Villa completed the 'double'. He scored on his only appearance for England, in the international at Goodison against Scotland, and despite being praised on his performance was unfortunate that England were served by an abundance of equally talented players in his favoured position on the left wing. He left Villa for Portsmouth in 1901 and helped his new club win the Southern League title at the end of his first season at Fratton Park. He then became player-manager of New Brompton (forerunners of the current Gillingham club) and held the position for two years before retiring from the game. His brother William was also a professional and played in the same side as Steve at Portsmouth, whilst his son Stephen Jr. played for a number of clubs during the 1920s.

Steve Smith

Tommy Smith

Thomas SMITH
Born: Liverpool, 5th April 1945
Role: Defender
Career: Liverpool, Swansea City
Debut: v Wales (h) 19-5-1971
Appearances: 1
Tommy Smith was spotted by Liverpool playing schools football and joined the Anfield ground staff in May 1960, subsequently turning professional in April 1962. Initially used as a centre-forward, despite the fact that he was only 5' 8" at the time, he was a regular in the reserve side by the time he was 15. The addition of a further three inches saw him become a regular for the first team, although he was switched to the midfield where his tough tackling was an important factor in Liverpool's domestic and European success during the 1960s and 1970s. Indeed, although Tommy has become legendary as one of the hardest men to have played football in recent memory, he possessed exceptional skills and could be guaranteed to weigh in with vital goals along the way. Whilst with Liverpool he helped the club win the European Cup once, the UEFA Cup twice, four League titles and the FA Cup twice as well as runners-up medals for the European Cup Winners' Cup, the FA Cup twice and the League Cup. After representing England at Youth level, Tommy went on to win 10 Under-23 caps and represented the Football League once, collecting his only full cap for England in 1971. In August 1978 he was allowed to leave Anfield, joining former Liverpool player John Toshack at Swansea City and was subsequently upgraded to player-coach in August 1979, although two months later he left following medical advice concerning his knees. He then had a spell coaching the juniors at Liverpool before leaving the game altogether in order to concentrate on his outside business interests.

Trevor SMITH
Born: Brierley Hill, 13th April 1936
Died: 9th August 2003
Role: Centre-Half
Career: Birmingham City, Walsall
Debut: v Wales (a) 17-10-1959
Appearances: 2
A talented schoolboy footballer, Trevor represented Staffordshire and Birmingham at that level and was taken on by Birmingham as an amateur in July 1952, turning professional in April 1953. He made his first team debut in October the same year and was a virtual regular in the side for the next eleven seasons, although national service caused some disruption! Trevor won numerous representative honours during his time with the club, including 15 caps at Under-23 level, one appearance in the B team and selection for the Football League twice as well as his two full caps for his country, the continued presence of Billy Wright preventing further selection for the side. A member of the side that won the Second Division championship in 1955 he helped Birmingham reach the FA Cup final a year later, although they lost to Manchester City. In 1963 however he collected a winners' medal in the League Cup as Birmingham beat local rivals Aston Villa. He was sold to Walsall for £17,000 in October 1964 having made 365 League appearances for the Blues, scoring just three goals. He made just 12 appearances for Walsall before injury forced his retirement in February 1966. He later became a licensee in the Lichfield area.

Trevor Smith

William Henry SMITH
Born: Tantobie, 23rd May 1895
Died: 13th April 1951
Role: Left-Winger
Career: Hobson Wanderers, Huddersfield Town, Rochdale
Debut: v Wales (h) 13-3-1922
Appearances: 3
One of the key players in the Huddersfield side that dominated the domestic game in the 1920s, Billy joined the club from Hobson Wanderers in October 1913 and was to spend more than twenty years patrolling the left wing, as well as earning four benefits from the club. A member of the side that won the League championship three years in succession, the first side to achieve the feat, in 1924, 1925 and 1926, Billy also collected a winners' medal in the 1922 FA Cup final and runners-up medals in 1928 and 1930. A scorer as a well as a creator of goals, Billy finally left Huddersfield in July 1934 to become player-manager of Rochdale, retiring from the playing side in the summer of 1935 and remaining as manager until November the same year. His son Conway later became a professional player with Huddersfield, QPR and Halifax Town, with the pair becoming the first father and son to net more than 100 League goals.

Thomas Heathcote SORBY
Born: Sheffield, 16th February 1856
Died: 13th December 1930
Role: Forward
Career: Thursday Wanderers, Sheffield FC, Sheffield FA
Debut: v Wales (h) 18-1-1879 (scored once)
Appearances: 1 (1 goal)
Thomas was a member of the Cheltenham College side and later played for Thursday Wanderers of Sheffield and then the more senior Sheffield club as well as representing the Sheffield FA. After retiring from playing he moved to Scarborough where he went into business.

Gareth SOUTHGATE
Born: Watford, 3rd September 1970
Role: Defender
Career: Crystal Palace, Aston Villa, Middlesbrough
Debut: v Portugal (h) (substitute) 12-12-1995
Appearances: 57 (2 goals)
Gareth joined Crystal Palace as a trainee and was upgraded to the professional ranks in 1989, helping the club win promotion to the top flight in 1994. At the end of the following season when they were relegated back, Southgate was transferred to Villa for £2.5 million and was switched from midfield to defence, subsequently forcing his way into the England side. He bounced back from a missed penalty in the European championship semi final in 1996 to retain his place in the side and was part of the foundation of the side that qualified for the 1998 World Cup finals in France. After appearing in the opening match he was injured during training and forced to sit out the rest of the tournament, returning to the team by the time qualification for the

Gareth Southgate

European Championships in 2000 came around. By then he had handed in a transfer request at Aston Villa, citing his wish to join a bigger club and eventually signed for Middlesbrough in 2001 for £6.5 million where he linked up again with former Villa team-mate Ugo Ehiogu. Gareth was made captain of the club in 2002-03 following the departure of Paul Ince and therefore got to lift the club's first major trophy, the Carling Cup, in 2004.

John SOUTHWORTH

Born: Blackburn, December 1866
Died: 16th October 1956
Role: Centre-Forward
Career: Blackburn Olympic, Blackburn Rovers, Everton
Debut: v Wales (h) 23-2-1889
Appearances: 3 (3 goals)

Jack began his career with Blackburn Olympic and switched to Rovers where he won two FA Cup winners' medals in 1890 and 1891. The following year he was awarded a testimonial by the club against Darwen and it cost Everton £400 to secure his signature in August 1893. Unfortunately he suffered with illness and injury whilst at Goodison Park and made only 32 appearances for the club, but still managed to net 36 goals. He seemed set for a blistering goalscoring career, but injury forced his retirement after just nine games of the 1894-95 season. He made 139 appearances for Rovers and Everton, scoring 139 goals, and also represented England on three occasions, scoring three goals! His ratio therefore is one of the best ever registered in League football. As well as his ability on the football field he was also an accomplished professional violinist, playing with the Hallé Orchestra!

Francis John SPARKS

Born: Billericay, 4th July 1855
Died: 13th February 1934
Role: Forward
Career: St. Albans Pilgrims, Brondesbury, Upton Park, Hertfordshire Rangers, Clapham Rovers, Essex County
Debut: v Scotland (h) 5-4-1879
Appearances: 3 (3 goals)

Francis played for St. Albans Pilgrims in 1873 and switched his allegiance later that year to join Brondesbury for the rest of the season. He also played for Upton Park between 1876 and 1878 but achieved greater success whilst associated with Herts Rangers and Clapham Rovers. He helped Clapham win the FA Cup in 1880 and also represented both Essex and London and served on the FA Committee from 1876 to 1880.

Joseph Walter SPENCE

Born: Throckley, 15th December 1898
Died: 31st December 1966
Role: Right-Winger
Career: Throckley Celtic, Scotswood, Manchester United, Bradford City, Chesterfield
Debut: v Belgium (a) 24-5-1926
Appearances: 2 (1 goal)

After starring in schools and army football, Joe was signed by Manchester United in March 1919 and made his League debut in August the same year. Joe remained at Old Trafford for fourteen years and made a then record 481 appearances in the League side, was regularly top scorer and was awarded two caps by England. In May 1933 he was released and joined Chesterfield, with whom he won his only major honour at club level; a Third Division North championship medal in 1934. He retired as a player in 1938 but retained his links with Chesterfield, scouting for them after the Second World War whilst working for the Chesterfield Tube Company until his retirement in 1965.

Dickie Spence

Richard SPENCE

Born: Platts Common, 18th July 1911
Died: March 1983
Role: Right-Winger
Career: Platts Common, Thorpe Colliery, Barnsley, Chelsea
Debut: v Austria (a) 6-5-1936
Appearances: 2

Dickie played for Thorpe Colliery and Platts Common Working Men's Club before being spotted by Barnsley and joining the Oakwell club in February 1933. He made his debut soon after and would go on to make 64 appearances and help them win the Third Division North championship in 1934 before a £4,000 move to Chelsea in October 1934. Although he joined with the season already under way, he soon settled into the side and proved a valuable acquisition, especially with his goalscoring, which brought 18 goals in his first season with the club. He remained on the club's books throughout the Second World War and when he finally retired from playing in 1950 had made 221 appearances, netting 62 goals. He then joined the training staff at Stamford Bridge and remained with the club until midway through the 1970s, having given the club more than forty years service.

Charles William SPENCER

Born: Washington, County Durham, 4th December 1899
Died: York, 9th February 1953
Role: Centre-Half
Career: Glebe Rovers, Washington Chemical Works, Newcastle United, Manchester United, Tunbridge Wells Rangers, Wigan Athletic
Debut: v Scotland (h) 12-4-1924
Appearances: 2

Charlie played minor League football in his native North East before being signed by Newcastle United in October 1921, going on to help the club win the FA Cup in 1924 and the League championship in 1927. It was in between these successes that his game changed, for he was said to have been something of an attack minded centre-half prior to 1925 and adopted a more defensive role, similar to that employed by Herbie Roberts at Arsenal, following the change in the offside rule. Charlie remained at Newcastle until July 1928 when he was sold to Manchester United for £3,250 but spent less than two years at Old Trafford before leaving League football to become player-manager of Tunbridge Wells Rangers in May 1930. He then joined Wigan Athletic in a similar capacity in August 1932 until his resignation in March 1937. Charlie was appointed manager of Grimsby Town in March 1937 and remained in charge throughout the Second World War, but ill health in May 1951 forced his resignation. He had recovered sufficiently by November 1952 to become manager of York City but died after only three months in charge.

Howard SPENCER

Born: Edgbaston, 23rd August 1875
Died: 14th January 1940
Role: Right-Back
Career: Stamford, Birchfield Trinity, Aston Villa
Debut: v Wales (h) 29-3-1897
Appearances: 6

Howard Spencer made his debut for Aston Villa in a 3-1 home win over West Bromwich Albion on 13th October 1894, thus beginning an association with the club that would stretch for 42 years. He made 294 appearances for the club and won four League titles and three FA Cups, captaining the 1905 winning side as well as six caps for England. He also represented the Football League on nine occasions and went through his career known as either 'The Prince of Full-Backs' or 'Gentle Howard', both a reference to his standing within the game and his noted fairness on the field. He retired as a player in November 1907 but returned to Villa Park in June 1909 when he joined the board and remained a director until May 1936. In his business career he was managing director of a coal and coke contracting company.

Howard Spencer

Frederick SPIKSLEY

Born: Gainsborough, 25th January 1870
Died: Goodwood, 28th July 1948
Role: Left-Winger
Career: Gainsborough Trinity, Sheffield Wednesday, Glossop, Leeds City, Southend United, Watford
Debut: v Wales (h) 13-3-1893
Appearances: 7 (5 goals)

Fred played for Jubilee Swifts before linking with Gainsborough Trinity in 1887, subsequently receiving the first of his representative honours when selected for Lincolnshire on three occasions. He joined Sheffield Wednesday in January 1891, going on to help them win the FA Cup in 1896, the Second Division championship in 1900 and the League title in 1903. The following year he joined Glossop but spent only a few months with the club before switching to Leeds City early in 1905. That summer he moved south to play for Southend United, linking with Watford later that season where he finished his playing career in the summer of 1906. Fred then moved to Germany to coach in Nuremberg and was still in the country at the outbreak of the First World War, being interred for the duration. At the end of the hostilities Fred coached for a while in Mexico and had a spell with Fulham until the summer of 1926 when he returned to Nuremberg, finally returning home for good in 1932. Fred later became a bookmaker and actually collapsed and died whilst at Goodwood racecourse.

Benjamin Ward SPILSBURY

Born: Finden, 1st August 1864
Died: Vancouver, 15th August 1938
Role: Inside-Right, Right-Winger
Career: Cambridge University, Corinthians, Derby County
Debut: v Ireland (h) 28-2-1885
Appearances: 3 (5 goals)

Educated at Repton School and a member of the school side between 1881 and 1883, captaining them in his final year, Ben was also proficient at cricket and athletics, representing the school at both these sports. He then attended Cambridge University and won a Blue in every year from 1884 to 1887, again captaining the side in his final year. By then Ben had also begun his association with both Derby County and Corinthians and therefore was probably also a cricketer with Derbyshire County Cricket Club, for it was they that were responsible for forming Derby County in 1884. Ben is certainly credited with having scored Derby's very first goal and had four years with the club before emigrating to Canada where he worked as a land agent in Vancouver.

Nigel Philip SPINK

Born: Chelmsford, 8th August 1958
Role: Goalkeeper
Career: Chelmsford City, Aston Villa, West Bromwich Albion, Millwall
Debut: v Australia (a) (substitute) 19-6-1983
Appearances: 1

He joined Aston Villa from Chelmsford City for £6,000 in 1977 and made his first team debut in 1979. In May 1982 he was thrown into the spotlight when called upon to replace the injured Jimmy Rimmer eight minutes into the European Cup Final in Rotterdam, but he performed heroics to ensure a Villa victory. By 1982-83 he had made the goalkeeper's position his own and at the end of the season won his only cap for England. He helped the club win the League Cup in 1994 before losing his place to Mark Bosnich and was subsequently allowed to join West Bromwich Albion on a free transfer in 1996 having made nearly 300 appearances for Villa. He is currently goalkeeping coach at Birmingham City.

Nigel Spink

William Alfred SPOUNCER

Born: Gainsborough, 1st July 1877
Died: 31st August 1962
Role: Left-Winger
Career: Gainsborough Trinity, Sheffield United, Nottingham Forest
Debut: v Wales (a) 26-3-1900
Appearances: 1

William attended Gainsborough Grammar School and played for the school team in 1889. He joined Gainsborough Trinity in 1893 and spent two years with the club before moving on to Sheffield United. Eighteen months later he cost Nottingham Forest £125 for his transfer and would go on to help the club win the FA Cup in 1898 and the Second Division championship in 1907. He remained at Forest until 1910 by which time he had made 338 appearances for the first team. He then switched to coaching throughout Europe, including a spell at Barcelona.

Ronald Derrick SPRINGETT

Born: Fulham, 22nd July 1935
Role: Goalkeeper
Career: Victoria United, Queens Park Rangers, Sheffield Wednesday, Queens Park Rangers, Ashford Town
Debut: v Northern Ireland (h) 18-11-1959
Appearances: 33

Spotted by QPR whilst playing for local side Victoria United, Ron signed with the Loftus Road club in February 1953 and made his debut two years later. His performances for the Division Three side were duly noted by bigger clubs and in March 1958 he was sold to Sheffield Wednesday for a fee variously reported to be between £9,000 and £15,000. His first season in the top flight was not a success, however, as Wednesday were relegated into the Second Division, but he proved to be one of the best goalkeepers in the country during 1959-60, keeping clean sheets in 13 out of the 32 matches he played, earning a call-up to the Football League and England sides the same season. He went on to collect a Second Division championship medal that season and established himself as England's first choice for the next four years. Following the arrival of Alf Ramsey as manager and defeat against France, Ron was replaced by Gordon Banks, although he still made a further four appearances for his country and was a member of the squad for the 1966 World Cup. That same year he helped Sheffield Wednesday reach the final of the FA Cup where they lost to Everton. In May 1967 a £16,000 deal saw him return to Loftus Road, with his brother Peter making the opposite journey, where he finished his League career having made a total of 478 appearances for the two clubs. Ron was later involved in a gardening business.

Ron Springett

Bert SPROSTON

Born: Ellworth, 22nd June 1915
Died: 27th January 2000
Role: Right-Back
Career: Sandbach Ramblers, Leeds United, Tottenham Hotspur, Manchester City
Debut: v Wales (a) 17-10-1936
Appearances: 11 + 2 War appearances

Bert played in the Cheshire League with Sandbach Ramblers and had a trial with Huddersfield Town before joining Leeds United in May 1933. He made 130 appearances for the Elland Road club before a £9,500 transfer took him to Spurs in June 1938, already an established England international. Bert made a further two appearances for his country whilst at White Hart Lane, but only nine for Spurs in five months. On 5th November 1938 he was due to have played for Spurs in the match against Manchester City, but having previously complained that he was unable to settle in London was transferred to City the day before the game

Bert Sproston

for £9,500 and therefore played for City against Spurs! He helped City win the Second Division championship in 1947 and made 125 appearances for the club before retiring in the summer of 1950. He then became trainer to Bolton Wanderers before switching to scouting, a position he retained into the 1980s.

Ralph Tyndall SQUIRE

Born: London, 10th September 1863
Died: 22nd August 1944
Role: Full-Back
Career: Cambridge University, Old Westminsters, Clapham Rovers, Corinthians
Debut: v Ireland (a) 13-3-1886
Appearances: 3

Educated at Westminster School and a member of the school side between 1880 and 1882, Ralph then attended Cambridge University where he won a Blue in 1884 and 1886 (he was unavailable in 1885 as he was secretary of the club at the time). After graduation Ralph played for Old Westminster and Clapham Rovers and also turned out for Corinthians between 1886 and 1892, later serving as treasurer for Corinthians from 1903 and also won representative honours with London. He also served on the FA Committee between 1884 and 1887.

Morris Hugh STANBROUGH

Born: Cleobury, 2nd September 1870
Died: Broadstairs, 15th December 1904
Role: Left-Winger
Career: Cambridge University, Old Carthusians, Corinthians
Debut: v Wales (h) 18-3-1895
Appearances: 1 + 1 unofficial appearance

Hugh attended Charterhouse School and was a member of the school team in 1889. He then continued his education at Cambridge University, earning a Blue in 1890, 1891 and 1892, being captain in 1892. After leaving university, Hugh played for Old Carthusians, helping them win the FA Amateur Cup in 1894 and reach the final the following year, as well as turning out for Corinthians between 1890 and 1904. He later played for Eastbourne before a knee injury brought his playing career to a halt. He was a schoolmaster by profession and was teaching at St. Peter's School in Broadstairs at the time of his death at the age of 34.

Ronald STANIFORTH

Born: Manchester, 13th April 1924
Role: Right-Back
Career: Newton Albion, Stockport County, Huddersfield Town, Sheffield Wednesday, Barrow
Debut: v Scotland (a) 3-4-1954 (WCQ)
Appearances: 8

After wartime service in the Royal Navy, Ron was playing non-League football with Newton Albion and working as a milkman when he wrote to Stockport County to ask for a trial. He duly impressed and was signed as an amateur in August 1946, being upgraded to the professional ranks barely six weeks later. Over the next six years Ron became a regular in the side, making 223 League appearances for the Hatters. When manager Andy Beattie left to take over at Huddersfield Town, he soon returned to Edgeley Park to lure Ron to Leeds Road, with a £1,000 transfer fee and another player being agreed between the two clubs in May 1952. Ron helped Huddersfield win promotion to the First Division in his time at Leeds Road, before moving on to Sheffield Wednesday in July 1955 and helped them win the Second Division championship in both 1956 and 1959. In October 1959 Ron became player-manager at Barrow, retiring from playing in 1961 and remaining manager until July 1964. At the end of the decade Ron rejoined Sheffield Wednesday, initially as assistant coach and then chief coach in March 1971, later having a spell as youth team coach. As well as eight caps for the full England side, Ron also played three times for the England B team.

Ron Staniforth

Ronald William STARLING

Born: Pelaw, 11th October 1909
Died: Sheffield, 17th December 1991
Role: Inside-Forward
Career: Washington Colliery, Hull City, Newcastle United, Sheffield Wednesday, Aston Villa
Debut: v Scotland (a) 1-4-1933
Appearances: 2

Although Ronnie was widely tipped for future stardom, he was ignored as a schoolboy and so took a job working down the coal mine at Unsworth Colliery and later Washington Colliery, turning out for the works side in his spare time. In 1927 he came to the attention of former Newcastle United defender turned Hull City manager, Bill McCracken, and offered immediate forms. As Ronnie was still unsure as to whether he might make the grade as a player, McCracken suggested he sign as an amateur and come to work at Boothferry Park as an office boy, a more than adequate compromise. This arrangement remained in force for the next two years before Newcastle United moved in with an offer of professional terms and a transfer fee of £3,750. His move to St. James' Park did not work out to be much of a success and in 1932 he was allowed to join Sheffield Wednesday. This move proved to be the making of Ronnie Starling, for he was captain when they won the FA Cup in 1935 against West Bromwich Albion and won his two caps for England. In January 1937 he was sold to Aston Villa for £7,500 and proved the inspiration behind the side that won the Second Division title in 1938 and a winners' medal in the League Cup (North) during the Second World War. Ronnie guested for Walsall during the war and made his final League appearance for Villa in April 1947 before retiring. In later years he ran a newsagents business in Sheffield.

Derek James STATHAM

Born: Wolverhampton, 24th March 1959
Role: Left-Back
Career: West Bromwich Albion, Southampton, Stoke City, Walsall
Debut: v Wales (h) 23-2-1983
Appearances: 3

Derek played schoolboy football in the Wolverhampton area before being taken on as an apprentice at West Bromwich Albion in July 1975, being upgraded to the professional ranks in April 1976. He made his League debut in December that year, going on to earn representative honours for England at Youth, Under-21 and B level before being called up for his first full cap in 1983. A succession of injuries meant he was restricted to just three caps and in August 1987 he was sold to Southampton for £100,000 having made 299 appearances for Albion. He was to enjoy two years at The Dell, making 64 appearances before returning to the Midlands to play for Stoke City and then Walsall before leaving League football to turn out for Telford United.

Derek Statham

Freddie Steele

Frederick Charles STEELE

Born: Stoke, 6th May 1916
Died: 23rd April 1976
Role: Centre-Forward
Career: Downings FC, Stoke City, Mansfield Town, Port Vale
Debut: v Wales (a) 17-10-1936
Appearances: 6 (8 goals)

Freddie joined Stoke City as an amateur in 1931 before being upgraded to the professional ranks in August 1933 and made his League debut as an inside-right at the age of 18. It was a switch to centre-forward during the 1935-36 season that attracted wider attention, for he would go on to net 140 goals in 224 League appearances for Stoke, including 33 in 35 matches in the 1936-37 season. Freddie also represented the Football League twice during his time at Stoke. He moved on to Mansfield Town for £750 as player-manager in July 1949 and hit 39 goals in 53 games before being appointed player-manager of Port Vale in December 1951. He retired from playing in May 1953, having made 25 appearances for the club (and scored 12 goals) and remained as manager until January 1957. Freddie then had a spell as a licensee before returning to Port Vale as manager in October 1962, a position he held until February 1965.

Brian STEIN

Born: Cape Town, South Africa, 19th October 1957
Role: Forward
Career: Edgware Town, Luton Town, Annecy, Luton Town, Barnet
Debut: v France (a) 29-2-1984
Appearances: 1

Brian was born in South Africa, one of nine children born to a father who was under house arrest because of his opposition to the apartheid system in the country. The family were allowed to leave South Africa in 1965 and came to London, with Brian going on to play for North London and North Paddington schools. He was spotted by Luton whilst playing for Edgware Town and cost the Kenilworth Road club £1,000 when he signed in October 1977. Brian was to enjoy fourteen years at the club, helping them win the Second Division championship in 1982 and the League Cup in 1988 where he scored two of their goals. That summer he left the club for Annecy in France but returned to Kenilworth Road in July 1991 for a season before moving on to Barnet where he finished his playing career. He is the elder brother of Mark Stein who played for England at Youth level.

Clement STEPHENSON

Born: New Delaval, 6th February 1890
Died: 24th October 1961
Role: Inside-Left
Career: West Stanley, New Delaval Villa, West Stanley, Blyth Spartans, Aston Villa, Stourbridge, Huddersfield Town
Debut: v Wales (h) 3-3-1924
Appearances: 1

One of three brothers taken on by Aston Villa (George, listed below and Jim being the other two), Clem joined the club in March 1910 for £165 from Blyth Spartans and was sent on loan to Stourbridge to continue his football education. Upon his return in February 1911 he became a regular in the first team and would go on to help Aston Villa win the FA Cup in 1913. During the First World War he guested for Leeds City and then returned to Villa Park to add a second FA Cup winners' medal in 1920. In March 1921 Huddersfield manager Herbert Chapman bought the player he had had under his wing at Leeds City for £3,000 and Clem became an integral part of the side that won the First Division championship in three consecutive seasons, 1924, 1925 and 1926. He also appeared in the FA Cup final either side of those title triumphs, collecting a third winners' medal in 1922 and a runners-up medal in 1928. Clem retired from playing in May 1929 and was appointed manager of the club, a position he held until June 1942.

George Ternant STEPHENSON

Born: New Delaval, 3rd September 1900
Died: 18th August 1971
Role: Inside-Left
Career: New Delaval Villa, Leeds City, Aston Villa, Stourbridge, Derby County, Sheffield Wednesday, Preston North End, Charlton Athletic
Debut: v France (a) 17-5-1928 (scored twice)
Appearances: 3 (2 goals)

The younger brother of Clement Stephenson (above), George's career mirrored that of his brother in many ways. He had played schools football in Northumberland and was signed by Leeds City in August 1919, although the FA ordered the club to disband for financial irregularities and he was sold to Aston Villa for £300 in November the same year. He too was sent out to Stourbridge on loan to continue his development before returning to Villa Park. He remained with the club until November 1927 when he moved on to Derby County and spent a little over three years with Derby before moving on to Sheffield Wednesday. Two years later George joined Preston North End and ten months on moved to Charlton Athletic where he won his only honour in the game, a Third Division South championship medal in 1935. Injuries then hampered his career and he was forced to retire in May 1937. After a spell on the coaching staff at Charlton, subsequently serving as assistant manager, he was appointed manager of Huddersfield Town in August 1947 and held the position until March 1952. His son Bobby played for Derby, Shrewsbury and Rochdale in the 1960s as well as cricket for Derbyshire and Hampshire.

Joseph Eric STEPHENSON

Born: Bexley Heath, September 1914
Died: Burma, 8th September 1944
Role: Inside-Left
Career: Harrogate, Leeds United
Debut: v Scotland (h) 9-4-1938
Appearances: 2

Eric played junior and schoolboy football in the Leeds area and joined Leeds United as an amateur from Harrogate in January 1933. He was upgraded to the professional ranks in September 1934 and would go on to make 115 appearances for the club, scoring 22 goals, before the outbreak of the Second World War. He joined the Ghurkha Rifles and had attained the rank of major when he was killed in action in Burma in September 1944.

Alexander Cyril STEPNEY

Born: Mitcham, 18th September 1944
Role: Goalkeeper
Career: Tooting & Mitcham United, Millwall, Chelsea, Manchester United
Debut: v Sweden (h) 22-5-1968
Appearances: 1

Signed by Millwall as an amateur from Tooting & Mitcham, Alex spent three seasons at Millwall before a £50,000 fee took him to Chelsea. Four months later he was on the move again as Matt Busby paid £55,000, then a record fee for a goalkeeper, to take him to Old Trafford. At the end of his first season with the club he won a championship medal, and in May 1968 appeared at Wembley twice within a week, collecting his one and only England cap on the 22nd and a European Cup winners' medal with United on the 29th. He was still firmly established as United's first choice goalkeeper the following decade when he won a Second Division championship medal and appeared in successive FA Cup finals, in 1976 (runners-up) and 1977 (winners). He left United in February 1979 and played for a spell in America, returning briefly to Altrincham as player-coach before finishing his playing career back in America. He, perhaps more than any other goalkeeper at Old Trafford, established the habit of shouting at defenders in order to keep them alert and was taken to hospital after one match having dislocated his jaw through shouting too loud!

Melvyn STERLAND

Born: Sheffield, 1st October 1961
Role: Full-Back
Career: Sheffield Wednesday, Glasgow Rangers, Leeds United
Debut: v Saudi Arabia (a) 16-11-1988
Appearances: 1

Mel joined Sheffield Wednesday as an apprentice and was upgraded to the professional ranks in October 1979 and made his initial appearances for the club in midfield. He was converted to full-back during the 1981-82 season and would go on to help the club win promotion to the top flight 1984, with his previous experiences as a midfield player proving especially useful when going forward, for he netted 11 goals during the 1985-86 season. He asked for a transfer in 1989 after he had been relieved of the captaincy and was subsequently sold to Glasgow Rangers for £800,000 in March of that year. He spent only four months at Ibrox but still managed to help Rangers win the

Scottish Premier League at the end of the season before a move back across the border to Leeds United in July 1989. He collected championship medals from the second Division in 1990 and the First Division in 1992 but injuries began to hamper his career. After four operations on an ankle injury, he finally retired during the 1993-94 season. He was given the nickname 'Zico' on account of his ferocious kick.

Trevor McGregor STEVEN

Born: Berwick-Upon-Tweed, 21st September 1963
Role: Midfield
Career: Burnley, Everton, Glasgow Rangers, Marseille (France), Glasgow Rangers
Debut: v Northern Ireland (a) 27-2-1985 (WCQ)
Appearances: 36 (4 goals)

Trevor rose through the ranks at Burnley, making his first team debut in 1981. In the space of two years he had become one of the brightest midfield prospects in the country, with Everton taking him to Goodison Park for £300,000 in the summer of 1983. He became a key player in the side that restored Everton to former glories, winning the FA Cup in 1984 and the League title and European Cup Winners' Cup in 1985 as well as finishing runners-up in the FA Cup final the same year. The Heysel Stadium disaster in 1985 robbed Trevor and his Everton team-mates of the chance to pit their wits against further European opposition, although he did win a further League championship medal in 1987. Trevor remained at Goodison Park until 1989 when, having made 299 appearances for the club, he was sold to Rangers for £1.5 million. In 1991 he spent a season with Marseille having cost the club £5.5 million, and helped them win the French League before returning to Rangers. During his time in Scotland he won four Scottish championships and played a bit part in two other championship-winning sides before retiring in 1997.

Trevor Steven

Gary Andrew STEVENS

Born: Hillingdon, 30th March 1962
Role: Defender, Midfield
Career: Brighton & Hove Albion, Tottenham Hotspur, Portsmouth
Debut: v Finland (h) (substitute) 17-10-1984 (WCQ)
Appearances: 7

Gary began his professional career with Brighton, signing for them in October 1979. He quickly established himself as a reliable performer, able to switch effortlessly between defence and midfield, and was an integral part of the side that reached the 1983 FA Cup final, and scored one of their goals in the 2-2 draw. Although they lost the replay, Spurs had seen enough to offer £350,000 for the utility player and he joined in June 1983. At the end of his first season at Spurs he helped them win the UEFA Cup, although as a utility player he was seldom played in the same position for any considerable length of time, although he excelled in midfield and was capped for England in October 1984. A serious knee injury in March 1985 kept him out of the side for six months. He fought back to full fitness, collecting a further six caps and went to Mexico in the World Cup, but then suffered another serious injury in November 1986. Thereafter he suffered a string of injuries and was loaned to Portsmouth in January 1990, with the move becoming permanent in March for a fee of £250,000. He retired as a player in 1992, still troubled by injuries, and became a media commentator and presenter.

Michael Gary STEVENS

Born: Barrow, 27th March 1963
Role: Defender
Career: Everton, Glasgow Rangers, Tranmere Rovers
Debut: v Italy (Mexico City) 6-6-1985
Appearances: 46

Signed by Everton as a schoolboy, he graduated through the ranks and became an integral part of the side that lifted the FA Cup in 1984 and the League and European Cup Winners' Cup the following year. Gary added a second League title in 1987 before joining Glasgow Rangers for £1 million in 1988, adding to his collection of honours north of the border. Indeed, in 1992 he became only the second Englishman to have won winners' medals in both the FA Cup and Scottish Cup and at the same time only the second player to have won both League and Cup medals on both sides of the border, Dave Mackay having been the first. He returned to England to play for Tranmere Rovers for £350,000 in September 1994.

Gary Stevens

James STEWART

Born: Newcastle-Upon-Tyne, 1883
Died: 23rd May 1957
Role: Inside-Forward
Career: Sheffield Wednesday, Newcastle United, Glasgow Rangers
Debut: v Wales (h) 18-3-1907 (scored once)
Appearances: 3 (2 goals)

Known as 'Tadger' from childhood, he joined Sheffield Wednesday in May 1902 having been spotted playing non-League football in the Newcastle area. A member of the side that won the FA Cup in 1907, he returned home to Newcastle United in August 1908, the undisclosed fee costing the St. James' Park club a four figure sum. He went on to collect a championship winning medal in 1909 and made a second appearance in the FA Cup final although he had to settle for a runners-up medal as Newcastle were beaten by Bradford City. Compensation, of sorts, was achieved when he received a recall into the England side for the first time in four years and scored England's goal in the 1-1 draw with Scotland at Goodison Park. He was sold to Rangers for £600 in September 1913 but returned south of the border the following May to become player-manager of North Shields. After the First World War he lived at Gateshead and worked as a commercial traveller.

Paul Andrew STEWART

Born: Manchester, 7th October 1964
Role: Midfield, Striker
Career: Blackpool, Manchester City, Tottenham Hotspur, Liverpool, Crystal Palace, Wolverhampton Wanderers, Burnley, Sunderland, Stoke City
Debut: v Germany (h) (substitute) 11-9-1991
Appearances: 3

Signed by Blackpool in October 1981, Paul scored 56 goals in 201 appearances for the Seasiders before transferring to Manchester City for £200,000 in 1987. In a little over twelve months, Paul found the net with regularity for City and was then signed by Spurs for £1,700,000, joining at the same time as Paul Gascoigne. A suspension incurred at City prevented him making his Spurs debut until October 1988 when he came on as substitute against Manchester United and promptly missed a penalty. That somehow set the scene for his first two years at Spurs, for as a striker who had thrived on scoring goals he found the going a little tough. Although Gary Lineker arrived to bolster the forward line, it was not until midway through the 1990-91 season that Paul's fortunes changed for the better. Switched to midfield in an emergency in the game with Luton (Spurs had had two players sent off) he took the game by the scruff of the neck and turned in one of the best individual performances seen in many a year, scoring both goals as Spurs came from behind. Thereafter he came to the fore in midfield, scoring Spurs' equalising goal in the 1991 FA Cup final against Nottingham Forest and winning a full England cap in September the same year. By the end of the 1991-92 season Paul's desire to return back to his native north had become too great and he was transferred to Liverpool for £2.3 million, subsequently appearing on loan for Crystal Palace and Wolves and later Sunderland and finishing his career with Stoke City.

Norbert Peter STILES

Born: Manchester, 18th May 1942
Role: Wing-Half
Career: Manchester United, Middlesbrough, Preston North End
Debut: v Scotland (h) 10-4-1965
Appearances: 28 (1 goal)

Nobby joined Manchester United as a junior in 1959 and made the first of 312 appearances for the Reds in 1960. Something of a slow developer, he wasn't firmly established in the side until the departure of his brother-in-law, Johnny Giles, to Leeds, but thereafter he made the wing-half berth his own, winning two League championship medals and a European Cup winners' medal. A tough-tackling defender, he was awarded his first England cap in 1965 and by the time the World Cup came around was an established member of the England team. His performances in the opening group games led to calls for his exclusion from the team, but Ramsey stuck by him and was rewarded with performances from the quarter final onwards that were little short of commanding. In May 1971 he joined Middlesbrough for £20,000 and then wound down his playing career with Preston in 1973 for similar fee of £20,000, retiring as a player in 1974. He was then appointed first team coach and remained in the position until July 1977 when he was promoted to manager. Nobby spent four years in the Deepdale hot seat before taking a coaching position with Vancouver Whitecaps, returning to England in 1984 when he was appointed assistant manager at West Bromwich Albion, with his brother-in-law Johnny Giles (the former Manchester United, Leeds United and Irish international player) as manager. Following Giles' departure in October 1985, Nobby spent three months as caretaker manager until the appointment of Ron Saunders, upon which Nobby rejoined the coaching staff. As well as his 28 full caps for England he also represented his country at schoolboy, Youth and Under-23 level and the Football League on three occasions. Although he did not play in the 1963 FA Cup Final he was awarded a medal in recognition of his performances in earlier rounds.

Nobby Stiles

Lewis STOKER

Born: Wheatley Hill, 31st March 1910
Died: 1979
Role: Right-Half
Career: Bear Park, West Stanley, Birmingham, Nottingham Forest
Debut: v Wales (a) 16-11-1932
Appearances: 3

Lewis was something of a late developer where football was concerned, for although he played schoolboy and junior football he was not a regular in his school side at Bear Park. On leaving school he worked as an electrician and played part-time for West Stanley before being spotted by Birmingham City and being invited along for a month's trial. He eventually signed professional forms with the club in September 1929 and spent nine years with them, collecting three caps for England and representing the Football League once. He moved to Nottingham Forest in 1938 but the outbreak of the Second World War brought his career to an end.

Steve Stone

Steven Brian STONE

Born: Gateshead, 20th August 1971
Role: Midfield
Career: Nottingham Forest, Aston Villa, Portsmouth
Debut: v Norway (a) (substitute) 11-10-1995
Appearances: 9 (2 goals) + 1 unofficial appearance

Steve initially joined Nottingham Forest as a youth trainee and signed professional forms in May 1989, going on to make his debut during the 1991-92 season. His all-action style in central midfield saw him break his leg on three occasions, but each time he bounced back and in October 1995 made the first of his nine appearances for England. A member of the side that won the First Division title in 1998, he was sold to Aston Villa for £5.5 million in March 1999 having successfully converted to a wider midfield position. His initial days at Villa Park were punctuated by injuries but he enjoyed an extended run in the side following the appointment of John Gregory as manager, but when Gregory left the club Steve's place was not assured. Sent on loan to Portsmouth in October 2002 he was eventually released on a free transfer by Aston Villa in December 2002 and promptly signed permanently for the Fratton Park club.

Harry STORER

Born: Liverpool, 2nd February 1898
Died: Derby, 1st September 1967
Role: Inside-Left
Career: Ripley Town, Eastwood, Grimsby Town, Derby County, Burnley
Debut: v France (a) 17-5-1924 (scored once)
Appearances: 2 (1 goal)

Harry had a spell as an amateur with Notts County during the 1918-19 season and joined Grimsby Town in February 1919 with the same status, subsequently signing professional forms in April 1920. In March 1921 he was sold to Derby County for £4,500 and spent eight years with the club, playing football for Derby during the winter and cricket for Derbyshire in the summer (he represented the county between 1920 and 1936). In February 1929 Burnley paid £4,250 to take him to Turf Moor where he finished his playing career in May 1931. Harry was then appointed manager of Coventry City, a position he was to hold until 1945, although he returned to Highfield Road in November 1948 until December 1953. He then became manager of Derby County in June 1955 and remained in the position until his retirement in May 1962 although he later scouted for Everton. He was known as a reliable opening batsman for Derbyshire, scoring 13,515 runs and an occasional wicketkeeper who took 242 catches. He was the nephew of Billy Storer, a Derbyshire and England wicketkeeper in the 1890s.

Peter Edwin STOREY

Born: Farnham, 7th September 1945
Role: Defender
Career: Arsenal, Fulham
Debut: v Greece (h) 21-4-1971 (ECQ)
Appearances: 19

Peter played schools football in Aldershot before being invited to join the Arsenal ground staff in May 1961, turning professional in September 1962. He first played for the first team during a pre-season tournament in Italy but impressed enough to quickly establish himself in the League side during the 1965-66 season. He was initially used as a full-back, replacing Don Howe and remained in this position until 1970 when, on the eve of the 1970-71 season, manager Bertie Mee switched him to midfield. His aggressive hard-tackling style was the launch pad for Arsenal's double success that season and also saw him break into the England side, a natural successor to the likes of Nobby Stiles. Having represented England at schoolboy level and played twice for the Football League, Peter went on to win 19 caps for England. In addition to the double success of 1971, Peter helped Arsenal to the Inter-Cities Fairs Cup in 1969 and the finals of the FA Cup in 1972 and the League Cup in 1968 and 1969. Peter remained at Arsenal until 1977, although he had been in and out of the side for the two previous seasons, and joined Fulham on transfer deadline day for £10,000. Six months later he was forced to retire owing to injury and his life since then has been a mixture of highs and lows, culminating in a spell in prison.

Peter Storey

Ian Storey-Moore

Ian STOREY-MOORE

Born: Ipswich, 17th January 1945
Role: Winger
Career: Ashby Juniors, Nottingham Forest, Manchester United
Debut: v Holland (h) 14-1-1970
Appearances: 1

Ian had a trial with Blackpool but joined Nottingham Forest as an amateur in August 1961, subsequently joining the professional ranks in May 1962. He made his debut in 1963 and became a regular in the side a short while later, going on to collect two caps for England at Under-23 level and also make two appearances for the Football League. Although he played as a winger he was a prolific goalscorer, finishing top goalscorer for Forest in four seasons and helping the club reach the FA Cup semi finals and finish second in the League in 1966-67. Alf Ramsey's policy of playing without wingers meant he was restricted to just one appearance for his country, and in March 1972 he was sold to Manchester United for £200,000 having scored 105 goals in 236 appearances for Forest. He made just 39 appearances for United, netting 11 goals, before an ankle injury brought a premature end to his career in December 1973.

Alfred Henry STRANGE

Born: Ripley, 2nd April 1900
Died: October 1978
Role: Right-Half
Career: Marehay Colliery, Portsmouth, Port Vale, Sheffield Wednesday, Bradford
Debut: v Scotland (h) 5-4-1930
Appearances: 20

Alf was spotted by Portsmouth whilst playing for Marehay Colliery and signed professional forms in December 1922, relatively late for a footballer at the time. Initially a centre-forward, Alf was unable to break into the first team on a regular basis and was sold to Port Vale in October 1924. There he had greater success and was eventually picked up by Sheffield Wednesday in February 1927 in a swap deal with another player. Here he was switched to right-half and his career blossomed, resulting in three appearances for the Football League, 20 full caps for England and championship medals in 1929 and 1930. Alf remained at Hillsborough until May 1935 when he moved on to Bradford Park Avenue, retiring from playing the following summer. He then settled in the Ripley area where he worked as a poultry farmer.

Alfred Hugh STRATFORD

Born: Kensington, London, 5th September 1853
Died: Newark, New Jersey (USA), 2nd May 1914
Role: Full-Back
Career: Wanderers, Old Malvernians, Swifts, Middlesex
Debut: v Scotland (a) 7-3-1874
Appearances: 1

Educated at Malvern College, Alfred played for the college team from 1871 to 1874 and was captain in his final year. He then played for Wanderers, collecting winners' medals in the FA Cup in 1876, 1877 and 1878, as well as assisting both Old Malvernians and the Swifts. He also won representative honours with Middlesex and also played for the county at cricket (he made 34 first class appearances for the county). Alfred also played cricket for the MCC, South of England and London United before emigrating to America in 1890, where he played cricket for the USA.

Bernard Reginald STRETEN

Born: Rochester, 14th January 1921
Died: 6th May 1984
Role: Goalkeeper
Career: Notts County, Shrewsbury Town, Luton Town, King's Lynn, Wisbech Town, Cambridge City, North Walsham
Debut: v Northern Ireland (h) 16-11-1949 (WCQ)
Appearances: 1

After playing junior football in Norfolk, Bernard signed as an amateur with Notts County and then Shrewsbury Town and during the Second World War guested for Wolverhampton Wanderers in the Football League (North). However, it was his performances for Shrewsbury Town in the Midland League that alerted a number of other clubs as to his abilities and he was signed by Luton Town, again as an amateur in January 1947. The following year he signed professional forms, by which time he had also won six caps for the England amateur side, and gave the club exceptional service over the next nine years. His performances for Luton Town earned him selection for the full England side in 1949 in the World Cup qualifier against Northern Ireland, which was won 9-2, although Bernard was unable to add to his tally of full caps owing to the exceptional form of Bert Williams. Two months after his only England appearance, Bernard lost his place in the Luton side to fellow England international Ron Baynham and was confined to the reserves. Bernard put in a transfer request, which was turned down, and he eventually won back his place and would go on to make a total of 301 appearances for the Hatters. He retired from the professional game in the summer of 1957 but continued to turn out as an amateur once again, appearing for King's Lynn, Wisbech Town and Cambridge City. His finished his playing career with the North Walsham club of Norfolk.

Albert STURGESS

Born: Stoke-on-Trent, 21st October 1882
Died: 16th July 1957
Role: Wing-Half
Career: Tunstall Crosswells, Stoke, Sheffield United, Norwich City
Debut: v Ireland (h) 11-2-1911
Appearances: 2

Albert played local football in the Stoke area before joining Tunstall Crosswells and subsequently signing for Stoke City in 1903. Five years later he moved on to Sheffield United and would go on to help the club win the FA Cup in 1915, the last season before organised football shut down for the duration of the First World War. Albert returned to Sheffield United at the end of the hostilities and remained a first team regular until July 1923 when he moved on to Norwich City, retiring from playing in the summer of 1925. He then returned to Staffordshire, opening up a crockery shop in Eccleshall.

Albert Sturgess

Michael George SUMMERBEE

Born: Cheltenham, 15th December 1942
Role: Forward
Career: Swindon Town, Manchester City, Burnley, Blackpool, Stockport County
Debut: v Scotland (a) 24-2-1968 (ECQ)
Appearances: 8 (1 goal)

Mike was spotted by Swindon whilst playing schools football in his native Cheltenham and signed amateur forms in August 1959, being upgraded to the professional ranks the following December. In August 1965 he became Joe Mercer's first signing for Manchester City, costing the Maine Road club £35,000. At the end of his first season with the club he had helped them win the Second Division championship and restored City to the top flight, and over

Mike Summerbee

the next four years was an integral part of the side that won virtually all of the game's top honours. These included the League title in 1968, the FA Cup in 1969 and League Cup in 1970, and although City also won the European Cup Winners' Cup the same season, Mike was absent from the final through injury (although as he had played in the earlier rounds he was given a medal in recognition of his contribution). He was first capped by England in 1968, although he had to wait three years before earning a second appearance for his country. He also won one Under-23 cap and represented the Football League on one occasion and collected a runners-up medal with City in the 1974 League Cup. In June 1975 he was sold to Burnley for £25,000, one of the last of Joe Mercer's and Malcolm Allison's great side to leave the club and having appeared in over 400 games for City. He made 51 League appearances for Burnley and then spent a brief spell with Blackpool before finishing his League career with Stockport County. He was player-manager at Edgeley Road between March 1978 and October 1979 and then finished his playing career with Mossley. At his height he was considered almost an equal to Manchester rival George Best and whilst there was seldom much quarter asked or given on the field whenever they came up against each other, off it they were the best of friends, jointly owning a boutique in the city!

Alan SUNDERLAND

Born: Mexborough, 1st July 1953
Role: Forward
Career: Wolverhampton Wanderers, Arsenal, Ipswich Town
Debut: v Australia (a) 31-5-1980
Appearances: 1

Alan joined Wolves as an apprentice and was upgraded to the professional ranks in June 1971. A member of the side that won the League Cup in 1974 and won the Second Division championship in 1977 he was sold to Arsenal for £240,000 in November 1977 and went on to help his new club reach the FA Cup final three years in succession. In 1979, the only one of the three that was won, Alan scored the winner against Manchester United and the following season helped Arsenal reach the final of the European Cup Winners' Cup, although they were beaten on penalties. As well as his one full cap, Alan also represented his country at B, Under-21 and Under-23 level. He joined Ipswich Town on loan in February 1984, the move becoming permanent in July the same year. He retired from playing at the end of the 1984-85 season.

Alan Sunderland

John William SUTCLIFFE

Born: Halifax, 14th April 1868
Died: Bradford, 7th July 1947
Role: Goalkeeper
Career: Bolton Wanderers, Millwall, Manchester United, Plymouth Argyle, Southend United
Debut: v Wales (h) 13-3-1893
Appearances: 5

John began his career as a centre-forward and was playing for Bolton Reserves in one match when the opposing goalkeeper came out to tackle him; John picked him up and threw him into the goal! After that Bolton decided he would be better off serving in goal and duly converted him. It turned out to be the making of John's career, for his safe and assured handling was sufficient to earn him five caps for England at football and a further cap for his country at Rugby Union; he is the last man to have represented England at the two codes. The closest he came to domestic honours with any of his clubs came in 1894 with Bolton when he helped them to the FA Cup Final where they were beaten by Notts County. When he finished his playing career at the age of 44 with Southend United he joined the coaching staff.

Christopher Roy SUTTON

Born: Nottingham, 10th March 1973
Role: Striker
Career: Norwich City, Blackburn Rovers, Chelsea, Celtic, Birmingham City
Debut: v Cameroon (h) (substitute) 15-11-1997
Appearances: 1

Chris joined Norwich City as a trainee and was upgraded to the professional ranks in July 1991. After just 102 League appearances, scoring 35 goals, he was targeted by Blackburn Rovers as the ideal partner for Alan Shearer and joined the Ewood Park club in a £5 million deal. At the end of his first season Rovers had won the Premier League and he

Chris Sutton

and Shearer were widely regarded as one of the most potent strike forces in the game. The subsequent departure of Shearer to Newcastle United did little to blunt Sutton's own goalscoring ability and he proved capable of playing equally effectively with a succession of partners in the Rovers side. However, having made his England debut in November 1997 he was expected to challenge for a place in the England squad for the 1998 World Cup Finals in France. Any chance he may have had disappeared with his refusal to turn out for the England B side in a friendly international, claiming he had little to gain or prove by playing in the match. Glenn Hoddle's immediate decision was to discount him from any England side whilst he remained in charge. A £10 million move took him to Chelsea in 1999 but he proved unable to win a regular place in the side, departing for Celtic for £6 million in the summer of 2000. After winning a succession of medals north of the border, he returned to England with Birmingham City on a free transfer in January 2006, having been unable to reclaim his place in the England side under any of Hoddle's successors.

Peter SWAN

Born: South Elmsall, 8th October 1936
Role: Centre-Half
Career: Sheffield Wednesday, Bury
Debut: v Yugoslavia (h) 11-5-1960
Appearances: 19

Peter represented Doncaster Schools before being signed by Sheffield Wednesday as an amateur in May 1952, being upgraded to the professional ranks in November 1953. He made his debut in November 1955 and the following year became a first team regular, a position he was to enjoy for some eight seasons. A member of the side that won the Second Division championship in 1959 and finished runners-up in the top flight in 1961, Peter also seemed set for a lengthy spell in the full England side. Unfortunately, he picked up a stomach bug in Chile with England for the World Cup in 1962 and, as the wrong treatment was given fell violently ill. He never played for his country again, for at the end of the 1963-64 season he was one of three First Division players named in a betting scandal, imprisoned and handed a life ban from the game. The ban was overturned in 1972 and Peter made a brief return to Hillsborough, making a further 15 appearances to take his League tally to 275 and then joined Bury in August 1973. In the summer of 1974 he was appointed player-manager of Matlock Town and guided them to victory in the FA Trophy over Scarborough at Wembley, his first appearance at the Twin Towers since May 1962. Peter later had spells as manager at Worksop Town, Buxton Town and a second spell at Matlock. Having been a licensee in Sheffield during his ban from the game, Peter later returned to the profession in Chesterfield.

Peter Swan

Harry Albermarle SWEPSTONE

Born: Stepney, London, 1st July 1859
Died: 7th May 1907
Role: Goalkeeper
Career: Clapton, Pilgrims, Ramblers, Corinthians, Essex County
Debut: v Scotland (a) 13-3-1880
Appearances: 6

Harry played for Chigwell School in his youth and would go on to play for Clapton, Pilgrims and Ramblers as well as earning representative honours with Essex. He was also a member of the committee that formed the Corinthians and it was he who gave the club its name as well as making two appearances for the club during the 1885 86 season. He also served on the FA Committee between 1883 and 1884. A solicitor by profession he was admitted in 1881 and worked in the Bethnal Green area until 1892 when he set up a practice in Bishopsgate.

Frank Victor SWIFT

Born: Blackpool, 26th December 1913
Died: Munich, 6th February 1958
Role: Goalkeeper
Career: Fleetwood, Manchester City
Debut: v Northern Ireland (a) 28-9-1946
Appearances: 19 + 14 War appearances + 3 unofficial appearances

After playing schoolboy and junior football in Blackpool, Frank was working in the local gasworks when he signed with Fleetwood in 1931 and then Manchester City as an amateur during the 1931-32 season. He was upgraded to the professional ranks in October 1932 and came to national prominence in the 1934 FA Cup Final. Frank was extremely nervous when he was told he was in the side and Sam Cowan, City's captain, took him under his wing the night before the game and made sure he kept his mind on matters by telling him stories of the previous year's final (City were beaten by Everton), although on the morning of the game Frank, as the junior player in the side, was still expected to go and buy the day's supply of chewing gum! Frank performed well in the final itself, helping City overcome Portsmouth 2-1, although at the end of the game the tension proved too much for Frank and he collapsed. Cowan helped him to his feet and made sure he got up to the Royal Box to collect his medal. After that there was no looking back for Frank and by the outbreak of the Second World War he was widely regarded as one of the best goalkeepers in the country. He helped Manchester City win the League title in 1937 and in 1939 earned his first call-up for England, albeit in a wartime international. He guested for Hamilton Academicals during the war and emerged at the end of hostilities as England's first choice 'keeper, adding 19 full caps to go with his 14 wartime appearances and also became England's first goalkeeper captain in the twentieth century. He was still very much a regular when he retired from playing in the summer of 1949, although he later changed his mind and returned to play a further four League matches for City during the 1949-50 season. He initially became a licensee in Manchester and later turned to journalism. Indeed, he was writing for the Sunday Empire News when he accompanied the Manchester United side to Belgrade for their European Cup match in 1958 and subsequently lost his life when the plane crashed at Munich. In addition to his full England appearances Frank turned out once for the B side and three times for the Football League and also helped Manchester City to the Second Division title in 1947. His brother Fred was also a professional goalkeeper, turning out for Bolton Wanderers during his career. Aside from the 1933 FA Cup final the only time Frank ever got flustered was during the Second World War, in which he served as a policeman. On his first day of traffic duty he got so confused he left his post and let the traffic sort itself out!

Frank Swift

T

TAIT, George
TALBOT, Brian Ernest
TAMBLING, Robert Victor
TATE, Joseph Thomas
TAYLOR, Edward Hallows
TAYLOR, Ernest
TAYLOR, James Guy
TAYLOR, Peter John
TAYLOR, Philip Henry
TAYLOR, Thomas
TEMPLE, Derek William
TERRY, John
THICKETT, Henry
THOMAS, Daniel Jospeh
THOMAS, David
THOMAS, Geoffrey Robert
THOMAS, Michael Lauriston
THOMPSON, Alan
THOMPSON, Peter
THOMPSON, Philip Bernard
THOMPSON, Thomas
THOMSON, Robert Anthony
THORNEWELL, George
THORNLEY, Irvine
TILSON, Samuel Frederick
TITMUSS, Frederick
TODD, Colin
TOONE, George
TOPHAM, Arthur George
TOPHAM, Robert
TOWERS, Mark Anthony
TOWNLEY, William J
TOWNROW, John Ernest
TREMELLING, Daniel Richard
TRESADERN, John
TUEART, Dennis
TUNSTALL, Frederick Edward
TURNBULL, Robert Joseph
TURNER, Arthur
TURNER, Hugh
TURNER, James Albert
TWEEDY, George Jacob

John Terry

George TAIT

Born: 1859
Died: 1882
Role: Forward
Career: Birmingham Excelsior
Debut: v Wales (h) 26-2-1881
Appearances: 1

George played junior football in the Birmingham area before joining Birmingham Excelsior where he appears to have spent his entire career. He owed his one appearance for England to the fact that the selection committee tended to honour players from all around the country in fixtures other than Scotland. According to reports, George was 'altogether outclassed in an international team' in a match that was lost 1-0, and was not picked again.

Brian Ernest TALBOT

Born: Ipswich, 21st July 1953
Role: Midfield
Career: Ipswich Town, Arsenal, Watford, Stoke City, West Bromwich Albion, Fulham, Aldershot
Debut: v Northern Ireland (a) (substitute) 28-5-1977
Appearances: 6

Taken on as an apprentice by Ipswich Town in July 1970, Brian turned professional in August 1972 and made his League debut in February 1974. Brian went on to earn representative honours at Under-21 and B level and helped Ipswich win the FA Cup in 1978 against Arsenal. In January 1979 he was sold to Arsenal for £450,000 and at the end of the season collected another winners' medal as Arsenal overcame Manchester United, the first player to win consecutive winners' medals with different sides since Lord Kinnaird achieved the feat the previous century. Brian then helped Arsenal reach the finals of both the FA Cup and European Cup Winners' Cup in 1980, although Arsenal suffered defeat in both. In June 1985 he was sold to Watford for £150,000, spending a little over a year at the club before moving on to Stoke City for £25,000 in October 1986. In January 1988 he joined West Bromwich Albion, being appointed player-manager in November the same year (resigning from his post as chairman of the PFA at the same time), a position he held until 1991. Brian then resumed his playing career with Fulham and Aldershot before returning to management with Rushden & Diamonds.

Brian Talbot

Bobby Tambling

Robert Victor TAMBLING

Born: Storrington, 18th September 1941
Role: Forward
Career: Chelsea, Crystal Palace
Debut: v Wales (h) 21-11-1962
Appearances: 3 (1 goal)

Bobby was spotted by Chelsea whilst playing for East Hampshire Schools, taken on as an apprentice in July 1957 and upgraded to the professional ranks in September 1958. He scored on his League debut for the club in February 1959 but it was to take the departure of Jimmy Greaves before Bobby was able to establish himself as a regular in the side. Thereafter he was a prolific goalscorer, netting a Chelsea record of 164 League goals over the course of 302 appearances, including a record equalling five in one match against Aston Villa in September 1966. A member of the side that won the League Cup in 1965 he also helped the club reach the FA Cup in 1967, netting Chelsea's goal in the 2-1 defeat by Spurs. Unfortunately for Bobby, by the time Chelsea had reassembled a side to challenge and win major honours, his career at Stamford Bridge had started to falter, hampered by injuries, and he was loaned to Crystal Palace in January 1970. The move became permanent during the summer, with Palace paying £40,000 to secure his services, and over the next three years Bobby made 68 League appearances and scored 12 goals. He wound down his playing career in Ireland, having spells with Cork Celtic (where he also served as a player-manager), Waterford and Shamrock Rovers before finally retiring.

Joseph Thomas TATE

Born: Old Hill, 4th August 1904
Died: 18th May 1973
Role: Left-Half
Career: Round Oak, Cradley Heath, Aston Villa, Brierley Hill Alliance
Debut: v France (a) 14-5-1931
Appearances: 3

Joe played in the Birmingham League with Cradley Heath before being signed by Aston Villa in April 1925, initially as an inside-left. He was moved into the half-back line whilst at Villa, forming a formidable trio with Jimmy Gibson and Alec Talbot and would go on to win representative honours with the Football League as well as collecting three caps for England. Joe remained at Villa Park until the summer of 1935 when he accepted the position of player manager of Brierley Hill Alliance. He was also a notable cricketer having been on the ground staff with Warwickshire and later became assistant coach at Rugby School.

Edward Hallows TAYLOR

Born: Liverpool, 7th March 1887
Died: 5th July 1956
Role: Goalkeeper
Career: Liverpool Balmoral, Oldham Athletic, Huddersfield Town, Everton, Ashton National, Wrexham
Debut: v Northern Ireland (h) 21-10-1922
Appearances: 8

Eddie had a trial for the England amateur side whilst playing for Liverpool Balmoral before signing professional forms with Oldham Athletic in February 1912. During the First World War he guested for Liverpool and Fulham and returned to Oldham at the end of the hostilities. He was sold to Huddersfield Town in June 1922 for £2,500 and was one of the key players that secured the League championship in three consecutive seasons, 1923-24, 1924-25 and 1925-26, although Eddie was hit by injury during the 1924-25 season and did not qualify for a medal. He did, however, get to represent the Football League on two occasions and collect eight caps for England. He moved to Everton in February 1927 and picked up a third championship medal in 1928, more than adequate compensation for missing out in 1925. In September 1928 he moved on to Ashton National but returned to League action with Wrexham in November 1928, remaining with the club until the end of the season when he retired. He then moved to Manchester where he worked in the cotton trade.

Ernest TAYLOR

Born: Sunderland, 2nd September 1925
Died: 9th April 1985
Role: Inside-Right
Career: Newcastle United, Blackpool, Manchester United, Sunderland, Altrincham, Derry City
Debut: v Hungary (h) 25-11-1953
Appearances: 1

Spotted whilst playing for Hylton Colliery Juniors, Ernie was signed by Newcastle United in September 1942. During the Second World War he served in the Royal Navy and returned to St. James' Park at the end of the hostilities to become a key player for the Magpies, helping them win the FA Cup in 1951. Six months later he was surprisingly sold to Blackpool for £25,000 but soon created a devastating right-wing partnership with Stanley Matthews. Whilst Matthews got most of the plaudits and Stan Mortensen most of the goals, Ernie Taylor was something of an unsung hero in Blackpool's march to the FA Cup final in 1953, where they recovered from being 3-1 down to win against Bolton Wanderers 4-3. Six months later Ernie played in his only match for England, the 6-3 defeat against Hungary, and along with several others who played in the match was discarded from the England setup. In February 1958, following the Munich air disaster, Ernie was sold to Manchester United for £7,500 where his experience was going to be vital to a club attempting to recover from such a heartbreaking incident – the younger players christened him 'Uncle Ernie'. After making his debut in the emotional first match after Munich, against Sheffield Wednesday in the FA Cup, Ernie played an important part in United's emotional charge towards Wembley. There, Ernie's hopes of winning FA Cup winners' medals with three different sides came to an end, with Bolton Wanderers winning 2-0. In December 1958 Ernie was sold to Sunderland for £7,500, having made just 22 League appearances for Manchester United. He remained at Roker Park until the summer of 1961 when he was released, promptly joining non-League Altrincham. In November 1961 he joined Derry City, where he finished his playing career in February 1962. Ernie later had a spell coaching in New Zealand and upon returning to England worked for Vauxhall Motors in Hooton, Cheshire.

Jim Taylor

James Guy TAYLOR

Born: Hillingdon, 5th November 1917
Role: Centre-Half
Career: Hillingdon Town, Fulham, Queens Park Rangers, Tunbridge Wells Rangers
Debut: v Argentina (h) 9-5-1951
Appearances: 2

Jim was playing non-League football for Hillingdon Town as an inside-right when he was spotted by Fulham, joining the Craven Cottage side in March 1938. The outbreak of the Second World War put his professional career on hold, although he did make 88 appearances for the club in wartime fixtures. At the end of hostilities he was successfully converted to centre-half and became something of an ever-present for Fulham for the next seven seasons, helping the club win the Second Division championship in 1948-49. Having represented the Football League in March 1948 and toured Canada with the FA in 1950, Jim earned his first full cap for England in May 1951 and in so doing became the first Fulham player to be afforded the honour. He remained at Craven Cottage until April 1953 when he joined Queens Park Rangers on a free transfer, spending a little over a season at Loftus Road before joining non-League Tunbridge Wells Rangers as player-manager. He later served Yiewsley FC in a similar capacity and then coached Uxbridge FC in the Corinthian League.

Peter Taylor

Peter John TAYLOR

Born: Southend, 3rd January 1953
Role: Forward
Career: Southend United, Crystal Palace, Tottenham Hotspur, Orient
Debut: v Wales (a) (substitute) 24-3-1976 (scored once)
Appearances: 4 (2 goals)

Although Peter was turned down by Spurs as a youngster he soon got fixed up with Southend and after two years was snapped up by Crystal Palace in October 1973. Whilst at Palace he developed into a winger of true potential, so much so that he became the last player to be capped by England whilst playing in the Third Division. As such it was not long before bigger clubs starting enquiring about his availability, and in September 1976 a fee of £400,000 brought him to White Hart Lane. Unfortunately his career at Spurs did not really take off, for although he was a regular in the side during his first season, the arrival of Ricky Villa and then a series of injuries limited his opportunities. In November 1980 he was sold to Orient for £150,000 and subsequently drifted into the non-League game. He later turned to coaching and management, being brought into the England setup by Glenn Hoddle as manager of the Under-21 side. He later managed Gillingham (guiding them to promotion), Leicester City and Hull City (also guiding them to promotion) before being brought back into the England setup. He also managed the England full side for one match.

Philip Henry TAYLOR

Born: Bristol, 18th September 1917
Role: Right-Half
Career: Bristol Rovers, Liverpool
Debut: v Wales (a) 18-10-1947
Appearances: 3 + 1 unofficial international

After representing Bristol schools, Phil joined the Bristol Rovers ground staff in 1932 and turned professional in 1935. At this time he was an inside-forward and it was his prowess in this position that prompted Liverpool to pay £5,000 for his services in March 1936, thus beginning a twenty-three year connection with the Anfield club. Like many of his generation he lost his best years to the Second World War, but at the end of hostilities Liverpool converted him to right-half and made him club captain. He responded by leading the club to the League championship in 1947 and the FA Cup final in 1950, although they were beaten by Arsenal at Wembley that year. With Liverpool suffering the ignominy of relegation to the Second Division at the end of the 1953-54 season, Phil retired from playing and joined the coaching staff. By May 1956 he was chief coach at Liverpool and when manager Don Welsh was taken ill that same month Phil was appointed caretaker manager. The following April he was appointed manager with a brief to get the club back into the top flight, but despite several near

Phil Taylor

misses Liverpool remained a Second Division outfit during his spell in charge. In November 1959 his own health began to suffer as a result of the pressure to obtain results and he left the club after being replaced by Bill Shankly. He severed all ties with football, becoming a sales representative. In addition to his three full caps for England Phil was also capped at schoolboy level, made two appearances for the England B team and represented the Football League on four occasions. He was also a gifted cricketer, making one appearance for Gloucestershire in 1938.

Tommy Taylor

Thomas TAYLOR

Born: Barnsley, 29th January 1931
Died: Munich, 6th February 1958
Role: Centre-Forward
Career: Barnsley, Manchester United
Debut: v Argentina (a) 17-5-1953 (match abandoned)
Appearances: 19 (16 goals)

Tommy joined Barnsley straight from school and turned professional in 1949, making an almost immediate impression at Oakwell, scoring a phenomenal 26 goals in 44 League appearances before Matt Busby lured him to Old Trafford in March 1953 for a fee of £29,999, a figure deliberately £1 short so as not to burden the player with the tag of £30,000 (it was claimed that Busby gave the £1 to a tea lady at Old Trafford). At Old Trafford Tommy was converted from inside-forward to centre-forward and proved an immense success, netting 112 League goals in only 166 appearances. He also scored five FA Cup and 11 European goals during his time at Old Trafford, helping United reach the final of the FA Cup in 1957 (he scored their only goal) and reach the European Cup semi final the same year. As well as winning two League championships with United, Tommy appeared in the 1954 World Cup tournament and helped England qualify for the 1958 finals, by which time he had replaced the great Nat Lofthouse in the England side. Widely tipped to help England achieve great things at the 1958 World Cup, Tommy never got a chance to fulfil his potential, for he was one of the Manchester United players killed in the Munich air crash of February 1958. Whilst the loss of Duncan Edwards, also killed in the crash, robbed England of its powerhouse midfield player, the goals of Tommy Taylor were just as sadly missed – he netted 138 goals in just 212 League matches for Barnsley and Manchester United, as well as 16 in 19 games for England. Tommy, who also won two caps for England at B level and represented the Football League on two occasions, was widely reckoned to be England's finest centre-forward since Tommy Lawton. After his untimely death, it was some considerable time before anyone quite as potent in front of goal emerged to take his place.

Derek William TEMPLE

Born: Liverpool, 13th November 1938
Role: Winger
Career: Everton, Preston North End, Wigan Athletic
Debut: v West Germany (a) 12-5-1965
Appearances: 1

Introduced into the Everton first team in March 1957, he went on to make nearly 300 appearances for the first team, helping them win the League title in 1963 and the FA Cup in 1966, scoring the winning goal in the final against Sheffield Wednesday. He was transferred to Preston in September 1967 for £35,000 and later played non-League football with Wigan Athletic.

John George TERRY

Born: Barking, 7th December 1980
Role: Defender
Career: Chelsea, Nottingham forest
Debut: v Serbia-Montenegro (h) 3-6-2003
Appearances: 21

John came through Chelsea's youth ranks, representing the club at youth and reserve level before being handed his first team debut in October 1998. A total of just six League appearances in two seasons prompted speculation that John might be better served trying his luck elsewhere and he had a spell on loan at Nottingham Forest, but in the 2000-01 season John began to break into the side on a more regular basis. The following season he had made the central defensive position largely his own, prompting calls for him to be included in the England World Cup squad for 2002, but an incident outside a nightclub led to him being charged with affray and banned from being selected for any England side until the matter was settled. He was subsequently cleared on all charges in August 2002. Over the next three years John Terry let his football do the talking, breaking into the fringes of the England side, initially as an obvious replacement for Rio Ferdinand or Sol Campbell but, for the last twelve months or so, as a first choice player himself, with Rio and Sol having to battle for the other slot. First handed the captain's armband at Chelsea during the 2003-04 season whenever Marcel Desailly was out of the side, John has since made the role his own and therefore collected the League Cup and FA Premiership in 2005. Largely seen as the rock upon which Chelsea built their championship winning side he superbly marshalled the defence through the season and also weighed in with one or two vital strikes at the other end.

John Terry

Henry THICKETT

Born: Hexthorpe, 1873
Died: 15th November 1920
Role: Right-Back
Career: Hexthorpe, Sheffield United, Rotherham Town, Sheffield United, Bristol City
Debut: v Wales (h) 20-3-1899
Appearances: 2

Harry played for Hexthorpe, a non-League side in the Doncaster area before being signed by Sheffield United in 1890. He did not make the grade first time around at Bramall Lane and left the club for Rotherham Town in 1891, although he was persuaded to return in December 1893. He enjoyed greater success the second time around, helping United win the Football League championship in 1898, the FA Cup the following season and again in 1902 and reach the final in 1901. He left to become player-manager of Bristol City in May 1904, retiring a year later in order to concentrate full time on management. Harry proved a success at this too, guiding Bristol City to the Second Division championship in 1906 and the FA Cup final in 1909. He resigned in 1910 and moved to Trowbridge where he became a licensee, a position he held until his death in 1920. Harry was known for being a bulky player during his career, weighing in at fourteen and a half stone at his prime, and this ballooned after his retirement – he was nearly 26 stone during his licensee days!

Daniel Joseph THOMAS

Born: Worksop, 12th November 1961
Role: Full-Back
Career: Coventry City, Tottenham Hotspur
Debut: v Australia (a) 11-6-1983
Appearances: 2

After failing trials with Sheffield United and Leeds United, Danny was signed by Coventry City in 1978 and soon developed into a full-back with the potential to break into the full England side, which he achieved during the England tour of Australia in 1983. Upon returning from international duty he was transferred to Spurs for £250,000 and earned a UEFA Cup winners' medal at the end of his first season with the club. In March 1987 he suffered a knee injury so serious it forced him to retire from the game, a decision he announced in January 1988. Although he was offered a position on the Spurs staff, he chose to pursue a career in physiotherapy and later linked with Ossie Ardiles at West Bromwich Albion in that position.

David THOMAS

Born: Kirkby, 5th October 1950
Role: Forward
Career: Burnley, Queens Park Rangers, Everton, Wolverhampton Wanderers, Vancouver Whitecaps (Canada), Middlesbrough, Portsmouth
Debut: v Czechoslovakia (h) (substitute) 30-10-1974 (ECQ)
Appearances: 8

Spotted by Burnley whilst playing schools football in the County Durham area, Dave was signed as an apprentice in February 1966 and upgraded to the professional ranks in October 1967. By then he had already made his first team debut, becoming Burnley's youngest debutant when he appeared in the final match of the 1966-67 season against Everton at the age of 16 years 220 days. Widely considered one of Burnley's brightest prospects, he would go on to earn caps at Youth and Under-23 level before a £165,000 move to QPR in October 1972. He helped his new club win promotion to the First Division in 1973 and finish runners-up in the top flight three years later, having already won his eight full caps for England in that spell. Dave was sold to Everton in August 1977 for £200,000 but stayed only two seasons before moving on to Wolves for £325,000 in October 1979. He had a spell in Canada with Vancouver Whitecaps in 1981 before returning to the UK to play for Middlesbrough, finishing his playing career with Portsmouth in 1985. He was later appointed youth coach at Fratton Park.

Geoffrey Robert THOMAS

Born: Manchester, 5th August 1964
Role: Midfield
Career: Rochdale, Crewe Alexandra, Crystal Palace, Wolverhampton Wanderers, Nottingham Forest, Barnsley, Notts County, Crewe Alexandra
Debut: v Turkey (a) 1-5-1991 (ECQ)
Appearances: 9

Geoff signed as a professional with Rochdale in August 1982 and made 11 appearances for the club before moving on to Crewe Alexandra in March 1984. Although not developed by the Crewe academy, he soon proved to be the perfect student and would go on to make 125 appearances for Dario Gradi's side before a £50,000 fee took him to Crystal Palace in June 1987. His progress at Selhurst Park was such he forced his way into the England side in 1991 and made nine appearances for his country, with England being unbeaten in all nine. An £800,000 move took him to Wolves in June 1993, but injuries meant he was unable to secure a permanent place in the side nor reclaim his England place and he then spent brief spells with Nottingham Forest, Barnsley, Notts County and returned to Crewe Alexandra before hanging up his boots in 2002.

Geoff Thomas

Michael Lauriston THOMAS

Born: Lambeth, 24th August 1967
Role: Midfield
Career: Arsenal, Portsmouth, Arsenal, Liverpool, Benfica (Portugal), Middlesbrough, Wimbledon
Debut: v Saudi Arabia (a) 16-11-1988
Appearances: 2

Michael joined Arsenal as an apprentice and was upgraded to the professional ranks in December 1984, the same time as his future midfield partner David Rocastle. Michael spent a spell on loan to Portsmouth before returning to Highbury and making his debut in the League Cup semi final against Spurs. It is, however, his exploits in the League that ensured him a lasting place in Arsenal folklore, for he scored the crucial second goal at Anfield that won the 1989 League championship. Michael added a second championship medal in 1991 before being surprisingly sold to Liverpool for £1.5 million in December 1991, and although his time at Anfield

Michael Thomas

was plagued by injuries he did score one of the goals that won the FA Cup against Sunderland in 1992. He was released on a free transfer in 1997 and joined Benfica but was unable to settle in Portugal, returning to the UK in February 1998 to play for Middlesbrough on loan and joining Wimbledon when his Benfica contract expired. He retired from playing in 2001. During his time with Arsenal Michael achieved something of a record in having represented his country at five levels – schoolboy, Youth, Under-21, B and full level.

Alan THOMPSON

Born: Newcastle-Upon-Tyne, 22nd December 1973
Role: Midfield
Career: Newcastle United, Bolton Wanderers, Aston Villa, Celtic
Debut: v Sweden (a) 31-3-2004
Appearances: 1

Born in Newcastle-Upon-Tyne, Alan joined Newcastle United from their youth system, signing professional forms in March 1991. Two years later he moved on to Bolton Wanderers for £250,000 and helped the club reach the final of the Coca Cola Cup in 1995 where they were beaten by Liverpool. Two years later however he was an integral part of the side that won the First Division championship and promotion to the Premiership. In June 1998 he was signed by Aston Villa in a £4.5 million deal and two years later switched north of the border in a £2.5 million deal for Celtic. At Celtic Park he has helped the club win the League title on three occasions, the Scottish Cup twice and the Scottish League Cup once as well as reaching the final of the UEFA Cup. Having represented England at Under-18 and Under-21 (on two occasions) he finally received his full call-up for the match against Sweden in 2004. He played for an hour before being substituted.

Peter THOMPSON

Born: Carlisle, 27th November 1942
Role: Winger
Career: Preston North End, Liverpool, Bolton Wanderers
Debut: v Portugal (a) 17-5-1964
Appearances: 16

Peter played schoolboy football in his hometown Carlisle before joining the Deepdale ground staff in August 1958, turning professional in November 1959. He went on to make 122 appearances for Preston, his trickery on the wing earning rave reviews and admiring glances from other clubs. Bill Shankly paid £37,000 to take him to Anfield in August 1963 and he became an integral part of the first great Liverpool side Shankly built, winning League championship medals in 1964 and 1966, an FA Cup winners' medal in 1965 and runners-up medals from the European Cup Winners' Cup in 1966 and the FA Cup in 1971, although he was a substitute in the latter final. Peter also won four caps for England at Under-23 level and represented the Football League on five occasions to add to the schoolboy caps he had won earlier. Although he was a regular in the England side in Alf Ramsey's first year or so, the eventual phasing out of wingers in favour of a more solid midfield meant his final four caps for his country took four years to accumulate, the first 12 having been awarded over just two years. He went on loan to Bolton Wanderers in December 1973, the move becoming permanent in January 1974 for £18,000 and he retired from playing in March 1978. Peter then became director of a garage business as well as having interests in a number of caravan parks.

Peter Thompson

Philip Bernard THOMPSON

Born: Liverpool, 21st January 1954
Role: Centre-Back
Career: Liverpool, Sheffield United, Liverpool
Debut: v Wales (a) 24-3-1976
Appearances: 42 (1 goal) + 1 unofficial international

After playing schools football in Kirkby, Phil was signed by Liverpool as an apprentice and turned professional in February 1971. He spent virtually his entire career at

Phil Thompson

Anfield, developing into a solid and hard-tackling centre-back. During his time with the club he won five League championship medals (1976, 1977, 1979, 1980 and 1982), the European Cup twice (1978 and 1981), the UEFA Cup once (1976), the FA Cup once (1974) and the League Cup twice (1981 and 1982) as well as finishing with a runners-up medal in the 1978 League Cup medal. Having represented England at Youth and B level he was awarded his first full cap in 1976 and went on to make 42 appearances for the full side as well as one unofficial appearance in America in 1976 against Team America. Liverpool also won the League title in 1983 and 1984, although Phil's first team opportunities had diminished by then and he was allowed to go on loan to Sheffield United in December 1984, the move becoming permanent in March 1985. He returned to Liverpool in July 1986 as player-coach under Kenny Dalglish, leaving the club in 1990 following the appointment of Graeme Souness as manager. In 1998 he returned once again, assisting Gerard Houllier and taking over on a temporary basis when Houllier was undergoing a heart bypass operation. Phil remained at Anfield until 2004 when Houllier's contract was not renewed, with the new manager preferring to build his own team around him.

Thomas THOMPSON

Born: Fencehouses, County Durham, 10th November 1928
Role: Inside-Right
Career: Newcastle United, Aston Villa, Preston North End, Stoke City, Barrow
Debut: v Wales (a) 20-10-1951
Appearances: 2

Tommy 'Topper' Thompson was spotted by Newcastle United whilst turning out for Langley YMCA and cost £15 to sign as a professional in August 1946. He made his debut during the club's successful promotion season of 1947-48 but made just 20 appearances in three years before being allowed to join Aston Villa in September 1950 for £12,500. A little over a year later Tommy was a regular in the Aston Villa side and had been selected for England, proof that he had the ability to play at the highest level. After 165 games and 76 goals, Tommy was on the move again, this time costing Preston North End £28,500 for his signature in June 1955. Here he linked up with Tom Finney and over the course of the next six years grabbed 117 goals in 188 appearances and earned his second cap for England, some six years after his first. The closest he came to club honours during this time, however, was helping Preston finish League runners-up in 1957-58 behind Wolverhampton Wanderers, with Tommy weighing in with 34 goals. Tom Finney's retirement in April 1960 left the club with something of a mountain to overcome and at the end of the next season they were relegated into the Second Division. Tommy was allowed to leave following relegation, signing for Stoke City in a transfer deal worth £1,500 and helping the club earn promotion to the First Division. In March 1963 Tommy moved on again, joining Barrow, where he finished his career the following year. Tommy later returned to Preston North End, running the club's junior sides whilst Bobby Charlton was manager. As well as his two full caps for England, Tommy won a further cap for the B team and represented the Football League twice.

Tommy 'Topper' Thompson

Bobby Thomson

Robert Anthony THOMSON

Born: Smethwick, 5th December 1943
Role: Left-Back
Career: Wolverhampton Wanderers, Birmingham City, Walsall, Luton Town, Port Vale
Debut: v Northern Ireland (h) 20-11-1963
Appearances: 8

After representing Birmingham Schools, Bobby Thomson was taken onto the Wolves ground staff in 1959, becoming a professional in July 1961. He made his debut the following year in an FA Cup tie and showed a maturity beyond his years, culminating in his England debut whilst still a teenager. He remained with Wolves until March 1969 when a £55,000 move took him to Birmingham City, spending two and a half years at St. Andrews before joining Walsall on loan. He then joined Luton in 1972 and spent four years at Kenilworth Road before going off to America to play in the NASL. Upon his return he was transferred to Port Vale and spent a season there before playing non-League football. In addition to his eight caps at full level Bobby also won 15 Under-23 caps and represented the Football League on four occasions. He later ran a sports shop in Sedgley.

George THORNEWELL

Born: Romiley, 8th July 1898
Died: 6th March 1986
Role: Right-Winger
Career: Nottingham Forest, Derby County, Blackburn Rovers, Chesterfield
Debut: v Sweden (a) 21-5-1923 (scored once)
Appearances: 4 (1 goal) + 1 unofficial appearance

Born in Romiley in Cheshire, George was the youngest of eight children and moved with his widowed mother to Derby when aged just eight months. He was apprenticed at Rolls Royce in Derby during the First World War and played for the works side, subsequently being invited to guest for Nottingham Forest during the hostilities. After the war, however, he was offered professional terms by Derby County, signing with the club in May 1919 and spending eight years at the Baseball Ground. He moved on to Blackburn Rovers in December 1927 and would go on to help his new club win the FA Cup at the end of his first season at Ewood Park. In August 1929 he joined Chesterfield and collected a Third Division North championship medal where he finished his League career in 1932 having made exactly 400 appearances for his three clubs. He then played non-League football for Newark Town before becoming a licensee at Duffield near Derby.

Irvine THORNLEY

Born: Glossop, 1883
Died: 24th April 1955
Role: Centre-Forward
Career: Glossop Villa, Glossop St. James, Glossop North End, Manchester City, South Shields, Hamilton Academicals, Houghton
Debut: v Wales (h) 18-3-1907
Appearances: 1

Irvine played for a number of local sides in Glossop before signing with Glossop North End during the 1901-02 season and soon established a reputation as a powerful centre-forward. He was sold to Manchester City in March 1904 and became an instant hit with the Hyde Road crowd, although all he had to show in the way of honours was a championship medal from the Second Division in 1910, two appearances for the Football League and a solitary cap for England. Such was his popularity, however, that his benefit from the club amounted to £1,036, then a record. Irvine moved on to South Shields in August 1912 and his League career came to an end with the outbreak of the First World War. He joined Hamilton Academicals in the summer of 1919 and spent a year in Scotland before joining non-League Houghton where he finished his playing career.

Samuel Frederick TILSON

Born: Barnsley, 19th April 1903
Died: 21st November 1972
Role: Centre-Forward, Inside-Left
Career: Barnsley, Manchester City, Northampton Town, York City
Debut: v Hungary (a) 10-5-1934 (scored once)
Appearances: 4 (6 goals)

Fred played schools football in Barnsley before joining his local senior side in March 1926 and becoming first choice as an inside-forward. In March 1928 he and Eric Brook, also a future England player, were sold to Manchester City for a joint fee of £4,000 and had a galvanising effect on City's fortunes. Although Fred played a large part in helping City reach the FA Cup final at Wembley in 1933, he missed the final itself owing to injury. Deprived of his goalscoring abilities, City slumped to a 3-0 defeat by Everton, but Fred bounced back and scored four times in the semi final and twice in the final itself to give City a 2-1 victory over Portsmouth the following year. Fred also helped the club win the Football League in 1937 and would go on to earn representative honours with the Football League. He remained at Maine Road until March 1938 when he joined Northampton Town and spent a little over a year with the club before moving on to York City in the summer of 1939. The outbreak of the Second World War brought his playing career to an end and at the end of the hostilities he returned to Maine Road to become coach, subsequently becoming assistant manager until 1965 and then chief scout.

Fred Tilson

Frederick TITMUSS

Born: Pirton, 15th February 1898
Died: 2nd October 1966
Role: Left-Back
Career: Pirton United, Hitchin Town, Southampton, Plymouth Argyle, St. Austell
Debut: v Wales (h) 13-3-1922
Appearances: 2

Fred played non-League football before the First World War and served in the Royal Garrison Artillery and Lancashire Fusiliers during the hostilities as well as playing representative football for the Army. This alerted Southampton who signed him in the summer of 1919 and after a season in the Southern League, Fred made his debut in the Football League in 1920. A member of the side that won the Third Division South in 1922, he was honoured with his first cap for England the same season against Wales, collecting a second cap the following year against the same opposition. He remained at The Dell until February 1926 when he moved along the coast to join Plymouth, collecting a second Third Division South championship medal in 1930. Fred retired in 1932 but later turned out as a part-time professional with St. Austell. He was also a licensee in Plymouth until his death in 1966.

Colin TODD

Born: Chester-le-Street, 12th December 1948
Role: Defender
Career: Sunderland, Derby County, Everton, Birmingham City, Nottingham Forest, Oxford United, Vancouver Whitecaps (Canada), Luton Town
Debut: v Northern Ireland (h) 23-5-1972
Appearances: 27 + 1 unofficial international

Colin was taken on as an apprentice by Sunderland at the age of 15, subsequently turning professional in December 1965 and making his League debut the following year. Although he began his career as a left-half he was later successfully converted to a more defensive role and in February 1971 Derby County paid £175,000 to take him to the Baseball Ground. Here Colin helped the club win two League titles, in 1972 and 1975, as well as breaking into the England setup. In September 1978 he was sold to Everton for £300,000 but spent only a year at Goodison Park before moving on to Birmingham City for £250,000. Brian Clough bought him for a second time in August 1982 (Clough had previously been manager of Derby County), with Nottingham Forest paying a cut price £65,000 for him, although his experience proved invaluable for the club. He then spent a couple of months with Oxford United before going to Canada to play for Vancouver Whitecaps. Upon his return to England in October 1984 he wound down his playing career with Luton Town and later accepted a coaching position with Middlesbrough. He was promoted to first team coach in September 1986 and manager in 1990, although his spell in charge lasted only a year before he linked with Bruce Rioch as assistant manager at Bolton Wanderers. He was appointed manager of Bolton in January 1996. In addition to his 27 full caps, Colin also represented his country at Youth and Under-23 level, making 14 appearances at the latter level, and also turned out three times for the Football League.

Colin Todd

George TOONE

Born: Nottingham, 10th June 1868
Died: 1st September 1943
Role: Goalkeeper
Career: Nottingham Jardine, Notts Rangers, Notts County, Bedminster, Bristol City, Notts County
Debut: v Wales (a) 5-3-1892
Appearances: 2

George played for numerous clubs in and around the Nottingham area before signing with Notts County in 1889, going on to help the club win the FA Cup in 1894 and the Second Division championship in 1897. He remained with the club for a further two years before moving on to Bedminster, subsequently joining Bristol City in the summer of 1900 and returning to sign for Notts County a second time in 1901. He retired a year later and then became a licensee in the city. His son George junior also played League football for Notts County, Sheffield Wednesday and Watford.

Arthur George TOPHAM

Born: Ellesmere, 19th February 1869
Died: 18th May 1931
Role: Right-Half
Career: Oxford University, Casuals, Eastbourne, Chiswick Park, Corinthians
Debut: v Wales (a) 12-3-1894
Appearances: 1 + 1 unofficial appearance

Educated at Oswestry School, Arthur attended Oxford University and won a Blue in 1890 before going on to assist Casuals, Eastbourne and Chiswick Park as well as turning out for Corinthians. He was known as an adaptable half-back, playing at left-half for his only full international and centre-half when he helped Casuals reach the FA Amateur Cup final in 1894. He was a schoolmaster by profession and was initially the co-proprietor of a school in Eastbourne before teaching at Ascham St. Vincent's in the town. His brother Robert (below) also played for England.

Robert TOPHAM

Born: Ellesmere, 3rd November 1867
Died: 31st August 1931
Role: Right-Winger
Career: Oxford University, Oswestry FC, Casuals, Chiswick Park, Corinthians
Debut: v Ireland (h) 25-2-1893
Appearances: 2

The elder brother of Arthur Topham (above), Robert was also educated at Oswestry School and attended Oxford University, although he did not win a Blue. He then played for Oswestry and helped them reach the Welsh Cup final in 1885, a performance that earned him an invitation to play for Wales against Scotland, although he declined. Instead he continued his playing career in England, joining Wolves in 1891 and helping them win the FA Cup in 1893, the same season he made his first appearance for England. Robert also played for a number of amateur sides during his spell with Wolves and was thus able to help Casuals reach the FA Amateur Cup final in 1894 and also made a number of appearances for Corinthians between 1894 and 1898, his Wolves association ending in 1896. Like his brother he was initially a schoolmaster by profession, teaching at Brighton College between 1892 and 1905. He then became a hop grower in Kent.

Mark Towers

Mark Anthony TOWERS

Born: Manchester, 13th April 1952
Role: Midfield
Career: Manchester City, Sunderland, Birmingham City, Montreal Manic (Canada), Tampa Bay Rowdies (USA), Vancouver Whitecaps (Canada), Rochdale
Debut: v Wales (a) 8-5-1976
Appearances: 3

A local lad who had represented Manchester, Lancashire and England at schoolboy level, Tony was signed as an apprentice by Manchester City in July 1967 and turned professional in April 1969. He would go on to collect further international honours at Youth and Under-23 level and he collected his first major honour in the game just a few days after his eighteenth birthday when he helped Manchester City win the European Cup Winners' Cup in 1970. In 1974 he collected a runners-up medal in the League Cup and in March of that year was sold to Sunderland for £100,000 where he became an influential player who helped them win the Second Division championship in 1976. He won his three England caps whilst at Roker Park before being sold to Birmingham City in July 1977 for £140,000, but failed to fully settle at St. Andrews, having a spell in North America before returning to England and playing on a non-contract basis for Rochdale.

William J. TOWNLEY

Born: Blackburn, 14th February 1866
Died: 30th May 1950
Role: Left-Winger
Career: Blackburn Olympic, Blackburn Rovers, Stockton, Darwen, Manchester City
Debut: v Wales (h) 23-2-1889
Appearances: 2 (2 goals)

William played junior football in the Blackburn area and was briefly signed to Blackburn Olympic before joining Blackburn Rovers in 1887. A member of the side that won the FA Cup in successive seasons 1890 and 1891, he was the first player to score a hat-trick in the final, a feat achieved in the 6-1 win over Sheffield Wednesday in 1890. He remained with Rovers until July 1892 when he joined Stockton, later having spells with Darwen and Manchester City until his retirement as a player in the summer of 1897. William had been a schoolteacher from 1890 (he was a part-time footballer) until 1909 when he moved to the continent to become a coach, coaching in Germany prior to the First World War and Holland, Sweden and Switzerland after the hostilities.

John Ernest TOWNROW

Born: West Ham, 28th March 1901
Died: 11th April 1969
Role: Centre-Half
Career: Fairbairn House, Clapton Orient, Chelsea, Bristol Rovers
Debut: v Scotland (a) 4-4-1925
Appearances: 2

John played representative football for West Ham schools and was working as an engineer at Becton Gasworks and playing part-time for non-League Fairbairn House when he was invited to sign for Clapton Orient in August 1919. He maintained his job at Becton Gasworks whilst playing for Clapton, performing well enough to earn two caps for England. He remained with Clapton until February 1927 when he was sold to Chelsea for £5,000 and spent almost five years with the club before moving on to Bristol Rovers in May 1932. He spent a year at Eastville before hanging up his boots, subsequently joining the licensed trade.

Richard Daniel TREMELLING

Born: Burton-on-Trent, 12th November 1897
Died: 1970
Role: Goalkeeper
Career: Shirebrook, Lincoln City, Birmingham, Bury
Debut: v Wales (h) 28-11-1927
Appearances: 1

Dan began his playing career with the Langwith Colliery Junction Wagon Works side before joining Shirebrook and assisting Lincoln City during the First World War. In June 1919 he joined Birmingham City and would go on to help the club win the Second Division championship in 1921 as well as making three appearances for the Football League. He was unable to gain more than one full cap for England, however, chiefly because the England selectors were unsure as to who was the best goalkeeper around at the time – they tried 21 different players in the position in 46 internationals before finally settling on a regular goalkeeper, who turned out to be Dan's original understudy at Birmingham, Harry Hibbs. It says much for Dan's abilities that Harry was unable to dislodge Dan for almost five years at St. Andrews. Dan left for Bury in May 1933 and spent three years with the club, returning to Birmingham as assistant trainer, a position he held until the outbreak of the Second World War.

Dan Tremelling

John TRESADERN

Born: Leytonstone, 26th September 1890
Died: 26th September 1959
Role: Left-Half
Career: Barking Town, West Ham United, Burnley, Northampton Town
Debut: v Scotland (a) 14-4-1923
Appearances: 2

Jack played for Barking Town before being invited along to West Ham United in July 1913, signing amateur forms before turning professional during the following season. During the First World War he served with the Royal Garrison Artillery and then resumed his playing career, helping West Ham reach the very first FA Cup final held at Wembley in 1923, although they lost 2-0 to Bolton. Jack remained with West Ham until October 1924 when he moved on to Burnley, but seven months later he was appointed player-manager of Northampton Town. He retired from playing in 1927 but remained manager until 1930, thus beginning a managerial career that was to last almost for the rest of his life. He was in charge at Crystal Palace (he was also secretary of the club at the same time) between October 1930 and June 1935, then at Spurs until April 1938 when he joined Plymouth Argyle, a position he retained until November 1947. Jack then had a spell scouting for Aston Villa before returning to management with Chelmsford City in June 1949. He was later in charge at Hastings United and Tonbridge, holding the latter position from April 1958 until his death in 1970.

Dennis TUEART

Born: Newcastle, 27th November 1949
Role: Forward
Career: Sunderland, Manchester City, New York Cosmos (USA), Manchester City, Stoke City, Burnley, Derry City
Debut: v Cyprus (a) (substitute) 11-5-1975 (ECQ)
Appearances: 6 (2 goals)

Dennis represented Newcastle schools and played junior football in the town before signing for local rivals Sunderland in August 1967. A member of the side that surprisingly won the FA Cup against Leeds United in 1973, Dennis was sold to Manchester City for £275,000 in March 1974. During his first spell at Maine Road he helped the club win the League Cup in 1976 (he scored the winning goal with an overhead kick) and finish runners-up in the League the following season. He was sold to New York Cosmos for £250,000 in February 1978 but returned to Manchester City for £150,000 almost two years later, going on to collect a runners-up medal in the FA Cup in 1981. He remained at Maine Road until July 1983 when he joined Stoke City, subsequently playing for Burnley and finishing his playing career with Derry City in Ireland. Dennis later served on the board of directors of Manchester City.

Dennis Tueart

Frederick Edward TUNSTALL

Born: Low Valley, 29th March 1900
Died: 18th November 1965
Role: Left-Winger
Career: Darfield St. George's, Scunthorpe United, Sheffield United, Halifax Town, Boston United
Debut: v Scotland (a) 14-4-1923
Appearances: 7

Known as 'Tunny' throughout his career, he joined then non-League Scunthorpe United in 1920 and made an immediate impact, so much so that Sheffield United swooped to pay a fee of £1,000 to take him to Bramall Lane in December 1920. He went on to represent the Football League on four occasions, collect seven caps for England and help Sheffield United win the FA Cup in 1925, scoring the only goal of the game in the 1-0 win over Cardiff City. Tunny remained at Bramall Lane until February 1933 when he joined Halifax Town, spending a little over three years at Halifax before moving on to Boston United. He finished his playing career at Boston but continued to assist the club after the Second World War, serving as trainer, coach and manager.

Frederick Tunstall

Robert Joseph TURNBULL

Born: South Bank, 17th December 1895
Died: 18 March 1952
Role: Right-Winger
Career: South Bank East End, Bradford, Leeds United, Rhyl Athletic
Debut: v Ireland (a) 25-10-1919
Appearances: 1 + 3 War appearances (1 goal)

Robert played schools football in South Bank, Middlesbrough and joined local club South Bank East End after he finished his education whilst also working as a steel worker. During the First World War he played football for the Army and subsequently signed for Bradford in January 1918. He made an immediate impact at Bradford, earning selection for the England side in the Victory International against Scotland at Everton in April 1919 and scored one of England's goals in the 2-2 draw. He played in a further two Victory Internationals and also appeared in the first official international against Ireland later the same year. The closest he came to similar honours was being selected to join the FA touring party that visited South Africa in 1920 and 1929, making a total of five appearances during the two tours. Robert remained at Bradford until May 1925 when he joined Leeds United, finishing his League career with the club in September 1932 and stepping into the non-League game with Rhyl Athletic. He retired from playing in 1933 and returned to his former occupation of steel worker.

Arthur Turner

Arthur TURNER

Born: Farnborough, June 1877
Died: Farnborough, 4th April 1925
Role: Right-Winger
Career: Aldershot North End, South Farnborough, Camberley St. Michaels, Southampton, Derby County, Newcastle United, Tottenham Hotspur, Southampton
Debut: v Ireland (a) 17-3-1900
Appearances: 2

Arthur played for a number of clubs before joining Southern League outfit Southampton in 1899 and was part of a three year burst of success that saw the club reach the FA Cup final twice, 1900 and 1902, and win the Southern League championship in 1901. In May 1902 he joined Derby County but less than a year later moved on to Newcastle United. He returned to the Southern League with Spurs in February 1904, costing the club £150 but made only 13 appearances for the White Hart Lane club before being released and rejoining Southampton. His second sojourn at The Dell was similarly short, for Arthur played for a single season, including one match on loan to Bristol City, before retiring at the age of 28 and joining his father's business in Farnborough.

Hugh TURNER

Born: Wigan, 6th August 1904
Died: 1997
Role: Goalkeeper
Career: Felling Colliery, High Fell, Huddersfield Town, Fulham
Debut: v France (a) 14-5-1931
Appearances: 2

Hugh was playing for Felling Colliery when he was offered amateur forms by Darlington in 1924 although he failed to make the grade for the club, subsequently signing for the High Fell club in Gateshead. Here he was spotted by Huddersfield Town and offered professional forms, signing in April 1926. He was unfortunate that Huddersfield's great side of the 1920s was already beginning to be eclipsed by others, although they finished runners-up in the First Division in consecutive seasons (having won the title for the previous three years) and reached the FA Cup Final in 1930 where they were beaten by Arsenal. The following year Hugh represented both the Football League and the full England side and remained at Leeds Road until May 1937. After 364 League appearances for Huddersfield he was allowed to join Fulham, making a further 68 appearances for the Cottagers before the outbreak of the Second World War effectively brought his career to an end, although he remained with the club during the hostilities.

James Albert TURNER

Born: Blackbull, 1866
Died: 9th April 1904
Role: Left-Half
Career: Black Lane Rovers, Bolton Wanderers, Stoke, Derby County, Stoke
Debut: v Wales (h) 13-3-1893
Appearances: 3

Signed by Bolton Wanderers from Black Lane Rovers early in 1889, James was known to be a versatile player in an era before the term was properly understood. Although he won all three of his England caps at left-half, he variously played on either flank as a winger during his career. He remained at Burnden Park until the summer of 1894 when he left to join Stoke but his career took off with his transfer to Derby County for £70 in June 1896. A member of the side that reached the FA Cup final in 1898 (in which he played at left-half), James finished the season with Derby before returning to Stoke in August and finishing his career in 1900. His three caps for England were achieved over a period of five years, during his time with Bolton, Stoke and Derby and he could be considered unlucky not to have won further caps during this period. After retiring from playing he worked as a clerk for a commercial firm.

George Jacob TWEEDY

Born: Willington Quay, 8th January 1913
Died: 23rd April 1987
Role: Goalkeeper
Career: Willington Town, Grimsby Town
Debut: v Hungary (h) 2-12-1936
Appearances: 1

George played schools football in the County Durham area before signing with Grimsby Town in August 1931. He was to spend his entire career with Grimsby, making 347 League appearances over the course of some twenty years, although seven seasons were lost owing to the Second World War. He initially retired from playing in the summer of 1950 and was appointed assistant manager in September, although he registered as a player again towards the end of 1951, finally retiring for good in April 1953. He was unfortunate not to have won further caps for England, but the form of Harry Hibbs and Vic Woodley restricted him to a single appearance. After leaving football George worked in the furniture trade in Grimsby.

U-V

UFTON, Derek Gilbert
UNDERWOOD, Alfred
UNSWORTH, David Gerald
UPSON, Matthew
URWIN, Thomas
UTLEY, George

VASSELL, Darius
VAUGHTON, Oliver Harold
VEITCH, Colin Campbell McKechnie
VEITCH, John Gould
VENABLES, Terence Frederick
VENISON, Barry
VIDAL, Reverend Robert Walpole Sealy
VILJOEN, Colin
VIOLLET, Dennis S
VON DONOP, Pelham George

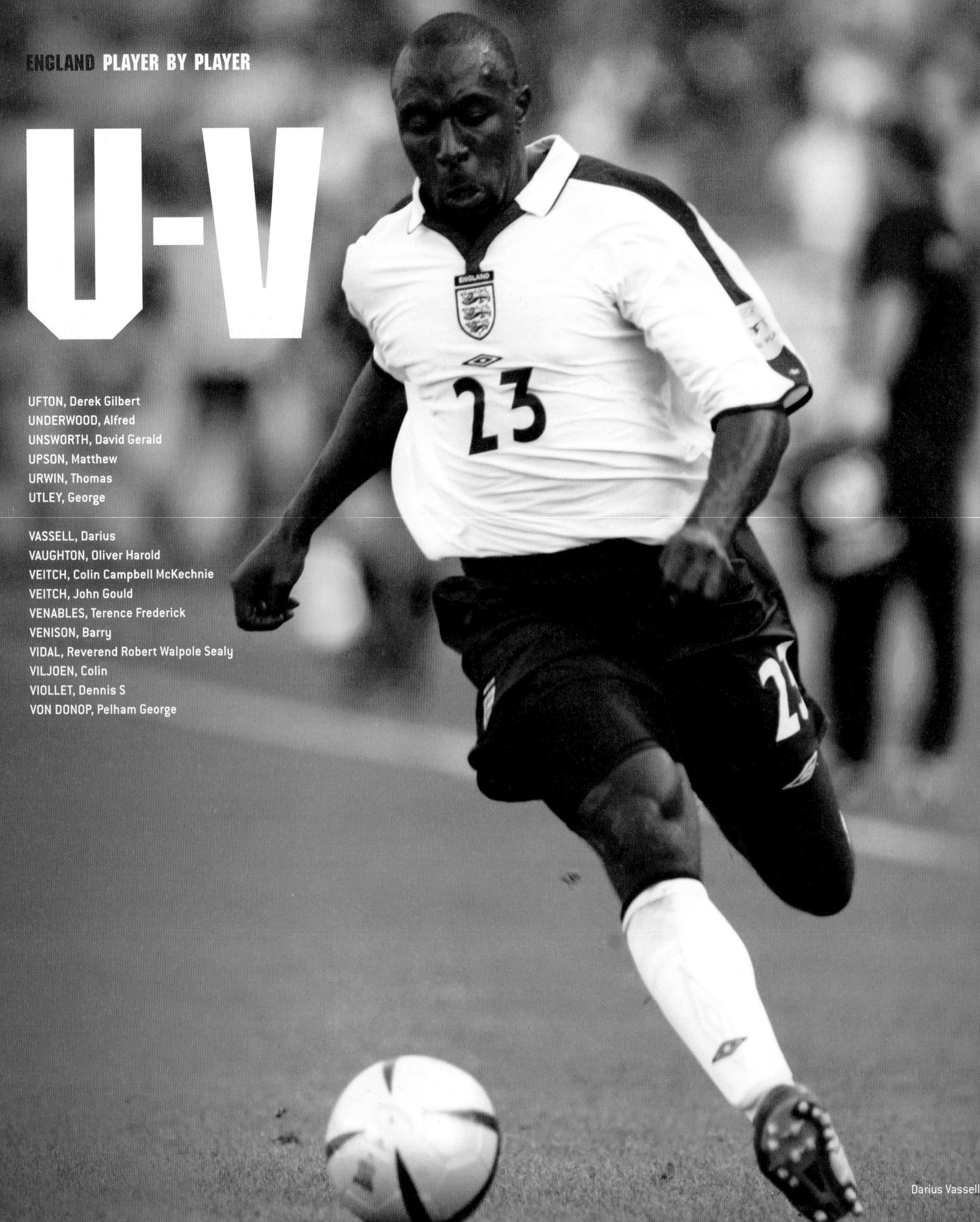

Darius Vassell

Derek Gilbert UFTON

Born: Crayford, 31st May 1928
Role: Left-Half
Career: Borough United, Dulwich Hamlet, Cardiff City, Bexleyheath & Welling, Charlton Athletic
Debut: v Rest of Europe (h) 21-10-1953
Appearances: 1

Derek played non-League football for Borough United, Dulwich Hamlet and Bexleyheath & Welling and was briefly on Cardiff City's books as an amateur before signing professional forms with Charlton Athletic in September 1948. Over the course of the next twelve years Derek gave the club exceptional service, amassing 263 League appearances at the heart of the Charlton defence. So concerned was he with preventing opposition goals, Derek failed to get his name on the scoresheet for Charlton! Having suffered twenty dislocations during his career, injury finally forced him into retirement in the summer of 1960. He then moved into coaching and management, initially with non-League Tooting & Mitcham before linking with Malcolm Allison at Plymouth Argyle in September 1964. Following Allison's departure for Manchester City, Derek was appointed caretaker manager in April 1965, his full-time appointment being confirmed the following month. Derek remained in charge at Home Park until January 1968 when he was sacked following poor results. Derek was also an accomplished cricketer, making 148 appearances for Kent between 1949 and 1962, scoring 3,919 runs and taking 314 wickets as wicketkeeper. Away from the game Derek managed a West End club and had a spell as a photographic model! In August 1984 Derek was appointed to the board of Charlton Athletic, a position he still holds, and is also president of Kent County Cricket Club.

Alfred UNDERWOOD

Born: Newcastle-under-Lyme, 1869
Died: 8th October 1928
Role: Left-Back
Career: Hanley Tabernacle, Etruria, Stoke
Debut: v Ireland (h) 7-3-1891
Appearances: 2

Alf played local football in the Stoke area before joining Stoke some time in the mid 1880s. A member of the side that won the Football Alliance championship in 1891, Alf had therefore played for the club before they became a founder member of the football League, had suffered the ignominy of not being re-elected and then earning promotion back into the League, all in the space of three years! Alf suffered a bad injury upon Stoke's return to League action and officially retired in the summer of 1892, although he made a number of sporadic appearances for some time after. According to contemporary reports, the injury was sufficient to leave him little more than an invalid by the turn of the century.

David Gerald UNSWORTH

Born: Chorley, 16th October 1973
Role: Defender
Career: Everton, West Ham United, Aston Villa, Everton, Portsmouth, Ipswich Town, Sheffield United
Debut: v Japan (h) 3-6-1995
Appearances: 1

Dave developed through the ranks at Everton and became a full professional in 1992. He went on to help the club win the FA Cup in 1995 and was also capped by England during the same summer, but thereafter seemed to lose his way a little as the club faced a continuous struggle against relegation. He was sold to West Ham in August 1997 but was unable to settle in London and the club reluctantly sold him to Aston Villa during the close season of 1998. Even that wasn't the end of the story, for less than a week later Dave informed Villa manager John Gregory that his family had been unable to settle in Birmingham either and had returned to Merseyside and he would need to join them! This prompted an enquiry from Everton, with the transfer eventually going through after protracted negotiations concerning how the £3 million fee was to be paid. In July 2004 he was released and joined Portsmouth on a free transfer, subsequently spending a spell on loan at Ipswich Town. At the start of the 2005-06 season he joined Sheffield United.

Dave Unsworth

Matthew James UPSON

Born: Hartismere, 18th April 1979
Role: Defender
Career: Luton Town, Arsenal, Nottingham Forest, Crystal Palace, Reading, Birmingham City
Debut: v South Africa (a) 27-5-2003
Appearances: 7

Matthew joined Luton as a trainee and won recognition for England at Youth level before he signed professional forms in April 1996. He was considered such a bright prospect for the future that Arsenal paid £1 million to take him to Highbury in May 1997, even though he had made only one substitute appearance for the Luton first team! Initially seen as cover for the aging Tony Adams, Martin Keown and Steve Bould, Matthew made the occasional first team appearance and forced his way into the England Under-21 side. A ruptured cruciate ligament sustained during 2000-01 ruled him out for most of the season and once recovered he had spells on loan with Nottingham Forest and Crystal Palace to prove his fitness. Upon returning to Highbury he had forced his way back into the first team when a broken fibula put him on the sidelines once again. He then went on loan to Reading before a permanent move to Birmingham City for £2 million in January 2003.

Matthew Upson

Thomas URWIN

Born: Haswell, 5th February 1896
Died: 7th May 1968
Role: Left-Winger
Career: Fulwell, Lambton Star, Shildon, Middlesbrough, Newcastle United, Sunderland
Debut: v Sweden (a) 21-5-1923
Appearances: 4

One of only a handful of players to have appeared for the big three North East clubs, Tom joined Middlesbrough from Shildon in May 1914 but had to wait until 1919 to make his League debut owing to the outbreak of the First World War. He won representative honours with the Football League before collecting his first England cap during the summer tour of Sweden in 1923. In August 1924 he was sold to Newcastle United for £3,200 and won his final cap against Wales in 1926 and the following year helped Newcastle win the League championship. A move to Sunderland in February 1930 for £525 followed, with Tom subsequently retiring from playing in the summer of 1936. He later coached the Roker Park junior side and worked as a clerk at a Sunderland hospital before retiring in 1962.

George UTLEY

Born: Elsecar, 1887
Died: 8th January 1966
Role: Left-Half
Career: Elsecar – Wentworth, Sheffield Wednesday, Elsecar, Barnsley, Sheffield United, Manchester City
Debut: v Ireland (a) 15-2-1913
Appearances: 1

George was spotted by Sheffield Wednesday playing for Wentworth and was signed on an amateur basis in the summer of 1906. A knee injury that required surgery meant he never got to play for the club, being released in early in 1907 and returning to Elsecar. He obviously recovered from his injury, for Barnsley signed him later the same year and he would go on to help them win the FA Cup in 1912, represent the Football League and collect his only cap for England. He was sold to Sheffield United for a then record fee of £2,000 in November 1913, eventually taking over a sports good shop in the city as part of the deal. George won a second FA Cup winners' medal in 1915 and remained at Bramall Lane until September 1922 when he joined Manchester City where he finished his playing career a year later. George then had spells on the coaching staff at Bristol City and Sheffield Wednesday as well as being cricket coach at Rossall, a public school in Lancashire.

Darius VASSELL

Born: Birmingham, 13th June 1980
Role: Forward
Career: Aston Villa – Manchester City
Debut: v Holland (a) 13-2-2002 (scored once)
Appearances: 22 (6 goals)

Darius grew up an Aston Villa fan and joined the club's School of Excellence at the age of 13 and rose through the ranks, netting 39 goals in one season with the youth side and signing professional forms in April 1998. He made his first team debut in August 1998, going on to represent England at Under-18 and Under-21 level, picking up 11 caps at the latter level. By 2000 he was a regular in the Aston Villa side and two years later made a scoring debut for the full England side. A member of the squad for the World Cup finals in 2002 and the European Championships two years later, Darius looked to revive his club career with a move to Manchester City for £2 million in July 2005.

Oliver Harold VAUGHTON

Born: Aston, 9th January 1861
Died: 6th January 1937
Role: Inside-Left
Career: Waterloo FC, Birmingham FC, Wednesbury Strollers, Aston Villa
Debut: v Ireland (a) 18-2-1882
Appearances: 5 (6 goals)

Howard joined Aston Villa in 1880 from Wednesbury Strollers and earned the accolade of being one of the club's first international players, a feat he achieved in the 13-0 win over Ireland in 1882. It is recorded that he scored five goals in this match, the first time an England player had scored as many as five goals in a single game, although there is still some considerable doubt as to whether or not he scored five, since it was not common practice to record the names of goalscorers at the time. At club level he was a member of the Aston Villa side that won their very first FA Cup in 1887, a year before injury forced his retirement. However Howard retained his connection with Villa, serving the club as vice-president in 1923 and in February 1933 was made a life member of the club. When he retired in 1888 he started a silversmith business and seven years later in 1895 when the FA Cup was stolen (whilst in Villa's safekeeping!) his was the company engaged to produce a new trophy.

Colin Campbell McKechnie VEITCH

Born: Newcastle-upon-Tyne, 22nd May 1881
Died: 26th August 1938
Role: Half-Back
Career: Newcastle United
Debut: v Ireland (a) 17-2-1906
Appearances: 6

Colin played all of his football in the Newcastle area, representing Newcastle schools and Rutherford College before signing for Newcastle United as an amateur in January 1899, turning professional four years later. He helped the club win three League championships, in 1905, 1907 and 1909 and reach the final of the FA Cup five times, although only one of these, in 1910, resulted in victory (Newcastle never won once at the final venue of Crystal Palace, their only victory coming in a replay at Goodison Park) with runners-up medals being collected in 1905, 1906, 1908 and 1911. Colin served as chairman of the Players' Union between 1909 and 1912 and remained a player with Newcastle United until retiring during the First World War. After the war he became secretary of Newcastle Swifts, United's nursery side, before a brief spell as secretary-manager of Bradford City between August 1926 and January 1928. A producer and actor and briefly chairman of Newcastle People's Theatre, Colin was a journalist from 1929 until his death in 1938.

John Gould VEITCH

Born: Kingston Hill, 19th July 1869
Died: 3rd October 1914
Role: Left-Winger
Career: Cambridge University, Old Westminsters, Corinthians
Debut: v Wales (a) 12-3-1894
Appearances: 1 (3 goals)

Educated at Westminster School and a member of the school side in 1887 he then attended Cambridge University and won a Blue in 1888, 1889, 1890 and 1891. He assisted Corinthians between 1889 and 1898, making a total of 72 appearances for the club and scoring 63 goals, a remarkable return for a winger. Indeed, it is John's goalscoring abilities that have ensured his place in England history, for in his one and only appearance for his country he netted a hat-trick, one of only five players to have netted as many goals in their only national appearance.

Terence Frederick VENABLES

Born: Bethnal Green, 6th January 1943
Role: Inside-Forward
Career: Chelsea, Tottenham Hotspur, Queens Park Rangers, Crystal Palace
Debut: v Belgium (h) 21-10-1964
Appearances: 2

The only man to have been capped by England at every possible level (schoolboy, youth, amateur, Under-23 and full), Terry made his name with Chelsea whom he joined as a junior straight from school. He made his League debut in 1959 and won a League Cup winners' medal in 1965 before joining Tottenham in May 1966. The following season he won an FA Cup winners' medal with Spurs (against Chelsea) although never really settled at the club and left to join Queens Park Rangers in June 1969. After five years with Rangers he moved on to Crystal Palace, but after only 14 appearances was persuaded by manager Malcolm Allison to move onto the coaching side. As coach and later manager Terry found his true vocation, producing a side that was acclaimed 'Team of the Eighties', although following his departure to Queens Park Rangers his former side suffered relegation. He built a side at Rangers good enough to reach the 1982 FA Cup final (lost to Spurs after a replay) and win the Second Division championship the following season. In 1984 QPR qualified for the UEFA Cup, but before Terry could attempt an assault on this competition he accepted an offer to become manager of Spanish giants Barcelona. They won the Spanish title in his first season as manager (their first Spanish title in eleven years) and the following season reached the final of the European Cup, losing on penalties to Steaua Bucharest. After a bad start to the 1987 - 88 season Barcelona dismissed him, but at the same time Spurs had parted company with David Pleat and Terry took over at White Hart Lane. In 1991, against a backdrop of financial problems and threatened bankruptcy, he led Spurs to the FA Cup, beating Nottingham Forest 2-1. During the summer he and colleague Alan Sugar completed the takeover of Tottenham, although the pair fell out spectacularly in 1993, with Terry being dismissed from his position as managing director. For the next six months he spent his time between courts and television panels until in January 1994 he accepted the offer he'd always yearned for; that of England manager. He held the England position until the end of the 1996 European Championships in England, guiding the host country to the semi-finals where they were beaten in a penalty shoot-out by Germany, and then returned to domestic football in the capacity of chairman of Portsmouth. By the end of the year he was also appointed manager of the Australian national side. In 1998 he became manager at Crystal Palace, although he later had spells as chief coach at Portsmouth and Middlesborough before returning to full time management with Leeds United in 2002, being relieved of his position the following year. Aside from his football activities over the years, Terry is an accomplished writer (his Hazell series was filmed for television) and singer.

Terry Venables

Barry Venison

Barry VENISON

Born: Consett, 16th August 1964
Role: Defender
Career: Sunderland, Liverpool, Newcastle United, Galatasaray (Turkey), Southampton
Debut: v USA (h) 7-9-1994
Appearances: 2

Barry joined Sunderland as a youngster and earned Youth and Under-21 caps for England during his time at Roker Park. A member of the side that reached the League Cup final in 1985, he chose not to extend his contract when it expired in 1986, instead writing to every club in the top division in search of a deal. He was eventually signed by Liverpool, who paid Sunderland £250,000 to secure the deal, and Barry helped the club win the FA Cup in 1989 and the League title in 1988 and 1990. Displaced from the first team through a succession of injuries, Barry joined Newcastle United for £250,000 in 1992 and was appointed club captain, although he was stripped of the post for breaking a club curfew. He then had a spell playing in Turkey under former Liverpool manager Graeme Souness at Galatasaray before finishing his career at Southampton through injury in 1997.

Reverend Robert Walpole Sealy VIDAL

Born: Cornborough, 3rd September 1853
Died: Abbotsham, 5th November 1914
Role: Forward
Career: Oxford University, Wanderers, Old Westminsters
Debut: v Scotland (h) 8-3-1873
Appearances: 1 + 5 unofficial appearance

Had any of England's first three matches at Kennington Oval against Scotland been deemed official, then Robert Vidal would have held the honour of being the youngest player to have represented the country, being only 16 when the first of these matches was played in 1870. As it was, Robert, who was educated at Westminster School, is surely the only player to have won an FA Cup winners' medal whilst still at school, for he was a member of the Wanderers side that won the first FA Cup final in 1872, although he was still studying at Westminster. He left the same year to continue his education at Oxford University and appeared in the next two FA Cup finals for his university, being on the losing side in 1873 and the winning side in 1874, the first player to collect winners' medals for more than one club. Despite his youth he was a member of the FA Committee between 1872 and 1874, earned a Blue at Oxford for rugby in 1873 (he won the football equivalent in 1874 and 1875 and was captain in the latter year) and was also a more than adequate golfer. Ordained in 1877 he became vicar of Abbotsham in Devon in 1881 and remained there to his death in 1914.

Colin VILJOEN

Born: Johannesburg, South Africa, 20th June 1948
Role: Midfield
Career: Ipswich Town, Manchester City, Chelsea
Debut: v Northern Ireland (a) 17-5-1975
Appearances: 2

Colin began his career with Southern Transvaal before joining Ipswich as an amateur in 1966, signing professional forms in March 1967. That same month he made his debut for the first team, netting a hat-trick against Portsmouth and instantly endearing himself to the Portman Road crowd. The following year he helped Ipswich win the Second Division championship and would go on to make 305 League appearances for the club, netting 45 goals. He became a British citizen in 1971 and went on to win two caps for his adopted country, although an Achilles tendon injury sustained soon after he had won his second cap caused him to miss the entire 1976-77 season, thus bringing an end to his international career. In August 1978 he was sold to Manchester City, making just 27 appearances for the club before a further move to Chelsea for £45,000 in March 1980. Colin appeared in just 20 games for Chelsea before retiring in the summer of 1982, subsequently becoming a licensee close to Heathrow Airport.

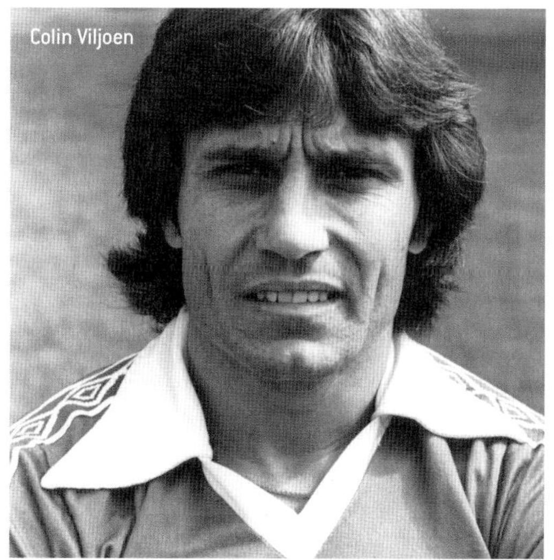
Colin Viljoen

Dennis Sydney VIOLLET

Born: Manchester, 20th September 1933
Died: Florida, America, 7th March 1999
Role: Inside-Forward
Career: Manchester United, Stoke City, Baltimore Bays (USA), Witton Albion, Linfield
Debut: v Hungary (a) 22-5-1960
Appearances: 2 (1 goal)

Dennis was signed by Manchester United straight from school, signing professional forms in September 1950 and

Dennis Viollet

making his debut three years later. He eventually went on to form a lethal partnership with Tommy Taylor and helped the club win successive League championships in 1956 and 1957. He survived the Munich air crash and had recovered sufficiently enough to take his place in the 1958 FA Cup final side, although he missed the 1957 final through injury. In 1959-60 he scored 32 League goals in 36 appearances, United's record haul by an individual in one season. In January 1962 he was surprisingly sold to Stoke City for £25,000, winning a Second Division championship medal in 1963 and a League Cup runners-up medal in 1964. After a brief spell in America he became player-coach at Linfield, collecting another medal as Linfield won the 1970 Irish Cup. Despite all of the goals he scored during his career (including 178 for United in 291 appearances) he won only two caps for England. He later turned to coaching, guiding Preston and Crewe before finishing his career with the Washington Diplomats in America and then retiring to Florida. He died in hospital in Florida some time after being diagnosed as suffering from a brain haemorrhage.

Pelham George VON DONOP

Born: Southsea, 28th April 1851
Died: 7th November 1921
Role: Forward
Career: Royal Military Academy Woolwich, Royal Engineers
Debut: v Scotland (h) 8-3-1873
Appearances: 2

Educated at Somerset College he played for the college and Bath before joining the Royal Military Academy at Woolwich. He entered the Royal Engineers with the rank of Lieutenant in December 1871 and was soon picked to represent the regiment at football, helping them reach consecutive FA Cup finals in 1874 and 1875, the latter of which was won against Old Etonians after a replay. The only Royal Engineer to win more than one cap for England, he was promoted to captain in December 1883, major in May 1890 and lieutenant colonel in November 1897, the rank he held when he left the regiment in 1899, having seen war service in the Sudan in 1884 and 1885. He then served as inspecting officer of Railways from 1899 until 1913 and then chief inspecting office until 1916.

W-Y

WACE, Henry
WADDLE, Christopher Roland
WADSWORTH, Samuel John
WAINSCOAT, William Russell
WAITERS, Anthony Keith
WALDEN, Frederick Ingram 'Fanny'
WALKER, Desmond Sinclair
WALKER, Ian Michael
WALKER, William Henry
WALL, George
WALLACE, Charles William
WALLACE, David L
WALSH, Paul Anthony
WALTERS, Arthur Melmoth
WALTERS, Mark Everton
WALTERS, Percy Melmoth
WALTON, Nathaniel
WARD, James Thomas
WARD, Peter David
WARD, Timothy Victor
WARING, Thomas 'Pongo'
WARNER, Conrad
WARREN, Benjamin
WATERFIELD, George Smith
WATSON, David
WATSON, David Vernon
WATSON, Victor Martin
WATSON, William
WATSON, Willie
WEAVER, Samuel
WEBB, George William
WEBB, Neil John
WEBSTER, Maurice
WEDLOCK, William John
WEIR, David
WELCH, Reginald de Courtenay
WELLER, Keith
WELSH, Donald
WEST, Gordon
WESTWOOD, Raymond William
WHATELEY, Oliver
WHEELER, John E
WHELDON, George Frederick

WHITE, David
WHITE, Thomas Angus
WHITEHEAD, James
WHITFIELD, Herbert
WHITHAM, Michael
WHITWORTH, Steven
WHYMARK, Trevor John
WIDDOWSON, Sam Weller
WIGNALL, Frank
WILCOX, Jason Malcolm
WILKES, Albert
WILKINS, Raymond Colin
WILKINSON, Bernard
WILKINSON, Leonard Rodwell
WILLIAMS, Bert Frederick
WILLIAMS, Owen
WILLIAMS, Steven Charles
WILLIAMS, William
WILLIAMSON, Ernest Clarke
WILLIAMSON, Reginald Garnet 'Tim'
WILLINGHAM, Charles Kenneth
WILLIS, Arthur
WILSHAW, Dennis J
WILSON, Charles Plumpton
WILSON, Claude William
WILSON, Geoffrey Plumpton
WILSON, George
WILSON, Ramon
WILSON, Thomas
WINCKWORTH, William Norman
WINDRIDGE, James Edwin
WINGFIELD-STRATFORD, Cecil Vernon
WINTERBURN, Nigel
WISE, Dennis Frank
WITHE, Peter
WOLLASTON, Charles Henry Reynolds
WOLSTENHOLME, Samuel
WOOD, Harry
WOOD, Raymond E
WOODCOCK, Anthony Stewart
WOODGATE, Jonathan
WOODGER, George 'Lady'
WOODHALL, George 'Spry'

WOODLEY, Victor Robert
WOODS, Christopher Charles Eric
WOODWARD, Vivian John
WOOSNAM, Maxwell
WORRALL, Frederick J
WORTHINGTON, Frank Stuart
WREFORD-BROWN, Charles
WRIGHT, Edward Gordon Dundee
WRIGHT, Ian Edward
WRIGHT, John Douglas
WRIGHT, Mark
WRIGHT, Richard
WRIGHT, Thomas James
WRIGHT, William Ambrose
WRIGHT-PHILLIPS, Shaun Cameron
WYLIE, John George

YATES, John
YORK, Richard Ernest
YOUNG, Alfred
YOUNG, Gerald Morton
YOUNG, Luke

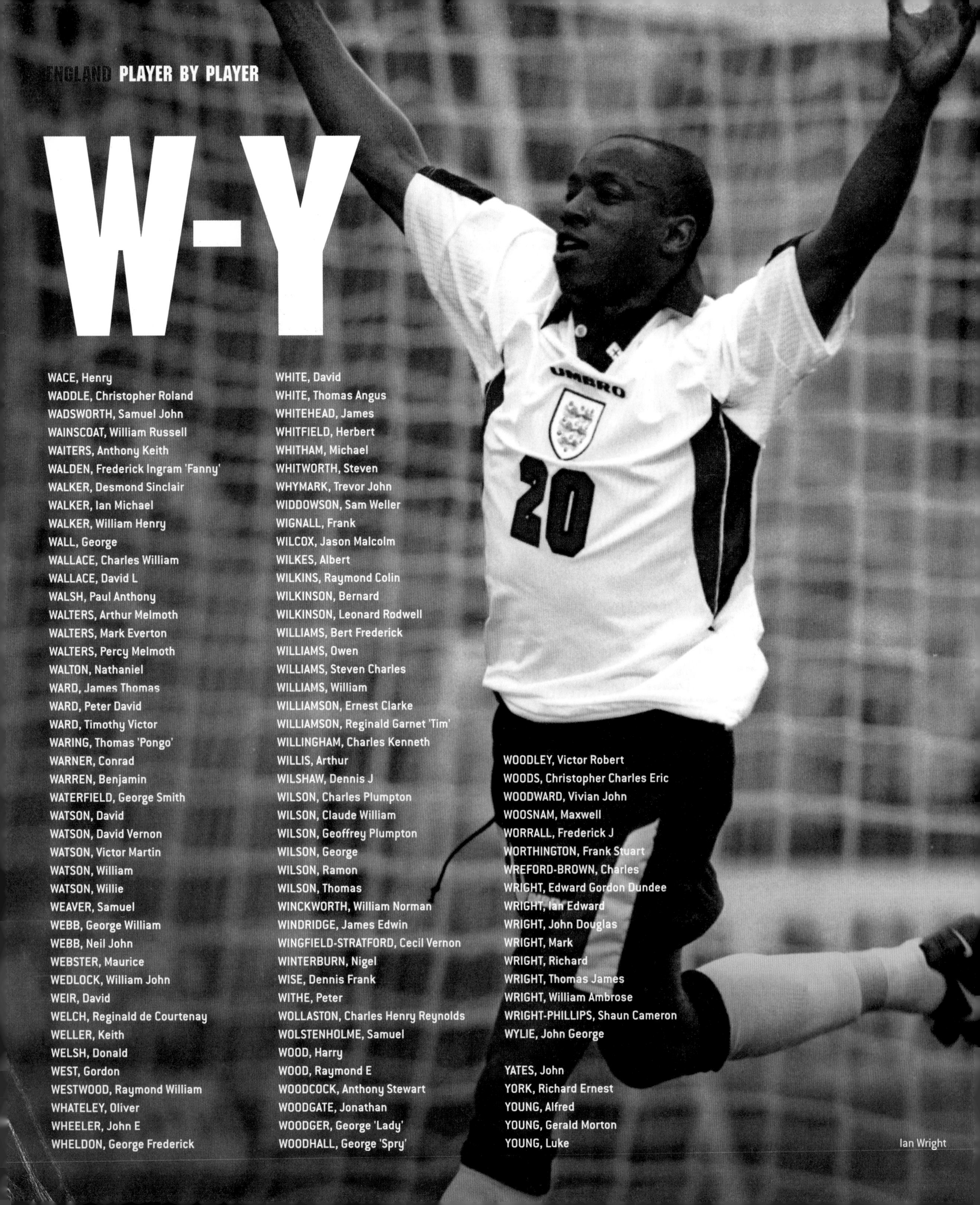

Ian Wright

Henry WACE

Born: Shrewsbury, 21st September 1853
Died: 5th November 1947
Role: Forward
Career: Cambridge University, Wanderers, Clapham Rovers, Shropshire Wanderers
Debut: v Scotland (a) 2-3-1878
Appearances: 3

Educated at Shrewsbury School, Henry continued his education at Cambridge University, winning a Blue in 1874 and 1875 and also winning Blues for rugby the same years. He then assisted Wanderers, Clapham Rovers and Shropshire Wanderers, helping Wanderers win the FA Cup in 1877 and 1878. He qualified as a barrister and was called to the bar in 1879 and became known as an authority on bankruptcy law.

Chris Waddle

Christopher Roland WADDLE

Born: Hepworth, 14th December 1960
Role: Midfield, Winger
Career: Newcastle United, Tottenham Hotspur, Marseille (France), Sheffield Wednesday, Falkirk, Bradford City, Sunderland, Burnley, Torquay United
Debut: v Republic of Ireland (h) 26-3-1985
Appearances: 62 (6 goals)

Having had various trials before signing with non-League Tow Law Town and one after, all unsuccessful, a professional career as a footballer seemed to have passed Chris Waddle by, with Chris finding full-time work in a sausage seasoning factory. In July 1980 he was given one last try and this time managed to impress Newcastle United, who signed him almost immediately and gave him his League debut in October that year. Guided by manager Arthur Cox and with the experience of Kevin Keegan and Peter Beardsley alongside, Chris soon developed into a winger of considerable talent. After representing England at Under-21 level he was selected for the full England side in March 1985. He joined Spurs for £650,000 in July 1985 and immediately formed a partnership with Glenn Hoddle both on the pitch for Spurs and England and off it too, the pair hitting the UK Top 20 with Diamond Lights. That year also saw Spurs reach the FA Cup Final (and the Top 40 of the charts with Hotshot Tottenham!), but lost out to Coventry City 3-2 after extra time. Following Glenn's departure for Monaco, Chris became the main creative player within the side and was given very much a free role. As such he developed into one of the most complete players in the country and a prized asset, and in July 1989 Olympique de Marseille offered £4.5 million to take him to France. There he helped the club win successive League titles and reach the final of the European Cup, and he returned home in 1992 with Sheffield Wednesday. He later played for Bradford City and Sunderland (the club he supported as boy) before taking the position of player-manager at Burnley in 1997. At the end of the 1997-98 season he left the club by mutual agreement, returning to playing with Torquay United.

Samuel John WADSWORTH

Born: Darwen, 13th September 1896
Died: 1st September 1961
Role: Left-Back
Career: Darwen, Blackburn Rovers, Nelson, Huddersfield Town, Burnley, Lytham
Debut: v Scotland (h) 8-4-1922
Appearances: 9

Sam began his career with Darwen before joining Blackburn Rovers in 1914, moving on to Nelson after the First World War in May 1919. It was a move to Huddersfield Town in March 1921, one of the first signings made by Herbert Chapman, that saw his career blossom, for the following year he helped Huddersfield win the FA Cup and then three consecutive League championships, in 1924, 1925 and 1926, the first time this feat had been achieved. Sam also made six appearances for the Football League as well as winning nine caps for England before a move to Burnley in September 1929. He finished his League career at Turf Moor and joined Lytham in 1931 where injury ended his career soon after. He then turned to coaching in Holland either side of the Second World War until his death in 1961.

Sam Wadsworth

William Russell WAINSCOAT

Born: Maltby, 28th July 1898
Died: July 1967
Role: Inside-Left
Career: Maltby Main Colliery, Barnsley, Middlesbrough, Leeds United, Hull City
Debut: v Scotland (a) 13-4-1929
Appearances: 1

A worker at the Maltby Main Colliery and member of the works side either side of the First World War, Russell was signed by Barnsley in March 1920. He moved on to Middlesbrough in December 1923 for £3,750 but didn't really settle at the club, being sold on to Leeds United for £2,000 in March 1925. Here he found his true form, earning selection for the FA touring party to Canada in 1926, where he scored five in one match. Despite this he had to wait a further three years before making his only appearance for England. He remained at Elland Road until October 1931 when he moved on to Hull City where he finished his playing career in 1934. After leaving football, Russell had a wide variety of jobs and occupations, including licensee, railway worker and shopkeeper.

Anthony Keith WAITERS

Born: Southport, 1st February 1937
Role: Goalkeeper
Career: Bishop Auckland, Macclesfield, Blackpool, Burnley
Debut: v Republic of Ireland (a) 24-5-1964
Appearances: 5

Tony played representative football for the RAF whilst doing his national service and was briefly associated with Middlesbrough before playing non-League football with Bishop Auckland and Macclesfield. He joined Blackpool as an amateur in July 1959, turning professional in October, by which time he had won a cap for England at amateur level. He eventually replaced Scottish International George Farm as Blackpool's first choice and won his first representative honour when selected for the Football League in 1963, the first of five such appearances. The following year he made the first of his five appearances for England, although he was always behind Gordon Banks as first choice for the national side. Tony retired from playing in May 1967 following Blackpool's relegation to the Second Division and became the FA's North West regional coach, a post he held for almost two years before joining Liverpool as coach in January 1969. He moved on to Burnley in July 1970 and was persuaded to come out of retirement that season following an injury to Peter Mellor. He went on to make 38 appearances for the Turf Moor club, following his 257 for Blackpool. He retired from playing again in 1971 and had a spell as director of coaching at Coventry City before becoming manager of Plymouth between October 1972 and April 1977. He then moved to Canada where he managed Vancouver Whitecaps and the Canadian Olympic team in 1984, subsequently taking Canada to the World Cup finals in Mexico in 1986.

Frederick Ingram 'Fanny' WALDEN

Born: Wellingborough, 1st March 1888
Died: Northampton, 3rd May 1949
Role: Right-Winger
Career: Wellingborough White Cross, Wellingborough All Saints, Wellingborough Redwell, Wellingborough Town, Northampton Town, Tottenham Hotspur, Northampton Town
Debut: v Scotland (a) 4-4-1920
Appearances: 2

After impressing for the local Wellingborough side, Fanny was signed by Northampton Town in 1909 and scored a hat-trick on his debut, even though he had been selected at centre-forward and stood only 5' 2" tall! Despite his lack of height he displayed intricate ball skills and was subsequently switched out on to the right wing, being selected for the Southern League in that position in a match against the Football League. When Northampton manager Herbert Chapman moved on to Leeds City he made enquiries about buying Fanny, but by then Northampton had already accepted a record bid of £1,700 from Spurs and Fanny came to White Hart Lane in April 1913. An instant crowd favourite, his progress continued unchecked and he won the first of his two England caps in April 1914. The outbreak of the First World War interrupted his career, although it did allow Herbert Chapman to get an opportunity of seeing Fanny in a Leeds City shirt, for Fanny enlisted during the war and guested on a number of occasions for the club managed by his previous boss. When League football resumed Fanny was a permanent fixture within the Spurs side, helping the club win the Second Division title in 1919-20 and reach the FA Cup final the following year, although Fanny had to miss the final owing to injury. He remained with Spurs until 1926 when he returned to Northampton Town, retiring the following year and subsequently coaching. He was also a more than useful cricketer who represented Northamptonshire between 1910 and 1929 in tandem with his football career and later became an umpire, attaining Test match level (he officiated eleven Tests between 1934 and 1939).

Desmond Sinclair WALKER

Born: Hackney, 26th November 1965
Role: Defender
Career: Nottingham Forest, Sampdoria (Italy), Sheffield Wednesday, Burton Albion, Nottingham Forest
Debut: v Denmark (h) (substitute) 14-9-1988
Appearances: 59

Des was spotted by Nottingham Forest whilst playing junior football in London and signed as an apprentice in 1982. Given a first team debut in March 1984 at the age of 18, Des made rapid progress at the club and was one of the brighter prospects from the youth academy, going on to help Forest win the League Cup in successive years, 1989 and 1990. The following year he made his first appearance in the FA Cup final but had the misfortune to head the winning goal into his own net! This slip aside, Des was seen as one of the best defenders in the country, having made his debut for England in 1988 and becoming a regular from March the following year. His performances for England in the 1992 European Championships prompted Italian club Sampdoria to pay £1.5 million for his transfer (they were coached by future England coach Sven Goran Eriksson) but after just one season he returned to England, signing for Sheffield Wednesday for £2.7 million. He remained an England regular until England failed to qualify for the 1994 World Cup finals, having made 59 appearances for his country. He made more than 300 appearances for Sheffield Wednesday before leaving in 2001 to link up with former Forest team-mate Nigel Clough at Burton Albion but subsequently returned to Nottingham Forest to help his former club. In his two spells with Forest, Des made 354 appearances and scored one goal against Luton Town on New Year's Day 1992. He retired from playing at the age of 38 and was appointed first team coach but left in 2005 following the arrival of Gary Megson.

Des Walker

Ian Walker

Ian Michael WALKER

Born: Watford, 31st October 1971
Role: Goalkeeper
Career: Tottenham Hotspur, Oxford United, Leicester City, Bolton Wanderers
Debut: v Hungary (h) (substitute) 18-5-1996
Appearances: 4

The son of former Watford goalkeeper and Norwich and Everton manager Mike Walker, there was little surprise when Ian also took up goalkeeping, signing with Spurs as a trainee in 1988 and being upgraded to professional level in October 1989. After loan spells with Oxford United, Gillingham and Ipswich Town he returned to Spurs as deputy for Erik Thorstvedt, initially replacing him when Erik was away on international duty and then when Erik was injured. The second time around Ian kept his place on merit, and by the mid-1990s was firmly established as Spurs' number one choice, a member of the England setup and widely regarded as a permanent fixture between the posts for the next ten years or so. In 1999 he won his first major domestic medal, helping Spurs win the Worthington Cup, although the subsequent arrival of Scottish goalkeeper Neil Sullivan restricted his first team opportunities and he left to join Leicester City in 2001 for £2.5 million. At the end of the 2004-05 season he was given a free transfer and subsequently joined Bolton Wanderers.

William Henry WALKER

Born: Wednesbury, West Midlands, 29th October 1897
Died: Sheffield, 28th November 1964
Role: Forward
Career: Hednesford Town, Darleston, Wednesbury Old Park, Aston Villa
Debut: v Ireland (h) 23-10-1920 (scored once)
Appearances: 18 (9 goals) + 1 unofficial appearance

Billy played schoolboy football in the West Midlands, made three appearances for Hednesford Town in 1912 and then was with Darleston and Wednesbury Old Park before sign-

Billy Walker

ing with Aston Villa as a part-time professional in 1915. He guested for Wednesbury Old Park and Birmingham during the First World War and signed as a professional at Villa Park in May 1919. He was made club captain during the first season after the war and guided the club to victory in the FA Cup in 1920, gaining his first cap for England later the same year. Billy remained a Villa player until 1933, making 531 appearances for the first team, including 480 in the League, both of which were records for the club until overtaken by Charlie Aitken in the 1970s. Originally a centre-forward, Billy later played inside-forward and netted 244 goals for his club. Seventeen of Billy's caps came between 1920 and 1927; he then had to wait six years before making his final appearance for his country, in the 1932 clash with Austria which England won 4-3. He retired from playing in December 1933 and immediately took over as manager of Sheffield Wednesday, taking them to victory in the 1935 FA Cup Final. He remained at Hillsborough until November 1937 and then had a spell with Chelmsford City before returning to the cut and thrust of League football with Nottingham Forest in March 1939. He was in charge at the City Ground until ill health forced his retirement in July 1960, although he then served on Forest's committee until his death. In 1959 he had taken them to the FA Cup Final, thus becoming the first manager to have steered two separate clubs to success in the FA Cup. As well as his 18 caps for England, Billy also represented the Football League on six occasions.

George WALL

Born: Boldon Colliery, 20th February 1885
Died: Manchester, 1962
Role: Left-Winger
Career: Bolden Royal Rovers, Whitburn, Jarrow, Barnsley, Manchester United, Oldham Athletic, Hamilton Academicals, Rochdale
Debut: v Wales (h) 18-3-1907
Appearances: 7 (2 goals)

George began his professional career with Barnsley in 1903 before a fee of £175 took him to Manchester United in April 1906. With George operating on the left wing and Billy Meredith on the right, United were one of the most potent attacking forces of the day. He helped United win two League championships (1908 and 1911) and the FA Cup (1909) as well as representing England, winning a total of seven caps during his career and touring South Africa with the FA in 1910. But for the First World War George might well have helped United to further honours, but in 1919, soon after his demobilisation from the Black Watch regiment, he was sold to Oldham for £200. He spent just over two years with Oldham before being sold to Hamilton Academicals and then returned to England with Rochdale in 1922 and by the time of his retirement from professional football had appeared in more than 500 League matches. Upon retiring he worked on the Manchester docks.

Charles William WALLACE

Born: Sunderland, 20th January 1885
Died: 7th January 1970
Role: Right-Winger
Career: Southwick, Crystal Palace, Aston Villa, Oldham Athletic
Debut: v Wales (h) 17-3-1913
Appearances: 3

Charlie Wallace joined Aston Villa in 1907 from Crystal Palace and went on to make 349 appearances for the club, despite losing four seasons to the First World War, and scored 57 goals before leaving for Oldham in 1921. Two years later he returned to Villa Park as a steward, a position he held until 1960. After making his England debut, the year of 1913 turned out to be one of mixed emotions, for the following month he missed a penalty in the FA Cup Final, the last to be missed until John Aldridge of Liverpool in 1988, but at least Charlie had the compensation of seeing Villa win the cup.

David Lloyd WALLACE

Born: London, 21st January 1964
Role: Forward
Career: Southampton, Manchester United, Millwall, Birmingham City, Wycombe Wanderers
Debut: v Egypt (a) 26-1-1986 (scored once)
Appearances: 1 (1 goal)

One of three brothers who played for Southampton, Danny became the club's then youngest debutant when he made his first team debut at the age of 16 years and 313 days against Manchester United in 1980. He became a regular in the side from 1982 and added England Under-21 honours to go with those he had won at Youth level and made 311 first team appearances before a £1.2 million move to Manchester United in September 1989. Although he won an FA Cup winners' medal in 1990, he was seldom a regular in the side and in March 1993 joined Millwall on loan before a permanent move to Birmingham City in October the same year for £250,000. Danny made one appearance on loan to Wycombe Wanderers before bringing his career to an end.

Paul Anthony WALSH

Born: Plumstead, 1st October 1962
Role: Centre-Forward
Career: Charlton Athletic, Luton Town, Liverpool, Tottenham Hotspur, Queens Park Rangers, Portsmouth, Manchester City, Portsmouth
Debut: v Australia (a) (substitute) 12-6-1983
Appearances: 5 (1 goal)

Paul was signed by Charlton Athletic as an apprentice and turned professional in October 1979. He quickly became noted as a bright prospect, with good close dribbling skills and in the course of 87 appearances for Charlton in the Second Division was frequently linked with a move up the League. He eventually joined Luton for £250,000 and another player in July 1982, a sizeable fee for a player who was still a teenager. He broke into the England side the following year and was eventually sold to Liverpool for £700,000 in May 1984, going on to help the club win the European Cup in 1985, the League in 1986 and reach the League Cup final in 1987. Despite these honours he was often left on the bench and was subsequently sold to Spurs for £500,000 in 1988. He picked up an FA Cup winners' medal in 1991 before having a spell on loan with QPR, subsequently joining Portsmouth in June 1992. He returned to the North West to sign for Manchester City in March 1994, spending eighteen months with the club before rejoining Portsmouth where a knee ligament injury ended his playing career.

Paul Walsh

Arthur Melmoth WALTERS

Born: Ewell, 26th January 1865
Died: 2nd May 1941
Role: Right-Back
Career: Cambridge University, Old Carthusians, East Sheen, Corinthians, Surrey
Debut: v Ireland (h) 28-2-1885
Appearances: 9

Educated at Charterhouse School, Arthur played for the school side in 1882 and 1883 before continuing his education at Cambridge University. He won a Blue in 1884, 1885, 1886 and 1887 and assisted the Corinthians between 1885 and 1893. He also won representative honours with Surrey and helped Old Carthusians reach successive FA Amateur Cup finals, winning the trophy in 1894 and finishing runners-up the following year. Known as 'Morning' (after his initials, with his elder brother being referred to as 'Afternoon'!), he qualified as a solicitor in 1889.

Mark Everton WALTERS

Born: Birmingham, 2nd June 1964
Role: Midfield
Career: Aston Villa, Glasgow Rangers, Liverpool, Stoke City, Wolverhampton Wanderers, Southampton, Swindon Town, Bristol Rovers
Debut: v New Zealand (a) 3-6-1991
Appearances: 1

First associated with Aston Villa as a schoolboy at the age of 14, Mark was taken on the ground staff as an apprentice in 1980 and joined the professional ranks in May 1982. That same year he made his first team debut and quickly became established as one of the brightest wing talents in the game, earning representative honours at schoolboy, Youth, Under-21 and B level for England. He was sold to Glasgow Rangers in December 1987 for £500,000, winning three League titles and two Skol cups during his time at Ibrox. He was then sold to Liverpool for £1.25 million in August 1991 (although his middle name is Everton!) as a full England international, having collected his only cap during the tour of Australia and New Zealand that summer. He won an FA Cup winners' medal in 1992 and after loan spells with Stoke and Wolves he joined Southampton on a permanent basis in January 1996. Mark then moved on to Swindon in July 1996 and finally Bristol Rovers in November 1999 where he finished his playing career.

Percy Walters

Percy Melmoth WALTERS

Born: Ewell, 30th September 1863
Died: 6th October 1936
Role: Left-Back
Career: Oxford University, Old Carthusians, East Sheen, Epsom, Corinthians, Surrey
Debut: v Ireland (h) 28-2-1885
Appearances: 13

The elder brother of Arthur Walters and known as 'Afternoon' because of his initials, Percy was also educated at Charterhouse School although he did not get to play for the school side. He then attended Oxford University where he won a Blue in 1885 and subsequently assisted Corinthians between 1885 and 1892 and won representative honours with Surrey. He also played for Old Carthusians and helped them reach the final of the FA Amateur Cup in 1895. A member of the FA Committee in 1886 and a vice-president between 1891 and 1892, he qualified as a barrister and was called to the bar in 1888.

Nathaniel WALTON

Born: Preston, 1867
Died: 3rd March 1930
Role: Inside-Forward
Career: Witton, Blackburn Rovers, Nelson
Debut: v Ireland (a) 15-3-1890
Appearances: 1

Nat played for Witton in a Blackburn League before being signed by Blackburn Rovers in 1885. He went on to help the club win the FA Cup three times, in 1886, 1890 and 1891, appearing in different positions in each of the three finals. He also played as a goalkeeper in an emergency but made his only appearance for England in his more usual inside-forward position. He remained at Ewood Park until the summer of 1893 when he joined Nelson, where he finished his playing career in 1898. He then returned to Blackburn where he was trainer for eight years and subsequently became a licensee in the town.

James Thomas WARD

Born: Blackburn, 28 March 1865
Role: Left-Back
Career: Little Harwood, Blackburn Olympic, Blackburn Rovers
Debut: v Wales (h) 14-3-1885
Appearances: 1

James worked in a cotton mill and played minor League football before being signed by Blackburn Olympic in 1881. Although Blackburn Olympic would eventually be eclipsed by the exploits of Blackburn Rovers, it was the Olympic club that first won the FA Cup for the town, a feat achieved in 1883 with James at right-back. Two years later he won his only cap for England playing at left-back and in 1886 moved across town to sign for Blackburn Rovers. He finished his career at Rovers without adding to his honours and subsequently became a licensee in the town.

Peter David WARD

Born: Derby, 27th July 1955
Role: Striker
Career: Brighton & Hove Albion, Nottingham Forest, Brighton & Hove Albion
Debut: v Australia (substitute) (a) 31-5-1980
Appearances: 1

Peter was playing non-League football with Burton Albion when Brighton bought him for £4,000 in May 1975 and he soon proved to be a sound investment. He became the club's top goalscorer in a single season, netting 32 in 1976-77 as the club won promotion to the Second Division and also helped them into the top flight in 1979. After a brief spell out with injuries he netted 18 goals in the First Division and was subsequently sold to Nottingham Forest for £400,000 in October 1980 but was unable to settle at the City Ground, rejoining Brighton on loan in October 1982. He then moved to America where he played in the indoor football League.

Tim Ward

Timothy Victor WARD

Born: Cheltenham, 17th October 1917
Died: 28th January 1993
Role: Wing-Half
Career: Cheltenham Town, Derby County, Barnsley
Debut: v Belgium (a) 21-9-1947
Appearances: 2

Tim played schools football as an outside-right in his native Cheltenham and was converted to his more usual wing-half position upon signing with Cheltenham Town, then a non-League side. Spotted almost immediately by Derby County, he was invited along for a trial by manager George Jobey and impressed right from the off, scoring with his first kick and being offered professional forms to sign for the Baseball Ground club. Derby paid £100 to secure his signature in April 1937 and he was almost ever-present in the side prior to the outbreak of the Second World War. After service in the Army, being wounded during the D-Day landings, Tim returned to Derby at the war's end and played in their opening FA Cup match against Luton. Unfortunately he had not been demobbed at the time, and whilst Derby County went on to win the FA Cup in 1946 for the first and only time in their history, Tim was stationed in Germany at the time the club lifted the cup. Upon returning to Derby on a more permanent basis, Tim was switched from left-half to right-half and impressed enough to earn an England call-up in September 1947, adding a second cap the following year against Wales. In March 1951 he was surprisingly sold to Barnsley where he became player-coach and replaced the Aston Villa-bound Danny Blanchflower. Tim retired from playing in March 1953 in order to accept the position of manager of Exeter City, but less than two weeks later he returned to Oakwell to take over as manager following the death of Angus Seed. At the time Tim was just 34 years of age and the youngest manager in the League. After suffering relegation to Division 3 North at the end of the 1952-53 season, Tim set about guiding the club back to the Second Division, finishing runners-up (at a time when only the champions were promoted) and then champions in 1954-55. In 1959 Barnsley were relegated back to Division 3 North and the following February Tim left to take over at Grimsby Town, lifting them to runners-up spot in the revamped Third Division in 1961-62 and promotion to Division Two. That summer Tim accepted an offer to take over at Derby County and remained in charge at the Baseball Ground for almost five years, all of which were spent struggling in the Second Division. When his contract was not renewed in May 1967 (he was subsequently replaced by Brian Clough) Tim moved on to Carlisle United as manager, remaining in charge until September 1968. That effectively ended Tim's involvement with football, although he had a brief spell scouting for Nottingham Forest and coaching junior sides, as well as working as a sales representative for an engineering company.

Thomas 'Pongo' WARING

Born: Birkenhead, 12th October 1906
Died: 20th December 1980
Role: Centre-Forward
Career: Tranmere Celtic, Tranmere Rovers, Aston Villa, Barnsley, Wolverhampton Wanderers, Tranmere Rovers, Accrington Stanley, Bath City, Ellesmere Port Town, Grayson's FC, Birkenhead Dockers, Harrowby
Debut: v France (a) 14-5-1931 (scored once)
Appearances: 5 (4 goals)

After representing Birkenhead schools and playing junior football for Tranmere Celtic, Pongo Waring became a professional with Tranmere Rovers in 1926. His goalscoring exploits soon attracted considerable interest, and when Villa scouts went to run the rule over him in January 1928 he scored six of Tranmere's goals in the 11-1 win over Durham. Not surprisingly, Villa agreed to pay £4,750 for him and he made his debut for the club in a reserve match in the Central League. His appearance in the side drew a crowd of 23,000 for the fixture and he went on to score a hat-trick. His appearances in the first team were no less impressive, rattling in 167 goals in 226 games, and when he was allowed to leave in November 1935 for Barnsley, a crowd of 5,000 showed themselves against the move by calling for his immediate return. After less than a year with Barnsley he joined Wolves and then back to Tranmere after three months. In 1938 he collected his only domestic honour in the game, helping Tranmere win the Third Division North championship. In November 1938 he joined Accrington Stanley, where he finished his League career. He did, however, continue to play well into middle age for a variety of junior clubs in the Merseyside area, including Ellesmere Port Town, Grayson's FC, Birkenhead Dockers and Harrowby, all of which coincided with his employment in the docks at Liverpool.

Pongo Waring

Conrad WARNER

Born: Cripplegate, London, 19th April 1852
Died: New York, America, 10th April 1890
Role: Goalkeeper
Career: Upton Park
Debut: v Scotland (a) 2-3-1878
Appearances: 1

Educated at a Quaker school in Tottenham, Conrad was something of an all-round sportsman, going on to play rugby for Cheshunt, hockey for Southgate (where he was captain) and was secretary of the Winchmore Hill Cricket and Lawn Tennis Club. He played for Upton Park at football and represented both London and Middlesex as well as earning one cap for England. Although he was widely regarded as one of the best goalkeepers in the country for a considerable time, his one appearance for England was little short of a disaster – he conceded seven goals in the 7-2 defeat! Away from the game he was a stationer with Partridge & Cooper and was on a business trip to New York when he died of pneumonia.

Benjamin WARREN

Born: Newhall, 1879
Died: 15th January 1917
Role: Right-Half
Career: Newhall Town, Newhall Swifts, Derby County, Chelsea
Debut: v Ireland (a) 17-2-1906
Appearances: 22 (2 goals)

After playing for a number of local sides in his native Newhall, Ben joined Derby County in May 1899 and would go on to help the club reach the FA Cup final in 1903 as well as making the first of his five appearances for the Football League. He broke into the England side in 1906 and appeared in 19 consecutive internationals, only one of which was lost, and netted both his goals against Austria, in 1908 and 1909. By then he was a Chelsea player, having cost the Stamford Bridge club £1,500 for his signature in August 1908. Ben earned a recall to the England side in 1911 but was forced to retire from playing in February 1912 on health grounds.

George Smith WATERFIELD

Born: Swinton, 2nd June 1901
Role: Left-Back
Career: Mexborough, Burnley, Crystal Palace
Debut: v Wales (a) 12-2-1927
Appearances: 1

George was playing as a left-winger for Mexborough and working as a miner when he was spotted by Burnley and signed by the Turf Moor club in October 1923. Although he made a number of appearances at his original position, it was a switch to left-back during the 1924-25 season that brought about a change in his fortunes, for he became one of the club's most consistent performers over the next ten years, making a total of 373 League appearances. He moved on to Crystal Palace in June 1935 and spent a season with the club before retiring.

David WATSON

Born: Liverpool, 20th November 1961
Role: Centre-Back
Career: Liverpool, Norwich City, Everton
Debut: v Brazil (a) 10-6-1984
Appearances: 12

Dave began his professional career with Liverpool but was unable to break into the first team, the presence of international players Phil Thompson and Alan Hansen proving an insurmountable hurdle. In 1980 he was therefore sold to Norwich City for an initial fee of £50,000 with an additional £50,000 being payable should he make 25 appearances for the Canaries. This he achieved with ease, helping the club win the League Cup in 1985, breaking into the England side and becoming one of the best defenders in the game. A £900,000 move in the summer of 1986 took him back to Merseyside, this time signing for Everton, and at the end of his first season with the club he had a League championship medal in his possession. His progress at Goodison Park continued and he returned to the England side, appearing in the 1988 European Championship finals in Germany. Still a permanent fixture in the side in the 1990s he was captain when they won the FA Cup in 1995 and in 1997 was appointed caretaker manager following the departure of Joe Royle. He announced his retirement from playing during the 2000-01 season and went into management with Tranmere Rovers although he was sacked after just one season in charge. His brother Alex also played professional football for Liverpool, although he found greater success at Bournemouth.

David Vernon WATSON

Born: Stapleford, 5th October 1946
Role: Centre-Back
Career: Notts County, Rotherham United, Sunderland, Manchester City, Werder Bremen (West Germany), Southampton, Stoke City, Vancouver Whitecaps (Canada), Derby County, Fort Lauderdale (USA), Notts County
Debut: v Portugal (a) 3-4-1974
Appearances: 65 (4 goals)

Dave began his career as a centre-forward with Notts County, joining the club as an amateur in 1965 and turning professional in January 1967. He was sold to Rotherham

Dave Watson

United for £8,000 and another player in December 1967 and it was manager Tommy Docherty that converted him to centre-half. Over the next three years he became acknowledged as one of the best centre-backs in the game, prompting a £100,000 transfer to Sunderland in December 1970. A member of the side that won the FA Cup in 1973, Dave broke into the England side the following year, the first of 65 caps for his country. In June 1975 he was sold to Manchester City for £175,000 and another player, helping them win the League Cup in 1976. In June 1979 he moved to Germany to play for Werder Bremen for £200,000 but returned to England and Southampton for a similar fee. Dave played in all England's matches during this year, thus becoming the first player to appear in three consecutive matches with three different clubs! He remained at Southampton until January 1982 when he joined Stoke for £50,000, winning the last of his England caps whilst with the Potteries club. He had a brief spell in Canada with Vancouver Whitecaps (although initially he was slated to appear on an illegal tour of South Africa) before joining Derby County in September 1983. The following summer he returned to North America to play for Fort Lauderdale for a couple of months before rejoining Notts County as player-coach in September 1984. He later played non-League football for Kettering Town.

Victor Martin WATSON

Born: Chesterton, 10th November 1897
Died: 3rd August 1988
Role: Centre-Forward
Career: Girton, Cambridge United, Peterborough & Fletton United, Brotherhood Engineering Works, Wellingborough Town, West Ham United, Southampton
Debut: v Wales (a) 5-3-1923 (scored once)
Appearances: 5 (4 goals)

Vic played non-League and minor League football for a number of sides and was working for the Brotherhood Engineering Works when he signed for Wellingborough Town. He cost West Ham United just £50 when he signed in March 1920, perhaps one of the biggest bargains the club ever captured. Over the next fifteen years Vic set most of the club's individual goalscoring records, including most goals in a season, 42 in 1929-30, most goals in one match, six against Leeds United in February 1929 and most goals in total aggregate, 298 League goals and 326 goals in total in 505 appearances for the club. The closest he came to winning domestic honours was an appearance in the 1923 FA Cup final, the first at Wembley, where Bolton kept him quiet throughout their 2-0 victory. He left West Ham in the summer of 1935 and spent one season with Southampton before retiring from playing, later working as a market gardener.

William WATSON

Born: Southport, 11th September 1890
Died: 1st September 1955
Role: Left-Half
Career: Blowick Wesleyans, Southport Central, Burnley
Debut: v Scotland (h) 5-4-1913
Appearances: 3 + 1 War appearance

William played schoolboy football in Southport before joining Southport Central as an amateur in 1907, turning professional the following year. In March 1909 he was sold to Burnley for £200, going on to help them win the FA Cup in 1914 and set something of a record in appearing in 112 consecutive matches for the club up to March 1913. First capped for England in 1913 he appeared in two consecutive matches and then was not called upon until the final Victory International match in 1919 and the first official international against Ireland the same year. In 1921 he won a League championship medal before officially retiring in the summer of 1926, although he later joined Blackburn Rovers as a coach and played for the club's A team. He then worked as an ironmonger and decorator and had two spells as a Liberal councillor on the Southport council.

Willie Watson

Willie WATSON

Born: Bolton-upon-Dearne, South Yorkshire, 7th March 1920
Died: Johannesburg, South Africa, 24th April 2004
Role: Right-Half
Career: Huddersfield Town, Sunderland, Halifax Town
Debut: v Northern Ireland (h) 16-11-1949 (WCQ)
Appearances: 4 + 1 War appearance + 1 unofficial appearance (1 goal)

Willie excelled at both football and cricket, representing his country at both sports during his long and illustrious career. Having played schoolboy and junior football in Huddersfield he signed to the local club in October 1937, the same club his father had played for between 1912 and 1927 and had won three League championship and two FA Cup medals. His performances during the Second World War earned him a call-up for England in a wartime international in 1945, although he had to wait a further four years before being officially capped. In April 1946 he was sold to Sunderland for approximately £8,000 and remained at Roker Park for eight years, making over 200 first team appearances and scoring 15 goals in the League. In November 1954 he was sold to Halifax Town for £4,000, becoming player-manager of the club, a position he retained until April 1956. He returned to Halifax Town as manager in September 1964 and two years later took over at Bradford City, holding the position until January 1968. As a cricketer Willie's record was no less impressive. In 1953 he scored 163 runs in 5 _ hours at Lord's to set England on the way to victory over Australia in the fifth Test and with it victory in the Ashes for the first time in fifteen years. He also appeared in Test matches against South Africa and the West Indies, scoring centuries against both, although he was in and out of the England side until 1959 and yet still managed to make 23 Test appearances. He moved from Yorkshire to become captain of Leicestershire in 1958, remaining captain until 1961, and was a Test selector himself between 1962 and 1964. In addition to his four full caps for England at football he also made three B team appearances. He emigrated to South Africa to coach the Wanderers club of Johannesburg.

Samuel WEAVER

Born: Pilsley, 8th February 1909
Died: 15th April 1985
Role: Left-Half
Career: Pilsley, Sutton Junction, Sutton Town, Hull City, Newcastle United, Chelsea, Stockport County
Debut: v Scotland (h) 9-4-1932
Appearances: 3

Sam played non-League football for Sutton before being signed by Hull City in March 1928, costing the club a £50 transfer fee. The following November he was transferred to Newcastle United for £2,500 having made just 48 appearances for the Anlaby Road club. He thrived in the higher League with Newcastle, helping them win the FA Cup in 1932 and made two appearances for the Football League as well as collecting three caps for England. He returned south to join

Sam Weaver

Chelsea for £4,100 in August 1936 and during the Second World War made a number of guest appearances for Leeds United. He made 116 appearances for the Stamford Bridge club and remained on their books until December 1945 when he joined Stockport County, where he finished his playing career in the summer of 1947. He then returned to Leeds to become coach for two years, subsequently serving Millwall and Mansfield in a similar capacity. He was appointed manager of Mansfield in June 1958, a position he retained until January 1960, reverting back to assistant trainer until 1967 when he was appointed chief scout. Sam was also a notable cricketer, playing twice for Somerset in 1939.

George William WEBB

Born: East London, 1888
Died: 28th March 1915
Role: Centre-Forward
Career: Ilford Alliance, Ilford, Wanstead, West Ham United, Manchester City
Debut: v Wales (h) 13-3-1911 (scored once)
Appearances: 2 (1 goal)

An amateur throughout his career, he joined West Ham during the 1908-09 season and would go on to earn representative honours with the Southern League as well as being capped at amateur level on seven occasions and twice for the full side. He moved on to Manchester City in the summer of 1912 but retired a year later.

Neil John WEBB

Born: Reading, 30th July 1963
Role: Midfield
Career: Reading, Portsmouth, Nottingham Forest, Manchester United, Nottingham Forest, Swindon Town, Grimsby Town
Debut: v West Germany (substitute) (a) 9-9-1987
Appearances: 26 (4 goals)

Like his father Doug Webb, Neil began his professional career with Reading and then was sold to Portsmouth in 1982 for £87,500. Having helped Portsmouth win the Third Division championship his abilities in midfield became known to a wider audience and Brian Clough paid £250,000 to take him to Nottingham Forest in 1985. There he developed into one of the best midfielders in the country, helping his club to win the League Cup in 1989 and receiving international recognition with England. He was sold to Manchester United in July 1989 for a fee fixed by the tribunal at £1.5 million and it seemed his career could only get better. Unfortunately an injury sustained whilst on international duty was far more serious than at first thought, and although he returned to the side in time to collect an FA Cup winners' medal in 1990, his real effectiveness had been blunted. He was sold back to Forest for £800,000 in November 1992. He later played on loan at Swindon before being released on a free transfer and subsequently signing for Grimsby.

Maurice WEBSTER

Born: Blackpool, 13th November 1899
Died: February 1978
Role: Centre-Half
Career: Bloomfield Villa, South Shore Wednesday, Fleetwood, Lytham, Stalybridge Celtic, Middlesbrough, Carlisle United
Debut: v Scotland (h) 5-4-1930
Appearances: 3

Maurice played for a number of non-League sides in the Lancashire area before being signed by Middlesbrough in March 1922. Although he would go on to help the club win the Second Division championship in 1929 and represent the Football League once, his time at Ayresome Park was punctuated by frequent spells out of the side owing to injury. He moved on to Carlisle in June 1935 but retired from playing the following year. He then returned to Middlesbrough to join the training staff and after a year went back to Carlisle to become trainer in May 1937. He later worked as a plumber.

Neil Webb

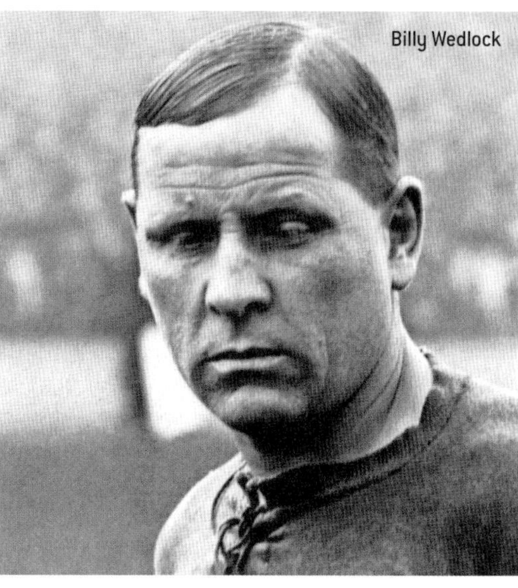

Billy Wedlock

William John WEDLOCK

Born: Bedminster, 28th October 1880
Died: 25th January 1965
Role: Centre-Half
Career: Masonic Rovers, Arlington Rovers, Abedare, Bristol City
Debut: v Ireland (h) 16-2-1907
Appearances: 26 (2 goals)

Born in the Bristol area, Billy spent four years playing for Arlington Rovers during which time he was first spotted by Bristol City and signed amateur forms with the Ashton Gate club. It was City's refusal to offer him professional forms that led him to join Abedare, helping them reach the Welsh FA Cup final in 1904 and 1905 and spending four years as a part-time professional with the Welsh club. Bristol realised their error in the summer of 1905, taking him back to Ashton Gate as a professional and were rewarded when he helped them win the Second Division championship and reach the FA Cup final in 1909. Known as either 'Fatty' (he only weighed 10st 7lbs at his peak) or the 'India Rubber Man', in recognition of his ability to recover quickly from injury, he remained a player at Bristol City until the summer of 1921. Originally a stonemason by trade, he later became a licensee close to City's ground, where the East End at Ashton Gate was named the Wedlock Stand in his honour.

David WEIR

Born: Aldershot, 1863
Died: November 1933
Role: Forward
Career: Maybole, Glasgow Thistle, Halliwell, Bolton Wanderers, Ardwick, Bolton Wanderers
Debut: v Ireland (h) 2-3-1889
Appearances: 2

The son of an officer's batman, David grew up in Scotland from the age of 12 and played for a number of clubs north of the border before joining Bolton Wanderers in the summer of 1888. He won both his caps for England whilst with the Burnden Park club and moved on to Ardwick in May 1890, returning to Bolton in January 1893. He retired from playing in the summer of 1895 and returned to Scotland to coach and occasionally play for Maybole, his original club. He was appointed manager of Glossop in 1909 and later coached in Stuttgart before the outbreak of the First World War.

Reginald de Courtenay WELCH

Born: Kensington, London, 1851
Died: 4th June 1939
Role: Full-Back, Goalkeeper
Career: Harrow Chequers, Wanderers, Remnants, Middlesex
Debut: v Scotland (a) 30-11-1872
Appearances: 2

Educated at Harrow School, he played for the school side in 1873 and assisted Old Harrovians, Harrow Chequers, Wanderers and Remnants and earned representative honours with Middlesex. An Army tutor between 1883 and 1895, he won FA Cup winners' medals with Wanderers in 1872 and 1873 and appeared as a full-back in the very first official England international. His second and last appearance, in 1874, saw him in goal in the 2-1 defeat! A member of the FA Committee between 1873 and 1875 and again from 1879 to 1890, he became principal of the Army College at Farnham in Surrey in 1895.

Keith WELLER

Born: Islington, 11th June 1946
Died: Seattle, USA, 13th November 2004
Role: Forward
Career: Tottenham Hotspur, Millwall, Chelsea, Leicester City
Debut: v Wales (a) 11-5-1974
Appearances: 4 (1 goal)

Keith joined Spurs as an amateur in August 1963 and signed professional forms the following January. He was initially used as little more than cover for established wingers Jimmy Robertson and Cliff Jones, but his inability to obtain regular first team action prompted a demand for a transfer. Reluctantly, just as they would later do with Graeme Souness, Spurs sold the player, collecting £18,000 from Millwall for his services in June 1967. At Millwall, Keith developed into one of the best midfield players of his era and three years later was sold to Chelsea for £100,000. He helped the club win the European Cup Winners' Cup in 1971 but was surprisingly sold to Leicester City for £100,000 in September of that year. Although Keith did not win any major honours during his time at Filbert Street he did break into the England side, winning all four of his caps whilst with the club. In February 1979 he was sold to New England Teaman for £40,000 and finished his playing career in America. He could also show a temperamental side, for during one match for Leicester City in 1974 he went on strike at half time and refused to appear for the second half! He died from cancer at his home in Seattle in November 2004.

Keith Weller

Donald WELSH

Born: Manchester, 25th February 1911
Died: Stevenage, 1989
Role: Left-Half, Inside-Left
Career: Torquay United, Charlton Athletic
Debut: v Germany (a) 14-5-1938
Appearances: 3 (1 goal) + 9 War appearances (11 goals) + 1 unofficial appearance (2 goals)

Don played schools football in Manchester and also represented the Royal Navy before signing amateur forms with Torquay United in 1933. He turned professional in July 1934 and soon attracted considerable interest, earning a £3,250 move to Charlton Athletic in February 1935 having made 79 appearances for Torquay. At The Valley he was used in a variety of positions, turning out as a centre-back and inside-forward, able to play either in the centre or left hand side of the field. It was on the left that he earned his full international caps, although the majority of his wartime appearances were at centre-forward. He was a member of the side that won the Third Division South Championship in 1935 and finished as runners-up in the Second Division and First Division in successive seasons. After the Second World War he appeared in consecutive FA Cup finals, captaining the side and collecting the cup in 1947. In November the same year he retired from playing upon being appointed secretary-manager of Brighton, a position he held until May 1956. Don later had spells in charge at Bournemouth and Wycombe Wanderers before returning to Charlton to join the administrative staff. In between his managerial appointments he was a licensee in Devon and manager of a youth centre.

Gordon WEST

Born: Barnsley, 24th April 1943
Role: Goalkeeper
Career: Blackpool, Everton, Tranmere Rovers
Debut: v Bulgaria (h) 11-12-1968
Appearances: 3

After making his name with Blackpool he cost Everton a then record fee for a goalkeeper, £27,000 to come to Goodison Park in March 1962. He immediately replaced Albert Dunlop and went on to win two League titles in 1963 and 1970 and the FA Cup in 1966, as well as representing England on three occasions. That figure might have been higher but he chose to opt out of the squad for the 1970 World Cup finals in Mexico, preferring to remain at home with his family. The arrival of David Lawson effectively brought his Everton career to an end, having made 399 appearances for the first team. Astonishingly, he played for Tranmere Rovers almost three years after having played his last game for Everton and finally retired for good in 1978. In addition to his three full caps Gordon won Youth and Under-23 caps and also represented the Football League once.

Gordon West

William Raymond WESTWOOD

Born: Brierley Hill, 14th April 1912
Died: January 1982
Role: Left-Winger
Career: Stourbridge, Brierley Hill Alliance, Bolton Wanderers, Chester, Darwen
Debut: v Wales (a) 29-9-1934
Appearances: 6 + 1 unofficial appearance (1 goal)

Ray played junior football in the Midlands and had an opportunity of signing for Aston Villa but opted to sign for Bolton Wanderers where his uncle had been a former player. He joined the Burnden Park club in February 1930 and would go on to make 301 appearances for the club, a figure that would have been considerably higher had he not lost seven seasons to the Second World War. Ray had also made five appearances for the Football League by the time he moved on to Chester in December 1947, making a further 38 appearances in Chester's colours before finishing his playing career with Darwen.

Oliver WHATELEY

Born: Birmingham, 1862
Died: October 1926
Role: Inside-Forward
Career: Gladstone Unity, Aston Villa
Debut: v Ireland (a) 24-2-1883 (scored twice)
Appearances: 2 (2 goals)

Olly played for Gladstone Unity in the Coventry area before linking with Aston Villa in 1880 and remained with the club for almost eight years after which he appears to have retired. Known as an artist, designer and draughtsman by profession, he underwent a major operation in 1911 but recovered enough to serve in Rouen, France with the YMCA during the First World War, too old for military service. At the end of the war he returned to the Birmingham area and, having been in continued ill health and struggling financially, was the beneficiary of a fund set up by Aston Villa to aid their former player.

John Edward WHEELER

Born: Liverpool, 26th July 1928
Role: Right-Half
Career: Carlton FC, Tranmere Rovers, Bolton Wanderers, Liverpool
Debut: v Northern Ireland (a) 2-10-1954
Appearances: 1

Johnny played in the Liverpool Combination for Carlton FC during the Second World War before being invited to join Tranmere Rovers as an amateur in 1944. He was upgraded to the professional ranks in April 1946 and remained at Prenton Park until February 1951, making a total of 101 appearances for the club before his move to Bolton Wanderers. A member of the side that reached the FA Cup final in 1953, he also earned representative honours with the Football League and turned out five times for the England B side. In November 1956 and after 189 appearances for the Burnden Park club he was sold to Liverpool for £9,000, remaining with the club until his retirement in 1962, although he played only one match in the 1961-62 Second division championship winning side. He was appointed player-manager of New Brighton in May 1963 but decided not to take up the post, opting instead to become assistant trainer at Bury. Promoted to head trainer in the summer of 1967 he became trainer and assistant trainer in September 1969, holding both roles until he left the club twelve months later.

George Frederick WHELDON

Born: Langley Green, 1st November 1869
Died: Worcester, 13th January 1934
Role: Inside-Left
Career: Road End White Star, Langley Green Victoria, Small Heath, Aston Villa, West Bromwich Albion, Queens Park Rangers, Portsmouth
Debut: v Ireland (h) 20-2-1897
Appearances: 4 (6 goals)

George joined Aston Villa from Small Heath (now Birmingham City) for £100 plus the proceeds of a testimonial and scored 22 goals in 37 appearances in the double-winning side of 1896-97. The 1897-98 campaign was even better, for he netted 23 goals in just 28 games and was top goalscorer for both the club and League. Known throughout his career as 'Diamond' he helped the club win the League title three times in just four seasons and also collected four caps for England. After 138 appearances for the Villa first team (scoring 78 goals) he was transferred to West Bromwich Albion, later going on to play for Queens Park Rangers, Portsmouth and Worcester City, finally ending his career with Coventry City. As well as his exploits on a football field he was also an accomplished cricketer for Worcestershire, smashing 4,938 runs in 138 matches between 1899 and 1906.

David WHITE

Born: Manchester, 30th October 1967
Role: Striker
Career: Manchester City, Leeds United, Sheffield United
Debut: v Spain (a) 9-9-1992
Appearances: 1

Taken on by Manchester City as an apprentice after leaving school, David was upgraded to the professional ranks in November 1985. Capped for England at Youth, Under-21 and B level he made his only appearance for England in 1992, although he was substituted by Paul Merson during the match. He helped Manchester City return to the top flight in 1988 before a £2 million move to Leeds United in December 1993. His time at Elland Road was not as successful as might have been hoped, for injuries blighted his stay and he was sold to Sheffield United for a knock down £500,000 in January 1996. His luck got no better at Bramall Lane, injuries finally bringing a halt to his career in 1997.

Thomas Angus WHITE

Born: Manchester, 29th July 1908
Died: Liverpool, 13th August 1967
Role: Centre-Half
Career: Southport, Everton, Northampton Town, New Brighton
Debut: v Italy (a) 13-5-1933
Appearances: 1

Tommy made his League debut for Everton in October 1927 deputising for the absent Dixie Dean and proved a worthy replacement, scoring twice in a 7-0 rout over West Ham. He had joined Everton from Southport earlier in the year as a centre-forward although he originally played at centre-half, a position he was later to return to during his Everton career (and even won a cap for England at centre-half!). This was his only game of the season but he went on to make 202 appearances for the first team, scoring 66 goals and collecting winners' medals for the First Division championship in 1932 and FA Cup in 1933. He left Everton for Northampton in October 1937 but stayed less than five months before returning to the Merseyside area and joining New Brighton. He retired at the end of the 1938-39 season, although football itself shut down soon after for the duration of the Second World War. He then went to work in the Liverpool docks, where he died following a fall in 1967.

James WHITEHEAD

Born: Church, 1870
Died: August 1929
Role: Inside-Right
Career: Peel Bank, Accrington, Blackburn Rovers, Manchester City
Debut: v Wales (h) 13-3-1893
Appearances: 2

James spent less than ten years in the first class game, joining Accrington in the summer of 1890 and retiring in the summer of 1899. In between time he spent three years at Accrington before moving along to Blackburn Rovers in the summer of 1893 and after a little over four years joined Manchester City in September 1897. His international appearances therefore came whilst he was on the books of Accrington and Blackburn Rovers.

Herbert WHITFIELD

Born: Lewes, 15th November 1858
Died: Chailey, 6th May 1909
Role: Winger
Career: Cambridge University, Old Etonians
Debut: v Wales (h) 18-1-1879 (scored once)
Appearances: 1 (1 goal)

Educated at Eton and a member of the college side in 1877, Herbert then attended Cambridge University and earned a Blue in 1879, 1880 and 1881. He also earned a Blue at cricket in every year between 1878 and 1881 and represented the university at athletics and real tennis. After university he went to work in a bank, attaining a high position within Barclays Bank as well as playing for Old Etonians, helping them win the FA Cup in 1879 and reach the final in 1881. Herbert also maintained his cricket career after university, making 75 first class appearances between 1878 and 1889 and scoring 2400 runs for Sussex.

Michael Whitham

Michael WHITHAM

Born: Ecclesfield, 6th November 1867
Died: London, 6th May 1924
Role: Left-Half
Career: Ecclesfield, Rotherham Swifts, Sheffield United
Debut: v Ireland (a) 5-3-1892
Appearances: 1

Michael played for Ecclesfield before turning professional with Rotherham Swifts, spending a year with the club before linking with Sheffield United in 1890. Whilst with the club he earned representative honours with the Sheffield FA against their counterparts at Glasgow and London as well as making one appearance for England. He retired from playing in 1898 and then became a trainer, holding positions at Gainsborough Trinity twice, Rotherham County, Huddersfield Town and Brentford, being on the staff at Griffin Park at the time of his death.

Stephen WHITWORTH

Born: Coalville, 20th March 1952
Role: Full-Back
Career: Leicester City, Sunderland, Bolton Wanderers, Mansfield Town, Barnet
Debut: v West Germany (h) 12-3-1975
Appearances: 7

Steve won representative honours for Leicester and England schoolboys before being taken on by Leicester City as an associate schoolboy and then apprentice, before signing professional forms in November 1969. He went on to win caps at Under-21 level and help the club win the Second Division championship in 1971 before earning selection for the full side in 1975. He was sold to Sunderland in March 1979 for £180,000 and helped them win promotion to the First Division in 1980, although he was on the move again to Bolton in October 1981. Following relegation to Division Three in 1983, Steve was released and joined Mansfield of the Fourth Division, where he finally got his name on the score sheet, netting two goals in his 80 League appearances for the Stags after drawing a blank in his 503 appearances for his previous clubs. Steve remained at Mansfield until 1985 when he joined Barnet as player-coach.

Steve Whitworth

Trevor John WHYMARK

Born: Burston, 4th May 1950
Role: Forward
Career: Ipswich Town, Vancouver Whitecaps (Canada), Sparta Rotterdam (Holland), Derby County, Grimsby Town, Southend United, Peterborough United, Colchester United
Debut: v Luxembourg (a) (substitute) 12-10-1977 (WCQ)
Appearances: 1

Trevor played for Diss Town before being discovered by Ipswich Town and proving a prolific goalscorer in their reserve side. Signed to professional forms in May 1969 he made his debut for the club at the start of the 1969-70 season and became a regular within the side three seasons later. His performances for Ipswich in the UEFA Cup were particularly impressive, eventually earning him a call-up to the full England side in the World Cup qualifier against Luxembourg in 1977, but a knee injury sustained over that Christmas blunted his effectiveness. He was sold to Vancouver Whitecaps for £150,000 in November 1978, returning to Europe to sign for Sparta Rotterdam in September 1979 and being sent on loan to Derby two months later. He returned permanently to England in December 1980 when signed by Grimsby for their record fee of £80,000 and later had spells with Southend United, Peterborough United and Colchester United before finishing his playing career in 1985.

Sam Weller WIDDOWSON

Born: Hucknall Torkard, 16th April 1851
Died: Beeston, 9th May 1927
Role: Centre-Forward
Career: Nottingham Forest
Debut: v Scotland (a) 13-3-1880
Appearances: 1

Sam played schoolboy and junior football in Nottingham before signing with Nottingham Forest in 1878. He remained a player with the club until 1885 and also served as club chairman between 1879 and 1884. He was also a member of the FA Committee between 1888 and 1892 and again from 1893 to 1894. Sam was also a more than useful cricketer, making one appearance for Nottinghamshire in 1878 and scoring 15 runs. He achieved greater fame, however, as the man who invented and took out a patent on shin pads.

Frank WIGNALL

Born: Chorley, 21st August 1939
Role: Centre-Forward
Career: Blackrod, Horwich RMI, Everton, Nottingham Forest, Wolverhampton Wanderers, Derby County, Mansfield Town
Debut: v Wales (h) 18-11-1964 (scored twice)
Appearances: 2 (2 goals)

Signed by Everton from Horwich RMI in May 1958 he found first team opportunities at Goodison severely restricted, although he could be relied upon to give a good account of himself whenever called up for service. Indeed, he scored 14 goals in 33 League appearances and seven in the League Cup in 1960-61. He was sold to Nottingham Forest in March 1963 for £20,000 and restored his reputation, representing the Football League twice and winning two caps for England. A £50,000 move took him to Wolves in March 1968 but less than a year later he joined Derby County in a £20,000 deal. He remained at the Baseball Ground until November 1971 when he moved on to Mansfield for £8,000 where he finished his League career. Frank then became player-manager of Kings Lynn in July 1973 and finished his playing career with Burton Albion. He then turned to coaching, serving as national coach to Qatar for five years.

Jason Malcolm WILCOX

Born: Farnsworth, 15th July 1971
Role: Winger
Career: Blackburn Rovers, Leeds United, Leicester City, Blackpool
Debut: v Hungary (h) 18-5-1996
Appearances: 3 + 1 unofficial appearance

Signed by Blackburn Rovers straight from school, Jason made his debut for the club during the 1989-90 season and spent almost nine seasons a first team regular, going on to make over 300 first team appearances. A member of the side that won the Premier League title in 1995, he was sold to Leeds United for £3 million in December 1999 and helped his new club reach the semi finals of the UEFA Cup and Champions League in successive seasons. After 106 appearances for the Elland Road club he was released on a free transfer in 2004 and promptly joined Leicester City. He made a good start to his career at Leicester but suffered a cruciate ligament injury in October 2004 and missed virtually the rest of the season, subsequently going on loan to Blackpool to prove his fitness.

Jason Wilcox

Albert WILKES

Born: Birmingham, 1874
Died: 9th December 1936
Role: Wing-Half
Career: Oldbury Town, Walsall, Aston Villa
Debut: v Wales (h) 18-3-1901
Appearances: 5 (1 goal) + 1 unofficial appearance

Albert began his career playing for Oldbury Town and was spotted by Walsall whilst playing against Villa in the Birmingham Charity Cup Final and offered professional terms. He joined Aston Villa in the summer of 1898 and helped the club win the League championship in 1900 and remained with the club until the summer of 1907 having made 157 games. He then joined Fulham but retired in July 1909 in order to concentrate on his photographic business. He did, however, become a Football League referee and returned to Aston Villa in 1934 when elected onto the board of directors.

Raymond Colin WILKINS

Born: Hillingdon, 14th September 1956
Role: Midfield
Career: Chelsea, Manchester United, AC Milan (Italy), Paris St. Germain (France), Glasgow Rangers, Queens Park Rangers, Crystal Palace, Queens Park Rangers, Wycombe Wanderers, Hibernian, Millwall, Orient, Fulham
Debut: v Italy (New York) 28-5-1976
Appearances: 84 (3 goals)

Known by his nickname of 'Butch' he was signed by Chelsea straight from school and was their youngest ever captain when appointed at the age of 18. In 1979 former Chelsea manager Dave Sexton, by this time occupying the hot seat at Old Trafford, paid £825,000 to take him to Manchester United. The highlight of his United career was the 1983 FA Cup final in which he won a winners' medal, and his performances in midfield alongside Bryan Robson

Ray Wilkins

were also repeated with England. In July 1984 he was sold to AC Milan for £1.5 million, where he remained for three years before spending a brief spell with Paris St. Germain. He returned to Britain with Glasgow Rangers and then came south of the border to play for QPR in 1989. After five years at Loftus Road he joined Crystal Palace but returned six months later as player-manager. He resigned from this position in September 1996 and after brief spells playing for Wycombe Wanderers, Hibernian, Millwall and Leyton Orient was appointed manager at Fulham, although he was sacked in May 1998.

Bernard WILKINSON

Born: Thorpe Hesley, 12th September 1879
Died: 28th May 1949
Role: Half-Back
Career: Shiregreen, Sheffield United, Rotherham Town
Debut: v Scotland (a) 9-4-1904
Appearances: 1

Bernard played junior football in Thorpe Hesley and had a brief association with Shiregreen before signing with Sheffield United in July 1899. It took him a while to break into the first team, with the result he missed the 1901 FA Cup final defeat but more than made amends the following year, helping them win the final against Southampton 2-1 in a replay. He remained at Bramall Lane until June 1913 when he left to play for Rotherham Town but retired during the First World War. He was also a more than capable cricketer, being invited to sign for Yorkshire County Cricket Club, but turned the offer down. He later became a successful businessman in Sheffield.

Leonard Rodwell WILKINSON

Born: Highgate, London, 15th October 1868
Died: 9th February 1913
Role: Goalkeeper
Career: Oxford University, Old Carthusians, Corinthians
Debut: v Wales (h) 7-3-1891
Appearances: 1

Educated at Charterhouse, Leonard played for the school side in 1887 and then went to Oxford University to continue his education. He won a Blue in 1889, 1890 and 1891 and also earned a Blue in athletics in 1890 and 1891. Leonard helped Old Carthusians reach three FA Amateur Cup finals, collecting winners' medals in 1894 and 1897 and a runner-up medal in 1895, alongside fellow England international players Morris Stanbrough and Charles Wreford-Brown. Leonard qualified as a barrister and was called to the bar in 1893.

Bert Williams

Bertram Frederick WILLIAMS

Born: Bilston, 31st January 1920
Role: Goalkeeper
Career: Thompsons FC, Walsall, Wolverhampton Wanderers
Debut: v France (a) 22-5-1949
Appearances: 24 + 4 War appearances

Educated in Bilston, Bert was playing for Thompsons FC of Wolverhampton when he was spotted by Walsall and signed as an amateur in April 1937. He turned professional in March 1939, by which time he had already made 25 first team appearances and was trained on a daily basis by Walsall trainer Harry Waite. After serving in the RAF during the Second World War, Bert was sold to Wolves in September 1945 for £3,500 and went on to become perhaps one of the most consistent and reliable goalkeepers to turn out for the Molineux club. A member of the side that won the FA Cup in 1949 he also collected a League championship medal in 1954. He made a total of 420 appearances for Wolves during his twelve years with the club. Having first been selected for England during the Second World War he won a total of 24 caps at full level, made one appearance at B level and represented the Football League five times. When his playing career came to an end he ran a sports shop in Bilston as well as opening a goalkeeping school in 1969.

Owen WILLIAMS

Born: Ryhope, 23rd September 1896
Died: 9th December 1960
Role: Left-Winger
Career: Manchester United, Easington Colliery, Clapton Orient, Middlesbrough, Southend United
Debut: v Northern Ireland (h) 21-10-1922
Appearances: 2

Owen played schools football in Sunderland and for Ryhope Colliery when he had a trial with Sunderland and then signed amateur forms with Manchester United, although he failed to make the grade at Old Trafford. He then played for Easington Colliery before being signed by Clapton Orient in July 1919, going on to win his two caps for England during his time with the club. He was sold to Middlesbrough for £3,000 in February 1924, helping them win the Second Division championship in 1927 and again in 1929. He moved on to Southend United in July 1930 where he finished his League career in September 1931, having made 361 appearances for his various clubs.

Steven Charles WILLIAMS

Born: London, 12th July 1958
Role: Midfield
Career: Southampton, Arsenal, Luton Town, Exeter City
Debut: v Australia (a) 12-6-1983
Appearances: 6

Steve was signed to Crystal Palace as a schoolboy but was offered apprentice forms by Southampton, turning professional in September 1974. Considered one of the best midfield prospects the club had produced in years, he went straight from the youth side into the first team, making his debut in April 1977 against local rivals Portsmouth. He helped the club reach the League Cup final in 1979 and finish runners-up in the First Division in 1984 and in December of that year he was sold to Arsenal for £550,000. He was hampered by injuries during his early days at Highbury, although he recovered and helped the club win the League Cup in 1987. The following July he was sold to Luton Town for £300,000 where he spent two seasons before moving on to Exeter City where he finished his career. In addition to his six full caps Steve also won 15 caps at Under-21 and four at B level.

Steve Williams

William Williams

William WILLIAMS
Born: Smethwick, 20th January 1876
Died: 22nd January 1929
Role: Full-Back
Career: West Smethwick, Old Hill Wanderers, West Bromwich Albion
Debut: v Ireland (h) 20-2-1897
Appearances: 6

William played schoolboy football in his hometown and for a number of local sides before signing with West Bromwich Albion in 1894. His potential was seen immediately, for he went straight into the first team and helped Albion reach the FA Cup final at the end of his first season at the club. Although he was unable to add further domestic honours he did break into the England side and seemed set for a lengthy stay at right-back until a niggling cartilage injury towards the end of the century saw him frequently out of the game. He eventually retired in June 1901 because of the injury, becoming trainer and later scout for West Bromwich Albion. He then became a licensee in the town for many years.

Ernest Clarke WILLIAMSON
Born: Murton Colliery, 24th May 1890
Died: Norwich, 30th April 1964
Role: Goalkeeper
Career: Murton Red Star, Wingate Albion, Croydon Common, Arsenal, Norwich City
Debut: v Sweden (a) 21-5-1923
Appearances: 2 + 1 War appearance + 1 unofficial appearance

Given the nickname 'Tim', in deference to the earlier England goalkeeper (see below), he was first spotted whilst playing football for the Royal Army Signal Corps during the First World War and made numerous guest appearances for Arsenal during the conflict. He officially signed with the club in the summer of 1919 and made his first England appearance in October that year in a Victory International against Wales. He had to wait four years before gaining an official cap, however, but appeared in both matches against Sweden in May 1923. The following month he moved on to Norwich City and spent two years at The Nest before retiring in 1925. He was then a licensee in the city for many years.

Reginald Garnet 'Tim' WILLIAMSON
Born: North Ormesby, 6th June 1884
Died: 1st August 1943
Role: Goalkeeper
Career: Redcar Crusaders, Middlesbrough
Debut: v Ireland (h) 25-2-1905
Appearances: 7

Tim joined Middlesbrough from Redcar Crusaders in 1903 and was to give the club more than twenty years service, making a club record of 563 League appearances in that time. He made his England debut in 1905 in the 1-1 draw with Ireland and then didn't feature in the side again until six years later, kept out of contention by the great Sam Hardy. Tim replaced Sam when recalled against Ireland in 1911 and appeared in six of the next seven internationals, his final tally of seven caps a truer reflection of his abilities. He retired in the summer of 1924 and became an engineering draughtsman.

Ken Willingham

Charles Kenneth WILLINGHAM
Born: Sheffield, 1st December 1912
Died: May 1975
Role: Right-Half
Career: Ecclesfield, Worksop Town, Huddersfield Town, Sunderland, Leeds United
Debut: v Finland (a) 20-5-1937 (scored once)
Appearances: 12 (1 goal) + 6 War appearances

An exceptional sportsman as a schoolboy, Ken was a county champion at the half mile and represented England at athletics. He also represented Yorkshire at football and was taken on to the Huddersfield Town ground staff in 1930, turning professional in November 1931. A member of the side that reached the FA Cup final in 1938, Ken represented the Football League on six occasions and made 247 appearances for the club before the outbreak of the Second World War. He made six appearances for England during the war, the last coming in 1942 and left Huddersfield for Sunderland in December 1945, making 14 outings for the Roker Park club. He was then appointed player-coach at Leeds United in March 1947, retiring from playing in May the following year but remaining on the coaching staff for a further two years. He later had a spell as coach at Halifax Town before becoming a licensee in Leeds.

Arthur WILLIS
Born: Denaby Main, 2nd February 1920
Died: Haverfordwest, 7th November 1987
Role: Left-Back
Career: Finchley, Tottenham Hotspur, Swansea Town, Haverfordwest
Debut: v France (h) 3-10-1951
Appearances: 1

Arthur was working as a miner and playing non-League football when he was offered contracts with Barnsley, Sunderland and Spurs, deciding on signing as an amateur with Spurs in 1938. He was farmed out to the club's nursery sides and then upgraded to the professional ranks in January 1944. Initially used as a right-back, he was switched to the opposite flank following the arrival of Alf Ramsey from Southampton. He finally broke into the first team in place of Charlie Withers as left full-back in the last two games of the 1949-50 season and kept his place the following season as Spurs lifted the First Division title for the first time. In October 1951 he was capped by England, but as he was similar in style to Withers, both he and Arthur tended to alternate the left-back position with the result Arthur could not add to his England tally. He was released in September 1954 and joined Swansea Town, becoming player/assistant trainer in November 1957 after helping the club reach the Welsh FA Cup Final in 1956. The following summer he retired as a player but remained on the staff as assistant trainer. Arthur resumed playing, briefly, when he joined Haverfordwest of the Welsh League in the summer of 1960.

Dennis James WILSHAW
Born: Stoke, 11th March 1926
Died: 10th May 2004
Role: Centre-Forward, Inside-Left, Left-Winger
Career: Wolverhampton Wanderers, Walsall, Wolverhampton Wanderers, Stoke City
Debut: v Wales (a) 10-10-1953 (scored twice) (WCQ)
Appearances: 12 (10 goals)

Dennis was a versatile player for both club and country, being able to play centre-forward, inside-left or on the left

Dennis Wilshaw

wing and give a good account of himself wherever selected. He attended the same Hanley High School as Ronnie Allen and played junior football for Packmoor Boys club before signing with Wolves in March 1944. He was sent on loan to Walsall in May 1946 and did so well he was recalled to Molineux, going on to earn selection for the England B side in 1949. He remained at Wolves until December 1957, during which time he made 211 League appearances and scored 105 goals, collecting a League championship medal in 1954. He was sold to Stoke for £12,000 in 1957 and spent nearly four years with the Potteries club before retiring after sustaining a broken leg. In total he made 378 matches for his three League clubs, scoring 172 goals and hit nine in his 12 appearances for England, including four in one match against Scotland. Upon retiring as a player he became a schoolteacher, subsequently becoming head of the Service and Community Studies Department at Alsager College of Education.

Charles Plumpton WILSON

Born: Roydon, Norfolk, 12th May 1859
Died: East Dereham, Norfolk, 9th March 1938
Role: Wing-Half
Career: Hendon, Casuals, Corinthians
Debut: v Scotland (a) 15-3-1884
Appearances: 2

Charles was educated at Uppingham and Marlborough schools before attending Cambridge University. An all-round sportsman, he won a Blue at cricket in 1880 and 1881 and rugby in 1878, 1879, 1880 and 1881, but surprisingly did not win one at football! Associated with the Hendon club when he won his two caps for England, Charles is one of only three players to have also been capped at rugby, sharing the distinction with John Sutcliffe and Reg Birkett. He was a schoolmaster by profession and was master at Elstree School from 1881 to 1898 and then joint headmaster of Sandroyd School in Cobham from 1898 until 1920.

Claude William WILSON

Born: Banbury, 9th September 1858
Died: 7th June 1881
Role: Full-Back
Career: Oxford University, Old Brightonians, Sussex
Debut: v Wales (h) 18-1-1879
Appearances: 2

Educated at Brighton College, Claude played for the college side in 1876 and 1877, being captain in the latter year. He then attended Oxford University, winning a Blue in 1879, 1880 and 1881 and helping the university reach the FA Cup final in 1880. He also represented Sussex at football and Surrey at cricket and was on the verge of winning a Blue at cricket before his untimely death.

Geoffrey Plumpton WILSON

Born: Bourne, 21st February 1878
Died: 30th July 1934
Role: Inside-Left
Career: Corinthians, Casuals, Southampton, London Hospital
Debut: v Wales (a) 26-3-1900 (scored once)
Appearances: 2 (1 goal)

The younger brother of Charles Wilson (above), Geoffrey was educated at Rossall School and played for the school side from 1894 to 1896, captaining the side in 1896. He was associated with the Corinthians from 1897 to 1902 and also made three appearances for Southampton in the Southern League during the 1901-02 season. He qualified as a physician and surgeon in 1902 and made a number of appearances for London Hospital thereafter.

George Wilson

George WILSON

Born: Blackpool, 14th January 1892
Died: Blackpool, 25th November 1961
Role: Centre-Half
Career: Morecambe, Blackpool, Sheffield Wednesday, Nelson
Debut: v Wales (a) 14-3-1921
Appearances: 12

George played schoolboy football in Preston and was spotted by Blackpool whilst playing for Morecambe in the West Lancashire League, signing with the Bloomfield Road club in February 1912. By the time League football resumed after the First World War, George was reckoned to be one of the best centre-halves in the game and this prompted a £3,000 move to Sheffield Wednesday in March 1920. A year later he won the first of his 12 caps for England and would also go on to make four appearances for the Football League. In July 1925 he was sold to Nelson for £2,000, a figure then a record fee paid by the Third Division club, and George gave the club five years service before retiring from playing in the summer of 1930. He then returned to Blackpool where he was a licensee for thirty years until his retirement in May 1961.

Ramon WILSON

Born: Shirebrook, 17th December 1934
Role: Left-Back
Career: Huddersfield Town, Everton, Oldham Athletic, Bradford City, Langwith Junction Imperials
Debut: v Scotland (a) 9-4-1960
Appearances: 63

Ray played junior football in Langworth before being taken on to the Huddersfield Town ground staff in May 1952, turning professional in August 1953. After making steady if unspectacular progress with Huddersfield he was awarded his first cap for England in 1960 at the age of 25 years and was virtually a regular for the next six years, adding 63 caps to his 10 appearances for the Football League. In June 1964, having made 265 appearances for Huddersfield he was transferred to Everton for £25,000 and another player. He was to spend five years at Goodison Park, with the 1965-66 season perhaps the pinnacle of his career, for in May he helped Everton win the FA Cup 3-2 against Sheffield Wednesday and in July was back at Wembley with England in the World Cup Final. Despite an uncustomary slip in the early stages that allowed Haller to open the scoring for West Germany, Ray gave a good performance throughout and thoroughly deserved his winners' medal. He made his last appearance for England in June 1968, a badly twisted knee later the same year costing him his international place and robbing him of some of his pace on the field. In June 1969 he was allowed to join Oldham Athletic, having made 117 appearances for Everton, and spent a year at Boundary Park before joining Bradford City as player-coach. He retired from playing in May 1971 and continued to serve City as assistant manager until the end of the year. He then went into business as an undertaker.

Ray Wilson

Thomas WILSON

Born: Seaham, 16th April 1896
Died: Barnsley, 2nd February 1948
Role: Centre-Half
Career: Seaham Colliery, Sunderland, Seaham Colliery, Huddersfield Town, Blackpool
Debut: v Scotland (h) 31-3-1928
Appearances: 1

Tom was spotted by Sunderland whilst playing for Seaham Colliery and signed with the Roker Park club during the 1913-14 season. When he reported back to the club at the end of the First World War, they thought he was overweight and so released him from contract. He returned to Seaham Colliery and showed his weight did not affect his play, for in June 1919 he was signed by Huddersfield Town. Tom's arrival at Leeds Road coincided with Huddersfield's rise to domination in the domestic game, winning the League championship in 1924, 1925 and 1926, the first time the League had been won three years in succession, and winning the FA Cup in 1922 as well as being runners-up in 1920, 1928 and 1930. Tom also made three appearances for the Football League but only one full appearance for England, a match that was lost 5-1 at Wembley to Scotland. Tom remained at Huddersfield until November 1931 when he moved on to Blackpool but retired the following summer and returned to Huddersfield to take up a training position. He remained associated with the club through to the end of the Second World War, joining Barnsley as trainer in 1945 and holding the position until his death in 1948.

William Norman WINCKWORTH

Born: London, 9th February 1870
Died: 9th November 1941
Role: Centre-Half, Inside-Left
Career: Old Westminsters, Corinthians
Debut: v Wales (a) 5-3-1892
Appearances: 2 (1 goal)

Educated at Westminster School, he represented the school in 1888 and then played for Old Westminsters as well as turning out for the Corinthians between 1890 and 1894. His playing career came to an end in 1894 when he emigrated to Calcutta where he was in business until 1914, returning to England and settling near Exeter in Devon.

James Edwin WINDRIDGE

Born: Birmingham, 21st October 1882
Died: Birmingham, 23rd September 1939
Role: Inside-Forward
Career: Small Heath, Chelsea, Middlesbrough, Birmingham
Debut: v Ireland (a) 15-2-1908
Appearances: 8 (7 goals)

James joined Small Heath (later to become Birmingham City) during the 1902-03 season and helped the club win promotion to the First Division at the end of his first season with the club. He was one of the first players signed by the newly formed Chelsea Football Club in April 1905, costing the Stamford Bridge club £190 for his transfer. He helped his new club win promotion to the top flight in 1907, although they were relegated back into the Second Division in 1910 and the following year he was signed by Middlesbrough. After three years at Ayresome Park he returned to Birmingham (they changed their name in 1905) where he finished his career during the First World War. James was also a noted cricketer, making seven first class appearances for Warwickshire between 1909 and 1913.

Cecil Vernon WINGFIELD-STRATFORD

Born: West Malling, 7th October 1853
Died: 5th February 1939
Role: Winger
Career: Royal Military Academy Woolwich, Royal Engineers, Kent
Debut: v Scotland (h) 3-3-1877
Appearances: 1

Cecil attended the Royal Military Academy in Woolwich before joining the Royal Engineers in 1873, playing in the FA Cup final two years later and helping the Royal Engineers beat Old Etonians 2-0 in a replay. He also represented Kent and remained in the Royal Engineers until 1910 when he retired with the rank of Brigadier. He was recalled to service during the First World War, being awarded the CMG in 1916 and the CB in 1918.

Nigel WINTERBURN

Born: Nuneaton, 11th December 1963
Role: Defender
Career: Birmingham City, Oxford United, Wimbledon, Arsenal, West Ham United
Debut: v Germany (substitute) (Detroit) 19-6-1993
Appearances: 2

Nigel began his professional career with Birmingham City but, despite earning caps for England at Youth level, never appeared in the first team at St. Andrews. After a spell at Oxford United he joined Wimbledon on a free transfer in 1983, going on to help the club win promotion to the First Division in 1986 as well as earning caps for his country at Under-21 level. In 1987 he was bought by Arsenal for £350,000 as an eventual replacement for Kenny Sansom, although Nigel made a number of appearances for the club on the opposite flank. He settled into the more natural left-back position following Sansom's departure in 1988 and went on to help the club win three League titles, two FA Cups, the League Cup and the European Cup Winners' Cup. Nigel was a regular in the Arsenal side until 2000 and was released on a free transfer during that summer. He then finished his career with three seasons at West Ham United, finally retiring in his fortieth year.

Nigel Winterburn

Dennis Wise

Dennis Frank WISE

Born: Kensington, 16th December 1966
Role: Midfield
Career: Southampton, Wimbledon, Chelsea, Leicester City, Millwall, Southampton, Coventry City
Debut: v Turkey (a) 1-5-1991 (scored once) (ECQ)
Appearances: 21 (1 goal)

Dennis joined Southampton as an apprentice straight from school but never made the grade at The Dell, being allowed to leave and subsequently joining Wimbledon in March 1985. He made his debut for The Dons before the season was out but made just four appearances during the 1985-86 season. The following season, Wimbledon's first in the First Division, saw Dennis become something of a regular and the heart, along with Vinnie Jones, of the so-called 'Crazy Gang'. Dennis was an integral part of the side that won the FA Cup in 1987-88, netting the winner in the semi final and responsible for crossing the ball over for the only goal of the final. One of the last of the original Crazy Gang left, Dennis moved on to Chelsea in July 1990 for £1.6 million. Over the course of the next ten years he gave Chelsea exceptional service, both on and off the pitch, and was the heartbeat and captain of the side that won two FA Cups and the European Cup Winners' Cup. The higher profile he enjoyed at Chelsea was rewarded with his first cap for England in 1991 and he would go on to win 12 caps for his country, scoring one goal. In June 2001, after 332 League appearances and 113 games in other competitions (he is fourth in the all-time list of Chelsea appearances), Dennis was allowed to join Leicester City, linking him once again with his former mentor Dave Bassett, but during the summer of 2002, an altercation with a team-mate saw him sacked by the club and he subsequently joined Millwall. Later elevated to player-manager, he guided them to their first FA Cup final (Dennis's fifth) in 2004, but at the end of the 2004-05 season he resigned and subsequently returned to Southampton. In January 2006 he linked up with former Leicester City manager Mickey Adams at Coventry City.

Peter WITHE

Born: Liverpool, 30th August 1951
Role: Striker
Career: Skelmersdale, Southport, Barrow, Port Elizabeth City (South Africa), Arcadia Shepherds (South Africa), Wolverhampton Wanderers, Portland Town (USA), Birmingham City, Nottingham Forest, Newcastle United, Aston Villa, Sheffield United, Birmingham City, Huddersfield Town
Debut: v Brazil 12-5-1981
Appearances: 11 (1 goal)

After an unsuccessful start to his career with Southport and Barrow, he went to America and South Africa in order to restore his confidence, arriving back in England in November 1973 and signing for Wolves. After just 12 games he was sold to Birmingham City, remaining at St. Andrews for a year before Brian Clough signed him for Nottingham Forest. Here he linked with Tony Woodcock and inspired the club to promotion from the Second Division and then the First Division title the following season. By the time Forest won the European Cup, Peter had already left, signed by Newcastle United in August 1978. Villa paid their then record fee of £500,000 to sign him in May 1980 and he proved the catalyst for the championship winning side, netting 20 goals during the course of the season. The following year he scored the winning goal in the European Cup Final and also collected five caps for England in his five seasons with the club. After Villa he had spells playing for Sheffield United, Birmingham City and Huddersfield before returning to Villa Park as Jozef Venglos' assistant. He later managed Wimbledon in his own right but was sacked and returned once again to Villa Park to serve the club as chief scout.

Peter Withe

Charles Henry Reynolds WOLLASTON

Born: Felpham, Sussex, 31st July 1849
Died: 22nd June 1926
Role: Inside-Forward
Career: Oxford University, Clapham Rovers, Wanderers, Middlesex
Debut: v Scotland (a) 7-3-1874
Appearances: 4 (1 goal) + 1 unofficial appearance

Charles Wollaston was educated at Lancing College and played for the college football team between 1864 and 1868, being captain of the side for the last two years. He then went on to Oxford University, although the annual match against Cambridge University had yet to be instituted and therefore had to content himself with turning out for Lancing Old Boys. He also played for Clapham Rovers and was with Wanderers in 1872, helping them win the inaugural FA Cup. In fact, Charles kept his place in the side that won the cup in five of the first seven seasons, thus becoming the first player to have won as many as five winners' medals in the FA Cup (the only two other players to have achieved the feat are James Forrest, with Blackburn Rovers, and the Hon. Alfred Kinnaird, with Wanderers and Old Etonians). Charles earned his first cap for England in 1874, although he was injured and therefore handicapped throughout the game, but he performed well enough to make a further three appearances for his country, scoring one of England's goals in the 2-2 draw with Scotland in 1875. That same year he was admitted as a solicitor and he later went on to become assistant secretary and then secretary to the Union Bank of London.

Samuel WOLSTENHOLME

Born: Little Lever, 1876
Role: Right-Half
Career: Farnworth Alliance, Horwich, Everton, Blackburn Rovers, Croydon Common, Norwich City
Debut: v Scotland (a) 9-4-1904
Appearances: 3

Sam joined Everton in 1897 and made one appearance in the 1897-98 season, but thereafter established himself as a regular in the side and soon won England recognition, making his debut in April 1904. Everton surprisingly sold him to Blackburn soon after, even though he was still only 25 years of age, and he went on to add to his tally of caps at Ewood Park. He had made 170 appearances for Everton at the time of his transfer, scoring eight goals. In 1908 he joined Croydon Common and later switched to Norwich City before retiring in 1913. He then turned to coaching and had the misfortune to be in Germany when the First World War broke out, being interned along with Steve Bloomer and Fred Spikesley, although the three persuaded the camp commandant to allow them to organise a league among the other prisoners! In addition to his three full caps for England Sam also represented the Football League twice.

Harry Wood

Harry WOOD

Born: Walsall, 26th June 1868
Died: Portsmouth, 5th July 1951
Role: Inside-Forward
Career: Walsall Town Swifts, Wolverhampton Wanderers, Walsall, Wolverhampton Wanderers, Southampton, Portsmouth
Debut: v Wales (a) 15-3-1890
Appearances: 3 (1 goal)

After leaving school, Harry linked with Walsall Town Swifts before signing with Wolverhampton Wanderers in 1885 and made his debut in the FA Cup the same year. He spent a brief spell back with Walsall before returning again to Wolves, helping them win the FA Cup in 1893 and finish runners-up in both 1889 and 1896. He left Wolves for Southampton in 1898 and helped them win the Southern League title on four occasions, 1899, 1901, 1903 and 1904 and also made two return appearances in the FA Cup Final, finishing on the losing side in both 1900 and 1902. He retired from playing in 1905 and then became trainer further along the south coast with Portsmouth. He was trainer at Fratton Park for seven years and then became landlord of the Milton Arms, some 200 yards from Fratton Park. Throughout his playing career, Harry was regarded as a perfect gentleman and model professional. He also made four appearances for the Football League during his career. His son Arthur later became a goalkeeper with Southampton and Clapton Orient.

Raymond Ernest WOOD

Born: Hebburn, 11th June 1931
Role: Goalkeeper
Career: Newcastle United, Darlington, Manchester United, Huddersfield Town, Bradford City, Barnsley
Debut: v Northern Ireland (a) 2-10-1954
Appearances: 3

Born in County Durham, Ray was signed by Newcastle United as an amateur but turned professional with Darlington in September 1949. After only 12 games for the Shakers he was sold to Manchester United for £5,000 in December 1949 and initially faced a battle with Jack Crompton and Reg Allen for the role of first choice goalkeeper. By 1953-54 the position was his and he won League championship medals in 1956 and 1957 and might have won an FA Cup winners' medal in 1957 but for an early collision with Peter McParland of Aston Villa which effectively put him out of the match. He spent some considerable time out on the wing before returning to goal for the final 10 minutes, but the disruption effectively cost United their chance of the double. He survived the Munich air crash a year later but once he had recovered from his injuries was unable to dislodge Harry Gregg from goal and in December 1958 he was sold to Huddersfield Town for £1,500. He went on to make over 200 appearances for Huddersfield and had spells with Bradford City and Barnsley before retiring in 1967. He then turned to coaching and has held positions all over the world.

Tony Woodcock

Anthony Stewart WOODCOCK

Born: Nottingham, 6th December 1955
Role: Forward
Career: Nottingham Forest, Lincoln City, Doncaster Rovers, Nottingham Forest, FC Cologne (West Germany), Arsenal, FC Cologne (West Germany)
Debut: v Northern Ireland (h) 16-5-1978
Appearances: 42 (16 goals)

A product of Nottingham Forest's youth policy, Tony was taken on as an apprentice in 1972, turning professional in January 1974. After spending loan spells with Lincoln City and Doncaster Rovers he became a regular in the Forest side in 1977 and helped the club win promotion to the First Division in 1977. Thereafter he won a League championship medal in 1978, the same year as collecting a League Cup winners' medal, the PFA Young Footballer of the Year award and his first England cap, and the following year added winners' medals in the League Cup again and the European Cup. His performances for Forest attracted interest from outside England and in November 1979 he was sold to FC Cologne for a then German record fee of £650,000. He proved just as successful on the continent as he had at home and settled in extremely well in Germany, although he was sold to Arsenal for £500,000 in June 1982. He returned to Cologne for a second spell with the club in July 1986, going on to make 131 appearances for Cologne in the Bundesliga during his two spells with the club. In 1994 he joined VfB Leipzig as trainer. As well as his 42 full appearances for England, Tony also represented the country at B and Under-21 level, making two appearances at the latter level.

Jonathan Woodgate

Jonathan WOODGATE

Born: Middlesbrough, 22nd January 1980
Role: Defender
Career: Leeds United, Newcastle United, Real Madrid (Spain)
Debut: v Bulgaria (a) 9-6-1999
Appearances: 5

Spotted by Leeds whilst playing for local side Marton, Jonathan was taken on as a junior and helped the club win the FA Youth Cup in 1997, making his debut for the League side the following November. He made his breakthrough into the England side in 1999 but the following year a court convicted him of affray outside a nightclub and his club and international careers suffered. He was sold to Newcastle United for £9 million in January 2003 but he struggled to overcome a series of injuries, further restricting his career. In August 2004 he was sold to Real Madrid, still injured and unable to make a single appearance for the club during the 2004-05 season. He finally made his debut in September 2005 but had the misfortune to score an own goal and get sent off for a second bookable offence! A later return also brought about a fresh injury to contend with.

George 'Lady' WOODGER

Born: Croydon, 3rd September 1883
Died: 1961
Role: Inside-Left
Career: Thornton Heath, Croydon Glenrose, Croydon Wanderers, Crystal Palace, Oldham Athletic, Tottenham Hotspur
Debut: v Ireland (h) 11-2-1911
Appearances: 1

George first earned representative honours with Surrey and was signed by Crystal Palace as an amateur in 1905, turning professional the following summer. He was described two years later as 'A player possessing a neat, clever, polished style which has earned for him the peculiar title of Lady'. He was sold to Oldham Athletic in September 1910 for £800 and earned selection for the England team a year later. He returned to the south to sign for Spurs in the summer of 1914 and retired during the First World War.

George 'Spry' WOODHALL

Born: West Bromwich, 5th September 1863
Role: Right-Winger
Career: West Bromwich Albion, Wolverhampton Wanderers
Debut: v Wales (h) 4-2-1888
Appearances: 2 (1 goal)

George played for a number of minor sides before joining West Bromwich Albion in May 1883 and was a member of the side that reached three consecutive FA Cup finals in 1886, 1887 and 1888. The first two, which saw George playing on the wing, were lost, but by the time they reached the final again in 1888 he was playing as an inside-forward and they beat Preston 2-1. In October 1892 George joined Wolves, spending a year with the club before leaving League football to turn out for Berwick Rangers and later Oldbury Town before retiring in 1898.

Victor Robert WOODLEY

Born: Slough, 26th February 1911
Died: Bradford-On-Avon, 23rd October 1978
Role: Goalkeeper
Career: Chippenham, Windsor & Eton, Bath City, Derby County, Bath City
Debut: v Scotland (a) 17-4-1937
Appearances: 19 + 2 War appearances

Vic played minor League football in Buckinghamshire before joining Windsor & Eton in the Spartan League, being spotted by Chelsea and signed as a professional in May 1931. He remained at Stamford Bridge until the end of the Second World War having made 252 appearances for the club and joined Bath City in December 1945, his League career seemingly over. In March 1946 Derby County were in desperate need of a goalkeeper, and in particular one who was not cup-tied as they were on their way to the FA Cup final, and barely a month later Vic was the proud owner of a winners' medal as Charlton were beaten 4-1. He made a total of 30 appearances for Derby before returning to Bath City, this time as player-manager in May 1947, finally retiring in December 1949. He then became a licensee in Bradford-On-Avon in Wiltshire. His 19 full appearances for England came in consecutive matches and he was also England's goalkeeper for their first wartime international in 1939. He was recalled into the side in May 1940 when Sam Bartram (later to be Vic's opposite number in the 1946 FA Cup final) was refused permission by the RAF to travel to Glasgow for the match against Scotland.

Christopher Charles Eric WOODS

Born: Boston, 14th November 1959
Role: Goalkeeper
Career: Nottingham Forest, Queens Park Rangers, Norwich City, Glasgow Rangers, Sheffield Wednesday, Reading, Colorado Rapids (USA), Southampton, Sunderland, Burnley
Debut: v USA (a) 16-6-1985
Appearances: 43

Chris was first thrust into the limelight in 1978, for despite having yet to make his League debut for Forest he collected a winners' medal in the League Cup, deputising for the cup-tied Peter Shilton. Chris had joined Forest as an apprentice and been upgraded to the professional ranks in December 1976 and performed well in the League Cup Final in 1978, although the continued form of Peter Shilton restricted Chris's opportunities at Forest and he was sold to Queens Park Rangers for £250,000 in June 1979. He spent less than two years at Loftus Road before going to Norwich City on loan, the deal becoming permanent in May 1981 for £225,000. He collected a second League Cup winners' medal in 1985, helping Norwich to victory over Sunderland, and collected his first cap for England later the same year. In July 1986 he was sold to Glasgow Rangers for £600,000, a then record fee paid by a Scottish club and the British record for a goalkeeper. As part of Rangers' growing English contingent he helped the club win the Premier League in 1987, 1989, 1990 and 1991 and the Scottish League Cup in 1987, 1989 and 1991. The retirement of Peter Shilton in 1990 gave Chris a chance at a regular place in the England side and he went on to make 43 appearances in the senior side. He was sold to Sheffield Wednesday for £1.2 million in August 1991 but was later affected by a mystery illness and lost both his club and national place. He spent a spell on loan to Reading in 1995 before being released on a free transfer, later playing in America and then returning back to England to turn out for Southampton, Sunderland and Burnley. During the 1986-87 season with Rangers, Chris set a British first class record, going 13 matches without conceding a goal, a record since surpassed. As well as his 43 full caps Chris also represented the country at Youth, B and Under-21 level, making six appearances for the Under-21 side.

Chris Woods

Vivian John WOODWARD

Born: South London, 3rd June 1879
Died: London, 31st January 1954
Role: Inside-Forward, Centre-Forward
Career: Clacton, Harwich & Parkeston, Chelmsford, Essex County, Tottenham Hotspur, Chelsea
Debut: v Ireland (h) 14-2-1903 (scored twice)
Appearances: 23 (29 goals)

One of the finest players of his or any other age, Vivian Woodward would have shone in any team. An amateur for his entire career, he began playing with local sides in Clacton and then signed with Chelmsford City. He signed with Spurs in March 1901 but did not become a regular in the side until 1902-03 as he had business commitments and also because he had no wish to let down Chelmsford. He was a regular feature of the Spurs side until 1909 and to him fell the honour of scoring their first goal as a Football League side, in the match against Wolves at White Hart Lane in September 1908. His amateur status saw him make 67 appearances for the England amateur team and he was good enough to also represent the full side on 23 occasions, scoring 29 goals. He was also captain of the United Kingdom teams that won consecutive Olympic titles in 1908 and 1912. He was appointed a director of Spurs in 1908 but the following year announced his retirement from the top level of the game in order to return playing for Chelmsford. Less than three months later he signed with Chelsea and remained on the playing staff until midway through the First World War. This of course included Chelsea's first appearance in the FA Cup final, and Woodward was given leave by the Army to play in the match against Sheffield United. However, Woodward's principles were such that if he had played, Bob Thomson (who had scored most of the goals that got Chelsea to the final) would have missed out and so Woodward declined Chelsea's offer and watched the match from the stands. He did however become a director of the club in 1922 and served them in this capacity until 1930. Having previously been an architect for most of his professional life he became a gentleman farmer.

Maxwell WOOSNAM

Born: Liverpool, 6th September 1892
Died: London, 14th July 1965
Role: Centre-Half
Career: Cambridge University, Chelsea, Corinthians, Manchester City, Northwich Victoria
Debut: v Wales (h) 13-3-1922
Appearances: 1

Like Vivian Woodward, Maxwell Woosnam won an Olympic gold medal during his lifetime, but whereas Woodward collected his at football, Max won gold at tennis. Indeed, Max Woosnam is perhaps the greatest all-round sportsman the country has ever produced, earning international recognition or playing at top-class level at football, lawn tennis, real tennis, rackets, cricket and golf. He was educated at Winchester College where he was captain of the cricket and golf sides and also played for the college at football and rackets. He then attended Trinity College in Cambridge and earned Blues at football, lawn tennis and real tennis, only missing out on cricket. He played for the college in every game leading up to the clash with Oxford at Lord's but was surprisingly dropped for the game, being named 12th man. Meanwhile Max had already linked with both Corinthians and Chelsea and accompanied the famous amateur side on their tour of Brazil in 1914. By the time the team arrived in South America news reached the continent that the First World War had broken out and the entire team boarded a ship for the journey home the following day! Upon arriving back in England, Max enlisted with the Montgomeryshire Yeomanry, later switching to the Royal Welsh Fusiliers. At the end of the war he returned to Cambridge and was elected captain of the cricket team, although once again he missed out on earning his Blue and decided to concentrate on lawn tennis and football. At the 1920 Olympic Games held in Antwerp he was entered into the men's doubles with Noel Turnbull and the mixed doubles with Kitty McKane, winning gold in the former and silver in the latter. He had also been selected for the United Kingdom football side at the same Olympics but decided he had spent too long away from home and withdrew from the squad. Later the same year he made his debut in the Davis Cup, partnering Randolph Lycett to victory over Spain, and the following year Woosnam and Lycett won the Wimbledon doubles title. The following year, in 1922, Max Woosnam's football abilities were fully recognised when he earned a full cap for England having already been capped by both England and Wales at amateur level! A broken leg sustained in 1922 brought his football career to an end, but he returned to the Olympics in 1924 (in Paris) for the tennis tournament, being eliminated early on in both the singles and doubles competitions. He had joined the ICI company in 1919 and remained in their employment for 31 years as well as serving as president of both the Isthmian League and Corinthian Casuals FC. His nephew Phil Woosnam later played professional football and was capped for Wales before moving to America where he has played a major role in helping establish football in that country.

Frederick WORRALL

Born: Warrington, 8th September 1910
Died: 13th April 1979
Role: Right-Winger
Career: Witton Albion, Nantwich, Oldham Athletic, Portsmouth, Crewe Alexandra, Stockport County
Debut: v Holland (a) 18-5-1935 (scored once)
Appearances: 2 (2 goals)

Fred first attracted attention when playing for Nantwich and was initially signed by Bolton Wanderers in December 1928. It was then discovered that the club was forbidden from signing him and he subsequently linked with Oldham Athletic the same month. Almost three years later he moved on to Portsmouth, going on to help the club reach the FA Cup final in 1934 and win the competition in 1939. He also made two appearances for the Football League and was a virtual ever-present at Fratton Park for the duration of his stay, making 313 League appearances and scoring 68 goals. He guested for Crewe Alexandra during the Second World War and joined Stockport County in September 1946 where he finished his League career after just six appearances. Fred then had spells coaching at Chester and as manager of Stockton Heath.

Frank Worthington

Frank Stuart WORTHINGTON

Born: Halifax, 23rd November 1948
Role: Forward
Career: Huddersfield Town, Leicester City, Bolton Wanderers, Birmingham City, Tampa Bay Rowdies (USA), Leeds United, Sunderland, Southampton, Brighton & Hove Albion, Tranmere Rovers, Preston North End, Stockport County
Debut: v Northern Ireland (h) (substitute) 15-5-1974
Appearances: 8 (2 goals)

A charismatic and hugely entertaining player, Frank delighted crowds and infuriated managers for virtually the whole of his twenty-year career. He began with Huddersfield Town, signing as an apprentice in 1963 and turning professional in November 1966. A member of the side that won the Second Division championship in 1970 he won two caps for England at Under-23 level and was also called up to represent the Football League. In 1972 he seemed set for a move to Liverpool for £150,000 but the medical revealed he had high blood pressure and Liverpool pulled out of the deal. Leicester City swooped to sign him for a cut price £80,000 in August 1972 and he became a mainstay of the side, making a total of 210 League appearances over the next five years. Initially joining Bolton on loan, he was signed permanently for £90,000 in October 1977 and helped them win the Second Division in 1978 before moving on again to Birmingham City for £150,000 in November 1979. Frank then had a spell in the American game with Tampa Bay Rowdies (an apt club for him to join!) before returning briefly to Birmingham and then on to Leeds United in March 1982. Frank continued his journeys around the Football League, finally reaching a figure of 757 appearances after turning out for Sunderland, Southampton, Brighton, Tranmere, Preston and Stockport County before retiring in 1988 just short of his fortieth birthday.

Charles WREFORD-BROWN

Born: Bristol, 9th October 1866
Died: London, 26th November 1951
Role: Centre-Half
Career: Oxford University, Old Carthusians, Corinthians
Debut: v Ireland (h) 2-3-1889
Appearances: 4

Educated at Charterhouse, Charles played for the school side between 1884 and 1886 and then went on to continue his education at Oxford University. Awarded a Blue in 1888 and 1889, being captain in the latter year, he also earned a Blue at cricket in 1887. He then played football for Old Carthusians, helping them win the FA Amateur Cup in 1894 and 1897 and assisted the Corinthians and Casuals and represented London. He served on the FA Committee in 1892 to 1893, 1895 to 1902 and again from 1903 until the following year. He was on the FA Council from 1919 to 1941 and was a vice president from 1941. He was also an exceptional cricketer, making 19 first class appearances for Gloucestershire between 1886 and 1898. A solicitor by profession he qualified in 1895 and is credited with coining the phrase 'soccer' – apparently when asked if he was off to play 'rugger' (instead of rugby) he replied 'No, soccer' (from the word 'association'). Whilst he played in four England matches he was part of the selection committee for many more.

Charles Wreford-Brown

Edward Gordon Dundee WRIGHT

Born: Earslfield Green, 3rd October 1884
Died: Johannesburg, South Africa, 5th June 1947
Role: Left-Winger
Career: Ramsgate, Cambridge University, Worthing, Reigate Priory, Leyton, Portsmouth, Hull City, Corinthians, Sussex
Debut: v Wales (a) 19-3-1906
Appearances: 1

The son of a clergyman, Gordon was educated at St. Lawrence College in Ramsgate and then went to Queen's College Cambridge where he earned his Blue. After leaving Cambridge in 1906 he accepted a post at Hymer's College in Hull teaching Natural History and Science, also continuing his football career with the local Hull City club, for whom he was subsequently made captain. Even though he had yet to be capped for England at amateur level he was selected for the full side, making his only appearance in the 1-0 win over Wales in 1906. He was subsequently honoured for England at amateur level in 1908, going on to win 20 caps by 1913 and was also a member of the United Kingdom side that won the 1912 Olympic Games in Stockholm, although he only played in one of the early round matches (against Finland) and not in the final itself. After collecting his degree at Cambridge he graduated from the Royal School of Mining and in 1913 went to live in South Africa, thus ending his playing career. He remained in South Africa for the rest of his life, apart from a brief spell spent in America.

Ian Edward WRIGHT

Born: Woolwich, 3rd November 1963
Role: Striker
Career: Greenwich Borough, Crystal Palace, Arsenal, West Ham United
Debut: v Cameroon (h) 6-2-1991
Appearances: 33 (9 goals)

Ian developed late as a footballer, having seemingly been lost to the professional game and playing part-time for Greenwich Borough. In 1985 he was recommended to Crystal Palace for a trial, initially for two weeks, but impressed enough in three days to be offered a contract. He averaged almost a goal every other game whilst with the club and played an integral part in Palace reaching the 1990 FA Cup Final against Manchester United. Ian had been injured and out of action in the run up to the final itself and was on the substitutes' bench on the big day, but called into action he scored twice to help Palace earn a replay. His enthusiasm for the game subsequently earned him a call-up to the England side and, in September 1991, a £2.5 million transfer to Arsenal. Over the next seven years he was the focal point of the Arsenal attack, overtaking Cliff Bastin's record of 178 goals for the club in September 1997 and helping them win the League in 1998, the League Cup in 1993 and the FA Cup in 1993 and 1998, although he did not play in the latter final. His all-action playing style sometimes led him into disciplinary problems and he missed the 1994 European Cup Winners' Cup Final which Arsenal won, although he was in the side twelve months later when Arsenal again reached the final, although this time they lost. Whilst he took time to settle into the England side and find his goalscoring touch, he remained a part of the setup despite his advancing years. In the summer of 1998 he was sold to West Ham for £750,000, linking up again with former Arsenal striker John Hartson.

Ian Wright

John Douglas WRIGHT

Born: Southend-on-Sea, 29th April 1917
Died: December 1992
Role: Left-Half
Career: Southend United, Newcastle United, Lincoln City, Blyth Spartans
Debut: v Norway (h) 9-11-1938
Appearances: 1

Doug played junior football in Southend before being signed by Southend United in August 1936, making a total of 31 appearances for the club before a £325 fee took him to Newcastle United in May 1938. The outbreak of the Second World War robbed him of seven seasons of League football, although he was able to make an appearance for England in 1938. He was sold to Lincoln City for £600 in December 1948 having made 72 appearances for Newcastle and went on to help Lincoln win the Third Division championship in 1952, having lost their Second Division status in 1949. Doug made 233 appearances for the Imps and was appointed player-manager in the summer of 1955, subsequently becoming secretary in May 1957 until November 1960.

Mark WRIGHT

Born: Dorchester, 1st August 1963
Role: Defender
Career: Oxford United, Southampton, Derby County, Liverpool
Debut: v Wales (a) 2-5-1984
Appearances: 45 (1 goal)

Mark joined Oxford United as a junior and graduated through the ranks to become a professional in August 1980. He made just 10 appearances for the first team before being sold to Southampton in March 1982 for £140,000 and another player, and went on to become one of the best defenders in the game. Having broken into the England setup in 1984, he seemed a certainty to accompany the team to the 1986 World Cup finals in Mexico, but a broken leg, sustained in an FA Cup semi final a few months before the tournament, cost him that chance. In August 1987 he was sold to Derby County for £760,000 and re-established himself in the England side, being one of the key performers during the 1990 World Cup finals in Italy, scoring the only goal of the game in the match against Egypt. He was sold to Liverpool in July 1991 for £2.2 million and collected an FA Cup winners' medal at the end of his first season with the club, but thereafter was affected by a succession of injuries, culminating in his retirement from the game in 1998 owing to a back injury. Mark also made four appearances for England at Under-21 level. He later went into management, taking over at Southport and then Oxford United before returning to the Conference with Chester City, guiding them back into the Football League, and in June 2005 he took over at Peterborough United.

Mark Wright

Billy Wright

Richard WRIGHT

Born: Ipswich, 5th November 1977
Role: Goalkeeper
Career: Ipswich Town, Arsenal, Everton
Debut: v Malta (a) 3-6-2001
Appearances: 2

Richard joined Ipswich Town from school and made his debut for the club whilst still only 17. He represented England at Youth, Under-21 and B level and was seen as one of the best young goalkeepers around, prompting a £6 million move to Arsenal in 2001, going on to help the club win the Premier League in 2001-02. Initially bought as an understudy for David Seaman, Richard felt he was worth a more permanent place in the first team and he moved on to Everton in July 2002. Although he subsequently earned a recall into the England side, he found it difficult to displace Nigel Martyn from the Everton goal. In his England debut he had to face two penalties, saving one.

Thomas James WRIGHT

Born: Liverpool, 21st October 1944
Role: Right-Back
Career: Everton
Debut: v USSR (Rome) 8-6-1968 (EC)
Appearances: 11 + 1 unofficial appearance

Tommy spent his entire career with Everton, joining the ground staff in 1961 and being elevated to the professional ranks in March 1963. He won seven caps for England at Under-23 level before going on to collect 11 full caps and was a member of the 1970 World Cup squad, appearing in the matches against Romania and Brazil. Originally an inside-forward, he was first converted to half-back and then full-back, where he enjoyed his greatest success, being a member of the Everton side that won the FA Cup in 1966 and the League championship in 1970 as well as reaching the FA Cup final in 1968. He retired through injury in February 1974 having made 370 appearances for the Everton first team.

William Ambrose WRIGHT C.B.E.

Born: Ironbridge, 6th February 1924
Died: Barnet, 3rd September 1994
Role: Inside-Forward, Wing-Half
Career: Wolverhampton Wanderers
Debut: v Northern Ireland (a) 28-9-1946
Appearances: 105 (3 goals) + 4 War appearances + 1 unofficial appearance

Billy Wright joined Wolves as a 15-year-old straight from school but did not impress early on - the club nearly sent him home because they felt he wasn't good enough or tall enough to make the grade! Luckily Major Frank Buckley had a change of mind and signed Billy to the ground staff in June 1938 for the princely sum of £2 per week. He was upgraded to the full professional ranks in February 1941 and was later sent to Leicester on loan in order to gain experience. In May 1942 he broke an ankle, an injury that at the time threatened to halt his career, but he recovered from his injury and was soon back in training. He enlisted in the Army in 1943 and became a Physical Training Instructor for the rest of the hostilities, returning to Molineux in 1945 in order to resume his football career. He was made captain of Wolves in 1947 and thereafter guided them to a host of honours, including three League titles in 1954, 1958 and 1959 and the FA Cup in 1949. He was named Footballer of the Year in 1952 and awarded the CBE in 1959, the same year he announced his retirement. By then Billy had amassed 491 League appearances for his club and 105 caps for his country (of which 90 were as captain), the first English player to have surpassed 100 caps. Never booked or sent off throughout his career, Billy was named manager of the England Youth team in 1960 and later assumed responsibility for the Under-23 side. In 1962 he was appointed manager of Arsenal but was felt by many to be too 'nice' to be a manager, leaving the club in June 1966. He then worked in the television industry as Head of Sport for one of the independent stations and served as a member of the Pilkington Commission on Television and Broadcasting. He was married to Joy Beverly, one of the famous Beverly Sisters and was later president of Wolves as well as an Honorary Life Member of the Football Association. Seventy of Billy's appearances were consecutive; a record run for an England international.

Shaun Cameron WRIGHT-PHILLIPS

Born: Greenwich, London, 25th October 1981
Role: Winger
Career: Nottingham Forest, Manchester City
Debut: v Ukraine (h) 18-8-2004 (scored once)
Appearances: 7 (1 goal)

The stepson of former Crystal Palace/Arsenal/West Ham United and England striker Ian Wright, Shaun has been widely tipped as one of the most exciting talents to emerge in the domestic game for many a year. Originally signed by Nottingham Forest as a trainee, Shaun was surprisingly released by the club who claimed he was too fragile to withstand the rigours of the modern game, but he eventually signed with Manchester City in July 1999 and set about

Shaun Wright-Philips

proving his detractors wrong. Something of a throwback to a bygone age, Shaun's prowess on the wing for Manchester City soon had pundits tipping him for England honours and he eventually earned a call-up for the match against the Ukraine in August 2004. He scored on his debut after a jinking run, confirming that he can more than hold his own in any company, be it at club or international level. Although there had been much speculation over his future during the course of the 2004-05 season, with Manchester City turning down a number of offers believed to be in the region of £8 million, during the summer of 2005 Shaun was considered one of the hottest properties in the game. Despite interest from his stepfather's old club Arsenal, Shaun finally settled on a move to League champions Chelsea in a deal worth £21 million.

John George WYLIE

Born: Shrewsbury, 1854
Died: 30th July 1924
Role: Forward
Career: Wanderers, Sheffield FC, Sheffield FA
Debut: v Scotland (a) 2-3-1878 (scored once)
Appearances: 1 (1 goal)

Educated at Shrewsbury School, John later played for the Wanderers and Sheffield and earned representative honours with the Sheffield FA. A member of the Wanderers side that won the FA Cup in 1878, he qualified as a solicitor the same year and joined a practice in London.

John YATES

Born: Blackburn, 1861
Died: 1st June 1917
Role: Left-Winger
Career: Accrington, Blackburn Olympic, Accrington, Burnley
Debut: v Ireland (h) 2-3-1889 (scored three times)
Appearances: 1 (3 goals)

Jack joined Accrington in 1879 and spent a year with the club before joining Blackburn Olympic, collecting an FA Cup winners' medal with the club in 1883. He returned to Accrington in February 1886 and spent a further two years with the club before linking with Burnley in 1888. Although he had represented Lancashire on a number of occasions he did not get to win an England cap until 1889, when he had already notched up ten years in the top flight game. He made the most of the opportunity, scoring a hat-trick in his one and only international, one of five players to have achieved the feat. He retired from playing in 1894 and then concentrated on his profession of cotton weaver.

Richard Ernest YORK

Born: Birmingham, 25th April 1899
Died: 9th December 1969
Role: Right-Winger
Career: Aston Villa, Port Vale, Brierley Hill Alliance
Debut: v Scotland (h) 8-4-1922
Appearances: 2

Richard represented Birmingham Schools before the First World War and at the outbreak of hostilities was commissioned into the Army, subsequently switching to the Royal Air Force and training to be a pilot as well as representing the force at football. At the end of the war he signed with Aston Villa and helped the club reach the FA Cup final in 1924 as well as representing the Football League twice. He remained on the books of Aston Villa until June 1931 when he joined Port Vale, spending a single season at Vale Park before finishing his playing career with Brierley Hill Alliance. He then returned to the Birmingham area where he ran his own plumbing and decorating business.

Alfred YOUNG

Born: Sunderland, 4th November 1905
Died: 30th August 1977
Role: Half-Back
Career: Durham City, Huddersfield Town, York City
Debut: v Wales (a) 16-11-1932
Appearances: 9

Alf had a brief spell with Durham City before being invited to join Huddersfield Town in January 1927 and remaining with the club for eighteen years. During that time he helped them reach the FA Cup final in 1938 and made two appearances for the Football League. He joined York City in November 1945 and retired the following year before going on to coach in Denmark until 1948. He then returned to Huddersfield to coach from July 1948 to May 1952. Alf later had spells as manager of Bradford Park Avenue and coaching again in Denmark before spending a third spell at Huddersfield as coach from December 1960 to 1964 and then chief scout until his retirement in July 1965.

Gerry Young

Gerald Morton YOUNG

Born: South Shields, 1st October 1936
Role: Wing-Half
Career: Newcastle United, Hawthorn Leslie Juniors, Sheffield Wednesday
Debut: v Wales (h) 18-11-1964
Appearances: 1

Gerry played schools football in the Jarrow area and was initially signed by Newcastle United at the age of 16, but unable to make the grade slipped back into non-League football. He then worked towards qualifying as an electrician and playing for the Hawthorn Leslie works side when he was spotted by Sheffield Wednesday and signed professional forms in May 1955. He was to spend sixteen years with the club, helping them earn promotion to the First Division twice and reach the FA Cup final in 1966, although it was his mistake in the final against Everton that led to Derek Temple scoring Everton's winning goal in the 3-2 win. He made 345 first team appearances for the club before hanging up his boots in 1971 and became second team trainer, later serving the club as chief coach until 1975 and having a brief spell on the staff at Barnsley.

Luke Paul YOUNG

Born: Harlow, 19th July 1979
Role: Defender
Career: Tottenham Hotspur, Charlton Athletic
Debut: v USA (a) 28-5-2005
Appearances: 7

Luke joined Spurs as a trainee and signed professional forms in the summer of 1997. Over the next four years he made more than 60 appearances for the first team, but it was his inability to establish himself in one position that prompted him to look for a move – whilst Spurs saw him as a versatile defender able to play either in the centre or flanks, he preferred to settle into one position. Charlton Athletic paid £3,000,000 for his signature in the summer of 2001 and over the next few years he settled into the right-back position. Capped for England 12 times at Under-21 level having previously represented his country at Youth level, Luke was called into the full squad for the American tour of 2005. Injury to regular right-back Gary Neville saw Luke add to his tally of caps, growing in confidence and stature with each successive game and helping the national side reach the World Cup finals of 2006.

Luke Young

APPENDIX 1
Victory Internationals following the First World War

Normal League football was halted at the end of the 1914-15 season and did not recommence until the 1919-20 season, although regional Leagues were in operation for the duration of the war. Four international matches, designated as Victory Internationals were staged between April and October 1919, although these were not classified as full internationals and accordingly no caps were awarded, although the players did receive gold medals. The following players, therefore, have represented England only in these matches.

William Ball (born in Dudley, Worcestershire on 9th April 1886, died 30th September 1942) made his name with Birmingham, joining the club in May 1911 from non-League Wellington Town. He remained with Birmingham until October 1921 when he left to join Cannock Town, later returning to Wellington before finishing his playing career in 1924. He was unfortunate to have lost the bulk of his playing career to the First World War and made just 165 first team appearances for Birmingham, even missing out on a championship medal in 1920-21 when the club won the Second Division title. His international career was little better, for he sustained an injury during the first half of his only appearance and did not return for the second half of the match against Wales in Cardiff. Even though England had both George Edmonds (of Watford) and Archie Mitchell (Queens Park Rangers) sitting on the bench, this was in the days before substitutes were allowed and England thus played with 10 men during the second period.
Appearances: 1

Horace Barnes (born in Wadsley Bridge in Sheffield on 3rd January 1890, died 12th September 1961) was a prolific goalscorer for Manchester City during the First World War, netting 73 goals in exactly 73 appearances. On 4th September 1915 he helped City win 3-1 in the Lancashire Principal Tournament and was subsequently fined by a Manchester magistrate for having absented himself from the munitions factory where he worked in order to play! He had begun his career with Sunday League side Birley Carr in Sheffield before commencing his League career with Derby County in October 1908, subsequently costing Manchester City a then record fee of £2,500 in May 1914. He remained at City until November 1924 when a fee of £2,759 took him to Preston North End, although a year later he was on the move again, this time costing Oldham Athletic £1,250. A little under two years later he left League football and signed for Ashton National where he finished his career in 1931. Aside from his single appearance for England he also represented the Football League twice and helped Derby win the Second Division championship in 1912.
Appearances: 1

Samuel Ernest Brooks (born in Brierley Hill on 28th March 1890, died in Wolverhampton circa 1955) was known as the 'Little Giant' within Molineux. Educated at Bent Street School, he turned professional with Wolves in August 1910 and spent twelve years with the club. During that time he helped reach the FA Cup Final in 1921 where they were beaten 1-0 by Spurs at Stamford Bridge and made one appearance in a Victory International before being transferred to Spurs in 1922. He spent two years with Spurs before returning to the Midlands in order to play for Cradley Heath and then Stourbridge, retiring in 1927.
Appearances: 1

Fred Duckworth (born in Blackburn in 1892) was a Blackburn man through and through, joining the local club in January 1910 from local football and remaining with them until injury forced his retirement in 1922. Interestingly, he did not become a regular in the Blackburn League side until after he had made his debut for England in a Victory International, mainly because of the continued good form of Bob Crompton and Arthur Cowell at club level. In April 1921 he was playing in an East Lancashire Charity Cup-tie when he broke his forearm in two places. The bone would not reset properly and he was eventually forced to retire the following year. He then resorted to his initial trade of plumber.
Appearances: 2

Tom Fleetwood (born in Toxteth Park, Liverpool on 6th December 1888, died 1945) made his name as a forward with Rochdale and was transferred to Everton in March 1911 for £460, later proving adaptable enough to turn out for the Goodison Park club as a centre-forward, half-back and centre-half. He joined Oldham Athletic in August 1923 having made two appearances for England, both of which came against Scotland in Victory Internationals in 1919. Although he was unable to break into the full England side, Tom did represent the Football League on five occasions during his career and won a League championship medal with Everton in 1915. He was transferred to Oldham Athletic for £750 in August 1923 and immediately appointed captain, but an injury sustained on his debut restricted his appearances for the club and he subsequently joined Chester in September 1924.
Appearances: 2

Alan Grenyer (born in North Shields, Northumberland on 31st August 1892, died in June 1953) began his career with North Shields and joined Everton in November 1910, sharing the left-half berth with the famous double international Harry Makepeace. Alan was able to help the club win the League championship in 1915 and also represented the Football League on one occasion. In November 1924 he joined South Shields and remained with the club until his retirement in 1929.
Appearances: 1

Elias Henry Hendren (born in Turnham Green in Middlesex on 5th February 1889, died on 4th October 1962) was known as 'Patsy' throughout his career which began with Brentford whom he joined from junior football during the summer of 1907. A little under a year later he joined Manchester City, although this move was always likely to prove problematical, for Patsy was also an exceptionally talented cricketer and had begun playing for Middlesex the same year. He therefore joined Coventry City in October 1909 and subsequently rejoined Brentford in August 1911, remaining with the club until his retirement in the summer of 1927. Aside from his one appearance in a Victory International, Patsy also represented the Southern League on one occasion, but his performances for England as a cricketer surpassed anything he achieved on a football field. First selected for a Test Match during the winter tour of Australia in 1920-21, he went on to appear in 51 Tests. During the visit to the West Indies in 1929-30 he hit four double centuries and scored a total of 1,765 runs to register an average of 137.76 runs, a record that still stands.
Appearances: 1

Clarence Hilditch (born in Hartford in Cheshire on 2nd June 1894, died on 31st October 1977) was known throughout the game as 'Lal' and signed for Manchester United in January 1916. He was appointed player-manager in October 1926, holding the position until the end of the season in April 1927. He then resumed his career as a player and finally retired in 1932. He made over 300 appearances for the club during his long association with them, sadly winning no medals, although he did represent England in a Victory International in 1919 and played for the Football League. At the end of his playing career he coached United's Colts team. Lal was a member of the FA touring party which visited South Africa in 1920.
Appearances: 1

Charles William Parker (born in Seaham Harbour in County Durham on 21st September 1891) played for the local Seaham Harbour club in the North Eastern League and was signed by Stoke in 1914. In September 1920 he cost Sunderland £3,300 but despite the hefty fee was not an automatic first choice at centre-half, even more so when the Roker Park club paid £5,250 to bring in Michael Gilhooley. Gilhooley was subsequently seriously injured and Charlie made the centre-half berth his own, linking exceptionally well with wing-halves Willie Clunas and Arthur Andrews and the three formed a solid club half-back line between 1923 and 1927. In May 1929 he was transferred to Carlisle United and a year later joined Chopwell Institute where he finished his career. Charlie also represented the Football League once during his career.
Appearances: 2

William Voisey (born on the Isle of Dogs on 19th November 1891, died on 19th October 1964) played schools football in Millwall before joining Millwall Athletic as an amateur during the 1908-09 season, subsequently being upgraded to the professional ranks the following season. Known as 'Banger' during his career he enlisted in the Army at the outbreak of the First World War and rose to the rank of battalion sergeant major, collecting the Distinguished Service Medal, the Military Medal and the Belgian Croix de Guerre during his service. Upon the resumption of his football career he won his only international honour when appearing in one Victory International and subsequently toured South Africa with the FA in 1920. He remained with Millwall until June 1923 when he joined Bournemouth and retired from playing a year later. He then switched to training and coaching, serving Leytonstone, Fulham and Millwall, joining the latter club in June 1939. He also served Millwall as manager between 1940 and November 1944 and then reverted back to trainer, a position he held until 1949. He was then chief scout until his retirement in 1962.
Appearances: 1

Robert Whittingham (born in Goldenhill in Stoke-on-Trent in 1889, died in June 1926) was briefly linked with Crewe Alexandra before joining the professional ranks with

Blackpool during the summer of 1907. In January 1909 he joined Bradford City and a little over a year later switched to Chelsea in a deal worth £1,300. He represented the Football League on one occasion and then, barely days after representing England in a Victory International, was transferred to Stoke in October 1919. By the summer of 1920 he was forced to retire owing to illness, although he did attempt a comeback with Wrexham in November 1922 without success. He died from tuberculosis in the summer of 1926 at the age of just 37.
Appearances: 1 (1 goal)

APPENDIX 2
Wartime and Victory Internationals during the Second World War

Unlike the First World War, when representative football was all but abandoned, a series of internationals were staged during and after the Second World War. The majority of these were for morale boosting purposes, and as with the Victory Internationals of the First World War, no caps were awarded. The longer duration of the war meant that there were considerably more players who made their only appearances for their country in these internationals, as can be seen below. Once again there were no actual caps awarded, although in April 1946 the Football Association did present each player with an illuminated address, containing the details of each and every match the player had taken part in between 1939 and 1946. Additionally, those who played in any of the six Victory International matches of season 1945-46 were presented with an embroidered blazer badge.

It should also be noted that the two matches played against Switzerland in July 1945 have also been included in this section. According to the Football Association, these matches were between two sides comprised of Combined Services XIs, not full international sides, but clearly there are mitigating circumstances for considering them as international matches, albeit unofficial ones. To begin with, the players chosen to represent the FA were all Englishmen and all of them had represented their country previously, either in full or wartime internationals. Secondly, the menu cards for the after match dinners clearly stated that they were for the Schweiz - England match, whilst pictures of the matches reveal the 'England' players to be wearing the distinctive white shirt with three lions on the badge. Finally, the players themselves had the details of the matches produced on the illuminated addresses they received giving details of all wartime internationals they had taken part in.

Giuseppe Luigi Davide Bacuzzi (born in London on 25th September 1916, died on 1st February 1995) was known as 'Joe' throughout his career, which began as an amateur with Fulham in the summer of 1935. He was upgraded to the professional ranks the following year and went on to remain with the club until his retirement in 1956, then serving as assistant trainer until 1965. In all he made 283 League appearances for the club and won a Second Division championship medal in 1949, and when his association with football ended he was employed by Sainsbury's as a cook. Joe is unfortunate not to have won a full cap for England, for he played in both the first and last wartime internationals for his country. His son Dave, a full-back with Arsenal, Manchester City and Reading during the 1960s, represented the country at Youth level.
Appearances: 13

John Balmer (born in Liverpool on 6th February 1916, died on 25th December 1984) represented Liverpool FA and County FA as a youngster and was also briefly on the books of Everton as an amateur. However, he chose to join Liverpool as an amateur in 1935 and was subsequently upgraded to the professional ranks the following year, remaining with the club until his retirement in the summer of 1952. By this time he had helped Liverpool win the League championship in 1947 and had scored 111 goals in 313 League games. He was a nephew of William and Robert Balmer, famous full-backs for Everton during Edwardian times.
Appearances: 1 (1 goal)

Sam Bartram (born in Simonside in County Durham on 22nd January 1914, died on 17th July 1981) is generally regarded as one of England's greatest ever goalkeepers and unlucky never to have won a full cap for England, a plethora of others in that position keeping him out. He joined Charlton from Boldon Colliery and had originally been an outfield player and would have been capped for England at schoolboy level but for the fact that the letter informing him of his selection arrived four days after he had left school in order to work down the pits! He took to goalkeeping when a works side regular was injured and did well enough to attract the attention of Charlton Athletic, going on to serve the club for some twenty years. He appeared in successive FA Cup Finals for Charlton, collecting a winners' medal in 1947 and finally retired from playing in March 1956, subsequently becoming manager of York City the same month. He remained in charge until July 1960 when he left to take over at Luton Town, staying at Kenilworth Road until June 1962. He then turned to journalism, writing for the Sunday People for many years.
Appearances: 3

Robert Albert John Brown (born in Great Yarmouth on 7th November 1915) was known as 'Sailor' during his career and joined Charlton from Gorleston in August 1934. He remained at Charlton until May 1946 when he cost Nottingham Forest £6,750, a then considerable fee, and in October 1947 he was on the move again, this time costing Aston Villa £10,000. Injury forced his retirement from playing in June 1949 by which time he had made 123 League appearances for his three clubs. After his retirement he undertook a number of jobs, including running a sports shop, a turf accountant, was a holiday camp sports organiser and then a timber merchant.
Appearances: 6 (4 goals) + 1 unofficial appearance (1 goal)

Victor Frederick Buckingham (born in South London on 23rd October 1915, died 21st January 1995) joined Spurs in 1935 and went on to make over 300 appearances for the first team before retiring in 1949. During the war he guested for Crewe, Fulham, Millwall and Portsmouth, even playing for Portsmouth against Spurs in one match in 1944. At the end of his playing career he turned to coaching and became one of the best in the game, taking the combined Oxford and Cambridge University side Pegasus to the FA Amateur Cup in 1951. He then turned to management, taking over at Bradford Park Avenue and West Bromwich Albion before trying his luck on the continent. One of the early British successes overseas, he coached Ajax of Amsterdam for two years (including Johann Cruyff) before returning to England as manager of Sheffield Wednesday in 1961. He remained at Hillsborough for two years before taking over at Craven Cottage where he remained for three years. A spell in Greece with Ethnikos followed and he then took over at Barcelona, taking them to victory in the 1971 Spanish Cup Final and finished his managerial career with Seville the following year.
Appearances: 2

Henry Clifton (born in Marley Hill on 28th May 1914, died 1998) was briefly signed as an amateur with West Bromwich Albion but began his professional career with Chesterfield in August 1933. After 122 League appearances and 66 goals he cost Newcastle United £8,000 when he signed in August 1938, having already collected a Third Division North championship medal with Chesterfield in 1936. The Second World War cost him a large slice of his career and he was able to make just 29 League appearances and score 15 goals before he was sold to Grimsby Town for £2,500 in January 1946. He made 69 League appearances for the Mariners before finishing his career with non-League Goole Town.
Appearances: 1 (1 goal)

Denis Compton (born in Hendon on 23rd May 1918, died 23rd April 1997) joined Arsenal from Hampstead Town, following exactly the footsteps of his elder brother Les who was also on Arsenal's books. Denis first broke into the England side in 1940 against Wales, operating on the left wing and made his final appearance three years later in the 8-0 drubbing of Scotland in Manchester. After the war he returned to Arsenal but was seldom a regular in the League side, making only 32 appearances in some three years. Much of the reason for this, of course, was his immensely successful cricket career for both Middlesex and England, although he was a member of the Arsenal side that won the FA Cup in 1950.
Appearances: 12 (3 goals)

Walter Crook (born in Whittle on 24th April 1913, died on 27th December 1988) began his career with Blackburn Rovers, signing professional forms in January 1931. He remained at Ewood Park for the next sixteen years, finally leaving after 218 League appearances to join Bolton Wanderers in May 1947. He helped Blackburn win the Second Division championship in 1939, the only domestic honour of his career. Injury brought his playing career to an end in the summer of 1948 and he then turned to coaching, taking over as manager and coach of Ajax in Amsterdam for a season. In March 1951 he was appointed trainer to Accrington Stanley, subsequently being upgraded to manager at Peel Park in June 1951. A year later he was appointed secretary-manager, holding the post until February 1953 when he returned to coaching in Holland. He was then manager of Wigan Athletic between October 1954 and the summer of 1955 and then served Preston North End as scout until his eventual retirement in April 1969.
Appearances: 1

Maurice Edelston (born in Hull on 27th April 1918, died on 30th January 1976) began his career as an amateur and turned out for Brentford and Fulham in such a capacity, as well as being capped by England at this level (he won a total of nine amateur caps). He also played for Great Britain in the Olympics of 1936, appearing in the match against China. He turned professional with Reading in 1947, with whom he was playing when he made his debut for the England side in 1941. At the end of the war he returned to Reading and made a further 202 League appearances before being sold to Northampton Town in 1952 where he finished his career. His father Joe had also been a noted footballer and later manager.
Appearances: 5 (1 goal)

William Elliott (born in Harrington on 6th August 1919, died in Birmingham on 24th November 1966) played left-wing for Carlisle United, Wolverhampton Wanderers, Dudley and Bournemouth before signing for West Bromwich Albion and made his debut for England in 1944. He remained with Albion until 1950 and joined Bilston United as player-manager, finally retiring in 1954. He then became a publican and was working in Birmingham at the time of his death in 1966.
Appearances: 2

Edward Benjamin Fenton (born in Forest Gate in London on 9th November 1914, died on 14th July 1992) played for West Ham schools and Colchester Town before linking with West Ham United as an amateur in 1930, turning professional in 1932. He remained at Upton Park until May 1946 (and was therefore at the club at the same time as his younger brother Benny) when he became player-manager of Colchester United. He returned to West Ham as manager in August 1950 and held the position until March 1961 when he took over as manager of Southend United. He remained at Roots Hall until May 1965 when he finished with football, working as a publican and later running a sports shop in Brentwood before retiring to Gloucestershire. In addition to his one wartime international, Ted also appeared for England in one unofficial match against Switzerland in 1945. He had also been a member of the FA touring party to South Africa in 1939, appearing in three matches.
Appearances: 1 + 1 unofficial appearance

Lester Charles Finch (born in Hadley in Hertfordshire on 26th August 1909) was a leading amateur player of his era, representing Great Britain in the 1936 Olympics and collecting 16 caps for England at amateur level. During the Second World War he turned out for Chelsea, Wolverhampton Wanderers, West Bromwich Albion, Nottingham Forest, Walsall and Bournemouth and at the time of his selection for England was associated with the Barnet club. He won a winners' medal in the FA Amateur Cup in 1946 and a runners-up medal two years later and in 1939 had been invited by the FA to join their touring party to South Africa, appearing twice. Lester spent his working life in the print trade.
Appearances: 1

Frederick William Fisher (born in Dodworth, Barnsley on 11th April 1910, killed in action over Europe in September 1944) began his professional career with Barnsley in November 1933 and remained with the club until a £500 transfer took him to Chesterfield in February 1938. By the end of the year he had transferred again, costing Millwall £1,600 when they signed him in November the same year. Unfortunately the outbreak of the Second World War brought his playing career to an effective end and he lost his life during the conflict whilst serving as a rear gunner in a bomber plane.
Appearances: 1

Reginald Flewin (born in Portsmouth on 28th November 1920) joined Portsmouth as a professional in November 1937 after playing for Ryde on the Isle of Wight. His only appearance for England came in the meeting with the Welsh at Anfield in 1944 and after the war he was captain as Portsmouth won successive League titles, in 1948-49 and 1949-50. He made 151 League appearances before retiring in 1953 and then served the club as coach and assistant manager until September 1960 when he was appointed manager at Stockport County. He remained at the club until July 1963 when he took over as manager at Bournemouth and was in charge until November 1965, when ill health forced his retirement. He then had a spell in charge of non-League Hastings United before taking over as manager of a holiday camp at Ventnor on the Isle of Wight. Reg had also served as team manager of the FA touring parties to Canada and Australia in 1950 and 1951 respectively.
Appearances: 1

Albert Henry Gibbons (born in West London on 10th April 1914) signed as an amateur with Spurs in 1937 and quickly proved to be an exceptionally good goalscorer, netting 18 goals in 33 senior outings in his first season and collecting the first of his six amateur caps for England. The following season, however, he elected to join Brentford and made 12 appearances for the Bees before returning to Spurs in August 1939. He appeared for the club regularly during the war, represented England in 1942 and Spurs were hopeful that they could persuade him to stay with them when normal football resumed in 1946. Instead he chose to move north for work reasons, later returning to the south to take over as manager at Brentford in 1949. He resigned from the post in August 1952 and thereafter coached all around the world, including Australia, South Africa and Europe.
Appearances: 1

Henry Goslin (born in Willington in Derbyshire on 9th November 1909, killed in action in Italy on 18th December 1943) was brought up in Nottingham and worked for the Boots company based in the city before signing professional forms with Bolton Wanderers in April 1930. He went on to make 334 first team appearances for the club prior to the outbreak of the Second World War, guesting for Norwich City and Chelsea during the hostilities. Having served in the Territorials for four years, Harry was called up for the regular army as soon as war was declared and after serving in the Royal Artillery in France and Africa, he lost his life in Italy.
Appearances: 4

Norman Greenhalgh (born in Bolton on 10th August 1914, died 1995) was initially signed by Bolton but made his name with New Brighton, joining them in 1935. After recovering from appendix trouble and rediscovering his form, he was sold to Everton, making his debut in the 1937-38 season and forming an effective partnership with Willie Cook. He helped Everton to the League title in 1939 and represented the Football League once but, like many of his generation, was unfortunate that the Second World War cut right across his career, although he remained at Goodison Park until 1949 when he was given a free transfer and joined Bangor City. He was once described by Stanley Matthews as the opponent he least enjoyed playing against!
Appearances: 1

Adolphe Jonathan Hanson (born in Bootle on 27th February 1912, died 1993) was briefly linked with Everton before signing with Liverpool in November 1931. In July 1938 Alf cost Chelsea £7,500 and by the time the Second World War broke out he had 220 first team outings for his two clubs to his credit, scoring 61 goals, a remarkable tally for a left-winger. In 1945 he was appointed player-manager of South Liverpool, moving over to Ireland the following year to take over as player-manager of Shelbourne. He returned home to take over a similar position at Ellesmere Port Town in February 1949. His younger brother Stan was also a professional footballer, serving Bolton Wanderers in goal.
Appearances: 1

Bernard Harper (born in Gawber in Barnsley on 23rd November 1912, died 1994) joined Barnsley in August 1932 from Barugh Green and successfully came through a trial period to be offered professional terms. He helped the club win the Third Division North championship in 1934 and 1939 and had made 228 League and cup appearances for the club by the time war broke out. At the end of the hostilities he became player-manager of Scunthorpe United, holding the position until 1948.

Herbert Johnson (born in Spennymoor on 4th June 1916) played schools and junior football in his native North East before signing with Charlton Athletic in March 1939, costing the club £400 from Spennymoor United. With the outbreak of the Second World War he guested for Bolton Wanderers, returning south to Charlton in 1946 and helping them reach successive FA Cup finals, collecting a winners' medal in the second of these in 1947. He remained at Charlton until July 1953 when he left to become player-manager of Bexleyheath & Welling, subsequently taking over at Cambridge United in November 1955 in a similar capacity. In June 1959 he became chief scout to Leicester City and was later to serve the club as assistant manager and chief coach. He also had spells scouting for Nottingham Forest, Derby County, Southampton and Walsall before retiring in the summer of 1981.
Appearances: 2

Harry Thomas Kinsell (born in Cannock on 3rd May 1921, died September 2000) joined West Bromwich Albion from schools football in Cannock, joining the ground staff in May 1935 and turning professional in June 1938. During the Second World War he guested for Blackpool, Grimsby Town and Middlesbrough and returned to West Bromwich at the end of the hostilities. He moved on to Bolton Wanderers in June 1949, costing a then club record fee of £12,000, although less than a year later he was on the move again, joining Reading. In January 1951 he joined West Ham United and remained at Upton Park for five years, joining non-League Bedford Town in July 1956. He retired from playing the following year.
Appearances: 2 + 1 unofficial appearance

James Lewis (born in Hackney in London on 21st December 1905, died in March 1976) was one of the leading amateur players of his era, winning 13 caps for England at that level. He was also a member of the FA touring party to South Africa in 1939, playing twice during the tour. As a player he played junior football prior to signing for Walthamstow Avenue in 1929, although he also spent a year on the books of Queens Park Rangers. He returned to Walthamstow in 1932 and remained with the club until retiring during the Second World War. He made his debut for England as a substitute, coming on for the injured Joe Bacuzzi in the very first wartime international and was thus the first substitution made in a British big match. His son, also christened James and an amateur with Walthamstow, was later a member of the Chelsea side that won the First Division championship in 1955.
Appearances: 1

John Mapson (born in Birkenhead on 2nd May 1917, died August 1999) moved to Swindon when he was a child and signed amateur forms with Swindon Town when aged 16 years. After a spell with Guildford City he joined Reading in April 1935, although he was loaned back to the non-League side for season 1935-36. After barely a handful of appearances for Reading he was sold to Sunderland for £1,000 in March 1936 and a year later was goalkeeper when they won the FA Cup. He toured with the FA party to South Africa, appearing in two games, and remained with Sunderland until his retirement in the summer of 1954. During the Second World War he worked in a Royal Ordnance engineering factory and at the end of his playing career worked in the furniture and upholstery trade. He was also selected to play for England in the wartime match against Wales in Cardiff in June 1941, but with Reading having reached the London War Cup Final on the same day opted to play for his club at Stamford Bridge. John was never selected by England again.
Appearances: 1

William George Marks (born in Figheldean on 9th April 1915, died on 1st February 1998) had joined Arsenal from Salisbury City and broke into the first team at the tail end of the 1938-39 season, keeping his place for the first three games of the 1930-40 season which were later expunged from the records. With the eventual return of international football, albeit on an unofficial basis, George replaced Frank Swift as England's goalkeeper and made eight appearances for England. Unfortunately, he suffered a head injury in a clash with Wales at Wembley and never fully recovered, thereby missing out on a proper international career. When League football resumed in 1946 he was transferred to Blackburn Rovers, making 67 appearances for the Ewood Park club before moving on to Bristol City in August 1948. Less than two months later he was on the move again, this time to Reading where he finished his career with 128 League outings.
Appearances: 8

John Rowland Martin (born in Birmingham on 5th August 1914, died in 1996) began his career with Hednesford Town and joined Aston Villa as an amateur in October 1934, upgrading to the professional ranks in 1935. He remained with Villa until the summer of 1949, although because of the war he had made only 81 appearances during his fourteen year association with the club. He returned to Hednesford Town at this time, later becoming manager of the club for a time. Upon retiring as a player he reverted to teaching and later served as a headmaster.
Appearances: 1 (1 goal)

George William Mason (born in Birmingham on 5th September 1913, died on 12th August 1993) represented South Birmingham schools and signed with Redhill Amateurs before joining Coventry City in November 1931. He went on to make 330 League appearances for the club before joining Nuneaton Borough in the summer of 1952. He retired in September 1953 but subsequently joined Bedworth Town in the summer of 1954 for a brief spell. George also represented England at schoolboy level, collecting one cap, and won a Third Division South championship medal with Coventry in 1936. Upon his retirement he became a publican, a vocation he maintained for virtually the remainder of his working life, although he did have a brief spell working for Jaguar.
Appearances: 2

Reginald Charles Mountford (born in Darlington on 16th July 1908, died 1994) represented Darlington at schools level and was working as a miner when he was invited to join Darlington during the 1928-29 season. Initially signed as an amateur, he became a professional with Huddersfield Town in May 1929 and remained with the club for the remainder of his playing career, finally retiring during the Second World War. He was a member of the side that reached the FA Cup final in 1938, finishing runners-up to Preston North End. During the war he guested for Brentford, Chelsea and Crystal Palace.
Appearances: 1

John Oakes (born in Winsford in Cheshire on 13th September 1905, died in Australia on 20th March 1992) had a remarkable career as a professional player, twice returning to the League game after seemingly dropping out of sight in the non-League game. He was signed by Nottingham Forest in August 1928 and made two League appearances before joining Crook Town in the summer of 1930. He then returned to League football with Southend United, joining the Roots Hall club in May 1931 and made two appearances for the club before returning to Crook Town in the summer of 1932. He made a third return to the League game with Aldershot in August 1934 and went on to make 61 League appearances, scoring 19 goals before a £650 move to Charlton in March 1936. He remained at The Valley until July 1947, by which time he had helped Charlton reach the FA Cup final in 1946 (he is one of the oldest players to have appeared in an FA Cup final). He then moved on to Plymouth Argyle and was still playing League football at the age of 44 years. After playing and managing in the non-League game he went to Sweden to coach for a number of years and later emigrated to first the United States and then Australia. He died in Perth in 1992.
Appearances: 1

Thomas Usher Pearson (born in Edinburgh on 6th March 1913, died 1st March 1999) cost Newcastle United just £35 when he was signed in March 1933 from Edinburgh Amateurs. He was exchanged with another player in February 1948 and returned north of the border to sign for Aberdeen, later becoming a sports journalist and coach. He was manager of Aberdeen between November 1959 and February 1965 and later served Newcastle United as their Edinburgh scout. Tommy owed his place in the England side to a car accident - on the day of the match between England and Scotland at Newcastle in December 1939, the car carrying England players Sam Barkas and Eric Brook was involved in a three car pile-up. This left England two players short and two Newcastle players (where the match between England and Scotland was taking place) were drafted in as replacements. That Tommy Pearson was up to the task is not in doubt, for he went on to win two full caps for his home country - Scotland, one of which was against England! He also represented the Scottish League on one occasion whilst with Aberdeen.
Appearances: 1

Joseph Richardson (born in Bedlington in Northumberland on 24th August 1908, died in 1977) first came to prominence with leading non-League side Blyth Spartans and cost Newcastle United £250 plus another player when he joined in April 1929. He was to remain associated with the club for the rest of his life, retiring as a player during the Second World War but serving the club thereafter as assistant trainer until his death in 1977.
Appearances: 1

Ronald Leslie Rooke (born in Guildford on 7th December 1911, died July 1985) played junior football in Guildford and had a trial with Stoke City before signing with non-League Woking. He then played for Guildford City before being spotted by Crystal Palace and was signed in March 1933. In October 1936 he moved across London to join Fulham, remaining at Craven Cottage until December 1946 when a £1,000 fee took him to Arsenal. Despite the fact that he was already 35 years of age, his experience proved invaluable and he was a member of the side that won the League title in 1948 (he finished top goalscorer that season with 33 goals). He returned to Crystal Palace in June 1949 as player-manager, retiring from playing in 1950 and remaining as manager until December 1950. He then moved on to non-League Bedford Town as player-manager in February 1951 and towards the end of the decade had a second spell in charge of the club.
Appearances: 1

Alexander White Roxburgh (born in Manchester on 19th September 1910, died on 5th December 1985) played junior football in Blackpool and first linked with the local club as an amateur in January 1931, having also been briefly signed with Manchester City. He made 62 appearances in goal for the club prior to the outbreak of the Second World War and at the end of hostilities joined Barrow, going on to make 69 appearances before he moved on to Hyde United. It was claimed that Alex was discovered whilst performing in a fairground booth in Blackpool, although this story has never been substantiated!
Appearances: 1

George Casper Smith (born in Poplar in London on 23rd April 1915, died on 31st October 1983) played in goal whilst at school and represented Hackney Schools in that position, although he was later converted to centre-half prior to joining Bexleyheath & Welling during the 1937-38 season.

He was then snapped up by Charlton Athletic in August 1938 but was able to make only one appearance for the League side before the outbreak of the Second World War. At the end of the hostilities he was transferred to Brentford for £3,000 and went on to make 41 appearances for the Griffin Park club during his eighteen months there. In May 1947 he was transferred to Queens Park Rangers and as captain guided them to the Third Division South championship at the end of his first season. In April 1949 he joined Ipswich Town as player-assistant manager, a position he held for eight months. George then spent spells managing and coaching Redhill and Eastbourne before returning to League football with Sheffield United, joining them as coach in September 1955. After a spell as manager and coach at Sutton United, George was appointed manager of Crystal Palace in June 1958 and held the position for two years. He was then chief coach at Sheffield United but returned to management with Portsmouth, taking over at Fratton Park in March 1961 and holding the reins until March 1970.
Appearances: 1

Frank Soo (born in Buxton on 8th March 1914, died on 25th January 1991) played schoolboy football in Liverpool and then for Prescot Cables before being discovered by Stoke City. He signed for the Potteries club in January 1933 and went on to make 173 League appearances for the club by the time of his departure for Leicester City in September 1945. Despite the fact that Leicester paid £4,600 for his signature he did not make a single League appearance for the club, subsequently joining Luton Town as player-coach in July 1946 for £3,000. He made 71 League appearances for the Kenilworth Road club before joining Chelmsford City in the summer of 1948. He subsequently coached in Israel and then Sweden for five years before returning to England as manager of Scunthorpe United in June 1959. He held this position for a year and was later in charge at St. Albans City. Although he played under the Christian name of Frank, his given name was in fact Hoing, attributable to his Chinese father and English mother. One assumes, therefore, that he could have played for China if he had so wished!
Appearances: 9 + 1 unofficial appearance

Albert Stubbins (born in Wallsend on 13th July 1919, died 28th December 2002) was brought up in America but returned to England and subsequently signed with Newcastle United in April 1937. He went on to make 27 League appearances for the club, scoring five goals, but his record during the war was little short of remarkable, for he ended with a tally of 240 goals in just 172 appearances. In September 1946 he was sold to Liverpool for £12,500 and at the end of the season had a League championship medal to look back on. He made 161 League appearances for the Anfield club, scoring 75 goals, and helped them reach the FA Cup final in 1950, although they were beaten by Arsenal at Wembley. He then joined non-League Ashington in September 1953 and subsequently retired from playing in 1954. After a spell scouting for Liverpool he returned to America and was appointed national coach in 1960. During the Second World War he had worked in a Royal Ordnance engineering factory.
Appearances: 1

Thomas Anderson Swinburne (born in Fencehouses in County Durham on 9th August 1915, died in 1969) was spotted by Newcastle United whilst playing for Herrington Colliery Welfare having already had trials with West Ham and Hull City. He joined the St. James' Park club in April 1934 and went on to make 77 League appearances for the club before joining Consett in June 1947. Both of his sons became professional goalkeepers as well, Trevor with Sunderland, Carlisle, Brentford, Leeds United, Doncaster and Lincoln, and Alan with Oldham Athletic.
Appearances: 1

Frank Taylor (born in Barnsley on 30th April 1916, died on 10th January 1970) was Wolves' regular full-back, along with his brother Jack, and a member of the side that reached the FA Cup Final in 1939. He had joined Wolves in 1933 and was a regular until a serious knee injury forced his retirement in 1944, subsequently being invalided out of the Army as well. He worked for Wolves on their training staff until 1947 when he left to join Hull City as assistant manager, a position he held until June 1948. He then served Scarborough as manager for two years and then became coach and subsequently assistant manager of Leeds United, remaining at Elland Road between 1950 and 1952. He was then appointed manager of Stoke City in June 1952 and had nearly eight years in charge, retiring in May 1960 and later becoming a publican. He also spent a brief spell on the coaching staff at Blackburn Rovers. He served under Major Frank Buckley, his former manager at Wolves, at both Hull and Leeds United.
Appearances: 1

Dennis Westcott (born in Wallasey on 2nd July 1917, died in Stafford on 13th July 1960) began his career with New Brighton as a youngster and represented England at schoolboy level. He joined Wolves in season 1936-37 as a right-winger but was later successfully converted to centre-forward and went on to become a feared striker. He scored 56 goals for Wolves in the three seasons before the Second World War and in 1938-39 established a record number of goals for a single season at the club, netting 43 times. The record stood until 1988 when Steve Bull notched 52. Dennis also scored four goals in the 1939 FA Cup semi final, a record tally for that stage of the competition, although he was unable to repeat the feat in the final. He remained with Wolves until April 1948 when he left to join Blackburn Rovers, later going on to play for Manchester City, Chesterfield and Stafford Rangers before retiring in 1957. He was generally regarded as unlucky not to have won a full cap for England, for his performances in the wartime internationals revealed him to be an exceptional goalscorer. He died suddenly at the age of 43 years in 1960.
Appearances: 4 (5 goals)

The pictures in this book were provided courtesy of the following:

GETTY IMAGES
101 Bayham Street, London NW1 0AG
www.gettyimages.com
EMPICS
www.empics.com

Design and Artwork by Newleaf Design & Media

Series Editor Vanessa Gardner

Proofread by Jane Pamenter

ACKNOWLEDGEMENTS

During the course of researching and writing this book, I had access to a vast number of newspapers, magazines, books and on-line sources, and would like to acknowledge the following as being of particular assistance during the creation of this work:

The Essential History of England *(Headline)*
England The Official FA History *(Virgin)*
England! England! *(Sutton Publishing)*
An English Football Internationalists' Who's Who *(Hutton Press)*
The PFA Footballers' Who's Who *(Queen Anne Press – various editions)*
The PFA Premier & Football League Players Records *(Queen Anne Press – various editions)*
Rothmans Football Yearbook *(Various publishers, various editions)*
The FA Yearbook *(Various publishers, various editions)*

In addition, numerous club histories and alphabets provided additional information on many of the players, but I would like to single out Bob Goodwin for also doing some additional research purely for this book.

Thanks also to Neil 'Cod' Cozens, Vanessa Cozens, Carlton 'Sid' Tucker, Andrew 'Charlie' Carlisle, Jim McKenna, James 'Plod' Devlin and Pete Horn for rekindling my interest in the national team.

Finally, a big thank you to my wife Caroline and children Jo and Steven, who had just about got used to my disappearances for Spurs matches and then had to deal with my watching England.